D0182309

Leadership

Leadership

Understanding the Dynamics of Power and Influence in Organizations

Robert P. Vecchio

Editor

Second Edition

University of Notre Dame Press
Notre Dame, Indiana

Copyright © 2007 by University of Notre Dame
Notre Dame, Indiana 46556
www.undpress.nd.edu
All Rights Reserved

Manufactured in the United States of America

Library of Congress Cataloging-in-Publication Data

Leadership : understanding the dynamics of power and influence in
organizations / Robert P. Vecchio, editor. — 2nd ed.
    p.   cm.
    Includes bibliographical references.
    ISBN-13: 978-0-268-04367-4 (pbk. : alk. paper)
    ISBN-10: 0-268-04367-1 (pbk. : alk. paper)
  1. Leadership.   2. Executive ability.   I. Vecchio, Robert P.
    HD57.7.L4373   2007
    658.4'092—dc22
                     2007017491

 This book is printed on recycled paper.

Contents

VI. Emerging Issues

Preface

Employees in both large and small organizations are experiencing tremendous personal and professional pressures which are a product of the changing context in which organizations operate today. Chief among these changes are growing globalization, down-sizing of organizations, the introduction of participative work-team structures, increasing diversity in the work force, and greater legal constraints. In order to cope with these forces, supervisors and administrators need a deeper understanding of how to marshal and manage human resources.

In response to these challenges, leadership training is frequently cited as an area warranting greater investment. Today, more and more universities are offering leadership classes—often as electives within colleges of business administration or departments of psychology and sociology. Leadership courses are also found in continuing education programs, such as those in executive development and management training. Despite growing recognition of this area within the curriculum, there is still a shortage of strong (i.e., academically grounded) college-level texts in this area. *Leadership*, an anthology of key writings by renowned contributors, is designed to meet the need for a text that encompasses the major theories in the field. Materials have been selected from journals and periodicals widely recognized for publishing in the areas of general management and leadership.

This book is aimed at upper-level undergraduate and graduate-level students in leadership and management, and would be appropriate for executive MBA courses. Portions of the text may also be useful for continuing education training programs of short duration (one to three days), with a reliance on assigned readings for participants. Departments of psychology, political science, sociology, public administration, nursing, safety, and education will also find it relevant. By going beyond a general introduction, *Leadership* fills a need at the university level for a text on leadership with an academic, critical focus which is rich with high quality writing and innovative, yet practical, material.

Leadership is divided into six sections. Part I provides an overview of the subject with readings that examine what leaders actually do, as well as the many myths surrounding the notion of leadership. Part II focuses on the fundamentals of leadership by taking a close look at the specific tactics people use to get their own way. These readings analyze the political games people play and the two-way nature of leader-subordinate influence. Part

III considers problems that can arise from leadership gone wrong—when power and influence are abused. The major, formal models of leadership that have been offered over the years are reviewed in Part IV. These articles include newer variations of the leadership-trait model, as well as behavioral and situational views. Part V looks at contemporary views of leadership, emphasizing reliance on maturity of subordinates for success. This area includes leadership in the context of self-directed work teams, entrepreneurial leadership, the notion of the leader as servant, and examples of leaders who are recognized for having empowered others or for providing moral leadership. The final section, Part VI, overviews the roles of societal and organizational cultures as they pertain to leadership. This section also considers gender issues that relate to managerial roles, as well as the problems inherent in situations where extreme emotions are present in the workplace.

Each of the six sections opens with a selection of interesting quotes on leadership. These quotes are drawn from a variety of business, popular, historical, and academic sources. They are intended to raise issues that are of relevance to the theme of each section, and may help serve as discussion starters.

In this second edition of *Leadership*, the selection of articles has been updated where appropriate, while popular classic materials have been retained. As before, there is a mix of scholarly and managerial writings.

I am grateful to Barbara Hanrahan, Lowell Francis, and Charles Van Hof of the Notre Dame Press for their enthusiastic support of the new edition of this text. Their strong belief in the importance of leadership as a topic and in the value of this book has helped to make it a reality. I am, as ever, indebted to the support of my staff assistants, Kim Brumbaugh and Jacqueline Marnocha, and my wife Betty for their help in the preparation of the final manuscript, and also to the support of Dean Carolyn Woo of the College of Business Administration.

Acknowledgments

The author and publisher are grateful to the following for permission to reprint:

The Free Press, publishers of Bass & Stogdill's *Handbook of Leadership*, for "Concepts of Leadership," (1990): 3–15.

Harvard Business School Press, publishers of *Harvard Business Review*, for "What Leaders Really Do," (May–June 1990): 103–105, 107, 111.

Harvard Business School Press, publishers of *Harvard Business Review*, for "The Manager's Job: Folklore and Fact," (July–August 1975): 49–61.

Harvard Business School Press, publishers of *Harvard Business Review*, for "Crucibles of Leadership," (September–October 2002): 39–46.

Thomson Learning, publishers of *Organizational Behavior*, Third Edition, for "Power, Politics, and Influence," Chapter 9, (1995): 298–322.

Harvard Business School Press, publishers of *Harvard Business Review*, for "Managing Your Boss," (January–February 1980): 92–100.

Sam Houston State University, publishers of *Journal of Business Strategies*, for "Effective Followership: Leadership Turned Upside Down," reprinted from vol. 4, 1 (1987): 39–47.

American Psychological Association, publishers of *Journal of Applied Psychology*, for "Intraorganizational Influence Tactics: Explorations in Getting One's Way," reprinted from vol. 65, 4 (1980): 440–452.

Academy of Management, publishers of *Academy of Management Review*, for "A Social Influence Interpretation of Worker Motivation," reprinted from vol. 7, 2 (1982): 177–186.

Sussex Publishers, Inc., publishers of *Psychology Today*, for "Groupthink," (November 1971): 43, 44, 46, 74–76.

Academy of Management, publishers of *The Academy of Management Executive*, for "The Long-Term Organizational Impact of Destructively Narcissistic Managers," reprinted from vol. 16 (2002): 127–138.

Elsevier, Inc., publishers of *Organizational Dynamics*, for "The Dark Side of Leadership," (1990): 44–55.

Elsevier, Inc., publishers of *Organizational Dynamics*, for "Leaders Who Self-Destruct: The Causes and Cures," (1989): 5–17.

Academy of Management, publishers of *Academy of Management Journal*, for "On the Folly of Rewarding A, While Hoping for B," reprinted from vol. 18, 4 (December 1975): 769–775, 779–783.

University of Washington, publishers of *Journal of Contemporary Business*, for "Path-Goal Theory of Leadership," reprinted from vol. 4, 3 (Autumn 1974): 81–97.

Elsevier, Inc., publishers of *Business Horizons*, for "Are You *In* or *Out* with Your Boss?" (November–December 1986): 76–78.

Elsevier, Inc., publishers of *Organizational Dynamics*, for "Can Leaders Learn to Lead?" (1975): 17–28.

Elsevier, Inc., publishers of *Academy of Management Learning and Education Journal*, for "WICS: A Model of Leadership in Organizations," reprinted from vol. 2 (2003): 386–401.

Elsevier, Inc., publishers of *Organizational Dynamics*, for "From Transactional to Transformational Leadership: Learning to Share the Vision," (1990): 19–31.

American Psychological Association, publishers of *Journal of Applied Psychology*, for "Situational Leadership Theory: An Examination of a Prescriptive Theory," reprinted from vol. 72, (1987): 444–451.

Elsevier Inc., publishers of *Leadership Quarterly*, for "The Contingency Model of Leadership Effectiveness: Its Levels of Analysis," reprinted from vol. 6, 2 (1995): 147–167.

Elsevier, Inc., publishers of *Organizational Dynamics*, for "Substitutes for Leadership: Effective Alternatives to Ineffective Leadership," (1990): 21–38.

Elsevier, Inc., publishers of *Organizational Dynamics*, for "SuperLeadership: Beyond the Myth of Heroic Leadership," (1991): 18–35.

Jim Collins (jimcollins@aol.com and www.jimcollins.com), author of "Level 5 Leadership," reprinted from *Harvard Business Review*, vol. 79 (2001): 67–76. © 2001 Jim Collins.

Paulist Press, publishers of *Servant Leadership*, for "The Servant as Leader," (1977): 7–17.

Robert J. Doyle, author of "The Case of a Servant Leader: John F. Donnelly, Sr."

The New Yorker and Terrence Rafferty for "A Man of Transactions," (December 1993): 83–88.

Elsevier, Inc., publishers for *Human Resources Management Review*, for "Entrepreneurship and Leadership," reprinted from vol. 13 (2003): 303–327.

Academy of Management, publishers of *Academy of Management Executive*, for "Cultural Constraints in Management Theories," reprinted from vol. 7, 1 (1993): 81–93.

Pittsburgh State University, publishers of *Journal of Managerial Issues*, for "Organizational Culture and Strategic Leadership: Issues in the Management of Strategic Change," reprinted from vol. 5, 1 (Spring 1993): 53–70.

Mary D. Zalesny, co-author of "Challenges to Leadership in the Implementation of Technological Change."

Elsevier, Inc., publishers of *Leadership Quarterly*, for "Leadership and Gender Advantage," reprinted from vol. 13 (2002): 643–671.

Elsevier, Inc., publishers of *Research in Personnel and Human Resources Management*, for "It's Not Easy Being Green: Jealousy and Envy in the Workplace," reprinted from vol. 13 (1995): 202–207, 213–216, 220–244.

PART I

Introduction and Overview

By working faithfully eight hours a day, you may eventually get to be a boss and work twelve hours a day.

Robert Frost

Management is the art of getting other people to do all the work.

Anonymous

It's not whether you get knocked down, it's whether you get back up.

Vince Lombardi

If I were truly lucky, I wouldn't have this job.

Ronald Reagan

Boy, the things I do for England.

Prince Charles (on sampling snake meat)

Leadership is always a fascinating topic. Although the subject goes in and out of vogue, it never ceases to draw the attention of both academic and business audiences. Perhaps this fascination stems from our admiration of the ability of others to reach their goals and to be influential, or out of our desire to be more effective in obtaining desired results ourselves. Academic areas that consider leadership to be a topic within their domain include business, politics, communication, sociology, and psychology. This breadth of interest reveals the allure of leadership. In this volume, we will examine a number of perennial questions. For example, is leadership a reality or is it merely a social construction that observers attribute to perceived and inter-preted events? Does leadership make a difference in a group's performance, or is the actual outcome more powerfully determined by the interaction of members and the force of contextual dynamics?

Part of our interest in leadership derives from our expectation that people who are nominal heads (such as managers and administrators)

1

should display leadership. In addition, we are concerned with our own abilities to successfully project strong leadership qualities over and above mere administrative competence. Individual interest in social dominance predates recorded history; however, only in the past century has serious attention been devoted to the study of leadership as a social phenomenon.

The first section opens with Bernard Bass's consideration of the origins of leadership concepts, from the most primitive to contemporary definitions of the construct. Professor Bass looks at various theories of leadership, and the questions which they raise and attempt to answer. Next, John Kotter of Harvard University examines the differences between management and leadership, and suggests that most organizations are overmanaged but underled. Henry Mintzberg, in a classic discussion of the manager's job, distinguishes between the folklore of a manager's presumed activities and the factual reality of a fragmented, reactive set of activities. Warren Bennis and Robert Thomas then explore the role of adversity in the development of leaders. Finally, Robert Vecchio considers whether (and, if so, to what extent) leadership can be taught.

Concepts of Leadership

Bernard M. Bass

Leadership is one of the world's oldest preoccupations. The understanding of leadership has figured strongly in the quest for knowledge. Purposeful stories have been told through the generations about leaders' competencies, ambitions, and shortcomings; leaders' rights and privileges; and the leaders' duties and obligations.

THE BEGINNINGS

Leaders as prophets, priests, chiefs, and kings served as symbols, representatives, and models for their people in the Old and New Testaments, in the Upanishads, in the Greek and Latin classics, and in the Icelandic sagas. In the *Iliad*, higher, transcendental goals are emphasized: "He serves me most, who serves his country best" (Book X, line 201). The *Odyssey* advises leaders to maintain their social distance: "The leader, mingling with the vulgar host, is in the common mass of matter lost" (Book III, line 297). The subject of leadership was not limited to the classics of Western literature. It was of as much interest to Asoka and Confucius as to Plato and Aristotle.

Myths and legends about great leaders were important in the development of civilized societies. Stories about the exploits of individual heroes (and occasionally heroines) are central to the Babylonian *Gilgamesh, Beowolf,* the *Chanson de Roland,* the Icelandic sagas, and the Ramayana (now they would be called cases). All societies have created myths to provide plausible and acceptable explanations for the dominance of their leaders and the submission of their subordinates (Paige, 1977). The greater the socioeconomic injustice in the society, the more distorted the realities of leadership—its powers, morality and effectiveness—in the mythology.

The study of leadership rivals in age the emergence of civilization, which shaped its leaders as much as it was shaped by them. From its infancy, the study of history has been the study of leaders—what they did and why they did it. Over the centuries, the effort to formulate principles of leadership spread from the study of history and the philosophy associated with it to all the developing social sciences. In modern psychohistory, there is still a search for generalizations about leadership, built on the in-depth analysis of the development, motivation, and competencies of world leaders, living and dead.

In 2300 B.C. in the Instruction of Ptahhotep, three qualities were attributed to the Pharoah. "Authoritative utterness is in thy mouth, perception is in thy heart, and thy tongue is the shrine of justice" (Lichtheim, 1973). The Chinese classics, written as early as the sixth century B.C., are filled with hortatory advice to the country's leaders about their responsibilities to the people. Confucius urged leaders to set a moral example and to manipulate rewards and punishments for teaching what was right and good. Taoism emphasized the need for the leader to work himself out of his job by making the people believe that successes were due to their efforts.

Greek concepts of leadership were exemplified by the heroes in Homer's *Iliad*. Ajax symbolized inspirational leadership and law and order. Other qualities that the Greeks admired and thought were needed (and sometimes wanting) in heroic leaders were (1) justice and judgment (Agamemnon), (2) wisdom and counsel (Nestor), (3) shrewdness and cunning (Odysseus), and (4) valor and activism (Achilles) (see Sarachek, 1968). (Shrewdness and cunning are not regarded as highly in contemporary society as they once were.) Later, Greek philosophers, such as Plato in the *Republic*, looked at the requirements for the ideal leader of the ideal state (the philosopher king). The leader was to be the most important element of good government, educated to rule with order and reason. In *Politics*, Aristotle was disturbed by the lack of virtue among those who wanted to be leaders. He pointed to the need to educate youths for such leadership. Plutarch, although he was involved with prosocial ideals about leadership, compared the traits and behavior of actual Greek and Roman leaders to support his point of view in *The Parallel Lives* (Kellerman, 1987).

A scholarly highlight of the Renaissance was Machiavelli's (1513/1962) *The Prince*. Machiavelli's thesis that "there is nothing more difficult to take in hand, more perilous to conduct, or more uncertain in its success, than to take the lead in the introduction of a new order of things" is still a germane description of the risks of leadership and the resistance to it. Machiavelli was the ultimate pragmatist. He believed that leaders needed steadiness, firmness, and concern for the maintenance of authority, power, and order in government. It was best if these objectives could be accomplished by gaining the esteem of the populace, but if they could not, then craft, deceit, threat, treachery, and violence were required (Kellerman, 1987). Machiavelli is still widely quoted as a guide to an effective leadership of sorts, which was the basis for a modern line of investigation with the Mach scale (Christie & Geis, 1970). A 1987 survey of 117 college presidents reported that they still found *The Prince* highly relevant.

In the same way, a fundamental principle at West Point today can be traced back to Hegel's (1830/1971) *Philosophy of Mind* which argued that by first serving as a follower, a leader subsequently can best understand his followers. Hegel thought that this understanding is a paramount requirement for effective leadership.

Universality

Leadership is a universal phenomenon in humans and in many species of animals.

Animal Origins

Leadership predates the emergence of humankind. Allee (1945, 1949, 1951) maintained that all vertebrates that live in groups exhibit social organization and leadership. High-ranking males feed more freely than do other members of the group and tend to have more ready access to females. In some cases, high status involves guard duty and protection of the herd.

Pecking Order

Individual animals dominate or submit their local spaces to others in the well-known pecking order. In one of the early experiments on animal social relations, Murchison (1935) placed roosters at opposite ends of a narrow runway and measured the distance that each advanced toward the other. As a result of successive pairings, he was able to determine a strict hierarchy of dominance. Rooster A invariably dominated all the remaining subjects. At the bottom of the hierarchy was the rooster who yielded to all the others.

Douglis (1948) removed hens from their home flocks and placed them in other flocks for short periods. The hen's pecking order in each flock was observed. It was found that a hen can become an assimilated member in at least five different flocks and have a different status in each. The hen can recognize and react to the status or esteem of as many as 27 individuals. Highly dominant hens become assimilated within three days, but hens that were not dominant required three to six weeks to become assimilated. Once established, a hierarchy tended to maintain itself.

Dominance Effects in Primates

Miller and Murphy (1956) and Warren and Maroney (1969) tested pairs of monkeys who were competing for food in an area and observed strict dominance hierarchies. Subordinate animals were more successful in obtaining low-preference, rather than middle- or high-preference, foods. Bernstein (1964) noted that when the dominant male was removed from a group of monkeys, the activities of other males increased. After the dominant male returned, he resumed his dominant status and the activities of other males decreased.

Carpenter (1963) studied societies of monkeys and apes. His general findings suggested that the leader tended to control the group's movement in its search for food and shelter, regulate intragroup status, defend the group, and maintain its integrity in its contacts with other organized groupings. When the dominant male was removed from the group, the territory covered by the group was markedly reduced. Thus, the leader enlarged the freedom of the group's movement. But the dominant male tended to be avoided by low-ranking males. In some bands, the one or two males that were next in rank stood by the leader to ward off intruders and were permitted to groom him on occasion.

Again, Mason (1964) reported that leaders among groups of monkeys and apes appeared to have the primary function of initiating progressions and determining the line of march. The dominant males quelled intragroup fights, protected the females and young, were attractive to all members, were sought out by females, and influenced the size of the group's territorial range.

Zajonc (1969) interpreted the fact that fighting disappears almost entirely in primate groups after a hierarchy of dominance has been established as evidence that such groups develop norms. The norms are learned by group members, are stable but can be changed, and are complied with by the majority of members. Koford (1963) observed that the relative dominance of two bands of monkeys that meet at an eating place is usually determined by the relative dominance of the leaders of the bands. Once the dominance of a band has been established, it is observed by the other group, even in the absence of the other leader. Experimentation and observation in natural settings suggest that groups of animals develop strongly differentiated status hierarchies that their members recognize and observe. In primate groups, leaders obtain privileges that tend to bolster their dominance. Their presence is an advantage to the group in gaining possession of a desired territory and in expanding the area of free movement for the group. However, whether these findings and similar results reported for packs of wolves and hyenas, elephant matriarchies, bands of gorillas, and pods of whales are relevant to understanding the human condition remains controversial.

Humans

Parenthood, a condition that unarguably cuts across cultural lines, makes for ready-made patterns of leadership. Nevertheless, the patterns of behavior that are regarded as acceptable in leaders differ from time to time and from one culture to another. Citing various anthropological reports on primitive groups in Australia, Fiji, New Guinea, the Congo, and elsewhere, H. L. Smith and Krueger (1933) concluded that leadership occurs among all people, regardless of culture, be they isolated Indian villagers, nomads of the Eurasian steppes, or Polynesian fisherfolk. Lewis (1974) concluded, from a more recent anthropological review, that even when a society does not have institutionalized chiefs, rules, or elected officials, there are always leaders who initiate action and play central roles in the group's decision making. No societies are known that do not have leadership in some aspects of their social life, although many may lack a single overall leader to make and enforce decisions.

Leaders, such as Abraham, Moses, David, Solomon, and the Macabees, were singled out in the Old Testament for a detailed exposition of their behavior and relations with God and their people. God was the supreme leader of his Chosen People who clarified, instructed, and directed what was to be done through the words of his Prophets and arranged for rewards for compliance and punishment for disobedience to the laws and rules He had handed down to Moses. In Islam, the ideal caliphate leadership was based on religious law (Rabi, 1967).

In *The Parallel Lives*, Plutarch (1932), in about A.D. 100, tried to show the similarities between 50 Greek and Roman leaders. Latin authors, such as Caesar, Cicero, and Seneca to name just a few, wrote extensively on the subject of leadership and administration. Their influence was considerable on the medieval and Renaissance periods, which looked back to the classics for guidance. Their influence on Thomas Jefferson and James Madison has an impact on the design of the U.S. government as we know it, as did such Renaissance scholars as Montesquieu in his *The Spirit of Laws* (1748).

Military writings about leadership stretch from the Chinese classics to the present. Napoleon listed 115 qualities that are essentials for a military leader. Meyer (1980) called for a renaissance in the concern for military leadership, in contrast to the focus on the "over-management" of logistics. Resources must be managed by the military leader but are no substitute for effective leadership.

The Importance of Leaders and Leadership

Napoleon expressed his feelings about the importance of leadership in his quip that he would rather have an army of rabbits led by a lion than an army of lions led by a rabbit. Surveys of job satisfaction from the 1920s onward illustrated the importance of leadership.[1] They uniformly reported that employees' favorable attitudes toward their supervisors contributed to the employees' satisfaction. In turn, employees' favorable attitudes toward their supervisors were usually found to be related to the productivity of the work group (see, for example, Lawshe & Nagle, 1953). Since then, countless surveys can be cited to support the contention that leaders make a difference in their subordinates' satisfaction and performance. Leaders also can make the difference in whether their organizations succeed or fail.

The usual efforts to estimate the number of leaders in the United States use census data on proprietors and officials. But Gardner (1988) noted that although owners, managers, and officials are in the position to do so, they do not necessarily act as leaders. Cleveland (1985) estimated the number of opinion leaders in the United States and how they grew in number between 1955 and 1985. In 1955, he estimated that there were 555,000 opinion leaders, whereas in 1971, he guessed that at least 1 million Americans could be classified as opinion leaders. He considered seven out of ten public executives to be opinion leaders—policymakers in public, philanthropic, voluntary, and large-scale "private" enterprises—in 1971. By 1985 he estimated the number to have multiplied to 1 out of every 200 Americans.

As Cleveland (1985, p. 4) stated: There are some 83,000 government units in the United States, and about 175,000 corporations each doing more than $1 million worth of business a year. The galloping rate of growth of

---

1. Bergen (1939), Houser (1927), Kornhauser and Sharp (1932), and Viteles (1953).

complexity means that a growth curve of the requirement for leaders (if anyone were clever enough to construct such an index) would show a steeper climb than any other growth rate in our political economy.

Is Leadership a Figment of the Imagination?

Some critics argue that all the effects of leadership are in the eyes of their beholders. Followers attribute effects that are due to historical, economic, or social forces to leadership, as in romantic fiction (Meindl & Ehrlich, 1987; Meindl, Ehrlich, & Dukerich, 1985). Other critics, such as Pandey (1976), regard leadership as a useless concept for understanding social influence. For Calder (1977), the objective contributions of the "leader" to outcomes may be more interesting than true. The extreme position taken by some attribution theorists is that organizational outcomes are determined primarily by other factors, but leaders are credited with what happened after the fact.

Organizational leaders who are perceived to be exerting leadership on organizational performance are merely the subjects of misperceptions, some critics contend. That is, organizational outcomes are objectively determined by environmental and organizational factors in which leadership, at best, can play only a minor role. For instance, M. C. Brown (1982, p. 1) concluded that "once other factors influencing effectiveness are accounted for, it is likely that leadership will have little bearing on organizational performance."

Pfeffer (1977) took a similar but not as extreme position: Leadership is a sense-making heuristic to account for organizational performance and is important primarily for its symbolic role in organizations. Leaders are selected or self-selected to fulfill the fate of the organization and are highly constrained by organization and external factors. Therefore, they can have only limited impact on organizational outcomes compared to external factors. Leaders are able only to react to contingencies, to facilitate the adjustment of the organization in its context, and to alter that environment to some limited extent. Also they have no control over many factors that affect organizational performance and they typically have unilateral control over few resources.

Despite these constraints, management and leadership seem to have a substantial effect on some organizational outcomes. Thus, when Lieberson and O'Connor (1972) examined the effects of top management on the success of 167 firms over a 20-year period, they found that the effects depended on which outcomes were considered. Managers had the greatest effect on profit margins but the least effect on sales; they also were of less consequence in capital-intensive industries. In the same way, Salancik and Pfeffer (1977) showed that the mayors of 30 U.S. cities had considerable influence only on those budgetary issues, such as libraries and parks, that were not in the domain of important special-interest groups, such as the police, fire fighters, and highway maintenance personnel. In all, Pfeffer concluded that since people want to achieve the feeling that they are in control of their environment, they find it useful to attribute outcomes of their group and organizational performance to leaders, rather than to the complex internal and external environmental forces that actually are most important. Meindl and Ehrlich (1987) showed that if performance outcomes of firms were attributed to the leadership of the top management, rather than to the employees, market conditions, or the government, the judges gave better evaluations of the outcomes. Meindl and Ehrlich attributed this finding to the judges' assumption that leaders have a reliable and potent impact on outcomes.

Even when the true causes of outcomes were logically not determinable, Meindl, Ehrlich, and Dukerich (1985) showed that there was a tendency to view leadership as the likely cause of the outcomes. This study and the one by Meindl and Ehrlich (1987) were thought to demonstrate that leadership is more of a romantic notion than a phenomenon that truly affects group and organizational outcomes.

Then there is evidence that would-be followers, subordinates, and groups of employees are so constrained by technology, rules, job requirements, and organizational policies that there is little discretionary room for a superior or leader to make much of a difference in how things get done (Katz & Kahn, 1966). Furthermore, subordinates may have much more effect on the behavior of their superiors than vice versa (Goodstadt & Kipnis, 1970).

Miner (1975, p. 200) was ready to abandon the concept of leadership, stating that "the concept of leadership itself has outlived its usefulness. Hence, I suggest that we abandon leadership in favor of some other, more fruitful way of cutting up the theoretical pie." In 1982, Miner recanted this statement but still maintained that the concept has limited usefulness because so much of the empirical research has been on emergent leadership in small groups, rather than within more complex organizations. For Miner, the fragile, distressed leadership that arises in the small, temporary group to develop, maintain, and enforce the norms of the group may have little relevance for leadership in the impersonal "task system" of the traditional organization.

Leaders Do Make a Difference

Despite the skepticism about the reality and importance of leadership, all social and political movements require leaders to begin them. As Tucker (1981, p. 87) put it, "in the beginning is the leadership act. A 'leaderless movement' is naturally out of the question." This does not mean that formal, institutionalized leadership is required. In fact, no leader in an institutional form appeared in the numerous peasant revolts from the sixteenth to nineteenth centuries in Southern Germany. The same was true for journeymen's strikes during the eighteenth century. Leadership remained informal and egalitarian. Only in the middle of the nineteenth century did definite leaders, such as Ferdinand Lasalle, emerge. Lasalle placed himself at the head of the German workers' movement and worked out its explicit ideology, along with the myth that he founded the movement (Groh, 1986). This behavior is consistent with most cases of institutional development: Leaders determine the direction they will take. The historical records of the early British Royal Society of the seventeenth century illustrate that its secretaries were responsible for who joined the society and what kinds of science were sponsored (Mulligan & Mulligan, 1981).

Indeed, leadership is often regarded as the single most critical factor in the success or failure of institutions. For instance, T. H. Allen (1981) argued that the school principal's leadership is the most important factor in determining a school's climate and the students' success. Sylvia and Hutchison (1985) concluded that the motivation of 167 Oklahoma teachers depended considerably on their perceptions of the quality of their relationships with their superiors. And Smith, Carson, and Alexander (1984) found that among the 50 Methodist ministers they studied, some were more effective leaders than were others. The effectiveness of these ministers was evidenced by the differential impact that their ministries had on church attendance, membership, property values, and contributions to the church.

In the business and industrial sector, Maccoby (1979, p. 313) concluded, from his observations of the manager as a game-playing politician, that the need of firms to survive and prosper in a world of increasing competition, of technological advances, of changing governmental regulations, of changing worker attitudes, requires "a higher level of leadership than ever before." When an organization must be changed to reflect changes in technology, the environment, and the completion of programs, its leadership is critical in orchestrating the process (Burke, Richley, & DeAngelis, 1985). Mintzberg and Waters (1982) examined the evolution of a retail firm over a 60-year period and found that a senior executive could successfully reorient the firm by intervening to change previous strategies and organizational structures. In the same way, Day and Lord (1986) noted that when confounding errors are controlled in studies of the effects of executive succession, differences in executive leaders can explain as much as 45 percent of their organizations' performance. Agreeing with Chandler (1962), they stated that historical analyses of changes of leadership over significant periods have shown that leadership has a profound influence on an organization. Concurrent correlational analyses of a sample of executives and their organizations at the same point in time reach similar conclusions, although the effects are not as strong.

In a review of experiments in the United States on the productivity of workers between 1971 and 1981, Katzell and Guzzo (1983) concluded that supervisory methods seemed particularly effective in increasing output. In Sweden, Westerlund (1952) observed that the high-quality performance of supervisors improved the attitudes and performance of telephone operators. Also in Sweden, Ekvall and Arvonen (1984) found that leadership styles accounted for 65 percent of the variance in organizational climate in the 25 units they studied. Virany and Tushman (1986) stated that the senior managers of better-performing minicomputer firms were systematically different from those of firms that performed poorly. The senior management in the better firms had had previous experience in the electronic industry and was more likely to include the founder of the firm who still served as chief executive officer. Although most attention has been paid to industrial leaders as developers and builders, Hansen (1974) pointed out that the success with which a firm, such as the Ford Motor Company, closed a plant without much human dislocation depended on effective leadership.

Leadership has been considered a critical factor in military successes since records have been kept; that is, better-led forces repeatedly have been victorious over poorly led forces. Thus, not unexpectedly, morale and cohesion among Israeli and U.S. enlisted soldiers correlated with measures of the soldiers' confidence in their company, division, and battalion commanders (Gal & Manning, 1987).

Personnel of the Mississippi Cooperative Extension reported that they felt less job stress if they saw their supervisors displaying more leadership in structuring the work to be done and showing concern for the subordinates' needs (Graham, 1982). In a study of 204 innovations in state programs, Cheek (1987) found that the governors came up with 55 percent of the innovations and the agencies with only 36 percent.

Studies by Tucker (1981), Hargrove and Nelson (1984), and Hargrove (1987) concluded that the style and performance of a U.S. president makes a big difference in what happens to legislation, policy, and programs. Successful presidents are more sensitive to the inherent politics of policy-making. They define and publicize the policy dilemmas facing the country and earn widespread public and Congressional support for their positions. They construct their policy agendas with the felt needs of the country in mind and create political support for their agendas; they also realize that timing is important (Tucker, 1981). But like Jimmy Carter, they can fail if they push for what they deem to be right but what is not politically feasible and if they favor comprehensive integrated solutions rather than incremental steps (Hargrove, 1987). Presidents can make decisions that are not implemented because they or their assistants do not follow them up. For example, as part of the agreement to resolve the Cuban missile crisis, President Kennedy ordered the removal of U.S. missiles from Turkey on the border of the Soviet Union. Six months later, he was astonished to learn that the missiles were still in place (Manchester, 1988). Although presidents spend relatively little time trying to make major reorientations in policy, they have an important impact on the smaller substantive decisions that affect the larger overall strategies (Neustadt, 1980). History may be drastically altered by a sudden change in presidents. Before leaving Washington, D.C., for his fateful trip to Texas in November 1963, Kennedy signed the first order for a phased withdrawal from Vietnam. On assuming office after Kennedy's assassination, Lyndon Johnson rescinded the order. The war continued for another decade.

According to Richard Nixon's "Silent Majority" speech in 1969, presidents may have to take an unpopular stand, but when they do, they can strengthen acceptance by explaining their reasons, soliciting support, and winning approval (Safire, 1975). Presidents also provide symbolic support for the development of norms, values, and beliefs that contribute to subsequent national and organizational development (Sayles, 1979). As Gardner (1988) noted, for a society to function, its people must share beliefs and values regarding the standards of acceptable behavior. Leaders can revitalize those shared beliefs and help keep the values fresh. "They have a role in creating the state of mind that is the society" (Gardner, 1988, p. 18). They conceive and articulate goals that move people from their own interests to unite for higher ends.

Often, the effects of leadership are indirect. For example, Katzell (1987) showed through a path analysis that although supervisors' direct influence on their subordinates was modest, they exerted indirect influence and increased the employees' morale by providing rewards, relating rewards to performance, and treating employees equitably; the increased morale, in turn, improved the employees' performance.

Jongbloed and Frost (1985) modified Pfeffer's (1977) reasoning to argue that leaders still have an important general role to play. What leaders really manage in organizations are the employees' interpretations or understanding of what goes on in the organizations. The leaders manage meanings and, therefore, exert a strong impact on organizational outcomes. Jongbloed and Frost showed how the laboratory director in one Canadian hospital, compared to another in a second hospital with the same formal assignments and the same absence of control of issues, successfully lobbied for the importance of pathology and convinced the hospital administrators to allocate more funds for operations and budget than were allocated in the second hospital.

· The importance of leadership is attested by academic and lay interest in leadership as a subject for development, training, and education (Campbell, 1977).[2] Although U.S. college presidents believe that our educational institutions are reluctant to incorporate leadership education into their curricula (Cronin, 1984), the college landscape is not bleak. Gregory's (1986) survey of all known U.S. degree-granting institutions of higher learning uncovered 53 that offered an academic course on leadership, 70 that made it possible to major or concentrate in the subject, 181 that incorporated the study of leadership in an academic course or a student-affairs program, and 81 that offered the subject in continuing education or professional programs.[3]

2. Recognition of the importance to the nation of leadership and its development for all types of organizations is witnessed by the Alliance for Leadership Development, which includes the following members: American Leadership Forum of Houston; Association of American Colleges of Washington, D.C.; Association of Governing Boards of Universities and Colleges; Center for Creative Leadership of Greensboro, N.C.; Coro Foundation of St. Louis; International Leadership Center of Dallas; National Association of Secondary School Principals of Reston, Va.; and the National Executive Service Corps of New York. The Alliance's programs include the promotion of research on and teaching of leadership, related conferences and publications, a clearinghouse of information on leadership programs at universities and secondary schools, leadership development programs in the community, and development programs for corporate executives.

3. Details about these can be found in Clark, Freeman, and Britt (1987).

Leadership as a Subject of Inquiry

The importance of leadership is also demonstrated by its place in social science research. According to Mitchell (1979) and DeMeuse (1986), leadership has been one of the frequent subjects of empirical research, concentrating on the antecedents of leaders' behavior and the factors that contribute to its effectiveness. Leadership is a featured topic in almost every textbook on organizational behavior. The scholarly books on leadership number in the hundreds, and articles, reports, and essays number in the thousands.

Several different schools of thought have prevailed simultaneously since leadership first was studied. The early sociological theorists tended to explain leadership in terms of either the person or the environment. Later researchers tended to view leadership as an aspect of role differentiation or as an outgrowth of social interaction processes. Recently, the naive theories of leadership we hold have been considered most important in explaining what is going on. But this is as it should be. Theory and empirical research should move forward together, each stimulating, supporting, and modifying the other. Neither can stand alone. An elegant theory without prospects of elegant data gathering makes for a sketchy theory. Early in a line of investigation, crude data and theory may be useful. Later, as understanding develops and practice improves, more stringent standards are required (Bass, 1974).

Assumptions

An almost insurmountable problem is the question of the extent to which we pour old wine into new bottles when proposing "new" theories. For instance, Julius Caesar's descriptions of his leadership style in the Gallic Wars in the first century B.C. are clear, succinct endorsements of the need for what Blake and Mouton (1964) conceived as "9-9" style—a style that Fleishman (1953) described in terms of high initiation and consideration and that in the year 2500 some new theorist will give a new name. When does a field advance? Are we beyond Caesar's understanding of how to lead infantry shock troops?

THE MEANING OF LEADERSHIP

The word leadership is a sophisticated, modern concept. In earlier times, words meaning "head of state," "military commander," "princeps," "proconsul," "chief," or "king" were common in most societies; these words differentiated the ruler from other members of society. A preoccupation with leadership, as opposed to headship based on inheritance, usurpation, or appointment, occurred predominantly in countries with an Anglo-Saxon heritage. Although the *Oxford English Dictionary* (1933) noted the appearance of the word "leader" in the English language as early as the year 1300, the word "leadership" did not appear until the first half of the nine-teenth century in writings about the political influence and control of British Parliament. And the word did not appear in most other modern languages until recent times.

Defining Leadership

There are almost as many different definitions of leadership as there are persons who have attempted to define the concept.[4] Moreover, as Pfeffer (1977) noted, many of the definitions are ambiguous. Furthermore, the distinction between leadership and other social-influence processes is often blurred (Bavelas, 1960; Hollander & Julian, 1969). The many dimensions into which leadership has been cast and their overlapping meanings have added to the confusion. Therefore, the meaning of leadership may depend on the kind of institution in which it is found (Spitzberg, 1986). Never-theless, there is sufficient similarity among definitions to permit a rough scheme of classification. Leadership has been conceived as the focus of group processes, as a matter of personality, as a matter of inducing com-pliance, as the exercise of influence, as particular behaviors, as a form of persuasion, as a power relation, as an instrument to achieve goals, as an ef-fect of interaction, as a differentiated role, as initiation of structure, and as many combinations of these definitions.

WORKS CITED

Allee, W. C. 1945. Social biology of subhuman groups. *Sociometry,* 8, 21–29.
———. 1951. *Cooperation among animals, with human implications.* New York: Schuman.

4. Different definitions and conceptions of leadership have been reviewed briefly by Mor-ris and Seeman (1950), Shartle (1951a, 1951b, 1956), L. F. Carter (1953), C. A. Gibb (1954, 1969), Bass (1960), Stogdill (1975), and Schriesheim and Kerr (1977).

————. Emerson, A. E., Park, O., Park, T., & Schmidt, K. P. 1949. *Principles of animal ecology.* Philadelphia: Saunders.

Allen, T. H. 1981. Situational management roles: A conceptual model. *Dissertation Abstracts International,* 42 (2A) 465.

Allport, F. H. 1924. *Social psychology.* Boston: Houghton Mifflin.

Babikan, K. 1981. The leader-entrepreneur in the public sector. In F. I. Khuri, ed., *Leadership and Development in Arab Society.* Beirut: American University of Beirut, Center for Arab and Middle East Studies.

Bass, B. M. 1960. *Leadership, psychology, and organizational behavior.* New York: Harper.

————. 1974. The substance and the shadow. *American Psychologist,* 29, 870–886.

Bavelas, A. 1960. Leadership: Man and function. *Administrative Science Quarterly,* 4, 491–498.

Bennis, W. G. 1970. *American bureaucracy.* Chicago: Aldine.

Bernard, L. L. 1926. *An introduction to social psychology.* New York: Holt.

————. 1927. Leadership and propaganda. In J. Davis & H. E. Barnes, *An introduction to sociology.* New York: Heath.

Bernstein, I. S. 1964. Group social patterns as influenced by removal and later reintroduction of the dominant male Rhesus. *Psychological Reports,* 14, 3–10.

Bingham, W. V. 1927. Leadership. In H. C. Metcalf, *The psychological foundations of management.* New York: Shaw.

Blackmar, F. W. 1911. Leadership in reform. *American Journal of Sociology,* 16, 626–644.

Blake, R. R., Mouton, J. S., Barnes, L. B., & Greiner, L. E. 1964. Breakthrough in organization development. *Harvard Business Review,* 42, 133–155.

Bowden, A. O. 1926. A study of the personality of student leaders in the United States. *Journal of Abnormal and Social Psychology,* 21, 149–160.

Brown, J. F. 1936. *Psychology and the social order.* New York: McGraw-Hill.

Brown, M. C. 1982. Administrative succession and organizational performance: The succession effect. *Administrative Science Quarterly,* 27, 1–16.

Bundel, C. M. 1930. Is leadership losing its importance? *Infantry Journal,* 36, 339–349.

Burke, W., Richley, E. A., & DeAngelis, L. 1985. Changing leadership and planning processes at the Lewis Research Center, National Aeronautics and Space Administration. *Human Resource Management,* 24(1), 81–90.

Burns, J. M. 1978. *Leadership.* New York: Harper & Row.

Calder, B. J. 1977. An attribution theory of leadership. In B. M. Staw and G. R. Salancik, eds., *New directions in organizational behavior.* Chicago: St. Clair.

Campbell, J. P. 1977. The cutting edge of leadership: An overview. In J. G. Hunt and L. L. Larson, eds., *Leadership: The cutting edge.* Carbondale: Southern Illinois University Press.

Carpenter, C. R. 1963. Societies of monkeys and apes. In C. H. Southwich, ed., *Primate social behavior.* Princeton, N.J.: Van Nostrand.

Carter, L. F. 1953. Leadership and small group behavior. In M. Sherif & M. O. Wilson, eds., *Group relations at the crossroads.* New York: Harper.

Cartwright, D. 1965. Influence, leadership, control. In J. G. March, ed., *Handbook of organizations.* Chicago: Rand McNally.

Chandler, A. D., Jr. 1962. Strategy and structure. *Chapters in the history of the industrial enterprises.* Cambridge, Mass.: M.I.T. Press.

Chapin, F. S. 1924b. Leadership and group activity. *Journal of Applied Sociology,* 8, 141–145.

Cheek, S. K. 1987. *Recent state initiatives: The governor as policy leader: The governor as chief administrator.* Paper, Academy of Management, New Orleans.

Christie, R., & Geis, F. L. 1970. *Studies in Machiavellianism.* New York: Academic Press.

Clark, M. B., Freeman, F. H., & Britt, S. K. 1987. *Leadership education '87: A source book.* Greensboro, N.C.: Center for Creative Leadership.

Cleeton, G. U., & Mason, C. W. 1934. *Executive ability—its discovery and development.* Yellow Springs, Ohio: Antioch Press.

Cleveland, H. 1985. *The knowledge executive: Leadership in an information society.* New York: Dutton.

Cooley, C. H. 1902. *Human nature and the social order.* New York: Scribners.

Copeland, N. 1942. *Psychology and the soldier.* Harrisburg, Pa.: Military Service Publishing.

Cronin, T. E. 1984. Thinking and learning about leadership. *Presidential Studies Quarterly,* 14(1), 22–34.

Day, D. V., & Lord, R. G. 1986. Executive leadership and organizational performance: Suggestions for a new theory and methodology. Paper, Academy of Management, Chicago. Also 1988. *Journal of Management,* 14, 453–464.

DeMeuse, K. P. 1986. A compendium of frequently used measures in industrial/organizational psychology. *The Industrial-Organizational Psychologist,* 23(2), 53–59.

Douglis, M. B. 1948. Social factors influencing the hierarchies of small flocks of the domestic hen; Interactions between resident and part-time members of organized flocks. *Physiological Zoology,* 21, 147–182.

Dyer, W. G., & Dyer, J. H. 1984. The M*A*S*H generation: Implications for future organizational values. *Organizational Dynamics,* 13(1), 66–79.

Ekvall, G., & Arvonen, J. 1984. *Leadership styles and organizational climate for creativity: Some findings in one company* (Report 1). Stockholm: Ferreted.

Ferris, G. O., & Rowland, K. M. 1981. Leadership, job perceptions, and influence: A conceptual integration. *Human Relations,* 34, 1069–1077.

Fiedler, F. E. 1967. *A theory of leadership effectiveness.* New York: McGraw-Hill.

Fleishman, E. A. 1953. The measurement of leadership attitudes in industry. *Journal of Applied Psychology,* 37, 153–158.

French, J. R. P. 1956. A formal theory of social power. *Psychological Review,* 63, 181–194.

Gal, R., & Manning, F. J. 1987. Morale and its components: A cross national comparison. *Journal of Applied Social Psychology,* 17, 369–391.

Gardner, J. W. 1988. *The task of motivating* (Leadership Paper No. 9). Washington, D.C.: Independent Sector.

Gerth, H., & Mills, C. W. 1953. *Character and social structure.* New York: Harcourt, Brace.

Gibb, J. R. 1954. *Factors producing defensive behavior within groups.* (Annual Tech. Report). Boulder: University of Colorado, Human Relations Lab.

————. 1969. Leadership. In G. Lindzey & E. Aronson, eds., *The handbook of social psychology,* 2d ed., vol. 4. Reading, Mass.: Addison-Wesley.

Graham, F. C. 1982. Job stress in Mississippi cooperative extension services county personnel as related to age, gender, district, tenure, position and perceived leadership behavior of immediate supervisors. *Dissertation Abstracts International,* 43(7A), 2180.

Goodstadt, B. E., & Kipnis, D. 1970. Situational influences on the use of power. *Journal of Applied Psychology,* 54, 201–207.

Gregory, R. A. 1986. *Leadership education in institutions of higher education: An assessment.* Greensboro, N.C.: Center for Creative Leadership.

Groh, D. 1986. The dilemma of unwanted leadership in social movements: The German example before 1914. G. F. Graumann & S. Moscovici, eds., *Changing conception of leadership.* New York: Springer-Verlag.

Haiman, F. S. 1951. Group leadership and democratic action. Boston: Houghton Mifflin.

Hansen, P. 1974. *Sex differences in supervision.* Paper, American Psychological Association, New Orleans.

Hargrove, E. C. 1987. Jimmy Carter as President. Paper, Conference on the Presidency, Princeton University, Princeton, N.J.

————, & Nelson, M. 1984. *Presidents, politics, and policy.* Baltimore: John Hopkins University Press.

Hemphill, J. K. 1949. The leader and his group. *Journal of Educational Research,* 28, 225–229, 245–246.

Hollander, E. P., & Julian, J. W. 1969. Contemporary trends in the analysis of leadership processes. *Psychological Bulletin,* 71, 387–397.

Iliad of Homer. 1720/1943. A. Pope, trans. New York: Heritage Press.

Jacobs, T. O., & Jaques, E. 1987. Leadership in complex systems. In J. Zeidner, ed., *Human productivity enhancement.* New York: Praeger.

Janda, K. F. 1960. Towards the explication of the concept of leadership in terms of the concept of power. *Human Relations,* 13, 345–363.

Jongbloed, L., & Frost, P. J. 1985. Pfeffer's model of management: An expansion and modification. *Journal of Management,* 11, 97–110.

Katz, D., & Kahn, R. L. 1966, 1978. *The social psychology of organizations.* New York: Wiley.

Katzell, R. 1987. *How leadership works.* Paper, Conference on Military Leadership: Traditions and Future Trends, United States Naval Academy, Annapolis, Md.

Katzell, R. A., & Guzzo, R. A. 1983. Psychological approaches to productivity improvement. *American Psychologist,* 38, 468–472.

Kellerman, B. 1987. *The politics of leadership in America: Implications for higher education in the late 20th century.* Paper, Invitational Interdisciplinary Colloquium on Leadership in Higher Education, National Center for Postsecondary Governance and Finance, Teachers College, Columbia University, New York.

Knickerbocker, I. 1948. Leadership: A conception and some implications. *Journal of Social Issues,* 4, 23–40.

Koford, C. B. 1963. Group relations in an island colony of Rhesus monkeys. In C. H. Southwick, ed., *Primate social behavior.* Princeton, N.J.: Van Nostrand.

Koontz, H., & O'Donnell, C. 1955. *Principles of management.* New York: McGraw-Hill.

Krech, D., & Crutchfield, R. S. 1948. *Theory and problems of social psychology.* New York: McGraw-Hill.

Larson, A. 1968. *Eisenhower: The president nobody knew.* New York: Popular Library.

Lawshe, C. H., & Nagle, B. F. 1953. Productivity and attitude toward supervisor. *Journal of Applied Psychology,* 37, 159–162.

Lewis, H. S. 1974. Leaders and followers: Some anthropological perspectives. *Addison-Wesley Module in Anthropology No. 50.* Reading, Mass.: Addison-Wesley.

Lichtheim, M. 1973. *Ancient Egyptian literature, Vol. 1: The old and middle kingdoms.* Los Angeles: University of California Press.

Lieberson, S., & O'Connor, J. F. 1972. Leadership and organizational performance: A study of large corporations. *American Sociological Review,* 37, 117–130.

Lippmann, W. 1922. *Public opinion.* New York: Harcourt, Brace.

Maccoby, M. 1979. Leadership needs of the 1980's. *Current Issues in Higher Education,* 2, 17–23.

Manchester, W. 1988. Manchester on leadership. *Modern Maturity,* 31(5), 40–46, 108–111.

Mason, W. A. 1964. Sociability and social organization in monkeys and apes. In L. Berkowitz, ed., *Advances in experimental social psychology.* New York: Academic Press.

Meindl, J. R., Ehrlich, S. B., & Dukerich, J. M. 1985. The romance of leadership. *Administrative Science Quarterly,* 30, 78–102.

Meindl, J. R., & Ehrlich, S. B. 1987. The romance of leadership and the evaluation of organizational performance. *Academy of Management Journal,* 30, 90–109.

Merton, R. K. 1969. The social nature of leadership. *American Journal of Nursing,* 69, 2614–2618.

Meyer, E. C. 1980. Leadership: A return to the basics. *Military Review,* 60(7), 4–9.

Miller, J. A. 1973. *Structuring/destructuring: Leadership in open systems.* (Tech. Rep. No. 64). Rochester, N.Y.: University of Rochester, Management Research Center.

Miller, R. E., & Murphy, J. V. 1956. Social interactions of Rhesus monkeys: I. Food-getting dominance as a dependent variable. *Journal of Social Psychology,* 44, 249–255.

Miner, J. B. 1975. The uncertain future of the leadership concept: An overview. In J. G. Hunt & L. L. Larson, eds., *Leadership frontiers.* Kent, Ohio: Kent State University Press.

Mintzberg, H., & Waters, J. A. 1982. Tracking strategy in an entrepreneurial firm. *Academy of Management Journal,* 25, 465–499.

Mitchell, T. R. 1979. Organizational behavior. *Annual Review of Psychology,* 30, 243–281.

Moore, B. V. 1927. The May conference on leadership. *Personnel Journal,* 6, 124–128.

Morris, R. T., & Seeman, M. 1950. The problem of leadership: An interdisciplinary approach. *American Journal of Sociology,* 56, 149–155.

Mulligan, L., & Mulligan, G. 1981. Reconstructing restoration science: Styles of leadership and social composition of the early royal society. *Social Studies of Science,* 11, 327–364.

Murchison, C. 1935. The experimental measurement of a social hierarchy in Gallus Domesticus. *Journal of General Psychology,* 12, 3–39.

Mumford, E. 1906/1907. Origins of leadership. *American Journal of Sociology,* 12, 216–240, 367–397, 500–531.

Munson, E. L. 1921. *The management of men.* New York: Holt.

Nash, J. B. 1929. Leadership. *Phi Delta Kappan,* 12, 24–25.

Neustadt, R. E. 1960. *Presidential power.* New York: Wiley.

———. 1980. *Presidential power: The politics of leadership from FDR to Carter.* New York: Wiley.

Odier, C. 1948. Valeur et valence du chef. *Schweizerisches Archiv für Neurologische Psychiatrie,* 61, 408–410.

Osborn, R. N., Hunt, J. G., & Jauch, L. R. 1980. *Organization theory: An integrated approach.* New York: Wiley.

Oxford English Dictionary. 1933. London: Oxford University Press.

Paige, G. G. 1977. *The scientific study of political leadership.* New York: Free Press.

Pandey, J. 1976. Effects of leadership style, personality characteristics and methods of leader selection on members' leaders' behavior. *European Journal of Social Psychology,* 6, 475–489.

Pfeffer, J. 1977. The ambiguity of leadership. *Academy of Management Review,* 2, 104–112.

Phillips, T. R. 1939. Leader and led. *Journal of the Coast Artillery,* 82, 45–58.

Plutarch. 1932. *Lives of the noble Grecians and Romans.* New York: Modern Library.

Rabi, M. M. 1967. *The political theory of Ibn Khaldun.* Leiden: Brill.

Raven, B. H., & French, J. R. P. 1958a. Group support, legitimate power, and social influence. *Journal of Personality,* 26, 400–409.

———. 1958b. Legitimate power, coercive power, and observability in social influence. *Sociometry,* 21, 83–97.

Redl, F. 1942. Group emotion and leadership. *Psychiatric,* 5, 573–596.

Safire, W. 1975. *Before the fall: An inside view of the pre-Watergate White House.* New York: Doubleday.

Salancik, G. R., & Pfeffer, J. 1977. Constraints on administrative discretion: The limited influence of mayors on city budgets. *Urban Affairs Quarterly,* 12, 475–498.

Sarachek, B. 1968. Greek concepts of leadership. *Academy of Management Journal,* 11, 39–48.

Sayles, L. 1979. *Leadership: What effective managers really do . . . and how they do it.* New York: McGraw-Hill.

Schenk, C. 1928. Leadership. *Infantry Journal,* 33, 111–122.

Schriesheim, C. A., & Kerr, S. 1977. Theories and measures of leadership. In J. G. Hunt & L. L. Larson, eds., *Leadership: The cutting edge.* Carbondale: Southern Illinois University Press.

Shartel, C. L. 1951a. Leader behavior in jobs. *Occupations,* 30, 164–166.

———. 1951b. Studies in naval leadership. In H. Guetzkow, ed., *Groups, leadership, and men.* Pittsburgh, Pa.: Carnegie Press.

———. 1956. *Executive performance and leadership.* Englewood Cliffs, N.J.: Prentice-Hall.

Smith, H. L., & Krueger, L. M. 1933. *A brief summary of literature on leadership.* Bloomington: Indiana University, School of Education Bulletin.

Smith, J. E., Carson, K. P., & Alexander, R. A. 1984. Leadership: It can make a difference. *Academy of Management Journal,* 27, 765–776.

Smith, M. 1934. Personality dominance and leadership. *Sociology and Social Research,* 19, 18–25.

Smith, M. 1948. Control interaction. *Journal of Social Psychology,* 28, 263–273.

Spitzberg, I. J., Jr. 1986. *Questioning leadership.* Unpublished manuscript.

Stark, S. 1970. Toward a psychology of charisma: III. Intuitional empathy, Vorbilder, Fuehrers, transcendence-striving, and inner creation. *Psychological Reports,* 26, 683–696.

Stogdill, R. 1950. Leadership, membership and organization. *Psychological Bulletin,* 47, 1–14.

Stogdill, R. M. 1975. The evolution of leadership theory. *Proceedings of the Academy of Management.* New Orleans, 4–6.

Sylvia, D., & Hutchinson, T. 1985. What makes Ms. Johnson teach? A study of teacher motivation. *Human Relations,* 38, 841–856.

Tannenbaum, R., Weschler, I. R., & Massarik, F. 1961. *Leadership and organization.* New York: McGraw-Hill.

Tead, O. 1929. The technique of creative leadership. In human nature and management. New York: McGraw-Hill.

———. 1935. *The art of leadership.* New York: McGraw-Hill.

Truman, H. S. 1958. *Memoirs.* New York: Doubleday.

Tucker, R. C. 1981. *Politics as leadership.* Columbia: University of Missouri Press.

Virany, B., & Tushman, M. L. 1986. *Executive succession: The changing characteristics of top management teams.* Paper, Academy of Management, Chicago.

Warren, J. M., & Maroney, R. J. 1969. Competitive social interaction between monkeys. In R. B. I. Zajonc, ed., *Animal social psychology.* New York: Wiley.

Warriner, C. K. 1955. Leadership in the small group. *American Journal of Sociology,* 60, 361–369.

Weiss, W. 1958. The relationship between judgments of communicator's position and extent of opinion change. *Journal of Abnormal and Social Psychology,* 56, 380–384.

Westerlund, G. 1952. *Behavior in a work situation with functional supervision and with group leaders.* Stockholm: Nordisk Rotogravyr.

Zajonc, R. B. 1969. *Animal social psychology: A reader of experimental studies.* New York: Wiley.

What Leaders Really Do

John P. Kotter

Leadership is different from management, but not for the reasons most people think. Leadership isn't mystical and mysterious. It has nothing to do with having "charisma" or other exotic personality traits. It is not the province of a chosen few. Nor is leadership necessarily better than management or a replacement for it.

Rather, leadership and management are two distinctive and complementary systems of action. Each has its own function and characteristic activities. Both are necessary for success in an increasingly complex and volatile business environment.

Most U.S. corporations today are overmanaged and underled. They need to develop their capacity to exercise leadership. Successful corporations don't wait for leaders to come along. They actively seek out people with leadership potential and expose them to career experiences designed to develop that potential. Indeed, with careful selection, nurturing, and encouragement, dozens of people can play important leadership roles in a business organization.

But while improving their ability to lead, companies should remember that strong leadership with weak management is no better, and is sometimes actually worse, than the reverse. The real challenge is to combine strong leadership and strong management and use each to balance the other.

Of course, not everyone can be good at both leading and managing. Some people have the capacity to become excellent managers but not strong leaders. Others have great leadership potential but, for a variety of reasons, have great difficulty becoming strong managers. Smart companies value both kinds of people and work hard to make them a part of the team.

But when it comes to preparing people for executive jobs, such companies rightly ignore the recent literature that says people cannot manage *and* lead. They try to develop leader-managers. Once companies understand the fundamental difference between leadership and management, they can begin to groom their top people to provide both.

THE DIFFERENCE BETWEEN MANAGEMENT
AND LEADERSHIP

Management is about coping with complexity. Its practices and procedures are largely a response to one of the most significant developments
of the twentieth century: the emergence of large organizations. Without
good management, complex enterprises tend to become chaotic in ways
that threaten their very existence. Good management brings a degree of
order and consistency to key dimensions like the quality and profitability of
products.

Leadership, by contrast, is about coping with change. Part of the reason
it has become so important in recent years is that the business world has
become more competitive and more volatile. Faster technological change,
greater international competition, the deregulation of markets, overcapac-
ity in capital-intensive industries, an unstable oil cartel, raiders with junk
bonds, and the changing demographics of the work force are among the
many factors that have contributed to this shift. The net result is that doing
what was done yesterday, or doing it 5% better, is no longer a formula for
success. Major changes are more and more necessary to survive and compete effectively in this new environment. More change always demands
more leadership.

Consider a simple military analogy: a peacetime army can usually survive with good administration and management up and down the hierarchy, coupled with good leadership concentrated at the very top. A wartime
army, however, needs competent leadership at all levels. No one yet has figured out how to manage people effectively into battle; they must be *led*.

These different functions—coping with complexity and coping with
change—shape the characteristic activities of management and leadership.
Each system of action involves deciding what needs to be done, creating
networks of people and relationships that can accomplish an agenda, and
then trying to ensure that those people actually do the job. But each accom-
plishes these three tasks in different ways.

Companies manage complexity first by *planning and budgeting*—setting
targets or goals for the future (typically for the next month or year), establishing detailed steps for achieving those targets, and then allocating resources to accomplish those plans. By contrast, leading an organization to
constructive change begins by *setting a direction*—developing a vision of
the future (often the distant future) along with strategies for producing the
changes needed to achieve that vision.

Management develops the capacity to achieve its plan by *organizing and staffing*—creating an organizational structure and set of jobs for accomplishing plan requirements, staffing the jobs with qualified individuals, communicating the plan to those people, delegating responsibility for carrying out the plan, and devising systems to monitor implementation. The equivalent leadership activity, however, is *aligning people*. This means communicating the new direction to those who can create coalitions that understand the vision and are committed to its achievement.

Finally, management ensures plan accomplishment by *controlling and problem solving*—monitoring results versus the plan in some detail, both formally and informally, by means of reports, meetings, and other tools; identifying deviations; and then planning and organizing to solve the problems. But for leadership, achieving a vision requires *motivating and inspiring*—keeping people moving in the right direction, despite major obstacles to change, by appealing to basic but often untapped human needs, values, and emotions.

A closer examination of each of these activities will help clarify the skills leaders need.

SETTING A DIRECTION VS. PLANNING AND BUDGETING

Since the function of leadership is to produce change, setting the direction of that change is fundamental to leadership.

Setting direction is never the same as planning or even long-term planning, although people often confuse the two. Planning is a management process, deductive in nature and designed to produce orderly results, not change. Setting a direction is more inductive. Leaders gather a broad range of data and look for patterns, relationships, and linkages that help explain things. What's more, the direction-setting aspect of leadership does not produce plans; it creates vision and strategies. These describe a business, technology, or corporate culture in terms of what it should become over the long term and articulate a feasible way of achieving this goal.

Most discussions of vision have a tendency to degenerate into the mystical. The implication is that a vision is something mysterious that mere mortals, even talented ones, could never hope to have. But developing good business direction isn't magic. It is a tough, sometimes exhausting process of gathering and analyzing information. People who articulate such visions aren't magicians but broad-based strategic thinkers who are willing to take risks.

Nor do visions and strategies have to be brilliantly innovative; in fact, some of the best are not. Effective business visions regularly have an almost mundane quality, usually consisting of ideas that are already well known. The particular combination or patterning of the ideas may be new, but sometimes even that is not the case.

For example, when CEO Jan Carlzon articulated his vision to make Scandinavian Airline Systems (SAS) the best airline in the world for the frequent business traveler, he was not saying anything that everyone in the airline industry didn't already know. Business travelers fly more consistently than other market segments and are generally willing to pay higher fares. Thus, focusing on business customers offers an airline the possibility of high margins, steady business, and considerable growth. But in an industry known more for bureaucracy than vision, no company had ever put these simple ideas together and dedicated itself to implementing them. SAS did, and it worked.

What's crucial about a vision is not its originality but how well it serves the interests of important constituencies—customers, stockholders, employees—and how easily it can be translated into a realistic competitive strategy. Bad visions tend to ignore the legitimate needs and rights of important constituencies—favoring, say, employees over customers or stockholders. Or they are strategically unsound. When a company that has never been better than a weak competitor in an industry suddenly starts talking about becoming number one, that is a pipe dream, not a vision.

One of the most frequent mistakes that over-managed and underled corporations make is to embrace "long-term planning" as a panacea for their lack of direction and inability to adapt to an increasingly competitive and dynamic business environment. But such an approach misinterprets the nature of direction setting and can never work.

Long-term planning is always time consuming. Whenever something unexpected happens, plans have to be redone. In a dynamic business environment, the unexpected often becomes the norm, and long-term planning can become an extraordinarily burdensome activity. This is why most successful corporations limit the time frame of their planning activities. Indeed, some even consider "long-term planning" a contradiction in terms.

In a company without direction, even short-term planning can become a black hole capable of absorbing an infinite amount of time and energy. With no vision and strategy to provide constraints around the planning process or to guide it, every eventuality deserves a plan. Under these circumstances, contingency planning can go on forever, draining time and attention from far more essential activities, yet without ever providing the clear sense of direction that a company desperately needs. After awhile, managers inevitably become cynical about all this, and the planning process can degenerate into a highly politicized game.

Planning works best not as a substitute for direction setting but as a complement to it. A competent planning process serves as a useful reality check on direction-setting activities. Likewise, a competent direction-setting process provides a focus in which planning can then be realistically carried out. It helps clarify what kind of planning is essential and what kind is irrelevant.

ALIGNING PEOPLE VS. ORGANIZING AND STAFFING

A central feature of modern organizations is interdependence, where no one has complete autonomy, where most employees are tied to many others by their work, technology, management systems, and hierarchy. These linkages present a special challenge when organizations attempt to change. Unless many individuals line up and move together in the same direction, people will tend to fall all over one another. To executives who are overeducated in management and undereducated in leadership, the idea of getting people moving in the same direction appears to be an organizational problem. What executives need to do, however, is not organize people but align them.

Managers "organize" to create human systems that can implement plans as precisely and efficiently as possible. Typically, this requires a number of potentially complex decisions. A company must choose a structure of jobs and reporting relationships, staff it with individuals suited to the jobs, provide training for those who need it, communicate plans to the work force, and decide how much authority to delegate and to whom. Economic incentives also need to be constructed to accomplish the plan, as well as systems to monitor its implementation. These organizational judgments are much like architectural decisions. It's a question of fit within a particular context.

Aligning is different. It is more of a communications challenge than a design problem. First, aligning invariably involves talking to many more individuals than organizing does. The target population can involve not only a manager's subordinates but also bosses, peers, staff in other parts of the organization, as well as suppliers, governmental officials, or even custom-ers. Anyone who can help implement the vision and strategies or who can block implementation is relevant.

Trying to get people to comprehend a vision of an alternative future is also a communications challenge of a completely different magnitude from organizing them to fulfill a short-term plan. It's much like the difference between a football quarterback attempting to describe to his team the next two or three plays versus his trying to explain to them a totally new ap-proach to the game to be used in the second half of the season.

Whether delivered with many words or a few carefully chosen symbols, such messages are not necessarily accepted just because they are under-stood. Another big challenge in leadership efforts is credibility—getting people to believe the message. Many things contribute to credibility: the track record of the person delivering the message, the content of the mes-sage itself, the communicator's reputation for integrity and trustworthi-ness, and the consistency between words and deeds.

Finally, aligning leads to empowerment in a way that organizing rarely does. One of the reasons some organizations have difficulty adjusting to rapid changes in markets or technology is that so many people in those companies feel relatively powerless. They have learned from experience that even if they correctly perceive important external changes and then initiate appropriate actions, they are vulnerable to someone higher up who does not like what they have done. Reprimands can take many different forms: "That's against policy" or "We can't afford it" or "Shut up and do as you're told."

Alignment helps overcome this problem by empowering people in at least two ways. First, when a clear sense of direction has been commu-nicated throughout an organization, lower level employees can initiate ac-tions without the same degree of vulnerability. As long as their behavior is consistent with the vision, superiors will have more difficulty reprimand-ing them. Second, because everyone is aiming at the same target, the prob-ability is less that one person's initiative will be stalled when it comes into conflict with someone else's.

MOTIVATING PEOPLE VS. CONTROLLING AND PROBLEM SOLVING

Since change is the function of leadership, being able to generate highly en-ergized behavior is important for coping with the inevitable barriers to change. Just as direction setting identifies an appropriate path for movement and just as effective alignment gets people moving down that path, successful motivation ensures that they will have the energy to overcome obstacles.

According to the logic of management, control mechanisms compare system behavior with the plan and take action when a deviation is detected. In a well-managed factory, for example, this means the planning process establishes sensible quality targets, the organizing process builds an organization that can achieve those targets, and a control process makes sure that quality lapses are spotted immediately, not in 30 or 60 days, and corrected.

For some of the same reasons that control is so central to management, highly motivated or inspired behavior is almost irrelevant. Managerial processes must be as close as possible to fail-safe and risk-free. That means they cannot be dependent on the unusual or hard to obtain. The whole purpose of systems and structures is to help normal people who behave in normal ways to complete routine jobs successfully, day after day. It's not exciting or glamorous. But that's management.

Leadership is different. Achieving grand visions always requires an occasional burst of energy. Motivation and inspiration energize people, not by pushing them in the right direction as control mechanisms do but by satisfying basic human needs for achievement, a sense of belonging, recognition, self-esteem, a feeling of control over one's life, and the ability to live up to one's ideals. Such feelings touch us deeply and elicit a powerful response.

Good leaders motivate people in a variety of ways. First, they always articulate the organization's vision in a manner that stresses the values of the audience they are addressing. This makes the work important to those individuals. Leaders also regularly involve people in deciding how to achieve the organization's vision (or the part most relevant to a particular individual). This gives people a sense of control. Another important motivational technique is to support employee efforts to realize the vision by providing coaching, feedback, and role modeling, thereby helping people grow professionally and enhancing their self-esteem. Finally, good leaders recognize and reward success, which not only gives people a sense of accomplishment but also makes them feel like they belong to an organization that cares about them. When all this is done, the work itself becomes intrinsically motivating.

The more that change characterizes the business environment, the more that leaders must motivate people to provide leadership as well. When this works, it tends to reproduce leadership across the entire organization, with people occupying multiple leadership roles throughout the hierarchy. This is highly valuable, because coping with change in any complex business demands initiatives from a multitude of people. Nothing less will work.

Of course, leadership from many sources does not necessarily converge. To the contrary, it can easily conflict. For multiple leadership roles to work together, people's actions must be carefully coordinated by mechanisms that differ from those coordinating traditional management roles.

Strong networks of informal relationships—the kind found in companies with healthy cultures—help coordinate leadership activities in much the same way that formal structure coordinates managerial activities. The key difference is that informal networks can deal with the greater demands for coordination associated with nonroutine activities and change. The multitude of communication channels and the trust among the individuals connected by those channels allow for an ongoing process of accommodation and adaptation. When conflicts arise among roles, those same relationships help resolve the conflicts. Perhaps most important, this process of dialogue and accommodation can produce visions that are linked and compatible instead of remote and competitive. All this requires a great deal more communication than is needed to coordinate managerial roles, but unlike formal structure, strong informal networks can handle it.

Of course, informal relations of some sort exist in all corporations. But too often these networks are either very weak—some people are well connected but most are not—or they are highly fragmented—a strong network exists inside the marketing group and inside R&D but not across the two departments. Such networks do not support multiple leadership initiatives well. In fact, extensive informal networks are so important that if they do not exist, creating them has to be the focus of activity early in a major leadership initiative.

CREATING A CULTURE OF LEADERSHIP

Despite the increasing importance of leadership to business success, the on-the-job experiences of most people actually seem to undermine the development of attributes needed for leadership. Nevertheless, some companies have consistently demonstrated an ability to develop people into outstanding leader-managers. Recruiting people with leadership potential is only the first step. Equally important is managing their career patterns. Individuals who are effective in large leadership roles often share a number of career experiences.

Perhaps the most typical and most important is significant challenge early in a career. Leaders almost always have had opportunities during their twenties and thirties to actually try to lead, to take a risk, and to learn from both triumphs and failures. Such learning seems essential in developing a wide range of leadership skills and perspectives. It also teaches people something about both the difficulty of leadership and its potential for producing change.

Later in their careers, something equally important happens that has to do with broadening. People who provide effective leadership in important jobs always have a chance, before they get into those jobs, to grow beyond the narrow base that characterizes most managerial careers. This is usually the result of lateral career moves or of early promotions to unusually broad job assignments. Sometimes other vehicles help, like special task-force assignments or a lengthy general management course. Whatever the case, the breadth of knowledge developed in this way seems to be helpful in all aspects of leadership. So does the network of relationships that is often acquired both inside and outside the company. When enough people get opportunities like this, the relationships that are built also help create the strong informal networks needed to support multiple leadership initiatives.

Corporations that do a better-than-average job of developing leaders put an emphasis on creating challenging opportunities for relatively young employees. In many businesses, decentralization is the key. By definition, it pushes responsibility lower in an organization and in the process creates more challenging jobs at lower levels. Johnson & Johnson, 3M, Hewlett-Packard, General Electric, and many other well-known companies have used that approach quite successfully. Some of those same companies also create as many small units as possible so there are a lot of challenging lower-level general management jobs available.

Sometimes these businesses develop additional challenging opportunities by stressing growth through new products or services. Over the years, 3M has had a policy that at least 25% of its revenue should come from products introduced within the last five years. That encourages small new ventures, which in turn offer hundreds of opportunities to test and stretch young people with leadership potential.

Such practices can, almost by themselves, prepare people for small- and medium-sized leadership jobs. But developing people for important leadership positions requires more work on the part of senior executives, often over a long period of time. That work begins with efforts to spot people with great leadership potential early in their careers and to identify what will be needed to stretch and develop them.

Again, there is nothing magic about this process. The methods successful companies use are surprisingly straightforward. They go out of their way to make young employees and people at lower levels in their organizations visible to senior management. Senior managers then judge for themselves who has potential and what the development needs of those people are. Executives also discuss their tentative conclusions among themselves to draw more accurate judgments.

Armed with a clear sense of who has considerable leadership potential and what skills they need to develop, executives in these companies then spend time planning for that development. Sometimes that is done as part of a formal succession planning or high-potential development process; often it is more informal. In either case, the key ingredient appears to be an intelligent assessment of what feasible development opportunities fit each candidate's needs.

To encourage managers to participate in these activities, well-led businesses tend to recognize and reward people who successfully develop leaders. This is rarely done as part of a formal compensation or bonus formula, simply because it is so difficult to measure such achievements with precision. But it does become a factor in decisions about promotion, especially to the most senior levels, and that seems to make a big difference. When told that future promotions will depend to some degree on their ability to nurture leaders, even people who say that leadership cannot be developed somehow find ways to do it.

Such strategies help create a corporate culture where people value strong leadership and strive to create it. Just as we need more people to provide leadership in the complex organizations that dominate our world today, we also need more people to develop the cultures that will create that leadership. Institutionalizing a leadership-centered culture is the ultimate act of leadership.

The Manager's Job: Folklore and Fact

Henry Mintzberg

If you ask managers what they do, they will most likely tell you that they plan, organize, coordinate, and control. Then watch what they do. Don't be surprised if you can't relate what you see to these words.

When a manager is told that a factory has just burned down and then advises the caller to see whether temporary arrangements can be made to supply customers through a foreign subsidiary, is that manager planning, organizing, coordinating, or controlling? How about when he or she presents a gold watch to a retiring employee? Or attends a conference to meet people in the trade and returns with an interesting new product idea for employees to consider?

These four words, which have dominated management vocabulary since the French industrialist Henri Fayol first introduced them in 1916, tell us little about what managers actually do. At best, they indicate some vague objectives managers have when they work.

The field of management, so devoted to progress and change, has for more than half a century not seriously addressed *the* basic question: What do managers do? Without a proper answer, how can we teach management? How can we design planning or information systems for managers? How can we improve the practice of management at all?

Our ignorance of the nature of managerial work shows up in various ways in the modern organization—in boasts by successful managers who never spent a single day in a management training program; in the turnover of corporate planners who never quite understood what it was the manager wanted; in the computer consoles gathering dust in the back room because the managers never used the fancy on-line MIS some analyst thought they needed. Perhaps most important, our ignorance shows up in the inability of our large public organizations to come to grips with some of their most serious policy problems.

Somehow, in the rush to automate production, to use management science in the functional areas of marketing and finance, and to apply the skills of the behavioral scientist to the problem of worker motivation, the

33

manager—the person in charge of the organization or one of its sub-units—has been forgotten.

I intend to break the reader away from Fayol's words and introduce a more supportable and useful description of managerial work. This description derives from my review and synthesis of research on how various managers have spent their time.

In some studies, managers were observed intensively; in a number of others, they kept detailed diaries; in a few studies, their records were analyzed. All kinds of managers were studied—foremen, factory supervisors, staff managers, field sales managers, hospital administrators, presidents of companies and nations, and even street gang leaders. These "managers" worked in the United States, Canada, Sweden, and Great Britain.

A synthesis of these findings paints an interesting picture, one as different from Fayol's classical view as a cubist abstract is from a Renaissance painting. In a sense, this picture will be obvious to anyone who has ever spent a day in a manager's office, either in front of the desk or behind it. Yet, at the same time, this picture throws into doubt much of the folklore that we have accepted about the manager's work.

FOLKLORE AND FACTS ABOUT MANAGERIAL WORK

There are four myths about the manager's job that do not bear up under careful scrutiny of the facts.

Folklore: The manager is a reflective, systematic planner. The evidence on this issue is overwhelming, but not a shred of it supports this statement.

Fact: Study after study has shown that managers work at an unrelenting pace, that their activities are characterized by brevity, variety, and discontinuity, and that they are strongly oriented to action and dislike reflective activities. Consider this evidence:

Half of the activities engaged in by the five chief executives of my study lasted less than nine minutes, and only 10% exceeded one hour.[1] A study of 56 U.S. foremen found that they averaged 583 activities per eight-hour shift, an average of 1 every 48 seconds.[2] The work pace for both chief executives and foremen was unrelenting. The chief executives met a steady stream of callers and mail from the moment they arrived in the morning until they left in the evening. Coffee breaks and lunches were inevitably work related, and ever-present subordinates seemed to usurp any free moment.

A diary study of 160 British middle and top managers found that they worked without interruption for a half hour or more only about once every two days.[3]

Of the verbal contacts the chief executives in my study engaged in, 93% were arranged on an ad hoc basis. Only 1% of the executives' time was spent in open-ended observational tours. Only 1 out of 368 verbal contacts was unrelated to a specific issue and could therefore be called general planning. Another researcher found that "in *not one single case* did a manager report obtaining important external information from a general conversation or other undirected personal communication."[4]

Is this the planner that the classical view describes? Hardly. The manager is simply responding to the pressures of the job. I found that my chief executives terminated many of their own activities, often leaving meetings before the end, and interrupted their desk work to call in subordinates. One president not only placed his desk so that he could look down a long hallway but also left his door open when he was alone—an invitation for subordinates to come in and interrupt him.

Clearly, these managers wanted to encourage the flow of current information. But more significantly, they seemed to be conditioned by their own work loads. They appreciated the opportunity cost of their own time, and they were continually aware of their ever-present obligations—mail to be answered, callers to attend to, and so on. It seems that a manager is always plagued by the possibilities of what might be done and what must be done.

When managers must plan, they seem to do so implicitly in the context of daily actions, not in some abstract process reserved for two weeks in the organization's mountain retreat. The plans of the chief executives I studied seemed to exist only in their heads—as flexible, but often specific, intentions. The traditional literature notwithstanding, the job of managing does not breed reflective planners; managers respond to stimuli, they are conditioned by their jobs to prefer live to delayed action.

Folklore: The effective manager has no regular duties to perform. Managers are constantly being told to spend more time planning and delegating and less time seeing customers and engaging in negotiations. These are not, after all, the true tasks of the manager. To use the popular analogy, the good manager, like the good conductor, carefully orchestrates everything in advance, then sits back, responding occasionally to an unforeseeable exception. But here again the pleasant abstraction just does not seem to hold up.

Fact: Managerial work involves performing a number of regular duties, including ritual and ceremony, negotiations, and processing of soft information that links the organization with its environment. Consider some evidence from the research:

A study of the work of the presidents of small companies found that they engaged in routine activities because their companies could not afford staff specialists and were so thin on operating personnel that a single absence often required the president to substitute.[5]

One study of field sales managers and another of chief executives suggest that it is a natural part of both jobs to see important customers, assuming the managers wish to keep those customers.[6]

Someone, only half in jest, once described the manager as the person who sees visitors so that other people can get their work done. In my study, I found that certain ceremonial duties—meeting visiting dignitaries, giving out gold watches, presiding at Christmas dinners—were an intrinsic part of the chief executive's job.

Studies of managers' information flow suggest that managers play a key role in securing "soft" external information (much of it available only to them because of their status) and in passing it along to their subordinates.

Folklore: The senior manager needs aggregated information, which a formal management information system best provides. Not too long ago, the words *total information system* were everywhere in the management literature. In keeping with the classical view of the manager as that individual perched on the apex of a regulated, hierarchical system, the literature's manager was to receive all important information from a giant, comprehensive MIS.

But lately, these giant MIS systems are not working—managers are simply not using them. The enthusiasm has waned. A look at how managers actually process information makes it clear why.

Fact: Managers strongly favor verbal media, telephone calls and meetings, over documents. Consider the following:

In two British studies, managers spent an average of 66% and 80% of their time in verbal (oral) communication.[7] In my study of five American chief executives, the figure was 78%.

These five chief executives treated mail processing as a burden to be dispensed with. One came in Saturday morning to process 142 pieces of mail in just over three hours, to "get rid of all the stuff." This same manager looked at the first piece of "hard" mail he had received all week, a standard cost report, and put it aside with the comment, "I never look at this."

These same five chief executives responded immediately to 2 of the 40 routine reports they received during the five weeks of my study and to 4 items in the 104 periodicals. They skimmed most of these periodicals in seconds, almost ritualistically. In all, these chief executives of good-sized organizations initiated on their own—that is, not in response to something else—a grand total of 25 pieces of mail during the 25 days I observed them.

An analysis of the mail the executives received reveals an interesting picture—only 13% was of specific and immediate use. So now we have another piece in the puzzle: not much of the mail provides live, current information—the action of a competitor, the mood of a government legislator, or the rating of last night's television show. Yet this is the information that drove the managers, interrupting their meetings and rescheduling their workdays.

Consider another interesting finding. Managers seem to cherish "soft" information, especially gossip, hearsay, and speculation. Why? The reason is its timeliness; today's gossip may be tomorrow's fact. The manager who misses the telephone call revealing that the company's biggest customer was seen golfing with a main competitor may read about a dramatic drop in sales in the next quarterly report. But then it's too late.

To assess the value of historical, aggregated, "hard" MIS information, consider two of the manager's prime uses for information—to identify problems and opportunities[8] and to build mental models (e.g., how the organization's budget system works, how customers buy products, how changes in the economy affect the organization). The evidence suggests that the manager identifies decision situations and builds models not with the aggregated abstractions an MIS provides but with specific tidbits of data.

Consider the words of Richard Neustadt, who studied the information-collecting habits of Presidents Roosevelt, Truman, and Eisenhower: "It is not information of a general sort that helps a President see personal stakes; not summaries, not surveys, not the *bland amalgams*. Rather . . . it is the odds and ends of *tangible detail* that pieced together in his mind illuminate the underside of issues put before him. To help himself he must reach out as widely as he can for every scrap of fact, opinion, gossip, bearing on his interests and relationships as President. He must become his own director of his own central intelligence."[9]

The manager's emphasis on this verbal media raises two important points. First, verbal information is stored in the brains of people. Only when people write this information down can it be stored in the files of the organization—whether in metal cabinets or on magnetic tape—and managers apparently do not write down much of what they hear. Thus the strategic data bank of the organization is not in the memory of its computers but in the minds of its managers.

Second, managers' extensive use of verbal media helps to explain why they are reluctant to delegate tasks. It is not as if they can hand a dossier over to subordinates; they must take the time to "dump memory"—to tell subordinates all about the subject. But this could take so long that managers may find it easier to do the task themselves. Thus they are damned by their own information system to a "dilemma of delegation"—to do too much or to delegate to subordinates with inadequate briefing.

Folklore: Management is, or at least is quickly becoming, a science and a profession. By almost any definition of *science* and *profession,* this statement is false. Brief observation of any manager will quickly lay to rest the notion that managers practice a science. A science involves the enaction of systematic, analytically determined procedures or programs. If we do not even know what procedures managers use, how can we prescribe them by scientific analysis? And how can we call management a profession if we cannot specify what managers are to learn? For after all, a profession involves "knowledge of some department of learning or science" *(Random House Dictionary).*[10]

Fact: The managers' programs—to schedule time, process information, make decisions, and so on—remain locked deep inside their brains. Thus, to describe these programs, we rely on words like *judgment* and *intuition,* seldom stopping to realize that they are merely labels for our ignorance.

I was struck during my study by the fact that the executives I was observing—all very competent—are fundamentally indistinguishable from their counterparts of a hundred years ago (or a thousand years ago). The information they need differs, but they seek it in the same way—by word of mouth. Their decisions concern modern technology, but the procedures they use to make those decisions are the same as the procedures used by nineteenth-century managers. Even the computer, so important for the specialized work of the organization, has apparently had no influence on the work procedures of general managers. In fact, the manager is in a kind of loop, with increasingly heavy work pressures but no aid forthcoming from management science.

Considering the facts about managerial work, we can see that the manager's job is enormously complicated and difficult. Managers are overburdened with obligations yet cannot easily delegate their tasks. As a result, they are driven to overwork and forced to do many tasks superficially. Brevity, fragmentation, and verbal communication characterize their work.

Yet these are the very characteristics of managerial work that have impeded scientific attempts to improve it. As a result, management scientists have concentrated on the specialized functions of the organization, where it is easier to analyze the procedures and quantify the relevant information.[11]

But the pressures of a manager's job are becoming worse. Where before managers needed to respond only to owners and directors, now they find that subordinates with democratic norms continually reduce their freedom to issue unexplained orders, and a growing number of outside influences (consumer groups, government agencies, and so on) demand attention. Managers have had nowhere to turn for help. The first step in providing such help is to find out what the manager's job really is.

BACK TO A BASIC DESCRIPTION OF MANAGERIAL WORK

Earlier, I defined the manager as that person in charge of an organization or subunit. Besides CEOs, this definition would include vice presidents, bishops, foremen, hockey coaches, and prime ministers. All these "managers" are vested with formal authority over an organizational unit. From formal authority comes status, which leads to various interpersonal relations, and from these comes access to information. Information, in turn, enables the manager to make decisions and strategies for the unit.

THE MANAGER'S ROLES

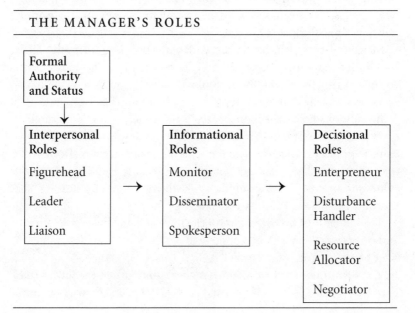

The manager's job can be described in terms of various "roles," or organized sets of behaviors identified with a position. My description, shown in "The Manager's Roles," comprises ten roles. As we shall see, formal authority gives rise to the three interpersonal roles, which in turn give rise to the three informational roles; these two sets of roles enable the manager to play the four decisional roles.

INTERPERSONAL ROLES

Three of the manager's roles arise directly from formal authority and involve basic interpersonal relationships. First is the *figurehead* role. As the head of an organizational unit, every manager must perform some ceremonial duties. The president greets the touring dignitaries. The foreman attends the wedding of a lathe operator. The sales manager takes an important customer to lunch.

The chief executives of my study spent 12% of their contact time on ceremonial duties; 17% of their incoming mail dealt with acknowledgments and requests related to their status. For example, a letter to a company president requested free merchandise for a crippled schoolchild; diplomas that needed to be signed were put on the desk of the school superintendent.

Duties that involve interpersonal roles may sometimes be routine, involving little serious communication and no important decision making. Nevertheless, they are important to the smooth functioning of an organization and cannot be ignored.

Managers are responsible for the work of the people of their unit. Their actions in this regard constitute the *leader* role. Some of these actions involve leadership directly—for example, in most organizations the managers are normally responsible for hiring and training their own staff.

In addition, there is the indirect exercise of the leader role. For example, every manager must motivate and encourage employees, somehow reconciling their individual needs with the goals of the organization. In virtually every contact with the manager, subordinates seeking leadership clues ask: "Does she approve?" "How would she like the report to turn out?" "Is she more interested in market share than high profits?"

The influence of managers is most clearly seen in the leader role. Formal authority vests them with great potential power; leadership determines in large part how much of it they will realize.

The literature of management has always recognized the leader role, particularly those aspects of it related to motivation. In comparison, until recently it has hardly mentioned the *liaison* role, in which the manager makes contacts outside the vertical chain of command. This is remarkable in light of the finding of virtually every study of managerial work that managers spend as much time with peers and other people outside their units as they do with their own subordinates—and, surprisingly, very little time with their own superiors.

In Rosemary Stewart's diary study, the 160 British middle and top managers spent 47% of their time with peers, 41% of their time with people inside their unit, and only 12% of their time with their superiors. For Robert H. Guest's study of U.S. foremen, the figures were 44%, 46%, and 10%. The chief executives of my study averaged 44% of their contact time with people outside their organizations, 48% with subordinates, and 7% with directors and trustees.

The contacts the five CEOs made were with an incredibly wide range of people: subordinates; clients, business associates, and suppliers; and peers—managers of similar organizations, government and trade organization officials, fellow directors on outside boards, and independents with no relevant organizational affiliations. Guest's study of foremen shows, likewise, that their contacts were numerous and wide-ranging, seldom involving fewer than 25 individuals, and often more than 50.

INFORMATIONAL ROLES

By virtue of interpersonal contacts, both with subordinates and with a network of contacts, the manager emerges as the nerve center of the organi-

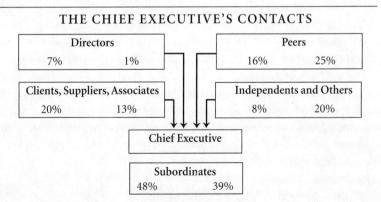

THE CHIEF EXECUTIVE'S CONTACTS

Directors		Peers	
7%	1%	16%	25%

Clients, Suppliers, Associates		Independents and Others	
20%	13%	8%	20%

Chief Executive

Subordinates	
48%	39%

Note: The first figure indicates the proportion of total contact time spent with each group and the second figure, the proportion of mail from each group.

zational unit. The manager may not know everything but typically knows more than subordinates do.

Studies have shown this relationship to hold for all managers, from street gang leaders to U.S. presidents. In *The Human Group,* George C. Homans explains how, because they were at the center of the information flow in their own gangs and were also in close touch with other gang leaders, street gang leaders were better informed than any of their followers.[12] As for presidents, Richard Neustadt observes: "The essence of [Franklin] Roosevelt's technique for information-gathering was competition. 'He would call you in,' one of his aides once told me, 'and he'd ask you to get the story on some complicated business, and you'd come back after a couple of days of hard labor and present the juicy morsel you'd uncovered under a stone somewhere, and *then* you'd find out he knew all about it, along with something else you *didn't* know. Where he got this information from he wouldn't mention, usually, but after he had done this to you once or twice you got damn careful about your information.'"[13]

We can see where Roosevelt "got this information" when we consider the relationship between the interpersonal and informational roles. As leader, the manager has formal and easy access to every staff member. In addition, liaison contacts expose the manager to external information to which subordinates often lack access. Many of these contacts are with other managers of equal status, who are themselves nerve centers in their own organization. In this way, the manager develops a powerful database of information.

Processing information is a key part of the manager's job. In my study, the CEOs spent 40% of their contact time on activities devoted exclusively to the transmission of information; 70% of their incoming mail was purely informational (as opposed to requests for action). Managers don't leave meetings or hang up the telephone to get back to work. In large part, communication *is* their work. Three roles describe these informational aspects of managerial work.

As *monitor,* the manager is perpetually scanning the environment for information, interrogating liaison contacts and subordinates, and receiving unsolicited information, much of it as a result of the network of personal contacts. Remember that a good part of the information the manager collects in the monitor role arrives in verbal form, often as gossip, hearsay, and speculation.

In the *disseminator* role, the manager passes some privileged information directly to subordinates, who would otherwise have no access to it.

When subordinates lack easy contact with one another, the manager may pass information from one to another.

In the *spokesperson* role, the manager sends some information to people outside the unit—a president makes a speech to lobby for an organization cause, or a foreman suggests a product modification to a supplier. In addition, as a spokesperson, every manager must inform and satisfy the influential people who control the organizational unit. For the foreman, this may simply involve keeping the plant manager informed about the flow of work through the shop.

The president of a large corporation, however, may spend a great amount of time dealing with a host of influences. Directors and shareholders must be advised about finances; consumer groups must be assured that the organization is fulfilling its social responsibilities; and government officials must be satisfied that the organization is abiding by the law.

DECISIONAL ROLES

Information is not, of course, an end in itself; it is the basic input to decision making. One thing is clear in the study of managerial work: the manager plays the major role in the unit's decision-making system. As its formal authority, only the manager can commit the unit to important new courses of action; and as its nerve center, only the manager has full and current information to make the set of decisions that determines the unit's strategy. Four roles describe the manager as decision maker.

As *entrepreneur,* the manager seeks to improve the unit, to adapt it to changing conditions in the environment. In the monitor role, a president is constantly on the lookout for new ideas. When a good one appears, he initiates a development project that he may supervise himself or delegate to an employee (perhaps with the stipulation that he must approve the final proposal).

There are two interesting features about these development projects at the CEO level. First, these projects do not involve single decisions or even unified clusters of decisions. Rather, they emerge as a series of small decisions and actions sequenced over time. Apparently, chief executives prolong each project both to fit it into a busy, disjointed schedule, and so that they can comprehend complex issues gradually.

Second, the chief executives I studied supervised as many as 50 of these projects at the same time. Some projects entailed new products or processes; others involved public relations campaigns, improvement of the cash position, reorganization of a weak department, resolution of a morale problem in a foreign division, integration of computer operations, various acquisitions at different stages of development, and so on.

Chief executives appear to maintain a kind of inventory of the development projects in various stages of development. Like jugglers, they keep a number of projects in the air; periodically, one comes down, is given a new burst of energy, and sent back into orbit. At various intervals, they put new projects on-stream and discard old ones.

While the entrepreneur role describes the manager as the voluntary initiator of change, the *disturbance handler* role depicts the manager involuntarily responding to pressures. Here change is beyond the manager's control. The pressures of a situation are too severe to be ignored—a strike looms, a major customer has gone bankrupt, or a supplier reneges on a contract—so the manager must act.

Leonard R. Sayles, who has carried out appropriate research on the manager's job, likens the manager to a symphony orchestra conductor who must "maintain a melodious performance,"[14] while handling musicians' problems and other external disturbances. Indeed, every manager must spend a considerable amount of time responding to high-pressure disturbances. No organization can be so well run, so standardized, that it has considered every contingency in the uncertain environment in advance. Disturbances arise not only because poor managers ignore situations until they reach crisis proportions but also because good managers cannot possibly anticipate all the consequences of the actions they take.

The third decisional role is that of *resource allocator*. The manager is responsible for deciding who will get what. Perhaps the most important resource the manager allocates is his or her own time. Access to the manager constitutes exposure to the unit's nerve center and decision maker. The manager is also charged with designing the unit's structure, that pattern of formal relationships that determines how work is to be divided and coordinated.

Also, as resource allocator, the manager authorizes the important decisions of the unit before they are implemented. By retaining this power, the manager can ensure that decisions are interrelated. To fragment this power encourages discontinuous decision making and a disjointed strategy.

There are a number of interesting features about the manager's authorization of others' decisions. First, despite the widespread use of capital budgeting procedures—a means of authorizing various capital expenditures at one time—executives in my study made a great many authorization decisions on an ad hoc basis. Apparently, many projects cannot wait or simply do not have the quantifiable costs and benefits that capital budgeting requires.

Second, I found that the chief executives faced incredibly complex choices. They had to consider the impact of each decision on other decisions and on the organization's strategy. They had to ensure that the decision would be acceptable to those who influence the organization, as well as ensure that resources would not be overextended. They had to understand the various costs and benefits as well as the feasibility of the proposal. They also had to consider questions of timing. All this was necessary for the simple approval of someone else's proposal. At the same time, however, the delay could lose time, while quick approval could be ill-considered and quick rejection might discourage the subordinate who had spent months developing a pet project.

One common solution to approving projects is to pick the person instead of the proposal. That is, the manager authorizes those projects presented by people whose judgment he or she trusts. But the manager cannot always use this simple dodge.

The final decisional role is that of *negotiator*. Managers spend considerable time in negotiations: the president of the football team works out a contract with the holdout superstar; the corporation president leads the company's contingent to negotiate a new strike issue; the foreman argues a grievance problem to its conclusion with the shop steward.

These negotiations are an integral part of the manager's job, for only he or she has the authority to commit organizational resources in "real time" and the nerve-center information that important negotiations require.

THE INTEGRATED JOB

It should be clear by now that these ten roles are not easily separable. In the terminology of the psychologist, they form a gestalt, an integrated whole. No role can be pulled out of the framework and the job be left intact. For example, a manager without liaison contacts lacks external information. As a result, that manager can neither disseminate the information that employees need nor make decisions that adequately reflect external conditions. (This is a problem for the new person in a managerial position, since he or she has to build up a network of contacts before making effective decisions.)

Here lies a clue to the problems of team management.[15] Two or three people cannot share a single managerial position unless they can act as one entity. This means that they cannot divide up the ten roles unless they can very carefully reintegrate them. The real difficulty lies with the informational roles. Unless there can be full sharing of managerial information—and, as I pointed out earlier, it is primarily verbal—team management breaks down. A single managerial job cannot be arbitrarily split, for example, into internal and external roles, for information from both sources must be brought to bear on the same decisions.

To say that the ten roles form a gestalt is not to say that all managers give equal attention to each role. In fact, I found in my review of the various research studies that sales managers seem to spend relatively more of their time in the interpersonal roles, presumably a reflection of the extrovert nature of the marketing activity. Production managers, on the other hand, give relatively more attention to the decisional roles, presumably a reflection of their concern with efficient work flow. And staff managers spend the most time in the informational roles, since they are experts who manage departments that advise other parts of the organization. Nevertheless, in all cases, the interpersonal, informational, and decisional roles remain inseparable.

TOWARD MORE EFFECTIVE MANAGEMENT

This description of managerial work should prove more important to managers than any prescription they might derive from it. That is to say, *the managers' effectiveness is significantly influenced by their insight into their own work.* Performance depends on how well a manager understands and responds to the pressures and dilemmas of the job. Thus managers who can be introspective about their work are likely to be effective at their jobs.

Let us take a look at three specific areas of concern. For the most part, the managerial logjams—the dilemma of delegation, the database centralized in one brain, the problems of working with the management scientist—revolve around the verbal nature of the manager's information. There are great dangers in centralizing the organization's data bank in the minds of its managers. When they leave, they take their memory with them. And when subordinates are out of convenient verbal reach of the manager, they are at an informational disadvantage.

The manager is challenged to find systematic ways to share privileged information. A regular debriefing session with key subordinates, a weekly memory dump on the dictating machine, maintaining a diary for limited circulation, or other similar methods may ease the logjam of work considerably. The time spent disseminating this information will be more than regained when decisions must be made. Of course, some will undoubtedly raise the question of confidentiality. But managers would be well advised to weigh the risks of exposing privileged information against having subordinates who can make effective decisions.

If there is a single theme that runs through this article, it is that the pressures of the job drive the manager to take on too much work, encourage interruption, respond quickly to every stimulus, seek the tangible and avoid the abstract, make decisions in small increments, and do everything abruptly.

Here again, the manager is challenged to deal consciously with the pressures of superficiality by giving serious attention to the issues that require it, by stepping back in order to see a broad picture, and by making use of analytical inputs. Although effective managers have to be adept at responding quickly to numerous and varying problems, the danger in managerial work is that they will respond to every issue equally (and that means abruptly) and that they will never work the tangible bits and pieces of information into a comprehensive picture of their world.

To create this comprehensive picture, managers can supplement their own models with those of specialists. Economists describe the functioning of markets, operations researchers simulate financial flow processes, and behavioral scientists explain the needs and goals of people. The best of these models can be searched out and learned.

In dealing with complex issues, the senior manager has much to gain from a close relationship with the organization's own management scientists. They have something important that the manager lacks—time to probe complex issues. An effective working relationship hinges on the resolution of what a colleague and I have called "the planning dilemma."[16] Managers have the information and the authority; analysts have the time and the technology. A successful working relationship between the two will be effected when the manager learns to share information and the analyst learns to adapt to the manager's needs. For the analyst, adaptation means worrying less about the elegance of the method and more about its speed and flexibility.

Analysts can help the top manager schedule time, feed in analytical information, monitor projects, develop models to aid in making choices, design contingency plans for disturbances that can be anticipated, and conduct "quick and dirty" analyses for those that cannot. But there can be no cooperation if the analysts are out of the mainstream of the manager's information flow.

The manager is challenged to gain control of his or her own time by turning obligations into advantages and by turning those things he or she wishes to do into obligations. The chief executives of my study initiated only 32% of their own contacts (and another 5% by mutual agreement). And yet to a considerable extent they seemed to control their time. There were two key factors that enabled them to do so.

First, managers have to spend so much time discharging obligations that if they were to view them as just that, they would leave no mark on the organization. Unsuccessful managers blame failure on the obligations. Effective managers turn obligations to advantages. A speech is a chance to lobby for a cause; a meeting is a chance to reorganize a weak department; a visit to an important customer is a chance to extract trade information.

Second, the manager frees some time to do the things that he or she—perhaps no one else—thinks important by turning them into obligations. Free time is made, not found. Hoping to leave some time open for contemplation or general planning is tantamount to hoping that the pressures of the job will go away. Managers who want to innovate initiate projects and obligate others to report back to them. Managers who need certain environmental information establish channels that will automatically keep them informed. Managers who have to tour facilities commit themselves publicly.

THE EDUCATOR'S JOB

Finally, a word about the training of managers. Our management schools have done an admirable job of training the organization's specialists—management scientists, marketing researchers, accountants, and organizational development specialists. But for the most part, they have not trained managers.[17]

Management schools will begin the serious training of managers when skill training takes a serious place next to cognitive learning. Cognitive learning is detached and informational, like reading a book or listening to a lecture. No doubt much important cognitive material must be assimilated by the manager-to-be. But cognitive learning no more makes a manager than it does a swimmer. The latter will drown the first time she jumps into the water if her coach never takes her out of the lecture hall, gets her wet, and gives her feedback on her performance.

In other words, we are taught a skill through practice plus feedback, whether in a real or a simulated situation. Our management schools need to identify the skills managers use, select students who show potential in these skills, put the students into situations where these skills can be practiced and developed, and then give them systematic feedback on their performance.

My description of managerial work suggests a number of important managerial skills—developing peer relationships, carrying out negotiations, motivating subordinates, resolving conflicts, establishing information networks and subsequently disseminating information, making decisions in conditions of extreme ambiguity, and allocating resources. Above all, the manager needs to be introspective in order to continue to learn on the job.

No job is more vital to our society than that of the manager. The manager determines whether our social institutions will serve us well or whether they will squander our talents and resources. It is time to strip away the folklore about managerial work and study it realistically so that we can begin the difficult task of making significant improvements in its performance.

REFERENCES

1. All the data from my study can be found in Henry Mintzberg, *The Nature of Managerial Work* (New York: Harper & Row, 1973).
2. Robert H. Guest, "Of Time and the Foreman," *Personnel*, May 1956, p. 478.
3. Rosemary Stewart, *Managers and Their Jobs* (London: Macmillan, 1967); see also Sune Carlson, *Executive Behaviour* (Stockholm: Strombergs, 1951).
4. Francis J. Aguilar, *Scanning the Business Environment* (New York: Macmillan, 1967), p. 102.
5. Unpublished study by Irving Choran, reported in Mintzberg, *The Nature of Managerial Work*.
6. Robert T. Davis, *Performance and Development of Field Sales Managers* (Boston: Division of Research, Harvard Business School, 1957); George H. Copeman, *The Role of the Managing Director* (London: Business Publications, 1963).
7. Stewart, *Managers and Their Jobs*; Tom Burns, "The Directions of Activity and Communication in a Departmental Executive Group," *Human Relations* 7, no. 1 (1954): 73.
8. H. Edward Wrapp, "Good Managers Don't Make Policy Decisions," *HBR* September–October 1967, p. 91. Wrapp refers to this as spotting opportunities and relationships in the stream of operating problems and decisions; in his article, Wrapp raises a number of excellent points related to this analysis.

9. Richard E. Neustadt, *Presidential Power* (New York: John Wiley, 1960), pp. 153–154; italics added.

10. For a more thorough, though rather different, discussion of this issue, see Kenneth R. Andrews, "Toward Professionalism in Business Management," *HBR* March–April 1969, p. 49.

11. C. Jackson Grayson, Jr., in "Management Science and Business Practice," *HBR* July-August 1973, p. 41, explains in similar terms why, as chairman of the Price Commission, he did not use those very techniques that he himself promoted in his earlier career as a management scientist.

12. George C. Homans, *The Human Group* (New York: Harcourt, Brace & World, 1950), based on the study by William F. Whyte entitled *Street Corner Society*, rev. ed. (Chicago: University of Chicago Press, 1995).

13. Neustadt, *Presidential Power*, p. 157.

14. Leonard R. Sayles, *Managerial Behavior* (New York: McGraw-Hill, 1964), p. 162.

15. See Richard C. Hodgson, Daniel J. Levinson, and Abraham Zaleznik, *The Executive Role Constellation* (Boston, Division of Research, Harvard Business School, 1965), for a discussion of the sharing of roles.

16. James S. Hekimian and Henry Mintzberg, "The Planning Dilemma," *The Management Review*, May 1968, p. 4.

17. See J. Sterling Livingston, "Myth of the Well-Educated Manager," *HBR* January–February 1971, p. 79.

Crucibles of Leadership

Warren G. Bennis and Robert J. Thomas

As lifelong students of leadership, we are fascinated with the notion of what makes a leader. Why is it that certain people seem to naturally inspire confidence, loyalty, and hard work, while others (who may have just as much vision and smarts) stumble, again and again? It's a timeless question, and there's no simple answer. But we have come to believe it has something to do with the different ways that people deal with adversity. Indeed, our recent research has led us to conclude that one of the most reliable indicators and predictors of true leadership is an individual's ability to find meaning in negative events and to learn from even the most trying circumstances. Put another way, the skills required to conquer adversity and emerge stronger and more committed than ever are the same ones that make for extraordinary leaders.

Take Sidney Harman. Thirty-four years ago, the then-48-year-old businessman was holding down two executive positions. He was the chief executive of Harman Kardon (now Harman International), the audio components company he had co-founded, and he was serving as president of Friends World College, now Friends World Program, an experimental Quaker school on Long Island whose essential philosophy is that students, not their teachers, are responsible for their education. Juggling the two jobs, Harman was living what he calls a "bifurcated life," changing clothes in his car and eating lunch as he drove between Harman Kardon offices and plants and the Friends World campus. One day while at the college, he was told his company's factory in Bolivar, Tennessee, was having a crisis.

He immediately rushed to the Bolivar factory, a facility that was, as Harman now recalls, "raw, ugly, and, in many ways, demeaning." The problem, he found, had erupted in the polish and buff department, where a crew of a dozen workers, mostly African-Americans, did the dull, hard work of polishing mirrors and other parts, often under unhealthy conditions. The men on the night shift were supposed to get a coffee break at 10 PM. When the buzzer that announced the workers' break went on the fritz, management arbitrarily decided to postpone the break for ten minutes, when another buzzer was scheduled to sound. But one worker, "an old black man with an almost biblical name, Noah B. Cross," had "an epiphany," as Harman describes it. "He said, literally, to his fellow workers, 'I don't work for no buzzer. The buzzer works for me. It's my job to tell me when it's ten o'clock. I got me a watch. I'm not waiting another ten minutes. I'm going on my coffee break.' And all 12 guys took their coffee break, and, of course, all hell broke loose."

The worker's principled rebellion—his refusal to be cowed by management's senseless rule—was, in turn, a revelation to Harman: "The technology is there to serve the men, not the reverse," he remembers realizing. "I suddenly had this awakening that everything I was doing at the college had appropriate applications in business." In the ensuing years, Harman revamped the factory and its workings, turning it into a kind of campus—offering classes on the premises, including piano lessons, and encouraging the workers to take most of the responsibility for running their workplace. Further, he created an environment where dissent was not only tolerated but also encouraged. The plant's lively independent newspaper, the *Bolivar Mirror*, gave workers a creative and emotional outlet—and they enthusiastically skewered Harman in its pages.

Harman had, unexpectedly, become a pioneer of participative management, a movement that continues to influence the shape of workplaces around the world. The concept wasn't a grand idea conceived in the CEO's office and imposed on the plant, Harman says. It grew organically out of his going down to Bolivar to, in his words, "put out this fire." Harman's transformation was, above all, a creative one. He had connected two seemingly unrelated ideas and created a radically different approach to management that recognized both the economic and humane benefits of a more collegial workplace. Harman went on to accomplish far more during his career. In addition to founding Harman International, he served as the deputy secretary of commerce under Jimmy Carter. But he always looked back on the incident in Bolivar as the formative event in his professional life, the moment he came into his own as a leader.

The details of Harman's story are unique, but their significance is not. In interviewing more than 40 top leaders in business and the public sector over the past three years, we were surprised to find that all of them—young and old—were able to point to intense, often traumatic, always unplanned experiences that had transformed them and had become the sources of their distinctive leadership abilities.

We came to call the experiences that shape leaders "crucibles," after the vessels medieval alchemists used in their attempts to turn base metals into gold. For the leaders we interviewed, the crucible experience was a trial and a test, a point of deep self-reflection that forced them to question who they were and what mattered to them. It required them to examine their values, question their assumptions, hone their judgment. And, invariably, they emerged from the crucible stronger and more sure of themselves and their purpose—changed in some fundamental way.

Leadership crucibles can take many forms. Some are violent, life-threatening events. Others are more prosaic episodes of self-doubt. But whatever the crucible's nature, the people we spoke with were able, like Harman, to create a narrative around it, a story of how they were challenged, met the challenge, and became better leaders. As we studied these stories, we found that they not only told us how individual leaders are shaped but also pointed to some characteristics that seem common to all leaders—characteristics that were formed, or at least exposed, in the crucible.

LEARNING FROM DIFFERENCE

A crucible is, by definition, a transformative experience through which an individual comes to a new or an altered sense of identity. It is perhaps not surprising then that one of the most common types of crucibles we documented involves the experience of prejudice. Being a victim of prejudice is particularly traumatic because it forces an individual to confront a distorted picture of him- or herself, and it often unleashes profound feelings of anger, bewilderment, and even withdrawal. For all its trauma, however, the experience of prejudice is for some a clarifying event. Through it, they gain a clearer vision of who they are, the role they play, and their place in the world.

Consider, for example, Liz Altman, now a Motorola vice president, who was transformed by the year she spent at a Sony camcorder factory in rural Japan, where she faced both estrangement and sexism. It was, says Altman, "by far, the hardest thing I've ever done." The foreign culture—particularly its emphasis on groups over individuals—was both a shock and a challenge to a young American woman. It wasn't just that she felt lonely in an alien world. She had to face the daunting prospect of carving out a place for herself as the only woman engineer in a plant, and nation, where women usually serve as low-level assistants and clerks known as "office ladies."

Another woman who had come to Japan under similar circumstances had warned Altman that the only way to win the men's respect was to avoid

becoming allied with the office ladies. But on her very first morning, when
the bell rang for a coffee break, the men headed in one direction and the
women in another—and the women saved her a place at their table, while
the men ignored her. Instinct told Altman to ignore the warning rather
than insult the women by rebuffing their invitation.

Over the next few days, she continued to join the women during breaks,
a choice that gave her a comfortable haven from which to observe the unfamiliar office culture. But it didn't take her long to notice that some of the
men spent the break at their desks reading magazines, and Altman determined that she could do the same on occasion. Finally, after paying close
attention to the conversations around her, she learned that several of the
men were interested in mountain biking. Because Altman wanted to buy a
mountain bike, she approached them for advice. Thus, over time, she established herself as something of a free agent, sometimes sitting with the
women and other times engaging with the men.

And as it happened, one of the women she'd sat with on her very first day,
the department secretary, was married to one of the engineers. The secretary took it upon herself to include Altman in social gatherings, a turn of
events that probably wouldn't have occurred if Altman had alienated her female coworkers on that first day. "Had I just gone to try and break in with
[the men] and not had her as an ally, it would never had happened," she says.

Looking back, Altman believes the experience greatly helped her gain a
clearer sense of her personal strengths and capabilities, preparing her for
other difficult situations. Her tenure in Japan taught her to observe closely
and to avoid jumping to conclusions based on cultural assumptions—invaluable skills in her current position at Motorola, where she leads efforts
to smooth alliances with other corporate cultures, including those of Motorola's different regional operations.

Altman has come to believe that she wouldn't have been as able to do the
Motorola job if she hadn't lived in a foreign country and experienced the
dissonance of cultures: ". . . even if you're sitting in the same room, ostensibly agreeing . . . unless you understand the frame of reference, you're probably missing a bunch of what's going on." Altman also credits her crucible
with building her confidence—she feels that she can cope with just about
anything that comes her way.

People can feel the stigma of cultural differences much closer to home,
as well. Muriel ("Mickie") Siebert, the first woman to own a seat on the
New York Stock Exchange, found her crucible on the Wall Street of the
1950s and 1960s, an arena so sexist that she couldn't get a job as a stockbro-
ker until she took her first name off her resumé and substituted a gender-

less initial. Other than the secretaries and the occasional analyst, women were few and far between. That she was Jewish was another strike against her at a time, she points out, when most of big business was "not nice" to either women or Jews. But Siebert wasn't broken or defeated. Instead she emerged stronger, more focused, and more determined to change the status quo that excluded her.

When we interviewed Siebert, she described her way of addressing anti-Semitism—a technique that quieted the offensive comments of her peers without destroying the relationships she needed to do her job effectively. According to Siebert, at the time it was part of doing business to have a few drinks at lunch. She remembers, "Give somebody a couple of drinks, and they would talk about the Jews." She had a greeting card she used for those occasions that went like this:

> Roses are reddish,
> Violets are bluish,
> In case you don't know,
> I am Jewish.

Siebert would have the card hand-delivered to the person who had made the anti-Semitic remarks, and on the card she had written, "Enjoyed lunch." As she recounts, "They got that card in the afternoon, and I never had to take any of that nonsense again. And I never embarrassed anyone, either." It was because she was unable to get credit for the business she was bringing in at any of the large Wall Street firms that she bought a seat on the New York Stock Exchange and started working for herself.

In subsequent years, she went on to found Muriel Siebert & Company (now Siebert Financial Corporation) and has dedicated herself to helping other people avoid some of the difficulties she faced as a young professional. A prominent advocate for women in business and a leader in developing financial products directed at women, she's also devoted to educating children about financial opportunities and responsibility.

We didn't interview lawyer and presidential adviser Vernon Jordan for this book, but he, too, offers a powerful reminder of how prejudice can prove transformational rather than debilitating. In *Vernon Can Read! A Memoir* (Public Affairs, 2001), Jordan describes the vicious baiting he was subjected to as a young man. The man who treated him in this offensive way was his employer, Robert Maddox. Jordan served the racist former mayor of Atlanta at dinner, in a white jacket, with a napkin over his arm. He also functioned as Maddox's chauffeur. Whenever Maddox could, he would derisively announce, "Vernon can read!" as if the literacy of a young African-American were a source of wonderment.

Subjected to this type of abuse, a lesser man might have allowed Maddox to destroy him. But in his memoir, Jordan gives his own interpretation of Maddox's sadistic heckling, a tale that empowered Jordan instead of embittering him. When he looked at Maddox through the rearview mirror, Jordan did not see a powerful member of Georgia's ruling class. He saw a desperate anachronism, a person who lashed out because he knew his time was up. As Jordan writes about Maddox, "His half-mocking, half-serious comments about my education were the death rattle of his culture. When he saw that I was . . . crafting a life for myself that would make me a man in . . . ways he thought of as being a man, he was deeply unnerved."

Maddox's cruelty was the crucible that, consciously or not, Jordan imbued with redemptive meaning. Instead of lashing out or being paralyzed with hatred, Jordan saw the fall of the Old South and imagined his own future freed of the historical shackles of racism. His ability to organize meaning around a potential crisis turned it into the crucible around which his leadership was forged.

PREVAILING OVER DARKNESS

Some crucible experiences illuminate a hidden and suppressed area of the soul. These are often among the harshest of crucibles, involving, for instance, episodes of illness or violence. In the case of Sidney Rittenberg, now 79, the crucible took the form of 16 years of unjust imprisonment, in solitary confinement, in Communist China. In 1949 Rittenberg was initially jailed, without explanation, by former friends in Chairman Mao Zedong's government and spent his first year in total darkness when he wasn't being interrogated. (Rittenberg later learned that his arrest came at the behest of Communist Party officials in Moscow, who had wrongly identified him as a CIA agent.) Thrown into jail, confined to a tiny, pitch-dark cell, Rittenberg did not rail or panic. Instead, within minutes, he remembered a stanza of verse, four lines recited to him when he was a small child:

> They drew a circle that shut me out,
> Heretic, rebel, a thing to flout.
> But love and I had the wit to win,
> We drew a circle that took them in!

That bit of verse (adapted from "Outwitted," a poem by Edwin Markham) was the key to Rittenberg's survival. "My God," he thought, "there's my strategy." He drew the prison guards into his circle, developing relationships that would help him adapt to his confinement. Fluent in Chinese, he persuaded the guards to deliver him books and, eventually, provide a candle so that he could read. He also decided, after his first year, to devote himself to improving his mind—making it more scientific, more pure, and more dedicated to socialism. He believed that if he raised his consciousness, his captors would understand him better. And when, over time, the years in the dark began to take an intellectual toll on him and he found his reason faltering, he could still summon fairy tales and childhood stories such as *The Little Engine That Could* and take comfort from their simple messages.

By contrast, many of Rittenberg's fellow prisoners either lashed out in anger or withdrew. "They tended to go up the wall. . . . They couldn't make it. And I think the reason was that they didn't understand . . . that happiness . . . is not a function of your circumstances; it's a function of your outlook on life."

Rittenberg's commitment to his ideals continued upon his release. His cell door opened suddenly in 1955, after his first six-year term in prison. He recounts, "Here was a representative of the central government telling me that I had been wronged, that the government was making a formal apology to me . . . and that they would do everything possible to make restitution." When his captors offered him money to start a new life in the United States or to travel in Europe, Rittenberg declined, choosing instead to stay in China and continue his work for the Communist Party.

And even after a second arrest, which put him in solitary confinement for ten years as retaliation for his support of open democracy during the Cultural Revolution, Rittenberg did not allow his spirit to be broken. Instead, he used his time in prison as an opportunity to question his belief system—in particular, his commitment to Marxism and Chairman Mao. "In that sense, prison emancipated me," he says.

Rittenberg studied, read, wrote, and thought, and he learned something about himself in the process: "I realized I had this great fear of being a turncoat, which . . . was so powerful that it prevented me from even looking at [my assumptions]. . . . Even to question was an act of betrayal. After I got out . . . the scales fell away from my eyes and I understood that . . . the basic doctrine of arriving at democracy through dictatorship was wrong."

What's more, Rittenberg emerged from prison certain that absolutely nothing in his professional life could break him and went on to start a company with his wife. Rittenberg Associates is a consulting firm dedicated to developing business ties between the United States and China. Today, Rittenberg is as commited to his ideals—if not to his view of the best way to get there—as he was 50 years ago, when he was so severely tested.

MEETING GREAT EXPECTATIONS

Fortunately, not all crucible experiences are traumatic. In fact, they can involve a positive, if deeply challenging, experience such as having a demanding boss or mentor. Judge Nathaniel R. Jones of the U.S. Court of Appeals for the Sixth Circuit, for instance, attributes much of his success to his interaction with a splendid mentor. That mentor was J. Maynard Dickerson, a successful attorney—and editor of a local African-American newspaper.

Dickerson influenced Jones at many levels. For instance, the older man brought Jones behind the scenes to witness firsthand the great civil rights struggle of the 1950s, inviting him to sit in on conversations with activists like Thurgood Marshall, Walter White, Roy Wilkins, and Robert C. Weaver. Says Jones, "I was struck by their resolve, their humor . . . and their determination not to let the system define them. Rather than just feel beaten down, they turned it around." The experience no doubt influenced the many important opinions Judge Jones has written in regard to civil rights.

Dickerson was both model and coach. His lessons covered every aspect of Jones's intellectual growth and presentation of self, including schooling in what we now call "emotional intelligence." Dickerson set the highest standards for Jones, especially in the area of communication skills—a facility we've found essential to leadership. Dickerson edited Jones's early attempts at writing a sports column with respectful ruthlessness, in red ink, as Jones remembers to this day—marking up the copy so that it looked, as Jones says, "like something chickens had a fight over." But Dickerson also took the time to explain every single mistake and why it mattered.

His mentor also expected the teenage Jones to speak correctly at all times and would hiss discreetly in his direction if he stumbled. Great expectations are evidence of great respect, and as Jones learned all the complex, often subtle lessons on how to succeed, he was motivated in no small measure by his desire not to disappoint the man he still calls "Mr. Dickerson." Dickerson gave Jones the kind of intensive mentoring that was tantamount to grooming him for a kind of professional and moral succession—and Jones has indeed become an instrument for the profound societal change for which Dickerson fought so courageously as well. Jones found life-changing meaning in the attention Dickerson paid to him—attention fueled by a conviction that he, too, though only a teenager, had a vital role to play in society and an important destiny.

Another story of a powerful mentor came to us from Michael Klein, a young man who made millions in Southern California real estate while still in his teens, only to lose it by the time he turned 20 and then go on to start several other businesses. His mentor was his grandfather, Max S. Klein, who created the paint-by-numbers fad that swept the United States in the 1950s and 1960s. Klein was only four or five years old when his grandfather approached him and offered to share his business expertise. Over the years, Michael Klein's grandfather taught him to learn from and to cope with change, and the two spoke by phone for an hour every day until shortly before Max Klein's death.

THE ESSENTIALS OF LEADERSHIP

In our interviews, we heard many other stories of crucible experiences. Take Jack Coleman, 78-year-old former president of Haverford College in Pennsylvania. He told us of one day, during the Vietnam War, when he heard that a group of students was planning to pull down the American flag and burn it—and that former members of the school's football team were going to make sure the students didn't succeed. Seemingly out of nowhere, Coleman had the idea to preempt the violence by suggesting that the protesting students take down the flag, wash it, and then put it back up—a crucible moment that even now elicits tremendous emotion in Coleman as he describes that day.

There's also Common Cause founder John W. Gardner, who died earlier this year at 89. He identified his arduous training as a Marine during World War II as the crucible in which his leadership abilities emerged. Architect Frank Gehry spoke of the biases he experienced as a Jew in college. Jeff Wilke, a general manager at a major manufacturer, told us of the day he learned that an employee had been killed in his plant—an experience that taught him that leadership was about much more than making quarterly numbers.

So, what allowed these people to not only cope with these difficult situations but also learn from them? We believe that great leaders possess four essential skills, and, we were surprised to learn, these happen to be the same skills that allow a person to find meaning in what could be a debilitating experience. First is the ability to engage others in shared meaning. Consider

Sidney Harman, who dived into a chaotic work environment to mobilize employees around an entirely new approach to management. Second is a distinctive and compelling voice. Look at Jack Coleman's ability to defuse a potentially violent situation with only his words. Third is a sense of integrity (including a strong set of values). Here, we point again to Coleman, whose values prevailed even during the emotionally charged clash between peace demonstrators and the angry (and strong) former football team members.

But by far the most critical skill of the four is what we call "adaptive capacity." This is, in essence, applied creativity—an almost magical ability to transcend adversity, with all its attendant stresses, and to emerge stronger than before. It's composed of two primary qualities: the ability to grasp context and hardiness. The ability to grasp context implies an ability to weigh a welter of factors, ranging from how very different groups of people will interpret a gesture to being able to put a situation in perspective. Without this, leaders are utterly lost, because they cannot connect with their constituents. M. Douglas Ivester, who succeeded Roberto Goizueta at Coca-Cola, exhibited a woeful inability to grasp context, lasting just 28 months on the job. For example, he demoted his highest-ranked African-American employee even as the company was losing a $200 million class-action suit brought by black employees—and this in Atlanta, a city with a powerful African-American majority. Contrast Ivester with Vernon Jordan. Jordan realized his boss's time was up—not just his time in power, but the era that formed him. And so Jordan was able to see past the insults and recognize his boss's bitterness for what it was—desperate lashing out.

Hardiness is just what it sounds like—the perseverance and toughness that enable people to emerge from devastating circumstances without losing hope. Look at Michael Klein, who experienced failure but didn't let it defeat him. He found himself with a single asset—a tiny software company he'd acquired. Klein built it into Transoft Networks, which Hewlett-Packard acquired in 1999. Consider, too, Mickie Siebert, who used her sense of humor to curtail offensive conversations. Or Sidney Rittenberg's strength during his imprisonment. He drew on his personal memories and inner strength to emerge from his lengthy prison term without bitterness.

It is the combination of hardiness and ability to grasp context that, above all, allows a person to not only survive an ordeal, but to learn from it, and to emerge stronger, more engaged, and more committed than ever. These attributes allow leaders to grow from their crucibles, instead of being destroyed by them—to find opportunity where others might find only despair. This is the stuff of true leadership.

Can Leadership Be Taught?

Robert P. Vecchio

Remarks delivered at Meeting of Southern Management Association,
San Antonio, Texas, November 5, 2004

The question under consideration by this symposium is an important one. It rests, arguably, at the heart of management education. A broader restatement of the question might be: Do we teach much that is of real value in schools of business? To be sure, there is a widespread perception that what we offer in business school curricula is of some value (just look at our enrollment numbers!). Although one sometimes hears people praise the merits of graduating from the "school of hard knocks," I vividly recall a conference that brought together highly successful entrepreneurs from across the nation, many of whom had very limited formal education, even a limited initial ability to speak English. I asked each entrepreneur if he or she would ultimately desire to someday complete an MBA degree at a university. They all said "yes," indicating that there was still much that they felt they could learn through exposure to formal business education. So even successful graduates of the "real-world" acknowledge that if the opportunity were available, they would pursue further knowledge of the type that we offer in our degree-granting programs. My sense is that their various contacts with more "knowledgeable" (more formally trained) managers created a sense of personal deficiency that they would like to have corrected.

As for the narrower question of whether we can actually teach leadership, I must mention that I often begin my leadership classes each semester by raising this very question. I point out that I (like other instructors) offer no warranties (written or implied) and that they will surely be "exposed" to educational content, but whether the course experience affects their subsequent behavior and success will be heavily influenced by other factors. If they become great leaders, it may not be because of what the course provides, as much as it is in spite of what the course provides to them (i.e., it is conceivable they may gain insights and understandings of other perspectives that lead them to be even less certain when adopting a course of action, and thereby less effective as a consequence of "over-analysis" of situations). Certainly, they should have, at a minimum, deeper insights on social dynamics at work and greater self-awareness after exposure to a leadership course.

The question of whether one can be taught to be a great or effective leader is a deceptive one. It seems that a simple dichotomous, yes/no, type of answer should exist. However, consider that we could also ask whether one can be taught to be a great swimmer or a great football wide-receiver. On deeper reflection, we would have to admit that it is really a matter of degree; that greatness/effectiveness is not definable in simple yes/no terms, but only in terms of gradations. Moreover, on still deeper reflection, we realize that there are separate performance dimensions that underlie greatness/effectiveness. So, a prospective wide-receiver may be very capable in terms of flat-out speed but lack needed strength for overcoming one-on-one blocking contact or lack needed coordination and dexterity to catch a pass while running at full speed. So too, a leader may have strong communication skills but lack detailed knowledge of the work at hand (and thereby lose credibility with followers who may know substantially more about the tasks they perform) or lack the ability to envision the future (and thereby fail to identify emerging threats and opportunities). Therefore, a person who aspires to be a leader must recognize the multidimensional nature of the role and the need for appraisal on each dimension. Furthermore, some dimensions are more critical than others, depending heavily on the context (unique character of circumstances). Exogenous factors can also undermine leaders. For example, consider one of my favorite quotes, "A person can do everything right, and do absolutely nothing wrong, and still fail!"

Subordinates, as part of the context, can also limit the effectiveness of a would-be leader in that they can withhold their support. Mutual dependency operates in leadership settings such that a person who appears to "have it all" on the dimensions that are seemingly critical for effectiveness in a given setting, may be undermined by subordinates who withhold their acceptance of that person. Moreover, followers are not uniform in their views, and followers are likely to vary in how accepting or supportive they are of a leader. With a sufficient cadre of loyal supporters, a leader may yet be effective. But without some minimal subgroup of key supporters, a leader cannot be effective.

While leadership can be viewed very broadly, we are most interested in the topic of *managerial* leadership (as distinct from political leadership, military leadership, sports leadership, etc.). Typically, we try to teach the major management functions, among which leadership is often listed and actually covered last (after planning, organizing, controlling, and staffing).

Perhaps it is often treated last because it is the murkiest of the management functions and does not lend itself to a summary list of "dos and don'ts." Fundamentally, education is essentially about "knowledge acquisition." For the topic of leadership, there is a "body of knowledge" that can be taught (consider the *Handbook of Leadership* as a useful compendium and starting point). There is also a "growing archive of research" (generated as a result of the scientific enterprise) that we can teach in terms of "how to contribute to it" by teaching research techniques and critical thinking skills. But it is the application of knowledge that is surely the tricky part. (Interestingly, we do not often ask instructors in, e.g., statistics or economics courses to demonstrate that their students will successfully apply what they have learned in class at a later point in a managerial career.) Unfortunately, we are still some distance away from developing a "science of leader development" (Day & Zaccaro, 2004).

In a review of the empirical evidence, Bass (1990, p. 856) concluded that "available evaluative studies have provided evidence that leadership and management training, education, and development are usually effective." One might more cautiously state that such experiences generally appear to "add value." However, a close examination of the relevant evidence shows that many studies rely on subjective criteria (such as participant satisfaction) to appraise the impact of developmental/training exercises. Also, a number of studies focus on demonstrating that participants gain in knowledge and its application relative to fairly narrow notions of leadership that are specified by certain models (e.g., Fiedler's Leader Match, the Vroom-Yetton Model, Hersey and Blanchard's Situational Leadership Theory, Mc-Clelland's achievement-motive imagery, etc.). On closer inspection, these criteria are not what we often envision when asking whether leadership can be taught. Furthermore, the training that is provided in undergraduate and MBA curricula may be very much in demand, by all economic indicators. Yet, my sense is that business schools do a far better job of teaching decision *making*, rather than decision *implementation* (i.e., we instruct, quite well, on how to calculate the Net Present Value of various courses of action and the selection of an appropriate statistical test; but we instruct less well, I believe, in how to build consensus, create and share a vision, or motivate others to pursue a course of action). Experience in the role of leader, or observing others in that role, is particularly valuable for understanding how to be successful in decision implementation.

In the realm of leadership education, I am impressed by three perspectives. These three perspectives relate to that portion of unexplained variance in leader effectiveness that remains after controlling for individual innate/trait propensities to be flexible, socially engaged, confident, etc. The first perspective is the cyclical notion of individualized assessment and learning. This involves the three steps of initially identifying individual strengths/weaknesses relative to a particular leadership role; then, designing developmental experiences that target deficiencies and maintain strengths (e.g., public speaking coupled with feedback, role-playing, and job-relevant training on the specifics of a task); and finally, re-appraisal and feedback. Unfortunately, this type of individualized assessment and learning, which identifies and targets relevant "gaps," is very labor-intensive (and especially not amenable to classes of 40–70 students, as are often found in university leadership courses). Moreover, this type of developmental exercise cannot be conducted even in small classes if we do not have a specific job in mind that we are targeting for individual appraisal. However, it is worth noting that the practice of "executive coaching" does, in fact, frequently follow this three-step process. Also, one can argue that "mentoring" implicitly incorporates this three-step process as well.

The second perspective that I find impressive is that of observational learning. Some might call it role-taking or mimicry. Yet, many people engage in this activity (often unconsciously) in that they have role models or exemplars whose style they, in fact, imitate. Because one's experiences are often limited to a certain range of people and settings, educators can try to broaden students' exposure to the range of styles that exist, thereby creating in students the useful sense that "I can do that," or "I can conduct myself like that." Beyond videos, structured simulation is another powerful tool for providing opportunities for active rehearsal and confidence-building.

The third perspective might be termed self-education. We can foster self-education (which includes experiences beyond the classroom) by emphasizing the continuing character of life-long education. Two pillars of self-education are self-managed ability and motivation. These constructs are compensatory, to a degree. However, the absence of either is fatal, while the presence of both in ample amounts can greatly enhance the likelihood of a leader's effectiveness.

But what should a person have as goals in terms of developing cross-situational abilities and motivation? Although it may seem overly broad in light of my earlier remarks, three often-cited critical dimensions of effectiveness that can be manifested by virtually anyone in a leader role are: knowing what one is talking about, being honest in dealings with others, and caring about the welfare of others (see Holtz & Mackay, 1999). "Knowing what one is talking about" is basic for possessing credibility with respect to followers and is a learnable skill. It requires (as Rudy Giuliani terms it in his 2003 book, *Leadership*) "relentless preparation"—a devotion to understanding as much as, if not more than, others know about the task at hand. Oddly, nearly all of our models of leadership omit this notion (perhaps because it is assumed to be self-evidently valid). "Honesty" is also an essential element of effectiveness, and the failure to maintain this standard can easily undermine any leader. And finally, "caring" is critical in that anything less than genuine concern for others will likely lead to a cynical interpretation of a leader's motives and actions. This cynicism, in turn, will have adverse consequences for follower loyalty and trust. Caring/concern for others, however, can often emerge as a result of circumstances that involve "mutual or shared fate" (i.e., "we are all in this together"). Those leaders who do not foster this sense of mutual dependency or sense of shared fate in themselves, as well as their followers, risk failure on this critical dimension.

So, bottom line: Can we teach leadership? The answer, like many answers in the realm of social relations, is both "yes," for certain aspects of leadership (such as an appreciation of obstacles to effectiveness, an awareness of different role models, greater self-awareness, and knowledge of frameworks for understanding/interpreting social influence processes); and "no," for certain aspects of leadership that are more situation-specific (such as whether to undertake a personal "makeover," to challenge one's own supervisors, or to join Toast-Masters). Traditionally, leadership has been analyzed in more general terms, such as personal style or demeanor of a nominal head, while the specifics of how a leader can influence others to achieve desired goals have not been treated in sufficient detail. The development of leader competencies (in the areas of cognitive and social skills), as well as the awareness of political/power realities, can provide a useful approach for more directly addressing these specifics.

REFERENCES

Bass, B. M. (1990). *Bass and Stogdill's Handbook of Leadership*. New York: Free Press.

Day, D. V. and Zaccaro, S. J. (2004). Toward a science of leader development. In D. V. Day, S. J. Zaccaro, and S. M. Halpin (eds.). *Leader Development for Transforming Organizations*. Mahwah, NJ: Lawrence Erlbaum.

Giuliani, R. W. (2003). *Leadership*. New York: Miramax.

Holtz, L. and Mackay, H. (1999). *Winning Every Day: The Game Plan for Success*. New York: Harper Business.

PART II

Power and Influence

Power does not corrupt men; fools, however, if they get into a position of power, corrupt power.

George Bernard Shaw

Nearly all men can stand adversity, but if you want to test a man's character, give him power.

Abraham Lincoln

One measure of leadership is the caliber of people who choose to follow you.

Dennis A. Peer

Charlatanism is to some degree indispensable to effective leadership.

Eric Hoffer

Power is the ultimate aphrodisiac.

Henry Kissinger

You can get more with a kind word and a gun, than with a kind word alone.

An American gangster

The first reading in this section, entitled "Power, Politics, and Influence," provides an overview of fundamental social dynamics. The reading initially defines power, authority, and influence, and then moves on to a description of bases of power and techniques people use to gain power and influence. The article concludes with a consideration of the ethics of exercising power and how people respond to influence exercised by legitimate authority.

The next article takes up the topic of how subordinates relate to authority figures, and suggests that subordinates have opportunities to project upward influence on their bosses. Authors John J. Gabarro and John Kotter underscore the mutual dependence that exists in work groups. The following article, on effective followership, considers the neglected topic of dimensions or styles of followership and argues for greater attention to appreciating how followers can dictate the responses of leaders.

David Kipnis, Stuart Schmidt and Ian Wilkinson then explore ways in which people try to influence others at work. Their results are most interesting in that their inductive approach identifies the tendency of people to choose among such tactics as assertiveness, ingratiation, rationality, sanctions, exchange, upward appeals, blocking, and coalitions when seeking to influence others.

The final article in this section, by Mario Sussmann and Robert Vecchio, integrates several major views of employee behavior in response to supervisory influence efforts. Their framework suggests that employee motivation can be understood in terms of employee acceptance or rejection of social influence efforts.

Power, Politics, and Influence

Robert P. Vecchio

DISTINGUISHING POWER AND INFLUENCE

Power is an essential feature of a manager's role. Without some degree of power, a manager would find it very difficult to direct the efforts of subordinates. Thus, power underlies a manager's effectiveness. Subordinates also possess forms and degrees of power. For example, subordinates can control the work flow or withhold support from their manager. Therefore, to some extent, each member of an organization possesses power.

Because power is intangible, it is very difficult to define clearly and precisely. Also, our language has several similar terms that we tend to confuse with power, such as authority and influence. In the interest of clarity, we shall define *power* as the ability to change the behavior of others. It is the ability to cause others to perform actions that they might not otherwise perform.[1]

Power is not always legitimate. Therefore, we speak of *authority* as the *right* to try to change or direct others. Authority includes the notion of legitimacy. It is the right to influence others in the pursuit of common goals that are agreed upon by various parties. Power, in contrast, does not always pursue common goals and may, at times, be clearly directed to pursuing only a single individual's goals.

Another term, *influence,* is also frequently used when discussing the notion of power. Influence tends to be subtler, broader, and more general than power. Although both influence and power can be defined as the ability to change the behavior of others, power embodies the ability to do so with regularity and ease. Influence is weaker and less reliable than power. Also, power rests on a number of specific sources or foundations, which will be examined in a subsequent section of this chapter. Influence relies on particular tactics and often employs face-to-face interactions. Thus, the exercise of influence tends to be more subtle than the exercise of power.

Interpersonal Influence Processes

In a classic article, Kelman distinguished among three primary reasons for an individual to yield to another person's attempt to be directive.[2] If an employee accepts a manager's influence attempt because she believes she will be rewarded or avoid being punished, her response is one of *compliance*. For example, an employee may skip lunch in order to finish typing a report for her supervisor. She may actually hope to receive an expression of appreciation from the supervisor or she may merely wish to avoid the hard feelings that will result if the report is not finished on time. The employee's behavior is strictly motivated by concern with rewards and punishments. Supervisors who strive for consistent compliance must (1) be certain that they can in fact deliver rewards or punishments and (2) be in a position to frequently monitor their subordinates' behavior.

A second influence process, *identification,* occurs when one person follows another's direction because of a desire to establish or maintain a personally satisfying relationship. When a subordinate admires his manager, seeks his approval, and perhaps tries to imitate him, we infer that the subordinate has a strong desire to identify with the manager. One example of this process occurs when a junior executive who greatly admires the CEO of his organization espouses the CEO's philosophy and beliefs when addressing the employees in his own work unit.

In both compliance and identification, the performance of an action in itself is not necessarily personally satisfying. Rather, the action may be due to a desire for specific outcomes (compliance) or an attraction to the source of influence (identification).

Sometimes employees' actions stem from a third reason: the belief that the behavior is congruent with their value systems. *Internalization* occurs when an employee accepts an influence attempt because he or she believes that the resulting behavior is correct and appropriate. For instance, assume that a high-level executive announces that the organization is participating in a United Way fund-raising campaign. Some of her managers may actively encourage subordinates to contribute to the fund because they strongly believe in the goals of United Way. These managers are not motivated by threats or rewards or admiration for their superior but rather by a personal commitment to a set of values.

The Five Bases of Power

Who gets what, when, and how are important concerns for every member of an organization. People at all levels are interested in and affected by the acquisition and distribution of rewards and resources. Of course, power plays a central role in such allocation processes. To explain how power operates, we will first examine the five distinct sources of power proposed by John French and Bertram Raven: reward power, coercive power, legitimate power, referent power, and expert power.[3]

Reward Power

Reward power is the ability to determine who will receive particular rewards. As long as the rewards are valued, a person who is able to distribute or withhold them can enjoy strong power over others' behavior. Granting promotions, giving raises, and conferring preferred job assignments are some typical rewards most managers can control. Unfortunately, this is not always the case. For example, when a work force is unionized, salary increases and job assignments are based more on seniority and the specifics of a labor contract than on the judgment of a manager or supervisor. The relationship between performance and rewards should always be clear. When a manager lacks the ability to administer both extrinsic and intrinsic rewards, it becomes extremely difficult to direct subordinates' behavior. Reward power gives a manager a distinct advantage in obtaining desired ends from his or her work group.

Coercive Power

If reward power can be termed "the carrot," then coercive power is "the stick." *Coercive power* stems from the capacity to produce fear in others. The threat of punishment can be a strong means of invoking compliance. The most obvious examples of punishments are demotions, salary cuts, suspension, removal of such perquisites as a company car or an expense account, and dismissal. However, coercive power can also be more subtle. For example, criticism and the denial of emotional support and friendship may also be effective forms of coercion.

The application of coercive power requires good social judgment. In some instances, a manager is actually expected to be coercive—as when a subordinate is extremely unproductive or interferes with the productivity of others. In such a situation, other employees and managers will rightly expect the supervisor to take firm action.

On the other hand, a manager must be careful when applying coercive power. If he or she is too heavy-handed and indiscriminately inflicts punishment on all employees, morale and productivity are likely to suffer. Such a manager may find that the unit's turnover rate is very high as people seek employment elsewhere. In addition, injured employees may retaliate by sabotaging the unit's operations or withholding useful suggestions for improving the unit's performance.

Despite its potentially negative effects, coercive power underlies much of the routine compliance that occurs in organizations. Decisions to arrive at work on time, meet deadlines, and so forth are often largely due to fear of being fired, ridiculed, or reprimanded. Rightly or wrongly, coercive power is frequently used in most organizations.

Legitimate Power

Legitimate power stems from the willingness of others to accept an individual's direction. They feel an obligation to follow the individual's lead and submit to his authority. There are two sources of legitimate power. The first is social conditioning: From early childhood, people are conditioned to accept the direction of authority figures. They learn that teachers and crossing guards, as well as foremen and managers, have the right to lead or direct others. The second source of legitimate power is designation: A person can gain power by being designated an authority figure by someone who already possesses legitimate authority. For example, the president of a company may assign a vice president the authority to make important decisions on the company's behalf. The president thus gives the vice president legitimate power to act as his representative and exercise authority accordingly.

Legitimate power can be effective only if it is accepted by the people it is intended to control. If the people withdraw their support from the system that is the basis of power, the power ceases to exist. Such withdrawals of support occur in revolutions, when ruling classes and their social systems are overthrown, and in riots, when a spontaneous but limited rebellion is made against authority.

Referent Power

People with attractive personalities or other special qualities possess a form of power. Their appearance, poise, interpersonal style, or values can inspire admiration and cause others to identify with them. The resulting ability to influence behavior is called *referent power*. It is often easy to identify an individual who possesses such power. For example, most people would agree that successful politicians, athletes, and entertainers—such as Bill Clinton, Michael Jordan, and Oprah Winfrey—have this attribute. However, it is extremely difficult to define exactly what gives these people their charisma. Usually, vigor and the appearance of success play important roles. But other characteristics that contribute to referent power can be very difficult to pinpoint (consider, for example, that Adolf Hitler was judged to be charismatic in the eyes of his countrymen).

Referent power derives from people's desire to identify with the qualities of an attractive individual. Advertising that uses a celebrity to endorse a product is based on referent power, since the sponsor hopes that the audience will buy the product in an attempt to imitate the celebrity's behavior and attitudes.

Expert Power

Individuals with *expert power* are able to direct others because they are perceived as knowledgeable or talented in a given area. Most of us readily seek and follow the advice of experts, such as our family physician or athletic coach. So too are we likely to follow the directions of a coworker who is seen as having expertise in our field of work. This form of power is usually limited to a fairly narrow and specific realm, however, and does not spread to other areas of social interaction.

Most subordinates presume that their superiors possess expert power in the form of understanding all jobs in the work unit. Generally, greater levels of experience and job-relevant knowledge do give a manager an edge in expertise. However, in highly technical job settings, it may happen that some subordinates have more expert knowledge about certain aspects of their jobs than do their managers. In fact, some managers may be highly dependent on the technical expertise of their subordinates in order to successfully manage their work units. In such a situation, expert power can lead to an atypical reversal of the usual manager-subordinate relationship.

Interplay among the Power Bases

A manager can possess each of the five sources of power to varying degrees, and his or her use of one power base can affect the strength of another. For example, a person can gain greater legitimacy by being promoted to a higher-level position. Of course, a position of greater legitimate power usually entails more opportunities to use rewards and coercion. The exercise of coercion, however, could reduce the manager's referent power because coercion tends to produce immediate compliance but may have negative side effects.

Above all, the manager should bear in mind that the tendency to use power can lead to greater effectiveness, while the failure to use power can have the opposite effect. Managers who exercise power with some frequency can be counted on to continue such behavior in future settings and are, therefore, given greater deference by subordinates. More passive managers may have difficulty if they suddenly decide to use their power because their subordinates will have become accustomed to their lack of assertiveness.

Distinctions can be drawn among the five power bases. Expert and referent power bases are more informal in nature, while legitimate, reward, and coercive power bases are more formal. The informal power bases have a greater capacity to affect overall employee satisfaction and performance. The formal power bases, in contrast, have potentially greater impact on immediate behavior. Although formal power can elicit a quick response from an employee, it will not necessarily produce agreement and commitment. For example, a worker may comply with a manager's order but still resent having been coerced.

Many centuries ago, the Italian philosopher Machiavelli contended that people who have formal power tend to remain in their positions of authority longer than people who rely on informal power. This observation makes some sense in that the informal bases of power can be more easily eroded, since they depend on people's perceptions. For example, a manager may lose his expertise due to changes in technology or his appeal may diminish following a series of unpopular actions or personnel changes. While expert power can be regained through technical training, there are no surefire ways of increasing referent power.

In general, informal power resides in the personal characteristics of the manager, whereas formal power resides in the position itself. It can be forcefully argued, however, that all sources of power can really be reduced to a single category: control over reinforcers. The most effective way to control others' behavior is to control when and how they receive reinforcement.

AN ORGANIZATIONAL ANALYSIS OF POWER

In his analysis of how complex organizations attempt to direct the behavior of their members, Etzioni identified three kinds of organizational power.[4] One type of organizational power can be characterized as coercive. Such organizations try to extract compliance from members through threats and punishment. Examples of coercive organizations include prisons, some mental institutions, and divisions within the military (such as boot camp).

Most business organizations, of course, do not rely on coercion, but instead offer contingent incentives: If employees follow directives, they can expect to be rewarded. Such organizations are said to use *utilitarian power* because of their emphasis on the utility of conforming to directives.

A third set of organizations relies on *normative power*. In this type of organization, members accept directives because of their sense of affiliation with the organization and its espoused values. Professional associations (such as the American Dental Association) and religious organizations typically use normative power to influence their members.

All three types of power can be useful in obtaining people's cooperation in organizations. However, the relative effectiveness of each approach depends on the organizational members' orientation or involvement. Etzioni contends that members' involvement can be broadly categorized as alienative, calculative, or moral. Members with *alienative involvement* have hostile, rejecting, and extremely negative attitudes. Members with *calculative involvement* are rational and oriented toward maximizing personal gain. And members with *moral involvement* are committed to the socially beneficial features of their organizations.

According to Etzioni, the three types of organizational power can be matched with the three types of involvement. According to this logic, only one type of power is most appropriate for each type of member involvement. Attempts to use types of power that are inappropriate for the type of involvement can reduce effectiveness. Figure 1 illustrates Etzioni's model of power and involvement.

TYING IT ALL TOGETHER

Sussmann and Vecchio formally compared the three models of power and influence put forth by French and Raven, Kelman, and Etzioni.[5] A good

Figure 1
Etzioni's Model of Power and Involvement

Types of Power

Types of Involvement	Coercive	Utilitarian	Normative
Alienative	x		
Calculative		x	
Moral			x

Table 1
A Comparison of Three Views of Power and Influence

Interpersonal Influence Process (Kelman)	Power Bases (French and Raven)	Organizational Power (Etzioni)
Internalization	Legitimate Power Expert Power	Normative
Identification	Referent Power	Normative
Compliance (reward-based)	Reward Power	Utilitarian
Compliance (punishment-based)	Coercive Power	Coercive

deal of similarity was identified among all three views. For example, French and Raven's concepts of reward and coercive power have a strong similarity to Kelman's notions of compliance. Referent power, in turn, is allied to Kelman's notion of identification, and legitimate and expert power overlap to a great extent with the process of internalization. Both Etzioni and Kelman identify three forms of power (or influence), but while Etzioni focuses on the organizational level of analysis, Kelman focuses on the interpersonal level. Table 1 summarizes the comparison of the three views.

In a sense, the multiple forms of power identified correspond to the need-level views of Maslow and others. The correspondence lies in the recognition that there are several levels of motivation or forms of influence. One level is fairly rudimentary: reward and punishment. A higher level is more social in nature: referent or identification. And the highest level is fairly psychological in nature: internalization or legitimacy.

A SOCIAL INFLUENCE VIEW OF SUPERVISOR BEHAVIOR

Sussmann and Vecchio also proposed that a supervisor's attempts to exert influence follow a cycle in which he or she tries one of three approaches to influence a subordinate in accordance with the three levels of needs and the three forms of power.[6] This view suggests that a supervisor (or evaluator) will attempt to use compliance, identification, or internalization to influence an individual. Respectively, he or she may try threats, appeals to a subordinate's sense of organizational membership or affiliation, or appeals to the subordinate's value system.

Such attempts will succeed or fail to the extent that the individual is disposed to accept incentives or threats, identity-related appeals, or value-related appeals. For certain types of subordinates, a particular type of disposition may be more prevalent, as is suggested by Etzioni's notion of involvement. Acceptance of the supervisor's influence attempt leads to behavioral intentions on the part of the subordinate to act in the desired direction. The actual behavior of the subordinate is then compared to the standards that are held in the mind of the supervisor. If the influence attempt is judged to have failed, the supervisor will likely try another attempt, but perhaps with a different type of influence (for example, appealing on a different level). This model suggests that supervisors need to be sensitive to differences in subordinates' preferences for inducement schemes. It is possible that supervisors who are aware of and make use of subordinate preferences for inducements are relatively more effective than other supervisors.

POLITICS: THE FACTS OF ORGANIZATIONAL LIFE

The terms *politics* and *power* are sometimes used interchangeably. Though they are related, they are nonetheless distinct notions. Pfeffer defines *organizational politics* as "those activities taken within organizations to acquire, develop, and use power and other resources to obtain one's preferred outcomes in a situation in which there is uncertainty or [disagreement] about choices."[7] In a sense, the study of organizational politics constitutes the study of power in action. It may also be said that politics involves the playing out of power and influence.

The word *politics* has a somewhat negative connotation. It suggests that someone is attempting to use means or to gain ends that are not sanctioned by the organization. Actually, political behavior, as we've defined it, is quite neutral. Similarly, power is not inherently negative. Whether a person views power and politics as unsavory topics depends on a number of considerations, most important perhaps being where the individual stands on a specific issue in a given situation. Nonetheless, most managers are reluctant to admit to the political character of their own work settings.

A further point is that all members of an organization may exhibit political behavior. In our previous discussion of power, we took a fairly formal and traditional approach to the topic of influence. Thus, we looked at power from the perspective of a supervisor or manager who directs others. Yet, in the area of politics, everyone is a player. Subordinates, as well as their managers, can engage in the give-and-take of organizational politics.[†]

Political Tactics

Several authors have identified a variety of political tactics used by employees at virtually all levels.[8] In this section, we will examine a number of these activities.

Ingratiation

This tactic involves giving compliments to or doing favors for superiors or coworkers. Most people have a difficult time rejecting the positive advances of others. Ingratiation usually works as a tactic insofar as the target often feels positive toward the source even if the ingratiation attempt is fairly blatant and transparent.

In the behavioral sciences, the notion of "social reciprocity" has been offered to help explain the process of ingratiation. In social reciprocity, there is a feeling of a social obligation to repay the positive actions of others with similar actions. For example, if someone pays you a compliment, there is a strong expectation that you should respond with a compliment of your own. If you fail to do so, you may be judged as being rude. Similarly, ingratiation involves giving positive strokes to a person with the expectation that he or she will feel obligated to return them in some form.

Forming Coalitions and Networks

Another political tactic consists of befriending important people. These people may not be in positions of any obvious political value. However, their jobs may provide them with information that could be useful to have. Some people find that forming friendships with people in upper-level management can help them gain access to important information. They

---

[†] Nonetheless, it is widely believed that political behavior is far less common and less intense among employees in lower-level positions than among employees in higher-level positions.

may also find that by being on good terms with their boss's secretary, they can sometimes gain inside information and easier access to the boss.

Impression Management

A simple tactic that virtually everyone uses from time to time is the management of their outward appearance and style. Generally, most organizations prefer a particular image that consists of being loyal, attentive, honest, neatly groomed, sociable, and so forth. By deliberately trying to exhibit this preferred image, an individual can make a positive impression on influential members of the organization.

Information Management

A further tactic consists of managing the information that is shared with others. The nature, as well as the timing, of information given out can have strong effects on others' conduct. Releasing good or bad news when it is likely to have its fullest impact can greatly promote one person's self-interest or defeat the hopes of others. Similarly, an individual can ask for information (such as sales data or a production report) when it is most likely to make things appear particularly good or bad. People who play the information management game are not likely to lie or spread misinformation, however, because their future credibility would be jeopardized. Instead, they rely on the carefully planned release of valid information to obtain their ends.

Promote the Opposition

It may sound strange, but one way to eliminate opposition is to aid political rivals. For example, it is possible to eliminate a political rival by helping that person become so successful that he or she is transferred to a desirable position someplace else in the organization. Recommending a rival for a new assignment or even a promotion within another division of the organization can make one's own work life easier.

Pursue Line Responsibility

Within virtually every organization, some positions are more closely tied to the primary mission of the organization; these jobs are called line positions. They are at the very heart of the organization. People who occupy support positions are said to be in staff positions. Examples of line positions include engineering, manufacturing, and sales in a customer-oriented firm. People in departments such as public relations, market research, and personnel are usually in staff positions. While staff people may come to wield great power within their own territories, it is the line people who usually "call the shots" on major issues. Line people not only make the more important decisions within the organization, they are also more likely to be promoted to top-level executive positions. In many organizations, there is a preferred department of origin and career path for top-level managers. These are usually line positions. Therefore, one way to gain influence within an organization is to be assigned initially to, or be transferred to a line position. It will often provide more visibility, influence, and upward mobility.

Devious Political Tactics

Some political tactics are quite honest in nature. For example, accumulating seniority, providing copies of your accomplishments to your boss, and hitching your wagon to yourself are all respectable means for gaining influence.[††] Some other tactics, however, are difficult to defend on moral grounds. In the interest of self-defense, it is worth examining several of these devious political tactics.[9]

Take No Prisoners

Sometimes it is necessary to do something unpopular or distasteful, such as demote or transfer someone or announce pay cuts. During corporate takeovers, many unpopular actions may be necessary. As a result, political enemies are likely to be made. One tactic for dealing with this potential problem is to ruthlessly eliminate *all* individuals who may resent your past actions by having them fired or transferred.

Divide and Conquer

This tactic involves creating a feud among two or more people so that they will be continually off balance and thus unable to mount an attack against

---

[††] Pure and simple performance remains an essential ingredient of a successful career in virtually all fields of endeavor.

you. This is a very old idea that is still practiced in some work settings. An unscrupulous individual who employs this tactic usually encourages bickering between possible rivals by spreading rumors or promoting competition between subordinates or factions. This is a risky tactic, however, as the opponents may eventually compare notes and conclude that someone else is really responsible for creating and maintaining their bad feelings.

Exclude the Opposition

Another devious tactic involves keeping rivals away from important meetings and social occasions. This can be done simply by scheduling important affairs when the opposition is out of town (on vacation or a business trip) or attending another meeting. With the opposition absent, it is possible to influence decision making or to take credit for a rival's efforts.

Political Blunders

Although certain tactics can promote desired ends, others can be costly political mistakes. Among the most common are violating the chain of command, losing your cool, saying no to top management, upstaging your supervisor, and challenging cherished beliefs. These activities constitute serious political blunders or mistakes.

Violating Chain of Command

Occasionally, a person will feel that it is his duty to see his boss's boss, either to complain about his treatment at the hands of his own boss or to serve as an informant. A person may even feel that such an "end run" is justified because he is fervently convinced of the rightness of his position. However, going over the boss's head is often a very strong organizational taboo. Generally, it is expected that an employee will ask the boss's permission before seeing his superior on any matter.

Losing Your Cool

Throwing temper tantrums and acting aggressively toward others are often seen as acceptable and sometimes effective tactics in settings such as sports events. But in office settings, these tactics do not work well at all. Fist pounding and snide remarks usually earn a person a reputation for being hard to deal with, a label that can be extremely difficult to overcome. One devious twist on this tactic is to goad a person who tends to be acerbic and aggressive into displaying these tendencies at the wrong times. In this way, such a person's peers help him or her to commit political suicide.

Saying No to Top Management

One of the surest ways to stop your own career progress is to reject a request from top-level management. Instead of feeling fortunate to be selected for an assignment, some individuals believe that they are overburdened and that they are being "dumped on," or that they can afford to defy top management because they are indispensable. This represents poor judgment on two counts: First, people in the lower ranks of an organization are rarely indispensable. Second, if workers are overburdened, they should explain the situation to the manager and try to arrange for additional help.

Upstaging Your Supervisor

Generally speaking, one should avoid publicly criticizing others. For example, it is not considered appropriate for a supervisor to criticize a subordinate in public view. However, the reverse is also true. A subordinate should refrain from implicitly criticizing the boss by upstaging him or her. Upstaging often takes the form of bragging about one's own accomplishments or claiming credit for a unit's success.

Challenging Cherished Beliefs

In many firms, there are a number of cherished beliefs about the nature of the organization, and it is generally considered "poor form" to criticize or challenge such folklore within earshot of company loyalists. Examples of such fond beliefs include "This organization is the best in its field," "Our founder was (or is) an outstanding individual," and "People who leave our organization are people that we are better off without." To be sure, all people are entitled to their own opinions, but it can be politically foolish to engage in an open debate about the truth of certain widely held beliefs.

Coping with Organizational Politics

Political gamesmanship, when carried to the extreme, has many dysfunctional effects: Morale is weakened, victors and victims are created, and energy and time are spent on planning attacks and counterattacks instead of on productivity. Thus, combating politics must be part of a manager's job.

Set an Example

When a manager plays political games, such as distorting the facts or manipulating people, he or she conveys to subordinates a message that such conduct is acceptable. A manager can create a climate either tolerant or intolerant of dirty tricks. Clearly, a department is better served by a manager who provides a positive role model by encouraging truthfulness and the even-handed treatment of others.

Give Clear Job Assignments

Politics seem to be more prevalent when overall purposes are unclear and it is difficult to assess the performance of individual employees.[§] One way to counter political activities is to give well-defined, discrete work assignments. When expectations are clear and subordinates understand how they will be assessed, game playing becomes less necessary as a device for gaining personal recognition.

Eliminate Coalitions and Cliques

Coalitions and cliques that are detrimental to unit performance can often be reduced in influence or eliminated. Although dismissal and transfer are two possible solutions, individuals may also be rotated through different job assignments. Job rotation encourages an employee's perception of the larger enterprise and helps to counter an us-them view of other departments.

Confront Game Players

Even in a climate of trust and openness, individuals may make suggestive comments or offer information that has an ulterior motive. A good response in such a situation is simply to ask, "Why are you telling me this about Sam?" or "Why don't you and I go see Sam's boss about this right

---

[§] The attributes of an open-ended purpose and difficulty in measuring individual performance are especially relevant to academic departments.

now? I think you should tell her what you've just told me." Another useful response is to offer to discuss questionable information in a public forum. A manager may say, for example, "I think I understand your concerns on this issue. Let's bring it up for discussion at our next department meeting." Using a public forum to discuss and choose a course of action is an excellent defense to most dubious suggestions. As a rule, a manager should not get involved in any scheme that he or she is unwilling to have discussed in public. Knowing that all suggestions are subject to open discussion invariably discourages people who hope to engage a manager in political games.

Machiavellianism

Niccolò Machiavelli, an Italian philosopher and statesman (1469–1527), was one of the earliest writers on the topic of political behavior. In his works, Machiavelli examined political effectiveness without regard for ethics or morality. Machiavelli simply ignored moral considerations in exploring not how people *should* behave, but how they actually do behave. Because of his uncompromising view of political reality, Machiavelli has sometimes been called the ultimate pragmatist. In recent years, his name has come to be synonymous with the use of political treachery and maneuvering. Thus, to say that someone is Machiavellian is a serious insult.**

Christie and Geis have tried to assess the extent to which an individual's personal style is Machiavellian in nature.[10] To do so, they converted certain basic tenets of Machiavelli's writings into an attitude scale that can be used to measure the extent to which an individual agrees with Machiavelli's views. The statements of the Machiavellian scale (or *Mach Scale* for short) focus on several factors. Chief among them are (1) the use of manipulative interpersonal tactics ("It is wise to flatter important people" and "Never tell anyone the real reason you did something unless it is useful to do so") and (2) an unfavorable view of human nature ("Generally speaking, people won't work hard unless they are forced to do so" and "Anyone who completely trusts anyone else is asking for trouble").

** Other world cultures have also had their own version of Niccolò Machiavelli. About 300 B.C., both Lord Shang of China and Koutilya, a prime minister in the south of India, wrote much the same philosophy as Machiavelli. All three writers shared several common themes: Humankind is basically weak, fallible, and gullible; therefore, a rational person takes advantage of situations and protects himself or herself from the implicit untrustworthiness of others.

A good deal is known about people who score high in agreement with Machiavelli's views.[11] Generally, they are able to control social interactions and effectively manipulate others. They are also especially effective in using their skills in face-to-face settings. A series of studies among college students found that highly Machiavellian students were more likely to be involved in medicine as a career and were more critical of their fellow students.[12] They also admitted to having strong feelings of hostility. In one contrived study, when students were induced to cheat and then accused of doing so, highly Machiavellian individuals looked their accuser in the eye and denied cheating longer than did less Machiavellian individuals.

Still other research indicates that Machiavellianism is positively correlated with occupational attainment (that is, job prestige and income) for individuals with above-average education, while for individuals with below-average education Machiavellianism is inversely related to occupational attainment. These results make sense in that highly Machiavellian individuals require situations that offer considerable latitude for improvisation and interpersonal manipulation (as is characteristic of white-collar jobs). Individuals in blue-collar jobs, where standards of performance are more objective and disciplinary measures are relatively coercive, may be penalized in proportion to their degree of Machiavellianism.[13]

In general, Machiavellian individuals are thought to be socially domineering and manipulative, and they are assumed to engage in political behavior more often than other organizational participants. They are lacking in (1) emotional display in interpersonal relations (that is, they remain cool and distant, and treat others as objects to be manipulated), (2) concern for traditional morality (that is, they find deceit useful rather than reprehensible), and (3) ideological commitments (that is, they prefer to maintain personal power in situations, rather than adhere to relatively inflexible ideals).

Consequences of Using Influence Tactics

Research on attempts to influence others has begun to focus on the specific techniques people use at work. After conversations with employees, David Kipnis and Stuart Schmidt developed a questionnaire for measuring six tactics for influencing others.[14] These tactics include:

1. Reason: relies on using data, logic, and discussion
2. Friendliness: interest, goodwill, and esteem are demonstrated to create a favorable impression

3. Coalition formation: other people in the organization are mobilized to support requests
4. Bargaining: relies on negotiation and exchanging favors
5. Assertiveness: relies on directness and forcefulness in communication
6. Appeal to higher authority: the influence of those higher in the organization is invoked to back up a request.

From responses to their questionnaire, Kipnis and Schmidt grouped employees into four influence styles:

1. Shotguns: people who refuse to take "no" for an answer and who use all of the preceding tactics to achieve their ends
2. Tacticians: people who try to influence others through reason and logic
3. Ingratiators: people who rely on ingratiation and flattery
4. Bystanders: people who watch the action rather than attempt to influence it[15]

Comparisons of performance evaluations for the four types of employees revealed that people who assertively attempted to influence their supervisors (Shotguns) were viewed less favorably. Both male and female Shotguns received equally low evaluations from their supervisors. Male supervisors tended to give the highest ratings to male Tacticians, who relied on reason and logic. Women who received the highest ratings were likely to be Ingratiators and Bystanders. In responding to these findings, male supervisors explained that both male Tacticians and female Ingratiators were seen as deferential and thoughtful.

Salary was also found to be associated with influence style. In a comparison of the income of 108 male CEOs, Tacticians earned the most ($73,240), followed by Bystanders ($60,270), Shotguns ($56,480), and Ingratiators ($52,700). Based on both evaluations and income, it seems that Tacticians are valued more than their peers who use other styles. Also, Shotgun-style individuals reported more job tension and personal stress than their counterparts.

Kipnis and Schmidt argue, from these and other findings, that books and training programs that are designed to "put people in charge" (in essence, teach a Shotgun style) are questionable. They contend that people should not be taught to be overly assertive as the best tactic for achieving their desires. Instead, training programs should emphasize less vigorous influence styles that rely on reason and logic.[16] Also, it is interesting to contrast managers' preferred styles when trying to influence superiors versus subordinates. Kipnis and Schmidt report that reason is preferred for trying to influence both superiors and subordinates. However, assertiveness is far more likely to be used with subordinates than with superiors, while coalition formation is more likely to be used to influence superiors than to influence subordinates.

Other Influence Techniques

Beyond the influence tactics discussed thus far are several other, more subtle, mechanisms by which people can be influenced. One effective technique is to create the appearance of higher *status*. Research has shown that people who merely appear to have higher status by virtue of their manner of dress or the use of titles exert greater influence. For example, in one study, a man violated the traffic light when crossing the street. In half the instances, the man was dressed in a well-tailored business suit, while in the remaining instances, he wore a work shirt and trousers. Of interest was the number of pedestrians who would cross the street with the man. As would be predicted from a status influence view, the well-dressed jaywalker influenced 3½ times as many people to cross the street with him.[17]

A second subtle form of influence is to create the appearance that a behavior is *normative*. For example, bartenders often place a few dollars into a tip glass to create the appearance that tipping is a proper action, and that greenbacks, not change, are commonly given. Also, "ringers" are sometimes planted in the audiences of preachers, with instructions to come forward on cue with donations or "cures." ‡ The apparent popularity of an action generally tends to induce compliance. For example, in one study, several individuals stared upward at the sky over New York City for a prolonged period of time. Within a short while, most passersby were also gazing at the empty sky.[18]

Lastly, people can sometimes be influenced to comply with a request for a sizable favor that they would otherwise not agree to, if they are first asked to do a small favor. This foot-in-the-door principle was once demonstrated in a study in which researchers asked people to install a large "Drive

‡ The use of ringers to induce behavior in others in a calculated fashion dates from Parisian opera houses in the 1820s, where members of the audience were paid to applaud or cheer on cue during the performance. The modem descendent of this practice is the television laugh track.

Carefully" sign in their front yards. Only 17 percent agreed to post a large sign. However, individuals who were initially asked to display a small 3-inch sign in their windows (which nearly all agreed to do) yielded 76 percent of the time when asked two weeks later to post the large sign.[19]

The Ethics of Organizational Politics

Figure 2 presents a model for incorporating ethical considerations into deciding whether to act in a political manner. This model, proposed by Gerald Cavanagh, Dennis Moberg, and Manuel Velasquez, provides guidance on whether a political behavior (PB), or course of action, should be followed in a particular situation.[20] From their perspective, a political behavior is ethical and appropriate only if (1) the behavior respects the rights of all affected parties and (2) the behavior respects the canons of justice— a self-evidently correct judgment of what is equitable and fair. In essence, the model encourages the adoption of nonpolitical behaviors (where such alternatives exist), and the rejection of behaviors that interfere with the canons of justice.

Figure 2

A Decision Tree for Incorporating Ethics into Political Behavior Decisions

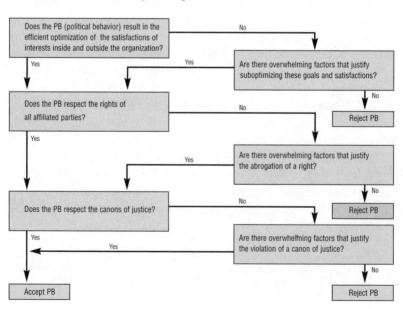

To illustrate their model, Cavanagh and his associates suggest a case in which two research scientists, Sam and Bill, are in competition in a new-product development lab. Each has prepared a proposal to win a significant cash award for the best new-product idea. Blind reviews of the proposals by other scientists indicate that both are equally meritorious. Sam inquires periodically about the outcome of the bidding process, while Bill wages an open campaign in support of his proposal. Specifically, Bill seizes every opportunity to point out the relative advantages of his proposal to individuals who may have some impact on the final decision. He does this after freely admitting his intention to Sam and others. His campaign of informal pressure is effective and his proposal is funded, while Sam's is not.

Using the decision tree, we first ask whether the outcome, in terms of the broad interests of society and the company, will be optimal. Since both proposals were judged to be equivalent in the blind reviews, we must answer yes to the first question. The second question focuses on whether Bill's behavior respected the rights of Sam. Because Bill told Sam he intended to campaign actively for his proposal, Bill cannot be accused of deceit. Also, Sam's inaction may be viewed as implied consent. The third question highlights the suspect nature of Bill's actions in pointing out irrelevant differences between the proposals. Given the equivalent merit of the proposals, other considerations (for example, which scientist was most qualified to implement the proposal, or other evidence of past performance) should have been incorporated in the funding decision.

RESPONDING TO AUTHORITY: OBEDIENCE

For managers to meet their goals, they must rely on their subordinates to obey their directions. Obedience to authority is a strongly ingrained predisposition for most people. Without this predisposition, society would not be able to function. Usually, the depth of our predisposition to obey orders can only be guessed at. Occasionally, we hear of instances of blind obedience to authority, as in the war-crime trials of Adolf Eichmann and Lieutenant William Calley, but we tend to discount such cases as extreme and unusual.

In the early 1960s, Stanley Milgram of Yale University conducted a series of studies to examine the extent to which people would obey, even if the demands of authority violated their moral responsibilities.[21] As part of this research, 40 adult males from a wide variety of occupations were paid to serve as subjects in a learning experiment. Each subject was told that he was participating in a study of the effects of punishment on learning. The subject was then asked to help another adult (actually the researcher's confederate) learn a lengthy list of word pairs by using electric shock as a penalty for each incorrect answer.

The subject (teacher) met with the alleged learner and then watched as the learner was strapped into an apparatus that looked like an electric chair. The experimenter then took the subject into the next room and showed him how to communicate with the learner through an intercom system. The experimenter also explained how to administer the punishment for any errors the learner might make in responding to stimulus words in the list of word pairs. The shock generator contained 30 switches, one for each of 30 different voltage levels ranging from 15 to 450 volts. The switches were also labeled in terms of the increasing strength of the voltage: slight shock, moderate shock, strong shock, very strong shock, intense shock, extreme intensity shock, danger: severe shock, and XXX.

After reading the list of word pairs to the learner, the teacher was to begin quizzing the learner. For each incorrect response, the teacher was to administer an electric shock, and for each additional incorrect response, the teacher was to apply the next higher voltage level on the generator.

The trials passed uneventfully until the learner began to make numerous mistakes. Then, in short order, the teacher found himself administering fairly high levels of voltage to the learner. At that point, the learner would begin to protest, saying that he wanted to drop out of the experiment because his heart was bothering him and the pain of the shocks was too much for him. If the teacher hesitated, the experimenter would encourage him to proceed, saying, for example, "Please go on" or "It is essential that you continue." If the teacher refused to proceed after four verbal encouragements, the experiment was discontinued.

As the voltage levels increased, the confederate (in accord with the experiment's protocol) would voice even stronger objections: He would pound on the wall and, at one point, scream loudly. Beyond a certain voltage level, the learner would no longer answer any of the teacher's questions, giving the impression that he was injured or dead. When this silence occurred, the experimenter would tell the teacher to treat the learner's failure to respond as an incorrect response, to administer the punishment, and to continue on with the next word pair.

Given these conditions, you would probably assume that very few subjects would obey the experimenter. But the actual results revealed that a majority of the subjects administered the maximum voltage on the shock generator and continued their participation in the experiment despite the learner's objections.

We should note, however, that although most subjects gave the maximum level of shock to the learner, they did not enjoy doing so. Typically, the subjects displayed strong signs of nervous tension, such as nail biting, trembling, and groaning. Many of them also laughed nervously whenever the learner protested or pleaded. However, the constraints of the situation compelled the subjects to continue their participation.‡‡

The high level of obedience displayed by Milgram's subjects suggests that the predisposition to follow authority is very strong. In this case, the experimenter relied on his expertise and legitimacy to give the subject orders. Despite the fact that all subjects received their pay in advance and participated voluntarily, most felt a strong desire to avoid disobeying authority, even in light of the suffering they inflicted on another person.

These results suggest that society may be too successful at socializing its members to obey authority. When people take on roles that prescribe obedience (such as those of research subject, student, soldier, or employee), the sense of responsibility for the outcomes of their own conduct is likely to be diminished. The evidence from Milgram's work implies that human conscience cannot be relied on to step in and halt activities that are injurious to others. It can be inferred that organizational members generally will carry out orders given by those in authority, regardless of the content or consequences of the actions. This suggests that forms of socialization that emphasize personal responsibility to others may be lacking in our society.

Milgram's findings have raised a number of questions. One of the more intriguing is whether there are cultural differences in the predisposition to obey authority. For example, considering the Holocaust—the persecution and extermination of European Jews by Nazi Germany—one might hypothesize that the level of obedience would be higher in Germany than in other countries. To test this notion, the conditions of Milgram's original study were recreated in several different countries: Canada, England, Jordan, and the former West Germany. The results yielded essentially similar findings, suggesting that the level of obedience to authority in the Milgram

---

‡‡ When each subject completed the experiment, he met with the learner and discovered that in fact no shocks had been given. The true purpose of the study was then explained to the subject.

condition is fairly constant across different societies.[22] By inference, the atrocities that occurred in Nazi Germany could happen elsewhere in the world.[§§]

In addition, the level of obedience in the Milgram study may have been near the "baseline" for injurious behavior. The victim (learner) in Milgram's original study was an innocent 47-year-old man. If the victim had been someone whom the subject disliked for any number of possible reasons (race, religion, or politics) or had the subject possessed a strong commitment to the purpose of the study in which he was involved, or expected to be continually involved with persons in the study, the level of obedience might well have been much higher.

The study of the personalities of participants in the Milgram experiments has yielded some interesting findings. Subjects who were relatively more obedient were significantly more authoritarian. This result confirms the notion that a major component of the authoritarian personality is one of uncritical submission to an idealized authority.[25] Individuals who defied the experimenter were at a higher stage of moral development than those who were obedient, as measured in Kohlberg's system of moral development. Yet another correlate of defiance of authority was social intelligence. In one study, it was found that subjects who did not comply fully with the experimenter's commands were individuals who scored higher on a measure of social intelligence.[26] People who are more socially intelligent (that is, who are more astute observers of others and who have the ability to effectively influence the outcomes of situations) are probably better able to understand and manage situations using available social cues.

Since the time of Milgram's studies, greater concern has arisen over research ethics and specifically the need to protect subjects from traumatic experiences. Because of these concerns about the rights of subjects, it has become exceedingly difficult to obtain peer approval to conduct and publish similar research. Therefore, something of a moratorium exists on con-

---

[§§] Such mass atrocities have in fact happened again—witness Cambodia, Uganda, Mao's China, and Stalin's Russia. In an interview with Morley Safer for the news program "Sixty Minutes," Milgram stated that "if a system of death camps were set up in the United States of the sort we had seen in Nazi Germany, one would be able to find sufficient personnel for those camps in any medium-sized American town".[23] However, other evidence from cross-national studies is somewhat suggestive of cultural differences. In a less well publicized self-decision condition (wherein the "teacher" was allowed to choose the shock level in each trial), various studies found extremely low levels of total shock administered by all national samples. However, the levels administered for German and Jordanian samples were somewhat higher than those observed for Australian and U.S. samples.[24]

ducting studies such as Milgram's that may involve unpleasant experiences for the subject. As a result, it cannot be determined whether the present level of obedience is lower than in the past. Some national experiences, such as the Watergate scandal and the Vietnam War protests, have certainly made it more socially acceptable to oppose authority. It is probably safe to say that it is now somewhat more difficult to extract conformity in a variety of settings (including work, school, and government) than it has been in the past.

In summary, Milgram's research suggests that people placed in a conflict situation pitting moral values against authority will tend to follow the dictates of authority. Perhaps the most sobering aspect of this discovery lies in how little real power an authority figure needs in order to succeed in directing others. Of course, opportunities for the abuse of authority also occur in business organizations. Because of this reality, it is essential that managers recognize the magnitude of their power over others and act in accordance with the responsibility that such power entails.

NOTES

1. D. C. McClelland, *Power: The Inner Experience* (New York: Irvington, 1975); D. C. McClelland, "Power Is the Great Motivation," *Harvard Business Review* 54 (1976): 100–110.

2. H. C. Kelman, "Processes of Opinion Change," *Public Opinion Quarterly* 25 (1961): 57–78.

3. J. R. P. French, Jr., and B. H. Raven, "The Bases of Social Power," in *Studies in Social Power,* ed. D. Cartwright (Ann Arbor: University of Michigan, Institute for Social Research, 1959); T. Hinkin and C. Schriesheim, "Development and Application of New Scales to Measure the French and Raven Bases of Social Power," *Journal of Applied Psychology* 74 (1989): 561–567.

4. A. Etzioni, *A Comparative Analysis of Complex Organizations,* rev. ed. (New York: Free Press, 1975); R. Mayer, "Understanding Employee Motivation through Organizational Commitment" (Ph.D. diss., Purdue University, 1989).

5. M. Sussmann and R. P. Vecchio, "A Social Influence Interpretation of Worker Motivation," *Academy of Management Review* 7 (1982): 177–186; R. P. Vecchio and M. Sussmann, "Preference for Forms of Supervisory Social Influence," *Journal of Organizational Behavior* 10 (1989): 135–143.

6. Ibid.

7. G. R. Ferris and K. M. Kacmar, "Perceptions of Organizational Politics," *Journal of Management* 10 (1992): 93–116; J. Pfeffer, *Power in Organizations* (Boston: Pitman Publishing Co., 1981).

8. R. W. Allen, D. L. Madison, L. W. Porter, et al., "Organizational Politics: Tactics and Characteristics of Its Actors," *California Management Review* 12 (Fall 1979):

77–83; A. J. DuBrin, *Winning at Office Politics* (New York: Ballantine, 1978); R. H. Miles, *Macro Organizational Behavior* (Santa Monica, Calif.: Goodyear, 1980), 174–175; Pfeffer, *Power in Organizations.*

9. DuBrin, *Winning at Office Politics.*

10. R. Christie and F. L. Geis, eds., *Studies in Machiavellianism* (New York: Academic Press, 1970).

11. G. R. Gemmil and W. J. Heisler, "Machiavellianism as a Factor in Managerial Job Strain, Job Satisfaction, and Upward Mobility," *Academy of Management Journal* 15 (1972): 53–67.

12. R. V. Exline, J. Thibaut, C. O. Hickey, et al., "Visual Interaction in Relation to Machiavellianism and an Unethical Act," in *Studies in Machiavellianism,* ed., R. Christie and F. L. Geis (New York: Academic Press, 1970), 53–75; D. Kipnis and S. M. Schmidt, *Profiles of Organizational Influence Strategies* (San Diego: University Associates, 1982); S. M. Schmidt and D. Kipnis, "The Perils of Persistence," *Psychology Today,* November 1987, 32–34; D. Kipnis, *The Powerholders* (Chicago: University of Chicago Press, 1976); P. Block, *The Empowered Manager* (San Francisco: Jossey-Bass, 1988).

13. C. F. Turner and D. C. Martinez, "Socioeconomic Achievement and the Machiavellian Personality," *Sociometry* 40 (1977): 325–336.

14. Kipnis and Schmidt, *Profiles of Organizational Influence Strategies;* C. Schriesheim and T. Hinkin, "Influence Tactics Used by Subordinates: A Theoretical and Empirical Analysis and Refinement of the Kipnis, Schmidt, and Wilkinson Subscales," *Journal of Applied Psychology* 75 (1990): 246–252; G. Yukl and J. B. Tracey, "Consequences of Influence Tactics Used with Subordinates, Peers, and the Boss," *Journal of Applied Psychology* 76 (1992): 525–535; C. Falbe and G. Yukl, "Consequences for Managers of Using Single Influence Tactics and Combinations of Tactics," *Academy of Management Journal* 35 (1992): 638–652; D. Brass and M. Burkhardt, "Potential Power and Power Use: An Investigation of Structure and Behaviors," *Academy of Management Journal* 36 (1993): 441–470.

15. Schmidt and Kipnis, "The Perils of Persistence."

16. Kipnis, *The Powerholders;* Block, *The Empowered Manager;* D. Kipnis, S. M. Schmidt, C. Swaffin-Smith, and I. Wilkenson, "Patterns of Managerial Influence: Shotgun Managers, Tacticians, and Bystanders," *Organizational Dynamics* (1984): 58–67; S. M. Farmer, D. B. Fedor, J. S. Goodman, and J. M. Maslyn, "Factors Affecting the Use of Upward Influence Strategies," *Proceedings of the Academy of Management* (1993): 64–68.

17. M. Lefkowitz, R. A. Blake, and J. S. Mouton, "Status Factors in Pedestrian Violation of Traffic Signals," *Journal of Abnormal and Social Psychology* 51 (1955): 704–706.

18. S. Milgram, L. Bickman, and L. Berkowitz, "Note on the Drawing Power of Crowds of Different Size," *Journal of Personality and Social Psychology* 13 (1969): 79–82.

19. J. C. Freedman and S. C. Fraser, "Compliance Without Pressure: The Foot-in-the-Door Technique," *Journal of Personality and Social Psychology* 4 (1966): 195–202.

20. G. F. Cavanagh, D. J. Moberg, and M. Velasquez, "The Ethics of Organizational Politics," *Academy of Management Review* 6 (1981): 363–374.

21. S. Milgram, "Behavioral Study of Obedience," *Journal of Abnormal and Social Psychology* 67 (1963): 371–378.

22. S. Milgram, *Obedience to Authority* (New York: Harper, 1974); M. E. Shanah and K. A. Yahya, "A Behavioral Study of Obedience in Children," *Journal of Personality and Social Psychology* 35 (1977): 530–536.

23. CBS News, Transcript of "Sixty Minutes" segment, "I Was Only Following Orders," (March 31, 1979): 2–8; D. M. Mantell, "The Potential for Violence in Germany," *Journal of Social Issues* 27 (1971): 101–112; M. E. Shanah and K. A. Yahya, "A Cross-Cultural Study of Obedience," *Bulletin of the Psychonomic Society* 11 (1978): 267–269; W. Kilham and L. Mann, "Level of Destructive Obedience as a Function of Transmitter and Executant Roles in the Milgram Obedience Paradigm," *Journal of Personality and Social Psychology* 29 (1974): 696–702; S. R. Shalala, "A Study of Various Communication Settings Which Produce Obedience by Subordinates to Unlawful Superior Orders" (Ph.D. diss., University of Kansas, 1974).

24. T. Blass, "Obedience to Authority: Some Issues and Significance," in *Perspectives on Stanley Milgram's Contributions to Social Psychology* (Symposium conducted at the Annual Meeting of the American Psychological Association, Boston, Mass., August 24, 1990).

25. A. C. Elms and S. Milgram, "Personality. Characteristics Associated with Obedience and Defiance toward Authoritative Command," *Journal of Experimental Research in Personality* 1 (1966): 282–289; A. C. Elms, *Social Psychology and Social Relevance* (Boston: Little, Brown, 1972); S. Milgram, *Obedience to Authority: An Experimental View* (New York: Harper and Row, 1974).

26. P. M. Burley and J. McGuiness, "Effects of Social Intelligence on the Milgram Paradigm," *Psychological Reports* 40 (1977): 767–770.

Managing Your Boss

John J. Gabarro and John P. Kotter

To many people, the phrase *managing your boss* may sound unusual or suspicious. Because of the traditional top-down emphasis in most organizations, it is not obvious why you need to manage relationships upward— unless, of course, you would do so for personal or political reasons. But we are not referring to political maneuvering or to apple polishing. We are using the term to mean the process of consciously working with your superior to obtain the best possible results for you, your boss, and the company.

Recent studies suggest that effective managers take time and effort to manage not only relationships with their subordinates but also those with their bosses. These studies also show that this essential aspect of management is sometimes ignored by otherwise talented and aggressive managers. Indeed, some managers who actively and effectively supervise subordinates, products, markets, and technologies assume an almost passively reactive stance vis-à-vis their bosses. Such a stance almost always hurts them and their companies.

If you doubt the importance of managing your relationship with your boss or how difficult it is to do so effectively, consider for a moment the following sad but telling story:

Frank Gibbons was an acknowledged manufacturing genius in his industry and, by any profitability standard, a very effective executive. One year, his strengths propelled him into the position of vice president of manufacturing for the second largest and most profitable company in its industry. Gibbons was not, however, a good manager of people. He knew this, as did others in his company and his industry. Recognizing this weakness, the president made sure that those who reported to Gibbons were good at working with people and could compensate for his limitations. The arrangement worked well.

Later, Philip Bonnevie was promoted into a position reporting to Gibbons. In keeping with the previous pattern, the president selected Bonnevie because he had an excellent track record and a reputation for being good with people. In making that selection, however, the resident neglected to notice that, in his rapid rise through the organization, Bonnevie had always had good-to-excellent bosses. He had never been forced to manage a relationship with a difficult boss. In retrospect, Bonnevie admits he had never thought that managing his boss was a part of his job.

Fourteen months after he started working for Gibbons, Bonnevie was fired. During that same quarter, the company reported a net loss for the first time in seven years. Many of those who were close to these events say that they don't really understand what happened. This much is known, however: while the company was bringing out a major new product—a process that required sales, engineering, and manufacturing groups to coordinate decisions very carefully—a whole series of misunderstandings and bad feelings developed between Gibbons and Bonnevie.

For example, Bonnevie claims Gibbons was aware of and had accepted Bonnevie's decision to use a new type of machinery to make the new product; Gibbons swears he did not. Furthermore, Gibbons claims he made it clear to Bonnevie that introduction of the product was too important to the company in the short run to take any major risks.

As a result of such misunderstandings, planning went awry: a new manufacturing plant was built that could not produce the new product designed by engineering, in the volume desired by sales, at a cost agreed on by the executive committee. Gibbons blamed Bonnevie for the mistake. Bonnevie blamed Gibbons.

Of course, one could argue that the problem here was caused by Gibbons's inability to manage his subordinates. But one can make just as strong a case that the problem was related to Bonnevie's inability to manage his boss. Remember, Gibbons was not having difficulty with any other subordinates. Moreover, given the personal price paid by Bonnevie (being fired and having his reputation within the industry severely tarnished), there was little consolation in saying the problem was that Gibbons was poor at managing subordinates. Everyone already knew that.

We believe that the situation could have turned out differently had Bonnevie been more adept at understanding Gibbons and at managing his relationship with him. In this case, an inability to manage upward was unusually costly. The company lost $2 million to $5 million, and Bonnevie's career was, at least temporarily, disrupted. Many less costly cases similar to this probably occur regularly in all major corporations, and the cumulative effect can be very destructive.

MISREADING THE BOSS-SUBORDINATE RELATIONSHIP

People often dismiss stories like the one we just related as being merely cases of personality conflict. Because two people can on occasion be psychologically or temperamentally incapable of working together, this can be an apt description. But more often, we have found, a personality conflict is only a part of the problem—sometimes a very small part.

Bonnevie did not just have a different personality from Gibbons, he also made or had unrealistic assumptions and expectations about the very nature of boss-subordinate relationships. Specifically, he did not recognize that his relationship to Gibbons involved *mutual dependence* between two *fallible* human beings. Failing to recognize this, a manager typically either avoids trying to manage his or her relationship with a boss or manages it ineffectively.

Some people behave as if their bosses were not very dependent on them. They fail to see how much the boss needs their help and cooperation to do his or her job effectively. These people refuse to acknowledge that the boss can be severely hurt by their actions and needs cooperation, dependability, and honesty from them.

Some people see themselves as not very dependent on their bosses. They gloss over how much help and information they need from the boss in order to perform their own jobs well. This superficial view is particularly damaging when a manager's job and decisions affect other parts of the organization, as was the case in Bonnevie's situation. A manager's immediate boss can play a critical role in linking the manager to the rest of the organization, making sure the manager's priorities are consistent with organizational needs, and in securing the resources the manager needs to perform well. Yet some managers need to see themselves as practically self-sufficient, as not needing the critical information and resources a boss can supply.

Many managers, like Bonnevie, assume that the boss will magically know what information or help their subordinates need and provide it to them. Certainly, some bosses do an excellent job of caring for their subordinates in this way, but for a manager to expect that from all bosses is dangerously unrealistic. A more reasonable expectation for managers to have is that modest help will be forthcoming. After all, bosses are only human. Most really effective managers accept this fact and assume primary responsibility for their own careers and development. They make a point of seeking the information and help they need to do a job instead of waiting for their bosses to provide it.

In light of the foregoing, it seems to us that managing a situation of mutual dependence among fallible human beings requires the following:

1. That you have a good understanding of the other person and yourself, especially regarding strengths, weaknesses, work styles, and needs.
2. That you use this information to develop and manage a healthy working relationship—one that is compatible with both people's work styles and assets, is characterized by mutual expectations, and meets the most critical needs of the other person. This combination is essentially what we have found highly effective managers doing.

UNDERSTANDING THE BOSS

Managing your boss requires that you gain an understanding of the boss and his or her context, as well as your own situation. All managers do this to some degree, but many are not thorough enough.

At a minimum, you need to appreciate your boss's goals and pressures, his or her strengths and weaknesses. What are your boss's organizational and personal objectives, and what are his or her pressures, especially those from his or her own boss and others at the same level? What are your boss's long suits and blind spots? What is the preferred style of working? Does your boss like to get information through memos, formal meetings, or phone calls? Does he or she thrive on conflict or try to minimize it?

Without this information, a manager is flying blind when dealing with the boss, and unnecessary conflicts, misunderstandings, and problems are inevitable.

In one situation we studied, a top-notch marketing manager with a superior performance record was hired into a company as a vice president "to straighten out the marketing and sales problems." The company, which was having financial difficulties, had recently been acquired by a larger corporation. The president was eager to turn it around and gave the new marketing vice president free rein—at least initially. Based on his previous experience, the new vice president correctly diagnosed that greater market share was needed for the company and that strong product management was required to bring that about. Following that logic, he made a number of pricing decisions that were aimed at increasing high-volume business.

When margins declined and the financial situation did not improve, however, the president increased pressure on the new vice president. Believing that the situation would eventually correct itself as the company gained back market share, the vice president resisted the pressure.

When by the second quarter, margins and profits had still failed to improve, the president took direct control over all pricing decisions and put all items on a set level of margin, regardless of volume. The new vice president began to find himself shut out by the president, and their relationship deteriorated. In fact, the vice president found the president's behavior bizarre. Unfortunately, the president's new pricing scheme also failed to increase margins, and by the fourth quarter, both the president and the vice president were fired.

What the new vice president had not known until it was too late was that improving marketing and sales had been only one of the president's goals. His most immediate goal had been to make the company more profitable—quickly.

Nor had the new vice president known that his boss was invested in this short-term priority for personal as well as business reasons. The president had been a strong advocate of the acquisition within the parent company, and his personal credibility was at stake.

The vice president made three basic errors. He took information supplied to him at face value, he made assumptions in areas where he had no information, and—what was most damaging—he never actively tried to clarify what his boss's objectives were. As a result, he ended up taking actions that were actually at odds with the president's priorities and objectives.

Managers who work effectively with their bosses do not behave this way. They seek out information about the boss's goals and problems and pressures. They are alert for opportunities to question the boss and others around him or her to test their assumptions. They pay attention to clues in the boss's behavior. Although it is imperative that they do this especially when they begin working with a new boss, effective managers also do this on an ongoing basis because they recognize that priorities and concerns change.

Being sensitive to a boss's work style can be crucial, especially when the boss is new. For example, a new president who was organized and formal in his approach replaced a subordinate who was informal and intuitive. The new president worked best when he had written reports. He also preferred formal meetings with set agendas.

One of his division managers realized this need and worked with the new president to identify the kinds and frequency of information and reports that the president wanted. This manager also made a point of sending background information and brief agendas ahead of time for their discussions. He found that with this type of preparation their meetings were very useful. Another interesting result was, he found that with adequate preparation his new boss was even more effective at brainstorming problems than his more informal and intuitive predecessor had been.

In contrast, another division manager never fully understood how the new boss's work style differed from that of his predecessor. To the degree that he did sense it, he experienced it as too much control. As a result, he seldom sent the new president the background information he needed, and the president never felt fully prepared for meetings with the manager. In fact, the president spent much of this time when they met trying to get information that he felt he should have had earlier. The boss experienced these meetings as frustrating and inefficient, and the subordinate often found himself thrown off guard by the questions that the president asked. Ultimately, this division manager resigned.

The difference between the two division managers just described was not so much one of ability or even adaptability. Rather, one of them was more sensitive to the boss's work style than the other and to the implications of the boss's needs.

UNDERSTANDING YOURSELF

The boss is only one-half of the relationship. You are the other half, as well as the part over which you have more direct control. Developing an effective working relationship requires, then, that you know your own needs, strengths and weaknesses, and personal style.

You are not going to change either your basic personality structure or that of your boss. But you can become aware of what it is about you that impedes or facilitates working with your boss and, with that awareness, take actions that make the relationship more effective.

For example, in one case we observed, a manager and the superior ran into problems whenever they disagreed. The boss's typical response was to harden his position and overstate it. The manager's reaction was then to raise the ante and intensify the forcefulness of his argument. In doing this, he channeled his anger into sharpening his attacks on the logical fallacies he saw in his boss's assumptions. His boss in turn would become even more adamant about holding his original position. Predictably, this escalating cycle resulted in the subordinate avoiding whenever possible any topic of potential conflict with his boss.

In discussing this problem with his peers, the manager discovered that his reaction to the boss was typical of how he generally reacted to counter-arguments—but with a difference. His response would overwhelm his peers but not his boss. Because his attempts to discuss this problem with his boss were unsuccessful, he concluded that the only way to change the situation was to deal with his own instinctive reactions. Whenever the two reached an impasse, he would check his own impatience and suggest that they break up and think about it before getting together again. Usually when they re-newed their discussion, they had digested their differences and were more able to work them through.

Gaining this level of self-awareness and acting on it are difficult but not impossible. For example, by reflecting over his past experiences, a young manager learned that he was not very good at dealing with difficult and emotional issues where people were involved. Because he disliked those is-sues and realized that his instinctive responses to them were seldom very good, he developed a habit of touching base with his boss whenever such a problem arose. Their discussions always surfaced ideas and approaches the manager had not considered. In many cases, they also identified specific ac-tions the boss could take to help.

Although a superior-subordinate relationship is one of mutual depen-dence, it is also one in which the subordinate is typically more dependent on the boss than the other way around. This dependence inevitably results in the subordinate feeling a certain degree of frustration, sometimes anger, when his actions or options are constrained by his boss's decisions. This is a normal part of life and occurs in the best of relationships. The way in which a manager handles these frustrations largely depends on his or her predisposition toward dependence on authority figures.

Some people's instinctive reaction under these circumstances is to resent the boss's authority and to rebel against the boss's decisions. Sometimes a person will escalate a conflict beyond what is appropriate. Seeing the boss almost as an institutional enemy, this type of manager will often, without being conscious of it, fight with the boss just for the sake of fighting. The subordinate's reactions to being constrained are usually strong and some-times impulsive. He or she sees the boss as someone who, by virtue of the role, is a hindrance to progress, an obstacle to be circumvented or at best tolerated.

Psychologists call this pattern of reactions counterdependent behavior. Although a counterdependent person is difficult for most superiors to manage and usually has a history of strained relationships with superiors, this sort of manager is apt to have even more trouble with a boss who tends to be directive or authoritarian. When the manager acts on his or her negative feelings, often in subtle and nonverbal ways, the boss sometimes does become the enemy. Sensing the subordinate's latent hostility, the boss will lose trust in the subordinate or his or her judgment and then behave even less openly.

Paradoxically, a manager with this type of predisposition is often a good manager of his or her own people. He or she will many times go out of the way to get support for them and will not hesitate to go to bat for them.

At the other extreme are managers who swallow their anger and behave in a very compliant fashion when the boss makes what they know to be a poor decision. These managers will agree with the boss even when a disagreement might be welcome or when the boss would easily alter a decision if given more information. Because they bear no relationship to the specific situation at hand, their responses are as much an overreaction as those of counterdependent managers. Instead of seeing the boss as an enemy, these people deny their anger—the other extreme—and tend to see the boss as if he or she were an all-wise parent who should know best, should take responsibility for their careers, train them in all they need to know, and protect them from overly ambitious peers.

Both counterdependence and overdependence lead managers to hold unrealistic views of what a boss is. Both views ignore that most bosses, like everyone else, are imperfect and fallible. They don't have unlimited time, encyclopedic knowledge, or extrasensory perception; nor are they evil enemies. They have their own pressures and concerns that are sometimes at odds with the wishes of the subordinate—and often for good reason.

Altering predispositions toward authority, especially at the extremes, is almost impossible without intensive psychotherapy (psychoanalytic theory and research suggest that such predispositions are deeply rooted in a person's personality and upbringing). However, an awareness of these extremes and the range between them can be very useful in understanding where your own predispositions fall and what the implications are for how you tend to behave in relation to your boss.

If you believe, on the one hand, that you have some tendencies toward counterdependence, you can understand and even predict what your reactions and overreactions are likely to be. If, on the other hand, you believe you have some tendencies toward overdependence, you might question the extent to which your overcompliance or inability to confront real differences may be making both you and your boss less effective.

DEVELOPING AND MANAGING THE RELATIONSHIP

With a clear understanding of both your boss and yourself, you can *usually* establish a way of working together that fits both of you, that is characterized by unambiguous mutual expectations, and that helps you both be more productive and effective. The "Checklist for Managing Your Boss" summarizes some things such a relationship consists of. Following are a few more.

Compatible Work Styles

Above all else, a good working relationship with a boss accommodates differences in work style. For example, in one situation we studied, a manager (who had a relatively good relationship with his superior) realized that during meetings his boss would often become inattentive and sometimes brusque. The subordinate's own style tended to be discursive and exploratory. He would often digress from the topic at hand to deal with background factors, alternative approaches, and so forth. His boss preferred to discuss problems with a minimum of background detail and became impatient and distracted whenever his subordinate digressed from the immediate issue.

Recognizing this difference in style, the manager became terser and more direct during meetings with his boss. To help himself do this, before meetings, he would develop brief agendas that he used as a guide. Whenever he felt that a digression was needed, he explained why. This small shift in his own style made these meetings more effective and far less frustrating for both of them.

Subordinates can adjust their styles in response to their bosses' preferred method for receiving information. Peter Drucker divides bosses into "listeners" and "readers." Some bosses like to get information in report form so they can read and study it. Others work better with information and reports presented in person so they can ask questions. As Drucker points out, the implications are obvious. If your boss is a listener, you brief him or her in person, *then* follow it up with a memo. If your boss is a reader, you cover important items or proposals in a memo or report, *then* discuss them.

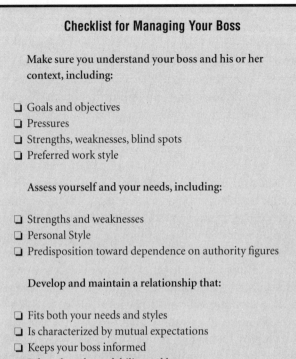

Checklist for Managing Your Boss

Make sure you understand your boss and his or her context, including:

❏ Goals and objectives
❏ Pressures
❏ Strengths, weaknesses, blind spots
❏ Preferred work style

Assess yourself and your needs, including:

❏ Strengths and weaknesses
❏ Personal Style
❏ Predisposition toward dependence on authority figures

Develop and maintain a relationship that:

❏ Fits both your needs and styles
❏ Is characterized by mutual expectations
❏ Keeps your boss informed
❏ Is based on dependability and honesty
❏ Selectively uses your boss's time and resources

Other adjustments can be made according to a boss's decision-making style. Some bosses prefer to be involved in decisions and problems as they arise. These are high-involvement managers who like to keep their hands on the pulse of the operation. Usually their needs (and your own) are best satisfied if you touch base with them on an ad hoc basis. A boss who has a need to be involved will become involved one way or another, so there are advantages to including him or her at your initiative. Other bosses prefer to delegate—they don't want to be involved. They expect you to come to them with major problems and inform them about any important changes.

Creating a compatible relationship also involved drawing on each other's strengths and making up for each other's weaknesses. Because he knew that the boss—the vice president of engineering—was not very good at monitoring his employees' problems, one manager we studied made a point of doing it himself. The stakes were high: the engineers and technicians were all union members, the company worked on a customer-contract basis, and the company had recently experienced a serious strike.

The manager worked closely with his boss, along with people in the scheduling department and the personnel office, to make sure that potential problems were avoided. He also developed an informal arrangement through which his boss would review with him any proposed changes in personnel or assignment policies before taking action. The boss valued his advice and credited his subordinate for improving both the performance of the division and the labor-management climate.

Mutual Expectations

The subordinate who passively assumes that he or she knows what the boss expects is in for trouble. Of course, some superiors will spell out their expectations very explicitly and in great detail. But most do not. And although many corporations have systems that provide a basis for communicating expectations (such as formal planning processes, career planning reviews, and performance appraisal reviews), these systems never work perfectly. Also, between these formal reviews, expectations invariably change.

Ultimately, the burden falls on the subordinate to find out what the boss's expectations are. They can be both broad (such as what kinds of problems the boss wishes to be informed about and when) as well as very specific (such things as when a particular project should be completed and what kinds of information the boss needs in the interim).

Getting a boss who tends to be vague or not explicit to express expectations can be difficult. But effective managers find ways to get that information. Some will draft a detailed memo covering key aspects of their work and then send it to their boss for approval. They then follow this up with a face-to-face discussion in which they go over each item in the memo. A discussion like this will often surface virtually all of the boss's expectations.

Other effective managers will deal with an inexplicit boss by initiating an ongoing series of informal discussions about "good management" and "our objectives." Still others find useful information more indirectly through those who used to work for the boss and through the formal planning systems in which the boss makes commitments to his or her own superior. Which approach you choose, of course, should depend on your understanding of your boss's style.

Developing a workable set of mutual expectations also requires that you communicate your own expectations to the boss, find out if they are realistic, and influence the boss to accept the ones that are important to you. Being able to influence the boss to value your expectations can be particularly important if the boss is an overachiever. Such a boss will often set unrealistically high standards that need to be brought into line with reality.

A Flow of Information

How much information a boss needs about what a subordinate is doing will vary significantly depending on the boss's style, the situation he or she is in, and the confidence the boss has in the subordinate. But it is not uncommon for a boss to need more information than the subordinate would naturally supply or for the subordinate to think the boss knows more than he or she really does. Effective managers recognize that they probably underestimate what their bosses need to know and make sure they find ways to keep them informed through processes that fit their styles.

Managing the flow of information upward is particularly difficult if the boss does not like to hear about problems. Although many people would deny it, bosses often give off signals they want to hear only good news. They show great displeasure—usually nonverbally—when someone tells them about a problem. Ignoring individual achievement, they may even evaluate more favorably subordinates who do not bring problems to them.

Nevertheless, for the good of the organization, the boss, and the subordinate, a superior needs to hear about failures as well as successes. Some subordinates deal with a good-news-only boss by finding indirect ways to get the necessary information to him or her, such as a management information system. Others see to it that potential problems, whether in the form of good surprises or bad news, are communicated immediately.

Dependability and Honesty

Few things are more disabling to a boss than a subordinate on whom he cannot depend, whose work he cannot trust. Almost no one is intentionally undependable, but many managers are inadvertently so because of oversight or uncertainty about the boss's priorities. A commitment to an optimistic delivery date may please a superior in the short term but become a source of displeasure if not honored. It's difficult for a boss to rely on a subordinate who repeatedly slips deadlines. As one president (describing a subordinate) put it: "I'd rather he be more consistent even if he delivered fewer peak successes—at least I could rely on him."

Nor are many managers intentionally dishonest with their bosses. But it is easy to shade the truth and play down issues. Current concerns often become future surprise problems. It's almost impossible for bosses to work effectively if they cannot rely on a fairly accurate reading from their subordinates. Because it undermines credibility, dishonesty is perhaps the most troubling trait a subordinate can have. Without a basic level of trust, a boss feels compelled to check all of a subordinate's decisions, which makes it difficult to delegate.

Good Use of Time and Resources

Your boss is probably as limited in his or her store of time, energy, and influence as you are. Every request you make of your boss uses up some of these resources, so it's wise to draw on these resources selectively. This may sound obvious, but many managers use up their boss's time (and some of their own credibility) over relatively trivial issues.

One vice president went to great lengths to get his boss to fire a meddlesome secretary in another department. His boss had to use considerable influence to do it. Understandably, the head of the other department was not pleased. Later, when the vice president wanted to tackle more important problems, he ran into trouble. By using up his chips on a relatively trivial issue, he had made it difficult for him and his boss to meet more important goals.

No doubt, some subordinates will resent that on top of all their other duties, they also need to take time and energy to manage their relationships with their bosses. Such managers fail to realize the importance of this activity and how it can simplify their jobs by eliminating potentially severe problems. Effective managers recognize that this part of their work is legitimate. Seeing themselves as ultimately responsible for what they achieve in an organization, they know they need to establish and manage relationships with everyone on whom they depend—and that includes the boss.

Effective Followership:
Leadership Turned Upside Down

Robert P. Vecchio

The twelve members of a professional association recently met to select a new president. Each member had a hand in pressuring the former president to resign. As a result of a number of minor actions and omissions of actions, the members had made the president's task so difficult that he had found it nearly impossible to function as the head of the association. Now, each member was prepared to fight for a preferred candidate for the presidential position. When the group's discussion came to the selection of a new president, one member observed, "Who can we find that will be able to lead us?" Unexpectedly, one clever member replied, "More importantly, who can we find that we will be able to follow?"

This wry reply provides an insight to a much neglected feature of the process of leadership: followership. Traditionally, studies of leadership have focused on leader behaviors and leader attributes. Omitted in these writings is a serious consideration of the impact of followership as a determinant of effective leadership. Yet, the activities of leadership and followership are inextricably related. The concepts are intertwined in Ying-Yang fashion: one concept implies (and, in fact, requires) the other. For example, consider the following propositions developed by Trudy Heller and Jon VanTil:[1]

- The leader must lead, and do it well to retain leadership; the follower must follow, and do it well to retain followership.
- Where all seek to lead, or all seek to follow, there can be no leadership or followership.
- Good leadership enhances followers, just as good followership enhances leaders.
- Leadership, and followership, may be an art in which people can become more highly skilled.

A good argument can be made that when we commonly speak of effective leadership, we are really speaking of effective followership. As evidence of this, consider that we typically measure a manager's effectiveness by examining the performance of his or her unit. The performance of a unit, however, is often more a function of the talents and desires of the followers than the leader. A given level of subordinate talent and motivation can have far more to do with the unit's performance than the leader's efforts.

As an essential element in the development and management of an effective business strategy, the human resources configuration of those units comprising an organization is critical. In this article, the importance and dynamics of effective followership will be explored. In addition, techniques for fostering and maintaining effective followership will be considered.

THE LIMITS OF LEADERSHIP

In many situations, it can be extremely difficult for a leader to influence, easily or directly, the performance of a unit. Social scientists have recently come to recognize that many factors can serve as "substitutes" for and "neutralizers" of a leader's efforts.[2] Substitutes for leadership include explicit rules and procedures, rigid reward structures which a leader cannot affect, and physical distance between a leader and his subordinates. For example, subordinates who are given explicit goals and rules for performing their jobs, will not need to be given direction by a leader. Characteristics of individuals can serve to neutralize a leader's influence. For example, subordinates who are highly experienced, possess sufficient training and knowledge, and have a high need for independence or a sense of professionalism will not need, or may even resent, a leader who tries to be directive. Task characteristics, such as routineness, frequent feedback, and a high degree of structure can also undercut a leader's potential influence.

What we typically think of as being failures in leadership, may also be rightly characterized as failures in followership. A degree of responsibility for unit performance rests squarely on subordinates. Superiors, where their influence can make a difference, cannot be effective if subordinates do not subscribe to unit goals, or exert sufficient effort. Subordinates have a responsibility to be conscientious, and to expend energies for unit goals. In an enlightened view, both leaders and followers share in the responsibility of being productive and effective.

LEADERSHIP AND FOLLOWERSHIP:
SOME POPULAR FICTIONS

The traditional view of leadership assumes that leaders are responsible for motivating subordinates and eliciting their commitment—that subordinates are initially lacking in responsibility and a willingness to commit. Of course, a leader's success at eliciting commitment depends on many factors. It is partly a function of individual differences in subordinates' willingness or predisposition to be committed, loyal, etc. An individual's upbringing can play an important role in determining the degree of his or her willingness to follow.[3] Whether or not, and to what degree, specific values are emphasized in a child's home can influence that individual's attitude toward superiors, as an adult. The emerging findings from the social sciences also suggest that managers are seldom fully in command (as frequently portrayed), and subordinates are rarely as submissive or faceless as is generally assumed.

Much has been made of the need to avoid being deceived by yes-men. A variation of this notion is popularly referred to as group-think, wherein a leader is surrounded by yea-sayers and devotees who contribute to the group's self-deception about its invulnerability.[4] In a unit that is victimized by the group-think phenomenon, the leader may make a disastrous decision because his or her followers have total conviction of the ultimate success of the group's efforts. Such a group will not seriously entertain the possibility of failure. The Bay of Pigs fiasco of the Kennedy Administration and the early escalation of U.S. military involvement in Vietnam by the Johnson Administration have often been attributed to group-think. In both the Bay of Pigs and Vietnam escalation decisions, the respective leaders and their supportive followers unconsciously conspired to create a mindset that inhibited their ability to foresee obstacles to the success of their plans.

The group-think phenomenon is most likely to occur in a highly cohesive work unit where the members are already strongly committed to their leader and the group's objectives. The message portrayed by the group-think examples is largely overstated since, in reality, the preconditions for group-think (i.e., extreme cohesion and total followership) are rare. More typically, managers must wrestle with a situation wherein their subordinates are far less loyal, and far less attracted to other members of the work unit than group-think requires. There is a good deal of *potential* followership held in reserve by subordinates.

Various anecdotal accounts of the group-think phenomenon have made it possible, and popular, to criticize the notion of followership. Similarly, well-publicized accounts of the predisposition of some individuals to blindly submit to authority in experimental settings have contributed to a criticism of followership. One famous study by Stanley Milgram[5] found that a majority of normal adults would administer seemingly painful electric shocks to another participant in a research study, even if the recipient of the shock protested and demanded to be set free. A related study by Phil Zimbardo[6] reported that college students who participated in role playing the job of prison guard would all too readily engage in the more cruel and sadistic activities stereotypically thought to characterize the treatment of prisoners by prison guards. In addition, the predisposition of some individuals to follow authority has been denigrated by the reports of social scientists in early research on the "obedient personality." Specifically, researchers during World War II sought to better understand the so-called "Nazi personality" and thus attempted to study fascist tendencies via a personality scale.[7] This research on the obedient (or fascist) personality, of course, represents an attempt to understand an aberrant style of behavior. Omitted in these classic studies were attempts to understand followership within normal settings (that is, hospitals, profit-oriented organizations, etc.).

While these studies provide fascinating insights into the more bizarre aspects of human behavior, their results do not have firm implications for life in organizations. Although laboratory experiments can offer insights to employee behavior, these popular studies often involved the creation of brief, transitory episodes, wherein people were placed in highly ambiguous and tension-charged settings of very short duration. Normal, adult behavior in the ongoing role of employee/subordinate does not readily lend itself to cruelty and blind obedience. The social norms and codes of personal conduct that exist in the real world (and are largely suspended in the temporary setting created in a research laboratory), inhibit tendencies toward excessive cruelty and blind obedience. In addition, most managers do not deliberately seek to be surrounded by blindly obedient and subservient individuals. The traits of good followership (that is, a sense of responsibility, adult-orientation, commitment, openness, and loyalty) are what most managers desire.

STYLES OF FOLLOWERSHIP

All managers are familiar with the notion of "styles of leadership." When this expression is used, we typically think of such terms as autocratic, participative, laissez-faire, etc. We can also extend this perspective to include styles of followership. Although a neglected topic, it is useful to consider the major dimensions along which subordinates differ, and to consider how follower styles may be developed and maintained.*

Figure 1 displays a framework for conceptualizing styles of followership. The framework incorporates two dimensions: compliance-defiance, and loyalty-hostility. The dimension of compliance-defiance is a behavioral dimension, and reflects the extent to which a follower conforms to the directives of a superior, versus undermines or counters the supervisor's desires. Loyalty-hostility is an attitudinal dimension which represents the degree to which a subordinate is supportive of, versus antagonistic toward, a supervisor and his or her goals. By crossing the two dimensions, we create a set of quadrants, each of which has a unique meaning.

In quadrant I (loyal, compliant), we are dealing with a supportive and conforming individual. Quadrant II refers to a compliant, but hostile individual. This would be the case of a subordinate who is maliciously obedient. Quadrant III is a person who is both hostile and defiant, while quadrant IV is a person who is defiant, but loyal (such as a conscientious objector would be). In the extremes of each quadrant (i.e., outside the circle), we are dealing with a form of mental illness. In their most exaggerated forms, the blindly obedient follower and the extremely hostile subordinate

Figure 1
Dimensions of Followership

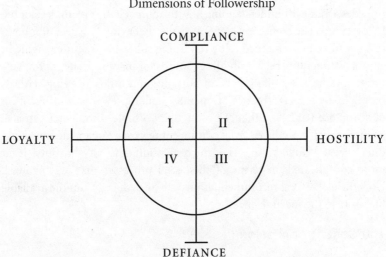

*One useful framework, which was developed by Zaleznik,[8] served as the starting point for developing the present scheme

(quadrants I and III) represent forms of illness. An extremely hostile but obedient individual is being logically inconsistent, and is perhaps only compliant because of external constraints (for example, fear of being terminated or having difficulty finding another position). An individual in quadrant III is also, in the extreme, experiencing distress. Such a person (who is simultaneously defiant, but committed to a supervisor's goals) may eventually be called to explain his or her actions, perhaps before a disciplinary board or a court. Eventual separation from the unit is the most likely outcome for an individual who is caught in the dilemma of supporting a supervisor, but defying his directives. At the extreme, this may be thought of as a situation which induces a form of mental illness. Finally, it should be noted that although the two dimensions are, in the "real world," likely to be highly correlated (such that loyal employees are likely to be compliant, and so on), there are certainly many occasions wherein attitudes and behaviors are not highly correlated.

DEVELOPING AND MAINTAINING EFFECTIVE FOLLOWERSHIP

Managers, of course, have a responsibility for developing and maintaining the followership of their subordinates (Note: being a follower and being a subordinate are not equivalent notions, as being a leader and being a supervisor also are not equivalent terms). The framework displayed in Figure 1 provides a guide for understanding how to approach the task of developing followership. The compliant-defiant (that is, behavioral) aspect of followership can be best attended to by rewarding subordinates for engaging in appropriate action and withholding rewards for inappropriate action. Volumes have been written on the importance and utility of tying rewards more closely to performance.[9] Generally, making rewards contingent on performance tends to enhance productivity. Simple compliance can also be more reliably predicted from contingent rewards. Enhancing the attitudinal aspect of followership (i.e., the dimension of loyalty-hostility) is far more complicated, in terms of the social processes that are involved. Nonetheless, several recommendations can be deduced from the available literature in the social sciences.

The Cost of Admission

Making the expense of attaining group membership more costly to the individual is a powerful means of inducing employee commitment. That is to say, individuals will have a more positive attitude toward group membership if they are compelled to expend more time, money, or effort to attain and maintain membership. A dramatic illustration of this phenomenon comes from a classic social science study by Eliott Aronson and Judson Mills.[10] As part of their research, these investigators had research subjects engage in an unpleasant activity as a prerequisite for admission to a group. Specifically, individual female college students, who were interested in joining a group that discussed topics related to human sexuality, were asked to read a written passage into a tape recorder (ostensibly to test their voice for maturity of reaction). Several groups of subjects were run in the study. One group was given a fairly innocuous passage to read (i.e., a mild initiation experience), while other groups read relatively more explicit and relatively sexually detailed passages in order to gain admission to the group (i.e., more severe initiation experience). All students were then asked to listen to a tape-recording of the group discussion (the group had allegedly already met several times). The discussion was deliberately staged so as to be extremely boring and unattractive (e.g., the members dryly and haltingly discussed the sexual habits of grasshoppers and other insects).

The investigators were primarily interested in how each applicant for group membership would evaluate the group. Intriguingly, the females who were put through the more difficult initiation experience rated the group more highly (i.e., gave higher ratings of the members' attractiveness, and intelligence, based on the tape). In a replication of this study by Gerard and Mathewson, subjects were required to demonstrate their ability to control their emotions by being given varying degrees of electric shock. The results were identical: the more electric shock a subject received, the more favorably she rated the group.[11] Thus, it appears that the more costly it is to individuals to gain admittance to a group, the more they will value their membership. This form of rationalization can be found in other varieties of group membership. For example, fraternities and sororities require "pledges" for membership to undergo a hazing period, where distasteful initiation experiences are forced on the would-be members. The resulting loyalty of the members of these organizations is well known.

Participation in Decision Making

A second method for inducing loyalty is to involve subordinates in the decision-making process. Participation in decision making increases an individual's sense of involvement and, thereby, dedication to the ultimate course of action. If the participation is genuine, participation can lead to a sense of "ownership" for a goal. A manager must be careful not to merely create an illusion of participation by asking for advice and input from subordinates which he or she does not intend to incorporate into the final decision. Many popular motivational schemes (e.g., MBO and quality circles) incorporate the notion of involving subordinates in planning, goal setting, and suggesting improvements in work methods.

Creating a Sense of Identification

A third device for soliciting loyalty is to create a sense of identity with a group or its leader. Many organizations try to elicit a sense of identity by having group members wear uniforms, or by emblazoning a company logo on paychecks, stationery, and I.D. cards. Beyond these simple techniques, a sense of identity can be fostered by first understanding the value system of employees. If employees value certain notions (such as the importance of being a part of a "family," or the importance of self-reliance), a manager can appeal to these notions by frequently relating to and highlighting these values as part of the theme of his or her administration. For example, as part of his election campaigns, President Reagan skillfully managed to identify his administration with the values of a strong defense and self-reliance (themes which were attractive to the American populace, especially at the end of President Carter's term in office). In short, a sense of identity can be achieved by frequent use of symbols (both tangible and verbal).

Accenting the Importance of Followership

Finally, a manager can enhance loyalty by demonstrating to his unit that loyalty and commitment are highly valued. For example, he or she can highlight the history of the organization and what makes for success and failure in the organization; a manager can stress the importance of loyalty and commitment in attaining both personal and corporate success. By their own conduct, managers communicate the extent to which loyalty is likely to be valued in their own units. If a manager is cynical and critical of superiors, he is more likely to create within his own unit a belief that sarcasm and second-guessing of superiors is an acceptable norm. That is not to say, of course, that a manager should be blindly devoted and praiseworthy of superiors. Rather, a manager should be respectful toward and considerate of the reputation of superiors (and all others) and predisposed to offer support and aid to help the organization achieve its goals.

To be sure, organizations would come to a grinding halt without a minimal degree of followership. Yet, the level of followership in the United States over the past two decades appears to be at an historically low level.[†] Our capacity for greater levels of effective followership is not completely utilized. Perhaps our readiness to follow is at a low ebb because the level of leadership (as distinct from headship) has not also been maximal. Our country has come through a difficult era for top-level leaders, a period characterized by assassinations and assassination attempts, near-impeachments, and questioning of traditional values. Also, employees are better educated, more outspoken, and more conscious of rights and entitlements than in the past. However, it is still popular to call for more effective leadership. Yet, organizational performance will not be maximal without the necessary condition of responsible followership.

The principle of followership is perhaps best understood at the U.S. Military Academy at West Point, where leadership is a central focus of the curriculum—the interrelated nature of leadership and followership is acknowledged. As they say at West Point, "(i)f you wish to develop people into leaders, you must begin by teaching them to be followers."[12]

REFERENCES

1. Heller, T. and VanTil, J. V. "Leadership and Followership: Some Summary Propositions." *Journal of Applied Behavioral Science,* vol. 18, pp. 405–414 (1982).

2. Kerr, S. and Jermier, J. "Substitutes for Leadership: Their Meaning and Measurement." *Organizational Behavior and Human Performance,* pp. 375–403 (1978).

3. McClelland, D. *The Achieving Society.* Princeton, NJ: VanNostrand (1961).

4. Janis, I. L. *Groupthink,* second edition. Boston, MA: Houghton Mifflin (1982).

5. Milgram, S. *Obedience to Authority.* London: Tavistock Publications (1974).

6. Zimbardo, P. G. "The Power and Pathology of Imprisonment." *Congressional Research, Serial No. 15,* Washington, DC: U.S. Government Printing Office (1971) 7.

7. Sanford, F. H. *Authoritarianism and Leadership.* Philadelphia, PA: Stephenson (1950).

8. Zaleznik, A. "The Dynamics of Subordinacy." *Harvard Business Review,* May–June 1965, pp. 119–131.

9. Lawler, E. E., III. "Whatever Happened to Incentive Pay?" *New Management,* vol. 1, pp. 37–41 (1984).

† Followership in the United States is also noticeably suboptimal when one considers the apparent level of followership in other industrialized nations, such as Japan and Germany.

10.   Aronson, E. and Mills, J. "The Effect of Severity of Initiation on Liking for a Group." *Journal of Abnormal and Social Psychology,* vol. 59, pp. 177–181 (1959).

11.   Gerard, H. B. and Mathewson, G. C. "The Effects of Severity of Initiation on Liking for a Group: A Replication." *Journal of Experimental Social Psychology,* vol. 2, pp. 278–287 (1966).

12.   Litzinger, W. and Schaeffer, T. "Leadership Through Followership." *Business Horizons* (1982).

Intraorganizational Influence Tactics: Explorations in Getting One's Way

David Kipnis, Stuart M. Schmidt, and Ian Wilkinson

Organizational psychologists have not been particularly interested in studying the ways in which people at work influence their colleagues and superiors to obtain personal benefits or to satisfy organizational goals. For the most part, interest has centered on the ways subordinates can be influenced to improve subordinate productivity and morale. This latter use of influence is customarily called the study of leadership, whereas the former can be called the study of organizational politics.

A consequence of this focus on leadership is that there is little systematic information available about how people use power to influence their colleagues or superiors. With but few exceptions (e.g., Izraeli, 1975; Schein, 1977), our thinking about this topic is guided by anecdotal evidence or armchair speculations that have been organized into rational classifications of power tactics (e.g., Etzioni, 1968, pp. 94–109; French & Raven, 1959). One problem with these classifications of power tactics, as Raven (1974) has pointed out, is that they overlap with each other, though each varies in the number of influence dimensions that are described. A further problem with existing classifications of power tactics is that when influence acts are actually studied, it is found that people do not exercise influence in ways predicted by rational classification schemes. This point was first explicitly made in a study by Goodchild, Quadrado, and Raven (Note 1) in which college students wrote brief essays on the topic "How I got my way." It was found that many of the influence tactics described by these students could not be classified into preexisting categories. Several tactics thought to be basic when classifying influence, such as the use of expert power, were not even mentioned by the students.

There is a need, therefore, for empirical studies of the use of influence within organizations. The purpose of this article is to report two studies that sought to examine the tactics of influence used by people at work when attempting to change the behavior of their superiors, co-workers, and subordinates. In the first study, the range of tactics that people use at work was identified by applying content analysis to written descriptions by managers of their attempts to influence their bosses, co-workers, or subordinates. The second study sought to identify through factor analysis the dimensions of influence underlying the specific tactics that were uncovered in the first study.

STUDY 1: DETERMINING INTRAORGANIZATIONAL INFLUENCE TACTICS

Method

The data for this study were collected from 165 respondents, 25% women and 75% men. All respondents were taking graduate business courses part-time, in the evening. They were told to refer to their current employment experience when supplying the requested information.

The respondents were employed mainly in managerial roles as engineers, technicians, and professionals. Since most respondents came from different organizations, there were almost as many organizations as respondents represented.

Respondents were asked to describe an incident in which they actually succeeded in getting either their boss, a co-worker, or a subordinate to do something they wanted; 62 described how they got their way with their boss, 49 with a co-worker, and 54 with a subordinate. The reason for the unequal distribution of respondents over status levels was that fewer respondents had subordinates or co-workers than had bosses.

In their description of an incident, each respondent wrote in essay form what they wanted from a target person, what they did, whether there was resistance from the target, and what further influence tactics were used in response to resistance from the target. Each respondent also completed a structured questionnaire containing demographic and specific organizational job-situation questions.

The incidents were sorted first in terms of the goal sought from the target person. This sorting yielded five general categories of goals: *assistance with own job*—obtaining the assistance of the target in helping the respondent do his or her job, when it was not part of the target's legitimate job duties; *get others to do their job*—getting the target to do his or her own work; *obtain benefits*—goals that personally benefited the respondent, such as salary increase, promotion, and improved work schedule; *initiate change*—

initiating new organizational programs and systems or improving the coordination of organizational activities (e.g., changing a scheduling procedure); and *improve performance*—improving the target's on-the-job performance.

These goals varied as a function of the target's job status, as shown in Table 1. Respondents sought mostly self-interest goals from their superiors. The primary goal sought from co-workers was to get assistance with the respondent's own job. The most prevalent reason for influencing subordinates was to get them to do their jobs. Finally, the goal of initiating change was sought both from bosses and from subordinates in almost equal proportion. However, the changes sought from superiors focused on job-related organizational changes, such as launching a new accounting procedure or starting a special project. But with subordinates, the changes sought dealt with job performance, such as changes in the way a job should be done or the manner of working in the organization.

Next, the influence tactics reported by the respondents in attempting to achieve these goals were identified. A total of 370 influence tactics were reported by the 165 respondents. The authors sorted these tactics into 14 categories (see Table 2). Consensus among the coders was used as the criterion for assigning a given tactic to a category. The 14 categories ranged from the use of administrative sanctions and personal threats through the use of logic and rational discussions to clandestine, dependency appeal, and ingratiating tactics. The individual tactics illustrating these 14 categories

Table 1

Reasons for Exercising Influence, by Target Status (Study 1) in Percentages

	Target status			
Reasons	*Boss* *(62)*	*Co-worker* *(49)*	*Subordinate* *(54)*	*Total* *(165)*
Obtain assistance on own job	3	48	9	18
Get others to do their jobs	13	23	46	27
Obtain personal benefits	58	10	0	25
Initiate change in work	26	15	28	23
Improve target's job performance	0	4	17	7

Note: Numbers in parentheses are *N*s.

Table 2

Classification of Influence Tactics by Category (Study 1)

Category/tactic	%[a]	Category/tactic	%[a]
Clandestine	8	Exchange	8
Challenged the ability of the target		Contributed in exchange for compliance	
Lied to the target		Compromised	
Acted in a pseudo-democratic manner		Offered to make sacrifice	
Puffed up the importance of the job		Offered help to get the job done	
Manipulated information		Invoked past favors	
Made the target feel important		Persistence	7
Cajoled the target		Repeated reminders	
Showed understanding (pretended)		Argued	
of the target's problem		Repeated previous actions	
Personal negative actions	8	Surveillance	
Fait accompli/went ahead on own		Training	6
Chastised the target		Explained how it was to be done	
Became a nuisance		Showed how to do it	
Slowed down on the job		Reward	2
Held personal confrontation with target		Verbal reinforcement	
Threatened withdrawal of help		Salary raise	
Expressed anger		Gave benefits	
Threatened to leave job		Self-presentation	5
Blocked target's actions		Demonstrated competence	
Ignored target		Performed well, then asked	
Administrative negative actions	3	Waited until target was in the right mood	
Filed a report with supervisor		Was humble	
Sent target to superior for conference		Was friendly	
Gave unsatisfactory performance		Direct request	10
evaluations		Weak ask	6
Gave no salary increase		Showed dependency	
Threatened with unsatisfactory		Weak request	
performance ratings		Demand	7
Threatened job security		Invoked rules	
Threatened loss of promotion		Ordered	
Explained rationale for request	17	Convened formal conference	
Gathered supporting data	6	Set time deadline	
Coalitions	7	Told target that it must be done as I said	
Obtained support from co-workers		or better proposed	
Obtained support informally		Obtained support from subordinates	
from superiors		Threatened to notify an outside agency	
		Made formal appeals to higher levels	

[a] Percentage of the 370 tabulated influence tactics reported by respondents.

are also shown in Table 2. To determine the reliability of the assignment of items to these 14 categories, three coders who were not associated with the research independently sorted the 370 influence tactics into the 14 categories. Raters 1 and 2 agreed on the placement of items 61% of the time; Raters 1 and 3 agreed 64% of the time; and Raters 2 and 3 agreed 65% of the time. Since there were 14 categories into which any item could be placed, the degree of agreement between the three raters suggests modestly high reliability for the classification scheme. The areas of disagreement between the raters involved primarily the three categories "weak ask," "explain," and "request."

In addition to identifying influence tactics, the analyses of Study 1 focused on the correlates of the 14 categories of influence. To this end, a unit weight of 1 was assigned if the respondent reported using any of the items comprising a given influence tactic category; a score of 0 was assigned if none of the items comprising a category were mentioned. Thus, each respondent had 14 scores of 1 or 0. Next, multivariate analyses of variance, which if significant were followed by univariate analyses, were carried out to examine the relationship among the 14 categories of influence, the status of the target person, and the goals sought by respondents in exercising influence.

The influence tactics used by the respondents varied with the goal sought from the target person. When the goal was self-interest, the most frequently reported tactics were self-presentation and personal negative actions; when the goal was to initiate change, the most frequently reported tactics were the use of logic and rational discussions; when the goal was to improve a target's performance, respondents reported using administrative sanctions, training, and simply demanding compliance. Finally, when the goal was to get others to do the respondent's own work, the most frequently reported tactic was the use of requests. All of the above findings were statistically reliable beyond the .05 level.

The kinds of influence tactics used by the respondents varied with the power of the target person. Respondents significantly more often used the tactics of self-presentation, supporting data, and coalitions when attempting to influence their bosses. Different tactics, however, were used to influence subordinates; then respondents significantly more often used clandestine tactics, administrative sanctions, training, demanding, and explaining. Finally, the data showed that only one tactic was significantly associated with influencing co-workers—the tactic of requesting help. At the .10 level, however, the tactics of exchange, requests, and rewards were also associated with influencing co-workers.

The use of influence tactics also varied with the amount of resistance shown by target persons. When the respondents stated that the target at first refused to comply, the subsequent actions of respondents included an increase in persistence and the use of personal negative actions. Additionally, when confronting resisting bosses and co-workers, the respondents reported an increase in the use of coalitions with fellow employees. If the person resisting was a subordinate, however, the respondents reported using more administrative sanctions such as giving unsatisfactory performance evaluations.

Results

The findings of the study suggest that in organizational settings the choice of influence tactics is associated with what the respondents are trying to get from the target person, the amount of resistance shown, and the power of the target person. Combining these findings suggests that administrative sanctions and personal negative actions are more likely to be used when the target is a subordinate who is actively resisting the request of the manager and when the reasons for exercising influence are based on the respondent's role in the organization (e.g., improve target's performance).

It is also important to note that many of the tactics reported by the respondents have received little mention in the organizational literature (e.g., the use of deceit, self-presentation, and clandestine tactics). In fact, the tactics shown in Table 2 represent a bewildering combination of several classification schemes from the exchange theories of Michener and Schwertfeger (1972) to the schemes described by French and Raven (1959) and by Cartwright (1965, pp. 1–47). It is clear that the many influence tactics described here do not fit easily into any single classification scheme currently found in the literature on power usage. Based on these findings, we believe that new ways of classifying such tactics are needed that use the actual influence behaviors of organizational members as the starting point. An effort in this direction is reported in the next study.

STUDY 2

Method

Many of the 14 categories of influence tactics in the first study overlapped either conceptually or empirically or both (e.g., "weak ask" vs. "request").

The purpose of Study 2 was to determine the factor structure of the tactics found in the previous study. To this end, 58 items were developed from Study 1's tactics. These items were included in a questionnaire administered to 754 employed respondents. Respondents were asked to describe on a 5-point scale how frequently during the past 6 months they had used each item to influence a target person at work. The 5-point scale had verbal anchors as follows: usually use this tactic to influence him/her (5), frequently use this tactic to influence him/her (4), occasionally use this tactic to influence him/her (3), seldom use this tactic to influence him/her (2), and never use this tactic to influence him/her (1).

There were three forms of the questionnaire: One asked respondents to describe how they influenced their bosses, another asked how they influenced their co-workers, and the third asked how they influenced their subordinates. The instructions read:

This questionnaire is a way of obtaining information about how you go about changing your boss's (or co-worker's or subordinate's) mind so that he or she agrees with you. Below are described various ways of doing this. Please do not answer in terms of what you would like to do.

Respondents were also told that if the tactics did not apply in their work to leave the space blank; blank responses were coded as "never used this tactic."

Sample. The respondents were drawn from the same managerial population as in Study 1 and were taking graduate business courses part-time: 690 were enrolled in evening courses at Temple University and 64 were enrolled at the Bernard Baruch Graduate Center in New York City. Of the 754 respondents, 225 described how they influenced their bosses, 285 described how they influenced co-workers, and 244 described how they influenced subordinates.

Reasons for exercising influence. In addition to describing how frequently each influence tactic was used, a separate scale presented respondents with five possible reasons for influencing the target person. These reasons were based on those found in Study 1 and read as follows: (a) have my boss (co-worker or subordinate) assist me on my job or do some of my work; (b) assign work to my boss (co-worker or subordinate) or tell him or her what to do; (c) have my boss (co-worker or subordinate) give me benefits, such as raises, better hours of work, time off, better job assignments, and so on; (d) have my boss (co-worker or subordinate) do his or her own work better or do what they are supposed to do; (e) have my boss (co-worker or subordinate) accept my ideas for changes, for example, to accept a new way of doing the work more efficiently or a new program or project.

For each of the five reasons, the respondents were asked to rate on a 5-point scale ranging from "very often" (5) to "never" (1) how frequently each reason had been the cause of their trying to influence the target person to do something.

Paralleling the findings of Study 1, the reasons for exercising influence varied with whether the target person was a superior, co-worker, or subordinate. Table 3 shows that the major reasons for influencing subordinates were that respondents more frequently attempted to assign them work, to improve their task performance, and to have them assist the respondents in their own work ($p < .01$ compared to co-workers or superiors). Superiors were influenced most frequently to receive personal benefits ($p < .01$). Finally, respondents reported that they attempted to influence both their subordinates and their superiors with almost equal frequency to convince them to initiate change. This last result was also found in Study 1.

Additional background data. The questionnaire also obtained information about the sex of the respondent, the sex of the respondent's boss, whether the organization was unionized, the number of persons employed in the respondent's work unit, and the job level of the respondent. Job level information was based on the respondent's description of his or her own work. This information was coded into four groups: clerical/sales, professional (e.g., engineer, computer technician), first-line and middle managers

Table 3

Mean Frequency of Reasons for Respondents Exercising Influence (Study 2)

Reason for exercising influence	Target status			F
	Subordinate (244)	Co-worker (285)	Superior (225)	
Assistance on own job	3.15_a	2.75_b	2.09_c	64.36**
Assign work	4.08_a	2.47_b	1.86_c	329.69**
Obtain benefits	1.33_a	1.65_b	2.42_c	90.41**
Improve performance	3.93_a	2.88_b	2.39_c	135.19**
Initiate change	3.54_a	3.27_b	3.47_a	6.66*

Note. Numbers in parentheses are Ns. Groups with different subscripts differ beyond the .05 level. High scores indicate that the goal was rated as a frequent reason for the respondent to influence the target person.
*$p < .05$ **$p < .01$.

(e.g., supervisor, manager of clerical unit, etc.), and top-level managers (e.g., vice president of marketing).

Results

The 58 influence tactic items were factor analyzed using a principal component factor solution, with iterations for communality and varimax rotation. Forced two-factor through eight-factor solutions were carried out to aid in interpreting the findings.

Factor analyses were carried out for the entire sample and separately for each of the three target status levels (superior, co-worker, subordinate). This was done to examine the possibility that dimensions of influence would emerge at each target status level that did not emerge in the overall analysis. A second reason for carrying out separate factor analyses at each target status level was to ensure that any factors that emerged in the combined analysis also appeared in at least one of the separate factor analyses. It was assumed that a factor that did not appear in any of the separate analyses, yet appeared in the overall analysis, only reflected differences between target status levels in the exercise of influence.

The factor analysis of the entire sample yielded six interpretable factors. These six factors accounted for 38% of the total item variance. Table 4 lists the tactics presented in the questionnaire. The data in Table 4 are based on the overall factor analysis utilizing all 754 respondents.

Factor 1 is identified by highest loadings on the influence tactics, including demanding, ordering, and setting deadlines. This factor is labeled *Assertiveness*. The factor emerged as a dimension of influence at all target status levels (superior, co-worker, and subordinate).

Factor 2 is described by the highest loadings on weak and nonobtrusive influence tactics. Included here were such tactics as "acting humble" and "making the other person feel important." This factor is labeled *Ingratiation*. The factor emerged as a dimension of influence at all levels of target status.

Factor 3 is characterized by loadings on the use of rationality influence tactics and is labeled *Rationality*. It includes such tactics as "writing a detailed plan" and "explaining the reasons for my request." This factor emerged at each target status level. In the analysis of tactics directed toward subordinates, however, additional items that involved group pressure also loaded highly on this factor. These latter items will be discussed subsequently.

Factor 4 involved the use of administrative sanctions to induce compliance. Tactics with high loadings included "prevented salary increases" and

Table 4
Rotated Factors and Items

Dimension of influence/tactic

Assertiveness

51. Kept checking up on him or her.
45. Simply ordered him or her to do what was asked.
18. Demanded that he or she do what I requested.
39. Bawled him or her out.
11. Set a time deadline for him or her to do what I asked.
19. Told him or her that the work must be done as ordered or he or she should propose a better way.
53. Became a nuisance (kept bugging him/her until he/she did what I wanted).
43. Repeatedly reminded him or her about what I wanted.
54. Expressed my anger verbally.
41. Had a showdown in which I confronted him or her face to face.
30. Pointed out that the rules required that he or she comply.

Ingratiation

46. Made him or her feel important ("only you have the brains, talent to do this").
9. Acted very humbly to him or her while making my request.
17. Acted in a friendly manner prior to asking for what I wanted.
28. Made him or her feel good about me before making my request.
37. Inflated the importance of what I wanted him or her to do.
36. Praised him or her.
3. Sympathized with him/her about the added problems that my request has caused.
44. Waited until he or she appeared in a receptive mood before asking.
10. Showed my need for their help.
29. Asked in a polite way.
22. Pretended I was letting him or her decide to do what I wanted (act in a pseudo-democratic fashion).

Rationality

40. Wrote a detailed plan that justified my ideas.
38. Presented him or her with information in support of my point of view.
31. Explained the reasons for my request.
13. Used logic to convince him or her.
24. Wrote a memo that described what I wanted.
42. Offered to compromise over the issue (I gave in a little).
16. Demonstrated my competence to him or her before making my request.

Sanctions

49. Gave no salary increase or prevented person from getting a pay raise.
26. Threatened his or her job security (e.g., hint of firing or getting him or her fired).

Table 4 *(continued)*

Dimension of influence/tactic

Dimension of influence/tactic

15. Promised (or gave) a salary increase.
6. Threatened to give him or her an unsatisfactory performance evaluation.
34. Threatened him or her with loss of promotion.

Exchange

35. Offered an exchange (e.g., if you do this for me, I will do something for you).
27. Reminded him or her of past favors that I did for them.
50. Offered to make a personal sacrifice if he or she would do what I wanted (e.g., work late, work harder, do his/her share of the work, etc).
55. Did personal favors for him or her.
7. Offered to help if he/she would do what I wanted.

Upward appeal

58. Made a formal appeal to higher levels to back up my request.
20. Obtained the informal support of higher-ups.
25. Filed a report about the other person with higher-ups (e.g., my superior).
33. Sent him or her to my superior.

Blocking

47. Threatened to notify an outside agency if he or she did not give in to my request.
48. Threatened to stop working with him or her until he or she gave in.
4. Engaged in a work slowdown until he or she did what I wanted.
5. Ignored him or her and/or stopped being friendly.
14. Distorted or lied about reasons he or she should do what I wanted.

Coalitions

12. Obtained the support of co-workers to back up my request.
56. Had him or her come to a formal conference at which I made my request.
32. Obtained the support of my subordinates to back up my request.

Unclassified items

52. Kept kidding him or her until they did what I wanted.
23. Ignored him or her and went ahead and did what I wanted.
8. Provided him or her with various benefits that they wanted.
1. Challenged his or her ability ("I bet you can't do that").
21. Pretended not to understand what needed to be done so that he or she would volunteer to do it for me.
2. Concealed some of my reasons for trying to influence him/her.

Note. $N = 754$. Item numbers denote the items' original position in the questionnaire.

"threatened job security." This factor is labeled *Sanctions*. It emerged as a dimension of influence at all levels of target status.

Factor 5 loaded on tactics involving the exchange of positive benefits. Included here were such tactics as "offering an exchange" and "offering to make personal sacrifices." This factor is labeled *Exchange of Benefits*. This factor only emerged in the factor analysis of influence tactics directed toward superiors.

Factor 6 is described by loadings on tactics that bring additional pressure for conformity on the target by invoking the influence of higher levels in the organization. Included here were such tactics as "making a formal appeal to higher levels" and "obtaining the informal support of higher-ups." This factor only emerged in the factor analysis of influence tactics directed toward superiors; it is labeled *Upward Appeal*.

Two additional factors (Factors 7 and 8) did not emerge in the overall factor analysis but were found in the subanalyses. It was decided to retain these factors for heuristic purposes.

Factor 7 emerged in the factor analysis of influence directed toward superiors. Items that loaded on this factor included "engaging in a work slowdown" and "threatening to stop working with the target person." Essentially, these tactics are attempts to stop the target person from carrying out some action by various kinds of blocking tactics. This factor is labeled *Blocking*.

Factor 8 emerged from the factor analysis of tactics directed toward subordinates. Items in this factor were part of the previously described factor *Rationality*. However, this subset of items described the use of steady pressure for compliance by "obtaining the support of coworkers" and by "obtaining the support of subordinates." This is labeled *Coalitions*.

Scale construction

To aid further analysis, scales were constructed whose items were selected to represent each of the eight dimensions of influence. Selection was made on the basis of two criteria. First, items were selected that loaded over .40 on a given dimension and did not load above .25 on any of the remaining dimensions. Second, from the pool of items that were selected to represent each dimension, items were selected based on an examination of each item's correlation with other items representing the factor and their correlations with items in the remaining factors. High item intercorrelation within a factor and low item intercorrelation with the remaining items were used as the final criteria for selecting items.

Correlates of Influence Tactics

Target status

Table 5 shows the means and standard deviations of each influence dimension as a function of the status of the target. Seven of the eight dimensions were significantly associated with the relative status of the target. Basically, the findings suggest that as the status of the target person increased, respondents placed more reliance on rationality tactics. An analysis using Duncan's multiple-range test found that Assertive tactics and Sanctions

Table 5

Target Status and Average Frequency of Tactic Use

Dimension	Target status			
of influence	Subordinate	Co-worker	Superior	F
Ingratiation				
M	15.92$_b$	16.08$_b$	14.52$_a$	16.69**
SD	3.97	4.73	4.48	
Rationality				
M	14.04$_b$	13.74$_b$	14.72$_a$	7.17**
SD	2.47	3.20	3.01	
Assertiveness				
M	12.04$_a$	8.06$_b$	6.94$_c$	243.91**
SD	3.00	2.67	2.25	
Sanctions				
M	6.39$_a$	5.27$_b$	5.16$_b$	68.18**
SD	1.95	0.91	0.62	
Exchange				
M	9.83$_b$	10.08$_b$	8.56$_a$	13.52**
SD	3.10	3.65	3.53	
Upward appeal				
M	7.05$_b$	6.83$_b$	5.43$_a$	37.16**
SD	2.31	2.29	1.99	
Blocking				
M	3.31$_a$	3.50$_b$	3.29$_a$	4.05*
SD	0.82	1.04	0.91	
Coalitions				
M	4.37	4.30	4.53	.08
SD	2.04	2.05	2.14	

Note. Groups with different subscripts differ beyond the .05 level.
*$p < .05$. **$p < .01$.

were used more often to influence subordinates than co-workers or superiors ($ps < .01$). The tactics of Ingratiation, Exchange of Benefits, and
Upward Appeal were used with equal frequency among subordinates and
co-workers but significantly less often when attempting to influence superiors ($p < .01$). Finally, respondents reported that they used Rationality tactics more frequently to convince superiors than co-workers or subordinates
($p < .01$). As will be shown later, these differences in choice of tactics in part
reflect the fact that respondents have different reasons for influencing target persons at different status levels.

Goals

It will be recalled that respondents in the present study rated the importance of five possible reasons for exercising influence. To determine
whether different combinations of tactics were used as the reasons for influencing varied, a set of stepwise regression analyses was performed. These
stepwise regression analyses examined the relation between the eight tactic
scores and the rated importance of each reason for exercising influence. A
restriction put on the analysis was that only tactics that correlated significantly ($p < .05$) with a given reason were entered into the regression analysis. Since we have already found that the type of tactic used and the reasons
for exercising influence both varied with the status of the target person,
separate regression analyses were carried out at each target status level.
Table 6 shows these findings in terms of the particular combination of influence tactics that best predicted each reason for exercising influence. In
addition, Table 6 presents the multiple correlations of these influence tactics with each reason for exercising influence.

Table 6 shows that at all target status levels, the respondent's choice of
influence tactics varied with the respondents' reasons for exercising influence. That is, respondents who frequently sought personal assistance from
target persons used Ingratiation tactics; respondents who frequently assigned work to target persons used Assertiveness; and respondents who frequently tried to improve a target person's performance used Assertiveness
and Rationality tactics. Finally, respondents who frequently tried to convince target persons to accept new ideas used Rationality tactics.

Another finding of interest in Table 6 is that respondents showed the
least variation in choice of tactics when attempting to influence their subordinates. No matter what the reason for influencing subordinates, the use
of Assertiveness was associated with each of the five reasons and accounted

Table 6

Multiple Correlations Between Tactics and Rated Importance
of Reasons for Exercising Influence

Reason for exercising influence/target	Tactic category used	R
Receive assistance on own job		
boss	Ingratiation	.20
co-worker	Ingratiation	.16
subordinate	Assertiveness	
	Ingratiation	.29
Assign work to target		
boss	Assertiveness	.51
co-worker	Assertiveness	.28
subordinate	Assertiveness	.31
Obtain benefits from target		
boss	Exchange	
	Ingratiation	.38
co-worker	Exchange	
	Blocking	
	Ingratiation	.32
subordinate	Assertiveness	
	Coalitions	.21
Improve target's performance		
boss	Assertiveness	
	Blocking	
	Rationality	.43
co-worker	Assertiveness	
	Exchange	
	Coalitions	
	Rationality	.46
subordinate	Assertiveness	
	Rationality	.34
Initiate change		
boss	Rationality	
	Coalition	
	Ingratiation	
	Exchange	.57
co-worker	Rationality	
	Coalitions	
	Exchange	.45
subordinate	Assertiveness	
	Rationality	.42

Note. Tactics are listed in order of their entry into the stepwise multiple regression equations.
All correlations are significant beyond the .05 level.

for the most variance for each reason. In contrast, when influencing co-workers and superiors, the use of Assertiveness was associated only with two of the five reasons.

Other Situational Factors

So far it has been shown that use of the eight dimensions of influence was associated with the relative power of the target person and the reasons why the respondents wanted to influence the target person. In this section we examine the relationship between the use of tactics and five personal or situational characteristics of the respondent: sex, level in the organization, whether the respondent's unit was unionized, number of people in respondent's work unit, and sex of respondent's boss.

The findings showed that the respondent's own level in the organization was closely associated with use of influence tactics. Compared to those with low job status, respondents with higher job status reported greater use of Rationality and Assertiveness tactics when influencing both their subordinates and their superiors ($ps < .01$). In addition, respondents with higher job status used Sanctions more frequently and sought aid from their superiors less frequently when influencing their subordinates ($ps < .01$). Thus, as the respondents' own job status rose, they were more likely to use more direct tactics of influence and be less dependent upon superiors.

Size of work unit also related to the use of tactics on subordinates. In large work units, respondents more frequently used Assertiveness ($p < .01$), Sanctions ($p < .01$), and Upward Appeal ($p < .05$) when influencing subordinates. These findings are consistent with the general idea that as the number of persons in a work unit increases, a greater reliance is placed on strong and impersonal means of control.

Finally, the presence of unions was associated with the use of certain tactics. If the organization was unionized, respondents were more likely to use Ingratiating tactics to influence subordinates ($p < .01$), to avoid the use of Assertiveness when influencing co-workers ($p < .05$), and to use Rationality tactics less frequently ($p < .01$) and Blocking tactics more frequently ($p < .01$) when influencing bosses.

There were no significant relations associated with the sex of the respondent and the sex of the respondent's boss in terms of the frequency of use of the eight dimensions of influence. Thus, in the present study men and women chose similar tactics when attempting to get their way.

DISCUSSION

In Study 1, influence tactics were sorted into 14 categories, but we suspected that a more parsimonious classification system was likely to exist. The results of Study 2 yielded eight dimensions of influence.

Four of these dimensions emerged at all status levels. These dimensions were Assertiveness, Sanctions, Ingratiation, and Rationality. The remaining dimensions were uniquely associated with influencing either superiors or subordinates. The tactics of Exchange of Benefits, Blocking, and Upward Appeal emerged when respondents described how they influenced their bosses. These dimensions did not appear in the analysis of influence tactics used among subordinates. Finally, the use of Coalitions tactics appeared only when respondents described how they influenced their subordinates.

Unfortunately, there are few studies available with which to compare the present findings. Within organizational settings, the major empirical studies of influence tactics have been based on the Ohio State–Navy leadership studies (Fleishman, 1973). These studies could identify only two dimensions of influence—consideration and initiating structure. However, this early program of research was only concerned with how leaders exercised influence over subordinates and was not concerned with the use of influence tactics among peers and bosses. Hence, the range of influence tactics used in that early research covered fewer areas than those included here.

Other factorial studies of influence tactics have focused on dimensions of influence in interpersonal settings (Falbo, 1977; Kipnis, Cohen, & Catalano, Note 2). These studies have uncovered only two or three dimensions of influence. For example, Kipnis et al. reported that dating couples used three dimensions of influence—strong, weak, and rational—as ways of changing their dating partner's behavior. The items loading on these three dimensions closely resemble the dimensions we have labeled *Assertiveness, Rationality,* and *Ingratiation* tactics. Thus, instead of acting "more loving" in order to influence, organizational members act "humble" and offer to "make sacrifices." The parallel is clearly there. The additional factors found in the present study suggest that organizational resources extend the range of tactics that organizational members can use. Thus, organizational members can invoke formal sanctions or the added authority of higher management as compliance-gaining strategies.

It is recognized, of course, that findings presented here are based on self-report measures and require replication using different methodologies. Nevertheless, the picture portrayed by these data is of organizational members actively seeking to influence peers, superiors, and subordinates for a variety of reasons, some personal and some based on their management roles. This picture supports the view of those who argue that organizational leadership is more complicated than is represented in organizational behavior textbooks (Kochan, Schmidt, & DeCotiis, 1976). Such texts mainly focus on the ways in which higher levels in the organization influence lower levels. This is called the leadership process. In fact, we would suggest that everyone is influencing everyone else in organizations, regardless of job title. People seek benefits, information, satisfactory job performance, the chance to do better than others, to be left alone, cooperation, and many other outcomes too numerous to mention.

In fact, there may be very little difference in the frequency with which people try to influence their bosses, co-workers, and subordinates, given all these various reasons for trying to influence others. What shows remarkable variation, however, are the kinds of tactics that are chosen when trying to obtain these various outcomes. The present article has shown that these tactics vary with the particular wants of the influencing agent and his or her degree of control over the target of influence. The implications of these findings for the understanding of organizational politics remain to be explored.

As a final point, the scales that have been developed to measure the various dimensions of influence can be useful in further research. Even though the use of influence within organizations is a topic of considerable interest, there have been few systematic attempts to develop a means of measuring such behavior. The present dimensions provide the potential for profiling the use of influence in a variety of organizational settings and at different levels as well as between various groups.

REFERENCE NOTES

1. Goodchild, J. D., Quadrado, C., & Raven, B. H. *Getting one's way.* Paper presented at the meeting of the Western Psychological Association, Sacramento, California, April 1975.

2. Kipnis, D., Cohen, E., & Catalano, R. *Power and affection.* Paper presented at the meeting of the Eastern Psychological Association, Philadelphia, April 1979.

REFERENCES

Cartwright, D. Influence, leadership and control. In J. G. March (Ed.), *Handbook of organizations.* Chicago: Rand McNally, 1965.

Etzioni, A. Organizational dimensions and their interrelationship. In B. Indik & F. K. Berrien (Eds.), *People, groups and organizations.* New York: Teachers College Press, 1968.

Falbo, T. The multidimensional scaling of power strategies. *Journal of Personality and Social Psychology,* 1977, *35,* 537–547.

Fleishman, E. A. Twenty years of consideration and structure. In E. A. Fleishman & J. G. Hunt (Eds.), *Current developments in the study of leadership.* Carbondale: Southern Illinois University Press, 1973.

French, J. R. P., & Raven, B. H. The bases of social power. In D. Cartwright (Ed.), *Studies in social power.* Ann Arbor: University of Michigan Press, 1959.

Izraeli, D. N. The middle manager and the tactics of power expansion. *Sloan Management Review,* 1975, *16,* 57–70.

Kochan, T. A., Schmidt, S. M., & DeCotiis, T. A. Superior-subordinate relations: Leadership and headship. *Human Relations,* 1976, *28,* 279–294.

Michener, A., & Schwertfeger, M. Liking as a determinant of power tactic preference. *Sociometry,* 1972, *35,* 190–202.

Raven, B. H. The comparative analysis of power and influence. In J. T. Tedeschi (Ed.), *Perspectives on social power.* Chicago: Aldine, 1974.

Schein, V. E. Individual power and political behavior. *Academy of Management Review,* 1977, *2,* 64–72.

A Social Influence Interpretation of Worker Motivation

Mario Sussmann and Robert P. Vecchio

When considering the topic of worker motivation, one is initially over-whelmed by the abundance of different theories and approaches that are present in the organizational literature (Adams, 1965; Campbell & Prit-chard, 1976; Campbell, Dunnette, Lawler, & Weick, 1970; Lawler, 1973; Porter & Lawler, 1968; Vroom, 1964). However, the major theories of worker motivation (both mechanistic and cognitive) have largely ignored a fundamental issue concerning the origins of worker behavior. Specifically, this omission stems from an assumption that factors which appear to pre-cede changes in behavior operate in a unilateral fashion, and workers (it is assumed) do not exercise an appreciable degree of personal volition, that is, they *do not decide to accept influence attempts.* This theoretical omission sidesteps the question of the process whereby influence attempts are ac-cepted/rejected as well as the varieties of influence that exist. Rather than define "influence processes," one can instead attempt to define the "basis of acceptance." However, the latter view does not present the worker as an ac-tive participant in the determination of his or her behavior. Presented in this paper is a process view of social influence that specifies the manner and nature of socially induced changes in worker behavior.

An influence attempt is defined here as a social occasion wherein one individual exhibits behaviors, emits verbal utterances, and so on, with the intent of altering the behavior of another or others to a desired end. The scope of this discourse is restricted to work related behaviors (especially, but not exclusively, behaviors related to worker productivity). Of concern here are occasions of socially dependent influence. That is to say, influence that originates from outside the target person can be distinguished from influence that originates primarily from within the target person (e.g., the socially independent process of a competency motive or exploratory mo-tive). Furthermore, it is recognized that influence is unlikely to be uni-lateral. Rather, it is most commonly a reciprocal process in that the target person's response to an influence attempt likely will alter the variety, frequency, intensity, and/or direction of future influence attempts.

For the moment, the focus is on the behavior (i.e., response to an influence attempt) of the person who occupies a "subordinate" position (i.e., in the formal, organizational sense of subordinate) because subordinate behavior traditionally has been the primary interest of theories of worker motivation. However, as will be illustrated, influence can be more broadly conceptualized so as to include the impact of subordinate behavior on supervisor behavior (specifically, supervisor's influence attempts).

SOCIAL INFLUENCE PROCESSES

Kelman's (1961) work on identifying qualitatively distinct processes of opinion change has particular relevance to the goals of this paper. These processes are termed compliance, identification, and internalization. If Kelman's terms are extended to work settings, it may be said that *compliance* is concerned with whether a worker accepts an influence attempt because of a desire to obtain a favorable outcome or to avoid an unfavorable outcome. *Identification* refers to whether a worker exhibits behaviors derived from another or others because these behaviors contribute to a person's self-image. The third type of influence process, *internalization,* refers to whether a worker accepts an influence attempt because the encouraged actions are congruent with a personal value system and/or are intrinsically rewarding to the individual.

French and Raven's (1959) view of social power suggests five major sources of influence: reward, coercive, legitimate, referent, and expert. Each of these five may be viewed as being relatively more closely aligned with one of the three processes proposed by Kelman. Specifically, French and Raven's reward and coercive power possesses a strong conceptual similarity with Kelman's notion of compliance. Also, the social power bases of referent power are most in allegiance with Kelman's process of identification. And, finally, legitimate power may be viewed as being potentially the power source for an internalization influence process. Therefore, French and Raven's analysis of social power may be viewed as overlapping with Kelman's typology such that French and Raven's power bases provide a more elaborate conceptual foundation for influence attempts. These influence attempts, in turn, are directed at (or, perhaps more properly, are translated into) specific psychological processes (Kelman, 1961) and succeed or fail in altering behavior as a function of individual and situational contingencies.

Etzioni (1975) has offered an approach that examines social power and worker response within the framework of a structurally oriented organizational analysis. Etzioni considered the influence-motivation problem as one of compliance, a term that indicates the relation between the influence agent's power and the influencee's involvement (by involvement is meant a cathectic-evaluative orientation of an actor to an object).

In Etzioni's typology of power, coercive power refers to the administration of pain or the threat to do so. Remunerative or utilitarian power refers to allocation of rewards such as pay, benefits, services, and commodities. Among two types of normative power, pure normative power refers to the allocation of symbolic rewards based on prestige, esteem, and ritualistic symbols, and social power refers to the apportionment of interpersonal rewards and acceptance. There also are four types of involvement: alienative (a negative and hostile orientation); calculative (based on the material gain in an economic relationship); and two types of moral involvement (devotion to ideas, groups, movements, organizations, leaders), with a distinction between "pure moral" commitment and "social" commitment, paralleling the distinction between pure normative and social power. In a proposal that anticipated contingency theories, congruent types of compliance are defined as occasions in which a type of power is paired with a corresponding type of involvement (coercive with alienative, remunerative-utilitarian with calculative, normative with moral); all other combinations are incongruent.

A comparison of Kelman's and Etzioni's typologies shows that Etzioni offers two types of relationship (coercive power and remunerative-utilitarian power) but Kelman writes only of compliance. On the other hand, Kelman's distinction between identification (social power, social commitment) and internalization (pure normative power—pure moral commitment) appears to be particularly useful because Kelman also postulates a cost difference between identification and internalization: the internalization process clearly is the one that does not require surveillance (in contrast with compliance) or the presence/salience (in contrast with identification) of the power agent and might be seen as the most effective and parsimonious means of control. Yet, an important difference remains: Kelman's three processes are located at the individual level of analysis, whereas Etzioni's compliance is defined as a relation between an individual process (involvement) and an organizational process (power).

INDIVIDUAL AND SITUATIONAL MODERATORS

Individual differences variables, one may reasonably assume, moderate the impact of influence attempts such that a given type of influence attempt will be more successful with a given group of individuals. Imagine, for example, the outcome of the use of coercive/reward power in order to bring about simple compliance. In such an instance, one would find that the influence attempt was or was not successful as a partial function of such predispositions as willingness to comply with incentives, intimidation, bribery, or threats. It would be suspected that animals, children, and those adults who possess little desire for autonomy would be most responsive to influence attempts that are designed to bring about simple compliance and that are based on coercive/reward power.

Some individual differences moderators that have been the focus of considerable organizational research include growth need strength (Hackman & Oldham, 1976), Protestant work ethic (Blood, 1969; Mirels & Garrett, 1971), and internal versus external locus-of-control (Rotter, 1966). It is suspected that these value system indices are likely to be most relevant for social influence attempts directed at an internalization process. That is to say, influence attempts that essentially are appeals to the target's value system will be differentially effective as a function of the target's value system.

A value system having implications across all three influence modes has been advanced by Kohlberg (1963, 1969). Kohlberg proposes that an individual passes through three identifiable stages of value maturity. At the first level, the preconventional, an individual is most concerned with the consequences of his or her behavior. At the second (conventional) level, an individual is most concerned with meeting the expectations of family, immediate group, or nation because it is valuable as an end in itself. The final, or postconventional, level is characterized by an individual's effort to define and apply these values or principles apart from external norms and potential sanctions.

It can be argued that Kohlberg's typology maps, aptly, into the social influence processes. Specifically, the more an influence attempt is based on simple reward/coercive power and seeks to evoke compliance, the more successful the influence attempt will be if it is directed towards individuals whose value system is best characterized as hedonistic/utilitarian. Influence attempts based on referent power should be most effective with individuals who have a strong desire for social conformity. And, finally, influence heavily directed toward appealing to an individual's values will be most effective with persons who are strongly concerned with value issues. It is worthy of note that a motivational study that employed the Kohlberg typology (Vecchio, 1981) reported support for the hypothesis that individual values moderate worker response to incentive schemes.

In addition to individual differences moderators, one might expect situational factors to play an important role in moderating the differential effectiveness of the various influence approaches. Situational attributes of possible importance include job autonomy and job challenge. Organizational level (a potentially significant situational factor) may be of particular importance to the influence process view of motivation. For example, one might find that different influence processes are used more frequently at different organizational levels, such that internalization influence attempts are used more frequently in higher organizational levels and compliance-based influence attempts are employed more commonly at lower organizational levels. Although such a finding would be of a purely descriptive nature, it should be possible to document the differential effectiveness of these influence processes at different levels.

At a still broader level of conceptualization, the organizational power types proposed by Etzioni offer a further framework for matching the type of influence attempt with situational attributes. That is to say, specific types of influence attempts may appear most appropriate (congruent) and be most effective within specific organizational power structures.

Up to this point, the importance has been shown of several situational and individual attributes as moderators of the relationship between influence attempts and individual motivation. However, the translation of individual motivation (often conceptualized as effort and/or strength of a behavioral intention) into performance requires the specification of individual and situational attributes that serve as moderators of the relationship between individual motivation and performance (Lawler, 1971; Porter & Lawler, 1968; Vroom, 1964). These specific attributes can be best summarized by the terms "ability" and "availability of the behavior."

The intersection of situational attributes, individual differences attributes, and influence attempts yields a complex and theoretically rich framework for hypothesizing specific interactions. However, before discussing such effects it is necessary to link the influence processes with clusters of relevant dependent variables. That is to say, not only is the presently proposed model deliberately explicit with respect to the impact of situational and individual differences moderators (and their interactions), but it also explicitly specifies theoretically relevant intermediate variables and it ties relevant dependent variables to associated processes. Therefore, it is suggested that each influence process is most directly relevant for only certain outcome/process variables.

RELEVANT VARIABLES

Before linking intermediary variables to their associated processes, one must consider the constructs and variables commonly investigated in the area of worker motivation. These constructs and variables have various conceptual commonalities that permit a simple clustering in the interest of parsimony.

The intermediary process variables may be defined as those dimensions that describe individuals' behaviors, intentions, and cognitive and emotional states within an organizationally relevant setting. These process variables appear to describe the specific details of Etzioni's "involvement." Two trends have emerged within the literature for identifying these variables. For the first approach, clusters of these variables are identified and relationships with their antecedents, concomitants, and consequents are explored (Porter & Steers, 1973). Alternatively, many authors have dropped the strict dichotomy between overt behaviors and attitudinal, conative, and cognitive antecedents/concomitants. These authors tend (implicitly) to conceive of acts as including both overt and covert aspects, and they describe work behavior as a process involving a sequence of stages (Mobley, 1977; Mobley, Homer, & Hollingsworth, 1978; Mobley, Griffith, Hand, & Meglino, 1979; Porter & Lawler, 1968; Steers & Rhodes, 1978). The second approach has the potential advantage of emphasizing the importance of individual processes that mediate overt actions and observable outcomes. Thus, the second route of viewing behavior as a unit of overt and covert processes (by covert is meant those latent processes that can reasonably be deduced from overt behaviors) has been adopted for this paper.

Based on a review of the recent literature, three sets of intermediary process variables and a suspected sequence were derived. The first set of variables centers on the issue of the extent to which work events and attributes are related to the individual's value system. Therefore, these variables are termed *value-related*. This set is similar to Katz's (1964) motivational patterns of intrinsic satisfaction, goal internalization, and acceptance of organizational rules. Four variables were identified for this set: (a) importance of success versus failure at work for a person's self-esteem—a variable identified by Rabinowitz and Hall (1977) as one conceptualization of job involvement; (b) the extent to which one's job and/or work is a "central life interest" (Dubin, 1956)—a variable also interpreted by Rabinowitz and Hall (1977) as a manifestation of the "importance of self-esteem" conceptualization of job involvement; (c) the worker's expectation of pleasant/unpleasant feelings as a result of success versus failure (Lawler, 1969)—a variable best summarized as intrinsic motivation; and (d) the extent of belief in and acceptance of values pertinent to the work role—these values can consist of organizational goals, but they may be specific to a particular profession or occupation (Gouldner, 1957). As "acceptance of organizational goals and values," this variable is identical to the first component of "organizational commitment" (Porter, Steers, Mowday, & Boulian, 1974).

The second set, which includes two variables, represents the extent to which work role, occupation, and organizational membership mark the individual's self-image and the degree to which the individual derives satisfaction from interpersonal relations and primary-group relationships (Katz, 1964) in organizations. This set therefore may be labeled *identity-related*. More specifically, the variables in this set may be termed: (a) importance of the job or the work role for a person's self-concept; and (b) social attachment to the organization. Importance of the job for self-concept is the second conceptualization of job involvement as elaborated by Rabinowitz and Hall (1977). According to these authors, this variable also can be understood as the degree of psychological identification with work. Social attachment refers to the desire to remain within one's organization and to remain a member of the organization. It corresponds therefore to the third component of "organizational commitment" (Porter et al., 1974).

The third set of variables is comprised of utility-related aspects of the job—for example Katz's (1964) instrumental system and individual rewards. These aspects will be referred to with the inclusive variable label of "job outcome utility." This variable consists of extrinsic factors and is reflected in terms such as role attraction (Mobley, Hand, Baker, & Meglino, 1979) and valence of the work role (Vroom, 1964). Also, it is parallel to satisfaction with specific extrinsic facets of the job (Lawler, 1973). Subjective evaluations of job outcomes are thought to be a function not only of the absolute attractiveness of outcomes, but also of social comparisons (Adams, 1965; Katzell, 1964; Locke, 1969).

These three sets of variables—value-related, identity-related, and utilitarian—may be understood as antecedents of those *behavioral intentions* that are, in turn, related to overt behavior. Thus, the variable now considered corresponds to Fishbein's (1967) "behavioral intentions" (BI). This variable is used in Mobley's turnover model (Miller, Katerberg, & Hulin, 1979; Mobley, 1977; Mobley et al., 1978). In the Porter et al. (1974) "organizational commitment" scheme, this variable appears as "willingness to exert effort on behalf of the organization." It must be noted that Porter et al.'s "willingness to exert effort" is far less specific than are such variables as intentions to quit, attend, and produce efficiently, which usually are criteria for prediction. Thus, willingness to exert effort might appear as an antecedent to specific intentions.

Lastly, the proposed process generates overt activity. Examples of this variable are production behavior, quitting, attending, and job performance (the latter is defined as production behavior projected on an evaluative dimension of effectiveness).

A SOCIAL INFLUENCE FRAMEWORK

The entire sequence, consisting of the influence attempts, the three sets of antecedent variables, BI, and overt behavior, is portrayed in Figure 1. Cardinal emphasis is placed on the concept that BI is determined by the three categories of antecedents identified herein. A major corollary of this

Figure 1
Influence Processes and Sequence

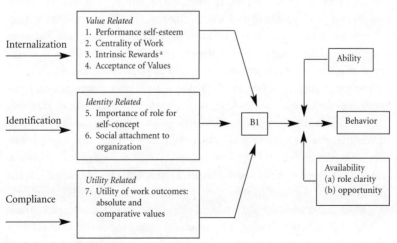

[a] Includes desire for competence, mastery.

contention is that in order to change motivation, one has to alter one, two, or all three of these categories. That is to say, motivation change is mediated by changes in the three sets of antecedent variables.

Logically, the question then must be asked as to how these antecedent variables can be modified. Kelman's (1961) aforementioned processes of influence appear to correspond closely to the character of the three BI-antecedent categories.

1. Compliance is defined by Kelman as acceptance of influence in order to gain specific rewards and to avoid punishments. It is a process wherein behavior is controlled by its contingencies; or, in the terminology of expectancy theory, by expectancies of differently valued outcomes. These notions are similar to the variable "utility of work outcomes." It is proposed here, therefore, that motivation is influenced through the mediary of *utility* by the process of *compliance.*

2. Identification refers to the process of accepting influence in order to engage in a satisfying role-relationship with another person or a group. It is behavior controlled by role acceptance, the involvement in the work role in terms of its importance for the self-concept, the commitment to a group, or the attractiveness of membership in an organization. Therefore, this variety of motivation is influenced through the mediary of *identity-related* variables (i.e., importance of the work role for the self-concept, and social attachment to the organization) by the process of *identification.*

3. Internalization refers to the acceptance of influence because it is congruent with a worker's value system and/or because it is intrinsically rewarding. With regard to the work behavior variables listed above, internalization can be understood to exert control through the importance of success and failure for self-esteem, the place of work as a central life interest, the importance of intrinsic rewards, and acceptance of organizational goals and values. Thus, in such cases, motivation is influenced through the mediary of *value-related* variables by the process of *internalization.*

The relationship between the Kelman influence processes and the dependent and process variables is shown at the left-hand side of Figure 1. The incorporation of the dependent and process variables within the Kelman scheme represents an important elaboration of Kelman's work. The proposed framework and inherent process may be summarized as follows: Among the three variables that influence overt behavior directly, BI is the motivational construct. Motivation, in turn, is a function of value-related, identity-related, and/or utility-related categories of person variables. These three categories are controlled by the interpersonal influence process of internalization, identification, and compliance, respectively.

A relationship exists between Kelman's interpersonal influence processes and Etzioni's types of organizational power. Pure normative organizational power (Etzioni) parallels an internalization interpersonal influence process (Kelman), social power corresponds to identification, and utilitarian and coercive power correspond to Kelman's compliance. In the present framework, this paper proposes to distinguish between *positive* (reward based) and *negative* (punitive oriented) compliance, in order to provide the connections with utilitarian and coercive power. Figure 2 portrays this integration of structural (macro-level) with interpersonal and individual (micro-level) processes. On the left-hand side of Figure 2 are Etzioni's types of power, which at the level of interpersonal influence attempts appear as Kelman-type influence processes (second column). The dependent and

Figure 2
An Expanded Motivation Framework[a]

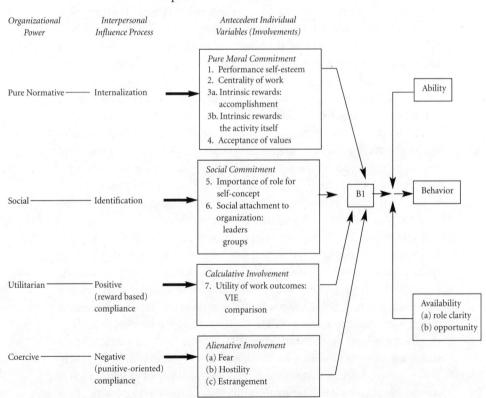

[a] Solid arrows indicate congruent (appropriate) links.

process variables are clustered, as in Figure 1, with the difference that now the corresponding involvement labels are: pure moral commitment for the value-related variables, social commitment for the identity-related variables, and calculative involvement for the utility-related variables. A cluster is added to describe alienative involvement (consisting of responses such as fear, hostility, and estrangement). These clusters are then seen as antecedents of BI. The right-hand side of Figure 2 is identical to the right-hand side of Figure 1.

The *validity* of the proposed view of social influence is suggested by a consideration of popular methods of motivating workers. For example, O. B. Mod and incentive-type schemes appear to be representative of influence attempts that are based on a simple compliance process. Such approaches seek to use extrinsic factors to bring about behavior change (with little or no attention given to appealing to higher order processes).

Identification-based motivational techniques are best represented by modeling techniques. For example, Goldstein and Sorcher (1974) proposed the use of behavioral modeling, which recently was tested by Latham and Saari (1979) and found to be an effective training technique. Also, studies reported by Burnaska (1976) and Kraut (1976) exemplify the social-learning theory approach to modifying work behavior (Davis & Luthans, 1980a).

Job enrichment, by contrast, appears to be directed toward altering the behavior of workers who are more seriously concerned with value-related issues (by offering opportunities for psychological rewards via job redesign). Job enrichment investigators have reported difficulty with respect to motivating individuals who are low on higher-order growth need strength (e.g., the case of the hard-core unemployed). This gives testimony to the validity of the proposition that an internalization influence attempt is most effective with only certain individuals (Hulin, 1971).

In summary, the major approaches to motivating workers (i.e., organizational intervention approaches) can be viewed as being aligned with each of the proposed influence processes. Although the effectiveness of the various intervention approaches is potentially *moderated* by individual and situational contingencies, the possibility exists that the simultaneous use of multiple approaches may result in relatively greater effectiveness (relative to employing a single motivational approach). This second, *additive* strategy is based on evidence—reviewed by Porras (1979) and Porras and Berg (1978)—that suggests that the number of OD techniques employed in intervention projects (or intervention mix) is positively related with effectiveness.

A SOCIALLY-INDEPENDENT MOTIVATIONAL PROCESS

There is a motivational process that has received little consideration in the organizational literature. This process has been ignored, perhaps, because it may be accurately described as a process that is somewhat socially independent. "Socially independent" here means that the relevant behavior originates within the worker with little (at least apparent) external inducement. Nonetheless, the behavior can be characterized as purposeful and seemingly goal-oriented, although the goal is totally internal to the worker. This socially independent motivational process has been termed a competence or mastery motive (White, 1959). This motivational process also encompasses exploratory behavior. Despite its generally socially independent nature, it nonetheless is possible to imagine an influence attempt directed at an individual's competence motive. Such an influence attempt would be one that offered novel and challenging job assignments.

In the vein of socially-independent motivational processes, the recently proposed concept of behavioral self-managment should be mentioned (Davis & Luthans, 1980b; Luthans & Davis, 1979; Manz & Sims, 1980). Based on concepts derived from cognitive behavior modification (Meichenbaum, 1977), behavioral self-management has been offered as a device for self-directing one's own behavior in desired directions.

IMPLICATIONS

By extending and elaborating the proposed framework, it is possible to deduce several implications for supervisory behaviors that would be directed toward motivating workers. For this extension, it is necessary to introduce a feedback loop from worker behavior to a supervisor or, more generally, an evaluator. In this process (see Figure 3), the supervisor compares the observed behavior of the worker with a standard or prior expectations. The supervisor then determines whether a further influence attempt is warranted. If so, the supervisor decides the nature of the influence attempt (compliance, internalization, and/or identification). From a purely descriptive standpoint, the framework represents a cyclical view of social influence, with the supervisor changing influence strategies as a function of worker behavior. It might be argued that this view places a substantial emphasis on worker behavior as a determinant of supervisor behavior. At first glance, this seems like supervision turned upside-down in that the

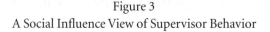

Figure 3
A Social Influence View of Supervisor Behavior

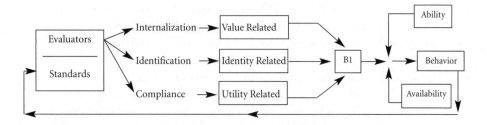

supervisor's influence attempts are "shaped" by the behavior of the worker. However, once the cycle begins, a reciprocal causation process is set in motion so that the question of primary control of one person over the other becomes pointless.

Taking the descriptive stance a bit further, it might be demonstrated empirically that different types of supervisors prefer different influence modes. For example, highly authoritarian supervisors might prefer to use compliance influence modes; human-relations oriented supervisors might prefer to use identification influence modes. Also, supervisors might be observed to use different modes of influence when operating in different levels of an organization.

From a prescriptive standpoint, the proposed influence framework suggests that supervisors should be attentive to individual worker differences for preferred inducements. For example, to increase worker motivation, a supervisor should be sensitive to differences in subordinates' preferences for compliance-identification-internalization inducement schemes. It might be possible to demonstrate that more effective supervisors are aware of and make use of subordinate's inducement preferences when attempting to influence the latter's behavior. Such a finding would have important implications for a prescriptive application of the proposed framework.

The above-mentioned extension to supervisor behavior is consistent with the currently popular contingency view of leadership. Clearly, the framework's implications for supervision point to an optimal "matching" of (a) supervisor's preferred style of influence, (b) individual predisposition to respond to specific influence modes, and (c) situational variables that dictate what is socially-appropriate (i.e., normative) for the employment of specific influence modes. The view of the supervisor within the proposed framework, in essence, is best summarized as a view of the supervisor "as motivator."

SUMMARY

This paper has outlined a viewpoint that argues that worker motivation cannot be adequately understood without relating the concept of motivation to attempts on the part of organizational agents to "motivate" people. Such attempts usually take place by means of manipulating outcomes that are made contingent on the actions of individuals. The variables were identified that operate at the individual level (motivation), the interpersonal level (influence), and the organizational level (power). A framework was presented for tying these variables together, and concepts from both micro-level and macro-level approaches were integrated in a relatively meso-level approach. Also, specific testable predictions were generated from a proposed theoretical integration.

REFERENCES

Adams, J. S. Inequity in social exchange. In L. Berkowitz (Ed.), *Advances in experimental social psychology* (Vol. 2). New York: Academic Press, 1965, 267–299.

Blood, M. R. Work values and job satisfaction. *Journal of Applied Psychology,* 1969, 53, 456–459.

Burnaska, R. F. The effects of behavior upon managers' behaviors and employees' perceptions. *Personnel Psychology,* 1976, 29, 329–335.

Campbell, J. P., & Pritchard, R. D. Motivation theory in industrial and organizational psychology. In M. Dunnette (Ed.), *Handbook of industrial and organizational psychology.* Chicago: Rand-McNally, 1976, 63–130.

Campbell, J. P., Dunnette, M. D., Lawler, E. E., & Weick, K. E. *Managerial behavior, performance, and effectiveness.* New York: McGraw-Hill, 1970.

Davis, T. R. V., & Luthans, F. A social learning approach to organizational behavior. *Academy of Management Review,* 1980a, 5, 281–290.

Davis, T. R. V., & Luthans, F. A social learning approach to training and development: Guidelines for application. *Proceedings of the 12th Annual Meeting of the American Institute for Decision Sciences,* 1980b, 1, 399–401.

Dubin, R. Industrial workers' worlds: A study of the "central life interests" of industrial workers. *Social Problems,* 1956, 3, 131–142.

Etzioni, A. *A comparative analysis of complex organizations* (Rev. ed.). New York: Free Press, 1975.

Fishbein, M. (Ed.). *Readings in attitude theory and measurement.* New York: Wiley, 1967.

French, J. R. P., & Raven, B. The bases of social power. In D. Cartwright (Ed.), *Studies in social power.* Ann Arbor, Mich.: Institute for Social Research, 1959, 150–167.

Goldstein, A. P., & Sorcher, M. *Changing supervisory behavior.* New York: Pergamon Press, 1974.

Gouldner, A. W. Cosmopolitans and locals: Toward an analysis of latent social roles. *Administrative Science Quarterly,* 1957, 2, 281–292.

Hackman, J. R., & Oldham, G. R. Motivation through the design of work: Test of a theory. *Organizational Behavior and Human Performance,* 1976, 16, 250–279.

Hulin, C. L. Individual differences and job enrichment: The case against general treatments. In J. R. Maher (Ed.), *New perspectives in job enrichment.* New York: Van Nostrand, 1971, 159–191.

Katz, D. The motivational basis of organizational behavior. *Behavioral Science,* 1964, 9, 131–146.

Katzell, R. A. Personal values, job satisfaction, and job behavior. In H. Borow (Ed.), *Man in a world of work.* Boston: Houghton Mifflin, 1964, 314–363.

Kelman, H. C. Processes of opinion change. *Public Opinion Quarterly,* 1961, 25, 57–78.

Kohlberg, L. Moral development and identification. In H. Stevenson (Ed.), *Child psychology,* 62nd Yearbook of the National Society for the study of Education. Chicago: University of Chicago Press, 1963, 383–431.

Kohlberg, L. The cognitive-developmental approach to socialization. In D. A. Goslin (Ed.), *Handbook of socialization theory and research.* Chicago: Rand-McNally, 1969, 347–480.

Kraut, A. I. Developing managerial skills via modeling techniques: Some positive research findings—a symposium. *Personnel Psychology,* 1976, 29, 325–369.

Latham, G. P., & Saari, L. M. Application of social-learning theory to training supervisors through behavioral modeling. *Journal of Applied Psychology,* 1979, 64, 239–246.

Lawler, E. E., III. Job design and employee motivation. *Personnel Psychology,* 1969, 22, 426–435.

Lawler, E. E., III. *Pay and organizational effectiveness.* New York: McGraw-Hill, 1971.

Lawler, E. E., III. *Motivation in work organizations.* Monterey, Cal.: Brooks/Cole, 1973.

Locke, E. A. What is job satisfaction? *Organizational Behavior and Human Performance,* 1969, 4, 309–336.

Luthans, F., & Davis, T. R. V. Behavioral self-management—the missing link in managerial effectiveness. *Organizational Dynamics,* 1979, 8, 42–60.

Manz, C. C., & Sims, H. P. Self-management as a substitute for leadership: A social learning theory perspective. *Academy of Management Review,* 1980, 5, 361–367.

Meichenbaum, D. *Cognitive behavior modification: An integrative approach.* New York: Plenum, 1977.

Miller, E. E., Katerberg, R., & Hulin, C. L. Evaluation of the Mobley, Horner, and Hollingsworth model of employee turnover. *Journal of Applied Psychology,* 1979, 64, 509–517.

Mirels, H. L., & Garrett, J. B. The Protestant ethic as a personality variable. *Journal of Consulting and Clinical Psychology,* 1971, 36, 40–44.

Mobley, W. H. Intermediate linkages in the relationship between job satisfaction and employee turnover. *Journal of Applied Psychology,* 1977, 62, 237–240.

Mobley, W. H., Horner, S. O., & Hollingsworth, A. T. An evaluation of precursors of hospital employee turnover. *Journal of Applied Psychology,* 1978, 63, 408–414.

Mobley, W. H., Griffeth, R. W., Hand, H. H., & Meglino, B. M. Review and conceptual analysis of the employee turnover process. *Psychological Bulletin,* 1979, 86, 493–522.

Mobley, W. H., Hand, H. H., Baker, R. L., & Meglino, B. M. Conceptual and empirical analysis of military recruit training attrition. *Journal of Applied Psychology,* 1979, 64, 10–18.

Porras, J. I. The comparative impact of different OD techniques and intervention intensities. *Journal of Applied Behavioral Sciences,* 1979, 15, 156–178.

Porras, J. I., & Berg, P. O. The impact of organization development. *Academy of Management Review,* 1978, 3, 249–266.

Porter, L. W., & Lawler, E. E., III. *Managerial attitudes and performance.* Homewood, Ill.: Irwin, 1968.

Porter, L. W., & Steers, R. M. Organizational, work and personal factors in employee turnover and absenteeism. *Psychological Bulletin,* 1973, 80, 151–176.

Porter, L. W., Steers, R. M., Mowday, R. T., & Boulian, P. V. Organizational commitment, job satisfaction and turnover among psychiatric technicians. *Journal of Applied Psychology,* 1974, 59, 603–609.

Rabinowitz, S., & Hall, D. T. Organizational research and job involvement. *Psychological Bulletin,* 1977, 84, 265–288.

Rotter, J. B. Generalized expectancies for internal versus external control of reinforcement. *Psychological Monographs,* 1966, 80, (1, Whole No. 609).

Steers, R. M., & Rhodes, R. S. Major influences on employee attendance: A process model. *Journal of Applied Psychology,* 1978, 63, 391–407.

Vecchio, R. P. An individual differences interpretation of conflicting predictions generated by equity theory and expectancy theory. *Journal of Applied Psychology,* 1981, 66, 470–481.

Vroom, V. H. *Work and motivation.* New York: Wiley, 1964.

White, R. Motivation reconsidered: The concept of competence. *Psychological Review,* 1959, 66, 297–334.

PART III

Dysfunctional Aspects of Leadership

I don't want any yes-men around me. I want everyone to tell me the truth even if it costs them their jobs.

> Samuel Goldwyn

The President doesn't want any yes-men and yes-women around him. When he says no, we all say no.

> Elizabeth Dole

Perpetual optimism is a force multiplier.

> Colin Powell

Treat others as if they are what they ought to be, and you help them become what they are capable of being.

> J. W. von Goethe

The secret of success is sincerity. Once you can fake that, you've got it made.

> Jean Giraudoux

Remember, you can do everything right, and do absolutely nothing wrong, and still fail.

> Captain Jean-Luc Picard

Although we tend to think of leadership in positive and heroic terms, many times leadership processes operate in a dysfunctional manner. In this set of readings, we explore social problems that arise and work to undermine a group's best interest. The initial reading considers how the drive for consensus in a group can result in the suppression of dissent and honest discussion of alternatives. In "Groupthink," Irving Janis provides concrete examples of how the tendency to internalize group norms and to seek approval has resulted in defective decision making. The power of expectations surrounding the principle of a self-fulfilling prophecy is then described in the next reading, by Robert Vecchio. The selection authored by executive coach Roy Lubit explores the self-destructive tendencies that reside in self-absorbed, narcissistic leaders. Jay Conger considers potential liabilities in a leader's skills that can simultaneously give rise to achievement while providing opportunities for self-destruction. The causes and cures of leader self-destruction are then examined in another article by Manfred Kets de Vries, who considers how leaders may unconsciously cause themselves to fail. Finally, Steven Kerr provides some interesting illustrations, from society in general and organizations in particular, on how reward systems that are thought to guide employee behavior toward one goal may, in fact, lead to unexpected and undesired consequences.

Groupthink

Irving L. Janis

"How could we have been so stupid?" President John F. Kennedy asked after he and a close group of advisers had blundered into the Bay of Pigs invasion. For the last two years I have been studying that question, as it applies not only to the Bay of Pigs decision-makers but also to those who led the United States into such other major fiascos as the failure to be prepared for the attack on Pearl Harbor, the Korean War stalemate and the escalation of the Vietnam War.

Stupidity certainly is not the explanation. The people who participated in making the Bay of Pigs decision, for instance, comprised one of the greatest arrays of intellectual talent in the history of American Government—Dean Rusk, Robert McNamara, Douglas Dillon, Robert Kennedy, McGeorge Bundy, Arthur Schlesinger Jr., Allen Dulles and others.

It also seemed to me that explanations were incomplete if they concentrated only on disturbances in the behavior of each individual within a decision-making body: temporary emotional states of elation, fear, or anger that reduce a person's mental efficiency, for example, or chronic blind spots arising from a person's social prejudices or idiosyncratic biases.

I preferred to broaden the picture by looking at the fiascos from the standpoint of group dynamics as it has been explored over the past three decades, first by the great social psychologist Kurt Lewin and later in many experimental situations by myself and other behavioral scientists. My conclusion after poring over hundreds of relevant documents—historical reports about formal group meetings and informal conversations among the members—is that the groups that committed the fiascos were victims of what I call "groupthink."

"Groupy"

In each case study, I was surprised to discover the extent to which each group displayed the typical phenomena of social conformity that are regularly encountered in studies of group dynamics among ordinary citizens. For example, some of the phenomena appear to be completely in line with findings from social-psychological experiments showing that powerful social pressures are brought to bear by the members of a cohesive group whenever a dissident begins to voice his objections to a group consensus. Other phenomena are reminiscent of the shared illusions observed in encounter groups and friendship cliques when the members simultaneously reach a peak of "groupy" feelings.

Above all, there are numerous indications pointing to the development of group norms that bolster morale at the expense of critical thinking. One of the most common norms appears to be that of remaining loyal to the group by sticking with the policies to which the group has already committed itself, even when those policies are obviously working out badly and have unintended consequences that disturb the conscience of each member. This is one of the key characteristics of groupthink.

1984

I use the term groupthink as a quick and easy way to refer to the mode of thinking that persons engage in when *concurrence-seeking* becomes so dominant in a cohesive ingroup that it tends to override realistic appraisal of alternative courses of action. Groupthink is a term of the same order as the words in the newspeak vocabulary George Orwell used in his dismaying world of *1984*. In that context, groupthink takes on an invidious connotation. Exactly such a connotation is intended, since the term refers to a deterioration in mental efficiency, reality testing and moral judgments as a result of group pressures.

The symptoms of groupthink arise when the members of decision-making groups become motivated to avoid being too harsh in their judgments of their leaders' or their colleagues' ideas. They adopt a soft line of criticism, even in their own thinking. At their meetings, all the members are amiable and seek complete concurrence on every important issue, with no bickering or conflict to spoil the cozy, "we-feeling" atmosphere.

Kill

Paradoxically, soft-headed groups are often hard-hearted when it comes to dealing with outgroups or enemies. They find it relatively easy to resort to dehumanizing solutions—they will readily authorize bombing attacks that kill large numbers of civilians in the name of the noble cause of persuading an unfriendly government to negotiate at the peace table. They are unlikely to pursue the more difficult and controversial issues that arise when alternatives to a harsh military solution come up for discussion. Nor are they inclined to raise ethical issues that carry the implication that *this fine group of ours, with its humanitarianism and its high-minded principles, might be capable of adopting a course of action that is inhumane and immoral.*

Norms

There is evidence from a number of social-psychological studies that as the members of a group feel more accepted by the others, which is a central feature of increased group cohesiveness, they display less overt conformity to group norms. Thus we would expect that the more cohesive a group becomes, the less the members will feel constrained to censor what they say out of fear of being socially punished for antagonizing the leader or any of their fellow members.

In contrast, the groupthink type of conformity tends to increase as group cohesiveness increases. Group-think involves nondeliberate suppression of critical thoughts as a result of internalization of the group's norms, which is quite different from deliberate suppression on the basis of external threats of social punishment. The more cohesive the group, the greater the inner compulsion on the part of each member to avoid creating disunity, which inclines him or her to believe in the soundness of whatever proposals are promoted by the leader or by a majority of the group's members.

In a cohesive group, the danger is not so much that each individual will fail to reveal objections to what the others propose but that the individual will think the proposal is a good one, without attempting to carry out a careful, critical scrutiny of the pros and cons of the alternatives. When groupthink becomes dominant, there also is considerable suppression of deviant thoughts, but it takes the form of each person's deciding that his or her misgivings are not relevant and should be set aside, that the benefit of the doubt regarding any lingering uncertainties should be given to the group consensus.

Stress

I do not mean to imply that all cohesive groups necessarily suffer from groupthink. All ingroups may have a mild tendency toward groupthink, displaying one or another of the symptoms from time to time, but it need not be so dominant as to influence the quality of the group's final decision. Neither do I mean to imply that there is anything necessarily inefficient or harmful about group decisions in general. On the contrary, a group whose members have properly defined roles, with traditions concerning the procedures to follow in pursuing a critical inquiry, probably is capable of making better decisions than any individual group member working alone.

The problem is that the advantages of having decisions made by groups are often lost because of powerful psychological pressures that arise when the members work closely together, share the same set of values and, above all, face a crisis situation that puts everyone under intense stress.

The main principle of groupthink, which I offer in the spirit of Parkinson's Law, is this: *The more amiability and esprit de corps there is among the members of a policy-making ingroup, the greater the danger that independent critical thinking will be replaced by groupthink, which is likely to result in irrational and dehumanizing actions directed against outgroups.*

Symptoms

In my studies of high-level governmental decision-makers, both civilian and military, I have found eight main symptoms of groupthink.

1 Invulnerability.   Most or all of the members of the ingroup share an *illusion* of invulnerability that provides for them some degree of reassurance about obvious dangers and leads them to become over optimistic and willing to take extraordinary risks. It also causes them to fail to respond to clear warnings of danger.

The Kennedy ingroup, which uncritically accepted the Central Intelligence Agency's disastrous Bay of Pigs plan, operated on the false assumption that they could keep secret the fact that the United States was responsible for the invasion of Cuba. Even after news of the plan began to leak out, their belief remained unshaken. They failed even to consider the danger that awaited them: a worldwide revulsion against the U.S.

A similar attitude appeared among the members of President Lyndon B. Johnson's ingroup, the "Tuesday Cabinet," which kept escalating the Vietnam War despite repeated setbacks and failures. "There was a belief," Bill Moyers commented after he resigned, "that if we indicated a willingness to use our power, they [the North Vietnamese] would get the message and back away from an all-out confrontation. . . . There was a confidence—it was never bragged about, it was just there—that when the chips were really down, the other people would fold."

A most poignant example of an illusion of invulnerability involves the ingroup around Admiral H. E. Kimmel, which failed to prepare for the possibility of a Japanese attack on Pearl Harbor despite repeated warnings. Informed by his intelligence chief that radio contact with Japanese aircraft carriers had been lost, Kimmel joked about it: "What, you don't know where the carriers are? Do you mean to say that they could be rounding Diamond Head (at Honolulu) and you wouldn't know it?" The carriers were in fact moving full-steam toward Kimmel's command post at the time. Laughing together about a danger signal, which labels it as a purely laughing matter, is a characteristic manifestation of groupthink.

2 Rationale. As we see, victims of groupthink ignore warnings; they also collectively construct rationalizations in order to discount warnings and other forms of negative feedback that, taken seriously, might lead the group members to reconsider their assumptions each time they recommit themselves to past decisions. Why did the Johnson ingroup avoid reconsidering its escalation policy when time and again the expectations on which they based their decisions turned out to be wrong? James C. Thompson Jr., a Harvard historian who spent five years as an observing participant in both the State Department and the White House, tells us that the policymakers avoided critical discussion of their prior decisions and continually invented new rationalizations so that they could sincerely recommit themselves to defeating the North Vietnamese.

In the fall of 1964, before the bombing of North Vietnam began, some of the policymakers predicted that six weeks of air strikes would induce the North Vietnamese to seek peace talks. When someone asked, "What if they don't?" the answer was that another four weeks certainly would do the trick.

Later, after each setback, the ingroup agreed that by investing just a bit more effort (by stepping up the bomb tonnage a bit, for instance), their course of action would prove to be right. *The Pentagon Papers* bear out these observations.

In *The Limits of Intervention,* Townsend Hoopes, who was acting Secretary of the Air Force under Johnson, says that Walt W. Rostow in particular showed a remarkable capacity for what has been called "instant rationalization." According to Hoopes, Rostow buttressed the group's optimism about being on the road to victory by culling selected scraps of evidence from news reports or, if necessary, by inventing "plausible" forecasts that had no basis in evidence at all.

Admiral Kimmel's group rationalized away their warnings, too. Right up to December 7, 1941, they convinced themselves that the Japanese would never dare attempt a full-scale surprise assault against Hawaii because Japan's leaders would realize that it would precipitate an all-out war which the United States would surely win. They made no attempt to look at the situation through the eyes of the Japanese leaders—another manifestation of groupthink.

3 Morality. Victims of groupthink believe unquestioningly in the inherent morality of their ingroup; this belief inclines the members to ignore the ethical or moral consequences of their decisions.

Evidence that this symptom is at work usually is of a negative kind—the things that are left unsaid in group meetings. At least two influential persons had doubts about the morality of the Bay of Pigs adventure. One of them, Arthur Schlesinger Jr., presented his strong objections in a memorandum to President Kennedy and Secretary of State Rusk but suppressed them when he attended meetings of the Kennedy team. The other, Senator J. William Fulbright, was not a member of the group, but the President invited him to express his misgivings in a speech to the policymakers. However, when Fulbright finished speaking, the President moved on to other agenda items without asking for reactions of the group.

David Kraslow and Stuart H. Loory, in *The Secret Search for Peace in Vietnam,* report that during 1966 President Johnson's ingroup was concerned primarily with selecting bomb targets in North Vietnam. They based their selections on four factors—the military advantage, the risk to American aircraft and pilots, the danger of forcing other countries into the fighting, and the danger of heavy civilian casualties. At their regular Tuesday luncheons, they weighed these factors the way school teachers grade examination papers, averaging them out. Though evidence on this point is scant, I suspect that the group's ritualistic adherence to a standardized procedure induced the members to feel morally justified in their destructive way of dealing with the Vietnamese people—after all, the danger of heavy civilian casualties from U.S. air strikes was taken into account on their checklists.

4 Stereotypes. Victims of groupthink hold stereotyped views of the leaders of enemy groups: they are so evil that genuine attempts at negotiating differences with them are unwarranted, or they are too weak or too stupid to deal effectively with whatever attempts the ingroup makes to defeat their purposes, no matter how risky the attempts are.

Kennedy's groupthinkers believed that Premier Fidel Castro's air force was so ineffectual that obsolete B-26s could knock it out completely in a surprise attack before the invasion began. They also believed that Castro's army was so weak that a small Cuban-exile brigade could establish a well-protected beach-head at the Bay of Pigs. In addition, they believed that Castro was not smart enough to put down any possible internal uprisings in support of the exiles. They were wrong on all three assumptions. Though much of the blame was attributable to faulty intelligence, the point is that none of Kennedy's advisers even questioned the CIA planners about these assumptions.

The Johnson advisers' sloganistic thinking about "the Communist apparatus" that was "working all around the world" (as Dean Rusk put it) led them to overlook the powerful nationalistic strivings of the North Vietnamese government and its efforts to ward off Chinese domination. The crudest of all stereotypes used by Johnson's inner circle to justify their policies was the domino theory ("If we don't stop the Reds in South Vietnam, tomorrow they will be in Hawaii and next week they will be in San Francisco," Johnson once said). The group so firmly accepted this stereotype that it became almost impossible for any adviser to introduce a more sophisticated viewpoint.

In the documents on Pearl Harbor, it is clear to see that the Navy commanders stationed in Hawaii had a naive image of Japan as a midget that would not dare to strike a blow against a powerful giant.

5 Pressure. Victims of groupthink apply direct pressure to any individual who momentarily expresses doubts about any of the group's shared illusions or who questions the validity of the arguments supporting a policy alternative favored by the majority. This gambit reinforces the concurrence-seeking norm that loyal members are expected to maintain.

President Kennedy probably was more active than anyone else in raising skeptical questions during the Bay of Pigs meetings, and yet he seems to have encouraged the group's docile, uncritical acceptance of defective arguments in favor of the CIA's plan. At every meeting, he allowed the CIA representatives to dominate the discussion. He permitted them to give their immediate refutations in response to each tentative doubt that one of the others expressed, instead of asking whether anyone shared the doubt or wanted to pursue the implications of the new worrisome issue that had just been raised. And at the most crucial meeting, when he was calling on each member to give his vote for or against the plan, he did not call on Arthur Schlesinger, the one man there who was known by the President to have serious misgivings.

Historian Thomson informs us that whenever a member of Johnson's ingroup began to express doubts, the group used subtle social pressures to "domesticate" him. To start with, the dissenter was made to feel at home, provided that he lived up to two restrictions: 1) that he did not voice his doubts to outsiders, which would play into the hands of the opposition; and 2) that he kept his criticisms within the bounds of acceptable deviation, which meant not challenging any of the fundamental assumptions that went into the group's prior commitments. One such "domesticated dissenter" was Bill Moyers. When Moyers arrived at a meeting, Thomson tells us, the President greeted him with, "Well, here comes Mr. Stop-the-Bombing."

6 *Self-censorship.* Victims of groupthink avoid deviating from what appears to be group consensus; they keep silent about their misgivings and even minimize to themselves the importance of their doubts.

As we have seen, Schlesinger was not at all hesitant about presenting his strong objections to the Bay of Pigs plan in a memorandum to the President and the Secretary of State. But he became keenly aware of his tendency to suppress objections at the White House meetings. "In the months after the Bay of Pigs, I bitterly reproached myself for having kept so silent during those crucial discussions in the cabinet room," Schlesinger writes in *A Thousand Days.* "I can only explain my failure to do more than raise a few timid questions by reporting that one's impulse to blow the whistle on this nonsense was simply undone by the circumstances of the discussion."

7 *Unanimity.* Victims of groupthink share an *illusion* of unanimity within the group concerning almost all judgments expressed by members who speak in favor of the majority view. This symptom results partly from the preceding one, whose effects are augmented by the false assumption that any individual who remains silent during any part of the discussion is in full accord with what the others are saying.

When a group of persons who respect each other's opinions arrives at a unanimous view, each member is likely to feel that the belief must be true. This reliance on consensual validation within the group tends to replace individual critical thinking and reality testing, unless there are clear-cut disagreements among the members. In contemplating a course of action such as the invasion of Cuba, it is painful for the members to confront disagreements within their group, particularly if it becomes apparent that there are widely divergent views about whether the preferred course of action is too risky to undertake at all. Such disagreements are likely to arouse anxieties about making a serious error. Once the sense of unanimity is shattered, the members no longer can feel complacently confident about the decision they are inclined to make. Each person must then face the annoying realization that there are troublesome uncertainties and he must diligently seek out the best information he can get in order to decide for himself exactly how serious the risks might be. This is one of the unpleasant consequences of being in a group of hardheaded, critical thinkers.

To avoid such an unpleasant state, the members often become inclined, without quite realizing it, to prevent latent disagreements from surfacing when they are about to initiate a risky course of action. The group leader and the members support each other in playing up the areas of convergence in their thinking, at the expense of fully exploring divergencies that might reveal unsettled issues.

"Our meetings took place in a curious atmosphere of assumed consensus," Schlesinger writes. His additional comments clearly show that, curiously, the consensus was an illusion—an illusion that could be maintained only because the major participants did not reveal their own reasoning or discuss their idiosyncratic assumptions and vague reservations. Evidence from several sources makes it clear that even the three principals—President Kennedy, Rusk and McNamara—had widely differing assumptions about the invasion plan.

8 Mindguards.   Victims of groupthink sometimes appoint themselves as mindguards to protect the leader and fellow members from adverse information that might break the complacency they shared about the effectiveness and morality of past decisions. At a large birthday party for his wife, Attorney General Robert F. Kennedy, who had been constantly informed about the Cuban invasion plan, took Schlesinger aside and asked him why he was opposed. Kennedy listened coldly and said, "You may be right or you may be wrong, but the President has made his mind up. Don't push it any further. Now is the time for everyone to help him all they can."

Rusk also functioned as a highly effective mindguard by failing to transmit to the group the strong objections of three "outsiders" who had learned of the invasion plan—Undersecretary of State Chester Bowles, USIA Director Edward R. Murrow, and Rusk's intelligence chief, Roger Hilsman. Had Rusk done so, their warnings might have reinforced Schlesinger's memorandum and jolted some of Kennedy's ingroup, if not the President himself, into reconsidering the decision.

Products

When a group of executives frequently displays most or all of these interrelated symptoms, a detailed study of their deliberations is likely to reveal a number of immediate consequences. These consequences are, in effect,

products of poor decision-making practices because they lead to inadequate solutions to the problems under discussion.

First, the group limits its discussions to a few alternative courses of action (often only two) without an initial survey of all the alternatives that
might be worthy of consideration.

Second, the group fails to reexamine the course of action initially preferred by the majority after they learn of risks and drawbacks they had not
considered originally.

Third, the members spend little or no time discussing whether there are
nonobvious gains they may have overlooked or ways of reducing the seemingly prohibitive costs that made rejected alternatives appear undesirable to
them.

Fourth, members make little or no attempt to obtain information from
experts within their own organizations who might be able to supply more
precise estimates of potential losses and gains.

Fifth, members show positive interest in facts and opinions that support
their preferred policy; they tend to ignore facts and opinions that do not.

Sixth, members spend little time deliberating about how the chosen policy might be hindered by bureaucratic inertia, sabotaged by political opponents, or temporarily derailed by common accidents. Consequently, they
fail to work out contingency plans to cope with foreseeable setbacks that
could endanger the overall success of their chosen course.

Support

The search for an explanation of why groupthink occurs has led me
through a quagmire of complicated theoretical issues in the murky area of
human motivation. My belief, based on recent social psychological research, is that we can best understand the various symptoms of groupthink
as a mutual effort among the group members to maintain self-esteem and
emotional equanimity by providing social support to each other, especially
at times when they share responsibility for making vital decisions.

Even when no important decision is pending, the typical administrator
will begin to doubt the wisdom and morality of past decisions each time
information is received about setbacks, particularly if the information is
accompanied by negative feedback from prominent people who originally
had been his supporters. It should not be surprising, therefore, to find that
individual members strive to develop unanimity and esprit de corps that
will help bolster each other's morale, to create an optimistic outlook about

the success of pending decisions, and to reaffirm the positive value of past policies to which all of them are committed.

Pride

Shared illusions of invulnerability, for example, can reduce anxiety about taking risks. Rationalizations help members believe that the risks are really not so bad after all. The assumption of inherent morality helps the members to avoid feelings of shame or guilt. Negative stereotypes function as stress-reducing devices to enhance a sense of moral righteousness as well as pride in a lofty mission.

The mutual enhancement of self-esteem and morale may have functional value in enabling the members to maintain their capacity to take action, but it has maladaptive consequences insofar as concurrence-seeking tendencies interfere with critical, rational capacities and lead to serious errors of judgment.

While I have limited my study to decision-making bodies in government, groupthink symptoms appear in business, industry and any other field where small, cohesive groups make the decisions. It is vital, then, for all sorts of people—and especially group leaders—to know what steps they can take to prevent groupthink.

Remedies

To counterpoint my case studies of the major fiascos, I have also investigated two highly successful group enterprises, the formulation of the Marshall Plan in the Truman Administration and the handling of the Cuban missile crisis by President Kennedy and his advisers. I have found it instructive to examine the steps Kennedy took to change his group's decision-making processes. These changes ensured that the mistakes made by his Bay of Pigs ingroup were not repeated by the missile-crisis ingroup, even though the membership of both groups was essentially the same.

The following recommendations for preventing groupthink incorporate many of the good practices I discovered to be characteristic of the Marshall Plan and missile-crisis groups:

1 The leader of a policy-forming group should assign the role of critical evaluator to each member, encouraging the group to give high priority to open airing of objections and doubts. This practice needs to be reinforced by the leader's acceptance of criticism of his own judgments in order to discourage members from soft-pedaling their disagreements and from allowing their striving for concurrence to inhibit critical thinking.

2   When the key members of a hierarchy assign a policy-planning mission to any group within their organization, they should adopt an impartial stance instead of stating preferences and expectations at the beginning. This will encourage open inquiry and impartial probing of a wide range of policy alternatives.

3   The organization routinely should set up several outside policy-planning and evaluation groups to work on the same policy question, each deliberating under a different leader. This can prevent the insulation of an ingroup.

4   At intervals before the group reaches a final consensus, the leader should require each member to discuss the group's deliberations with associates in the same unit of the organization—assuming that those associates can be trusted to adhere to the same security regulations that govern the policymakers—and then to report back their reactions to the group.

5   The group should invite one or more outside experts to each meeting on a staggered basis and encourage the experts to challenge the views of the core members.

6   At every general meeting of the group, whenever the agenda calls for an evaluation of policy alternatives, at least one member should play devil's advocate, functioning as a good lawyer in challenging the testimony of those who advocate the majority position.

7   Whenever the policy issue involves relations with a rival nation or organization, the group should devote a sizable block of time, perhaps an entire session, to a survey of all warning signals from the rivals and should write alternative scenarios on the rivals' intentions.

8   When the group is surveying policy alternatives for feasibility and effectiveness, it should from time to time divide into two or more subgroups to meet separately, under different discussion leaders and then come back together to hammer out differences.

9   After reaching a preliminary consensus about what seems to be the best policy, the group should hold a "second-chance" meeting at which every member expresses as vividly as possible all residual doubts, and rethinks the entire issue before making a definitive choice.

How

These recommendations have their disadvantages. To encourage the open airing of objections, for instance, might lead to prolonged and costly debates when a rapidly growing crisis requires an immediate solution. It also could cause rejection, depression and anger. A leader's failure to set a norm might create cleavage between leader and members that could develop into a disruptive power struggle if the leader looks on the emerging consensus as anathema. Setting up outside evaluation groups might increase the risk of security leakage. Still, inventive executives who know their way around the organizational maze probably can figure out how to apply one or another of the prescriptions successfully, without harmful side effects.

They also could benefit from the advice of outside experts in the administrative and behavioral sciences. Though these experts have much to offer, they have had few chances to work on policy-making machinery within large organizations. As matters now stand, executives innovate only when they need new procedures to avoid repeating serious errors that have deflated their self-images.

The Power of Leader Expectations: Self-Fulfilling Prophecies in Organizations

Robert P. Vecchio

All of us hold expectations, or future-oriented beliefs, for the behavior of others.[1] We also communicate our expectations to one another via verbal and nonverbal channels. Not uncommonly, we convey cues that reveal our approval or disapproval of another's conduct. Because we generally convey these expectations without any deliberate or conscious intent, the interpersonal dynamics can be relatively subtle in nature (in comparison to more direct attempts to change the behavior of others via incentives or threats).

Two of the more recognizable examples of how the power of expectations operates can be witnessed in the reactions of children to the expectations of parents and teachers. Within some families and classrooms, certain children are labeled as the "little devils" or the "stars," who then respond in accordance with these labels. By and large, individuals tend to respond to the expectations of others in a manner that supports the initial beliefs of the person who is transmitting the various cues.

Robert Rosenthal of Harvard University, in a well-known investigation of the power of expectations, examined the role of elementary school teachers' prior beliefs for the performance of their students.[2] Specifically, Rosenthal gave each pupil an academic aptitude test at the start of the school term, and then gave false feedback to the teachers, labeling 20 percent of the students in each class as likely to have a "great leap forward" in the coming year. In reality, the "bright" students had been selected at random for the honorific title. At the close of the school year, a retesting revealed, however, that the "star" students had indeed excelled, as indicated by significant gains in IQ scores compared to their classmates. Because the only independent (or manipulated) variable in the study was the expectation held by each teacher for each individual student, one is inclined to conclude that the students' test performance was a function of how the teachers varied the quality of their relations with the students (by subtly encouraging and being more positive toward the "stars," and by being less encouraging to all others). The students likely sensed these cues and responded by fulfilling the expectation (or prophecy) of the teacher. This social dynamic can be termed a self-fulfilling prophecy (or SFP).

AN ANCIENT TALE

In a published summary of this classroom research, Rosenthal entitled his work *Pygmalion in the Classroom.* The Greek mythological character of Pygmalion is an apt one for describing this social process. According to the ancient author Ovid (in the tenth book of *Metamorphoses*), a sculptor by the name of Pygmalion, who was a prince of Cyprus, carved an ivory statue of the ideal woman. He then fell in love with his creation, and was rescued from his frustrated love by the intervention of Venus, the goddess of love, who infused life into the statue. The now-animated statue was named Galatea, and the couple enjoyed a "happy ever after" life. Today, we use the term "Pygmalion effect" to refer to a person whose strong wishes or preferences are ultimately fulfilled. In a sense, the teachers in Rosenthal's classroom study acted as Pygmalions who were able to have their personal prophecies fulfilled.

ORGANIZATIONAL EXAMPLES

It is easy to see the relevance of the SFP dynamic for organizational life. Employees (in analogous fashion to students) desire approval from their superiors. And supervisors commonly hold initial beliefs for their unit members, either positive or negative. To some extent, these supervisors (acting in the role of Pygmalion) send cues, or expectations, concerning whether they believe a given employee will succeed or fail. In response to these cues, employees then typically conform to the transmitted prophecy. Furthermore, the "star" employee has a difficult time being seen as doing anything wrong and is generally given the benefit of the doubt in an ambiguous situation, while the employee for whom negative or low expectations are held can seldom seem to do anything right. For those employees who anticipate a harsh evaluation from their superior, the mental and emotional distraction of possible failure can also contribute to a poor performance outcome.

In another well-publicized study of the SFP dynamic, King studied a group of hard-core unemployed men who had enrolled in an adult training program devoted to learning the fundamentals of welding.[3] At the outset, the men were given a test of mechanical aptitude. Then, the classroom supervisors were given false feedback on each student's test performance. As in the Rosenthal study, a small group of individuals were randomly selected for the label of "high-aptitude" students. In truth, these students were comparable to their classroom colleagues. At the completion of the training program, all of the men were given a test of welding knowledge. The results revealed that the allegedly "high-aptitude" men did actually learn more about welding in the course than did their classmates. Also, the "high-aptitude" individuals had better attendance (i.e., missed fewer classes) and completed most of the class exercises ahead of the others. When a confidential vote was later taken to determine which class members were "most preferred to be assigned with on a job site" (in essence, a type of popularity contest), it was the "high-aptitude" individuals who were singled out most often.

In a more rigorous research study of SFP, Eden and Shani found that soldiers in the Israeli army who were randomly labeled as having "high command potential" had superior performance evaluations during their boot camp training experience (relative to other trainees who were in the same cohort).[4] Moreover, the researchers found that the magnitudes of the SFP effects were quite substantial. For example, the variance in later military career performance that could be attributed to the labeling process was nearly 75 percent, and roughly two-thirds of the variability in their attitudes (e.g., satisfaction with life in the military) could be attributed to an SFP phenomenon. And on the ultimate measure of the impact of the SFP phenomenon for these soldiers, the so-called "high-command potential" soldiers re-enlisted in the military for another tour of duty at a much higher rate than their peers.

There are numerous other examples of SFPs in everyday life. Consider the occasion of a bank run, where a bank's depositors descend on a bank based on a rumor of insolvency and thereby fulfill their own expectation by making the bank insolvent. In essence, collective behavior by the depositors turns the rumor into reality. It can also be argued that a component of economic inflation is driven by an SFP dynamic. For example, collective bargaining agents who represent unions may expect that inflation will be around 3 percent in the next year or so. With this in mind, these union reps will feel the necessity to demand a minimum increase of 3 percent from their employer. The employer, in turn, will feel the necessity to set prices 3 percent higher for the coming time period, and so a "wage-price spiral" is driven. In short, the expectation that everything will go up a certain percentage in the coming time frame is partially guaranteed by collective action based on the starting assumption.

A final set of intriguing illustrations of SFPs is given by research conducted by Rosenthal and his associates, wherein they told college students that specific laboratory rats had been previously trained to run in a maze and had displayed varying aptitude for maze-running (i.e., each rat was either maze-bright or maze-dull).[5] In fact, the rats were labeled at random, and were even genetically similar in that the rats were litter mates. When each college student later ran his or her allegedly bright or dull rat in a maze, the performance of the "bright" rats (as measured by blind observers' scorings of films of the rats' behaviors) exceeded that of the "dull" rats (e.g., 29 percent of the "dull" rats refused to leave the maze's starting point, versus 11 percent of the "bright" rats). This finding suggests three points: (1) SFPs are important potential nuisance variables for researchers (i.e., observed behavioral results obtained by researchers may partly reflect the researchers' own expectations if safeguards are not taken, as may also be true for supervisors in the workplace); (2) we probably find it more comfortable to interact with others who meet our expectations, whether high or low; and (3) it is apparently possible to convey subtle cues across animal species. A good illustration of this third point is found in instances when we encounter a strange dog for the very first time. Typically, the dog takes its cues on how to behave from our own behavior (or expectation). That is to say, the dog is often picking up our cues that we expect the dog to be aggressive (as evidenced by our nervousness or backing away) or that we expect the dog to be friendly (by our relaxed posture and gentle, reassuring tone of voice). In essence, whether the strange dog behaves in a vicious or friendly manner is not so much a function of the dog's personality as our expectation for the dog's behavior in that setting.

THE POSITIVE MANAGEMENT OF SFPS

Perhaps more often than we might care to acknowledge, we fall victim to an SFP, either as a cue sender or as a cue recipient (i.e., as a perpetrator or a benefactor, respectively). Instead of allowing SFPs to bandy us about, it is far wiser to try to take control of the SFP process and use it to achieve mutually beneficial, positive ends. Because cue sending is an inevitable facet of social life, we need to be conscious of the cues that we send, in order to encourage others to attain maximal performance. Supervisors, therefore, must be aware of how their degree of eye contact, tone of voice, smiling, nodding, physical proximity, relative detail in the nature of formal feedback that is provided, and the phrasing of sentences can convey expectations, and take active control of these elements of their self-presentation. Also, the active management of SFPs can foster motivation by displaying enthusiasm for a group's goals. This enthusiasm can then operate in a contagious fashion to enhance overall unit performance.

SFPs probably play an important role in the dynamics that surround performance appraisal systems. Typically, appraisal systems are the settings for surfacing expectations. Unfortunately, appraisal systems are often highly subjective, and the opportunity for personal bias to enter the picture can be quite real. When negative or positive bias enters the process, then a cycle of events can be initiated that has a relatively foreordained outcome (i.e., success or failure). In short, performance appraisal systems do not merely summarize past performance, they are also responsible for determining future performance.

Many times, managers and employees will suggest that a better approach to performance appraisal is to rely on more objective measures of performance. Sales figures, units of output per day, customer complaints, etc., might be offered as potentially less biased indices of performance. However, even these measures are still subject to the SFP dynamic in that the perception of allegedly simple objective indices, such as those noted above, can be influenced by strong prior expectations.

An intriguing study that demonstrates the power of expectations for tainting perception can be found in the field of extrasensory perception (ESP) research.[6] Specifically, researchers surveyed a class of college students on their beliefs of ESP and related phenomena (e.g., clairvoyance, precognition, psychokinesis, etc.). The survey responses showed that the students could be assigned to one of two groups: "believers" or "skeptics" (or as they are known to ESP researchers, "sheep" and "goats"). Both groups of students were then asked to participate in an alleged research project where a well-known psychic would try to influence a set of gambling dice to turn up a large number of 6s. In reality, the dice spilling was handled by a random-event generating machine, and no psychic was involved during a filming of the outcome of 20 dice spillings. Before viewing the resulting film in a large auditorium, the student groups ("sheep" and "goats") were reminded that a suspected psychic's ability was being tested, and their job, as observers, was to count the number of 6s that appeared during the showing of the film on an auditorium screen. A third group of student observers served as a control group in the study (wherein no questions were posed about their belief in ESP-related phenomena and no psychic was mentioned).

A comparison of the average number of 6s counted by the three groups showed that (1) the "sheep" found clear evidence of psychokinesis (i.e., they reported an average number of 6s that exceeded chance expectations, based on statistical theory); (2) the "goats" found clear evidence of a *reverse* psychokinetic effect (i.e., they reported that the presumed psychic actually made the number 6 come up less often than one could reasonably expect based on chance alone); and (3) the control group found that the number of 6s was within the bounds of chance expectation. Therefore, prior expectations do apparently influence the perception of simple, so-called, objective events! The arousal of strong priors can distort one's perceptions. Clearly, expectations are not only prevalent, they are also powerful.

CONCLUSION

In summary, our prior expectations influence both our perception of others and our interpretation of their behavior. To enhance the performance of employees and work groups, managers must recognize the existence of SFPs and manage the impressions they convey to employees. Without advocating the active manipulation of others, we can advocate trying to solicit the very best that others are capable of by deliberately treating others in a positive, optimistic, and supportive fashion. As observed by management consultant J. S. Livingston, a manager who is unskilled will leave scars on the careers of young people, cutting deeply into their self-esteem and distorting their self-image. But a skillful manager will have high positive expectations for subordinates, thereby increasing subordinate self-confidence, capabilities, and ultimately performance. More often than one realizes, "a manager is Pygmalion."[7]

REFERENCES

1. R. A. Jones (1977). *Self-fulfilling prophecies: Social, psychological and physiological effects of expectancies.* Hillsdale, NJ: Erlbaum Associates.
2. R. Rosenthal and I. Jacobsen (1968). *Pygmalion in the classroom: Teachers' expectations and pupil intellectual development.* New York: Holt, Rinehart & Winston.

3. A. S. King (1970). *Managerial relations with disadvantaged workgroups: Supervisory expectations of the underprivileged worker,* (Doctoral dissertation, Texas Tech University).

4. D. Eden and A. B. Shani (1982). Pygmalion goes to boot camp: Expectancy, leadership, and trainee performance. *Journal of Applied Psychology, 67,* 194–199; D. Eden (1990). Pygmalion without interpersonal contrast effects: Whole groups gain from raising manager expectations. *Journal of Applied Psychology, 75,* 394–400.

5. R. Rosenthal and K. Fode (1963). The effect of experimental bias on the performance of the Albino rat. *Behavioral Science, 8,* 183–189.

6. B. S. Kaufman and E. D. Sheffield (1952). A methodological flaw in ESP experiments. Paper presented at the annual meeting of the Eastern Psychological Association.

7. J. S. Livingston (1988). Retrospective commentary on Pygmalion in management. *Harvard Business Review, 47,* 81–89.

The Long-Term Organizational Impact of Destructively Narcissistic Managers

Roy Lubit

A significant number of managers have a degree of destructive narcissism (DN) in their personalities. One reason is that certain personality traits commonly but not exclusively found in DN help people to rise within management structures. These traits include high levels of expressed self-confidence, magnetic enthusiasm, and unrelenting drive to attain prestige and power,[1] DN managers are also frequently good at organizational politics. They can charm superiors, manipulate people, and forge quick, superficial relationships.[2] Their ruthlessness, drive, ability to make tough decisions quickly, and ability to generate enthusiasm in others help them to climb the rungs of power and to be effective in some aspects of leadership.

When the DN of managers reaches high levels, however, many problems arise.[3] Their grandiosity, devaluation of subordinates, sense of entitlement, lack of values, and search for excitement can do significant damage to an organization. They can compromise their business unit's long-term performance by driving away the most talented people. They divert people's energies away from their real work, foster a problematic culture, and sometimes make reckless business decisions.

This article begins by examining the behavioral tendencies of DN individuals. It moves on to discuss two possible origins of DN, how DN individuals are able to rise to power, the effects they have on the business units they lead, and what situations are likely to evoke the most detrimental aspects of their personalities. The article then discusses how to recognize DN managers before they cause significant damage to their organizations and how organizations can most effectively deal with them.

NARCISSISM: DEFINITION AND IMPACT

The term narcissism comes from the Greek myth of a beautiful youth who callously spurned the affection of others until he fell in love with his own reflection in a fountain. He stayed by the water in a futile attempt to possess the reflection he saw and pined away. In modern usage by social scientists, narcissism concerns our feelings about ourselves and how we regulate our self-esteem.

Healthy versus Destructive Narcissism

Healthy narcissism is based on relatively secure self-esteem that can survive daily frustrations and stress. Failure to attain desired goals, criticism, and seeing the success of others may cause disappointment, but it does not threaten the self-image of healthy individuals as worthwhile, valuable people. In addition to the self-confidence it provides, we need self-esteem to tolerate frustrations, stand up for our beliefs, and maintain commitment to values. Secure self-esteem and healthy narcissism are also necessary to relate in a healthy manner with others, i.e., empathize with others, enjoy true friendship and intimacy, and inspire confidence in others.

Although both healthy and destructive narcissism provide outward self-confidence, they are very different phenomena. The grandiosity of DN managers may appear to be due to high levels of self-confidence, but it is not so. Rather, it is frequently a reaction to (an attempt to seal over) fragile self-esteem. Lacking healthy, stable self-esteem, DN individuals tend to devalue and envy others and sometimes develop a grandiose self-image. When under stress that threatens their fragile self-esteem, they can suffer a serious decline in functioning and become depressed or enraged. While the solid self-esteem and healthy narcissism supports concern for the rights and well-being of others, DN managers do not respect others' rights and are frequently arrogant, devaluing, and exploitive in their interaction with others. Finally, a person with healthy narcissism may enjoy power, wealth, and admiration but is not obsessed with them, as is the DN manager. While both healthy narcissism and DN support an individual's ability to appear confident, they are fundamentally very different.

Destructive Narcissism: Defining Characteristics

The defining characteristics of destructive narcissists[4] are (1) grandiosity (inflated sense of self-importance, arrogance, preoccupation with power and wealth, excessive seeking of admiration), (2) a sense that they are entitled to have whatever they want, including a willingness to exploit others to get it, and (3) lack of concern for and devaluation of others. Frequently accompanying these traits are a lack of enduring attachment to a set of values and an inner emptiness that leads them to seek excitement despite high risks. DN individuals often do not realize that their behavior is a problem for others and are not concerned about their behavior's detrimental impact on others if they are aware.

Interpersonal relations are markedly compromised by destructive narcissism. DN individuals lack real empathy for others and are unable to understand others in depth. Rather than relating to others as human beings with rights and needs, DN individuals are concerned only with how others serve their own needs for admiration, support, and idealized figures to identify and merge with. While DN individuals may transiently idealize people with power who support them, they generally disparage and exploit others, including former idols. Constantly hungry and envious, they seek what is not theirs, simply because it has intrinsic value for them. Preoccupied with reinforcing their self-esteem, they greedily extract admiration from others. Devaluation of others helps them to avoid envy but leaves them feeling empty. They believe they deserve special treatment and are entitled to be served. They see nothing wrong with their behavior, since they feel they are special and are entitled to better treatment than they give to others. Devaluation of others, a sense of entitlement, and lack of concern for the rights of others color almost all of their relationships.

The overwhelming focus of DN individuals on reinforcing their self-esteem undercuts any deep attachment to values and leads them to betray convictions in the pursuit of self-interest. The inability to form true caring bonds to others or to a set of values, in combination with their lack of true self-love, leaves them with a sense of emptiness and underlying feelings of inferiority.

DN individuals sometimes have a strong paranoid streak. In order to ameliorate their sense of shame, they devalue others and project their bad self-image onto them. They can be suspicious, mistrustful, hypersensitive, argumentative, and prone to ascribe evil motives to others. They are preoccupied with the hidden motives of others and exaggerate threats. They look for signs of shameful conduct in others in order to support the projection of their own shameful self-image onto others. Since almost anyone placed under a microscope can be found to have faults, DN individuals can generally find reasons with a grain of truth for devaluing someone they dislike. Viewing the world as hostile and forbidding, they trust only a few chosen subordinates, cater to them to keep their loyalty, and demand total devotion in return. Lacking real connections to people, they often use new allies to betray old ones. When DN managers slide from simple devaluation of others to a paranoid stance, their ability to contribute productively to their organizations markedly deteriorates.

The aging process with its decrease in abilities and attractiveness is particularly difficult for DN individuals. In middle age they typically devalue things they once liked, since inevitably these things have failed to bring the narcissistic gratification they hoped for. They have no gratitude for the joys of younger years and resent the fact that these pleasures are no longer available to them. They feel aggression and rage over present and past frustrations. They also devalue the work of people who still have hopes and those things that they cannot have or be. They feel humiliation, suspicion, and anger toward people they depend on, rather than gratitude. Especially destructive to their organizations is their tendency to cling to power rather than hand it over to the next generation in a timely fashion. Table 1 compares the characteristics of healthy and destructive narcissism.

Adaptive and Nonadaptive Aspects of Destructive Narcissism

Although destructive in many ways to a manager's job performance, DN can help a manager rise in an organization. The high levels of expressed self-confidence found in DN can be useful in gaining the confidence of others. People often assume that self-confidence flows from competence and therefore trust those with great self-confidence. Moreover, by selecting subservient lieutenants and eschewing independent ones, DN managers can surround themselves with loyalty and praise, furthering the impression of competence.

DN also leads to driving ambition that enables a DN manager to make the sacrifices necessary to rise in an organization and frees the person from normal restraints on behavior. The ruthlessness and Machiavellianism of DN managers, which arise from lack of concern for others and lack of attachment to values, can help them rise through the ranks. They are willing to manipulate others to achieve their goals, steal credit for the work of others, and scapegoat others. Although lacking empathic concern for others, DN individuals may have "street smarts" that enable them to assess whom they can manipulate and what levers to pull to manipulate them. They can feign interest in others and play up to their bosses. Their driving ambition and lack of restraint can make them masters of organizational politics.

Table 1. Comparison of Healthy and Destructive Narcisissm

Characteristic	Healthy Narcissism	Destructive Narcissism
Self-confidence	High outward self-confidence in line with reallity	Grandiose
Desire for power, wealth, and admiration	May enjoy power	Pursues power at all costs, lacks normal inhibitions in its pursuit
Relationships	Real concern for others and their ideas; does not exploit or devalue others	Concern limited to expressing socially appropriate response when convenient; devalues and exploits others without remorse
Attitude toward authority	Variable	Submits to authority transiently, either when temporarily idealizing a superior or believing that submitting will lead to concrete benefit; believes he/she should be in charge; sees self as exempt from normal rules
Ability to follow a consistent path	Has values; follows through on plans	Lacks values; easily bored; often changes course
Foundation	Healthy childhood with support for self-esteem and appropriate limits on behavior toward others	Traumatic childhood undercutting true sense of self-esteem and/or learning that he/she doesn't need to be considerate of others

Being able to rise through the managerial ranks is not synonymous with being a good manager. A multi-decade study by the Gallup Organization found that for workers to be most productive, managers need to be clear on what they expect people to do, provide workers with the materials needed to do their work well, provide them with an opportunity each day to do what they do best, provide recognition or praise at least once a week, demonstrate concern for them as people, and encourage their development.[5] Because they lack concern for others, DN managers are likely to be weak on the first three of these characteristics and very weak on the last three. As a result, their subordinates generally do not function up to their capabilities.

Destructive narcissism particularly limits the ability of managers to work effectively with colleagues and subordinates. Their arrogance, sense of entitlement, lack of concern for others' feelings, devaluation of others' abilities, and desire for the limelight generally seriously compromise their ability to work in teams. Moreover, they not only do a poor job of developing people but alienate subordinates as a result of their devaluation of others, insistence on having their own way, lack of empathy, and willingness to exploit others. Obsequious individuals working for a DN manager are likely to be promoted; the best people are likely to leave. Furthermore, the good ideas of subordinates are likely to be disparaged lest they draw attention away from the narcissistic manager. Meanwhile, no one dares to criticize the DN manager's ideas, so both creativity and critical assessment of ideas are crippled. In sum, DN managers are markedly compromised in their ability to work with subordinates and peers.

They are also frequently weak at implementing programs. Their desire for excitement to fill their sense of boredom and emptiness, along with their lack of attachment to a set of values, leads to rapid changes in interests. As a result, DN managers tend to make sudden and repeated changes in organizational plans, never finishing the process of building needed core competencies or finishing projects. Moreover, the DN manager may fail to pay attention to details, being interested primarily in the grand plans. The DN manager's failure to follow through on projects can markedly undercut a business unit's performance.

In summary, destructive narcissism in managers has widespread and complex effects. At the same time that DN personality traits may help managers rise within an organization, these same traits impair their ability to lead effectively. As we shall discuss later, the characteristics of a specific organization are also important in determining whether DN managers can rise within its ranks.

CASE STUDIES OF DESTRUCTIVE NARCISSISM

The foregoing general description of the DN manager's characteristics is brought into focus in the following two case studies.

Study One: William Agee

Newspaper and magazine articles describing the alleged behavior of William Agee, former CEO of Morrison Knudsen, provide good illustrations of destructively narcissistic behavior.[6] One cannot credibly analyze someone's personality from a distance without ever interviewing the person. One can, however, say that actions described in published accounts are illustrative of destructively narcissistic behavior. Therefore, the following paragraphs are not meant as an analysis of William Agee but are simply a recounting of newspaper descriptions of managerial behavior often associated with DN.

Agee's career took off quickly. A Harvard MBA, he became CFO of Boise Cascade at age 31 and then CEO of Bendix (a $4 billion-per-year auto-parts manufacturer) in 1976 at age 38. He ran into trouble at Bendix as a result of rapidly promoting his assistant to VP and allegedly having an affair with her; they were later married. His attempt to buy out Martin Marietta backfired, leading to the sale of Bendix to Allied Corp. Despite his difficulties at Bendix, he became CEO of Morrison Knudsen (a dam, bridge, and factory builder) in 1988.

Newspapers reported grandiose and entitled behavior. He converted the company's massive boardroom into his own office. In addition to arranging a high salary and oversized bonuses for himself and living unusually lavishly, he reportedly misused company funds to such an extent that company employees reported it to the IRS. Agee was alleged to have used company money for personal legal fees, Waterford Crystal for himself, and petunia beds at his home. He ran the company from his home in Pebble Beach, rather than from corporate headquarters, flying executives back and forth to his house. In a particularly remarkable self-glorifying act, he replaced portraits of the company's founders with a life-sized portrait of himself and his wife that he commissioned at company expense.

Agee allegedly devalued others and got rid of people who threatened to detract from his prestige. He treated subordinates badly and undercut talented people who might take away some of the glory he sought. Agee was described as having a "high and mighty manner." He fired people with little or no warning, including high-ranking, talented managers. When the board of directors seemed to view people favorably, Agee was reported to have stated that they were not good performers, and then horror stories about them would appear. A company executive reported that Agee's "inner circle was made up of sycophants and yes men. People at the next level down caught hell. . . . He was afraid to have talent around."

Descriptions of Agee's behavior show little attachment to values and a willingness to be unusually deceptive in order to give the impression that he was doing a good job. He treated the corporate board to lavish meetings away from company headquarters, making it hard for board members to have access to other company officials. Moreover, information provided to the board about the company's financial condition was reported to be markedly skewed, and accounting practices were deceptive to shareholders. For example, it is alleged that Agee reported money from the sale of businesses as operating rather than nonrecurring income, giving the false impression that the company's construction and rail businesses were going well. When the company filed claims to recover unexpected costs on construction projects, the money was often immediately booked as revenues even though the claims might never be paid.

Accounts of Agee's behavior illustrate the excessive risk taking in which destructively narcissistic individuals often engage. For example, he moved into areas where he and the company lacked expertise, such as large, risky construction contracts. Similarly, without commissioning research (as far as a company top executive knew), he moved the company into building a new locomotive and arranged to build new passenger railroad cars without building a prototype. The company's initial success with railroad cars came when another firm did the design and engineering for the cars. In time the contracts Agee entered into for locomotive manufacturing led to large losses. He was finally fired after Morrison Knudsen lost $310 million in 1994.

Agee's behavior so alienated people at Morrison Knudsen that when he was fired as CEO, the employees gathered in the parking lot of company headquarters and cheered. A shareholder lawsuit cost him his severance pay and much of his pension.

Newspaper accounts of Agee's behavior illustrate many characteristics of the destructive narcissism syndrome. They portray the grandiosity, sense of entitlement, lack of values, risk taking, devaluation and abuse of others, need to surround oneself with sycophants, and inability to tolerate people more talented than oneself common in destructively narcissistic people.

Study Two: The Fortune 500 Executive

A second story involves a relatively high-level businessman whom I will call Mark. I came to know him and the people around him, and to witness their interactions, when I was consulting to their Fortune 500 company. Mark was loquacious. He spent far more time chatting with people and talking about himself than he spent actually working. He repeatedly boasted that he was skilled in fields besides business and that he had taught at a prestigious institution. He frequently claimed to know eminent individuals and said that he had written some of their papers.

Although solicitous to superiors and to peers who did his work for him, Mark was controlling and constantly critical of subordinates. For example, he frequently criticized one of his junior managers whom I will call Larry, falsely accusing him of failing to hand in deliverables. If Larry tried to explain what he had and had not done, Mark became enraged and stated that he did not want a response. On one occasion when Mark asked Larry to download files on various subjects, Larry said he thought that some of the work had already been done. Mark became angry, accusing Larry of suggesting that he was stupid.

While outwardly expressing the desire to help this new junior manager, Mark had no real concern for Larry's well-being. For example, without asking permission, Mark borrowed a key piece of Larry's computer equipment and then went out to lunch without telling Larry where he could find it. On several occasions, when asked to return borrowed equipment, Mark failed to do so. Particularly striking, after typing late one night for several hours while Mark dictated, Larry said that his hands were cramping and he needed a two-minute break. Mark refused to allow it.

Mark was often envious. He complained that Larry got far more time with their mutual superior than junior people normally received. Mark also complained about how close Larry was to his superior and said he intended to wean Larry away from him. Angry about being given an office in the basement, Mark insisted that Larry work there as well, although there was no desk for him in that location. When Larry said he could work more efficiently at his own desk, Mark angrily accused Larry of feeling that he was better than Mark was, since Larry did not want to work in the basement. When Larry needed to stop working with Mark for a day in order to do an assignment for their mutual superior, Mark became infuriated, initially refusing to talk to Larry, and threatening to put a damaging note in his file.

After a couple of weeks, Larry told Mark that the current set-up was uncomfortable for him and he thought it would be best if he could move on to another assignment. Mark complained that Larry was insulting him. Mark said he treated Larry no differently than he treated others and insisted that he, Mark, was being perfectly appropriate. In fact, Mark did treat other subordinates in a similarly abusive manner. Eventually, his poor work, particularly his arrogant and insensitive treatment of clients, caught up with him and he was fired.

This brief snapshot illustrates several typical traits of the DN person: the need to be admired, self-glorification, taking credit for the work of others, repressive control, critical and devaluing behavior, envy, lack of empathy, and lack of self-insight.

THE ORIGINS OF DESTRUCTIVE NARCISSISM

What leads to destructive narcissism? Psychodynamic theory and social learning theory provide different explanations. They will be discussed in turn.

Psychodynamic Theories

Psychodynamic theories of behavior focus on the effects of early childhood experiences on a person's psychological make-up, i.e., conscious and un-conscious models of the world, psychological conflicts, and defense mech-anisms. Psychodynamic theories hold that DN arises from growing up in a house with chronically cold, covertly aggressive parents. The primary par-enting figure functions well on the surface and maintains a superficially well-organized home. The primary parent, however, is callous and indiffer-ent to the child's desires and exhibits nonverbalized, spiteful aggression that injures the child's sense of self. At the same time, the child possesses some quality that others can envy which provides the child with a refuge against feelings of being unloved. People who grow up in such households fre-quently reinforce their fragile self-esteem by devaluing others and behaving in a grandiose way.

The defense mechanism that dominates the functioning of DN indi-viduals is splitting. They see people and situations in black-and-white terms, all bad or all good, with no shades of gray. Their black-and-white images of others lead them either to idealize or to fear and hate others. Moreover, the person they idealized yesterday may be devalued and hated tomorrow. Projection is another of their important defense mechanisms. To maintain a positive image of themselves, they project all their negative qualities onto others and therefore devalue others. Since their self-esteem is fragile and cannot handle responsibility for mistakes, they deny any re-sponsibility for problems and blame other people.

Social Learning Theory

Bandura's social learning theory provides another explanation for the development of destructively narcissistic behavior.[7] This theory argues that much of our behavior is learned by observing others. People try out behaviors that they have seen in others and then refine these behaviors based on the feedback they receive. Internalization of observed behavior is particularly likely if the persons imitated have high status. Behavior is also influenced by the inner standards one develops about appropriate behavior. These standards arise from the experience of having limits prescribed during childhood and by seeing how peers and adults limit their own actions. In other words, according to social learning theory, people's behavior is affected by direct reinforcement (being rewarded or punished for a behavior), by vicarious reinforcement (seeing others rewarded or punished for a given behavior), and by self-imposed standards.

From the perspective of social learning theory, DN behavior arises when someone sees others get away with grandiose and self-centered behavior, then also gets away with such behavior. People with great power or glamour often learn to be grandiose and self-centered because those around them treat them with great deference, fawn on them, and do not provide negative feedback when they fail to be diplomatic or concerned about the needs of others. It has been said that if you have power, you are probably not as smart, funny, or good looking as people say you are.

The Theories Compared

Social learning theory and psychodynamic theory are meant to be general theories of human behavior. Social learning theory, in particular, sees itself as an alternative to psychodynamic explanations of personality. In understanding human behavior, psychoanalytic theorists focus their attention on the individual's inner experience, the meaning given to events, and how one's inner experience is affected by experiences during the first few years of life when defense mechanisms develop, fixations lay the foundations for unconscious conflicts, and internalized object relations develop.

In contrast, social learning theorists focus their attention on how environmental contingencies (experiences of positive and negative reinforcement and observation of others) mold the behavior of people. Despite their focus on vastly different underpinnings of behavior, there is no logical reason that both cannot hold part of the key to understanding human behavior. Both early childhood developmental experiences and the reinforcement of our behavior throughout life can lead to the behavior pattern we recognize as destructive narcissism. Both may be contributing to an individual's DN behavior.

Destructive Narcissists Compared

From simple observation it may be impossible to differentiate individuals with learned destructive narcissism from those with psychodynamically based destructive narcissism. There are, however, important differences. The fragile self-esteem of individuals with psychodynamically based narcissism leaves them liable to "narcissistic rage" when challenged or criticized. Narcissistic rage is marked by its high intensity and loss of judgment in which the individual strikes out in ways that can be very damaging to self and others. Individuals with learned narcissism do not necessarily have fragile self-esteem and therefore are not as liable to narcissistic rages when challenged. They may, however, not learn to limit their angry outbursts since people have failed to give them negative feedback. People with psychodynamically based narcissism will have far less ability to empathize with others and to observe the problems in their own behavior than will individuals with learned narcissism. Moreover, the grandiosity of psychodynamically based narcissistic individuals will be much further out of line with reality than that of individuals with learned narcissism. The latter will lack the more malignant aspects of destructive narcissism such as paranoia.

The most important difference is that learned narcissism is not as locked in as psychodynamically based narcissism. When confronted with the problems in their behavior, individuals with learned narcissism can often make significant changes. In contrast, individuals with psychodynamically based narcissism are likely to become enraged, and perhaps paranoid, when confronted with their behavior problems.

HOW CAN DESTRUCTIVELY NARCISSISTIC INDIVIDUALS RISE IN ORGANIZATIONS?

Despite their troublesome behavior and weaknesses in performing their work, DN managers can rise and prosper in firms. Part of the reason is their ability to cover over their weaknesses with their outward self-confidence, enthusiasm, drive, ability to charm and manipulate people, glibness, and skill at selling themselves. In addition, their skill at organizational politics, the hesitancy of many people to complain about them to superiors, and their ability to restrain their behavior when dealing with superiors partially shield them from the normal consequences of their behavior. The most serious DN behavior is directed at subordinates and not at the superiors who determine the manager's fate. Moreover, subordinates are generally loath to complain about a DN manager, fearing that the complaint might reflect badly on them, or that their DN manager will find out and take revenge, or that complaining will lower them to the DN manager's level. People also tend to believe that eventually the information will come out and the manager will self-destruct without their taking steps to inform superiors about the problems that the DN manager creates. Since everyone is hesitant to share the negative information, no one person realizes how widespread the problem is, so its extent remains unknown to those with the power to do something about it.

The most powerful factors permitting DN managers to survive and even prosper in a company are organizational ones: the organization's hiring and transfer practices, culture, performance-measurement system, leadership, and work processes.

Hiring and Transfer Practices

Weaknesses in organizational hiring practices permit DN managers to attain jobs despite having had serious problems elsewhere. Leaders making hiring and promotion decisions often lean heavily on recommendations from people they know or rely on their impression from an interview, rather than adequately performing and using background checks. During interviews, DN managers are likely to perform particularly well as a result of their outward confidence, willingness to distort their history, and glibness that enables them to convincingly claim accomplishments they do not have. Similarly, many DN managers survive and prosper because the influential contacts who supported their elevation to their present positions continue to support them despite evidence of problems. Some DN managers survive by transferring from one position to another and burying their mistakes before their bad work catches up with them. When personal relationships are more important than objective performance, organizations will make problematic hiring and promotion decisions.

Even more surprising than the ability of DN managers to survive and rise within a firm is the ability of CEOs who brought companies down to get second and third chances as a result of their glibness, ability to sell themselves, and a lack of due diligence on the part of those making hiring decisions.[8] Frank Lorenzo, after plunging two airlines into bankruptcy three times, convinced investors to give him millions of dollars to start a new airline. James Baughman, while superintendent of the San Jose Unified School District in California in 1992, admitted to lying about having earned a Ph.D. from Stanford University. He was later found to have stolen money from student body funds and spent several months in prison. Despite his record, he rose to the rank of director of recruiting at Lucent where he served until he died of a heart attack in September 2000. Al Dunlap, after being fired from Max Philips and Son in 1973, was hired and later fired as president of Nitek Paper when the company's board accused him of overseeing a large accounting fraud. Nitek's chief executive stated that virtually all of the company's senior management threatened to resign if Dunlap remained at Nitek. Despite these serious difficulties, Dunlap was chosen to lead Scott Paper and then Sumbeam.

The Organizational Culture

An organization's culture—norms of behavior, values, and beliefs—is forged from the role models that leaders provide, the myths and stories leaders tell, what the organization measures and rewards, the criteria used for hiring and promoting people, and the organization's historical norms of behavior and values. Some organizational cultures are tolerant of DN behavior, and some are not. Those not tolerant force DN managers to change or leave.

Performance Measurement and Reward System

Many organizations focus overwhelmingly on short-term profits, rather than on a balanced scoreboard, and pay little or no attention to the human costs of how managers achieve financial results. If DN managers get results, the organization's hierarchy may not measure or even notice their failure to develop subordinates, encourage teamwork, support morale, and treat others well. Many organizations either do not have 360-degree feedback or do not make significant use of it in promotion and compensation decisions. Rather, making the numbers and political skill in grabbing credit for short-term profitability or sales increases are rewarded.

The Leadership's Narcissism

The leadership's narcissism will also have a considerable impact upon the presence of destructive narcissism at the managerial level. DN leaders tend not to care about the well-being of subordinates and tolerate DN managers who make the numbers but do not treat people well. They are particularly tolerant of DN managers who feed their own narcissism with flattery. Also very important, the organization's leaders serve as role models that managers emulate. If leaders exhibit DN behavior, managers who have DN tendencies are more likely to act out that behavior.

The Work Processes

Finally, the organization's work processes affect the ability of DN managers to succeed. For example, DN managers have difficulty prospering in organizations that use teams extensively, because their teamwork skills tend to be particularly weak.

DESTRUCTIVELY NARCISSISTIC MANAGERS AND ORGANIZATIONAL DETERIORIZATION

The behavior of destructively narcissistic leaders creates serious problems for organizations. The higher they are in an organization, the more power and opportunity they have to do harm. Even mid-level DN managers, however, can have serious harmful effects on morale, development, and retention of employees, and the long-term performance of their business units.

DN managers tend to neglect the functional requirements of leadership, the needs of others, and usual constraints on the pursuit of self-interest. One of the most destructive attributes of DN managers is their selective neglect of the needs of people who work for them. They may do nice things for others or engage in social pleasantries when it is convenient. But if they dislike a task, such as providing support, responding to questions, dealing with organizational problems, seeing to it that people have the tools they need to succeed, or writing performance evaluations, they won't do it. As a result, the morale of their subordinates flags, and people in the business unit begin to focus their energies on political survival and dealing with their frustration with the DN manager, rather than on doing their best work.

DN managers drive the most capable people away. They cannot tolerate the success of a subordinate who threatens to outshine them. Although they may support young colleagues for a while, in time they are likely to undercut them, especially if the colleagues show any signs of independence. Interested primarily in increasing their own power, and tending toward authoritarian leadership styles, they do not adequately delegate authority. Nor do they want the real interchanges of ideas needed for optimal decision-making. Capable junior managers are unlikely to remain in a DN manager's department if they can help it, since they will not have the opportunities for decision-making that they want and deserve.

The grandiosity of DN managers leads them to focus their attention and energy on increasing their own power and prestige, rather than on the work of the organization. In addition, their subordinates need to expend considerable energy feeding the manager's ego and dealing with the complex political situation and frustrations inherent in working under a DN manager. This massive drain on the energies of the manager and subordinates can seriously compromise the department's productivity.

Destructively narcissistic CEOs also tend to make more than their share of disastrous business decisions. They have the power and the inclination to squander large amounts of company money on extravagances. Seeking glory, they may try to build an empire rather than prudently growing a company. Their need for excitement may lead them to change course rapidly and to neglect the details of plans, causing confusion and poor follow-through. Destructively narcissistic CEOs often make destructive decisions because their personal agendas take precedence over the company's best interests.

DEALING WITH DESTRUCTIVELY NARCISSISTIC MANAGERS

The first practical issue for dealing with the problem of DN managers is being able to identify them before they rise to positions of high power. On the way up in the organization, they are not likely to evidence their full potential for grandiosity and lack of respect for others to their superiors, since they will have some internal inhibitions against acting grandiosely and only limited power to do so. Nevertheless, there are often significant warning signs. They include:

- devaluing and exploiting others,
- lack of concern for the needs of subordinates unless convenient,
- trying to take all credit for success,
- undermining competitors for promotion
- excessively criticizing others,
- scapegoating,
- excessive self-promotion and attention-seeking behavior,
- seeing all events in terms of significance to their own careers,
- being highly defensive when criticized,
- harboring unfounded beliefs that others want to hurt them,
- currying favor with superiors while failing to support and develop those below them.

One of the best tools for early recognition of DN managers is 360-degree feedback, since they are unlikely to contain their problematic behaviors when dealing with subordinates and colleagues. A potential difficulty is that subordinates may fail to give accurate assessments, out of fear that their negative comments about a manager will get back to the manager, be traced to them, and lead to retaliation. Therefore, 360-degree feedback needs to be a regular part of the organization's routine, with all people expected to provide anonymous, confidential feedback on superiors. For problematic managers to change, however, the content of subordinate concerns must be transmitted to them. To get around this conflict, one can make it clear to employees that negative comments about their manager will not be forwarded unless the negative feedback can be given in a way that protects the anonymity of the people who provided it. In addition to supporting the use of 360-degree feedback, executives should foster an organization in which communication across multiple levels of the hierarchy is supported.

How a company can best deal with a DN manager depends upon how destructive the narcissistic behavior is to the organization, what redeeming talent the DN manager has, and the likelihood that the person can change. Some self-aggrandizement and desire for attention can be a small price to pay for a dynamic, insightful, effective problem solver who knows the business.

If a DN manager is replaceable, without critical knowledge or contacts, then confronting the behavior in hopes of ameliorating it is a good place to begin. If the manager's DN is primarily of the learned variety, confrontation and executive coaching are usually helpful. Confrontation can even ameliorate moderate psychodynamically based narcissism by strongly reminding DN managers that they are subordinate to others. If the destructive narcissism is severe and based on psychodynamic problems and fragile self-esteem, however, confrontation may lead to rage and paranoia and make matters worse. These individuals may be helped to function better by providing them with copious emotional support from consultants and superiors, to reinforce their fragile self-esteem. In the graphic terms of self-psychology, the consultant becomes a mirroring object. A skilled executive coach providing a combination of empathic support and training in how to work with others can help a DN manager contain some of the most damaging manifestations of DN.

Managers and executives can often be helped to be more open to confrontation and change if their anxiety and depression are treated. These states decrease self-esteem, thereby increasing vulnerability to stress and ultimately increasing the rigidity of the DN manager's problematic personality traits. Treating their depression and anxiety with appropriate medication and cognitive behavioral therapy can help them to be less defensive, more responsive to others, and better able to make progress in therapy or executive coaching.

The management of an executive with destructive narcissism can be very challenging. The situation becomes particularly complicated when the executive is difficult to replace in the near future, since confrontation of the behavior in the hope of ameliorating it can precipitate a crisis and be counterproductive. Calling in a consultant skilled in dealing with problems of narcissism, and who can provide a complex mix of confrontation, coaching and support, can significantly ameliorate the situation.

COPING WITH DESTRUCTIVELY NARCISSISTIC BOSSES

Working for, or with, destructively narcissistic people brings considerable stress. Their devaluation, exploitation, arrogance, criticism, micromanagement, and failure to fulfill their responsibilities to you are inherently very stressful. Nevertheless, your attitude and actions can significantly affect your stress level when dealing with such people. Attempts to change their behavior toward you, by standard methods such as telling them how their behavior makes you feel, will not work. In general, trying to change the behavior of DN individuals will primarily lead to frustration. It is best to accept that they were so damaged in their emotional development that they lack the ability to empathize and behave reasonably. Keeping this in mind will help you avoid taking their criticism personally or arguing with them about it. Disagreeing with their critical statements will only enrage them.

There are other things you can do to avoid problematic situations. One is to pay attention to those things that lead to problems and avoid them when possible. Avoid gossiping with DN managers, borrowing from them, or lending to them. It makes you vulnerable. Try to obtain written directions whenever possible, since they decrease the room for uncertainty and complaint about you. Document your work so you can defend yourself if they criticize you for failing to do your job properly. Document interactions and the course of events so that if you need to defend yourself to someone higher up, you have the means to do so.

Moving to another position within the company in order to avoid the DN manager is generally the best long-term strategy. This is particularly important for very capable individuals, whom a DN manager will see as a threat and will therefore try to undercut. Once you are out of their unit, report to superiors how they treat people. If possible, do this in collaboration with others who can validate your statements. Informing superiors of the problem will help the company as a whole and improve the working environment for all.

It was noted earlier that confrontation can sometimes work with individuals with learned DN. This confrontation, however, needs to come from above, or possibly from a peer, not from below. If subordinates attempt to confront superiors about their behavior, whether their DN is mostly learned or mostly psychodynamic, the reaction will generally be anger and retaliation. It is safest for subordinates to behave in an admiring manner, which tends to decrease tensions.

DEALING WITH DESTRUCTIVELY NARCISSISTIC PEERS

Working with destructively narcissistic peers is also difficult. They take credit for your work, disparage you to others, incessantly boast, lie, and mislead people often for no other reason than the perverse pleasure of being able to deceive. They also act as if they know the best way to do everything, discount others' input, do not respect boundaries (enter your office and borrow things without permission), expect favors but rarely do any in return, and give you instructions as if they were your boss.[9]

These behaviors are serious problems. There are no perfect solutions, only courses of action that do not make things worse and are better than doing nothing. If they make disparaging remarks about you, simply state that you do not agree with the criticism. Avoid getting into arguments or retaliatory attacks. They can make you look bad to others and provoke the destructively narcissistic person to launch further attacks. To avoid having credit for your work stolen, avoid sharing ideas with DN individuals until after you have told your supervisor and team of your ideas in writing. When asked for ideas, respond in writing with your name attached. Boasting is best handled by ignoring it. Do not ask a DN person for favors, and do not borrow or lend anything. If given orders by a destructively narcissistic colleague, either ignore them or write to your boss to ask for clarification on responsibilities. Meet boundary violations with clear, consistent statements about what you do not want this individual to do.

ORGANIZATIONS AND DESTRUCTIVELY NARCISSISTIC MANAGERS: SOME FINAL QUESTIONS

Destructively narcissistic executives and managers are a significant problem for organizations. Their behavior is in stark contrast to what productive workplaces need. They damage the morale of subordinates, undercut their motivation, divert their energies from useful tasks, and drive away the most talented workers. If they rise to the CEO's office, they can lead an organization into disaster.

This article presents some steps that organizations and employees can take to decrease the negative impact of DN managers. Most important is being aware of the problem and its symptoms. Armed with this understanding, organizations can confront DN managers about their behavior and then either arrange for coaching or remove them.

Organizations also need to question the elements of their culture and procedures that tolerate or even celebrate destructive narcissism. Does the culture support or inhibit DN? Is 360-degree feedback used and analyzed in promotion decisions? Do leaders reach down into the organization to find out what is happening throughout the company? Are managers measured primarily on short-term profits, rather than on a balanced scorecard including how well they develop subordinates and cooperate with others? What role model does senior management provide? Are high levels of confidence, to the point of grandiosity, equated with competence? Are superiors automatically believed over subordinates?

We also need to be aware of our own vulnerability to letting ourselves fall into learned DN behavior. Most of us could do so if given power, placed under great pressure, and denied feedback from subordinates. If we do not pay attention to this potential in ourselves, we may inadvertently behave in damaging ways. If we are vigilant about our own behavior, provide a good role model for others to follow, foster an organizational culture opposed to destructively narcissistic behavior, and respond appropriately to abuses that others commit, we can make major strides in improving the productivity and well-being of people in our organization.

REFERENCES

1   Kernberg, O. 1998. *Ideology, conflict and leadership in groups and organizations.* New Haven: Yale University Press; Kohut, H. 1971 *The analysis of the self.* New York: International Universities Press.

2   Kets de Vries, M. 1993. *Leaders, fools and imposters.* San Francisco: Jossey-Bass Publishers.

3   The term destructive narcissism comes from Brown, N. 1998. *The destructive narcissistic pattern.* Westport: Praeger.

4   Kernberg, O. 1975. *Borderline conditions and pathological narcissism.* New York: Jason Aronson; Kernberg, O. 1985. *Borderline conditions and pathological narcissism.* Northvale: Jason Aronson. Kernberg, O. 1986. Factors in the psychoanalytic treatment of narcissistic personalities. In A. Morrison (Ed.), *Essential papers on narcissism.* New York: NYU Press; Kernberg, O. 1986. Further contributions to the treatment of narcissistic personalities. In A. Morrison, op. cit.; Kohut, H., & Wolf, E. 1978. The disorders of the self and their treatment: An outline. *The International Journal of Psychoanalysis,* 59: 413–426.

5   Buckingham, M., & Coffman, C. 1999. *First, break all the rules.* New York: Simon & Schuster.

6   Information on the career of Mr. Agee, as described in the text, comes from the following sources: O'Reilly, B. Agee in exile. *Fortune,* 29 May 1995, 50–61; Hopkins, J. Morrison Knudsen fires its extravagant CEO. *USA Today,* 13 February 1995, 2B; Groves, M. The corporate hero derailed. *LA Times,* 3 February 1995, D1; Chief exec gets red carpet as his company bleeds red ink. *Denver Rocky Mountain News,* 26 March 1995, 102A; Rigdon, J., & Lublin, J. Management: Call to duty: Why Morrison board fired Agee. *Wall Street Journal,* 13 February 1995, B1; Feder, B. Agee leaving Morrison Knudsen. *New York Times,* 2 February 1995, D1; Groves, M., & Sanchez, J. Morrison Knudsen chief Agee forced to step down. *Los Angeles Times,* 11 February 1995, D1; Hopkins, J. Ex-CEO surrounded himself with security. *USA Today,* 21 February 1995; Rigdon, J. William Agee will leave Morrison Knudsen. *Wall Street Journal,* 2 February 1995, B1; Henriques, D. A celebrity boss

faces exile from 2nd corporate kingdom. *New York Times,* 10 February 1995, A1; and Morrison Knudsen agrees to settle shareholder suits. *New York Times,* 21 September 1995, D4.

7 Bandura, A. 1977. *Social learning theory.* Englewood Cliffs: Prentice-Hall.

8 Bennett, A., & Lublin, J. Teflon big shots: Failure doesn't always damage the careers of top executives. *Wall Street Journal,* 31 March 1995. Romero, S., with Atlas, R. Lucent investigates record of former high-ranking executive. *New York Times,* 21 February 2001, C1; Norris, F. 2001. An executive's missing years: papering over past problems. *New York Times,* 16 July 2001, 1.

9 Brown, N., op. cit.

The Dark Side of Leadership

Jay A. Conger

In recent years, business leaders have gained great popularity: Lee Iaccoca and Steven Jobs, for example, have stepped into the limelight as agents of change and entrepreneurship. But though we tend to think of the positive outcomes associated with leaders, certain risks or liabilities are also entailed. The very behaviors that distinguish leaders from managers also have the potential to produce problematic or even disastrous outcomes for their organizations. For example, when a leader's behaviors become exaggerated, lose touch with reality, or become vehicles for purely personal gain, they may harm the leader and the organization.

How do leaders produce such negative outcomes—and why? Three particular skill areas can contribute to such problems. These include leaders' strategic vision, their communications and impression-management skills, and their general management practices. We will examine each to discover its darker side.

PROBLEMS WITH THE VISIONARY LEADER

As we know, there have been tremendous changes in the world's competitive business environment. Previously successful organizations that had grown huge and bureaucratic were suddenly faced with pressures to innovate and alter their ways. Out of these turbulent times came a new breed of business leader: the strategic visionary. These men and women, like Ross Perot of Electronic Data Systems and Mary Kay Ash of Mary Kay Cosmetics, possessed a twofold ability: to foresee market opportunities and to craft organizational strategies that captured these opportunities in ways that were personally meaningful to employees. When their success stories spread, "vision" became the new byword. Yet though many of these leaders led their organizations on to great successes, others led their organizations on to great failures. The very qualities that distinguished the visionary leader contained the potential for disaster.

Generally speaking, unsuccessful strategic visions can often be traced to the inclusion of the leaders' personal aims that did not match their

199

constituents' needs. For example, leaders might substitute personal goals for what should be shared organizational goals. They might construct an organizational vision that is essentially a monument to themselves and therefore something quite different from the actual wishes of their organizations or customers.

Moreover, the blind drive to create this very personal vision could result in an inability to see problems and opportunities in the environment. Thomas Edison, for example, so passionately believed in the future of direct electrical current (DC) for urban power grids that he failed to see the more rapid acceptance of alternating power (AC) systems by America's then-emerging utility companies. Thus the company started by Edison to produce DC power stations was soon doomed to failure. He became so enamoured of his own ideas that he failed to see competing and, ultimately, more successful ideas.

In addition, such personal visions encourage the leader to expend enormous amounts of energy, passion, and resources on getting them off the ground. The higher their commitment, the less willing they are to see the viability of competing approaches. Because of the leader's commitment, the organization's investment is also likely to be far greater in such cases. Failure therefore will have more serious consequences.

Fundamental errors in the leader's perceptions can also lead to a failed vision. Common problems include (1) an inability to detect important changes in markets (e.g., competitive, technological, or consumer needs); (2) a failure to accurately assess and obtain the necessary resources for the vision's accomplishment; and (3) a misreading or exaggerated sense of the needs of markets or constituents. For example, with a few exceptions like the Chrysler minivan, Lee Iacocca inaccurately believed that automobile style rather than engineering was the primary concern of automotive buyers. At Chrysler, he relied on new body styles and his charisma to market cars built on an aging chassis (the K car). The end result was that, after several initial years of successful sales, Chrysler's sales plunged 22.8%. Today, the future of Chrysler looks equally cloudy.

Ultimately, then, the success of a leader's strategic vision depends on a realistic assessment of both the opportunities and the constraints in the organization's environment and a sensitivity to constituents' needs. If the leader loses sight of reality or loses touch with constituents, the vision becomes a liability. Visions may fail for a wide variety of reasons; Exhibit 1 outlines some of the more significant ones. We will examine several of these categories and illustrate them with the experiences of some prominent business leaders.

Making the Leader's Personal Needs Paramount

As mentioned, one of the most serious liabilities of a visionary leader occurs when he or she projects purely personal needs and beliefs onto those of constituents. A common example is the inventor with a pet idea who acquires sufficient resources to initiate a venture that fails to meet the market's needs. When a leader's needs and wishes diverge from those of constituents, the consequences can be quite costly. Consider, for example, Edwin Land, inventor of the Polaroid camera. Dr. Land's experiences with a camera he developed called the SX-70 illustrate how a leader can get sidetracked by his own personal goals.

As we know, Land's company, Polaroid, held a monopoly on the instant photography market for some three decades and became the household word for such cameras. Throughout the 1960s and 1970s, Polaroid's sales climbed with astonishing speed. By 1973, four million of the company's Colorpack cameras were being sold annually at $30 a piece. But Dr. Land was not content. His dream was to create what he called "absolute one-step photography;" the SX-70 camera was to embody his dream. "Photography will never be the same . . . With the gargantuan effort of bringing SX-70 into being, the company has come fully of age," Land remarked on the day of the camera's inauguration.

In setting the parameters for his new vision, Land outlined several demanding criteria: The camera was to be totally automatic and would have to fold to fit into a purse or pocket, possess a single-lens reflex-viewing system, and focus from less than a foot to infinity. It was to be a radically new design, making earlier versions of instant photography obsolete.

The SX-70 also represented a major strategic shift for the company. Before its advent, the manufacturing of Polaroid products, especially films,

Exhibit 1
The Sources of Failed Vision

The vision reflects the internal needs of leaders rather than those of the market or constituents.

The resources needed to achieve vision have been seriously miscalculated.

An unrealistic assessment or distorted perception of market and constituent needs holds sway.

A failure to recognize environmental changes prevents redirection of the vision.

---

was subcontracted to outsiders. Plant and equipment were usually leased or rented. But Land's dream of the SX-70 required total integration of the company. A color-negative and camera-assembly plant were designed and built, and the company's existing chemical production and films-packaging facilities were expanded.

Although the total cost of the SX-70 strategy was never formally disclosed, Land responded in an interview that it was a half-billion-dollar investment. Other estimates have put it higher. In any case, the SX-70 was a design masterpiece. It was estimated that the reflex-viewing system cost millions of dollars and required more than two-and-a-half years of engineering effort. Engineering for the eye-piece alone cost $2 million.

Land's expectations of the camera's success were as lavish as his investment in the camera. At $180 per camera, company projections were that first-year sales would reach several million. By some accounts, sales of 5,000,000 units were predicted. Yet despite such optimism, the camera met with only limited public support. By the end of its first year in 1973, only 470,000 SX-70 cameras had been sold. It would take several years, many design changes, and significant price cuts before the camera would gain widespread market acceptance—all at the cost of sacrificing many of the camera's original features. Land's personal vision of the instant camera had missed what the market wanted.

Most important, in his quest for the perfect instant camera he had failed to take into account lessons that his company had already learned about consumers' needs. Before the SX-70, Polaroid's experience with both its black-and-white and its color cameras was that demand was intimately tied to price. Consumers wanted an inexpensive, easy-to-use, instant camera. Their foremost desire was not a perfect picture but a relatively good instant picture at a low price.

In the 1960s, the marketplace had powerfully demonstrated its needs to Polaroid after the company first introduced its color system in 1963. When the Colorpack cameras priced at $100 met with only limited market interest, Polaroid introduced a version at $75 and, by 1969, a $30 Colorpack. At the $30 price level, volume dramatically expanded, and 4,000,000 units were sold by 1973. Consumers wanted instant photography but only at an inexpensive price. So how could 5,000,000 SX-70s at $180 a piece be sold when only 4,000,000 Colorpack cameras had been sold at $30 each? Clearly they could not. Dr. Land's vision was a personal ideal, one that was not shared by consumers at a price of $180 per camera.

What happened to Land that he failed to learn from the past? There are several possible explanations. For one, his initial vision of instant photography had been correct; people really did want instant photographs. This initial success, however, may have convinced him of the invincibility of his ideas. Second, Land was an engineer at heart; he loved the technology more than the marketing of the product. His very background made him product- and technology-driven, not so much marketplace-driven. Finally and most important, I believe that Land, like other leaders, came to identify with his vision to an unhealthy extreme: The vision personified him.

A similar example is seen in Henry Ford, who was willing to build a Model T of any color as long as it was black. The vision in essence becomes so much a part of the leader's personality that he or she is unwilling or unable to consider information to the contrary from staff members or from the marketplace. Convinced by past successes of their invincibility, such leaders plow ahead without considering other viewpoints—a sure course toward failure.

Becoming a "Pyrrhic Victor"

In the quest to achieve a vision, a leader may be so driven as to ignore the costly implications of his strategic aims. Ambition and the miscalculation of necessary resources can lead to a "Pyrrhic victory" for the leader. The term "Pyrrhic victory" comes from an incident in Ancient Greece: Pyrrhus, the King of Epirus, sustained such heavy losses in defeating the Romans that despite his numerous victories over them, his entire empire was ultimately undermined. Thus the costs of a "Pyrrhic" victory deplete the resources that are needed for future success.

In this scenario, the leader is usually driven by a desire to expand or accelerate the realization of his vision. The initial vision appears correct, and early successes essentially delude or weaken the leader's ability to realistically assess his resources and marketplace realities. The costs that must be paid for acquisitions or market share ultimately become unsustainable and threaten the long-term viability of the leader's organization.

Robert Campeau is the quintessential Pyrrhic victor. After amassing a fortune as a real estate developer, he proceeded to expand his empire into retailing with a series of purchases in the mid-1980s totalling $13.4 billion. He did this despite the fact that he knew little about the business of retailing itself. His celebrated purchase of the Allied and Federated Department Stores alone cost him some $400 million in bankers' and lawyers' fees and added $11.7 billion of debt to the Campeau Corporation. They also transformed him overnight into the most powerful retailer in the world. The price of course was an enormous amount of debt—much of it in the form of high-interest junk bonds that would soon demand most of the company's operating cash to service.

When asked how he planned to successfully integrate and enhance the profitability of these new and unrelated acquisitions, Campeau explained that it was only a matter of consolidating various operations, selling off assets to pay off company debt, and motivating management by giving them stock options. With an air of great confidence, he commented: "I own the best department stores in the world, and they will be damned profitable." He also envisioned enormous potential for synergy between his retailing and real estate operations. His plans included the building of some 50 U.S. shopping malls anchored by his newly acquired retail stores. These projects, which included 17 new Bloomingdale's stores, were estimated at a cost of $1.5 billion. In comments to the press, he stated: "Most retail managements don't know much about real estate and finance . . . [but] real estate is the gravy on top of these great retailing deals." For Campeau, his newly acquired stores sat on prime land—ripe for future deals. It was an intriguing and untried dream.

Ironically, these bold strategic moves were all made during a sales slow-down in the department store industry and in a country glutted with shopping malls. As well, the two chains he had acquired were prestigious but also notoriously inefficient. None of these factors seemed to impede Campeau, who was intent on building an empire.

Despite his rosy projections for the future, Campeau's kingdom quickly unraveled within a few years. After struggling to meet a crushing debt load, Campeau's retail operations ran out of operating cash in August 1989. By January 1990 his company stood on the edge of bankruptcy, and so did Campeau himself. The projections of great profitability for the retail operations had never materialized. New and last-minute junk-bond financing to keep the company alive came at a dear price, with interest rates as high as 17.75%. But this would not save the company as soaring debt-servicing costs forced Campeau to sell off company stock to others and to default on company loans. Even the company's crown jewel—Bloomingdale's—was soon put up for sale. Campeau's own personal fortune of $500 million was said to have all but evaporated by February 1990.

Campeau's tragic error in this case was tied as much to blind ambition as it was to poor strategic and financing decisions. His history of successes in the real estate field, in combination with an ambitious personality, led this visionary leader to dream of ever-greater expansion, but in new and unfamiliar territories. The idea of an "empire" became more important than the satisfaction of enjoying his present successes. Failing to see that he lacked the long-term resources or skills needed to sustain his grand plan, he continued to acquire companies and debt at an alarming rate.

Then, too, in wishing to maintain an image of self-confidence, he may have denied or minimized the existence of any problems. Already an autocratic leader, Campeau became even more autocratic. For example, he himself assumed the position of chairman of the board at both Federated and Allied, a job he had originally and sensibly promised to an executive of a highly successful retail chain. He wanted to run his new and glamorous acquisitions personally. Sadly, this scenario is all too typical of the Pyrrhic victor whose ambitions stymie his ability to assess goals and resources realistically. Investment bankers and subordinates may further encourage visions of grandeur. As serious problems emerge, their importance is minimized. Once a crisis stage is reached, the leader exerts greater personal control and becomes less able to hear the counsel of advisors or staff members who might be helpful. In the worst case, such as Campeau's, the organization's resources are exhausted and the company fails.

Chasing a Vision Before Its Time

Sometimes a leader's perceptions of the market are so exaggerated or so significantly ahead of their time that the marketplace fails to sustain the leader's venture. The organization's resources are mobilized and spent on a mission that ultimately fails to produce the expected results. In this case, the leader is perhaps too visionary or too idealistic. He or she is unable to see that the time is not ripe, so the vision goes on to failure or, at best, a long dormancy.

Robert Lipp, former president of Chemical Bank, is an example of a visionary charismatic who in one project was essentially too far ahead of his time. He had championed a vision of home banking in the early 1980s. Sensing that the personal computer was revolutionizing many aspects of everyday life, Lipp and others at Chemical Bank expected personal banking to be the next beneficiary of the personal computer revolution. Through a modem, phone line, software supplied by the bank, and a personal computer at home, individuals could instruct their banks to carry out certain transactions. A service fee of $8 to $15 a month was charged for personal users and $20 to $50 a month for small businesses. From the user's viewpoint, home banking provided convenience in bill paying and ease of access to accounts. While on travel, the user could instruct the system to pay bills on exact due dates.

For banks, electronic home banking was very appealing. The printing, processing, and return of some 41 billion checks annually in the United States amounted to $41 billion. This figure represented 20% of the annual revenues of banks belonging to the Federal Reserve System. Home banking offered the possibility of a tremendous reduction in operating costs.

In 1983, Chemical Bank under Lipp's guidance introduced a home banking system called the Pronto Two with a goal of four million customers within several years. By 1988, however, the total nationwide users of home banking systems had reached only 100,000 people. An article in *Business Week* (February 29, 1988) remarked: "When Chemical Bank unveiled the idea of home banking in 1983, it projected that 10% of its customers would eventually pay bills and make banking transactions from their home computer. Talk about misplaced optimism. Today, if you're among those who deal with any bank by personal computer, you're in a minority of a mere 100,000 people—and that includes a number of small business operators." Only 30 banks were offering the service by 1988, out of a total of 14,000 banks nationwide.

What Chemical and others later discovered was that several inherent problems with home banking led to consumer resistance. First, customers were reluctant to give up the "float" between when they wrote a check and when it was cashed. With home banking, once the computer authorizes a payment, it is immediately debited from the customer's account.

Second, some investment—for a computer and a modem—was required on the customer's part. It is estimated that only 10% of personal computer owners had modems—and the number of personal computers in homes was limited. Finally, it was a matter of opinion whether writing a paper check was not just as simple and convenient as paying bills by personal computer. Given the costs of such computer systems, it was believed that only by providing a wider range of services, such as home shopping services, would home banking's appeal increase—and that a period of 10 to 15 years was required for market acceptance.

In Lipp's case, his vision was essentially premature for its market. Part of the problem could be attributed to the difficulty of trying to predict a future event for which there is no history. It is extremely difficult to accurately estimate the demand for a particular product or service; the leader is essentially relying on his or her forecast of resources and market trends. The margin for error in these situations is high, and the costs and time horizons for introducing a new product or service are often underestimated. Such miscalculations can forestall a vision.

Two other factors may play important roles. In their own excitement over an idea, leaders may fail to adequately test-market a new product or service, or fail to hear naysayers or overlook contrary signs from the environment. Again, because of successes in other projects (Lipp had had several outstanding ones), they may delude themselves into believing they know their markets more accurately than they actually do. Or their spellbinding ability to lead may not be backed up by an adequate understanding of marketplace trends.

HOW LEADERS COME TO DENY FLAWS
IN THEIR VISIONS

All three of these cases share certain characteristics that cause leaders to deny the flaws in their visions. Often, for example, leaders will perceive that their course of action is producing negative results, yet they persist. Why this happens can be explained by a process called "cognitive dissonance," which prevents the leader from changing his course. Simply put, individuals act to keep the commitments they have made because failing to do so would damage their favorable perceptions of themselves. For example, studies have found that executives will sometimes persist in an ineffective course of action simply because they feel they have committed themselves to the decision. This same process, I suspect, occurs with leaders.

Others in the organization, who tend to become dependent on a visionary leader, may perpetuate the problem through their own actions. They may idealize their leader excessively and thus ignore negative aspects and exaggerate the good qualities. As a result, they may carry out their leader's orders unquestioningly—and leaders may in certain cases encourage such behavior because of their needs to dominate and be admired. The resulting sense of omnipotence encourages denial of market and organizational realities. The danger is that leaders will surround themselves with "yes people" and thus fail to receive information that might be important but challenging to the mission. Their excessive confidence and the desire for heroic recognition encourages them to undertake large, risky ventures—but because of their overreliance on themselves and their cadre of "yes people," strategic errors go unnoticed. Bold but poorly thought-out strategies will be designed and implemented. The leader's vision, in essence, becomes a vehicle for his or her own needs for attention and visibility.

Finally, problems with "group-think" can occur where the leader's advisors delude themselves into agreement with the leader or dominant others. In such a case, decision-making becomes distorted, and a more thorough and objective review of possible alternatives to a problem are all but precluded. This is especially true of groups that are very cohesive, highly committed to their success, under pressure, and possessing favorable opinions of themselves—common characteristics in the organizations of powerful and charismatic leaders. When group-think occurs, the opinions of the leader and advisors with closely allied views come to dominate decision making. Doubts that others might have are kept hidden for fear of disapproval. It is more important "to go along to get along" rather than to consider contrary viewpoints.

John DeLorean is an example of a leader who may have purposely created group-think situations. One executive of the DeLorean Motor Company, after being dismissed by DeLorean from the company board, commented: "He told me he knew how some of the things the board was doing bothered my conscience. He said he wanted me to keep a clear conscience and not to worry as much as I did, so he had dropped me from the board. . . . When I told him he couldn't bear having anyone disagree with him so he had to stack the board his way, John . . . just nodded and said, 'That's right. It's my company and I'm going to do what I want to do—when you get your own company, you can do the same'" (Hill Levin, *Grand Delusions,* Viking, 1983, pg. 248).

MANIPULATION THROUGH IMPRESSION MANAGEMENT AND COMMUNICATION SKILLS

Because some leaders are gifted at communicating, it may be quite easy for them to misuse this ability. For instance, they may present information that makes their visions appear more realistic or more appealing than the visions actually are. They may also use their language skills to screen out problems in the larger environment or to foster an illusion of control when, in reality, things are out of control. Exhibit 2 highlights a number of these possible problem areas.

While at General Motors John DeLorean was particularly adept at employing skills of articulation and impression management to promote him-

Exhibit 2
Potential Liabilities in the Leader's Communications
and Impression Management Skills

Exaggerated self-descriptions.

Exaggerated claims for the vision.

A technique of fulfilling stereotypes and images of uniqueness to manipulate audiences.

A habit of gaining commitment by restricting negative information and maximizing positive information.

Use of anecdotes to distract attention away from negative statistical information.

Creation of an illusion of control through affirming information and attributing negative outcomes to external causes.

---

self. For example, he would often claim responsibility for projects without acknowledging the contributions of others. His aim was simply to manipulate information so that he appeared as the originating genius. In the case of the highly successful Pontiac GTO, DeLorean claimed to be the engineer at Pontiac who conceived the idea of combining a lighter version of the Tempest body with a powerful engine to create the GTO. In reality, the idea was suggested by a GM colleague.

In *Current Biography*, DeLorean is described as owning "more than 200 patents, including those for the recessed windshield wipers and the overhead-cam engine." However, Hill Levin in his biography of DeLorean reported that the U.S. Patent Office listed a total of 52 patents, none for the wipers or for the overhead cam. Exaggeration of personal deeds was perhaps DeLorean's way of building the legend. What we see with some leaders is that their need for personal recognition and visibility is so high that they feel compelled to distort reality to enhance their own image.

When leaders rely greatly on their impression management skills in communicating, they do themselves a disservice. For instance, research in impression management indicates not only that one's self-descriptions are effective in deceiving an audience, but also that they may deceive the presenter as well. This is especially true when an audience reinforces and approves of the individual's image. Such positive responses encourage leaders to internalize their own self-enhancing descriptions. Especially when exaggeration is only moderate, leaders tend to internalize and believe such claims. So DeLorean may ultimately have come to believe in his own responsibility for the Pontiac GTO.

Considerable research has also been performed on people who are in-gratiators—people who play to their audiences by telling them what they want to hear. Two particular tactics that I suspect charismatic leaders use to ingratiate themselves with their audiences are to (1) fulfill stereotypes and (2) create an image of uniqueness.

Research shows that if individuals behave in ways that fulfill the positive stereotypes of an audience, they are more likely to interact successfully with them. This can be achieved by espousing the beliefs, values, and behaviors associated with the stereotype and appearing as the stereotype is expected to look. For example, DeLorean supposedly went to great efforts to present the image of a young, highly successful executive with an entrepreneurial spirit. He underwent cosmetic surgery, dieted from 200 pounds to 160, lifted weights, dyed his grey hair black. He flew only first class. When he ate out, he always obtained the best table. To many, his image fulfilled the stereotype of the successful businessman.

DeLorean used the second tactic—to demonstrate uniqueness—through his unconventional actions while working at General Motors and his tales of innovations at the automobile giant. These stories created the image of a highly successful, unique individual excelling in the corporate world.

In terms of how or what a leader communicates, according to Charles Schwenk, there are several tactics that individuals can use to gain commit-ment from others even when the circumstances are unethical. Because our ability to process information is limited, we rely on simple biases to reduce the amount of information needed to make a decision. By playing on these biases, a leader can create or heighten commitment to a course of action. They may manipulate information so as to encourage biases in others that will increase confidence in and commitment to the leader's strategic choices. For example, leaders can withhold information that is not favor-able to a cause and present instead more positive information. Or they may relate anecdotes designed to draw attention away from statistical informa-tion that reflects negatively on their plans.

DeLorean's management of investors in his automobile venture offers one example of this process. If investors had looked at history, they would have found that the odds of his succeeding were slim. Not since the found-ing of the four major auto companies had a new automobile company suc-ceeded, and there had been many attempts in the interim. Moreover, there was negative statistical information in the company prospectus that might have dissuaded investors. But instead of focusing on such important statistical information, the investors allowed themselves to be swayed by De-Lorean's personal character and his impressive press coverage while at General Motors. Could it be that DeLorean aimed to create a flashy image in the minds of investors in order to draw their attention away from other sources of information?

Anecdotal information may be used by the leader not only to influence decision makers' choices, but also to increase their confidence in a choice. The sheer amount of information the leader provides may act to build overconfidence. Various studies of decision making indicate that more information apparently permits people to generate more reasons for justifying their decisions and, in turn, increases the confidence of others in the decisions. Leaders might also create an illusion of control by selectively providing information that affirms they are in control and attributes failures or problems to external causes. All of these tactics may be used by leaders to mislead their direct reports and their investors.

MANAGEMENT PRACTICES THAT BECOME LIABILITIES

The managerial practices of leaders also have certain inherent liabilities. Some leaders are known for their excessively impulsive, autocratic management style. Others become so disruptive through their unconventional behavior that their organizations mobilize against them. Moreover, leaders can at times be poor at managing their superiors and peers. In general, some of the very management practices that make leaders unique may also lead to their downfall.

Leaders' liabilities fall into several categories: (1) the way they manage relations with important others, (2) their management style with direct reports, and (3) their thoroughness and attention to certain administrative detail. Typical problems associated with each of these categories are shown in Exhibit 3. We will start with the first category: managing relations with important others.

Managing Upwards and Sideways

Some leaders—particularly charismatic leaders in large organizations—seem to be very poor at managing upwards and sideways. Because they are

Exhibit 3
Potential Liabilities of a Leader's Management Practices

Poor management of people networks, especially superiors and peers.
Unconventional behavior that alienates.
Creation of disruptive "in group/out group" rivalries.
An autocratic, controlling management style.
An informal/impulsive style that is disruptive and dysfunctional.
Alternation between idealizing and devaluing others, particularly direct reports.
Creation of excessive dependence in others.
Failure to manage details and effectively act as an administrator.
Attention to the superficial.
Absence from operations.
Failure to develop successors of equal ability.

---

usually unconventional advocates of radical reform, they may often alienate others in the organization, including their own bosses. The charismatic leader's unconventional actions may trigger the ire of forces within the organization which then act to immobilize him or her. Leaders' aggressive style may also alienate many potential supporters and ultimately leave them without sufficient political support for their ambitious plans. This problem is common when charismatic leaders are brought in from the outside; their radically different values and approaches may alienate the rest of the organization.

This kind of situation occurred at General Motors when Ross Perot was made a board member. Once on the board, Perot became one of the company's most outspoken critics. As an entrepreneur, he was quite naturally accustomed to running his own show, and after his company, Electronic Data Systems (EDS), merged with GM he insisted that any changes made in EDS procedures be cleared through him. His style and outspokenness were so much at odds with the General Motors culture that the company offered Perot $700 million in stock to step down from the board—an offer he finally accepted.

A second problem related to managing relations within large organizations is the tendency of certain leaders to cultivate a feeling of being "special" among members of their operating units. This practice is often accompanied by a corresponding depreciation of other parts of the corporation. In short, the leader creates an "us versus them" attitude. Although this heightens the motivation of the leader's group, it further alienates other groups that may be important for resources or political support. Steven Jobs did this with the Macintosh division at Apple Computer. Even though the company's Apple II Computer provided the profits, Jobs consistently downplayed that division's importance. He essentially divided the company into two rivals. He was fond of telling people in the Macintosh division, "This is the cream of Apple. This is the future of Apple." He even went so far as telling marketing managers for Apple II that they worked for an outdated, clumsy organization. Jobs's later departure from Apple stemmed in part from morale problems he created within the company by using this tactic.

In another case, the charismatic president of a division in a large corporation used as his group's emblem a mascot symbol of the TV cartoon character Roadrunner. (In the cartoons, Roadrunner was particularly adept at outwitting a wily coyote.) To him, his division managers were the "roadrunners" who were smarter and faster than the corporate "coyotes" who laid roadblocks in their path. He also had a habit of ignoring corporate staff requests for reports or information, and he returned their reports with "STUPID IDEA" stamped on the front cover. Although such behaviors and tactics fostered a sense of camaraderie and aggressiveness within the charismatic leader's division, they were ultimately detrimental both to the leader and to the organization. In this case, the executive eventually stepped down from the organization.

Relationships with Subordinates

Highly directive and visionary leaders are often described as autocratic. Jobs, for example, has been described as dictatorial. I suspect that in many cases the vision is such a personification of the leader that he or she becomes obsessed about its perfection or implementation. Leaders' natural impatience with the pace of the vision's achievement exacerbates the problem and encourages them to be more hands-on, more controlling.

There also appears to be, at times, an impulsive dynamic at work in the way leaders manage—and at such times they will override subordinates' suggestions or insights. Again, this occurs especially in relation to accomplishing the vision. DeLorean is described as increasing his production of the DeLorean car by 50% in the belief that his product would become an overnight sensation. Production went to an annual rate of 30,000 cars. This was done in spite of market research that showed total annual sales of between 4,000 and 10,000 cars. A company executive lamented, "Our fig-ures showed that this was a viable company with half the production. If the extravagence had been cut out of New York, we could have broken even making just 6,000 cars a year. But that wasn't fast enough for John. First he had to build his paper empire in the stock market. A creditable success was not enough for him" (ibid., pg. 282).

Steven Jobs is known to have darted in and out of operations causing havoc: "He would leap-frog back and forth among various projects, dictat-ing designs, with little or no knowledge of whether or not the technology even existed to make his ideas work" (L. Butcher, *Accidental Millionaire*, Paragon House, 1988, pp. 140–141).

Another potential problem can arise from a style of informality when managing the hierarchy of an organization—this is especially true of charismatic leaders. Advantages of this style are that leaders are highly visi-ble, approachable, and able to react quickly to issues and problems. The drawback is that they often violate the chain of command by going around direct reports and thus undercut their direct reports' authority. If a partic-ular project or idea interests them, they do not hesitate to become involved, sometimes to the detriment of the project managers' responsibilities. De-Lorean would drop in on his engineers to suggest what seemed trivial ideas. One company engineer said: "He came in one day to say we should hook into the cooling system and make a little icebox for a six-pack of beer be-hind the driver's seat. Or, another time, he told us to work on a sixty-watt radio speaker that could be detached and hung outside the car for picnics" (H. Levin, ibid., pg. 267).

Administrative Skills

Some visionary leaders are so absorbed by the "big picture" that they fail to understand essential details—except for "pet" projects in which they be-come excessively involved. Iaccoca, for instance, turned over most of the day-to-day operations to others as he became increasingly famous. As a re-sult, he lost touch with new model planning. He himself admitted: "If I made one mistake, it was delegating all the product development and not going to a single meeting" (ibid., pg. 267). A DeLorean executive com-plained: "He [John DeLorean] just didn't have time for the details of the project. But attention to detail is everything" (ibid., p. 267). Then, too, lead-ers may get so caught up in corporate stardom that they become absentee leaders. Again, Iaccoca is an example. His success at Chrysler led to his becoming a best-selling author, a U.S. presidential prospect, and the head of the $277 million fund-raising campaign for the Statue of Liberty—all of which distracted him from the important task of leading Chrysler.

Because these individuals are often excited by ideas, they may at times be poor implementors. Once an idea begins to appear as a tangible reality, I suspect they feel the need to move on to the next challenge, thereby leaving subordinates scrambling to pick up the pieces. Furthermore, because some leaders have high needs for visibility, they gravitate toward activities that afford them high people contact and recognition. Such activities are generally not performed at a desk while paying careful attention to the details.

Succession Problems

A true leader is usually a strong figure and, as noted, often one upon whom subordinates develop dependencies. Thus it is difficult for others with leadership potential to develop fully in the shadow of such leaders. For while they may actively coach their subordinates, I suspect that it is extremely difficult for them to develop others to be leaders of *equal power*. Leaders simply enjoy the limelight too much to share it, so when they ultimately depart, a leadership vacuum is created. Moreover, under charismatic leadership authority may be highly centralized around the leader—and this is an arrangement that, unfortunately, weakens the authority structures that are normally dispersed throughout an organization.

It's clear that many of the qualities of a strong leader have both a positive and a negative face. That's why the presence of leaders entails risks for their direct reports, their organizations, and at times their societies. They must be managed with care. The negatives, however, must always be weighed in light of the positives. For companies and society, the need for organizational change and strategic vision may be so great that the risks of confrontation, unconventionality, and so on may seem a small price to pay. It is also possible that organizations and educational institutions can train, socialize, and manage future leaders in ways that will minimize their negative qualities.

Leaders Who Self-Destruct: The Causes and Cures

Manfred F. R. Kets de Vries

Why do some people derail when they reach the top? What psychological forces affect executives when they attain a position of power? Why does an executive who seems bright, likeable, and well adjusted, suddenly resort to strange behavior when he or she becomes chief executive officer?

There are no simple answers to these questions. In order to address them, we must deepen our understanding of the psychodynamics of leadership and the vicissitudes of power. A number of clinical insights from dynamic psychiatry and psychoanalysis may help in our analysis.

First, however, consider an example that illustrates the kind of irrational behavior described above. Before Robert Clark[1] assumed the presidency of the Solan Corporation, he had always been well liked. His supervisors had been impressed by his capacity for work, his helpful attitude, his dedication, and his imaginative method of solving problems. He eventually crowned his seemingly brilliant career by being selected to succeed Solan's former CEO.

In the period immediately after Clark took over, he received many accolades for his role in taking a number of long overdue steps. Gradually, however, after the initial enthusiasm had cleared up, many of his old colleagues concluded that he had apparently undergone a personality change. He had become less accessible; his once widely acclaimed open-door policy and advocacy of participative management had disappeared. He had become increasingly authoritarian, impatient, and careless of the feelings of others.

The organizational effects of Clark's transformation were quickly forthcoming. In their desire to please him, key executives would jostle for his attention and waste time and energy on power games and intracompany

---

1. "Robert Clark" is a pseudonym, and the name "the Solan Corporation" is fictitious. The following individuals and organizations mentioned in this article are also identified by pseudonyms or fictitious names: Peter Harris and the Noro Corporation; Ted Howell and the Larix Corporation; and Ted Nolan and the Dalton Corporation.

squabbles rather than on strategic decisions. Company morale sank to an all-time low, and the financial results were predictably dismal.

What happened to Clark—and *why* did it happen? Certain psychological forces—his own and those of his followers—came into play, creating a multitude of problems. Here are three reasons why this occurred:

- Succession to the top leadership position in an organization is necessarily isolating in that it separates leaders from others (who now directly report to them) and leaves them without peers. As a result, their own normal dependency needs for contact, support, and reassurance rise up and overwhelm them.
- Whether consciously or unconsciously, employees expect their organization's leaders to be infallible and even gifted to some degree with "magical" powers.
- Troubled by guilt feelings about their success and fearful that it may not last, leaders may unconsciously cause themselves to fail.

To some degree, every human being suffers from these reactions and feelings. History has provided us with many examples of leaders whose behavior became pathological in the extreme once they attained power: political leaders such as King Saul, Caligula, Adolf Hitler, and Colonel Quaddafi, or business leaders such as Howard Hughes.

I am not suggesting that each business leader will resort to pathological behavior upon reaching the top of his or her organization. What differentiates those who "crash" from those who don't is the latter's ability to stay in touch with reality and take these psychological forces in stride. Many leaders are very good at handling the pressures that leadership brings; indeed, some individuals who may previously have been rather colorless turn into great leaders when they attain positions of power. However, some leaders just can't manage; the regressive pulls simply become too strong. Since we are all susceptible to these psychological forces, I will discuss their dynamics.

ISOLATION FROM REALITY

On June 18, 1982, the body of Roberto Calvi, Chairman of Ambrosiano, Italy's largest private bank, was found hanging under Black-friars Bridge in London. The exact circumstances of his death may never be known;

however, this was certainly an ignominious ending for one of Italy's most prominent bankers. It was also one of the saddest developments in modern Italy's largest financial scandal.

Although the extent of Calvi's involvement may never be known, he certainly carried a heavy responsibility. His secretive, control-oriented management style didn't help, and his remoteness was an added complication. In newspaper accounts of that time, Calvi was described as the most private of financiers, an individual who was very reserved and formal, a man for whom communication was a difficult task. From the various descriptions we have of him, he was apparently a person who would internalize his problems rather than confide in anyone. Here was an individual who had a very detached way of dealing with others.

Why did Calvi get himself into this situation? We cannot really answer this question; however, we do know that, in spite of the sea of executives reporting to Calvi, he apparently ended up very much alone in dealing with his problems. There was apparently no one he could turn to, which seems paradoxical in light of his contacts and his very active life. Unfortunately, this kind of isolation seems all too common among people who head organizations, and it can affect their sense of reality.

The term "loneliness of command" has been used frequently in the context of leadership. The inability to test one's perceptions, the tendency to lose touch with reality because one occupies a top position, is a danger anyone can fall victim to when in a leadership position.

For example, when Peter Harris became president of the Noro Corporation, he thought that his personal and professional lives would continue more or less as they had before. The appointment had been very routine; as one of the senior vice-presidents of his company, he had been the logical choice for the job.

In reality, however, Harris had to deal with more changes in his lifestyle than he had expected. Soon after he assumed the presidency, he realized that, in spite of his efforts to maintain his previous amicable working style, he was creating more distance between himself and his employees. Although he tried for a while to be one of the boys, he discovered that this was no longer possible. In short, Harris now had difficulty socializing with and having to make tough career decisions about the same person; life seemed much simpler if he retained some distance. He had also discovered that friendliness to an employee was quickly interpreted by others as favoritism; attempts at closeness by an employee were similarly viewed as a lobbying effort.

Although Harris simplified matters by keeping his distance, this had a price. He increasingly felt a sense of isolation, a loss of intimacy. He could talk to his wife, but that didn't seem to be enough. He wanted to confide in someone more familiar with what happened in the business, someone on whom he could test his ideas.

Sometimes he would think nostalgically of the time before he became president. Occasionally, he found himself longing for a way to resurrect the broken network of relationships, searching for a way of sharing, but this had become impossible. A side-effect was that he was becoming increasingly irritated about having gotten himself into this position; it was not what he had expected. He began to wonder if his increasing aloofness was affecting his ability to make decisions.

The examples of Roberto Calvi and Peter Harris show us one of the pitfalls of assuming the position of CEO; for some it becomes a mixed blessing. The organization's leaders are supposed to take care of their organization's existing strategic and structural needs; they are expected to articulate a vision of the future and show others how to achieve it. But there are a number of other aspects to leadership; one of these is that leaders should take care of the dependency needs of their employees. Given the universal nature of these needs, however, one must ask who takes care of the *leaders'* dependency needs? When no such person is available, some leaders may suffer from anxiety associated with loneliness and disconnectedness; some may even lose touch with reality.

When leaders reach the top of their organizations, they may be dismayed to learn that their network of complex mutual dependencies has been changed forever. Some leaders can overcome this and find other forms of gratification; others may even enjoy experiencing a certain degree of detachment. However, many leaders become upset at finding themselves in this situation and may react accordingly. They may feel frustrated and angry and may even experience a seemingly irrational desire to "get even" with those who have not fulfilled their dependency needs. The resulting scapegoating behavior can create a very politicized organization torn by interdepartmental rivalry.

However, aggression can also be turned inward, which can lead to depression and to alcohol and drug abuse. If these extreme responses continue, they can have dire consequences for the organization.

THE DANGERS OF TRANSFERENCE

Apart from acting as catalysts in the achievement of their organizations' objectives, leaders can also become the embodiment of their employees' ideals, wishes, feelings, and fantasies. By transforming their subjective fantasies into objective reality, employees may imbue their leaders with mystical qualities—a phenomenon that may occur despite their leaders' attempts to resist it. Employees may consciously or unconsciously perceive and respond to their leaders not according to objective reality, but as though the leader were a significant authority figure from their past, such as a parent or teacher. When this occurs, the boundaries between the past and present may disappear.

As with any authority figure, leaders are a prime outlet for such emotional reactions. Given their position, they can easily retrigger in their employees previously unresolved conflicts with significant figures from their past. When this happens, regressive behavior may occur: Employees may endow their leaders with the same omniscience that they attributed in childhood to parents or other significant figures.

This psychological process—the distortion of the whole context of one's relationship—is called *transference* and is present in all meaningful human interactions. Although leaders may find it hard to accept, all interpersonal exchanges involve both realistic *and* transference reactions—and leaders are particularly susceptible to this kind of confusion.

Transference reactions can be acted out in several ways and can affect both leaders and their employees. One common manifestation is for employees to "idealize" their leaders in an attempt to recreate the sense of security and importance they felt in childhood, when they were cared for by apparently omnipotent and perfect parents. As authority figures, leaders fall easily into an employee's subconscious definition of a "parent" role. Employees may therefore want to endow their leaders with unrealistic powers and attributes, which in turn can inflate their leaders' self-esteem.

During periods of organizational upheaval such as cutbacks or expansions, employees are particularly anxious to cling to their beliefs in their leaders' powers as a way of maintaining their own sense of security and identity. For this reason, employees will do anything to please or charm their leaders—including giving in to their extravagant whims. Thus, in times of organizational crisis, leaders may conceivably be surrounded by "yes-men." This lack of critical opinion can obviously have dire consequences for their organizations. If leaders get too much uncritical admiration from their employees, they may begin to believe that they really are as perfect, intelligent, or powerful as others think. Losing one's grasp on reality in this way is a common human failing, but it can be particularly dangerous for leaders since they often have the power to act on their delusions of grandeur. When a CEO stops listening to criticism and embarks on an overambitious expansion or orders the unnecessary construction of a new company headquarters, this process may indeed be at work.

As a result of their grandiose delusions, some leaders will favor highly dependent employees who are in search of an all-knowledgeable, all-powerful leader. However, such leaders can be very callous about these employees' needs; they may exploit them and then drop them when they no longer serve their purposes.

Such employees may legitimately react angrily to this type of behavior. However, another less obvious process may also be at work: Employees may subconsciously blame their leaders for failing to live up to their own exaggerated expectations. Angry about this, and perhaps aggravated by callous, exploitative behavior, these employees may find their attitudes quickly turning from admiration to hostility and rebellion. Like children, such people tend to divide all experiences, perceptions, and feelings into unambiguously "good" and "bad" categories. Thus, although new CEOs may initially have been welcomed as messiahs, they may be surprised to find out how suddenly their employees' mood can shift. After one setback, employees may view their leader as being responsible for all the company's problems, even if these problems developed long before his or her arrival.

Faced with this transition in employee attitudes from admiration to rebellion and anger, leaders may become irritated and even develop slight feelings of persecution. But leaders have to realize that this is to a certain extent inevitable and that they must exert a certain amount of self-control.

Some leaders, however, may be tempted to retaliate—possibly by firing their critics. There are some leaders who tend to mentally divide their employees into those who are "with" them and those who are "against" them; such an outlook is liable to breed an organizational culture of fear and suspicion. Employees who are "with" their leaders share their outlooks and support them even if they engage in unrealistic, grandiose schemes or imagine the existence of malicious plots, sabotage, and enemies. Effective leaders, however, know how to contain their excessive emotional reactions and avoid being caught up in groundless fears.

The Case of Ted Howell

To illustrate how these psychological forces can affect a leader, consider the following incident. As a result of the unexpected death of his predecessor, Ted Howell was appointed president of the Larix Corporation, a company in the electronics equipment field. Howell had been found with the help of a headhunter who had highly recommended him. He had previously held a senior staff position in a company in the same line of business; Howell's knowledge of the industry had been a key factor in convincing Larix's board to take him on.

Soon after his arrival, Larix's board members saw signs that Howell was having difficulties dealing with the pressures of the job. A number of rash decisions made in his first week at the office were the first indications of trouble. But in spite of these mistakes, everything initially turned out better than expected. First, one of the company's main competitors went out of business, which freed up an important segment of the market. In addition, one of Howell's employees came up with an excellent marketing idea that he quickly adopted and that proved very successful. Some executives were disturbed because their colleague never received credit for it; nevertheless, these two factors helped to get Larix back into the black.

Unfortunately, this success apparently went to Howell's head. After the turnaround, he embarked on a dramatic expansion program, ignoring cautionary remarks made by his employees, consultants, and bankers. Other steps were taken, including the relocation of the company's headquarters to what Howell thought were more suitable surroundings and the acquisition of an expensive company plane. These two actions put a heavy strain on the company's finances. Those executives who expressed disagreement or concern about the new moves were fired; consultants who suggested that Howell change course suffered the same fate. In the end, only sycophants who were willing to share his grandiose ideas and accept his aggressive outbursts were left.

As expected, the unrealistic plans and high expenditures put the company into the red. However, Howell was unwilling to admit his role in the debacle. When questioned at directors' meetings, he would become defensive and deny any responsibility for the losses; instead, he would blame them on faulty moves made by his predecessor or on vindictive action by executives no longer in his employ. In his opinion, a turnaround was just around the corner. To an increasing number of board members, however, Howell's behavior was becoming unacceptable. Eventually, having become impatient with the continuing losses and with Howell's imperious, paranoid behavior, they managed to remove him.

As in the case of Robert Clark, here was an individual who was apparently well adjusted and who had performed well in his previous job. After his promotion, however, when he was subjected to the pressures of being a leader, this same individual began to behave irrationally.

One contributing factor was apparently the excessively high expectations that Howell's employees had for him. Overwhelmed by all the attention that he was suddenly receiving, he apparently allowed his sense of reality to become distorted. Perhaps because he couldn't withstand these psychological pressures, he may have assumed that some of the qualities ascribed to him were true and behaved accordingly. When his grandiose actions backfired and he couldn't deliver, his employees reacted with anger. Howell began to show signs of paranoid behavior and retaliated by putting the blame on others.

This distortive reaction pattern is another factor that contributes to this strange, irrational behavior we sometimes find in leaders. These reaction patterns are semidormant tendencies with which we all have to deal and which arise easily in leadership situations. As I have indicated, some leaders find it very difficult to withstand these pressures.

THE FEAR OF SUCCESS

In a success-oriented society, failure is looked upon as a catastrophe, and to some extent we all fear it. But while the fear of failure is quite understandable as a reactivating mechanism for feelings of incompetence, fear of success is more of a mystery. In fact, Sigmund Freud tried to demystify some of the dynamics behind this fear in an article entitled "Those Wrecked by Success" (1916). He noted that some people become sick when a deeply rooted and longed-for desire comes to fulfillment. He gave as an example a professor who cherished a wish to succeed his teacher. When this wish eventually came true, the professor became plagued by feelings of depression and self-deprecation and found that he was unable to work.

The Case of Ted Nolan

Sometimes we can see how top executives fall victim to this form of anxiety. Reflecting on his career, Ted Nolan recalled being surprised when he was asked to succeed Larry Fulton as president of the Dalton Corporation. Like many of his colleagues, he had thought that the vice-president of marketing was the person most likely to be chosen by the board; however, he certainly didn't protest when asked.

When his appointment came through, however, Nolan noticed that he felt slightly ill at ease, a feeling that didn't go away when he took over. He became increasingly preoccupied with the question of whether he could hack it. He began to have difficulties sleeping at night, tormenting himself by wondering whether his previous day's actions had been correct. He often felt like an impostor, having just been "lucky" to get the job. To make matters worse, he also developed a full-fledged drinking problem. At work he found it increasingly difficult to concentrate and make decisions. He wondered how many of his problems in handling the top job were noticed by his board members. When were they going to realize that they had made a mistake, and that he was really an incompetent fake?

However, as Nolan said himself, he had been fortunate. His wife had been a great support to him. Because of the changes in his behavior, she had encouraged him to see a psychotherapist. As he explored the underlying causes of his anxiety with the therapist, he began to realize that he had always been anxious whenever he was put in a position of responsibility; previously, however, he had handled it better because there had always been others in a similar situation with whom he could talk. This time, however, he was really on his own.

With the psychotherapist's help, Nolan discovered the relationship between his past and his present feelings. In reviewing his life, he realized how successful he had been, having overcome tremendous handicaps to work himself up to a position far above those held by his parents and siblings. He also recognized that this success had come with feelings of guilt and betrayal of his origins. Having risen so far above his roots apparently contributed to his current anxiety. He had explored these feelings with his psychotherapist and had succeeded in becoming more objective by integrating these feelings with his current situation. Being able to see those connections and working through these insights had brought him greater peace of mind. What's more, he felt he was now doing a fairly good job in his new position.

What Nolan's experience exemplifies is that some people believe, whether consciously or unconsciously, that success can only be attained by displacing someone else. For them, success is perceived as a symbolic victory over the parents or siblings of childhood. This is particularly true for those individuals who have never resolved rivalrous feelings towards the latter. If this is the case, to be successful and to have tangible accomplishments in adulthood can turn into a Pyrrhic victory.

In a case like this, success becomes symbolically equated with betrayal. Success makes these individuals stand out and be noticed; it becomes a provocative, hostile act that not only leads to feelings of guilt but also invites retribution. As in childhood, being in such a position may arouse the envy and resentment of others. Retaliation will be feared from those individuals with whom the person is competing. Thus unresolved competitive feelings from the past become confused with present-day reality. Since success is feared to have negative consequences, these successful individuals may downgrade their accomplishments or even view themselves as impostors. They may have difficulty believing that they have achieved success through their own abilities.

In management situations, these irrational thoughts and behavior patterns may not become evident as long as the executive in question is one out of many. As long as such patterns are not particularly noticeable, the problem may be subdued. But as soon as these people reach a leadership position, they may become anxious, deprecate their accomplishments, and even engage in self-defeating behavior.

STAYING ON COURSE

I have described some of the more problematic aspects of leadership, as well as depicted a number of psychological forces that can negatively affect individuals in leadership positions. Many of these forces will often be brought to bear simultaneously; leaders who cannot withstand them will be the ones who cannot manage. Stress reactions may follow, and such individuals may lose touch with reality.

Leaders should be aware of the psychological forces and should be able to identify potential signs of trouble. To prevent stress reactions and irrational behavior from coming to the fore, leaders should engage in a regular process of critical self-evaluation. Those who are interested in the vicissitudes of leadership may want to reflect on the following questions:

- How accessible is the leader?
- How does the leader react to bad news or criticism from an employee?
- Is the leader able to discuss any problems or ideas with colleagues?
- Does the leader think of employees in terms of those who are "with" and those who are "against" him or her?
- How realistic is the leader's vision of the company's future? Is there a large discrepancy between his or her own and others' points of view?
- Is the leader willing to accept responsibility if things go wrong, or does he or she blame "the others"?

- Is the leader quick to take offense and feel unfairly treated? Does he or she have a great need to "blow his or her own horn"?
- Does the leader feel anxious and guilty when he or she is successful and have difficulties believing that his or her professional success is caused by his or her own accomplishments and not by sheer luck?

In considering these questions, we should not forget that the ability to change fantasy into reality, given the power leaders have, can be like the mythological siren's call and may cause an individual to change as soon as he or she attains a leadership position. The potential for losing touch with reality and behaving irrationally is dormant in all of us.

Paradoxically enough, it is sometimes this very irrational quality that is needed to make some leaders effective. Paranoid reactions and visionary experiences may feed very well into certain types of situations, and many political and religious leaders have acted in just this way (consider Joseph Stalin or the Ayatollah Khomeini).

However, in spite of what may have been an initially enthusiastic reception, there is a dark side to this behavior. To evoke regressive tendencies in others and to provoke aggression is to set in motion that which may be impossible to stop.

What Organizations—and Their Leaders—Can Do

This cautionary note—on a somewhat lesser scale—is also true in business situations. Here, however, it may be somewhat easier to set up safeguards against the excess of leadership. Leaders in contemporary society have to deal with the government, unions, banks, or other stakeholders that may take on the role of a countervailing power, helping to keep the leaders in touch with reality. In many large organizations, leaders will inherit an organizational structure with different checks and balances in the form of distribution of key policy decisions over a number of individuals and various agencies that will circumscribe their behavior. Moreover, in large organizations, organizational processes find their own momentum and are resistant to dramatic change. Social systems have their own way of providing a "safety belt" for individuals through their inherent structure.

Apart from the various external checks on leaders' actions that may prevent these irrational manifestations from coming to the fore, leaders themselves can take preventive action. Encouraging frank feedback from outsiders such as external directors, bankers, and consultants is one way of preventing these regressive forces from gaining the upper hand. Individuals from outside the organization usually possess a very different frame of reference, and their vision will be considerably less distorted by the existing organizational dynamics. They can provide more of an overall view and warn about potential sources of trouble. Board members in particular can play a critical role; selecting a strong, independent board that is really willing to enforce its auditing role rather than just acting as a rubber stamp is one of the best ways to keep an organization on course and prevent it from losing touch with reality.

Another useful countervailing force can be participation in top executive training programs. These programs can provide a nonthreatening environment in which leaders can discuss their working experience with colleagues and professionals exposed to similar problems; such situations will enhance reality testing. Mutual comparison of potential problem areas may provide leaders with a revelation, and insight is the first step toward constructive change.

A SHARED RESPONSIBILITY

Leaders and their employees are like partners in a dance: The experience can be very exhilarating, but the dancers can also fall over each others' feet. Both parties carry a heavy responsibility for the interchange to work. To make this possible, they must be willing to listen and have respect for each other's point of view. This requires a certain amount of self-knowledge and a preparedness to reflect on their actions. Empathetic listening becomes a *sine qua non* to a real understanding of the leader-employee dialogue. Thus in spite of all the countervailing forces mentioned, in the end it is the relationship of equity, consistency, and trust that will make for frank interchange between leaders and employees and will constitute the strongest force in preventing regressive behavior in leadership. And given the nature of power in organizations, making this relationship work is the real challenge for all concerned.

On the Folly of Rewarding A, While Hoping for B

Steven Kerr

Whether dealing with monkeys, rats, or human beings, it is hardly controversial to state that most organisms seek information concerning what activities are rewarded, and then seek to do (or at least pretend to do) those things, often to the virtual exclusion of activities not rewarded. The extent to which this occurs of course will depend on the perceived attractiveness of the rewards offered, but neither operant nor expectancy theorists would quarrel with the essence of this notion.

Nevertheless, numerous examples exist of reward systems that are fouled up in that behaviors which are rewarded are those which the rewarder is trying to *discourage*, while the behavior he desires is not being rewarded at all.

In an effort to understand and explain this phenomenon, this paper presents examples from society, from organizations in general, and from profit making firms in particular.

SOCIETAL EXAMPLES

Politics

Official goals are "purposely vague and general and do not indicate . . . the host of decisions that must be made among alternative ways of achieving official goals and the priority of multiple goals . . ." (6, p. 66). They usually may be relied on to offend absolutely no one, and in this sense can be considered high acceptance, low quality goals. An example might be "build better schools." Operative goals are higher in quality but lower in acceptance, since they specify where the money will come from, what alternative goals will be ignored, etc.

The American citizenry supposedly wants its candidates for public office to set forth operative goals, making their proposed programs "perfectly clear," specifying sources and uses of funds, etc. However, since operative goals are lower in acceptance, and since aspirants to public office need acceptance (from at least 50.1 percent of the people), most politicians prefer to speak only of official goals, at least until after the election. They of course would agree to speak at the operative level if "punished" for not doing so. The electorate could do this by refusing to support candidates who do not speak at the operative level.

Instead, however, the American voter typically punishes (withholds support from) candidates who frankly discuss where the money will come from, rewards politicians who speak only of official goals, but hopes that candidates (despite the reward system) will discuss the issues operatively. It is academic whether it was moral for Nixon, for example, to refuse to discuss his "secret plan" to end the Vietnam war, his operative goals concerning the lifting of price controls, the reshuffling of his cabinet, etc. The point is that the reward system made such refusal rational.

It seems worth mentioning that no manuscript can adequately define what is "moral" and what is not. However, examination of costs and benefits, combined with knowledge of what motivates a particular individual, often will suffice to determine what for him is "rational."[1] If the reward system is so designed that it is irrational to be moral, this does not necessarily mean that immorality will result. But is this not asking for trouble?

War

If some oversimplification may be permitted, let it be assumed that the primary goal of the organization (Pentagon, Luftwaffe, or whatever) is to win. Let it be assumed further that the primary goal of most individuals on the front lines is to get home alive. Then there appears to be an important conflict in goals—personally rational behavior by those at the bottom will endanger goal attainment by those at the top.

But not necessarily! It depends on how the reward system is set up. The Vietnam war was indeed a study of disobedience and rebellion, with terms such as "fragging" (killing one's own commanding officer) and "search and evade" becoming part of the military vocabulary. The difference in subordinates' acceptance of authority between World War II and Vietnam is

---

1. In Simon's (8, pp. 76–77) terms, a decision is "subjectively rational" if it maximizes an individual's valued outcomes so far as his knowledge permits. A decision is "personally rational" if it is oriented toward the individual's goals.

reported to be considerable, and veterans of the Second World War often have been quoted as being outraged at the mutinous actions of many American soldiers in Vietnam.

Consider, however, some critical differences in the reward system in use during the two conflicts. What did the GI in World War II want? To go home. And when did he get to go home? When the war was won! If he disobeyed the orders to clean out the trenches and take the hills, the war would not be won and he would not go home. Furthermore, what were his chances of attaining his goal (getting home alive) if he obeyed the orders compared to his chances if he did not? What is being suggested is that the rational soldier in World War II, *whether patriotic or not*, probably found it expedient to obey.

Consider the reward system in use in Vietnam. What did the man at the bottom want? To go home. And when did he get to go home? When his tour of duty was over! This was the case *whether or not* the war was won. Furthermore, concerning the relative chance of getting home alive by obeying orders compared to the chance if they were disobeyed, it is worth noting that a mutineer in Vietnam was far more likely to be assigned rest and rehabilitation (on the assumption that fatigue was the cause) than he was to suffer any negative consequence.

In his description of the "zone of indifference," Barnard stated that "a person can and will accept a communication as authoritative only when . . . at the time of his decision, he believes it to be compatible with his personal interests as a whole" (1, p. 165). In light of the reward system used in Vietnam, would it not have been personally irrational for some orders to have been obeyed? Was not the military implementing a system which *rewarded* disobedience, while *hoping* that soldiers (despite the reward system) would obey orders?

Medicine

Theoretically, a physician can make either of two types of error, and intuitively one seems as bad as the other. A doctor can pronounce a patient sick when he is actually well, thus causing him needless anxiety and expense, curtailment of enjoyable foods and activities, and even physical danger by subjecting him to needless medication and surgery. Alternately, a doctor can label a sick person well, and thus avoid treating what may be a serious, even fatal ailment. It might be natural to conclude that physicians seek to minimize both types of error.

Such a conclusion would be wrong.[2] It is estimated that numerous Americans are presently afflicted with iatrogenic (physican *caused*) illnesses (7). This occurs when the doctor is approached by someone complaining of a few stray symptoms. The doctor classifies and organizes these symptoms, gives them a name, and obligingly tells the patient what further symptoms may be expected. This information often acts as a self-fulfilling prophecy, with the result that from that day on the patient for all practical purposes is sick.

Why does this happen? Why are physicians so reluctant to sustain a type 2 error (pronouncing a sick person well) that they will tolerate many type 1 errors? Again, a look at the reward system is needed. The punishments for a type 2 error are real: guilt, embarrassment, and the threat of lawsuit and scandal. On the other hand, a type 1 error (labeling a well person sick) "is sometimes seen as sound clinical practice, indicating a healthy conservative approach to medicine" (7, p. 69). Type 1 errors also are likely to generate increased income and a stream of steady customers who, being well in a limited physiological sense, will not embarrass the doctor by dying abruptly.

Fellow physicians and the general public therefore are really *rewarding* type 1 errors and at the same time *hoping* fervently that doctors will try not to make them.

GENERAL ORGANIZATIONAL EXAMPLES

Rehabilitation Centers and Orphanages

In terms of the prime beneficiary classification (2, p. 42) organizations such as these are supposed to exist for the "public-in-contact," that is, clients. The orphanage therefore theoretically is interested in placing as many children as possible in good homes. However, often orphanages surround themselves with so many rules concerning adoption that it is nearly impossible to pry a child out of the place. Orphanages may deny adoption unless the applicants are a married couple, both of the same religion as the child, without history of emotional or vocational instability, with a specified minimum income and a private room for the child, etc.

---

2. In one study (4) of 14,867 films for signs of tuberculosis, 1,216 positive readings turned out to be clinically negative; only 24 negative readings proved clinically active, a ratio of 50 to 1.

If the primary goal is to place children in good homes, then the rules ought to constitute means toward that goal. Goal displacement results when these "means become ends-in-themselves that displace the original goals" (2, p. 229).

To some extent these rules are required by law. But the influence of the reward system on the orphanage's management should not be ignored. Consider, for example, that the:

1. Number of children enrolled often is the most important determinant of the size of the allocated budget.
2. Number of children under the director's care also will affect the size of his staff.
3. Total organizational size will determine largely the director's prestige at the annual conventions, in the community, etc.

Therefore, to the extent that staff size, total budget, and personal prestige are valued by the orphanage's executive personnel, it becomes rational for them to make it difficult for children to be adopted. After all, who wants to be the director of the smallest orphanage in the state?

If the reward system errs in the opposite direction, paying off only for placements, extensive goal displacement again is likely to result. A common example of vocational rehabilitation in many states, for example, consists of placing someone in a job for which he has little interest and few qualifications, for two months or so, and then "rehabilitating" him again in another position. Such behavior is quite consistent with the prevailing reward system, which pays off for the number of individuals placed in any position for 60 days or more. Rehabilitation counselors also confess to competing with one another to place relatively skilled clients, sometimes ignoring persons with few skills who would be harder to place. Extensively disabled clients find that counselors often prefer to work with those whose disabilities are less severe.

Universities

Society *hopes* that teachers will not neglect their teaching responsibilities but *rewards* them almost entirely for research and publications. This is most true at the large and prestigious universities. Cliches such as "good research and good teaching go together" notwithstanding, professors often find that they must choose between teaching and research oriented activities when allocating their time. Rewards for good teaching usually are limited to outstanding teacher awards, which are given to only a small percentage of good teachers and which usually bestow little money and fleeting prestige. Punishments for poor teaching also are rare.

Rewards for research and publications, on the other hand, and punishments for failure to accomplish these, are commonly administered by universities at which teachers are employed. Furthermore, publication oriented resumés usually will be well received at other universities, whereas teaching credentials, harder to document and quantify, are much less transferable. Consequently it is rational for university teachers to concentrate on research, even if to the detriment of teaching and at the expense of their students.

By the same token, it is rational for students to act based upon the goal displacement which has occurred within universities concerning what they are rewarded for. If it is assumed that a primary goal of a university is to transfer knowledge from teacher to student, then grades become identifiable as a means toward that goal, serving as motivational, control, and feedback devices to expedite the knowledge transfer. Instead, however, the grades themselves have become much more important for entrance to graduate school, successful employment, tuition refunds, parental respect, etc., than the knowledge or lack of knowledge they are supposed to signify.

It therefore should come as no surprise that information has surfaced in recent years concerning fraternity files for examinations, term paper writing services, organized cheating at the service academies, and the like. Such activities constitute a personally rational response to a reward system which pays off for grades rather than knowledge.

BUSINESS RELATED EXAMPLES

Ecology

Assume that the president of XYZ Corporation is confronted with the following alternatives:

1. Spend $11 million for antipollution equipment to keep from poisoning fish in the river adjacent to the plant; or
2. Do nothing, in violation of the law, and assume a one-in-ten chance of being caught, with a resultant $1 million fine plus the necessity of buying the equipment.

Under this not unrealistic set of choices it requires no linear program to determine that XYZ Corporation can maximize its probabilities by flouting the law. Add the fact that XYZ's president is probably being rewarded (by creditors, stockholders, and other salient parts of his task environment) according to criteria totally unrelated to the number of fish poisoned, and his probable course of action becomes clear.

Evaluation of Training

It is axiomatic that those who care about a firm's well-being should insist that the organization get fair value for its expenditures. Yet it is commonly known that firms seldom bother to evaluate a new GRID, MBO, job enrichment program, or whatever, to see if the company is getting its money's worth. Why? Certainly it is not because people have not pointed out that this situation exists; numerous practitioner-oriented articles are written each year to just this point.

The individuals (whether in personnel, manpower planning, or wherever) who normally would be responsible for conducting such evaluations are the same ones often charged with introducing the change effort in the first place. Having convinced top management to spend the money, they usually are quite animated afterwards in collecting arigorous vignettes and anecdotes about how successful the program was. The last thing many desire is a formal, systematic, and revealing evaluation. Although members of top management may actually *hope* for such systematic evaluation, their reward systems continue to *reward* ignorance in this area. And if the personnel department abdicates its responsibility, who is to step into the breach? The change agent himself? Hardly! He is likely to be too busy collecting anecdotal "evidence" of his own, for use with his next client.

Miscellaneous

Many additional examples could be cited of systems which in fact are rewarding behaviors other than those supposedly desired by the rewarder. A few of these are described briefly below.

Most coaches disdain to discuss individual accomplishments, preferring to speak of teamwork, proper attitude, and a one-for-all spirit. Usually, however, rewards are distributed according to individual performance. The college basketball player who feeds his teammates instead of shooting will not compile impressive scoring statistics and is less likely to be drafted by the pros. The ballplayer who hits to right field to advance the runners will win neither the batting nor home run titles, and will be offered smaller raises. It therefore is rational for players to think of themselves first, and the team second.

In business organizations where rewards are dispensed for unit performance or for individual goals achieved, without regard for overall effectiveness, similar attitudes often are observed. Under most Management by Objectives (MBO) systems, goals in areas where quantification is difficult often go unspecified. The organization therefore often is in a position where it *hopes* for employee effort in the areas of team building, interpersonal relations, creativity, etc., but it formally *rewards* none of these. In cases where promotions and raises are formally tied to MBO, the system itself contains a paradox in that it "asks employees to set challenging, risky goals, only to face smaller paychecks and possibly damaged careers if these goals are not accomplished" (5, p. 40).

It is *hoped* that administrators will pay attention to long-run costs and opportunities and will institute programs which will bear fruit later on. However, many organizational reward systems pay off for short-run sales and earnings only. Under such circumstances it is personally rational for officials to sacrifice long-term growth and profit (by selling off equipment and property, or by stifling research and development) for short-term advantages. This probably is most pertinent in the public sector, with the result that many public officials are unwilling to implement programs which will not show benefits by election time.

As a final, clear-cut example of a fouled-up reward system, consider the cost-plus contract or its next of kin, the allocation of next year's budget as a direct function of this year's expenditures. It probably is conceivable that those who award such budgets and contracts really hope for economy and prudence in spending. It is obvious, however, that adopting the proverb "to him who spends shall more be given," rewards not economy, but spending itself.

CONCLUSIONS

Modern organization theory requires a recognition that the members of organizations and society possess divergent goals and motives. It therefore is unlikely that managers and their subordinates will seek the same outcomes. Three possible remedies for this potential problem are suggested.

Selection

It is theoretically possible for organizations to employ only those individuals whose goals and motives are wholly consonant with those of management. In such cases the same behaviors judged by subordinates to be rational would be perceived by management as desirable. State-of-the-art reviews of selection techniques, however, provide scant grounds for hope that such an approach would be successful (for example, see Ref. 10).

Training

Another theoretical alternative is for the organization to admit those employees whose goals are not consonant with those of management and then, through training, socialization, or whatever, alter employee goals to make them consonant. However, research on the effectiveness of such training programs, though limited, provides further grounds for pessimism (for example, see Ref. 3).

Altering the Reward System

What would have been the result if:

1. Nixon had been assured by his advisors that he could not win reelection except by discussing the issues in detail?
2. Physicians' conduct was subjected to regular examination by review boards for type 1 errors (calling healthy people ill) and to penalties (fines, censure, etc.) for errors of either type?
3. The President of XYZ Corporation had to choose between (a) spending 11 million dollars for antipollution equipment, and (b) incurring a fifty-fifty chance of going to jail for five years?

Managers who complain that their workers are not motivated might do well to consider the possibility that they have installed reward systems which are paying off for behaviors other than those they are seeking. This, in part, is what happened in Vietnam, and this is what regularly frustrates societal efforts to bring about honest politicians, civic-minded managers, etc.

A first step for such managers might be to find out what behaviors currently are being rewarded. In fact, such undesirable behavior by organizational members as they have observed may be explained largely by the reward systems in use.

This is not to say that all organizational behavior is determined by formal rewards and punishments. Certainly it is true that in the absence of formal reinforcement some soldiers will be patriotic, some presidents will be ecology minded, and some orphanage directors will care about children. The point, however, is that in such cases the rewarder is not *causing* the behaviors desired but is only a fortunate bystander. For an organization to *act* upon its members, the formal reward system should positively reinforce desired behaviors, not constitute an obstacle to be overcome.

It might be wise to underscore the obvious fact that there is nothing really new in what has been said. In both theory and practice these matters have been mentioned before. Thus, in many states Good Samaritan laws have been installed to protect doctors who stop to assist a stricken motorist. In states without such laws it is commonplace for doctors to refuse to stop, for fear of involvement in a subsequent lawsuit. In college basketball additional penalties have been instituted against players who foul their opponents deliberately. It has long been argued by Milton Friedman and others that penalties should be altered so as to make it irrational to disobey the ecology laws, and so on.

By altering the reward system the organization escapes the necessity of selecting only desirable people or of trying to alter undesirable ones. In Skinnerian terms (as described in 9, p. 704), "As for responsibility and goodness—as commonly defined—no one . . . would want or need them. They refer to a man's behaving well despite the absence of positive reinforcement that is obviously sufficient to explain it. Where such reinforcement exists, 'no one needs goodness.'"

REFERENCES

1. Barnard, Chester I. *The Functions of the Executive* (Cambridge, Mass.: Harvard University Press, 1964).
2. Blau, Peter M., and W. Richard Scott. *Formal Organizations* (San Francisco: Chandler, 1962).
3. Fiedler, Fred E. "Predicting the Effects of Leadership Training and Experience from the Contingency Model," *Journal of Applied Psychology,* Vol. 56 (1972), 114–119.
4. Garland, L. H. "Studies of the Accuracy of Diagnostic Procedures," *American Journal of Roentgenological, Radium Therapy, and Nuclear Medicine,* Vol. 82 (1959), 25–38.

5. Kerr, Steven. "Some Modifications in MBO as an OD Strategy," *Academy of Management Proceedings,* 1973, pp. 39-42.

6. Perrow, Charles. "The Analysis of Goals in Complex Organizations," in A. Etzioni (Ed.), *Readings on Modern Organizations* (Englewood Cliffs, N.J.: Prentice-Hall, 1969).

7. Scheff, Thomas J. "Decision Rules, Types of Error, and Their Consequences in Medical Diagnosis," in F. Massarik and P. Ratoosh (Eds.), *Mathematical Explorations in Behavioral Science* (Homewood, Ill.: Irwin, 1965).

8. Simon, Herbert A. *Administrative Behavior* (New York: Free Press, 1957).

9. Swanson, G. E. "Review Symposium: Beyond Freedom and Dignity," *American Journal of Sociology,* Vol. 78 (1972), 702–705.

10. Webster, E. *Decision Making in the Employment Interview* (Montreal: Industrial Relations Center, McGill University, 1964).

PART IV

Models of Leadership

Being in politics is like being a football coach, you have to be smart enough to understand the game, and dumb enough to think it's important.

Eugene McCarthy

We have, I fear, confused power with greatness.

Stuart Udall

To be clever enough to gain real power over others, one must be dumb enough to want it.

G. K. Chesterton

Rank times IQ equals a mathematical constant.

Anonymous

This section overviews some of the major models of leadership that have been developed during the past several decades. Path-goal theory, by Robert House and Terence Mitchell, suggests that a manager's behavior is motivating to the extent that the behavior increases a subordinate's goal attainment and helps to clarify the paths to these goals. The next article, "Are You *In* or *Out* with Your Boss?" reviews an approach created by George Graen. This approach contends that each subordinate develops a unique working relationship with the leader, and the varying quality of these relationships influences individual responses to work, such as individual motivation and individual emotional reactions. This approach is quite distinct from early views of leadership as it argues for examining leadership as a dyadic process (i.e., between two people), rather than as a group-wide process. The following article, by Victor Vroom of Yale University, demonstrates that the ideal type of leader style depends on aspects of the situation and offers a model for understanding the requirements of a situation, including ways to modify one's style to satisfy these requirements. Robert Sternberg of Tufts University presents a three-part theory of managerial intelligence that is intuitively appealing and supported by data. His theory is gaining attention from academics and practitioners, in part because of its suggestion that the early trait approach to studying leadership may have some merit if suitably modified to take account of job demands and a more refined understanding of mental abilities. The article by Bernard Bass asks us to consider the topic of charismatic leadership, by offering terms and a framework for analyzing the potential influence of charisma on leader effectiveness.

The role of situational influences is examined in the final two readings of this section. The first, by Robert Vecchio, investigates the validity of one of the more popular models used in today's leadership training programs and suggests that the model may require some modification. Next, Roya Ayman, Martin Chemers, and Fred Fiedler review the research literature that relates to the Contingency Model of Leadership. The model has had a stormy history and has been the subject of substantial debate. Nonetheless, the model is worth some consideration because of the related effort to better understand how the situation in which a person operates as head may dictate the appropriate style of leadership.

Path-Goal Theory of Leadership

Robert J. House and Terence R. Mitchell

The path-goal approach has its roots in a more general motivational theory called expectancy theory.[1] Briefly, expectancy theory states that an individual's attitudes (e.g., satisfaction with supervision or job satisfaction) or behavior (e.g., leader behavior or job effort) can be predicted from: (1) the degree to which the job, or behavior, is seen as leading to various outcomes (expectancy) and (2) the evaluation of these outcomes (valences). Thus, people are satisfied with their job if they think it leads to things that are highly valued, and they work hard if they believe that effort leads to things that are highly valued. This type of theoretical rationale can be used to predict a variety of phenomena related to leadership, such as why leaders behave the way they do, or how leader behavior influences subordinate motivation.[2]

This latter approach is the primary concern of this article. The implication for leadership is that subordinates are motivated by leader behavior to the extent that this behavior influences expectancies (e.g., goal paths) and valences (e.g., goal attractiveness).

Several writers have advanced specific hypotheses concerning how the leader affects the paths and the goals of subordinates.[3] These writers focused on two issues: (1) how the leader affects subordinates' expectations that effort will lead to effective performance and valued rewards, and (2) how this expectation affects motivation to work hard and perform well.

While the state of theorizing about leadership in terms of subordinates' paths and goals is in its infancy, we believe it is promising for two reasons. First, it suggests effects of leader behavior that have not yet been investigated but which appear to be fruitful areas of inquiry. And, second, it suggests with some precision the situational factors on which the effects of leader behavior are contingent.

The initial theoretical work by Evans asserts that leaders will be effective by making rewards available to subordinates and by making these rewards contingent on the subordinate's accomplishment of specific goals.[4] Evans argued that one of the strategic functions of the leader is to clarify for subordinates the kind of behavior that leads to goal accomplishment and valued rewards. This function might be referred to as path clarification. Evans also argued that the leader increases the rewards available to subordinates by being supportive toward subordinates, i.e., by being concerned about their status, welfare, and comfort. Leader supportiveness is in itself a reward that the leader has at his or her disposal, and the judicious use of this reward increases the motivation of subordinates.

Evans studied the relationship between the behavior of leaders and the subordinates' expectations that effort leads to rewards and also studied the resulting impact on ratings of the subordinates' performance. He found that when subordinates viewed leaders as being supportive (considerate of their needs) and when these superiors provided directions and guidance to the subordinates, there was a positive relationship between leader behavior and subordinates' performance ratings.

However, leader behavior was only related to subordinates' performance when the leader's behavior also was related to the subordinates' expectations that their effort would result in desired rewards. Thus, Evans' findings suggest that the major impact of a leader on the performance of subordinates is clarifying the path to desired rewards and making such rewards contingent on effective performance.

Stimulated by this line of reasoning, House, and House and Dessler advanced a more complex theory of the effects of leader behavior on the motivation of subordinates.[5] The theory intends to explain the effects of four specific kinds of leader behavior on the following three subordinate attitudes or expectations: (1) the satisfaction of subordinates, (2) the subordinates' acceptance of the leader and (3) the expectations of subordinates that effort will result in effective performance and that effective performance is the path to rewards. The four kinds of leader behavior included in the theory are: (1) directive leadership, (2) supportive leadership, (3) participative leadership and (4) achievement-oriented leadership. Directive leadership is characterized by a leader who lets subordinates know what is expected of them, gives specific guidance as to what should be done and how it should be done, makes his or her part in the group understood, schedules work to be done, maintains definite standards of performance, and asks that group members follow standard rules and regulations. Supportive leadership is characterized by a friendly and approachable leader who shows concern for the status, well-being, and needs of subordinates. Such a leader does little things to make the work more pleasant, treats members as equals, and is friendly and approachable. Participative leadership is characterized by a leader who consults with subordinates, solicits their suggestions, and takes these suggestions seriously into consideration before making a decision. An achievement-oriented leader sets challenging goals, expects subordinates to perform at their highest level, continuously seeks improvement in performance *and* shows a high degree of confidence that the subordinates will assume responsibility, put forth effort, and accomplish challenging goals. This kind of leader constantly emphasizes excellence in performance and simultaneously displays confidence that subordinates will meet high standards of excellence.

A number of studies suggest that these different leadership styles can be shown by the same leader in various situations.[6] For example, a leader may show directiveness toward subordinates in some instances and be participative or supportive in other instances.[7] Thus, the traditional method of characterizing a leader as either highly participative and supportive or highly directive is invalid; rather, it can be concluded that leaders vary in the particular fashion employed for supervising their subordinates. Also, the theory, in its present stage, is a tentative explanation of the effects of leader behavior—it is incomplete because it does not explain other kinds of leader behavior and does not explain the effects of the leader on factors other than subordinate acceptance, satisfaction, and expectations. However, the theory is stated so that additional variables may be included in it as new knowledge is made available.

PATH-GOAL THEORY

General Propositions

The first proposition of path-goal theory is that leader behavior is acceptable and satisfying to subordinates to the extent that the subordinates see such behavior as either an immediate source of satisfaction or as instrumental to future satisfaction.

The second proposition of this theory is that the leader's behavior will be motivational, i.e., increase effort, to the extent that (1) such behavior makes satisfaction of subordinates' needs contingent on effective performance and (2) such behavior complements the environment of subordinates by providing the coaching, guidance, support, and rewards necessary for effective performance.

These two propositions suggest that the leader's strategic functions are to enhance subordinates' motivation to perform, satisfaction with the job, and acceptance of the leader. From previous research on expectancy theory of motivation, it can be inferred that the strategic functions of the leader consist of: (1) recognizing and/or arousing subordinates' needs for outcomes over which the leader has some control, (2) increasing personal payoffs to subordinates for work-goal attainment, (3) making the path to those payoffs easier to travel by coaching and direction, (4) helping subordinates clarify expectancies, (5) reducing frustrating barriers and (6) increasing the opportunities for personal satisfaction contingent on effective performance.

Stated less formally, the motivational functions of the leader consist of increasing the number and kinds of personal payoffs to subordinates for work-goal attainment and making paths to these payoffs easier to travel by clarifying the paths, reducing road blocks and pitfalls, and increasing the opportunities for personal satisfaction en route.

Contingency Factors

Two classes of situational variables are asserted to be contingency factors. A contingency factor is a variable which moderates the relationship between two other variables such as leader behavior and subordinate satisfaction. For example, we might suggest that the degree of structure in the task moderates the relationship between leaders' directive behavior and subordinates' job satisfaction. Figure 1 shows how such a relationship might look. Thus, subordinates are satisfied with directive behavior in an unstructured task and are satisfied with nondirective behavior in a structured task. Therefore, we say that the relationship between leader directiveness and subordinate satisfaction is contingent upon the structure of the task.

The two contingency variables are *(a)* personal characteristics of the subordinates and *(b)* the environmental pressures and demands with which subordinates must cope in order to accomplish the work goals and to satisfy their needs. While other situational factors also may operate to determine the effects of leader behavior, they are not presently known.

With respect to the first class of contingency factors, the characteristics of subordinates, path-goal theory asserts that leader behavior will be acceptable to subordinates to the extent that the subordinates see such behavior as either an immediate source of satisfaction or as instrumental to future satisfaction. Subordinates' characteristics are hypothesized to determine this perception partially. For example, Runyon[8] and Mitchell[9] show that the subordinate's score on a measure called Locus of Control moder-

Figure 1
Hypothetical Relationship Between Directive Leadership and
Subordinate Satisfaction with Task Structure as a Contingency Factor

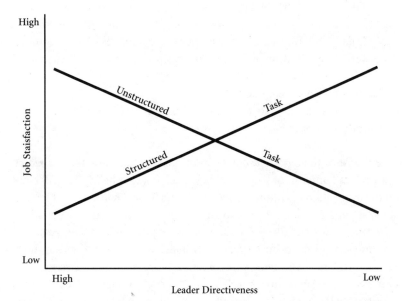

ates the relationship between participative leadership style and subordinate satisfaction. The Locus of Control measure reflects the degree to which an individual sees the environment as systematically responding to his or her behavior. People who believe that what happens to them occurs because of their behavior are called internals; people who believe that what happens to them occurs because of luck or chance are called externals. Mitchell's findings suggest that internals are more satisfied with a participative leadership style and externals are more satisfied with a directive style.

A second characteristic of subordinates on which the effects of leader behavior are contingent is subordinates' perception of their own ability with respect to their assigned tasks. The higher the degree of perceived ability relative to task demands, the less the subordinate will view leader directiveness and coaching behavior as acceptable. Where the subordinate's perceived ability is high, such behavior is likely to have little positive effect on the motivation of the subordinate and to be perceived as excessively close control. Thus, the acceptability of the leader's behavior is determined in part by the characteristics of the subordinates.

The second aspect of the situation, the environment of the subordinate, consists of those factors that are not within the control of the subordinate but which are important to need satisfaction or to ability to perform effectively. The theory asserts that effects of the leader's behavior on the psychological states of subordinates are contingent on other parts of the subordinates' environment that are relevant to subordinate motivation. Three broad classifications of contingency factors in the environment are:

The subordinates' tasks.
The formal authority system of the organization.
The primary work group.

Assessment of the environmental conditions makes it possible to predict the kind and amount of influence that specific leader behaviors will have on the motivation of subordinates. Any of the three environmental factors could act upon the subordinate in any of three ways: first, to serve as stimuli that motivate and direct the subordinate to perform necessary task operations; second, to constrain variability in behavior. Constraints may help the subordinate by clarifying expectancies that effort leads to rewards or by preventing the subordinate from experiencing conflict and confusion. Constraints also may be counterproductive to the extent that they restrict initiative or prevent increases in effort from being associated positively with rewards. Third, environmental factors may serve as rewards for achieving desired performance, e.g., it is possible for the subordinate to receive the necessary cues to do the job and the needed rewards for satisfaction from sources other than the leader, e.g., coworkers in the primary work group. Thus, the effect of the leader on subordinates' motivation will be a function of how deficient the environment is with respect to motivational stimuli, constraints, or rewards.

With respect to the environment, path-goal theory asserts that when goals and paths to desired goals are apparent because of the routine nature of the task, clear group norms or objective controls of the formal authority systems, attempts by the leader to clarify paths and goals will be both redundant and seen by subordinates as imposing unnecessary, close control. Although such control may increase performance by preventing soldiering or malingering, it also will result in decreased satisfaction (see Figure 1). Also with respect to the work environment, the theory asserts that the more dissatisfying the task, the more the subordinates will resent leader behavior directed at increasing productivity or enforcing compliance to organizational rules and procedures.

Finally, with respect to environmental variables the theory states that leader behavior will be motivational to the extent that it helps subordinates cope with environmental uncertainties, threats from others or sources of frustration. Such leader behavior is predicted to increase subordinates' satisfaction with the job context and to be motivational to the extent that it increases the subordinates' expectations that their effort will lead to valued rewards.

These propositions and specification of situational contingencies provide a heuristic framework on which to base future research. Hopefully, this will lead to a more fully developed, explicitly formal theory of leadership.

Figure 2 presents a summary of the theory. It is hoped that these propositions, while admittedly tentative, will provide managers with some insights concerning the effects of their own leader behavior and that of others.

EMPIRICAL SUPPORT

The theory has been tested in a limited number of studies which have generated considerable empirical support for our ideas and also suggest areas in which the theory requires revision. A brief review of these studies follows.

Figure 2
Summary of Path-Goal Relationships

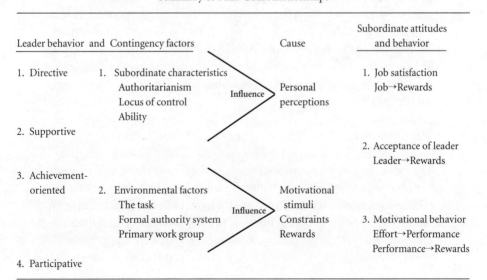

Leader Directiveness

Leader directiveness has a positive correlation with satisfaction and expectancies of subordinates who are engaged in ambiguous tasks and has a negative correlation with satisfaction and expectancies of subordinates engaged in clear tasks. These findings were predicted by the theory and have been replicated in seven organizations. They suggest that when task demands are ambiguous or when the organization procedures, rules, and policies are not clear, a leader behaving in a directive manner complements the tasks and the organization by providing the necessary guidance and psychological structure for subordinates.[10] However, when task demands are clear to subordinates, leader directiveness is seen more as a hindrance.

However, other studies have failed to confirm these findings.[11] A study by Dessler[12] suggests a resolution to these conflicting findings—he found that for subordinates at the lower organizational levels of a manufacturing firm who were doing routine, repetitive, unambiguous tasks, directive leadership was preferred by closed-minded, dogmatic, authoritarian subordinates and nondirective leadership was preferred by nonauthoritarian, open-minded subordinates. However, for subordinates at higher organizational levels doing nonroutine, ambiguous tasks, directive leadership was preferred for both authoritarian and nonauthoritarian subordinates. Thus, Dessler found that two contingency factors appear to operate simultaneously: subordinate task ambiguity and degree of subordinate authoritarianism. When measured in combination, the findings are as predicted by the theory; however, when the subordinate's personality is not taken into account, task ambiguity does not always operate as a contingency variable as predicted by the theory. House, Burill, and Dessler recently found a similar interaction between subordinate authoritarianism and task ambiguity in a second manufacturing firm, thus adding confidence in Dessler's original findings.[13]

Supportive Leadership

The theory hypothesizes that supportive leadership will have its most positive effect on subordinate satisfaction for subordinates who work on stressful, frustrating, or dissatisfying tasks. This hypothesis has been tested in 10 samples of employees,[14] and in only one of these studies was the hypothesis disconfirmed.[15] Despite some inconsistency in research on supportive leadership, the evidence is sufficiently positive to suggest that managers should be alert to the critical need for supportive leadership under conditions where tasks are dissatisfying, frustrating, or stressful to subordinates.

Achievement-Oriented Leadership

The theory hypothesizes that achievement-oriented leadership will cause subordinates to strive for higher standards of performance and to have more confidence in the ability to meet challenging goals. A recent study by House, Valency, and Van der Krabben provides a partial test of this hypothesis among white-collar employees in service organizations.[16] For subordinates performing ambiguous, nonrepetitive tasks, they found a positive relationship between the amount of achievement orientation of the leader and subordinates' expectancy that their effort would result in effective performance. Stated less technically, for subordinates performing ambiguous, nonrepetitive tasks, the higher the achievement orientation of the leader, the more the subordinates were confident that their efforts would pay off in effective performance. For subordinates performing moderately unambiguous, repetitive tasks, there was no significant relationship between achievement-oriented leadership and subordinate expectancies that their effort would lead to effective performance. This finding held in four separate organizations.

Two plausible interpretations may be used to explain these data. First, people who select ambiguous, nonrepetitive tasks may be different in personality from those who select a repetitive job and may, therefore, be more responsive to an achievement-oriented leader. A second explanation is that achievement orientation only affects expectancies in ambiguous situations because there is more flexibility and autonomy in such tasks. Therefore, subordinates in such tasks are more likely to be able to change in response to such leadership style. Neither of the above interpretations have been tested to date; however, additional research is currently under way to investigate these relationships.

Participative Leadership

In theorizing about the effects of participative leadership, it is necessary to ask about the specific characteristics of both the subordinates and their situation that would cause participative leadership to be viewed as satisfying and instrumental to effective performance.

Mitchell recently described at least four ways in which a participative leadership style would impact on subordinate attitudes and behavior as predicted by expectancy theory.[17] First, a participative climate should increase the clarity of organizational contingencies. Through participation in decision making, subordinates should learn what leads to what. From a path-goal viewpoint participation would lead to greater clarity of the paths to various goals. A second impact of participation would be that subordinates, hopefully, should select goals they highly value. If one participates in decisions about various goals, it makes sense that this individual would select goals he or she wants. Thus, participation would increase the correspondence between organization and subordinate goals. Third, we can see how participation would increase the control the individual has over what happens on the job. If our motivation is higher (based on the preceding two points), then having greater autonomy and ability to carry out our intentions should lead to increased effort and performance. Finally, under a participative system, pressure towards high performance should come from sources other than the leader or the organization. More specifically, when people participate in the decision process, they become more ego-involved; the decisions made are in some part their own. Also, their peers know what is expected and the social pressure has a greater impact. Thus, motivation to perform well stems from internal and social factors as well as formal external ones.

A number of investigations prior to the above formulation supported the idea that participation appears to be helpful,[18] and Mitchell presents a number of recent studies that support the above four points.[19] However, it is also true that we would expect the relationship between a participative style and subordinate behavior to be moderated by both the personality characteristics of the subordinate and the situational demands. Studies by Tannenbaum and Allport and Vroom have shown that subordinates who prefer autonomy and self-control respond more positively to participative leadership in terms of both satisfaction and performance than subordinates who do not have such preferences.[20] Also, the studies mentioned by Runyon[21] and Mitchell[22] showed that subordinates who were external in orientation were less satisfied with a participative style of leadership than were internal subordinates.

House also has reviewed these studies in an attempt to explain the ways in which the situation or environment moderates the relationship between participation and subordinate attitudes and behavior.[23] His analysis suggests that where participative leadership is positively related to satisfaction, regardless of the predispositions of subordinates, the tasks of the subjects appear to be ambiguous and ego-involving. In the studies in which the subjects' personalities or predispositions moderate the effect of participative leadership, the tasks of the subjects are inferred to be highly routine and/or nonego-involving.

House reasoned from this analysis that the task may have an overriding effect on the relationship between leader participation and subordinate responses, and that individual predispositions or personality characteristics of subordinates may have an effect only under some tasks. It was assumed that when task demands are ambiguous, subordinates will have a need to reduce the ambiguity. Further, it was assumed that when task demands are ambiguous, participative problem solving between the leader and the subordinate will result in more effective decisions than when the task demands are unambiguous. Finally, it was assumed that when the subordinates are ego-involved in their tasks they are more likely to want to have a say in the decisions that affect them. Given these assumptions, the following hypotheses were formulated to account for the conflicting findings reviewed above:

When subjects are highly ego-involved in a decision or a task and the decision or task demands are ambiguous, participative leadership will have a positive effect on the satisfaction and motivation of the subordinate, *regardless* of the subordinate's predisposition toward self-control, authoritarianism, or need for independence.

When subordinates are not ego-involved in their tasks and when task demands are clear, subordinates who are not authoritarian and who have high needs for independence and self-control will respond favorably to leader participation and their opposite personality types will respond less favorably.

These hypotheses were derived on the basis of path-goal theorizing, i.e., the rationale guiding the analysis of prior studies was that both task characteristics and characteristics of subordinates interact to determine the effect of a specific kind of leader behavior on the satisfaction, expectancies, and performance of subordinates. To date, one major investigation has supported some of these predictions[24] in which personality variables, amount of participative leadership, task ambiguity, and job satisfaction were assessed for 324 employees of an industrial manufacturing organization. As expected, in nonrepetitive, ego-involving tasks, employees (regardless of their personality) were more satisfied under a participative style than a nonparticipative style. However, in repetitive tasks which were less ego-involving, the amount of authoritarianism of subordinates moderated the relationship between leadership style and satisfaction. Specifically, low authoritarian subordinates were *more satisfied* under a participative style.

These findings are exactly as the theory would predict; thus, it has promise in reconciling a set of confusing and contradictory findings with respect to participative leadership.

SUMMARY AND CONCLUSIONS

We have attempted to describe what we believe is a useful theoretical framework for understanding the effect of leadership behavior on subordinate satisfaction and motivation. Most theorists today have moved away from the simplistic notions that all effective leaders have a certain set of personality traits or that the situation completely determines performance. Some researchers have presented rather complex attempts at matching certain types of leaders with certain types of situations . . . But, we believe that a path-goal approach goes one step further. It not only suggests what type of style may be most effective in a given situation—it also attempts to explain *why* it is most effective.

We are optimistic about the future outlook of leadership research. With the guidance of path-goal theorizing, future research is expected to unravel many confusing puzzles about the reasons for and effects of leader behavior that have, heretofore, not been solved. However, we add a word of caution: the theory, and the research on it, are relatively new to the literature of organizational behavior. Consequently, path-goal theory is offered more as a tool for directing research and stimulating insight than as a proven guide for managerial action.

REFERENCES

1. T. R. Mitchell, "Expectancy Model of Job Satisfaction, Occupational Preference and Effort: A Theoretical, Methodological and Empirical Appraisal," *Psychological Bulletin* (1974).
2. D. M. Nebeker and T. R. Mitchell, "Leader Behavior: An Expectancy Theory Approach," *Organization Behavior and Human Performance,* 11(1974): 355–67.
3. M. G. Evans, "The Effects of Supervisory Behavior on the Path-Goal Relationship," *Organization Behavior and Human Performance,* 55(1970): 277–98; T. H. Hammer and H. T. Dachler, "The Process of Supervision in the Context of Motivation Theory," Research Report no. 3 (University of Maryland, 1973); F. Dansereau, Jr., J. Cashman, and G. Graen, "Instrumentality Theory and Equity Theory as Complementary Approaches in Predicting the Relationship of Leadership and Turnover among Managers," *Organization Behavior and Human Per-*

formance, 10(1973): 184–200; R. J. House, "A Path-Goal Theory of Leader Effectiveness," *Administrative Science Quarterly*, 16, 3(September 1971): 321–38; T. R. Mitchell, "Motivation and Participation: An Integration," *Academy of Management Journal*, 16, 4(1973): 160–79; G. Graen, F. Dansereau, Jr., and T. Minami, "Dysfunctional Leadership Styles," *Organization Behavior and Human Performance*, 7(1972): 216–36; G. Graen, F. Dansereau, Jr., and T. Minami, "An Empirical Test of the Man-in-the-Middle Hypothesis among Executives in a Hierarchical Organization Employing a Unit Analysis," *Organization Behavior and Human Performance*, 8(1972): 262–85; R. J. House and G. Dessler, "The Path-Goal Theory of Leadership: Some Post Hoc and A Priori Tests," to appear in J. G. Hunt, ed, *Contingency Approaches to Leadership* (Carbondale, Ill.: Southern Illinois University Press, 1974).

4. M. G. Evans, "Effects of Supervisory Behavior"; M. G. Evans, "Extensions of a Path-Goal Theory of Motivation," *Journal of Applied Psychology*, 59 (1974): 172–78.

5. R. J. House, "A Path-Goal Theory"; R. J. House and G. Dessler, "Path-Goal Theory of Leadership."

6. R. J. House and G. Dessler, "Path-Goal Theory of Leadership"; R. M. Stogdill, *Managers, Employees, Organization* (Ohio State University, Bureau of Business Research, 1965); R. J. House, A. Valency, and R. Van der Krabben, "Some Tests and Extensions of the Path-Goal Theory of Leadership" (in preparation).

7. W. A. Hill and D. Hughes, "Variations in Leader Behavior as a Function of Task Type," *Organization Behavior and Human Performance*, 11, 1(1974): 83–96.

8. K. E. Runyon, "Some Interactions between Personality Variables and Management Styles," *Journal of Applied Psychology*, 57, 3(1973): 288–94; T. R. Mitchell, C. R. Smyser, and S. E. Weed, "Locus of Control: Supervision and Work Satisfaction," *Academy of Management Journal*, 18, 3(1975): 623–31.

9. T. R. Mitchell, "Locus of Control."

10. R. J. House, "A Path-Goal Theory"; R. J. House and G. Dessler, "Path-Goal Theory of Leadership"; A. D. Szalagyi and H. P. Sims, "An Exploration of the Path-Goal Theory of Leadership in a Health Care Environment," *Academy of Management Journal* (in press); J. D. Dermer, "Supervisory Behavior and Budget Motivation" (Cambridge, Mass.: unpublished, MIT, Sloan School of Management, 1974); R. W. Smetana, "The Relationship between Managerial Behavior and Subordinate Attitudes and Motivation: A Contribution to a Behavioral Theory of Leadership" (Ph.D. dissertation, Wayne State University, 1974).

11. S. E. Weed, T. R. Mitchell, and C. R. Smyser, "A Test of House's Path-Goal Theory of Leadership in an Organizational Setting" (paper presented at Western Psychological Assn., 1974); J. D. Dermer and J. P. Siegel, "A Test of Path-Goal Theory: Disconfirming Evidence and a Critique" (unpublished, University of Toronto, Faculty of Management Studies, 1973); R. S. Schuler, "A Path-Goal Theory of Leadership: An Empirical Investigation" (Ph.D. dissertation, Michigan State University, 1973); H. K. Downey, J. E. Sheridan, and J. W. Slocum, Jr., "Analysis of Relationships among Leader Behavior, Subordinate Job Performance and Satisfaction: A Path-Goal Approach" (unpublished mimeograph, 1974); J. E. Stinson and T. W. Johnson, "The Path-Goal Theory of Leadership: A Partial Test and

Suggested Refinement," *Proceedings* (Kent, Ohio: 7th Annual Conference of the Midwest Academy of Management, April 1974): 18–36.

12. G. Dessler, "An Investigation of the Path-Goal Theory of Leadership" (Ph.D. dissertation, City University of New York, Bernard M. Baruch College, 1973).

13. R. J. House, D. Burrill, and G. Dessler, "Tests and Extensions of Path-Goal Theory of Leadership, I" (unpublished, in process).

14. R. J. House, "A Path-Goal Theory"; R. J. House and G. Dessler, "Path-Goal Theory of Leadership"; A. D. Szalagyi and H. P. Sims, "Exploration of Path-Goal"; J. E. Stinson and T. W. Johnson, *Proceedings;* R. S. Schuler, "Path-Goal: Investigation"; H. K. Downey, J. E. Sheridan, and J. W. Slocum, Jr., "Analysis of Relationships"; S. E. Weed, T. R. Mitchell, and C. R. Smyser, "Test of House's Path-Goal."

15. A. D. Szalagyi and H. P. Sims, "Exploration of Path-Goal."

16. R. J. House, A. Valency, and R. Van der Krabben, "Tests and Extensions of Path-Goal Theory of Leadership, II" (unpublished, in process).

17. T. R. Mitchell, "Motivation and Participation."

18. H. Tosi, "A Reexamination of Personality as a Determinant of the Effects of Participation," *Personnel Psychology,* 23(1970): 91–99; J. Sadler "Leadership Style, Confidence in Management and Job Satisfaction," *Journal of Applied Behavioral Sciences,* 6(1970): 3–19; K. N. Wexley, J. P. Singh, and G. A. Yukl, "Subordinate Personality as a Moderator of the Effects of Participation in Three Types of Appraisal Interviews," *Journal of Applied Psychology,* 83 1(1973): 54–59.

19. T. R. Mitchell, "Motivation and Participation."

20. A. S. Tannebaum and F. H. Allport, "Personality Structure and Group Structure: An Interpretive Study of Their Relationship through an Event-Structure Hypothesis," *Journal of Abnormal and Social Psychology,* 53(1956): 272–80; V. H. Vroom, "Some Personality Determinants of the Effects of Participation," *Journal of Abnormal and Social Psychology,* 59(1959): 322–27

21. K. E. Runyon, "Some Interactions between Personality Variables and Management Styles," *Journal of Applied Psychology,* 57, 3(1973): 288–94.

22. T. R. Mitchell, C. R. Smyser, and S. E. Weed, "Locus of Control."

23. R. J. House, "Notes on the Path-Goal Theory of Leadership" (University of Toronto, Faculty of Management Studies, May 1974).

24. R. S. Schuler, "Leader Participation, Task Structure, and Subordinate Authoritarianism" (unpublished mimeograph, Cleveland State University, 1974).

Are You *In* or *Out* with Your Boss?

Robert P. Vecchio

At one time or another, each of us has had the feeling of being relatively *in* or *out* with an immediate supervisor. Perhaps more than anything else, the sense of being accepted or rejected by your boss makes or breaks your confidence. The tendency of supervisors to divide their subordinates into in-group members and out-group members is only beginning to be understood. Researchers are reporting insights that are important to both supervisor and subordinate.[1]

Until recently, the literature on how to be an effective manager has argued that there is one appropriate style of management for most situations, or that there is a best style for any given specific situation. Regardless of the theory of supervision you consider, it is generally assumed that a manager can and does display a uniform style of supervision toward all subordinates.

However, this assumption is in error. Different subordinates often report far different views of the same immediate supervisor. And supervisors do not describe their individual subordinates or relate to them in the same way. Often, they differentiate among subordinates by the kinds of assignments they entrust and the degree of freedom from supervision that they allow. Although such popular views of supervision as Theory X and Y, Managerial Grid, and Fiedler's Contingency Model assume that a leader exhibits a particular dominant style, recent research suggests that a given supervisor will show a far different "face" to certain subordinates.

THE INS AND OUTS

The existence of in-groups and out-groups within a given department or work unit is easy to document. Studies show that subordinates can readily

1. See, for example, Fred Dansereau, Jr., George Graen, and William J. Haga, "A Vertical Dyad Linkage Approach to Leadership within Formal Organizations: A Longitudinal Investigation of the Role Making Process," *Organizational Behavior and Human Performance* 13 (February 1975): 46–78; John B. Miner, *Theories of Organizational Behavior* (Hinsdale, Ill.: Dryden, 1980); Robert P. Vecchio and Bruce C. Gobdel, "The Vertical Dyad Linkage Model of Leadership: Problems and Prospects," *Organizational Behavior and Human Performance* 34 (August 1984): 5–20.

agree on who is relatively in or out with the boss. And the boss can quickly list which employees are currently in or out of favor.

By and large, in-groups can be labeled as the boss's *trusted assistants*. Out-group members can best be termed *hired hands*. *Trusted assistants* are given considerable freedom in their jobs. They are asked to give their opinions about various matters and have ready access to their supervisors. *Hired hands,* in contrast, are treated with courtesy and perhaps respect, but they are not considered loyal or capable of handling critical assignments. In a sense, the *hired hands,* in accordance with a written or unwritten labor contract, are merely supervised. In-groupers are given considerable responsibility, support, and encouragement. Out-groupers are denied valuable opportunities and displays of confidence.

WHY DO IN-GROUPS AND OUT-GROUPS DEVELOP?

The origins of in-groups and out-groups are not completely understood. It is likely, however, that something occurs fairly early in the relationship between each new employee and a supervisor.

The boss tries out each new employee by offering small but challenging assignments. The subordinate's reaction to these additional responsibilities is then closely watched. If the employee reacts negatively (by saying, "It's not *my* job") or positively (by replying, "I'm happy to help"), then a cycle of trust or distrust is begun. In short, supervisors learn quickly who is reliable and who is not. Frequently, this discovery process is not even conscious or intentional; supervisors may be unaware that this process is occurring.

In addition to these displays of loyalty and cooperation, a certain degree of personal bias may play a role in determining who is in or out. Supervisors may be more willing to offer desirable job assignments and be more available to subordinates whom they find attractive, or regard as similar to themselves in terms of attitudes, sex, and/or race. Still, though personal bias may play a role, it is perhaps more likely that employee competence and early manifestations of cooperation are the major determinants in most superior-subordinate relations.

Performance appraisal systems can create or cement a person's membership in an in-group or an out-group. The annual or semiannual task of sorting out employees for purposes of making decisions on raises or sending employees to training programs influences a supervisor's beliefs about the merit of a given employee. If a supervisor is unduly influenced by the realization that a given employee did not fare well in a performance assessment, and if the supervisor does not try to help in that employee's development, then the supervisor's later behavior may be influenced by the negative appraisal.

Lastly, it appears that some employees *want* to be out. Apparently not everyone wants to have a good working relationship with the boss. Some people are antagonistic to authority figures. For such people, this negative predisposition is present regardless of who their supervisor happens to be. Such individuals will take a relatively defiant and uncooperative stance as long as their jobs are secure (thanks to a union contract, the threat of a lawsuit, longevity, or being relatively indispensable because of their expert knowledge).

No one has yet offered a solution on how to reach or turn around such extremely negative individuals. Perhaps the only practical advice for coping with them is to try to arrange for their transfer to another unit or to redefine their job responsibilities so that their negative influence is minimized.

THE CONSEQUENCES OF BEING IN OR OUT

Studies of the in-out phenomenon show that in-groupers are more satisfied with their bosses and their jobs than are out-groupers. In-groupers may be less likely to quit than out-group members (although this finding of reduced turnover is less reliable than the findings for employee satisfaction).

Furthermore, in-group members have higher performance levels than out-group members. Regardless of how performance is measured (that is, by hard, objective measures of performance or by subjective ratings), in-groupers are generally better performers. These findings suggest that real gains may result from creating a sense of in-ness among subordinates. Marginal employees may be motivated to become superior performers.

IN OR OUT: WHAT TO DO ABOUT IT

In truth, the best time to manage the in or out phenomenon is very early in a person's employment. If you are a new employee or if you are developing a relationship with a newly assigned boss, it is a good idea to offer your loyalty and provide expressions of cooperativeness.

If your status as an out-member is already well established, it may be difficult or impossible to break the status quo. Short of confronting the supervisor and asking for a new start, an out-group employee's only options are to:

- Accept the current situation;
- Try to become an in-group member by being cooperative and loyal (this is an unattractive option for many out-groupers because they may have to swallow their pride); or
- Quit.

Out-group members typically—but resentfully—come to accept the status quo.

Supervisors should be mindful that in-groups and out-groups exist within their work units, and they should control potential conflict between the two divisions. Supervisors should consciously try to expand their in-groups. This means not giving up on people who may gradually be coming to see themselves as marginal members of the work unit. Supervisors who create a greater sense of in-ness among their subordinates can expect to have more effective work units.

Can Leaders Learn to Lead?

Victor H. Vroom

Like my fellow authors, I start with certain preconceptions. These preconceptions—some may call them biases—influence the way in which I view issues of leadership, particularly leadership training. I have tried to depict these preconceptions in Figure 1.

The central variable in this figure is the behavior of the leader, which I believe is determined by two classes of variables, attributes of the leader and attributes of the situation. Furthermore, I assume that many of the differences in the behavior of leaders can be explained only by examining their joint effects, including interactions between these two classes of variables.

The left-hand portion of the diagram is the descriptive side of the leader behavior equation. Much of my research has focused on these relationships in an attempt to understand the ways in which managers actually respond to situations that vary in a number of dimensions. If you examine the right-hand side of Figure 1, however, you encounter issues that are potentially normative or prescriptive in character. They deal with the consequences of leader behavior for the organization and here I share with Fiedler (and probably disagree with Argyris) a conviction that a contingency model is required. I do not see any form of leader behavior as optimal for all situations. The contribution of a leader's actions to the effectiveness of the organization cannot be determined without considering the nature of the situation in which that behavior is displayed.

WORKING WITH THE CONTINGENCY MODEL

I am going to assume that most of you are familiar with the model that Phil Yetton and I developed and have described in detail in our recent book. As a normative model, it deals with the right-hand side of Figure 1, but it is a limited model because it deals with only one facet of leadership behavior—the extent to which the leader shares decision-making power with subordinates.

Figure 1
Schematic Representation of Variables Used in Leadership Research

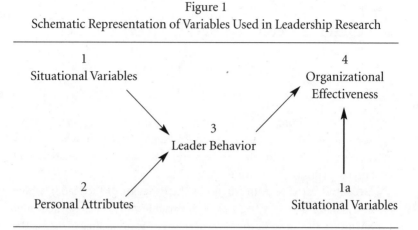

Figure 2 shows the latest version of our model. For purposes of simplicity, the presentation here is restricted to the model for group problems, that is, problems or decisions that affect all or a substantial portion of the manager's subordinates. At the top of the figure are problem attributes—that is, situational variables that ought to influence the decision process used by the leader—specifically, the amount of opportunity that the leader gives his or her subordinates to participate in the making of a decision. To use the model, one first selects an organization problem to be solved or decision to be made. Starting at the left-hand side of the diagram, one asks oneself the question pertaining to each attribute that is encountered, follows the path developed, and finally determines the problem type (numbered 1 through 12). This problem type specifies one or more decision processes that are deemed appropriate to that problem. These decision processes are called the "feasible set" and represent the methods that remain after a set of seven rules has been applied. The first three of these rules eliminate methods that threaten the quality of the decisions, while the last four rules eliminate methods that are likely to jeopardize acceptance of the decision by subordinates.

For those who are unfamiliar with the Vroom-Yetton model, let me point out that the decision processes are described here in a kind of code. AI and AII are variants of an autocratic process. In AI the manager solves the problem alone using whatever information is available at that time; in AII the manager obtains any necessary information of a specific nature from subordinates before making the decision alone. CI and CII are variants of a

Figure 2
Decision Process Flowchart (Feasible Set)

A. Does the problem possess a quality requirement?
B. Do 1 have sufficient information to make a high-quality decision?
C. Is the problem structured?
D. Is acceptance of the decision by subordinates important for effective implementation?
E. If I were to make the decision by myself, am I reasonably certain that it would be accepted by my subordinates'?
F. Do subordinates share the organizational goals to be attained in solving this problem?
G. Is conflict among subordinates likely in preferred solutions?

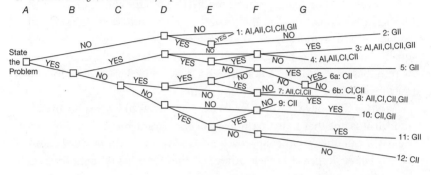

consultative process. In CI the manager shares the problem with relevant subordinates individually, getting their ideas and suggestions before making the decision; CII is similar, but the consultation takes place within the context of a group meeting. Finally, GII corresponds with Norman Maier's concept of group decision in which the manager's role is that of chairperson of a group meeting aimed at reaching consensus on the action to be taken.

The part of the model described so far specifies how decisions should *not* be made, not how they should be made. For most problem types, there exists more than one decision process consistent with the rules and therefore contained in the feasible set. We have also been concerned with the consequences of various ways of choosing from these alternatives. There is considerable evidence that the time required to make the decision (defined either as the elapsed time or the number of work hours needed to make the decision) increases with the intensity of involvement or participation of subordinates. Thus a time-efficient model (which we term Model A) would select the most autocratic alternative within the feasible set, a choice that would be clearly indicated in crisis or emergency situations, and in situations in which one seeks to minimize the number of work-hours that enter into making the decision.

Of course, time is not the only dimension to include in deciding the degree to which the leader should encourage the participation of subordinates in decision making. In addition to the possibilities that participation may increase decision quality or its acceptance (considerations that are incorporated into the rules referred to previously), there are also grounds for believing that participation contributes to individual and team development and is likely to result in more informed and responsible behavior by subordinates in the future. Hence Model B, which could be thought of as a time-investment or developmental model, dictates the choice of the most participative process within the feasible set. It is important to note that Models A and B are consistent with the same rules (to protect decision quality and acceptance) but represent extremely different ways of operating within these rules. Model A maximizes a short-run value—time; Model B maximizes a long-run value—development

What is the image of the effective leader portrayed by this normative model? It is one that is neither universally autocratic nor universally participative but utilizes either approach in response to the demands of a situation *as he or she perceives them.* Above all, the leader has thought through his or her values and has a repertoire of skills necessary to execute effectively each of the decision processes.

VALIDATING THE MODEL

When Philip Yetton and I wrote our book, we had no evidence validating the model other than the consistency of our rules with existing empirical evidence concerning the consequences of alternative approaches. During the past six months, Art Jago and I have been working to remedy this deficiency. We have asked managers, all of whom were unfamiliar with the model, to select two decisions that they had made—one that proved to be successful and one that proved to be unsuccessful. Each manager wrote up each decision situation as a case and specified the decision process he used in solving the problem. Later these managers were trained in the problem attributes and went back over each of these two cases, coding each in a manner that would permit the researcher to determine the problem type and the feasible set of methods for that problem type.

The data for this study are still coming in. To date, we have written accounts of 46 successful decisions and 42 unsuccessful ones. (It seems that some managers have difficulty in recalling the decisions they made that did not turn out too well!) Figure 3 shows the results available so far. These results clearly support the validity of the model. If the manager's method of dealing with the case corresponded with the model, the probability of the decision's being deemed successful was 65 percent; if the method disagreed with the model, the probability of its being deemed successful was only 29 percent.

It is important to note, however, that behavior that corresponds with the model is no guarantee that the decision will ultimately turn out to be successful—nor is behavior outside the feasible set inevitably associated with an unsuccessful decision.

To create a model of decision processes that completely predicts decision outcomes (that is, which generates 100 percent observations in upper left and lower right cells) is an impossibility. Any fantasies that we may have entertained about having created a model of process that would completely determine decision outcomes have been permanently dashed against the rocks of reality! Insofar as organizations are open systems and decisions within them are made under conditions of risk and uncertainty, it will be impossible to generate complete predictability for a model such as ours. To be sure, we may be able to use the data from the study I have described to improve the "batting average" of the model, but the limit of success must be less than perfection.

IMPLICATIONS FOR TRAINING

I would now like to turn to a central issue, the use of the model in leadership training. Over the past few years, several thousand managers have received training in the concepts underlying the model. The workshops have

Figure 3

Relationship Between Model Agreement and Decision Outcome

	Percent Successful	*Percent Unsuccessful*	*Total*
Method used agrees with feasible set	65	35	100%
Method used disagrees with feasible set	29	71	100%

ranged from two to over five days in length, and the participants have included admirals, corporation presidents, school superintendents, and senior government officials. I have been personally involved in enough of this training to have learned some important things about what to do and what not to do. And because I believe that there are substantial but understandable misconceptions about how training based on the Vroom and Yetton model works, I would like to describe the things I have learned.

It would have been possible to build a training program around the model that was completely cognitive and mechanistic. Participants would be sold on the model and then trained in its use through intensive practice—first on standardized cases and later on real problems drawn from their own experiences. Such an approach would represent a new domain for Taylorism and could even be accomplished through Skinnerian programmed learning. I believe that, at best, this behavioral approach would influence what Argyris calls espoused theories and would not have any long-lasting behavioral effects.

Our methods have been much more influenced by Carl Rogers than by B. F. Skinner. We have assumed that behavioral changes require a process of self-discovery and insight by each individual manager.

One method of stimulating this process is to provide the participants with a picture of their leadership style. This picture includes a comparison of one's style with that of others, the situational factors that influence one's willingness to share power with others, and similarities and differences between one's own "model" and the normative models.

In advance of the training program, each participant sits down with a set of cases, each of which depicts a leader confronted with an actual organizational problem. We call these cases "problem sets," and the number of cases in different problem sets ranges from 30 to 54. The common feature in each of the eight or nine problem sets that have been developed is that the cases vary along each of the situational dimensions used in the construction of the normative model. The set is designed so that the variation is systematic and that the effects of each situational attribute on a given manager's choice of decision process can be readily determined. This feature permits the assessment of each of the problem attributes in the decision processes used by a given manager.

The manager's task is to select the decision process that comes closest to depicting what he or she would do in each situation. Responses are recorded on a standardized form and processed by computer along with other participants' responses in the same program.

Instead of writing about information contained on a printout, I thought that it might be more efficient to let you see what it looks like. The next figure reproduces several pages of feedback that a manager recently received. Examine the first page of the printout shown in Figure 4. Consider A first in that figure. The first row opposite "your frequency" shows the proportion of cases in which the manager indicated he would use each of the five decision processes. The next row (opposite "peer frequency") shows the average use of these processes by the 41 managers constituting his training group. A comparison of these two rows indicates the methods the manager used more and less frequently than average.

The third row shows the distribution of decision processes that would be used by a manager using Model A, the time-efficient model in the 30 cases. The final row shows a distribution for Model B, the developmental or time-investment model.

To obtain an overall picture of how participative this manager's responses are in relation to other members of the training group and to

Figure 4
Page 1 of Printout

NAME OR I.D. -- JOHN DOE

A -- PROPORTION OF CASES IN WHICH
    EACH DECISION PROCESS IS USED

B -- SCALED PARTICIPATION SCORES

	AI	AII	CI	CII	GII		MEAN	SD
YOUR FREQUENCY	43%	3%	23%	30%	0%	YOUR RESPONSES	3.60*	3.48
PEER FREQUENCY	25%	14%	19%	27%	15%	PEER AVERAGE	4.73	3.66
MODEL A (MINIMIZE PARTICIPATION)	40%	13%	3%	23%	20%	MODEL A	4.17	4.31
MODEL B (MAXIMIZE PARTICIPATION)	0%	0%	0%	40%	60%	MODEL B	9.20	0.98

* - YOUR SCORE IN FIGURE 1

C -- FREQUENCY DISTRIBUTION OF SCALE SCORES
    (MEAN LEVELS OF PARTICIPATION)

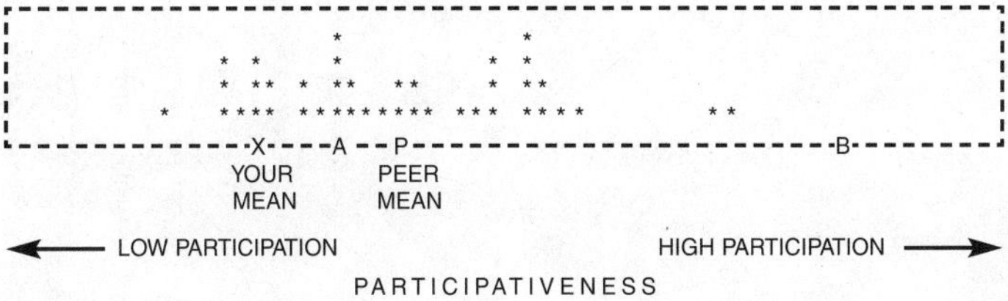

```
 ---------------------------------------------------------
|               *                        *                |
|        *  *         *               *  *                |
|        *  **  *  **     **          *  **               |
|     *  ****  *********  ***  ****         **            |
 ----------X---A--P---------------------------B----------
          YOUR    PEER
          MEAN    MEAN
```

◄—— LOW PARTICIPATION   HIGH PARTICIPATION ——►
              P A R T I C I P A T I V E N E S S

Figure 4 (*continued*)

D — BEHAVIOR BY PROBLEM TYPE

PROBLEM TYPE	PROBLEM NUMBERS	MODEL "A"	MODEL "B"	FEASIBLE SET	YOUR BEHAVIOR
1	14, 15, 17, 28	AI	GII	AI,AII,CI,CII,GII	AI AI AI AI
2	3, 5	GII	GII	GII	AI
3	2, 22, 27, 30	AI	GII	AI,AII,CI,CII,GII	AI AI CII
4	12, 25, 26, 29	AI	CII	AI,AII,CI,CII	AI CI CI CII AI
5	7, 8, 20	GII	GII	GII	CII CII CI
6A	1, 10	CII	CII	CII	CII CI
6B	11	CI	CII	CI,CII	CII AI
7	21, 24	AII	CII	AII,CI,CII	CII AII
8	19, 23	AII	CII	AII,CI,CII,GII	AI AII
9	4, 16	CII	CII	CII,	CII CI
10	6, 9	CII	CII	CII,GII	AI CI
11	13	GII	GII	CII	CII
12	18	CII	CII	CII	CII

E — FREQUENCY OF AGREEMENT WITH THE NORMATIVE MODEL

	YOUR MEAN	PEER AVERAGE
AGREEMENT WITH FEASIBLE SET	17 (57%)	20.8 (69%)
AGREEMENT MODEL A (MINIMUM PARTICIPATION)	12 (40%)	12.1 (40%)
AGREEMENT WITH MODEL B (MAXIMUM PARTICIPATION)	4 (13%)	6.3 (21%)

F — FREQUENCY OF RULE VIOLATIONS

	RULE	REPSONSES IN VIOLATION	YOUR FREQUENCY	PEER AVERAGE	PROBLEM NUMBERS
1	LEADER INFORMATION RULE	AI	3.0 (25%)*	0.7 (6%)	6 19 24
2	GOAL CONGRUENCY RULE	GII	0.0 (0%)	1.3 (10%)	0
3	UNSTRUCTURED PROBLEM RULE	AI,AII,CI	3.0 (50%)	2.8 (47%)	6 9 16
4	ACCEPTANCE RULE	AI,AII	1.0 (10%)	1.3 (13%)	5
5	CONFLICT RULE	AI,AII,CI	3.0 (60%)	1.9 (39%)	1 5 10
6	FAIRNESS RULE	AI,AII,CI,CII	2.0 (100%)	1.3 (63%)	3 5
7	ACCEPTANCE PRIORITY RULE	AI,AII,CI,CII	4.0 (100%)	2.9 (72%)	7 8 13 20

*---- PROBABILITY OF RULE VIOLATION (THAT IS, FREQUENCY OF VIOLATION EXPRESSED AS A PERCENTAGE OF RULE APPLICABILITY)

Figure 4 (*continued*)

YOUR MEAN = X		MODEL A MEAN = A
PEER MEAN = P		MODEL B MEAN = B

G ----- MAIN EFFECTS OF PROBLEM ATTRIBUTES

PARTICIPATIVENESS ON PROBLEMS WITH ATTRIBUTE
< LOW PARTICIPATION   HIGH PARTICIPATION >

PROBLEM ATTRIBUTES		Scale	PROBLEMS WITH ATTRIBUTE
IMPORTANCE OF THE QUALITY OF THE FINAL SOLUTION (ATTRIBUTE A)	HIGH X=4.17 P=4.97 A=4.38	------------XA----P-------------B	(1,2,4,6,7,8,9,10,11,12,13, 16,18,19,20,21,22,23,24,25, 26,27,29,30)
	LOW X=1.33 P=3.75 A=3.33	---X----A--P----------B	(3,5,14,15,17,28)
ADEQUACY OF MANAGER'S INFORMATION AND EXPERTISE (ATTRIBUTE B)	HIGH X=3.67 P=4.24 A=2.75	--------A---X----P------------B	(1,2,8,11,12,20,22,25,26, 27,29,30)
	LOW X=4.67 P=5.71 A=6.00	-----------X------P-A---------B	(4,6,7,9,10,13,16,18,19, 21,23,24)
DEGREE OF STRUCTURE IN PROBLEM (ATTRIBUTE C)	HIGH X=3.67 P=4.97 A=3.67	--------X-------P------------B	(7,10,19,21,23,24)
	LOW X=5.67 P=6.46 A=8.33	---------X----P----A----B	(4,6,9,13,16,18)
IMPORTANCE OF SUBORDINATE ACCEPTANCE (ATTRIBUTE D)	HIGH X=3.80 P=5.30 A=5.35	--------X-------------P-------B	(1,3,5,6,7,8,10,11,12,13,14, 15,16,18,19,20,22,24,29,30)
	LOW X=3.20 P=3.59 A=1.80	----A-----X--P-----------B	(2,4,9,17,21,23,25,26,27,28)
PROBABILITY OF LEADER'S SELLING HIS OWN SOLUTION (ATTRIBUTE E)	HIGH X=1.30 P=3.68 A=1.80	X--A-------P-----------------B	(6,11,12,14,15,16,19,22,24,29,30)
	LOW X=6.30 P=6.91 A=8.90	------------X--P----------A--B	(1,3,5,7,8,10,11,13,18,20)
DEGREE TO WHICH SUBORDINATES SHARE GOALS (ATTRIBUTE F)	HIGH X=3.58 P=5.45 A=4.83	-------X-------A----P--------B	(2,6,7,8,9,13,19,20,22, 23,27,30)
	LOW X=4.75 P=4.49 A=3.92	------A--P--X----------------B	(1,4,10,11,12,16,18,21,24, 25,26,29)
PROBABILITY OF CONFLICT AMONG SUBORDINATES (ATTRIBUTE G)	HIGH X=3.27 P=3.99 A=4.27	----X---P--A-----------------B	(1,2,5,8,9,10,13,15,16,19, 21,22,26,28,29)
	LOW X=3.93 P=5.47 A=4.07	----------X------P----------B	(3,4,6,7,11,12,14,17,18, 20,23,24,25,27,30)

NOTE: THE THREE ATTRIBUTES WITH THE GREATEST EFFECT ON YOUR RESPONSES ARE A, C, AND E.

Models A and B, it is necessary to assign scale values to each of the five decision processes. The actual numbers used for this purpose are based on research on the relative amounts of participation perceived to result from each process. AI is given a value of 0; AII a value of 1; CI a value of 5; CII a value of 8; and GII a value of 10.

With the aid of these scale values, a mean score can be computed for the manager, peers, and both models. These are obtained by multiplying the percentage of times each process is used by its scale value and dividing by 100. These mean scores are shown in B along with the standard deviation (SD), a measure of dispersion around the mean—that is, an indicator of how much behavior is varied over situations.

These mean scores are shown graphically in the figure at the bottom. Each asterisk is the mean score of one of the group members. The symbol X is printed underneath this manager's mean score, the symbol P under the group average, and the symbols A and B show the location on the scale of Models A and B respectively.

D through F in Figure 4 are on the second page of the printout. As we previously mentioned, the normative model identifies 12 problem types corresponding to the terminal nodes of the decision tree shown in Figure 2. There is at least one case within the set of 30 problems that has been designated by the authors and most managers as representative of each type. The problem types and corresponding problem numbers are shown in the two left-hand columns of D. In the third and fourth columns, the prescriptions of Models A and B are given, and the fifth column shows the feasible set for that problem type. The last column, marked "your behavior," indicates the manager's responses to each of the cases of the indicated problem type. If there is more than one case of that type, the methods used are shown in the same order as the problem numbers at the left-hand side.

E reports the frequency with which the manager's behavior agreed with the feasible set, with Model A, and with Model B. For comparison purposes, the average rates of agreement for members of the manager's training group are also presented.

Each time our manager chose a decision process that was outside the feasible set, he violated at least one of the seven rules underlying the model. F in Figure 4 reports the frequencies with which each rule was violated both by this manager and by his or her peer group. The right-hand column shows the specific cases in which the rule violations occurred. It should be noted that each manager understands the seven rules by the time he or she receives the feedback, and it is possible to reexamine the problems with the appropriate rule in mind.

We have previously noted that the cases included in a problem set are selected in accordance with a multifactorial experimental design. Each of the problem attributes is varied in a manner that will permit the manager to examine its role in his or her leadership style. Figure 4 (page 3 of printout) depicts these results. Consider problem attribute A—the importance of the quality of the final solution. The problem set contains cases that have a high quality requirement and those without a quality requirement (the identifying numbers of these cases are shown at the right-hand side of this table).

The mean scores for the manager's behavior on these two sets of cases are specified at the left-hand side of each row and are designated by the symbol X. They are also designated by the symbol X on each of the scales, and the slope of the line made by connecting the two letters (X) provides a visual representation of that difference.

If the score opposite "high" is greater (that is, more toward the right-hand side of the scale), it means that the manager encourages more participation from his subordinates on important decisions than on so-called "trivial" ones. However, if the score opposite "high" is lower, it means that the manager is willing to use more participative methods on problems for which the course of action adopted makes little difference and is more autocratic on "important" decisions.

The letter P shown on both scales designates the average effects of this attribute on the manager's peer group, and the letters A and B designate the effects on Models A and B respectively.

A similar logic can be used in interpreting the effects of each of the other attributes in the model. At the bottom of the page, the computer prints out the three attributes that have the greatest effect on the manager's behavior—magnitude of effect referring to the amount of difference the attribute makes in willingness to share decision-making power with subordinates.

The results shown in Figure 4 pertain to only one manager and to his or her peer group. Similar data have been obtained from several thousand managers, a sufficient number to provide the basis for some tentative generalizations about leadership patterns. One of our conclusions is that differences among managers in what might be termed a general trait of participativeness or authoritarianism are small in comparison with differences within managers. On the standardized cases in the problem sets, no manager has indicated that he or she would use the same decision process on all problems or decisions—and most use all methods under some circumstances.

It is clear that no one score computed for a manager and displayed on the printout adequately represents one's leadership style. To begin to understand one's style, the entire printout must be considered. For example, two managers may appear to be equally participative or autocratic on the surface, but a close look at the third page of the printout (Figure 4) may reveal crucial differences. One manager may limit participation by subordinates to decisions where the quality element is unimportant, such as the time and place of the company picnic, while the other manager may limit participation by subordinates to those decisions with a demonstrable impact on important organizational goals.

In about two-thirds of the cases we have examined—both those used in the problem sets and those reported to us by managers from their experiences—the manager's behavior was consistent with the feasible set of methods given by the model. Rules that helped ensure the acceptance of or commitment to a decision tend to be violated much more frequently than rules that protect the quality of the decision. Our findings suggest strongly that decisions made by typical managers are more likely to prove ineffective because subordinates don't fully accept decisions than because decision quality is deficient.

Let me now turn to another thing that we have learned in the design of this training—the usefulness of the small, informal group as a vehicle in the change process. The first four or five hours in the training process are spent in creating six- to eight-person teams operating under conditions of openness and trust. Each participant spends more than 50 percent of the training time with his or her small group before receiving feedback. Group activities include discussing cases in the problem set and trying to reach agreement on their mode of resolution, practicing participative leadership styles within their own groups, analyzing videotapes of group problem-solving activities; then group members give one another feedback on the basis of predictions of one another's leadership styles.

After feedback, group members compare results with one another and with their prior predictions and share with one another what they have learned as well as their plans to change. The use of small, autonomous groups greatly decreases the dependence of participants on the instructor for their learning and increases the number of people who can undergo the training at the same time. I have personally worked with as many as 140 managers at the same time (22 groups), and 40 to 50 is commonplace.

One criticism that has been correctly leveled at the Vroom and Yetton work stems from the fact that the data on which the feedback is based are, at best, reports of intended actions rather than observations of actual behavior. While we have evidence that most managers honestly try to portray what they think they would do in a particular situation rather than what they think they should do, I am persuaded by Argyris's evidence that many people are unaware of discrepancies between their espoused theories and their actions. Small groups can be helpful in pointing out these discrepancies. I have seen managers who were universally predicted by other group members to have a highly autocratic style, who were provided with very specific evidence of the ground for this assumption by other group members, but who later received a printout reflecting a much more participative style. I am less concerned about the relative validity of these discrepant pieces of data than I am about the fact that they are frequently confronted and discussed in the course of the training experience.

In fact, we have begun using a different source of potential inconsistencies, and it is logical to assume that this source will have more information about a manager's behavior than do the other members of his or her small group. I am referring to the manager's subordinates.

In a recent variant of the training program, subordinates were asked to predict their manager's behavior on each of the cases in the problem set. These predictions were made individually and processed by computer, which generated for each manager a detailed comparison of perceptions of leadership style with the mean perception of his or her subordinates. Not surprisingly, these two sources of information are not always in perfect agreement. Most managers, as seen by their subordinates, are substantially more autocratic (about one point on the 10-point scale) and in substantially less agreement with the model. Once again, I am less concerned with which is the correct description of the leader's behavior than I am with the fact that discrepancies generate a dialogue between the manager and subordinates that can be the source of mutual learning.

We are still experimenting with methods of using the Vroom-Yetton model in leadership training and, I believe, still learning from the results of this experimentation. How effective is the training in its present form? Does it produce long-lasting behavioral changes? I must confess that I do not know. Art Jago and I are in the first stages of designing an extensive follow-up study of almost 200 managers in 20 different countries who have been through a four-or five-day version of the training within the past two and one-half years. If we can solve the incredible logistical and methodological problems in a study of this kind, we should have results within a year.

On the basis of the evidence, I am optimistic on two counts: first, as to the leader's potential to vary style to meet the requirements of a situation; second, as to the leader's ability, through training and development, to enlarge the repertoire of his or her styles. In short, like Argyris and unlike Fiedler, I believe that managers can learn to become more effective leaders. But like Fiedler (and unlike Argyris), I believe that such effectiveness requires matching of one's leadership style to the demands of the situation. I also am confident that 50 years from now both contingency models will be found wanting in detail if not in substance. If we are remembered at that time, it will be for the kinds of questions we posed rather than the specific answers we provided.

WICS: A Model of Leadership in Organizations

Robert J. Sternberg

THREE COMPONENTS OF LEADERSHIP

If traditional models of leadership (see Antonakis, Cianciolo, & Sternberg, in press, for a comprehensive review) are too narrow, what model would be broader and more encompassing? One possible answer is WICS (an acronym for wisdom, intelligence, and creativity, synthesized; Sternberg, 2003; see also Sternberg & Vroom, 2002).

According to this model, the three key components of leadership are *wisdom, intelligence,* and *creativity,* synthesized (WICS). The basic idea is that one needs these three components working together (synthesized) in order to be a highly effective leader (see Figure 1).

One is not "born" a leader. Rather, wisdom, intelligence, and creativity are, to some extent, forms of developing expertise (Sternberg, 1998a, 1999a). One interacts with the environment in ways that utilize, to varying degrees, one's innate potentials. The environment strongly influences the extent to which we are able to utilize and develop whatever genetic potentials we have (Grigorenko & Sternberg, 2001; Sternberg & Grigorenko, 1997, 2001). Many people with substantial innate potential fail to take advantage of it; whereas others with lesser potential do take advantage of it.

Some scholars deal with the question of whether leadership is anything more than good management. Intuitively, leadership seems related to management, but perhaps it involves something more. The relationship between leadership and management has been debated for decades by academics and practitioners. Two alternative positions have emerged: that the concepts are distinct or that they are interrelated.

According to the first position, management and leadership are qualitatively different concepts. Often the semantics are shifted to make the distinction between *managers* and *leaders* rather than *management* and *leadership*. For example, Zaleznik (1977) proposed that managers and leaders are different types of people in terms of their motivation, personal history, thoughts, and behaviors. Managers are problem solvers who create goals in

Figure 1
The WICS Model of Leadership

Wisdom

Leadership

Intelligence   Creativity

order to maintain the stability of the organization. Leaders are visionaries who inspire workers to take part in their own and the organization's development and change. Bennis and Nanus (1985) also propose that leaders and managers differ qualitatively in their perspectives and willingness to implement change. Managers have a narrow perspective that is concerned with mastering routines to ensure the efficiency of daily operations. Leaders, in contrast, have a broad perspective that allows them to assess the organization's needs, envision the future, and implement change.

Kotter (1987) makes a distinction between leadership and management in terms of the processes involved rather than the personalities of individuals. Management tends to be a formal, scientific, and present-oriented process; whereas leadership tends to be an informal, flexible, inspirational, and future-oriented process.

There are others, however, who view leadership and management as overlapping processes that fulfill the functions or expectations of an organizational role. Mintzberg (1975), for example, suggests that one of the functions of the manager's role is to be a leader. According to this perspective, the term *manager* is a role label, while *leader* is a role function. Leadership is a process associated with the function of a leader. Yukl (1989) and Lau and Shani (1992) suggest that the functions associated with supervisory positions in organizations require the incumbent to be both a leader and a manager. Bass (1990) similarly suggests that leaders must manage and managers must lead. These researchers consider the terms *leader* and *manager* to be interchangeable.

In the following I review our work on intelligence, creativity, and wisdom, as they have relevance for leadership (as well as for management). I concentrate on intelligence, because it is a base for creativity and wisdom, and because we have collected the most data investigating it.

Intelligence

Intelligence would seem to be important to leadership, but how important? Indeed, if the conventional intelligence of a leader is too much higher than that of the people he or she leads, the leader may fail to connect with those people and become ineffective (Williams & Sternberg, 1988). Intelligence, as conceived of here, is not just intelligence in its conventional narrow sense—some kind of general factor (g) (Demetriou, 2002; Jensen, 1998, 2002; Spearman, 1927; see essays in Sternberg & Grigorenko, 2002) or IQ (Binet & Simon, 1905; Kaufman, 2000; Wechsler, 1939), but rather, is intelligence in terms of the theory of successful intelligence (Sternberg, 1997, 1999c, 2002c). *Successful intelligence* is defined as the ability to succeed in life, given one's conception of success, within one's sociocultural environment. Two aspects of the theory are especially relevant: academic and practical intelligence (see also Neisser, 1979). (A third aspect of the theory of successful intelligence, creative intelligence, will be dealt with below.)

Academic intelligence refers to the memory and analytical abilities that in combination largely constitute the conventional notion of intelligence— the abilities needed to recall and recognize but also to analyze, evaluate, and judge information. A long history of research on the relation between these abilities and leadership goes back at least to Stogdill (1948), and the results are ambiguous. Although there seems to be a modest correlation between these abilities and leadership effectiveness (Stogdill, 1948; see also essays in Riggio, Murphy, & Pirozzolo, 2002), the correlation is moderated by factors such as the stress experienced by the leader (Fiedler, 2002; Fiedler & Link, 1994), which apparently even can change the direction of the correlation.

These abilities matter for leadership, because leaders need to be able to retrieve information that is relevant to leadership decisions (memory abilities) and to analyze and evaluate different courses of action, whether proposed by themselves or by others (analytical abilities). But a good analyst is not necessarily a good leader.

Academic Intelligence

The long-time primary emphasis on *academic* intelligence (IQ) in the literature relating intelligence to leadership perhaps has been unfortunate. Presumably, some measure of academic intelligence is an ingredient of successful leadership. However, recent theorists have been emphasizing other aspects of intelligence in their theories, such as emotional intelligence (e.g., Caruso, Mayer, & Salovey, 2002; Goleman, 1998a, 1998b) or multiple intelligences (Gardner, 1995). These constructs of intelligence do not replace conventional academic intelligence: They supplement it. Here the emphasis is on practical intelligence (Sternberg et al., 2000; Sternberg & Hedlund, 2002), which has a somewhat different focus from emotional intelligence. Practical intelligence is a part of successful intelligence. Practical intelligence is a core component of leadership, and thus will receive special attention here.

Practical Intelligence

Practical intelligence is the ability to solve everyday problems by utilizing knowledge gained from experience in order to purposefully adapt to, shape, and select environments. It thus involves changing oneself to suit the environment (adaptation), changing the environment to suit oneself (shaping), or finding a new environment within which to work (selection). One uses these skills to (a) manage oneself, (b) manage others, and (c) manage tasks.

Effectiveness in "transactional leadership" (Avolio, Bass, & Jung, 1999; Bass, 1985, 1998, 2002; Bass, Avolio, & Atwater, 1996) derives, in large part although not exclusively, from the adaptive function of practical intelligence. Transactional leaders are for the most part adapters. They work with their followers toward the mutual fulfillment of essentially contractual obligations. These leaders typically provide contingent rewards, specifying role and task requirements and rewarding desired performance. Or they may manage by exception, in which case they monitor the meeting of standards and intervene when these standards are not met.

Different combinations of intellectual skills engender different types of leadership. Leaders vary in their memory, analytical, and practical skills. A leader particularly strong in memory skills but not in analytical and practical ones may have a vast amount of knowledge at his or her disposal, but be unable to use it effectively. A leader particularly strong in analytical skills as well as memory skills may be able to retrieve information and analyze it effectively, but be unable to convince others that his or her analysis is correct. A leader who is strong in memory, analytical, and practical skills is most likely to be effective in influencing others. But, of course, there exist leaders who are strong in practical skills but not in memory and analytical skills (Sternberg, 1997; Sternberg et al., 2000). In conventional terms they are "shrewd" but not "smart." Although they may be effective in getting others to go along with them, they may be leading them down the garden path.

My colleagues and I (Sternberg et al., 2000; Sternberg & Wagner, 1993; Sternberg, Wagner, & Okagaki, 1993; Sternberg, Wagner, Williams, & Horvath, 1995; Wagner & Sternberg, 1985; Wagner, 1987) have taken a knowledge-based approach to understanding practical intelligence. Individuals draw on a broad base of knowledge in solving practical problems, some of which is acquired through formal training and some of which is derived from personal experience. Much of the knowledge associated with successful problem solving can be characterized as tacit.

The term *tacit knowledge* has roots in works on the philosophy of science (Polanyi, 1966), ecological psychology (Neisser, 1976), and organizational behavior (Schön, 1983), and has been used to characterize the knowledge gained from everyday experience that has an implicit, unarticulated quality. Such notions about the tacit quality of the knowledge associated with everyday problem solving also are reflected in the common language of the workplace, as people attribute successful performance to "learning by doing" and to "professional intuition" or "instinct."

Tacit knowledge often is not openly expressed or stated; thus, individuals must acquire such knowledge through their own experiences. Furthermore, although people's actions may reflect their knowledge, they may find it difficult to articulate what they know. Research on expert knowledge is consistent with this conceptualization. Experts draw on a well-developed repertoire of knowledge in responding to problems in their respective domains (Scribner, 1986). That knowledge tends to be procedural in nature and to operate outside of focal awareness (see Chi, Glaser, & Farr, 1988). It also reflects the structure of formal, disciplinary knowledge (Groen & Patel, 1988).

My colleagues and I (Sternberg, 1997; Sternberg & Horvath, 1999; Sternberg et al., 2000; Wagner & Sternberg, 1985) have viewed tacit knowledge as an aspect of practical intelligence that enables individuals to adapt to, select, and shape real-world environments. It is knowledge that reflects the practical ability to learn from experience and to apply that knowledge in pursuit of personally valued goals. Our research (see e.g., Sternberg,

1997; Sternberg, Wagner, & Okagaki, 1993; Sternberg & Horvath, 1999; Sternberg et al., 1995; Sternberg et al., 2000) has shown that tacit knowledge has relevance for understanding successful performance in a variety of domains. I present below the conceptualization of tacit knowledge we have used in our research and our methodology for measuring tacit knowledge. I then review findings from a program of research aimed at understanding tacit knowledge and practical intelligence.

Measuring tacit knowledge. Because people often find it difficult to articulate their tacit knowledge, we rely on observable indicators of its existence. That is, we measure tacit knowledge in the responses individuals provide to practical situations in which tacit knowledge is expected to provide an advantage. The measurement instruments used to assess tacit knowledge typically consist of a series of situations and associated response options, which have been characterized in the literature as situational-judgment tests (SJTs; Schmitt & Chan, 1998; Legree, 1995; Motowidlo, Dunnette, & Carter, 1990). These types of tests generally are used to measure interpersonal and problem-solving skills (Hanson & Ramos, 1996; Motowidlo et al., 1990) or behavioral intentions (Weekley & Jones, 1997). In a situational-judgment or tacit-knowledge test, each question presents a problem relevant to the domain of interest (e.g., a manager intervening in a dispute between two subordinates) followed by a set of options (i.e., strategies) for solving the problem (e.g., meet with the two subordinates individually to find out their perspective on the problem; hold a meeting with both subordinates and have them air their grievances). Respondents are asked either to choose the best and worst alternatives from among a few options, or to rate on a Likert scale the quality or appropriateness of several potential responses to the situation.

Tacit-knowledge (TK) tests have been scored in one of three ways: (a) by correlating participants' ratings with an index of group membership (i.e., expert, intermediate, novice); (b) by judging the degree to which participants' responses conform to professional "rules of thumb;" or (c) by computing a profile match or difference score between participants' ratings and an expert prototype. We (Sternberg et al., 1993, 1995, 2000; Wagner, 1987; Wagner & Sternberg, 1985; Wagner et al., 1999) have used TK tests to study academic psychologists, salespersons, college students, civilian managers, and military leaders, among other occupations.

Tacit knowledge and experience. Tacit knowledge by definition is knowledge gained primarily from experience performing practical, everyday problems. The common phrase "experience is the best teacher" reflects the view that experience provides opportunities to develop important knowledge and skills related to performance. Several meta-analytic reviews indicate that the estimated mean population correlation between experience and job performance falls in the range of .18 to .32 (Hunter & Hunter, 1984; McDaniel, Schmidt, & Hunter, 1988; Quinones, Ford, & Teachout, 1995). Additional research suggests that this relationship is mediated largely by the direct effect of experience on the acquisition of job knowledge (Borman, Hanson, Oppler, & Pulakos, 1993; Schmidt, Hunter, & Outerbridge, 1986).

Consistent with this research, we (Sternberg et al., 2000; Wagner, 1987; Wagner & Sternberg, 1985; Wagner et al., 1999) have found that tacit knowledge generally increases with experience. Wagner and Sternberg (1985) found a significant correlation between tacit knowledge and a manager's level within the company. In a follow-up study, Wagner (1987) found differences in tacit-knowledge scores among business managers, business graduate students, and general undergraduates, with the managers exhibiting the highest scores. Comparable results were found for a TK test for academic psychologists when comparing psychology professors, psychology graduate students, and undergraduates.

For three levels of military leadership, TK scores were not found to correlate with the number of months leaders had served in their current positions (Hedlund et al., in press), presumably because successful leaders spent less time in a job before being promoted than did less successful leaders. Subsequent research, however, found that TK scores did correlate with leadership rank such that leaders at higher levels of command exhibited greater tacit knowledge than did those at lower ranks (Hedlund et al., 2003).

The research conducted to date generally supports the relationship between tacit knowledge and experience. The correlations tend to be moderate, falling in the range of .20 to .40, which suggests that although tacit knowledge has some basis in experience, it is not simply a proxy for experience. I propose directions for future research to enhance our understanding of the relationship between experience and the acquisition of tacit knowledge below.

Tacit knowledge and general cognitive ability. General cognitive ability (g) is considered by many to be the best single predictor of job performance (e.g., Hunter, 1986; Ree, Earles, & Teachout, 1994; Schmidt & Hunter, 1998). The relationship between g and performance is attributed largely to the direct influence of g on the acquisition of job-related knowledge (Borman et al., 1993; Hunter, 1986; Schmidt et al., 1986). Many job-knowledge tests, however, assess primarily declarative knowledge of facts and rules (McCloy, Campbell, & Cudeck, 1994). They consist of abstract, well-defined problems that are similar to the types of problems found on traditional intelligence tests, thus explaining the observed correlations between measures of job knowledge and cognitive ability tests. Tacit-knowledge tests, however, consist of problems that are poorly defined and context-specific. We consider performance on these tests to be a function of practical rather than of abstract, general intelligence.

In the research reviewed here, TK tests exhibit trivial-to-moderate correlations with measure of g. Scores on TK tests for academic psychologists and for managers yielded nonsignificant correlations (–.04 to .16) with a test of verbal reasoning in undergraduate samples (Wagner, 1987; Wagner & Sternberg, 1985). Scores on a TK test for managers also exhibited a non-significant correlation with an IQ test for a sample of business executives (Wagner & Sternberg, 1990). Similar findings were obtained with a test of tacit knowledge for sales in samples of undergraduates and salespeople (Wagner, Sujan, Sujan, Rashotte, & Sternberg, 1999).

In a study by Eddy (1988), the Armed Services Vocational Aptitude Battery (ASVAB) was administered along with a TK test for managers to a sample of Air Force recruits. The ASVAB is a multiple-aptitude battery measuring verbal, quantitative, and mechanical abilities and has been found to correlate highly with other cognitive ability tests. Scores on the TK test exhibited near-zero correlations with factor scores on the ASVAB. In research with military leaders, leaders at three levels of command completed Terman's (1950) Concept Mastery Test along with a TK test for their respective level. TK scores exhibited trivial and nonsignificant-to-moderate and significant correlations (.02 to .25) with verbal reasoning ability (Hedlund et al., 2003). Finally, Grigorenko and I (Sternberg & Grigorenko, 1999) found that a test of common sense for the workplace (e.g., how to handle oneself in a job interview) predicted self-ratings of practical abilities but not of academic abilities. The research reviewed above supports the contention that TK tests measure abilities that are distinct from those assessed by traditional intelligence tests. Additional research, discussed below, shows that TK tests measure something unique beyond g.

Tacit knowledge and perfomance. Tacit-knowledge tests have been found to predict performance in a number of domains, typically correlating generally in the range of .2 to .5 with criteria such as rated prestige of business or institution, salary, performance-appraisal ratings, number of publications, grades in school, and adjustment to college (Sternberg et al.,

1995, 2000; Wagner, 1987; Wagner & Sternberg, 1985). Some of these findings are reviewed below in more detail.

In studies with general business managers, TK scores correlated in the range of .2 to .4 with criteria such as salary, years of management experience, and whether the manager worked for a company at the top of the Fortune 500 list (Wagner, 1987; Wagner & Sternberg, 1985). Compared with the correlations reported by Schmidt and Hunter (1998), these correlations are uncorrected for attenuation due to restriction of range. In a study with bank managers, Wagner and I (Wagner & Sternberg, 1985) obtained significant correlations between TK scores and average percentage of merit-based salary increase ($r = .48$, $p < .05$) and average performance rating for the category of generating new business for the bank ($r = .56$, $p < .05$).

Additional findings regarding tacit knowledge. Some additional findings regarding tacit knowledge are worth noting because they further enhance our understanding of practical intelligence.

First, tacit knowledge, as a cognitive-ability variable, is viewed as distinct from personality measures. Wagner and I (Wagner & Sternberg, 1990) found that TK scores generally exhibited nonsignificant correlations with several personality-type tests, including the California Psychological Inventory, the Myers-Briggs Type Indicator, and the Fundamental Interpersonal Relations Orientation-Behavior (FIRO-B) given to a sample of business executives. The exceptions were the Social Presence factor of the California Psychological Inventory and the Control Expressed factor of the FIRO-B, which correlated with TK scores .29 and .25, respectively. In hierarchical regression analyses, TK scores consistently accounted for a significant increment in variance beyond the personality measures.

Second, tacit-knowledge measures tend to correlate among themselves and to show a general factor among themselves (Sternberg et al., 2000; Wagner, 1987) that is distinct from the general factor of tests of general ability. In one study, correlations between scores on a tacit-knowledge test for academic psychologists and business managers was at the .6 level (Wagner, 1987).

Third, tacit-knowledge measures have been found, in at least one instance, to yield similar results across cultures. Patterns of preferences for the quality of responses to a tacit-knowledge measure for the workplace were compared between workers in the United States and Spain. The correlation between the two patterns of preferences for responses to problems was at the .9 level (Cianciolo, Grigorenko, Jarvin et al., 2003).

Finally, traditional intelligence tests often are found to exhibit group differences in scores as a function of gender and race (for reviews see Loehlin, 2000; Neisser et al., 1996). TK tests, because they are not restricted to abilities developed in school, may be less susceptible to these differences. In Eddy's (1988) study of Air Force recruits, correlations were reported between dummy coded variables for race and gender and TK scores. Comparable levels of performance on the TK test were found among majority and minority group members and among males and females as indicated by nonsignificant correlations between tacit knowledge and both race (.03) and gender (.02). The same effects were not found for scores on the ASVAB. The dummy variables for race and gender exhibited significant correlations ranging from .2 to .4 with scores on the ASVAB subtest. Therefore, there is preliminary support for the notion that TK tests do not exhibit the same group differences found for traditional intelligence tests. Of course, additional research would be necessary to substantiate this claim.

The research conducted thus far indicates that tacit knowledge generally increases with experience; that it is distinct from general intelligence and personality traits; that TK tests predict performance in several domains and do so beyond tests of general intelligence; that scores on TK tests appear to be comparable across racial and gender groups; and that practical intelligence may have a substantial amount of generality that is distinct from the generality of psychometric g. These findings add support to the importance of considering practical intelligence in attempting to understand the competencies needed for real-world success.

Attempts to measure practical abilities are not unique to TK tests. The use of simulations and situational-judgment tests (SJTs) represents a set of attempts to capture real-world problem-solving ability. Simulations involve observing people in situations that have been created to represent aspects of the actual job situation. Responses to these simulations are considered to represent the actual responses (or close approximations of them) that individuals would exhibit in real situations. Simulations can take the form of in-basket tests, situational interviews, group discussions, assessment centers, and situational-judgment tests. Motowidlo et al. (1990) distinguished between high-fidelity and low-fidelity simulations. In high-fidelity simulations, the stimuli presented to the respondent closely replicate the actual situation, and the individual has an opportunity to respond as if he or she were in the actual situation. In low-fidelity simulations, the stimuli are presented in written or oral form, and the individual is asked to describe how he or she would respond to the situation, rather than actually to carry out the behavior.

Tacit knowledge and leadership. Two studies showed the incremental validity of TK tests over traditional intelligence tests in predicting performance. In a study with business executives attending the Leadership Development Program at the Center for Creative Leadership, Wagner and I (Wagner & Sternberg, 1990) obtained a correlation of .61 between scores on a TK test for managers and performance on a managerial simulation. Furthermore, TK scores explained 32% of the variance in performance beyond scores on a traditional IQ test, and also explained variance beyond measures of personality and cognitive style. In a study with military leaders, Hedlund et al. (2003) found TK scores to correlate significantly at all three levels of command with ratings of leadership effectiveness made by subordinates, peers, or superiors, with correlations ranging from .14 to .42 (Hedlund et al., 2003). More important, TK scores accounted for small (4–6%), but significant variance in leadership effectiveness beyond scores on tests of general verbal intelligence and tacit knowledge for managers. These studies provide evidence that tacit knowledge accounts for variance in performance that is not accounted for by traditional tests of abstract, academic intelligence.

Other researchers, using TK tests or similar measures, also have found support for the relationship between practical intelligence and performance (e.g., Colonia-Willner, 1998; Fox & Spector, 2000; Pulakos, Schmitt, & Chan, 1996). Colonia-Willner administered the Tacit Knowledge Inventory for Managers (TKIM; Wagner & Sternberg, 1991) to bank managers along with measures of psychometric and verbal reasoning. She found that scores on the TKIM significantly predicted an index of managerial skill, whereas psychometric and verbal reasoning did not. Thus, there is growing evidence to suggest that tests of TK and related tests not only explain individual differences in performance but also measure an aspect of performance that is not explained by measures of general intelligence. We consider that aspect to represent practical intelligence.

Creativity

Creativity refers to skill in generating ideas and products that are (a) relatively novel, (b) high in quality, and (c) appropriate to the task at hand. Creativity is important for leadership because it is the component whereby one generates the ideas that others will follow. A leader who is practically intelligent may get along and get others to go along—but with inferior or stale ideas. Many leaders are academically and even practically intelligent, but uncreative; they lead people through their ability to influence rather than through their agenda.

A confluence model of creativity (Sternberg & Lubart, 1995, 1996) suggests that creative people show a variety of characteristics. These characteristics represent not innate abilities, but rather, largely, decisions (Sternberg, 2000). In other words, to a great extent, people decide to be creative. They exhibit a creative attitude toward life. Attributes associated with creativity include (but are not limited to) proclivities to (a) redefine problems; (b) recognize how knowledge can both help and hinder creative thinking (see also Frensch & Sternberg, 1989; Sternberg, 1985a); (c) take sensible risks; (d) surmount obstacles that are placed in one's way; (e) believe in one's ability to accomplish the task at hand (self-efficacy [Bandura, 1996]); (f) tolerate ambiguity; (g) find intrinsic rewards for the things one is intrinsically motivated to do; and (h) continue to grow intellectually rather than to stagnate.

Research within the proposed framework has yielded support for this model (Lubart & Sternberg, 1995; Sternberg & Lubart, 1995). It has used tasks such as (a) writing short stories using unusual titles (e.g., The Octopus' Sneakers); (b) drawing pictures with unusual themes (e.g., the earth from an insect's point of view); (c) devising creative advertisements for boring products (e.g., cufflinks); and (d) solving unusual scientific problems (e.g., how we could tell if someone had been on the moon in the past month?). This research showed creative performance to be moderately domain-specific and to be predicted by a combination of intelligence, knowledge, thinking styles, personality, and motivation. Fluid intelligence was modestly-to-moderately correlated with performance on the creative tasks.

In a more recent study (Sternberg & The Rainbow Collaborators, in press), my colleagues and I used a variety of multiple-choice and performance measures to assess creativity in college students. The multiple-choice measures required participants to complete tasks such as solving counterfactual analogies ('Suppose sparrows played hopscotch . . . What would be the solution to the following analogy?') and to solve numerical problems with novel number operations (such as flix, which requires one to add $a + b$ when a is greater than b and to subtract a from b when a is less than or equal to b). Additional performance-based tasks included writing short stories, telling short stories, and captioning cartoons. The tests significantly increased prediction of college grades and also substantially reduced ethnic-group differences relative to analytical tests such as the SAT.

The creative ideas one proposes can be of different kinds (Sternberg, 1999b, 2002a; Sternberg, Kaufman, & Pretz, 2002):

(a) replications, which are recycled versions of already existing ideas, largely in their original form, in somewhat new situations. Leaders who are replicators basically work from someone else's script. They imitate someone or otherwise do as has been done in the past. They provide the minimal limiting case of creativity work.

(b) redefinitions, which involve using already existing ideas in a new form or way. Redefiners pretty much accept the status quo, but may give it a new name or a new description. They may also view existing ideas in a way that is different from the way others view these ideas, or use it for a new reason. Redefiners are sometimes referred to as presenting old wine in new bottles, because their ideas repackage already existing ideas.

(c) forward incrementations, which involve moving things the next step along the way they already are going. Forward incrementers take things one or two steps further, adhering to old patterns, but go beyond these patterns. Leaders who are forward incrementers take their followers further down a path set by previous leaders.

(d) advance forward incrementations, which involve moving things forward in the way they already are going, but several steps forward, often beyond where others are ready to follow. Advance forward incrementers try to move things very far, very fast, and sometimes lose their followers in the process.

(e) redirections, which involve changing the direction in which things are going, starting from where things are at the given time. Redirectors are unhappy with where things are going, so they attempt to steer their followers somewhere else. Such leaders change the direction that their organization or other group is pursuing.

(f) regressive redirections, which involve changing the direction in which things are going, but starting at a point that most people had long ago abandoned. Regressive redirectors look to the past. They argue that things once were better and that it is time to move back to the way things were and to move forward from there.

(g) reinitiations, which involve starting over from a new point beyond where things are, and moving forward in a different direction from there. Reinitiators not only do not accept the direction in which things are moving; they also do not accept the starting point or basic assumptions. They shake things up in a major way. Such leaders accept practically nothing from the past and move in a direction that they, alone, have set.

(h) syntheses, which involve putting together ideas from different paradigms or ways of thinking that have not previously been integrated. Synthesizers see value in multiple existing ways of doing things, and integrate these ways of doing things to form a new way of doing things unlike what has been done before. Such leaders integrate the approaches of other leaders to form their own unique approach.

Various forms of creative contributions engender different kinds of leadership. In particular, some leaders transform the nature of an organization or other institution, whereas others do not. At a given time, in a given place, transformation may or may not be called for. So transformation is not necessarily needed in every leadership situation. But the leaders who tend to be remembered over the course of history are probably, in most cases, those who transform organizations or, more generally, ways of thinking.

In the terms of Bass and Avolio (Avolio, Bass, & Jung, 1999; Bass, 1985, 1998, 2002; Bass, Avolio, & Atwater, 1996), transactional leaders are more likely to pursue Options a to c. Transformational leaders, on the other hand, are more likely to pursue any of Options e to h (and possibly d). They are crowd-defiers. In terms of Kuhn's (1970) theory of scientific revolutions, which applies to ideas outside the sciences as well, these are the leaders who revolutionize ways of thinking.

Different combinations of intelligence and creativity also can lead to different styles of leadership. Someone who is high in creativity but not in analytical or practical intelligence may be able to generate a number of ideas, some of them good, but not have the analytical skill to know which are good ideas, nor the practical skill to know how to persuade others of their value. In contrast, someone who is high in practical intelligence but not analytical intelligence or creativity may be able to persuade people to follow ideas, but ideas that are not of his or her own making and not ones that have been rigorously evaluated. Finally, someone who is high in creativity but not analytical or practical intelligence may be a frustrated leader who comes up with ideas that seem lost on Cloud Nine: They are neither rigorous nor practical; and so forth.

A transformational leader will always be creative in some degree, but may or may not be particularly wise. Transformational leaders who are low in or even who lack wisdom are not in any sense "pseudotransformational" as opposed to being "authentically transformational." They genuinely may effect transformations. These transformations simply are not very wise. For example, some African leaders in the latter half of the twentieth century adopted Marxist-Leninist ideas that, poorly implemented, drove countries that already were economically marginal into profound impoverishment. The leaders authentically transformed their countries, but for the worse, as have many unwise corporate leaders. Wise transformational leaders are probably not altogether common. One such uncommon leader, for example, Nelson Mandela, implemented a largely successful policy of forgiveness and reconciliation that is practically unique among modern heads of state.

Our research on creativity (Lubart & Sternberg, 1995; Sternberg & Lubart, 1995) has yielded several conclusions. First, creativity often involves defying the crowd, or as we have put it, "buying low and selling high" in the world of ideas. Creative leaders are good investors: They do what needs to be done, rather than just what other people or polls tell them to do. Second, creativity is relatively domain-specific. Third, creativity is weakly related to academic intelligence, but certainly is not the same thing as academic intelligence. In general, it appears that there is a threshold of IQ for creativity, but it is probably about 120 or even lower (see review in Sternberg & O'Hara, 2000).

Wisdom

A leader can have all of the above attributes and still lack an additional quality that, arguably, is the most important quality a leader can have, but perhaps, also the rarest. This additional quality is wisdom.

Over time, a number of philosophical and psychological approaches to wisdom have emerged, only a few of which can be mentioned briefly here. The approaches underlying some of these attempts are summarized elsewhere (Sternberg, 1990a), and a more detailed review of some of the major approaches to wisdom can be found in Baltes and Staudinger (2000) or in Sternberg (1990b, 1998a, 2000).

The main approaches can be classified as *philosophical, implicit-theories,* and *developmental* approaches.

Philosophical approaches have been reviewed by Robinson (1990; see also Robinson, 1989, with regard to the Aristotelian approach in particular, and Labouvie-Vief, 1990, for a further review). Robinson notes that the study of wisdom has a history that long antedates psychological study, with the Platonic dialogues offering the first intensive analysis of the concept of wisdom. Robinson points out that, in these dialogues, there are three different senses of wisdom: wisdom as (a) *sophia,* which is found in those who seek a contemplative life in search of truth; (b) *phronesis*, which is the kind of practical wisdom shown by statesmen and legislators; and (c) *episteme*, which is found in those who understand things from a scientific point of view.

Implicit-theoretical approaches to wisdom have in common the search for an understanding of people's folk conceptions of what wisdom is. Thus, the goal is not to provide a "psychologically true" account of wisdom, but rather an account that is true with respect to people's beliefs, whether these beliefs are right or wrong. Some of the earliest work of this kind was done by Clayton (1975, 1976, 1982; Clayton & Birren, 1980), who multi-dimensionally scaled ratings of pairs of words potentially related to wisdom for three samples of adults differing in age (younger, middle-aged, older). In her earliest study (Clayton, 1975), the terms that were scaled were ones such as *experienced, pragmatic, understanding,* and *knowledgeable.*

Holliday and Chandler (1986) also used an implicit-theories approach to understanding wisdom. Principal-components analysis of one of their studies revealed five underlying factors: exceptional understanding, judgment and communication skills, general competence, interpersonal skills, and social unobtrusiveness.

I have reported a series of studies investigating implicit theories of wisdom (Sternberg, 1985b, 1990c). In one study, 200 professors each of art, business, philosophy, and physics were asked to rate the characteristicness of each behavior obtained in a prestudy from the corresponding population with respect to the professors' ideal conception of each of an ideally wise, intelligent, or creative individual in their occupation. Laypersons were also asked to provide these ratings but for a hypothetical ideal individual without regard to occupation. Correlations were computed across the three ratings. In each group except philosophy, the highest correlation was between wisdom and intelligence; in philosophy, the highest correlation was between intelligence and creativity. The correlations between wisdom and intelligence ratings ranged from .42 to .78 with a median of .68. For all groups, the lowest correlation was between wisdom and creativity (which ranged from −.24 to .48 with a median of .27). The negative correlation was for business professors.

In a second study, 40 college students were asked to sort three sets of 40 behaviors each into as many or as few piles as they wished. The 40 behaviors in each set were the top-rated wisdom, intelligence, and creativity behaviors from the previous study. The sortings then each were subjected to nonmetric multidimensional scaling. For wisdom, six components emerged: *reasoning ability, sagacity, learning from ideas and environment, judgment, expeditious use of information,* and *perspicacity.*

In a third study, 50 adults were asked to rate descriptions of hypothetical individuals for wisdom, intelligence, and creativity. Correlations were computed between pairs of ratings of the hypothetical individuals' levels of the three traits. Correlations between the ratings were .94 for wisdom and intelligence, .62 for wisdom and creativity, and .69 for intelligence and creativity, again suggesting that wisdom and intelligence are highly correlated in people's implicit theories, at least in the United States.

Explicit-theoretical approaches have in common a formal theory of wisdom that is proposed to account for wisdom. The most extensive program of research has been that conducted by Baltes and his colleagues. This program of research is related to Baltes's long-standing program of research on intellectual abilities and aging. For example, Baltes and Smith (1987, 1990) gave adult participants life-management problems, such as "A fouteen-year-old girl is pregnant. What should she, what should one, consider and do?" and "A fifteen-year-old girl wants to marry soon. What should she, what should one, consider and do?" This same problem might be used to measure the pragmatics of intelligence, about which Baltes has written at length. Baltes and Smith tested a five-component model of wisdom on participants' protocols in answering these and other questions, based on a notion of wisdom as expert knowledge about fundamental life matters (Smith & Baltes, 1990) or of wisdom as good judgment and advice in important but uncertain matters of life (Baltes & Staudinger, 2000).

Three kinds of factors—general person factors, expertise-specific factors, and facilitative-experiential contexts—were proposed to facilitate wise judgments. These factors are used in life planning, life management, and life review. Wisdom is in turn then reflected in five components: (a) rich factual knowledge (general and specific knowledge about the conditions of life and its variations); (b) rich procedural knowledge (general and specific knowledge about strategies of judgment and advice concerning matters of life); (c) life span contextualism (knowledge about the contexts of life and their temporal [developmental] relationships); (d) relativism (knowledge about differences in values, goals, and priorities); and (e) uncertainty (knowledge about the relative indeterminacy and unpredictability of life and ways to manage). An expert answer should reflect more of these components, whereas a novice answer should reflect fewer of them. The data collected to date generally have been supportive of the model. These factors seem to reflect the pragmatic aspect of intelligence but to go beyond it, for example, in the inclusion of factors of relativism and uncertainty.

Over time, Baltes and his colleagues (e.g., Baltes, Smith, & Staudinger, 1992; Baltes & Staudinger, 2000) have collected a wide range of data showing the empirical utility of the proposed theoretical and measurement approaches to wisdom. For example, Staudinger, Lopez, and Baltes (1997) found that measures of intelligence (as well as of personality) overlap with but are nonidentical to measures of wisdom in terms of constructs measured, and Staudinger, Smith, and Baltes (1992) showed that human-services professionals outperformed a control group on wisdom-related tasks. They also showed that older adults performed as well on such tasks as did younger adults, and that older adults did better on such tasks if there was a match between their age and the age of the fictitious characters about whom they made judgments. Baltes, Staudinger, Maercker, and Smith (1995) found that older individuals nominated for their wisdom performed as well as did clinical psychologists on wisdom-related tasks. They also showed that up to the age of 80, older adults performed as well on such tasks as did younger adults. In a further set of studies, Staudinger and Baltes (1996) found that performance settings that were ecologically relevant to the lives of their participants and that provided for actual or "virtual" interaction of minds increased wisdom-related performance substantially.

Wisdom is viewed here according to a proposed balance theory of wisdom (Sternberg, 1998b, 2000), according to which an individual is wise to the extent he or she uses successful intelligence, creativity, and experience as moderated by values to (a) seek to reach a common good, (b) by balancing intrapersonal (one's own), interpersonal (others'), and extrapersonal (organizational/institutional/spiritual) interests, (c) over the short and long terms, to (d) adapt to, shape, and select environments.

Wise leaders do not look out just for their own interests, nor do they ignore these interests. Rather, they skillfully balance interests of varying kinds, including their own, those of their followers, and those of the organization for which they are responsible. They also recognize that they need to align the interests of their group or organization with those of other groups or organizations because no group operates within a vacuum. Wise leaders realize that what may appear to be a prudent course of action over the short term does not necessarily appear so over the long term.

Leaders who have been less than fully successful often have been so because they have ignored one or another set of interests. For instance, Richard Nixon and Bill Clinton, in their respective cover-ups, not only failed to fulfill the interests of the country they led, but also failed to fulfill their own interests. Their cover-ups ended up bogging down their administrations in scandals rather than allowing them to make the positive accomplishments they had hoped to make. Freud was a great leader in the fields of psychiatry and psychology, but his insistence that his followers (disciples) conform quite exactly to his own system of psychoanalysis led him to lose those disciples and the support they might have continued to lend to his efforts. He was an expert in interpersonal interests, but not as applied to his own life. Napoleon lost sight of the extrapersonal interests that would have been best for his own country. His disastrous invasion of Russia, which appears to have been motivated more by hubris than by France's need to have Russia in its empire, partially destroyed his reputation as a successful military leader, and paved the way for his later downfall.

Leaders can be intelligent in various ways and creative in various ways; neither trait guarantees wisdom. Indeed, probably relatively few leaders at any level are particularly wise. Yet the few leaders who are notably so—perhaps Nelson Mandela, Martin Luther King, Mahatma Gandhi, Winston Churchill—leave an indelible mark on the people they lead and, potentially, on history. It is important to note that wise leaders are probably usually charismatic, but charismatic leaders are not necessarily wise, as Hitler, Stalin, and many other charismatic leaders have demonstrated over the course of time.

Unsuccessful leaders often show certain stereotyped fallacies in their thinking. Consider five such flaws (Sternberg, 2002b, 2002d). The first, the *unrealistic optimism fallacy* occurs when they think they are so smart and effective that they can do whatever they want. The second, *egocentrism fallacy*, occurs when successful leaders start to think that they are the only ones that matter, not the people who rely on them for leadership. The third, *omniscience fallacy*, occurs when leaders think that they know everything, and lose sight of the limitations of their own knowledge. The fourth, *omnipotence fallacy*, occurs when leaders think they are all-powerful and can do whatever they want. And the fifth, *invulnerability fallacy*, occurs when leaders think they can get away with anything, because they are too clever to be caught; and even if they are caught, they figure that they can get away with what they have done because of who they imagine themselves to be.

Can wisdom be measured? My colleagues and I are currently engaged in a study to validate the balance theory. An example of a kind of problem we are using is the following:

Charles and Margaret are both engineers and have been married for 5 years. Three years ago Charles was offered a job in Europe. Margaret agreed to quit her job in the United States and move to Europe with Charles. The job was an excellent career move for Charles. Soon after the move, they had a baby boy. After the birth, Margaret decided to start working again and, with effort, found a very exciting job that paid well and promised real security. Meanwhile, Charles was offered a transfer back to the United States. Margaret feels she needs another year or two in her new job to meaningfully advance her career. She is also tired of moving. She has already given up a lot of time following Charles around. Charles knows that his wife's job is as important as his own, but he thinks returning to the United States would help both their careers in the end. What should Charles do?

Synthesis

There probably is no model for leadership that will totally capture all of the many facets—both internal and external to the individual—that make for a successful leader. The WICS model may come closer to some models, however, in capturing dimensions that are important.

The final element of the WICS model is *synthesis*. How do the various elements of the model interrelate in leadership?

The base of WICS is successful intelligence. A leader needs:

- Creative skills to generate new ideas;
- Analytical skills to evaluate whether the ideas are good ones;
- Practical skills to implement ideas and to persuade others of the value of the ideas.

A leader may have creative skills, but end up rarely or even never exercising them because of a lack of creative disposition, in particular, the willingness to decide for creativity. For example, the leader may not have the courage to defy the crowd, or the willingness to surmount difficult obstacles, or the insight to see how his or her entrenched thinking is blocking progress. Thus, creativity involves quite a bit more than just the creative skills involved in successful intelligence. It involves as well the personal dispositions that activate these skills.

A leader may be intelligent and/or creative but not wise because of his or her unwillingness to use intelligence and creativity for a common good. Certainly the business leaders of Enron, Arthur Andersen Accounting, WorldCom, and other organizations whose leaders drove them into bankruptcy were intelligent and creative. They were not wise.

An effective leader needs creative ability to come up with ideas, academic ability to decide whether they are good ideas, practical ability to make the ideas work and convince others of the value of the ideas, and wisdom to ensure that the ideas are in the service of the common good rather than just the good of the leader or perhaps some clique of family members or followers. A leader lacking in creativity will be unable to deal with novel and difficult situations, such as a new and unexpected source of hostility. A leader lacking in academic intelligence will not be able to decide whether his or her ideas are viable, and a leader lacking in practical intelligence will be unable to implement his or her ideas effectively. An unwise leader may succeed in implementing ideas, but may end up implementing ideas that are contrary to the best interests of the people he or she leads.

The WICS model is of course related to many other models. It incorporates elements of transformational as well as transactional leadership (Bass, 1998; Bass & Avolio, 1994; Bass, Avolio, & Atwater, 1996), emotionally intelligent leadership (Goleman, 1998b), visionary leadership (Sashkin, 1988), and charismatic leadership (Conger & Kanugo, 1998; Weber, 1968). Eventually a model of leadership will appear that integrates all the strengths of these various models. In the meantime, the WICS model seems like a start.

DEVELOPING WICS-BASED LEADERSHIP SKILLS

Developing WICS might seem like an insurmountable challenge. The opposite is true. To a large extent, the elements of WICS are based on decisions. Teaching for WICS, therefore, is in large part teaching students to make certain decisions rather than others. What are these decisions? I mention three critical ones for each of the three elements.

Intelligence

For intelligence, there is one decision corresponding to each of its analytical, creative, and practical elements.

For the analytical element, the decision is to make a serious effort to be a critical thinker. Many mistakes in judgment are made because people react mindlessly, or on the basis of what feels comfortable to them. They fail seriously to consider all serious and viable options, and to project the possible gains and losses associated with each.

For the creative element, the decision is not to become entrenched, or stuck in conventional ways of thinking. Often, expertise exacerbates rather than ameliorates the situation because experts are especially susceptible to becoming stuck in conventional ways of thinking that have worked for them in the past (Sternberg & Lubart, 1995). They cease "thinking outside the box" simply because they have had so much success thinking within it. Then, at some point, the success stops, and they cannot understand that it is because somewhere along the line, they sacrificed flexibility for comfort.

For the practical element, the decision is to realize that good ideas are not really good enough if one cannot convince others of their value and implement them effectively. The value of an idea inheres not just in how good it sounds in the abstract, but in how well it works. Academics sometimes forget this, resulting in their teaching ideas and techniques that do not work in real-life settings.

Creativity

With regard to creativity, the first decision is that one is willing to defy the crowd. Creativity requires, above all else, courage. It is usually much easier to follow the crowd than to defy it. The result is that most people are content to follow rather than lead; or if they lead, they simply adopt others' ideas as though they were their own.

The second decision is willingness to persevere in the face of obstacles. Few truly creative ideas receive a positive reception when they are first proposed. On the contrary, the ideas are often scorned, and sometimes, the person who proposes them as well. Almost all creative people have been so in spite of, rather than because of, the reception they initially receive from others (Sternberg & Lubart, 1995).

The third decision is willingness to take sensible risks. Creativity does not happen in the absence of risk taking. To the extent that our schools discourage risk taking, or encourage students merely to mimic ideas of their teachers, the schools discourage students' deciding for creativity.

Wisdom

For wisdom, the first and foremost decision is to use one's intelligence, creativity, and experience for a common good. This means that one extends one's field of vision beyond oneself, one's immediate family, or the particular groups with which one identifies. Many managers fail not because they cannot decide for the good, but because they simply do not choose to. Managers at Enron, Arthur Andersen, WorldCom, and other bankrupt companies knew better. They chose not to use their knowledge.

The second decision is to balance one's own, others', and institutional interests over the long and short terms. In today's world, there is a great deal of pressure to give in to short-term decision making. The result is often that managers win the battles but lose the wars. One may save this year's balance sheet at the expense of next year's. Or one may go for a quick profit in place of the investment that would result in longer term gains. In the long run, one loses, and so does the company.

The third decision is to make a genuine effort to understand other people's points of view and incorporate them into one's thinking (so-called dialogical thinking). One cannot do what is good for others if one does not understand what they think, why they think it, and how they came to think it. Many negotiations fail because neither side makes a serious effort to understand the other side. Rather, they see the other side as simply ill-motivated. The result is that whatever the problem is, it never gets solved.

In sum, WICS can be developed by teaching students about the decisions they can make. There are three good ways to teach them. First is to model them. Second is to illustrate them concretely. And third is to reward them. We all can develop leaders by teaching for WICS. WICS requires making certain decisions. But the first decision is the teacher's or mentor's: to teach for it.

REFERENCES

Antonakis, J., Ciancíolo, A., & Sternberg, R. J. (Eds.). In press. *Leadership: A concise review.* Thousand Oaks, CA: Sage.

Avolio, B. J., Bass, B. M., & Jung, D. I. 1999. Reexamining the components of transformational and transactional leadership using the Multifactor Leadership Questionnaire. *Journal of Occupational and Organizational Psychology,* 72: 441–462.

Baltes, P. B., & Smith, J. 1987, August. *Toward a psychology of wisdom and its ontogenesis.* Paper presented at the Ninety-Fifth Annual Convention of the American Psychological Association, New York.

Baltes, P. B., & Smith, J. 1990. Toward a psychology of wisdom and its ontogenesis. In R. J. Sternberg (Ed.), *Wisdom: Its nature, origins, and development:* 87–120. New York: Cambridge University Press.

Baltes, P. B., Smith, J., & Staudinger, U. 1992. Wisdom and successful aging. In T. B. Sonderegger (Ed.), *Psychology and aging:* 123–167. Lincoln, NE: University of Nebraska Press.

Baltes, P. B., & Staudinger, U. M. 2000. Wisdom: A metaheuristic (pragmatic) to orchestrate mind and virtue toward excellence. *American Psychologist,* 55: 122–135.

Baltes, P. B., Staudinger, U. M., Maercker, A., & Smith, J. 1995. People nominated as wise: A comparative study of wisdom-related knowledge. *Psychology and Aging.* 10: 155–166.

Bandura, A. 1996. *Self-efficacy: The exercise of control.* New York: Freeman.

Bass, B. M. 1985. *Leadership and performance beyond expectations.* New York: Free Press.

Bass, B. M. 1990. *Bass and Stogdill's handbook of leadership: Theory, research, and managerial applications.* New York: The Free Press.

Bass, B. M. 1998. *Transformational leadership: Industrial, military, and educational impact.* Mahwah, NJ: Lawrence Erlbaum Associates.

Bass, B. M. 2002. Cognitive, social, and emotional intelligence of transformational leaders. In R. E. Riggio, S. E. Murphy, & F. J. Pirozzolo, (Eds.), *Multiple intelligences and leadership:* 105–118. Mahwah, NJ: Lawrence Erlbaum Associates.

Bass, B. M., & Avolio, B. J. (Eds.). 1994. *Improving organizational effectiveness through transformational leadership.* Thousand Oaks, CA: Sage.

Bass, B. M., Avolio, B. J., & Atwater, L. 1996. The transformational and transactional leadership of men and women. *International Review of Applied Psychology,* 45: 5–34.

Bennis, W., & Nanus, B. 1985. *Leaders: The strategies for taking charge.* New York: Harper and Row.

Binet, A., & Simon, T. 1905. Méthodes nouvelles pour le diagnostic du niveau intellectuel des anormaux. *L'Année Psychologique,* 11: 191–336.

Borman, W. C., Hanson, M. A., Oppler, S. H., & Pulakos, E. D., et al. 1993. Role of early supervisory experience in supervisor performance. *Journal of Applied Psychology,* 78 (3): 443–449.

Caruso, D. R., Mayer, J. D., & Salovey, P. 2002. Emotional intelligence and emotional leadership. In R. E. Riggio, S. E. Murphy, & F. J. Pirozzolo, (Eds.), *Multiple intelligences and leadership:* 55–74. Mahwah, NJ: Lawrence Erlbaum Associates.

Chi, M. T. H., Glaser, R., & Farr, M. J. (Eds.). 1988. *The nature of expertise.* Hillsdale, NJ: Erlbaum.

Cianciolo, A. T., & Grigorenko, E. L., Jarvin, L., Gil, G., Drebot, M., & Sternberg, R. J. 2003. *Tacit knowledge and practical intelligence: Advancements in measurement and construct validity.* Manuscript in preparation.

Clayton, V. 1975. Erickson's theory of human development as it applies to the aged: Wisdom as contradictory cognition. *Human Development,* 18: 119–128.

Clayton V. 1976. *A multidimensional scaling analysis of the concept of wisdom.* Unpublished doctoral dissertation, University of Southern California.

Clayton, V. 1982. Wisdom and intelligence: The nature and function of knowledge in the later years. *International Journal of Aging and Development,* 15: 315–321.

Clayton, V., & Birren, J. E. 1980. The development of wisdom across the life-span: A reexamination of an ancient topic. In P. B. Baltes, & O. G. Brim (Eds.), *Life-span development and behavior,* 3: 103–135. New York: Academic Press.

Colonia-Willner, R. 1998. Practical intelligence at work: Relationship between aging and cognitive efficiency among managers in a bank environment. *Psychology and Aging,* 13: 45–57.

Conger, J. A., & Kanugo, R. N. 1998. *Charismatic leadership in organizations.* Thousand Oaks, CA: Sage Publications.

Demetriou, A. 2002. Tracing psychology's invisible g_{iant} and its visible guards. In R. J. Sternberg & E. L. Grigorenko (Eds.), *The general factor of intelligence: How general is it?* 3–18. Mahwah, NJ: Erlbaum.

Eddy, A. S. 1988. *The relationship between the Tacit Knowledge Inventory for Managers and the Armed Services Vocational Aptitude Battery.* Unpublished masters thesis, St. Mary's University, San Antonio, TX.

Fiedler, F. E. 2002. The curious role of cognitive resources in leadership. In R. E. Riggio, S. E. Murphy, F. J. Pirozzolo, (Eds.), *Multiple intelligences and leadership:* 91–104. Mahwah, NJ: Lawrence Erlbaum Associates.

Fiedler, F. E., & Link, T. G. 1994. Leader intelligence, interpersonal stress, and task performance. In R. J. Sternberg & R. K. Wagner (Eds.), *Mind in context: Interactionist perspectives on human intelligence:* 152–167. New York: Cambridge University Press.

Fox, S., & Spector, P. E. 2000. Relations of emotional intelligence, practical intelligence, general intelligence, and trait affectivity with interview outcomes: It's not all just *g. Journal of Organizational Behavior,* 21: 203–220.

Frensch, P. A., & Sternberg, R. J. 1989. Expertise and intelligent thinking: When is it worse to know better? In R. J. Sternberg (Ed.), *Advances in the psychology of human intelligence.* Hillsdale, NJ: Erlbaum.

Gardner, H. 1995. *Leading Minds.* New York: Basic Books.

Goleman, D. 1998a. *Working with emotional intelligence.* New York: Bantam.

Goleman, D. 1998b. What makes a good leader? *Harvard Business Review,* November/December: 93–102.

Grigorenko, E. L., & Sternberg, R. J. (Eds.). 2001. *Family environment and intellectual functioning: A life-span perspective.* Mahwah, NJ: Lawrence Erlbaum Associates.

Groen, G. J., & Patel, V. L. 1988. The relationship between comprehension and reasoning in medical expertise. In M. T. H. Chi, & R. Glaser, et al. (Eds.), *The nature of expertise:* 287–310. Hillsdale, NJ: Lawrence Erlbaum Associates.

Hanson, M. A., & Ramos, R. A. 1996. Situational judgment tests. In R. S. Barrett (Ed.), *Fair employment strategies in human resource management:* 119–124. Westport, CT: Greenwood Press.

Hedlund, J., Forsythe, G. B., Horvath, J. A., Williams, W. M., Snook, S., & Sternberg, R. J. 2003. Identifying and assessing tacit knowledge: Understanding the practical intelligence of military leaders. *Leadership Quarterly,* 14: 117–140.

Holiday, S. G., & Chandler, M. J. 1986. *Wisdom: Explorations in adult competence.* Basel, Switzerland: Karger.

Hunter, J. E. 1986. Cognitive ability, cognitive aptitude, job knowledge, and job performance. *Journal of Vocational Behavior,* 29(3): 340–362.

Hunter, J. E., & Hunter, R. F. 1984. Validity and utility of alternative predictors of job performance. *Psychological Bulletin,* 96: 72–98.

Jensen, A. R. 1998. *The g factor.* Westport, CT: Greenwood/Praeger.

Jensen, A. R. 2002. Psychometric *g:* Definition and substantiation. In R. J. Sternberg & E. L. Grigorenko (Eds.), *The general factor of intelligence: How general is it?* 39–53. Mahwah, NJ: Erlbaum.

Kaufman, A. 2000. Tests of intelligence. In R. J. Sternberg (Ed.), *Handbook of intelligence:* 445–476. New York: Cambridge University Press.

Kotter, J. 1987. *The leadership factor.* New York: Free Press.

Kuhn, T. S. 1970. *The structure of scientific revolutions* (2nd ed.). Chicago: University of Chicago Press.

Labouvie-Vief, G. 1990. Wisdom as integrated thought: Historical and developmental perspectives. In R. J. Sternberg (Ed.), *Wisdom: Its nature, origins, and development:* 52–83. New York: Cambridge University Press.

Lau, J., & Shani, A. 1992. *Behavior in organizations: An experimental approach* (5th ed.). Homewood, IL: Irwin.

Legree, P. J. 1995. Evidence for an oblique social intelligence factor established with a Likert-based testing procedure. *Intelligence,* 21(3): 247–266.

Loehlin, J. C. 2000. Group differences in intelligence. In R. J. Sternberg (Ed.), *Handbook of intelligence:* 176–193. New York: Cambridge University Press.

Lubart, T. I., & Sternberg, R. J. 1995. An investment approach to creativity: Theory and data. In S. M. Smith, T. B. Ward, & R. A. Finke (Eds.), *The creative cognition approach:* 269–302. Cambridge, MA: MIT Press.

McCloy, R. A., Campbell, J. P., & Cudeck, R. 1994. A confirmatory test of a model of performance determinants. *Journal of Applied Psychology,* 79(4): 493–505.

McDaniel, M. A., Schmidt, F. L., & Hunter, J. E. 1988. A meta-analysis of the validity of methods for rating training and experience in personnel selection. *Personnel Psychology,* 41(2): 283–314.

Mintzberg, H. 1975. The manager's job: Folklore and fact. *Harvard Business Review,* 4: 49–61.

Motowidlo, S. J., Dunnette, M. D., & Carter, G. W.1990. An alternative selection procedure: The low-fidelity simulation. *Journal of Applied Psychology,* 75(6): 640–647.

Neisser, U. 1976. General, academic, and artificial intelligence. In L. Resnick (Ed.), *Human intelligence: Perspectives on its theory and measurement:* 179–189. Norwood, NJ: Ablex.

Neisser, U. 1979. The concept of intelligence. In R. J. Sternberg & D. K. Detterman (Eds.), *Human intelligence: Perspectives on its theory and measurement:* 179–189. Norwood, NJ: Ablex.

Neisser, U., Boodoo, G., Bouchard, T. J., Boykin, W. A., & Brody, N., Ceci, S. J., Halpern, D. F., Loehlin, J. C., Perloff, R., Sternberg, R. J., & Urbina, S. 1996. Intelligence: Knowns and unknowns. *American Psychologist,* 51(2): 77–101.

Polanyi, M. 1966. *The tacit dimensions.* Garden City, NY: Doubleday.

Pulakos, E. D., Schmitt, N., & Chan, D. 1996. Models of job performance ratings: An examination of ratee race, ratee gender, and rater level effects. *Human Performance,* 9(2): 103–119.

Quinones, M. A., Ford, J. K., & Teachout, M. S. 1995. The relationship between work experience and job performance: A conceptual and meta-analytic review. *Personnel Psychology,* 48(4): 887–910.

Ree, M. J., Earles, J. A., & Teachout, M. S. 1994. Predicting job performance: Not much more than *g. Journal of Applied Psychology,* 79(4): 518–524.

Riggio, R. E., Murphy, S. E., & Pirozzolo, F. J. 2002. *Multiple intelligences and leadership.* Mahwah, NJ: Lawrence Erlbaum Associates.

Robinson, D. N. 1989. *Aristotle's psychology.* New York: Columbia University Press.

Robinson, D. N. 1990. Wisdom through the ages. In R. J. Sternberg (Ed.), *Wisdom: Its nature, origins, and development:* 13–24. New York: Cambridge University Press.

Sashkin, M. 1988. The visionary leader. In J. A. Conger & R. N. Kanugo (Eds.), *Charismatic Leadership: The elusive factor in organizational effectiveness:* 122–160. San Francisco: Jossey-Bass.

Sashkin, M. In press. Transformational leadership approaches: A review and synthesis. In R. J. Sternberg, J. Antonakis, & A. T. Cianciolo (Eds.), *The nature of leadership.* Thousand Oaks, CA: Sage.

Schmidt, F. L., & Hunter, J. E. 1998. The validity and utility of selection methods in personnel psychology. Practical and theoretical implications of 85 years of research findings. *Psychological Bulletin,* 124: 262–274.

Schmidt, F. L., Hunter, J. E., & Outerbridge, A. N. 1986. Impact of job experience and ability on job knowledge, work sample performance, and supervisory ratings of job performance. *Journal of Applied Psychology,* 71(3): 432–439.

Schmitt, N., & Chan, D. 1998. *Personal selection: A theoretical approach.* Sage Publications.

Schön, D. A. 1983. *The reflective practitioner.* New York: Basic Books.

Scribner, S. 1986. Thinking in action: Some characteristics of practical thought. In R. J. Sternberg & R. K. Wagner (Eds.), *Practical Intelligence: Nature and origins of competence in the everyday world:* 13–30. New York: Cambridge University Press.

Smith, J., & Baltes, P. B. 1990. Wisdom-related knowledge: Age/cohort differences in response to life-planning problems. *Developmental Psychology,* 26: 494–505.

Spearman, C. 1927. *The abilities of man.* London: Macmillan.

Staudinger, U. M., & Baltes, P. B. 1996. Interactive minds: A facilitative setting for wisdom-related performance? *Journal of Personality and Social Psychology,* 71: 746–762.

Staudinger, U. M., Lopez, D. F., & Baltes, P. B. 1997. The psychometric location of wisdom-related performance: Intelligence, personality, and more? *Personality and Social Psychology Bulletin,* 23: 1200–1214.

Staudinger, U. M., Smith, J., & Baltes, P. B. 1992. Widsom-related knowledge in life review task: Age differences and the role of professional specialization. *Psychology and Aging,* 7: 271–281.

Sternberg, R. J. 1985a. *Beyond IQ: Toward a triarchic theory of intelligence.* New York: Cambridge University Press.

Sternberg, R. J. 1985b. Implicit theories of intelligence, creativity, and wisdom. *Journal of Personality and Social Psychology,* 49(3): 607–627.

Sternberg, R. J. 1988. The intellect: Three portraits unveiled. *Gifted Children Monthly:* 9, 1–3.

Sternberg, R. J. 1990a. Understanding wisdom. In R. J. Sternberg (Ed.), *Wisdom: Its nature, origins, and development:* 3–9. New York: Cambridge University Press.

Sternberg, R. J. (Ed.). 1990b. *Wisdom: Its nature, origins, and development.* New York: Cambridge University Press.

Sternberg, R. J. 1990c. Wisdom and its relation to intelligence and creativity. In R. J. Sternberg (Ed.), *Wisdom: Its nature, origins, and development.* New York: Cambridge University Press.

Sternberg, R. J. 1997. *Successful intelligence.* New York: Plume.

Sternberg, R. J. 1998a. Abilities are forms of developing expertise. *Educational Researcher,* 27: 11–20.

Sternberg, R. J. 1998b. A balance theory of wisdom. *Review of General Psychology,* 2(4): 347–365.

Sternberg, R. J. 1999a. Intelligence as developing expertise. *Contemporary Educational Psychology,* 24: 259–375.

Sternberg, R. J. 1999b. A propulsion model of types of creative contributions. *Review of General Psychology,* 3: 83–100.

Sternberg, R. J. 1999c. The theory of successful intelligence. *Review of General Psychology,* 3: 292–316.

Sternberg, R. J. 2000. Creativity is a decision. In B. Z. Presseisen (Ed.), *Teaching for intelligence II: A collection of articles:* 83–103. Arlington Heights, IL: Skylight Training and Publishing Inc.

Sternberg, R. J. 2002a. Creativity is a decision. *American Psychologist,* 57(5): 376.

Sternberg, R. J. 2002b. Smart people are not stupid, but they sure can be foolish: The imbalance theory of foolishness. In R. J. Sternberg (Ed.), *Why smart people can be so stupid.* New Haven: Yale University Press.

Sternberg, R. J. 2002c. Successful intelligence: A new approach to leadership. In R. E. Riggio, S. E. Murphy, & F. J. Pirozzolo (Eds.), *Multiple intelligences and leadership:* 9–28. Mahwah, NJ: Lawrence Erlbaum Associates.

Sternber, R. J. (Ed.). 2002d. *Why smart people can be so stupid.* New Haven: Yale University Press.

Sternberg, R. J. 2003. *Wisdom, intelligence, and creativity, synthesized.* New York: Cambridge University Press.

Sternberg, R. J., Forsythe, G. B., Hedlund, J., Horvath, J., Snook, S., Williams, W. M., Wagner, R. K., & Grigorenko, E. L. 2000. *Practical intelligence in everyday life.* New York: Cambridge University Press.

Sternberg, R. J., & Grigorenko, E. L. (Eds.) 1997. *Intelligence, heredity, and environment.* New York: Cambridge University Press.

Sternberg, R. J., & Grigorenko, E. L. 1999. A smelly 113° in the shade, or, why we do field research. *APS Observer,* 12: 1, 10–11, 20–21.

Sternberg, R. J., & Grigorenko, E. L. (Eds.). 2001. *Environmental effects on cognitive abilities.* Mahwah, NJ: Lawrence Erlbaum Associates.

Sternberg, R. J., & Grigorenko, E. L. (Eds.). 2002. *The general factor of intelligence: How general is it?* Mahwah, NJ: Erlbaum.

Sternberg, R. J., & Hedlund, J. 2002 Practical intelligence, g, and work psychology. *Human Performance,* 15: 143–160.

Sternberg, R. J., & Horvath, J. A. (Eds.). 1999. *Tacit knowledge in professional practice.* Mahwah, NJ: Lawrence Erlbaum Associates.

Sternberg, R. J., Kaufman, J. C., & Pretz, J. E. 2002. *The creativity conundrum: A propulsion model of kinds of creative contributions.* Philadelphia, PA: Psychology Press.

Sternberg, R. J., & Lubart, T. I. 1995. *Defying the crowd: Cultivating creativity in a culture of conformity.* New York: Free Press.

Sternberg, R. J., & Lubart, T. I. 1996. Investing in creativity. *American Psychologist,* 51(7): 677–688.

Sternberg, R. J., & O'Hara, L. A. 2000. Intelligence and creativity. In R. J. Sternberg (Ed.), *Handbook of intelligence:* 609–628. New York: Cambridge University Press.

Sternberg & The Rainbow Collaborators. In press. Augmenting the SAT through assessments of analytical, practical, and creative skills. In W. J. Camara & E. W. Kimmel (Eds.), *Choosing students: Higher education tools for the 21ˢᵗ century.* Mahwah, NJ: Lawrence Erlbaum Associates.

Sternberg, R. J., & Vroom, V. H. 2002. The person versus the situation in leadership. *Leadership Quarterly,* 13: 301–323.

Sternberg, R. J., & Wagner, R. K. 1993. The g-ocentric view of intelligence and job performance is wrong. *Current Directions in Psychological Science,* 2(1): 1–4.

Sternberg, R. J., Wagner, R. K., & Okagaki, L. 1993. Practical intelligence: The nature and role of tacit knowledge in work and at school. In H. Reese & J. Puckett (Eds.), *Advances in lifespan development:* 205–227. Hillsdale, NJ: Lawrence Erlbaum Associates.

Sternberg, R. J., Wagner, R. K., Williams, W. M., & Horvath, J. A. 1995. Testing common sense. *American Psychologist,* 50(11): 912–927.

Stogdill, R. M. 1948. Personal factors associated with leadership: A survey of the literature. *Journal of Psychology,* 25: 35–71.

Terman, L. M. 1950. *Concept Mastery Test.* New York: The Psychological Corporation.

Wagner, R. K. 1987. Tacit knowledge in everyday intelligent behavior. *Journal of Personality & Social Psychology,* 52(6): 1236–1247.

Wagner, R. K., & Sternberg, R. J. 1985. Practical intelligence in real-world pursuits: The role of tacit knowledge. *Journal of Personality and Social Psychology,* 49: 436–458.

Wagner, R. K., & Sternberg, R. J. 1990. Street smarts. In K. E. Clark & M. B. Clark (Eds.), *Measures of leadership:* 493–504. West Orange, NJ: Leadership Library of America.

Wagner, R. K., & Sternberg, R. J. 1991. Tacit knowledge: Its uses in identifying, assessing, and developing managerial talent. In J. Jones, B. Steffy, & D. Bray (Eds.), *Applying psychology in business: The manager's handbook:* 333–344. New York: Human Sciences Press.

Wagner, R. K., Sujan, H., Sujan, M., Rashotte, C. A., & Sternberg, R. J. 1999. Tacit knowledge in sales. In R. J. Sternberg & J. A. Horvath (Eds.), *Tacit knowledge in professional practice:* 155–182. Mahwah, NJ: Lawrence Erlbaum Associates.

Weber, M. 1968. *Max Weber on charisma and institutional building* (S. N. Eisenstadt, Ed.). Chicago: University of Chicago Press.

Wechsler, D. 1939. *The measurement of adult intelligence.* Baltimore, MD: Williams & Wilkins.

Weekley, J. A., & Jones, C. 1997. Video-based situational testing. *Personnel Psychology,* 50(1): 25–49.

Williams, W. M., & Sternberg, R. J. 1988. Group intelligence: Why some groups are better than others. *Intelligence,* 12: 351–377.

Yukl, G. 1989. Managerial leadership: A review of theory and research. *Journal of Management,* 15: 251–289.

Zaleznik, A. 1977. Managers and leaders: Are they different? *Harvard Business Review,* 55: 67–78.

From Transactional to Transformational Leadership: Learning to Share the Vision

Bernard M. Bass

Sir Edmund Hillary of Mount Everest fame liked to tell a story about one of Captain Robert Falcon Scott's earlier attempts, from 1901 to 1904, to reach the South Pole. Scott led an expedition made up of men from the Royal Navy and the merchant marine, as well as a group of scientists. Scott had considerable trouble dealing with the merchant marine personnel, who were unaccustomed to the rigid discipline of Scott's Royal Navy. Scott wanted to send one seaman home because he would not take orders, but the seaman refused, arguing that he had signed a contract and knew his rights. Since the seaman was not subject to Royal Navy disciplinary action, Scott did not know what to do. Then Ernest Shackleton, a merchant navy officer in Scott's party, calmly informed the seaman that he, the seaman, was returning to Britain. Again the seaman refused—and Shackleton knocked him to the ship's deck. After another refusal, followed by a second flooring, the seaman decided he would return home. Scott later became one of the victims of his own inadequacies as a leader in his 1911 race to the South Pole. Shackleton went on to lead many memorable expeditions; once, seeking help for the rest of his party, who were stranded on the Antarctic Coast, he journeyed with a small crew in a small open boat from the edge of Antarctica to South Georgia Island.

LEADERSHIP TODAY

Most relationships between supervisors and their employees are quite different today. Few managers depend mainly on their legitimate power, as Scott did, or on their coercive power, as Shackleton did, to persuade people to do as they're told. Rather, managers engage in a transaction with their employees: They explain what is required of them and what compensation they will receive if they fulfill these requirements.

A shift in management style at Xerox's Reprographic Business Group (RBG) provides a good example. In the first step toward establishing management in which managers take the initiative and show consideration for others, 44 specific, effective management behaviors were identified. Two factors that characterize modern leadership were found in many of these behaviors. One factor—initiating and organizing work—concentrates on accomplishing the tasks at hand. The second factor—showing consideration for employees—focuses on satisfying the self-interest of those who do good work. The leader gets things done by making, and fulfilling, promises of recognition, pay increases, and advancement for employees who perform well. By contrast, employees who do not do good work are penalized. This transaction or exchange—this promise and reward for good performance, or threat and discipline for poor performance—characterizes effective leadership. These kinds of transactions took place in most of the effective 44 leadership behaviors identified at Xerox's RBG. This kind of leadership, which is based on transactions between manager and employees, is called "transactional leadership."

In many instances, however, such transactional leadership is a prescription for mediocrity. This is particularly true if the leader relies heavily on passive management-by-exception, intervening with his or her group only when procedures and standards for accomplishing tasks are not being met. My colleagues and I have arrived at this surprising but consistent finding in a number of research analyses. Such a manager espouses the popular adage, "If it ain't broken, don't fix it." He or she stands in back of the caboose of a moving freight train and says, "Now I know where we are going." This kind of manager may use disciplinary threats to bring a group's performance up to standards—a technique that is ineffective and, in the long run, likely to be counterproductive.

Moreover, whether the promise of rewards or the avoidance of penalties motivates the employees depends on whether the leader has control of the rewards or penalties, and on whether the employees want the rewards or fear the penalties. In many organizations, pay increases depend mainly on seniority, and promotions depend on qualifications and policies about which the leader has little to say. The breaking of regulations may be the main cause of penalties. Many an executive has found his or her hands tied by contract provisions, organizational politics, and inadequate resources.

TRANSFORMATIONAL LEADERSHIP

Superior leadership performance—transformational leadership—occurs when leaders broaden and elevate the interests of their employees, when they generate awareness and acceptance of the purposes and mission of the group, and when they stir their employees to look beyond their own self-interest for the good of the group. Transformational leaders achieve these results in one or more ways: They may be charismatic to their followers and thus inspire them; they may meet the emotional needs of each employee; and/or they may intellectually stimulate employees. Exhibit 1 lists the characteristics of transformational and transactional leadership; these listings are based on the findings of a series of surveys and on clinical and case evidence.

Attaining charisma in the eyes of one's employees is central to succeeding as a transformational leader. Charismatic leaders have great power and influence. Employees want to identify with them, and they have a high degree of trust and confidence in them. Charismatic leaders inspire and excite their employees with the idea that they may be able to accomplish great things with extra effort. Further, transformational leaders are individually considerate, that is, they pay close attention to differences among their em-

Exhibit 1

Characteristics of Transformational and Transactional Leaders

---

Transformational Leader

Charisma: Provides vision and sense of mission, instills pride, gains respect and trust.

Inspiration: Communicates high expectations, uses symbols to focus efforts, expresses important purposes in simple ways.

Intellectual Stimulation: Promotes intelligence, rationality, and careful problem solving.

Individualized Consideration: Gives personal attention, treats each employee individually, coaches, advises.

Transactional Leader

Contingent Reward: Contracts exchange of rewards for effort, promises rewards for good performance, recognizes accomplishments.

Management by Exception (active): Watches and searches for deviations from rules and standards, takes corrective action.

Management by Exception (passive): Intervenes only if standards are not met.

Laissez-Faire: Abdicates responsibilities, avoids making decisions.

---

ployees; they act as mentors to those who need help to grow and develop. Intellectual stimulation of employees is a third factor in transformational leadership. Intellectually stimulating leaders are willing and able to show their employees new ways of looking at old problems, to teach them to see difficulties as problems to be solved, and to emphasize rational solutions. Such a leader was Lorenz Iversen, a former president of the Mesta Machine Company, who said to his employees, "We got this job because you're the best mechanics in the world!" He practiced management-by-walking-around and stimulated the development of many of Mesta's patented inventions. He is remembered for instilling pride and commitment in his employees.

THE BIG PAYOFF

Managers who behave like transformational leaders are more likely to be seen by their colleagues and employees as satisfying and effective leaders than are those who behave like transactional leaders, according to their colleagues', supervisors', and employees' responses on the Multifactor Leadership Questionnaire (MLQ). Similar results have been found in various organizational settings. Leaders studied have come from an extremely broad variety of organizations: chief executive officers and senior and middle level managers in business and industrial firms in the United States, Canada, Japan, and India; research and development project leaders; American, Canadian, and British Army field grade officers; United States Navy senior officers and junior surface fleet officers; Annapolis midshipmen; educational administrators; and religious leaders.

Moreover, various types of evaluations—including performance ratings by both supervisors and direct reports, as well as standard financial measures—have produced a similar correlation between transformational behavior and high ratings. Managers tagged as high performers by their supervisors were also rated, in a separate evaluation by their followers, as more transformational than transactional. Their organizations do better financially. The same pattern emerged between followers' descriptions of shipboard Naval officers and those officers' supervisors' performance appraisals and recommendations for early promotion. And among Methodist ministers, transformational—not transactional—leadership behavior was positively related to high church attendance among congregants and growth in church membership.

Results were the same for evaluation of team performance in complex business simulations. Considerable credit for Boeing's turn-around since its 1969 crisis can be given to its chief executive, T. A. Wilson, who has emphasized technological progress, aggressive marketing, and a willingness to take calculated business risks. The confidence that Boeing employees have in Wilson, and their respect for him as a brilliant engineer and an outstanding leader, have instilled in them great pride in the company and its products.

EXTRA EFFORT FROM BELOW

Transformational leaders have better relationships with their supervisors and make more of a contribution to the organization than do those who are only transactional. Moreover, employees say that they themselves exert a lot of extra effort on behalf of managers who are transformational leaders. Organizations whose leaders are transactional are less effective than those whose leaders are transformational—particularly if much of the transactional leadership is passive management-by-exception (intervening only when standards are not being met). Employees say they exert little effort for such leaders. Nevertheless, leader-follower transactions dependent on contingent reward may also work reasonably well if the leaders can provide rewards that are valued by the followers.

Exhibit 2 illustrates the effect that transformational, as compared with transactional, leadership has on employee effort. The data were collected from 228 employees of 58 managers in a large engineering firm. The managers were ranked according to their leadership factor scores, which were based on descriptions of leaders by their employees and colleagues on the Multifactor Leadership Questionnaire. "Four-star" leaders were those who ranked in the top 25% on a leadership factor score; "one-star" leaders were among the bottom 25% of managers on the leadership factor score. From 75% to 82% of the "four-star" transformational managers had employees who indicated they frequently exerted extra effort on their jobs. Of the "one-star" transformational managers, only 22% to 24% had employees who said they frequently exerted extra effort.

It is interesting to note that, as Exhibit 2 illustrates, being rated as "four-star" rather than "one-star" in *transactional* leadership did not have the same impact on employees' extra effort as a high rating had for the transformational leaders. Similar findings have emerged from studies of leaders

Exhibit 2
Employees' Efforts Under Various Leaders

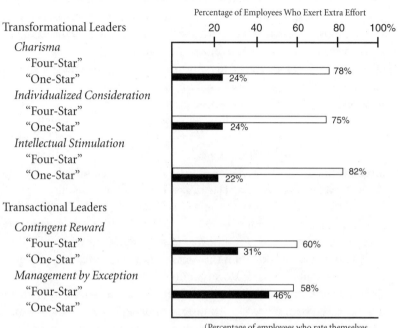

(Percentage of employees who rate themselves
3 or 4 on a 0–4 scale of extra effort.)

and their immediate employees at a diverse range of organizations, including Digital Equipment Corporation and Federal Express.

DIFFERENT STYLES OF
TRANSFORMATIONAL LEADERSHIP

As noted earlier, certain types of behavior characterize the transformational leader. Yet transformational leaders vary widely in their personal
styles. H. Ross Perot is self-effacing: "I don't look impressive," he says. "To
a lot of guys I don't look like I could afford a car." But Perot created the
$2.5 billion EDS organization from his vision, initiative, emphasis on hard
work, and a special organizational culture with strict codes of morality and
dress and quasi-military management. His personal involvement in the
rescue of two of his employees trapped as hostages in Iran in 1979 is an

extreme example of individualized consideration, a transformational factor. Leslie Wexner of The Limited, Inc. enjoys a more flamboyant lifestyle. But like Perot, Wexner converted his vision of a nationwide chain of women's sportswear stores into a reality through his own hard work. He stimulates employee participation in discussions and decisions and encourages them to share his vision of the company's future.

Many on *Fortune*'s list of the ten toughest bosses would not live up to modern behavioral science's prescriptions for the good leader: one who initiates the structure for interaction among his colleagues, and who does so with consideration for their welfare. Nevertheless, these tough bosses are highly successful as a consequence of the transformational qualities they display; Boeing's Wilson is a case in point. Although they do initiate structure and may be considerate of their employees, these leaders succeed through such transformational factors as charisma and the ability and willingness to treat different subordinates differently, as well as by providing intellectual stimulation for the employees. They frequently raise standards, take calculated risks, and get others to join them in their vision of the future. Rather than work within the organizational culture, they challenge and change that culture, as Roger Smith of General Motors Corporation did. Self-determination and self-confidence are characteristic of them. They succeed because of these transformational elements—even if they, like Wilson, have authoritarian tendencies.

TRANSFORMATIONAL LEADERS MAKE THE DIFFERENCE BETWEEN SUCCESS AND FAILURE

Fighting with far fewer men and tanks than his enemy had, against superior equipment, Ernst Rommel, the Desert Fox, won a series of victories in 1941 and 1942 against the British in North Africa, until he was overwhelmed at El Alamein. Because he was up front at the scene of the action, he could make more rapid assessments and decisions than could his British counterparts, who stayed 20 miles back in headquarters. This, and his willingness to accept calculated risks, contributed to his legendary speed, surprise, and boldness, as well as to the continuing high morale of his troops.

Napoleon declared that an army of rabbits commanded by a lion could do better than an army of lions commanded by a rabbit. He was not far from the truth. With all due respect to social, economic, political, and market forces, and to human resources policies that affect an organization's health, having a lion—or, in Rommel's case, a fox—in command rather than a rabbit frequently means success for the organization. Lee Iacocca of Chrysler Corporation and John Welch of General Electric, who have become folk heroes (or folk devils, to some), are contemporary examples of the importance of transformational leaders to their organizations.

Leadership makes its presence felt throughout the organization and its activities. We have found that employees not only do a better job when they believe their supervisors are transformational leaders, but they also are much more satisfied with the company's performance appraisal system. Likewise, mass communications directed toward individual employees are much more likely to have an impact if the messages are reinforced face-to-face by their supervisors at all organizational levels.

Transformational leadership should be encouraged, for it can make a big difference in the firm's performance at all levels. Managers need to do more than focus on the exchange of material, social, and personal benefits for services satisfactorily rendered. The charismatic leader, like the flamboyant Ted Turner of Turner Broadcasting System, Inc. can instill a sense of mission; the individually considerate leader, like the shy and self-effacing Roberto Goizueta of the Coca Cola Corporation, can lead employees to take an interest in higher-level concerns; the intellectually stimulating leader, like the innovative Roger Smith at General Motors Corporation, can articulate a shared vision of jointly acceptable possibilities. This is not to say that transformational leaders are always prosocial in their efforts, for some fulfill grandiose dreams at the expense of their followers.

Despite the many successes with management development programs and the leadership development programs in our military academies, many executives still feel that leadership is like the weather—something to talk about, but about which not much can be done. Others say leadership ability is mystical—one needs to be born with it.

In fact, much can be done to improve leadership in an organization and to change the presiding style from transactional to transformational. The overall amount of transformational leadership in an organization can be increased substantially by suitable organizational and human resources policies. The new model of transformational leadership presents opportunities for enhancing a corporation's image and for improving its success in recruitment, selection, and promotion. This model also has implications for the organization's training and development activities and for the design of its jobs and organizational structure.

Implications for Corporate Image

It is no accident that many of the firms identified in Tom Peters and Robert Waterman's *In Search of Excellence* (Warner Books, 1982) as excellently managed have large numbers of transformational leaders. Conversely, the poorly managed "dinosaurs" among the firms they describe need to implement a lot more transformational leadership. A firm that is permeated with transformational leadership from top to bottom conveys to its own personnel as well as to customers, suppliers, financial backers, and the community at large that it has its eyes on the future; is confident; has personnel who are pulling together for the common good; and places a premium on its intellectual resources and flexibility and on the development of its people.

Implications for Recruiting

Increasing transformational leadership within the organization may help in recruitment. Candidates are likely to be attracted to an organization whose CEO is charismatic and enjoys a public image as a confident, successful, optimistic, dynamic leader. In addition, prospects are likely to be attracted by interview experiences with other members of management who exhibit individualized consideration. More intelligent prospects will be particularly impressed with intellectually stimulating contacts they make during the recruiting and hiring process.

Implications for Selection, Promotion, and Transfer

Since we can identify and measure the factors associated with transformational leadership, these factors should be incorporated into managerial assessment, selection, placement, and guidance programs—along with related assessments of relevant personal dimensions and individual differences. Somewhat more transformational leadership is generally expected and found as managers move to successively higher levels in the organization, but it is reasonable to expect that an individual's performance at one level will be similar to his or her performance at the next. Direct reports, peers, and/or supervisors can be asked to describe the manager's current leadership with the Multifactor Leadership Questionnaire; their responses should be considered when decisions are made regarding a manager's promotion or transfer into a position of greater supervisory responsibility. Feedback from these results can also be used for counseling, coaching, and mentoring.

Further, the organization can tap the personal characteristics and strengths that underlie the manager's transformational behavior. Charismatic leaders are characterized by energy, self-confidence, determination, intellect, verbal skills, and strong ego ideals. Each of these traits can be assessed in individual managers. Similarly, we can assess some of the traits underlying individualized consideration, such as coaching skills; preference for two-way, face-to-face communication; and willingness to delegate. Again, in the area of intellectual stimulation, candidates for promotion could be assessed with an eye toward the type of intellectual stimulation—general, creative, or mathematical—that would be most effective at the higher level of management. Appropriate intelligence tests may be used to select intellectually stimulating candidates.

Research findings indicate that when employees rate their managers on the MLQ, they describe new business leaders as significantly more transformational than established business leaders. Thus MLQ scores can be used profitably to identify executives to head new ventures.

Implications for Development

A management trainee's first supervisor can make a big difference in his or her subsequent career success. For example, six years after they joined Exxon, many managers who were highly rated by their supervisors reported that they had been given challenging assignments by their initial supervisor (i.e., they had received individualized consideration). Many had been assigned to supervisors with good reputations in the firm. It is important to note that managers tend to model their own leadership style after that of their immediate supervisors. Thus if more higher-ups are transformational, more lower-level employees will emulate transformational behavior—and will be likely to act as transformational leaders as they rise in the organization.

Organizational policy needs to support an understanding and appreciation of the maverick who is willing to take unpopular positions, who knows when to reject the conventional wisdom, and who takes reasonable risks. For example, when R. Gordon McGovern took over as president of Campbell Soup, he introduced the "right to fail" policy, which shook up the stodgy organization. On the other hand, the fine line between self-confidence and obstinacy needs to be drawn. The determined Winston Churchill who contributed so much to the survival of Britain in 1940 was the same Churchill whose obstinacy contributed to the mistakes in 1941 of failing to prepare Singapore adequately and of committing British troops to unnecessary disaster in Crete and Greece.

Intellectual stimulation also needs to be nurtured and cultivated as a way of life in the organization. The "best and the brightest" people should be hired, nourished, and encouraged. Innovation and creativity should be fostered at all levels in the firm.

Implications for Training

Despite conventional wisdom to the contrary, transformational leadership is a widespread phenomenon. True, more of it occurs at the top than at the bottom of an organization; but it has also been observed by many employees in their first-level supervisors. Transformational leadership can be learned, and it can—and should—be the subject of management training and development. Research has shown that leaders at all levels can be trained to be charismatic in both verbal and nonverbal performance. Successful programs have been conducted for first-level project leaders in hi-tech computer firms as well as for senior executives of insurance firms.

That transformational leadership can be increased through training was verified in an experiment when Multifactor Leadership Questionnaire scores were obtained on shop supervisors from their trainees, who were inmates in minimum, medium, and maximum security prisons. The supervisors worked directly with the inmates in industrial shops to produce various products for sale within and outside the prison system. The experiment compared four groups of supervisors on their pre- and post-training effectiveness in various industrial and vocational shops in the prison. One group was trained in transformational leadership, one group was trained in transactional leadership, one was untrained but measured "before and after," and one was untrained and measured only "after." The performances of both trained groups improved, but in comparison to the three other groups of supervisors, those who were trained in transformational leadership did as well or better at improving productivity, absenteeism, and "citizenship" behavior among the inmates; they also won more respect from the inmates.

TRAINING MANAGERS

Practical training that teaches people how to be transformational is similar to that used in the Xerox RPG strategy to modify management style. A counselor, mediator, or supervisor gives a manager a detailed, standardized description of his or her transformational and transactional leadership performance as rated by the manager's employees and/or colleagues. The Multifactor Leadership Questionnaire is used for this purpose. The manager also sees a chart showing the effects of his or her leadership on employee satisfaction, motivation, and perception of organizational effectiveness. Anonymity is maintained, although the manager sees the individual differences among the responses.

Participating managers complete a parallel questionnaire about their own leadership. The discrepancies between how they rate themselves and how their employees rate them may be examined scale-by-scale and item-by-item. The counselor may pose such questions as: "Why do you think you gave yourself a much higher score than your employees gave you in individualized consideration?" and "Why did your employees disagree with you on how rapidly you get to the heart of complex problems or the extent to which they trust you to overcome any obstacles?" It is important for managers to be aware of and accept their employees' view of their performance. A study of United States Naval officers found that those who agreed with their direct reports about their transformational leadership behavior were also likely to earn higher fitness ratings and recommendations for early promotion from their supervisors.

The manager and the counselor discuss in detail why certain results may have appeared and what can be done to improve ratings. For example, a manager may be asked: "What specific behavior on your part makes your employees say they are proud to work with you?" or "What have you done that results in your colleagues' saying you foster a sense of mission?" The collected responses to these questions can create a useful picture of what the manager can do to raise his or her performance on particular items.

In addition to working individually with a counselor, the manager also may participate in a workshop with other managers who are working toward becoming more transformational leaders. Workshop participants who received high ratings from their employees on a particular item are asked what they, the participants, specifically did to achieve these ratings. Questions might include: "Why did all of your employees say that you frequently enabled them to think about old problems in new ways?" or "Why did they all say that you increased their optimism for the future?"

Conversely, questions may focus on why a participant's employees varied widely in their ratings. If the data printout shows a wide divergence of opinion about whether a manager made the employees enthusiastic about assignments, he or she might be asked to suggest possible reasons for such differences of opinion among the employees.

Other Approaches to Training

Several other approaches to teaching transformational leadership make use of the specific data gathered in the workshop. For instance, participants are asked to think of an effective leader they have known and the behavior the leader displayed. Many examples of charisma, individualized consideration, and intellectual stimulation are usually noted. The effective leaders who are mentioned typically come from many levels inside and outside the organization; the workshop leader may point out that transformational leadership is neither particularly uncommon nor limited only to world class leaders. Moreover, these leaders' specific behaviors can be described, observed, and adopted. After viewing videotapes of charismatic, individually considerate, and intellectually stimulating managers in action, workshop participants may be asked to create their own scenarios and videotapes, in which they emulate the transformational leaders they have observed. The other participants may then offer critiques and suggest improvements.

The workshop also aims to increase other aspects of transformational leadership. The transformational leader develops and changes the organizational culture, and to show participants that they have such capabilities, the workshop leader asks them to imagine what the organization might be like in two to five years if it were fully aligned with their own ideas and interests. Then, in small teams based on their actual functions at work, they proceed to redesign the organization.

Similarly, training in mentoring can be used to promote the transformational factor of individualized consideration. For example, one participant can counsel another while a third acts as an observer and a source of feedback about the performance. And many creativity exercises show a manager how he or she can be more intellectually stimulating. Action plans emerge from workshop sessions. Examples include the following:

- I am going to sit down with all my employees and review these data with them.

- I am going to ask for another "reading" in a year; in the meantime I will try to reduce the discrepancies between where I am and where I should be.
- I'm going to talk with my mentor about these results and ask what I should do about them.

Implications for Leadership Education

Military academies have traditionally emphasized leadership education, and today we are seeing a surge of interest in leadership courses in liberal arts colleges as well. At least 600 such courses were being offered, according to a recently completed survey of colleges. The Center for Creative Leadership holds conferences on leadership courses in undergraduate education, most recently in the summer of 1986. The subject of transformational leadership also has been added to leadership courses at the U.S. Air Force Academy at Colorado Springs. In one such course, both faculty and students examined how Air Force officers who are transformational leaders serve as role models for cadets. Scales from the Multifactor Leadership Questionnaire were used to show that the transformational leaders among the instructors and staff provided role models for their students. The faculty and students discussed the questionnaire results and their implications.

Clearly, training cannot turn a purely transactional leader into a transformational leader. Moreover, some managers, while striving to be transformational leaders, misuse their training; their pseudotransformational efforts only further the manager's self-interest and values. Under the influence of such a manager, employees can be misdirected away from their own best interests and those of the organization as a whole. In one such case, Donald Burr of People's Express Airlines displayed many transformational qualities that rapidly built and then rapidly ruined the firm.

For too long, leadership development has been seen as mainly a matter of skill development. But leadership—particularly transformational leadership—should be regarded as an art and a science. It is encouraging to see that the Council for Liberal Learning of the Association of American Colleges now sponsors week-long conferences on leadership for scholars, prominent citizens, and national leaders.

Implications for Job Design and Job Assignment

As we have noted earlier, the results of a study of Exxon managers showed that highly rated managers had had challenging tasks delegated to them by their supervisors when they first joined the company. Jobs can—and should—be designed to provide greater challenges. Delegation with guidance and follow-up can become an individualizing and developmental way of life in a firm.

Transformational leaders show individualized consideration by paying attention to the particular development needs of each of their employees. Employees' jobs are designed with those needs in mind, as well as the needs of the organization. One employee needs experience leading a project team. Another needs an opportunity to reinforce what she has learned in an advanced computer programming class. Their transformational leader assigns them tasks accordingly.

Leaders can be intellectually stimulating to their employees if their own jobs allow them to explore new opportunities, to diagnose organizational problems, and to generate solutions. Leaders whose jobs force them to focus on solving small, immediate problems are likely to be less intellectually stimulating than those who have time to think ahead and in larger terms.

Implications for Organizational Structure

Transformational leadership is not a panacea. In many situations, it is inappropriate and transactional processes are indicated. In general, firms that are functioning in stable markets can afford to depend on their "one-minute" managers to provide the necessary, day-to-day leadership. If the technology, workforce, and environment are stable as well, then things are likely to move along quite well with managers who simply promise and deliver rewards to employees for carrying out assignments. And in stable organizations, even management-by-exception can be quite effective if the manager monitors employee performance and takes corrective action as needed. Rules and regulations for getting things done, when clearly understood and accepted by the employees, can eliminate the need for leadership under some circumstances.

But when the firm is faced with a turbulent marketplace; when its products are born, live, and die within the span of a few years; and/or when its current technology can become obsolete before it is fully depreciated; then transformational leadership needs to be fostered at all levels in the firm. In order to succeed, the firm needs to have the flexibility to forecast and meet new demands and changes as they occur—and only transformational leadership can enable the firm to do so.

Problems, rapid changes, and uncertainties call for a flexible organization with determined leaders who can inspire employees to participate enthusiastically in team efforts and share in organizational goals. In short, charisma, attention to individualized development, and the ability and willingness to provide intellectual stimulation are critical in leaders whose firms are faced with demands for renewal and change. At these organizations, fostering transformational leadership through policies of recruitment, selection, promotion, training, and development is likely to pay off in the health, well-being, and effective performance of the organization.

Situational Leadership Theory: An Examination of a Prescriptive Theory

Robert P. Vecchio

Hersey and Blanchard's (1982) Situational Leadership Theory (SLT) embodies one of the more widely known and, at the same time, least researched views of managerial effectiveness. Throughout this article, the term *managerial* will be used interchangeably with the term *leadership* as SLT focuses on the effectiveness of nominal heads rather than on emergent or incremental forms of power and influence (i.e., leadership per se). As noted by Graeff (1983), the theory is often cited in academically oriented management textbooks. However, we can offer little advice to our students, or to practicing managers, on the utility of the theory. Before we can endorse or critique the theory to our constituencies, a rigorous test of the theory's propositions is, of course, required. In this article, the origins and central elements of the theory, the available evidence of the theory's validity, and the requirements for a rigorous test of the theory's propositions are considered.

ORIGINS AND ELEMENTS OF SITUATIONAL LEADERSHIP THEORY

Situational Leadership Theory developed from the writings of Reddin (1967). Reddin's 3-Dimensional Management Style Theory posits the importance of a manager's relationship orientation and task orientation in conjunction with effectiveness. From the interplay of these dimensions, Reddin proposed a typology of management styles (e.g., the autocrat, the missionary, the deserter). Although Reddin suggested that his framework explained effectiveness as a function of matching style to situation, his approach did not identify specific situational attributes that could be explicitly incorporated into a predictive scheme.

Building on Reddin's (1967) suggestion that leader or manager effectiveness varies according to style, Hersey and Blanchard (1969) proposed a life-cycle theory of leadership. According to life-cycle theory, degrees of task orientation and relationship orientation must be examined in conjunction with the dimension of follower maturity to account for leader effectiveness. The central precept of life-cycle theory (Hersey and Blanchard, 1969, p. 29) is that as the level of follower maturity increases, effective leader behavior will involve less structuring (task orientation) and less socio-emotional support (relationship orientation). However, the decline in need for both of these leader behaviors is not straightforward. During the early stages of an employee's tenure, a low level of relationship orientation coupled with high task orientation is considered to be ideal. As an employee (or group of employees of roughly equal maturity) gains in maturity, the need for supervisory social-emotional support increases, while the need for structuring declines. Beyond a certain level of maturity, the need for both social-emotional support and structuring declines. At the highest levels of employee maturity, supervisory task and social behaviors become superfluous to effective employee performance.

In a popular text (evidenced by its being in multiple editions) Hersey and Blanchard (1982) attempted to provide still greater precision to these precepts. They suggested that follower maturity can be broken into benchmark categories of high, moderate, and low, and that appropriate leader style can be summarized in terms of a leader primarily telling, selling, participating, or delegating in relations with subordinates.

EVIDENCE OF THE MODEL'S VALIDITY

At a purely theoretical level, SLT has been suggested as having a good deal of overlap with other popular views of leader and group behavior. In a comparison of their views with those offered by other perspectives, Hersey and Blanchard (1982, chap. 13) achieved a synthesis of their concepts with those contained in McGregor's (1960) Theory X and Y, Argyris's (1957) maturity-immaturity continuum, Likert's (1967) management systems, Maslow's (1954) need hierarchy, Herzberg's (1966) two-factor theory, McClelland's (1961) achievement theory, Schein's (1970) assumptions of human nature, transactional analysis (Berne, 1964; Harris, 1969), French and Raven's (1959) power bases, parent effectiveness training concepts (Gordon, 1970), Greiner's (1972) phases of organizational growth, Lewin's (1947) views of achieving behavioral change, behavior modification (Skinner, 1953), and force field analysis (Lewin, 1947). Although one can cynically argue that this high degree of overlap suggests that SLT is not saying much that is new or original, it can also be contended that many of the above theories can also be shown to contain a high degree of overlap. More positively, one can argue that SLT is focusing on critical features of behavior that have been previously identified.

The fact that SLT can be shown to overlap to varying degrees with other theories is not in itself sufficient evidence of SLT's validity. This point is of clear importance when one considers that many of the previously cited theories have not achieved a high degree of empirical support (e.g., Herzberg's two-factor theory), despite a fair amount of attention in the academic literature. In terms of internal theoretical coherence, Graeff (1983) has provided the most comprehensive critique of the theory. In his review of SLT, Graeff argued that the theory may actually have been derived from a passage in an article by Korman (1966), in which the suggestion of curvilinear relationships between dimensions of leader behavior and other variables was taken to mean that a curvilinear relationship may exist between dimensions of leader behavior. In addition, Graeff (1983) suggested that the manner in which components of dimensions in SLT are combined and the manner of graphic presentation of a four-dimensional model (task orientation, relationship orientation, follower maturity, and effectiveness) in only two dimensions are critical problems for the theory. Also, he has suggested that the popularly advocated measurement device for studying leader behaviors (the LEAD instrument) possesses unknown psychometric qualities. In the theory's favor, Graeff argued, however, that SLT correctly focuses on issues of leader flexibility and the importance of subordinate attributes as the key situational determinant of appropriate leader behavior.

At an empirical level, the theory has received little attention. One of the earliest published studies devoted to SLT concepts focused on the development of a measure of follower maturity, yet it did not use the measure in a test of the model (Moore, 1976). In a study that approximated a test of the theory, Hambleton and Gumpert (1982) asked managers to select at random 4 of their subordinates to complete a survey instrument. For 65 participating managers (of 159 who were contacted), manager ratings of subordinate maturity were coded in conjunction with manager self-assessments of leadership style (high vs. low task and relationship orientation). From this coding, matches and mismatches were identified. Matches occurred in only 29% of the cases. A comparison of mean performance ratings—given for each employee by the managers—for the matches and mismatches revealed that the matches received somewhat higher mean evaluations ($t = 6.47$, $p < .01$).

Although the findings of Hambleton and Gumpert (1982) are the only available supportive evidence for the model, they raise several concerns. First, the sample suffered severe attrition (i.e., less than half of the managers provided data). Second, the managers provided self-assessments of their own style. Such self-assessments of leader behavior are not regarded as being highly accurate (Schriesheim & Kerr, 1974). In addition, these assessments were taken on a version of the LEAD instrument, rather than on a more widely studied and accepted measure of leader behavior. Last, the respondents were highly cognizant of SLT precepts (as evidenced by their having been asked to rate their knowledge of SLT and to assess the extent to which they used SLT in their work). This awareness of SLT principles on the part of the participants may have induced some respondents to attempt to complete their surveys in conformity with the theory (i.e., in order to appear to be applying their knowledge of the theory). Also, all of the respondents reported at least fair knowledge of and some use of SLT.

The most recently reported study of SLT (Blank, Weitzel, & Green, 1986) involved 27 hall directors and 353 resident advisors (subordinates) at two large universities. Respondents completed the Leader Behavior Description Questionnaire (LBDQ-XII; Stogdill & Coons, 1957) and a measure of maturity. Directors provided performance ratings of resident advisors, and each resident advisor completed subscales of the Job Description Index (JDI) satisfaction measure (Smith, Kendall, & Hulin, 1969). In their analysis of these data, Blank, Weitzel, and Green did not report the results of matching subordinate maturity and leader behaviors to predict subordinate performance and satisfaction, but instead examined interactions between maturity and each of the two leader behavior dimensions (consideration and structuring) in an attempt to predict subordinate performance and satisfaction. In general, their search for two-way interactions did not reveal support for the theory. However, it should be noted that the theory predicts a three-way interaction, and not separate two-way interactions, among the key variables (i.e., the interaction of maturity with structuring should not be examined independently of consideration, but jointly).

In summary, investigations of the theoretical and empirical robustness of SLT have been rare. Although the theory contains strong intuitive appeal, the veracity of the theory has not been assessed via a rigorous empirical test.

ISSUES SURROUNDING A TEST OF THE SITUATIONAL
LEADERSHIP THEORY

In order to test SLT, several issues must be addressed that relate to the clarity of the theory's prediction. One major issue surrounds the unit of analysis for SLT: the individual versus the group. Although the theory is often stated in terms of group maturity, there are also many references to individual maturity as well. For example, in their definition of maturity, Hersey and Blanchard (1982, p. 151) stated that an "individual or a group" is their focus. They also recognized that when one relates to an entire group (e.g., a teacher speaking to a class of students), it is the maturity level of the group that is important. However, when one deals with an employee in a one-to-one setting (e.g., a teacher speaking with a single student), the maturity level of the individual is most important. This recognition of the need for leaders to behave differently with individual group members than when they relate to an entire group is an important statement. Much of the recent research in the area of leadership has, in fact, focused on the issue of universal versus differential leadership style (cf. research on the Vertical Dyad Linkage Model; Liden & Graen, 1980). That the dynamics of SLT are presumed to operate at both levels is an important feature of the SLT framework. In the context of a test of SLT, it is necessary to specify and be consistent in studying leadership phenomena at a given level (and not across levels) of analysis. It seems likely—in light of the preponderance of research at the individual level and the suspicion that group processes may mask individual process—that SLT will be most robust at the individual level of social dynamics (i.e., leadership behavior that is in accord with the prescriptions of SLT will be more effective when it is targeted to a given individual's level of maturity).

An extended issue that is beyond the present investigation is whether individual maturity interacts with group maturity in determining leader effectiveness. It is easy to envision a situation in which a subordinate is significantly more mature than his or her peers in a given position, yet the leader's behaviors (if they are often displayed for the benefit of the group) may be grossly inappropriate. In such settings, the incongruent subordinate will likely be dissatisfied with the leader's directions and may be resentful of the limits that his peers indirectly set via the leader's actions.

Perhaps the least clear feature of SLT surrounds the definition of effectiveness. In their book, Hersey and Blanchard (1982, pp. 96–99) define effectiveness and ineffectiveness as occurring when a leader's style is appropriate and inappropriate, respectively. Although they recognize that effectiveness can be viewed as a continuum, they do not acknowledge the multifaceted nature of the concept. Also, the definition of effectiveness in terms of appropriateness of leader style is somewhat circular in its use of logic. In order to test SLT, it is useful to define effectiveness in broader, more traditional terms. For example, effectiveness can be defined in terms of output, cost reduction, enhancement of employee motivation, morale, and so forth. This restatement of effectiveness implies that SLT should be restated so that effectiveness is a possible outcome of appropriateness of leader behavior. The use of the word *possible* is important in the foregoing sentence because an appropriate combination of leader style (in terms of SLT's prescription) may still not enhance subordinate behavior and attitudes. As noted by Kerr and Jermier (1978), situational attributes can offset and substitute for leader behaviors. In a sense, subordinate maturity in SLT is a substitute for leadership, in that subordinates of higher maturity need less attention or direction from leaders. Increases in subordinate self-sufficiency (maturity), which likely result from relevant work experience and training, can make leader behaviors increasingly irrelevant to subordinate performance and morale. Therefore, SLT's prediction that highly mature employees require a low-structure-low-consideration style of supervision may be partially misstated. It may be more correct to say that supervisory style is comparatively more irrelevant, in terms of its impact on highly mature subordinates. In short, the conduct of highly mature subordinates may simply be less predictable than that of other employees, from supervisory attributes.

A further issue centers on how to test in a statistical sense, the predictive accuracy of SLT. At its heart, the theory forecasts a three-way interaction of leader consideration, leader structuring, and subordinate maturity. If one imagines the form of this hypothesized interaction by trying to graph the hyperplane that is predicted, it becomes apparent that the predicted interaction does not satisfy the statistical assumption of homoscedascity. That is to say, the regression-based assumption of equal variance around the regression plane does not hold, by definition, for SLT as the predictions of superior performance only hold for specific points in the multidimensional space. In all other locations in the space, the data are free to vary. Therefore, the theory only makes predictions for specific combinations of variables. For all other combinations, the theory is silent. In essence, a test of the theory that uses the statistical technique of multiple regression may lead, erroneously, to the conclusion that the theory is incorrect for a given data set (i.e., a Type II error). To more fairly test the theory, it would be worthwhile to examine the predictions in the manner proposed by the theory's developers (i.e., to compare the effectiveness of leaders whose styles are "appropriate" for given settings to leaders whose styles are predicted to be "inappropriate" for the same settings). Although one may test whether a given data set violates the requirement of homoscedascity, the results of such a test would not, of course, shed light on the validity of Situational Leadership Theory, per se.

The purpose of the present investigation was (a) to test SLT in a study that was designed to capture the critical variables proposed by the theory and (b) to explore SLT with analytic techniques that reflect traditional practice in organizational research (i.e., regression) as well as accommodate the need to study leadership as a situation-specific phenomena (i.e., subgrouping analysis).

METHOD

Subjects and Procedure

Subjects were 303 full-time high school teachers, who represented 14 high schools in a large midwestern city and provided data in response to a confidential survey. Because of the support of the head of the school district, cooperation was readily obtained from the principals of all 14 schools in the district. During monthly meetings with faculty, the principals distributed surveys to their teachers. At the meetings, time was devoted to the completion of the surveys. Both teachers and principals completed similar surveys, which focused on the behavior of the school principal (leader) and the individual teacher (subordinate). To ensure anonymity for the teachers, the surveys were coded with ID numbers. In addition, the completed surveys of both teachers and principals were collected at the meeting, placed in an envelope, and mailed directly to the author. With the exception of 34 teachers who did not attend their school's monthly meeting in January 1986, all of the principals and teachers responded to the survey.

Measures

Each teacher provided responses to the following scales: (a) JDI, satisfaction with supervision (Smith et al., 1969); (b) Leader-Member Exchange, quality of leader-member relationship (Liden & Graen, 1980); (c) LBDQ-XII, leader consideration (Stogdill & Coons, 1957); and (d) LBDQ-XII, leader initiating structure (Stogdill & Coons, 1957). Modified versions of the LBDQ-XII measures of leader behavior were used in place of the LEAD instrument because of the relative psychometric advantages of the LBDQ-XII (i.e., its reliability and construct validity have received more attention than the LEAD instrument, and it is a more widely accepted index of leader behavior than the LEAD instrument). In addition, the stems of the items in the LBDQ-XII used in this study were modified to incorporate an individualized format (cf. Vecchio & Gobdel, 1984): sample item, "My principal acts without consulting me." Furthermore, each teacher was asked to complete a follower maturity index that contained items related to both task-relevant (e.g., understanding of job requirements) and psychological (e.g., commitment) forms of maturity (Hambleton, Blanchard, & Hersey, 1977).

Principals provided ratings for each teacher on dimensions of follower maturity and performance. Maturity was assessed on items related to task-relevant and psychological maturity, whereas performance was assessed by summing ratings across dimensions of dependability, planning, know-how, present performance, and expected performance (Liden & Graen, 1980).

Analytic Techniques

The accuracy of the principles of SLT was examined with several statistical techniques. As will be shown, each technique represents a somewhat different phrasing of the central research question. The first technique used was hierarchical regression analysis, in which a three-way multiplicative interaction term was created (Maturity × Consideration × Structuring). This interaction term was entered into a regression equation following the inclusion of main effects and two-way interaction terms to determine whether the inclusion of the three-way interaction term appreciably increased the variance accounted for in the performance criterion. As was noted earlier, the use of multiple regression for testing SLT can be critiqued on the grounds that certain assumptions of regression cannot be met when the principles of SLT are, in fact, correct. Nonetheless, the robustness of regression techniques and our present uncertainty as to just what would result with the use of the technique warrant the exploratory use of multiple regression to test the theory.

A second approach to testing SLT involves the creation of subgroups of employees for whom the theory is expected to hold or not to hold. This requires the creation of subgroups based on the combination of consideration, structuring, and maturity. For employees whose situations are designated "matches," their mean performance should be superior to that of subordinates for whom the situations are "mismatches." This comparison of matches and mismatches represents an omnibus test of SLT in that it ignores differences within specific categories of maturity in favor of an overall test.

It can be argued, however, that an omnibus test is not the best possible device for assessing SLT. If the distribution of cases is not uniform across categories, then the results of the omnibus test may be biased. For example, no (or very few) cases may exist for some combinations of maturity and leader behavior. The peculiarities of these distributions and the possible associated mean differences for the categories could, thereby, produce spurious results. A third, more direct, assessment of SLT involves the creation of several categories on the dimension of follower maturity. After creating these categories, comparisons could then be made within categories to determine whether subordinates who match on the leader dimensions are superior performers, relative to those who do not match on these dimensions. The need to first create categories of maturity is perhaps critical in that different levels of follower maturity are likely to be related to different levels of overall performance (although SLT does not directly address this critical issue). Therefore, the likely correlation of maturity with performance needs to be controlled by conducting comparisons within levels of maturity.

To be sure, only the third, partitioned, technique is the most defensible approach to assessing SLT. However, we presently know so little about SLT-related phenomena that all three techniques are reported here in the interest of completeness and in order to gain further understanding.

RESULTS

The internal consistency coefficients for the measures of interest were all of reasonable magnitude (ranging from .82 to .94). Evidence that the maturity measure at least partially taps work-relevant experience was obtained by correlating individual maturity with self-reported years of teaching experience. The obtained correlation suggested that years of experience was related to the index ($r = .15$, $p < .01$). It should also be noted that the range of professional teaching experience for the sample was substantial (range = 1–31 years; $M = 20.5$ years).

The results of the hierarchical regression analyses are presented in Table 1 for the criteria of supervisor rating, leader-member exchange, and satisfaction with supervision. For each analysis, the three predictors of consideration, structuring, and maturity were entered simultaneously at the first step. Next, the two-way interaction terms were entered into the equation. Last, the three-way interaction term was included. The increment in R^2 at each step (i.e., in variance accounted for) was calculated and tested for significance (Cohen & Cohen, 1975). As the results in Table 1 indicate, none of the three criteria tested yielded support for a three-way interaction.

Omnibus tests of mean differences on the criteria were also conducted. For these analyses, the distribution of follower maturity was trichotomized into high, moderate, and low maturity by cutting at the values of 44 and 40. Three categories, rather than four, of maturity were created to ensure a sufficient number of cases for each subgroup. The predictions for the middle-range groups on maturity are identical (i.e., high consideration coupled with moderate structuring is prescribed). Next, the dimensions of consideration and structuring were trichotomized and dichotomized, respectively. Cuts on the structuring dimension were made at the values of 19 and 15. On the consideration dimension, the split was made at the value of 19.

Table 1
Summary of Regression Analyses

Source	Performance		Leader-member quality		Satisfaction	
	R^2	ΔR^2	R^2	ΔR^2	R^2	ΔR^2
Consideration (C), structuring (S), maturity (M)	.743**		.686**		.639**	
C × S, C × M, S × M	.744**	.001	.697**	.011*	.641**	.012*
C × S × M	.744**	.000	.697**	.000	.641**	.000

*$p < .05$. **$p < .01$.

This resulted in a 3 x 2 cross tabulation, in accord with the SLT model. Employees whose values on maturity coincided with the prescribed levels of consideration and structuring were designated matches; all remaining employees were designated mismatches. It is, of course, predicted that mean values for the outcome variables will be higher for the matched group, relative to the mismatched group.

As Table 2 reveals, a large percentage of the employees were in the mismatched group (i.e., their situations were those for which the theory predicts lower effectiveness). This finding, in itself, is of some importance in that it suggests that the positive SLT prescriptions may have little relevance to a majority of employees (i.e., the natural occurrence of the preferred combinations may be fairly low). Alternatively, it can be argued that there is a great untapped potential or significant need for creating circumstances that the theory prescribes. To test this latter point, mean differences were tested for significance for the matched versus mismatched groups. If the theory is correct, we can expect the matched group (albeit a smaller group) to have higher values on the outcome measures.

As the results reported in Table 2 indicate, the means were in the predicted direction for all three comparisons. In two of these comparisons, the means were significantly different (although the estimates of the effects' sizes were not substantial). The results suggest that employees who describe their superiors' behavior on the dimensions of consideration and structur-

Table 2
Results of Omnibus Tests

Group	M	SD	n	F	p	Estimated effect size
Performance						
Match	30.4	3.91	50	1.61	.21	.002
Mismatch	29.5	5.03	252			
Leader-member quality						
Match	22.8	22.80	50	5.25	.02	.014
Mismatch	21.2	21.18	245			
Satisfaction with supervision						
Match	51.0	6.25	46	7.35	.01	.022
Mismatch	46.3	11.52	238			

ing in accord with SLT prescriptions, given their specific level of maturity, tend to have somewhat higher performance ratings, and to report higher quality relationships with their supervisor, as well as greater satisfaction with their supervisor.

Although the omnibus tests provided evidence of the accuracy of SLT, they do not tell us precisely where these differences are occurring in the framework. Also, the supportive results of the omnibus tests may have capitalized on unique, sample-specific differences that are correlated with uneven distributions of attributes. Therefore, sets of partitioned tests of the theory were conducted. These tests involved making mean difference comparisons within maturity groups. That is to say, matches and mismatches were designated within each of the three levels of maturity. The results of these comparisons (see Table 3) indicate that the mean differences were in the correct direction in six of nine comparisons. Of these six, four were significantly different. The effect sizes for these differences ranged from .032 to .160. In one instance, the mean difference was significant in the reverse direction of that which was hypothesized. Also, the results were more generally supportive in the low-maturity category, somewhat mixed in the moderate-maturity category, and generally nonsignificant in the high-maturity category. This suggests a very different picture of the results, in which the theory is only correct for low-maturity employees and less correct for more mature employees. The implication is that low consideration coupled with high structuring is a superior combination for low-maturity employees. For moderate- and especially high-maturity employees, it is not clear that the combinations prescribed by SLT are associated with superior outcomes. Furthermore, it is worth noting that the mismatched groups (Tables 2 and 3) were somewhat more variable than the matched groups. This is evidenced by the often larger standard deviations for the mismatched groups. This difference in variability confirms the earlier suggestion that the more stringent assumptions of parametric statistical tests (e.g., regression analysis) may not be satisfied by the data generated by—as well as the logic attendant to—tests of Situational Leadership Theory.

DISCUSSION

The present study represents one of the first comprehensive tests of Situational Leadership Theory. As such, it is not possible to contrast the current findings with those obtained in other investigations. Therefore, the present

Table 3
Summary of Partitioned Tests

Group	M	SD	n	F	p	Estimated effect size
Low maturity						
Performance						
Match	27.3	3.50	21	4.68	.03	.032
Mismatch	25.0	4.54	92			
Leader-member quality						
Match	24.2	3.06	21	22.18	.00	.160
Mismatch	19.1	4.79	92			
Satisfaction with supervision						
Match	53.4	3.86	19	16.80	.00	.129
Mismatch	41.3	12.68	88			
Moderate maturity						
Performance						
Match	32.1	2.37	15	5.65	.02	.048
Mismatch	30.1	3.11	78			
Leader-member quality						
Match	19.6	3.20	15	4.18	.04	.034
Mismatch	22.1	4.54	75			
Satisfaction with supervision						
Match	47.0	7.51	13	<1		
Mismatch	48.6	9.84	72			
High maturity						
Performance						
Match	33.4	2.10	14	1.20	.28	.002
Mismatch	33.9	1.70	82			
Leader-member quality						
Match	24.1	2.81	14	1.65	.20	.007
Mismatch	22.7	3.89	80			
Satisfaction with supervision						
Match	51.4	6.15	14	<1		
Mismatch	49.6	9.66	78			

evidence must be taken, for the moment, as providing the best available test of the theory's principles. In general, the present study provides partial support for the theory in that the omnibus tests and several of the partitioned tests point to the theory being partially accurate in its prescriptions. The results of the regression analyses are perhaps suspect in that various assumptions of regression analysis are contrary to the essential features of SLT. Furthermore, the predictor variables that were used in the regression analysis were intercorrelated. This may be more than a common source effect problem because the predictor constructs may not be logically or empirically independent of one another.

The finding that SLT was most strongly supported in the low-maturity condition appears reasonable in that employees who are relatively lacking in task-relevant knowledge or commitment should require more structuring on the part of their supervisor. Displays of considerateness by superiors for low-maturity subordinates would be tantamount to sending improper signals to such subordinates. For subordinates of moderate maturity, it is not clear what style of supervision works best. The present data suggest that performance is greater for these same employees if moderate structuring is combined with high consideration. However, the same sample provides evidence that the quality of leader-member relationships may be significantly lower when this particular combination of styles is reported.

For high-maturity employees, the theory appears to be unable to predict. Perhaps the theory needs to be rephrased to accommodate such high-maturity types. As it stands, the theory seems to suggest that highly mature employees can be relatively free from direction and do not need to receive "strokes" from their supervisors. Such a scenario is highly doubtful, as most employees probably appreciate supervisor considerateness and occasional signs of supervisor interest (as manifested by supervisor direction or structuring). In addition, the measurement of maturity poses a unique problem for testing Situational Leadership Theory. Self-reports of maturity are highly suspect. Similarly, peer ratings may largely reflect popularity rather than task orientation. Yet, the construct is so broad that a rating seems the most appropriate technique for addressing it. It is interesting that in the present sample, years of teaching was somewhat associated with supervisor ratings of maturity. However, experience can still be regarded as independent of supervisor ratings. This makes sense as long-tenured employees may be, on the average, more competent than are more recently hired individuals. Yet, the job-relevant maturity of long-tenured employees can still be quite variable (i.e., years of experience and job-relevant maturity are not likely to be highly correlated across situations). Of further interest, the correlation of teachers' self-ratings of maturity were significantly correlated with their superiors' ratings on the same instrument ($r = .28$, $p < .01$).

It is possible that SLT is not well suited to making predictions in any given job category, in that a full range of maturity and leader behaviors may not be manifested in one job classification. Perhaps SLT is better viewed as being prescriptive across job categories. In this view, high to low maturity represents various classes of jobs (e.g., professional to unskilled). For professional (high-maturity) jobs, supervisors should display relatively less consideration and less structuring. Professionals, as the reasoning goes, should be capable and desirous of greater self-direction. For unskilled (low-maturity) jobs, supervisors should provide significantly greater structuring and less consideration. Unskilled workers perhaps expect, and may prefer, greater direction and less social-emotional attention on the part of supervisors (cf. Vroom & Mann, 1960). This restatement of SLT suggests that the underlying principles of SLT may be valid but that the theory may be improperly conceptualized, such that the current focus is on maturity differences within jobs rather than across jobs.

An across-jobs perspective offers possibly greater ranges of maturity and, therefore, a greater likelihood of identifying systematic relationships. However, this across-jobs perspective requires a modification of the term *maturity*. As it is used in a within-job perspective, its meaning is fairly clear (i.e., employee level of task-relevant knowledge and commitment). In an across-jobs perspective, maturity may have to be replaced with a more level-appropriate concept such as normative expectations. This across-jobs view suggests that job prestige (or job quality) dictates specific norms for preferred styles of supervision. To be effective, a supervisor should be conscious of and responsive to these norms. The above viewpoint also can be seen as incorporating notions from Kerr and Jermier's (1979) suggestion of substitutes for leadership. In professional and highly skilled positions, experience and knowledge can make a supervisor's influence less important. In less skilled positions in which employees lack experience and acquired knowledge, supervisory influences can be of far greater importance. However, a testing of an across-jobs perspective should perhaps not be undertaken without further testing of the within-job view of Situational Leadership Theory. In addition, future tests of the theory should, to the degree possible, use independent measures of predictors.

In summary, the present study provided partial support for principles contained in Situational Leadership Theory. As is not uncommon in organizational research, an initial, seemingly simple research question yielded a complex set of results that only substantiated a portion of a set of propositions. Furthermore, the results underscored the somewhat disheartening observation that the approach taken in analyzing a theory determines, to an extent, the form and degree of support that is obtained for the propositions. The present results most strongly suggest that more recently hired employees may require greater structuring from their superior. Nonetheless, the present results are sufficiently intriguing so as to suggest that SLT be studied further, with an across-jobs perspective and with a recognition that high-maturity conditions may obviate the need for supervision, rather than specify a particular style of supervision.

REFERENCES

Argyris, C. (1957). *Personality and organizations.* New York: Harper & Row.

Berne, E. (1964). *Games people play.* New York: Grove Press.

Blank, W., Wietzel, J., & Green, S. G. (1986). Situational leadership theory: A test of underlying assumptions. *Proceedings of the Academy of Management, 384.*

Cohen, J., & Cohen, P. (1975). *Applied multiple regression/correlation analysis for the behavioral sciences.* Hillsdale, NJ: Erlbaum.

French, J. R. P., & Raven, B. (1959). The bases of social power. In D. Cartwright (Ed.), *Studies in social power* (pp. 150–167). Ann Arbor, MI: Institute for Social Research.

Gordon, T. (1970). *Parent effectiveness training.* New York: P. H. Wyden.

Graeff, C. L. (1983). The situational leadership theory: A critical view. *Academy of Management Review, 8,* 285–291.

Greiner, L. E. (1972, July–August). Evolution and revolution as organizations grow. *Harvard Business Review,* 37–46.

Hambleton, R. K., Blanchard, K. H., & Hersey, P. (1977). *Maturity Scale—Self-rating form.* San Diego, CA: Learning Resources Corporation.

Hambleton, R. K., & Gumpert, R. (1982). The validity of Hersey and Blanchard's theory of leader effectiveness. *Group and Organization Studies, 7,* 225–242.

Harris, T. (1969). *I'm OK—You're OK: A practical guide to transactional analysis.* New York: Harper & Row.

Herzberg, F. (1966). *Work and the nature of man.* New York: World Publishing.

Hersey, P., & Blanchard, K. (1969). Life-cycle theory of leadership. *Training and Development Journal, 23,* 26–34.

Hersey, P., & Blanchard, K. (1982). *Management of organizational behavior* (4th ed.). Englewood Cliffs, NJ: Prentice-Hall.

Kerr, S., & Jermier, J. M. (1978). Substitutes for leadership: Their meaning and measurement. *Organizational Behavior and Human Performance, 22,* 375–403.

Korman, A. K. (1966). Consideration, initiating structure, and organization criteria—A review. *Personnel Psychology, 19,* 349–361.

Lewin, K. (1947). Frontiers in group dynamics: Concept, method, and reality in social science, social equilibria and social change. *Human Relations, 1,* 5–41.

Liden, R. C., & Graen, G. (1980). Generalizability of the vertical dyad linkage model of leadership. *Academy of Management Journal, 23,* 451–465.

Likert, R. (1967). *The human organization.* New York: McGraw-Hill.

Maslow, A. (1954). *Motivation and personality.* New York: Harper & Row.

McClelland, D. C. (1961). *The achieving society.* Princeton, NJ: Van Nostrand.

McGregor, D. (1960). *The human side of enterprise.* New York: McGraw-Hill.

Moore, L. I. (1976). The FMI: Dimensions of follower maturity. *Group and Organization Studies, 1,* 203–222.

Reddin, W. J. (1967). The 3-D Management Style Theory. *Training and Development Journal, 21,* 8–17.

Schein, E. H. (1970). *Organizational psychology* (2nd ed.). Englewood Cliffs, NJ: Prentice-Hall.

Schriesheim, C. A., & Kerr, S. (1974). Psychometric properties of the Ohio State leadership scales. *Psychological Bulletin, 81,* 756–765.

Skinner, B. F. (1953). *Science and human behavior.* New York: Macmillan.

Smith, P., Kendall, L., & Hulin, C. L. (1969). *The measurement of satisfaction in work and retirement.* Chicago: Rand-McNally.

Stogdill, R., & Coons, A. (1957). *Leader behavior: Its description and measurement* (Research Monograph No. 88). Columbus: Ohio State University, Bureau of Business Research.

Vecchio, R. P., & Gobdel, B. C. (1984). The vertical dyad linkage model of leadership: Problems and prospects. *Organizational Behavior and Human Performance, 34,* 5–20.

Vroom, V. H., & Mann, F. C. (1960). Leader authoritarianism and employee attitudes. *Personnel Psychology, 13,* 125–140.

The Contingency Model of Leadership Effectiveness: Its Levels of Analysis

Roya Ayman, Martin M. Chemers, and Fred Fiedler

The contingency model of leadership effectiveness was presented in its most complete form in Fiedler (1967) and Fiedler and Chemers (1974). The evolution of the model and the development of its constructs covers three decades of research. This article examines the model from a theoretical and methodological perspective. It focuses on the levels of analysis used to determine the various components of the model, to measure effective leadership, and to define the sources of information for its central variables.

The model predicts that a leader's effectiveness is based on two main factors: a leader's attributes, referred to as task or relationship motivational orientation (formerly referred to as style), and a leader's situational control (formerly referred to as situational favorability). The model predicts that leaders who have a task motivational orientation compared to those who have a relationship orientation or motivation will be more successful in high- and low-control situations. Relationship-oriented leaders compared to task-oriented leaders will be more effective in moderate control situations (Fiedler, 1978). A leader is designated as "in match" in situations where the model predicts high group performance and "out of match" in situations of low group performance (Fiedler & Chemers, 1984).

The model is, by design, multi-level and multi-source. That is, measures of the leader's motivational orientation are based on the leader's responses (individual level); characteristics of the situation have been measured by the leader's report and/or that of subordinates and experimenters (multi-level and multi-source), and outcomes have been assessed at the group level, primarily group performance (Fiedler, 1978) as determined by objective measures, supervisor ratings, and averaged follower satisfaction (Rice, 1981). A few studies used outcomes related to the leader as an individual (e.g., stress, performance). A few studies have examined the model at the dyadic, leader-subordinate level (e.g., Fiedler, Potter, Zais, & Knowlton,

1979). Most generally, the model has defined the leadership effectiveness at the group level of analysis. In fact, it may be appropriate to say that this is the first model in leadership effectiveness research that was designed in a multi-level-of-analysis framework (Dansereau, personal communication).

The model has been the target of numerous criticisms through its evolution (e.g., Ashour, 1973; Graen, Alvares, Orris, & Martella, 1971; Graen, Orris, & Alvares, 1971; Schriesheim & Kerr, 1977; Vecchio, 1977) and has been an impetus for over 200 empirical studies. After three decades of research, two meta-analyses (i.e., Peters, Hartke, & Pohlmann, 1985; Strube & Garcia, 1981) have tested its criteria-related validity. The results, overall, have supported the model. Both meta-analyses agreed that the laboratory studies yielded stronger support than the field studies, and both provided recommendations for improvement. Most of the recommendations suggested a need to expand and refine the definitions of situational control and of the factors that contribute to situational control.

This article defines the constructs which determine the model and reviews the operational definitions. Although there have been several reviews of the model, it has been about 16 years since the last complete review (Fiedler, 1978). Confusion still exists regarding the model's components and their relationship with each other. In this article, new and old evidence is discussed to clarify these misunderstandings. The model's constructs are: (1) leader's characteristics, (2) situational control, and (3) leadership effectiveness. Table 1 gives a summary of the way each of these variables in the model has been defined and measured.

This article seeks to demonstrate that the strength of the contingency model lies in its use of a multi-level and multiple-sources approach in defining leadership effectiveness. Specifically, as presented in Table 1, measures of the leader's orientation are drawn from the leader; outcome measures are typically taken from sources independent of the leader, such as supervisor ratings or objective performance measures. Situational variables have been specified in a number of ways, many of which are conceptually and operationally independent both from leader variables and sources of the outcome criteria (e.g., experimental manipulations, observer ratings of organizational characteristics).

The independence of the theoretical variables reduces the model's vulnerability to validity threats attendant to single-source ratings and overlapping common-method variance. Furthermore, even when leader's characteristics and situational and outcome variables are provided by leader ratings, as in studies of leader stress (Chemers, Hays, Rhodewalt, & Wy-

Table 1

Summary of Contingency Model's Variables with Their Conceptual Level
of Analysis, Measure, and Source of Information

Variables	*Level*	*Measure*	*Source*
Leader's Motivational Orientation	Individual	Least Preferred Coworker (LPC) Scale	Leader
Situational Control			
Group Climate	Group	Group Atmosphere (GA) Leader-Member Relation Sociometric Method	Leader or Averaged Group Score
Task Structure	Individual	Task Structure Scale or Type of Job	Leader or Experimenter
Authority	Individual	Position Power Scale	Leader Experimenter Superior
Effectiveness			
Satisfaction	Group or Dyadic	Job Descriptive Index (JDI)	Subordinate
Performance	Group	Supervisory Rating Archival Data	Superior Experimenter Org. Records
Stress	Individual	Fiedler's Job Stress Scale	Leader

socki, 1985), the predicted interactions among the variables are of a nature (i.e., both complex and counterintuitive) such that the interactions are unlikely to be the result of consistency factors or demand characteristics (Orne, 1962).

In the sections that follow, we address the levels of analysis and sources of information with respect to: (1) the leader's motivational orientation, (2) the variables that contribute to the leader's situational control, (3) various individual, group, and organizational outcomes, (4) the new directions, and (5) the applications of the contingency model.

LEADERSHIP MOTIVATIONAL ORIENTATION

Although past reviews (e.g., Rice 1978a, 1978b) have been quite thorough, there are a few issues regarding the conceptualization of the scale and its use that were not clarified. In order to address these points, this section presents key evidence that elucidates these issues. The leader's orientation is measured by a scale referred to as "least preferred coworker" (LPC) scale. The scale's instructions ask the respondent to identify within the context of all the persons with whom the respondent has ever worked:

> the one person in your life with whom you could work least well. This in-dividual may or may not be the person you also dislike most. It must be the one person with whom you had the most difficulty getting a job done, the one single individual with whom you would least want to work—a boss, a subordinate, or a peer (Fiedler & Chemers, 1984, p. 17).

Various closely related forms of the LPC scale have consisted of from 16 to 22, eight-point, bipolar adjective scales on which the respondent's least preferred coworker is described. Regardless of the version, the respondent's score is calculated by summing across all items. When the LPC score has been treated categorically, the cutoff points to categorize the score have not always been consistent across studies. In some cases, extreme scores have been used (cutoffs usually have been based on a standard deviation on each side of the mean or the top and bottom 10% or thirds of the distribution). In other cases, a median or mean split has been used to categorize high and low LPC scores. In recent years, a few studies have used the LPC score as a continuous score, examining the magnitude of its relation to outcome vari-ables.

Psychometric Questions Concerning the LPC Scale

This section discusses the validity and reliability of the LPC scale, with the special intent of clarifying past misconceptions with respect to the meas-urement and meaning of the construct. We address both the psychometric properties of the scale and its validity and utility as a research tool. Rather than measuring a leader's attitudes, expectations, and self-reported behav-iors, the LPC scale seeks to infer a respondent's (leader's) investment in task accomplishment through his/her reactions to a coworker who thwarts ac-complishment. The degree to which the respondent gives a negative rating of the "least preferred coworker" presumably reflects the respondent's frustration or anger.

Two terms in the instructions are especially important—that is, "least" and "coworker." The term "least" demands that the person rated is not just any undesirable coworker in the rater's experience but the single worst ever encountered. The intent is to create a strong stimulus that will draw the greatest level of reaction from the respondent. Asking a respondent to describe two different coworkers as a means of assessing the reliability of the measure is not appropriate. For each rater, there should be only one appropriate stimulus: the least preferred coworker.

The term "coworker" rather than "subordinate" or "follower" is intentionally vague, allowing the respondent to rate a peer, superior, or subordinate. Finally, the frame of reference for identifying this poor coworker is the respondent's entire working history, avoiding an emphasis on the current situation. Here, the attempt is to obtain a stable, affective reaction. The items on which the least preferred coworker are rated are not descriptors of particular behaviors or task-related abilities. They are global, evaluative adjectives. The ratings of the stimulus thus reflect a general evaluative response (i.e., an attitude) toward a person who has interfered with the attainment of a more or less highly valued goal (e.g., task accomplishment). In sum, the LPC reflects a broad emotional reaction to a poor coworker, revealing how important the rater considers task success to be.

The LPC score clearly has been the most controversial component of the contingency model. It has been interpreted as a measure of psychological distance, leader orientation, and motivational hierarchy. All of these interpretations apply to some extent. This lack of consensus has been very disturbing to those with a low tolerance for ambiguity. Whether we now call LPC a measure of leader orientation, the term favored by Ayman and Chemers (1991), or a motivational index, the term favored by Fiedler (1978), is not of critical importance. As we shall see, the difference in operational terms turns out to be one of emphasis rather than of substance.

Questions of the construct validity of the LPC scale have engendered debates and controversies. Three approaches have been taken to respond to these debates. One has examined the scale's item content. A second has addressed issues of convergent and divergent validity, and a third has studied the relationship between the LPC score and leader behavior. Each of these approaches is now considered.

Item Content

The discussion surrounding the nature of the adjectives included in the scale has been concerned with the different number of adjectives that were descriptors of work-related traits (e.g., lazy or industrious) versus the number of relationship-relevant descriptors (e.g., friendly or close). Rice (1978b) referred to a series of studies (published and unpublished) demonstrating that the scale has two factors (task and people orientation). He also demonstrated that the structure has varied for high and low LPC respondents, and the intercorrelation between the factors across studies has also varied. Edwards, Rode, and Ayman (1989) compared the responses of ROTC cadets to the leader behavior questionnaire (LBDQ), leader opinion questionnaire (LOQ or LEAD), and LPC scale, using confirmatory factor analyses. They found that the three scales of LBDQ, LOQ, and LEAD had similar two-factor structures (consideration and initiation of structure) and that the LPC scale did not match this factor structure.

Rice (1978b) argued that "the potential importance of these factor analytic data is indicated by examining the relationship between LPC factor scores and external criteria" (p. 110). Rice and Seaman (1981) explored the relationship of task versus relationship adjective sets with outcome variables. Using a 22-item scale, they found that an overall score and a score based only on task items seemed to have quite similar relationships to outcome criteria. Apparently, the variations in item content of the scale do not threaten the criterion-related validity of the total LPC scale.

Convergent-Divergent Validity

During the past 30 years of research on LPC, several studies have examined the LPC scale's construct validity through convergent and divergent validity studies in which LPC scores are associated with other trait measures. The earlier studies reported correlations below .30 between the various traits and the LPC scale, establishing the LPC scale as an independent construct (Fiedler, 1967). Recent studies have shown that respondents' self-monitoring score (Ayman & Chemers, 1991; Ayman & Abenate, 1994), gender (Powell, Butterfield, & Mainiero, 1981; Schneier, 1978), values and intelligence (Kennedy, Houston, Korsgaard, & Gallo, 1987) are non-linearly related to the LPC scale.

Rice (1978a) reported a low negative linear relationship between the LPC score (that is, a low LPC person scoring higher) and measures of self-evaluation, including intelligence (Bons, Bass, & Komorita, 1970), achievement (Burke, 1965), and being agreeable (Shima, 1968). He also reported a positive relationship (that is, high LPC person scoring higher) with social cognitive complexity. A pattern of results relating the LPC score to measures of confidence, attention, and cognitive complexity, revealed that low LPC persons were more interested in, and knowledgeable about, variables in the task domain, whereas high LPC persons evidenced a similar involvement with aspects of the interpersonal or relationship domain. Rice concluded that the LPC scale reflects a basic value orientation (toward task achievement in low LPCs and toward interpersonal relations in high LPCs) and these values influence attitudes toward various factors in the leadership environment.

Two studies of job satisfaction provide direct support of the value-attitude interpretation of the LPC construct. In both a laboratory experiment (Rice, Marwick, Chemers, & Bentley, 1982) and an organizational survey (Chemers & Ayman, 1985), low LPC leaders showed a significantly stronger relationship between performance measures and job satisfaction than did high LPC leaders. The high LPCs showed a stronger relationship than the lows between job satisfaction and measures of group atmosphere and interpersonal harmony. Consistent with other studies that have demonstrated a moderating effect of work values (e.g., growth need strength, need for achievement) on satisfaction-performance relationships (e.g., Abdel-Halim, 1980), these findings reinforce the view of LPC as a measure of values or motivational orientations of the respondents.

Leader Behavior

The third construct validity technique involves relating the LPC scale to leader behavior measures. Fiedler and Chemers (1974) referred to the LPC score as a measure of the leader's style. Whereas it may have seemed rational then to relate the LPC score to leader behavior, several issues of concern need to be addressed. First, as already established, the LPC scale measures a respondent's attitudes, values, and motivational orientation, not his or her behavior. Although attitudes and values may be the basis for an individual's behavior, attitude/values and behavior do not bear an isomorphic relationship, and therefore, the relationship between a leader's LPC score and a particular leader behavior is an empirical question. Second, recognition of the strong effect of cognitive and information processing biases in the perception of leader behavior (Lord & Maher, 1991) has called into question the role of behavioral measures as valid indicators of "actual" leader behavior.

Given these caveats related to the measurement of leader behavior, the relationship between the LPC and leaders' behaviors is important not only from a leadership-process perspective but also because it can assist in clarifying two dominant hypotheses about the LPC: the Value-Attitude (Rice, 1978a) and the Motivational Hierarchy (Fiedler, 1978) hypotheses. For the value-attitude hypothesis to be supported, the research should show significant and consistent main effects for the LPC scale and measures of leader behavior. For the motivational hierarchy hypothesis to be validated, the results should have demonstrated an interaction effect of a leader's LPC score with his or her situational control predicting the leader's behavior. Rice (1978a), by including main effects that were present in studies with significant interaction effects, concluded that across studies there were an equal number of findings supporting both hypotheses. This conclusion may have been premature because some of these main effects were part of results that supported interaction effects.

We argued earlier that the LPC scale is an attitude measure with a strong emphasis on the affective component. However, evidence also supported the fact that although the LPC reflects the respondent's reaction to a person in a situation, it also reflects the respondent's values and goals (i.e., emphasis on task accomplishment or relationship with people), which are the motivational forces behind his/her actions. The results of the interaction effects of leader's LPC score and situational control on measures of leader behavior demonstrate that the relationship of the leader's LPC score to the leader's behavior is moderated by the situation (e.g., Bons & Fiedler, 1976; Borden, 1980; Chemers, 1969; Frost, 1981; Fiedler, 1967, 1972; Fiedler & Garcia, 1987; Larson & Rowland, 1973; Sample & Wilson, 1965). For example, high LPC leaders behaved more considerately toward group members in moderately stressful conditions than low LPC leaders; low LPC leaders behaved more considerately than highs in situations where they felt in control. On the other hand, high LPC leaders behaved with more emphasis on the task than low LPC leaders in situations where they felt in control, and the low LPC leaders behaved with more focus on the task than high LPC leaders when they were in moderately stressful conditions. These shifts in behavioral manifestations of LPC score may be indicative of a hierarchy of the leaders' goals motivating them to act. That is, in situations where individuals feel that their primary values, goals, or motivational orientations are not met, they act in a way to satisfy them, and if they are satisfied, their secondary goals or values will direct their behavior. It is important to note that in several of the above-mentioned studies, leader's behavior was measured by objective techniques—for example, in-basket exercise responses (Larson & Rowland, 1973).

In summary, the value-attitude and motivational hierarchy are not incompatible hypotheses. Rather, one focuses on the measure of LPC and the other on the construct it represents. They both agree that LPC measures values or goals. However, the former assumed that individual's values will always be manifested in specific behaviors (Rice, 1978a) and the latter (Fiedler, 1978) assumed that values or goals may or may not be manifested in a particular behavior. In the latter case, the vehicle that moderates the behavioral manifestation is the situation. The motivational hierarchy is more in line with other social-psychological views on the relationship between attitude and behavior (Ajzen, 1987; Fazio, 1990).

In addition, the relationship of the LPC score and leader behavior can only be studied when the issues of measurement of leader behavior are considered with great care. Therefore, although we concur with Rice's position that research on this relationship may provide a better understanding of the LPC score, the path is not as smooth and clear as it may seem.

Although the evidence on the construct validity of the LPC scale is not conclusive, some conclusions do seem reasonable. A low LPC score is a reflection of a negative affect emanating from frustration with the inability to complete the task at hand. A low score may represent those individuals who have a self-concept that is strongly associated with accomplishment. The evidence suggests that LPC is a measure of a respondent's inner state, not a measure of his/her behavior patterns.

Reliability

As a final note to the review of the LPC scale's psychometric properties, its reliability is now discussed. The reliability of the LPC scale has been measured both by examining its internal consistency and test-retest reliability. The internal consistency of the scale has always been fairly high. The average internal consistency coefficient reported is .88 (Rice, 1978b), and more recently, Ayman and Chemers (1991) reported Cronbach's alpha of .90. The test-retest reliability of the scale parallels other personality measures with a median stability coefficient of .67 (Rice, 1978b; Fiedler, 1978). Rice's (1978b) review included 23 studies on test-retest reliability of the scale. The time lapse in these studies ranged from two days to two-

and-a-half years. The scale seems to meet the established criteria for reliability.

Summary of the Review on the LPC Scale

Overall, the findings about the psychometric properties of the LPC scale have demonstrated that the nature of the adjectives included in the scale may affect its structure, but it is not critical to the scale's functionality. Based on the existing evidence, it is safe to say that the LPC scale is a measure of the internal state of the leader. Whether it measures values, motivation attitude, or goals is not totally resolved. However, based on Markus and Wurf (1987), all of these concepts are variables that operate in determining the working self, though they vary in their level of specificity.

The LPC scale is a measure whose history and approach creates unique advantages and disadvantages. As an indirect measure of values and/or motivational orientation, it is less susceptible to demand characteristics or social desirability effects. On the other hand, the lack of a clear theoretic-deductive explanation makes the LPC construct appear mysterious and unscientific. The predictive utility of the construct as evidenced in the comprehensive meta-analyses (Strube & Garcia, 1981; Peters, Hartke, & Pohlmann, 1985) does encourage us to continue attempts to understand the concept better.

SITUATIONAL CONTROL

The other central construct in contingency model research, situational control, has been operationalized in various ways. It is conceptually defined as the leader's sense of influence and control afforded by the situation (Fiedler, 1978). In most of the research, three components of the situation have been identified as contributors to a sense of predictability and control: Leader-Member Relationship (formerly referred to as Group Atmosphere), Task Structure, and Position Power.

In the following sections, each of the three components of situational control is discussed. Each component is defined both theoretically and methodologically. From a methodological perspective, both the measurements and the source of information for the component across studies are examined. Finally, the relationship among the three components is presented, as well as their relationship with the leader's motivational orientation.

Leader-Member Relations

This construct refers to the amount of cohesiveness in the work team and the support of the team for the leader. Leader-member relations is the most important aspect of the situation, because if the leader lacks group support, energy is diverted to controlling the group rather than toward planning, problem-solving, and productivity. Under these conditions, the leader's influence is weakened, and he or she can not rely on the team to achieve and implement the goal.

In early laboratory research of the model, the group-atmosphere scale (Fiedler, 1967) was used to assess either experimentally manipulated or naturally occurring work team cohesion. The measure was completed by all participants. The scale consisted of 10 eight-point bipolar items. In studies where sociometric choice was used to manipulate group cohesion, the statistical relationship between the score on the group atmosphere scale and sociometric manipulation was positive and substantial (e.g., Chemers & Skrzypek, 1972).

More recently, the Leader-Member Relations (LMR) scale has been used to assess this construct. This measure was first introduced as a training tool (Fiedler, Chemers, & Mahar, 1976). It consists of eight five-point scale items describing the relationship of the team members with each other and their loyalty and responsiveness to the leader. The LMR scale has good internal reliability—Cronbach's alpha of .80 (e.g., Ayman & Chemers, 1991).

Leader-member relations is theoretically conceptualized at the group level. In much of the experimental and field studies a group average on Group Atmosphere scale was used to determine group cohesion (e.g., Chemers & Skrzypek, 1972, Geyer & Julian, 1973, Csoka & Fiedler, 1972). In some of the more recent field studies, the leader has been the source of information about this construct. However, the leaders' scores represented their experiences with their group as a whole, not with individual subordinates in dyadic relationships (e.g., Ayman & Chemers, 1991).

The leader-member relations scale has shown strong construct validity. The Group Atmosphere scale and the Leader-Member Relation scale are highly correlated—$r = .88$ (Fiedler, 1978). Neither of the scales has shown a correlation with the leader's LPC scale (e.g., Chemers, Hays, Rhodewalt, & Wysoki, 1985; Fiedler, 1978; McNamara, 1968). However, Group Atmosphere has been correlated with some outcome variables like leader's experience of stress with the subordinates (Chemers et al., 1985). The construct validity of the Leader-Member Relations scale demonstrates that it is a valid measure depicting the group's cohesion and loyalty to the leader. The test of validity has been ascertained by high correlations between two different measures and from multiple sources (i.e., the group and/or the leader). It is independent of the leader's orientation even when the leader has been the source of information for both the LPC score and the leader-member relation score. This is a significant strength in the model because in field studies, the leader is typically the source of this information.

Task Structure

This second component of Situational Control represents the clarity and certainty in task goals and procedures that allow the leader confidently to guide the group's activities. In laboratory studies, the variable was usually manipulated by the choice of assigned tasks that varied on Shaw's (1963) criteria for task structure (Fiedler, 1978). In field studies, task structure ratings can be provided by a knowledgeable observer, such as a superior. A scale for rating task structure by a supervisor or investigator was developed by Hunt (1967).

More recent field research has employed the Task Structure Rating Scale developed as part of the "Leader Match" training program (Fiedler, Chemers, & Mahar, 1976; Fiedler & Chemers, 1984). The self-report scale consists of 10 items incorporating Shaw's (1963) dimensions of goal clarity, goal-path multiplicity, solution specificity, and outcome quantifiability. Based on research that indicated that task-relevant experience and training enhanced task structure (Fiedler, 1970; Chemers, Rice, Sundstrom, & Butler, 1975), an additional two-item subscale assessing the leader's experience and training was added to the scale. Information on the total scale's reliability is not available. However, Ayman and Chemers (1991) reported a Cronbach's alpha of .81 for the first section of the scale.

In studies where the measure of task structure has been based on the leader's perception, the intercorrelation of LPC score and task structure score has not been reported. Part of the reason may be due to the fact that task structure is a single component of the situational control dimension and only the correlations between situational control and other variables are usually reported. In addition, until recently, task structure was objectively rated by the experimenter or the leader's supervisor in most studies.

The sense of predictability and certainty provided by a task with clear goals and procedures contributes to the overall level of situational control experienced by the leader. Conceptually, task structure is a group-level variable. The task being measured includes all the activities that the leader must accomplish to move the group toward its collective goal. In contrast to some models, the task being measured is the leader's task, not the task of individual subordinates being supervised by the leader. For example, a task requiring high levels of interdependence among subordinates might increase complexity and reduce task structure for the leader.

Operationally, task structure has been defined by leader self-reports, by ratings of observers or superiors, or by manipulation of assigned tasks. Although the measurement of the variable sometimes occurs at the individual level, in combination with other situational control variables, it represents an aspect of the group environment in which the leader functions. As shown in Table 1, however, it is an individual-level variable about the Leader's Task.

Position Power

This component of situational control is defined as the administrative authority bestowed on the leader by the organization or other source of authority—for example, the experimenter. Fiedler (1978) advised that position power assessments should be supplied by the leader's supervisor, due to the possibility of distortion of information by self-report. However, in most field studies, the leader's self-report has been used (Fiedler & Chemers, 1984). This is a five-item scale that measures the leader's discretionary power to reward and punish, job-relevant expertise, and official status. Internal reliability data are available for only one study (Ayman & Chemers, 1991), where it had a low Cronbach's alpha of .31. While a single reliability coefficient is not conclusive, it may be that the low internal consistency is the result of the multidimensional nature of the scale, which measures several bases of power. In most field research, leaders are chosen from a single organizational level with similar position power. No relationship has been found between leader's LPC score and the leader's reported Position Power score.

Similar to the Task Structure, Position Power has been defined at the individual level, for the leader. It has been manipulated by experimental design, described by the leader's supervisor, or measured through the leader's perception (see Table 1). Like Task Structure, it contributes to the overall level of control in the leader's situation, and may be conceptualized as either a group- or individual-level variable depending on the analysis.

Summary of Situational Control and Social Power

The three components of situational control parallel French and Raven's (1959) five bases of power. Power has been defined as the ability to influence others. Situational Control has also been defined as providing the leader with the ability to influence and gain control (Bass, 1991). French and Raven identified the expert and referent sources of power as sources based on knowledge and expertise regarding the task and the strength or solidity of the social relationships. Research has indicated that these two sources of power have the most efficacious and lasting effects in social influence (Podsakoff & Schriesheim, 1985; Yukl & Taber, 1983). Referent power based on the quality of the social relationship is most similar to the contingency model variable of "Leader-Member Relations." Expert power with its emphasis on task knowledge bears much in common with "Task Structure." The three other sources of power—coercive, reward, and legitimate—reflect on an individual's authority. These three sources have shown to be inter-correlated to the point that some have referred to it as position power (Bass, 1991). Their effects have been debated. Thus, they do not seem to have as robust and lasting an effect as the referent and expert sources (Podsakoff & Schriesheim, 1985). In the contingency model, these power sources are given the least weight in the assessment of situational control.

The weighting of the three components of situational control was originally ordinal. Fiedler (1967) specified Group Atmosphere (leader-member relations) to be most important. Task Structure came second, and Position Power was third. The analytic strategy typically involved dividing groups at the median on each variable and combining the resultant designations into one of eight cells, or "octants." This approach had the ad hoc effect of weighting Leader-Member Relations twice as strongly as Task Structure, which was weighted twice as strongly as Position Power (i.e., 4:2:1 weighting ratio). Later empirical research related measures of each variable to a rating of overall control and predictability and found that the inductively derived weights were very close to the 4:2:1 ratios (Nebeker, 1975).

The self-rating Leader Match scales (Fiedler & Chemers, 1984) are adjusted for the prescribed weights by the maximum number of points possible on each scale (i.e., LMR scale, 40 points; TS scale, 20; PP scale, 10). The summed scale values provide a measure of overall Situational Control, which can be compared to the cutting points for high, moderate, and low levels of control. Recent field studies have used the normative cutoff points (e.g., Gifford & Ayman, 1989) or median (e.g., Ayman & Chemers, 1991) or tripartite splits (e.g., Chemers et al., 1985) of sample distributions to assign leaders to conditions.

THE RELATIONSHIP AMONG THE INDEPENDENT
VARIABLES WITHIN THE CONTINGENCY MODEL

The variables that define the leader's personal characteristic (the LPC) and the leader's situational control (leader-member relations, task structure, and position power) are both conceptually and psychometrically independent. This is one of the most valuable and unique properties of the contingency model. In studies where the leader is the only source of information for both personal and situational variables, or where the situation is defined by an independent observer, the LPC and situational control scores are not statistically related. Problems of multi-colinearity and single-source biases, which bedevil much current leadership-research methodology (Podsakoff & Organ, 1986; Spector, 1987), are not a serious problem for contingency model research. Although LPC and situational control are uncorrelated, some dependency does appear among the three situational variables.

In laboratory experiments, the situational control variables were manipulated and their relationship was, by design, independent. In field studies, task structure and position power have been found to be correlated between $r = .75$ (Chemers & Fiedler, 1986) and $r = .33$ (Chemers et al., 1985). The actual level of interdependence of the three factors may have varied from study to study because of the level of the manager, the type of company, or the source of information on each factor. Overlap among the situational control variables provides a strong rationale for employing the composite situational control score.

Relationship of the Model to Outcome (Dependent) Variables

The contingency model of leadership effectiveness has defined its criterion of effectiveness primarily as work group performance. However, some studies have examined effects on other criteria, such as subordinate satisfaction or leader's reported symptoms of stress.

The operational definition of performance has been based partially on the nature of task and the level of the leader's position. Wherever possible, productivity was defined by objective measures, such as win-lose records for basketball teams, tons per person-hour for steel production crews, and accuracy for bombing crews. In cases where the nature of the tasks required a subjective evaluation, at least two raters evaluated the quality of performance. Such tasks typically consisted of composing a story, developing a report, or recommending a program. In most of the organizational field studies, the manager's performance was rated by a superior.

The important point to note is that the contingency model has used a variety of performance measures that have been relevant to the work group objective. However, regardless of whether the performance was measured subjectively or objectively and whether it was a measure of quality or quantity, it was always assessed by an agent outside of the work team.

We pointed out earlier that the contingency model was designed primarily to predict work team performance. The empirical development of the model made clear that only the interaction of personal and situational parameters could predict group performance. One of the most important premises of the contingency principle is that neither leader characteristics nor situational factors alone can predict performance. The reviews and meta-analyses have established the essential validity of that premise. Person-situation match, but neither person nor situation alone, has been consistently predictive of performance outcomes.

In the early stages of the development of the model, Fiedler (1967) argued that group productivity was the most important and appropriate outcome variable in leadership research. He pointed out that chief executive officers, football coaches, and symphony conductors are not retained and rewarded for making their subordinates happy and satisfied but for making them productive and profitable. This point is still apt today, but organizational theorists and practitioners have come to recognize that variables such as commitment, loyalty, and satisfaction can have important implications for organizational performance and profitability.

In 1977, Schriesheim and Kerr criticized the contingency model for its lack of attention to subordinate satisfaction. If we turn our attention to the prediction and explanation of subordinate satisfaction and other attitudinal and affective states, what might be the most useful ways to proceed? A logical approach might be to look for the same confluence of person and situational variables that are effective in the prediction of performance— that is, leader-situation match.

In 1981, Rice responded to Schriesheim and Kerr's (1977) criticism with a review of existing studies examining the relationship of the contingency model variables to job satisfaction. Although some inconsistencies exist across studies, Rice concluded that the bulk of the evidence supports the view that subordinate satisfaction is highest when leaders are in match. Subsequent studies of managers in the United States (Giffort & Ayman, 1989) and in Mexico (Ayman & Chemers, 1991) have supported Rice's conclusions. Subordinates of low LPC managers in high-control situations and of high LPC managers in moderate-control situations were more satisfied than their "out-of-match" counterparts.

Job satisfaction is a multi-faceted construct. The contingency model effects reported here occur primarily on measures of satisfaction with the superior or satisfaction with coworkers (i.e., measures of work team cohesion) rather than on measures of satisfaction with pay or promotion which are variables frequently outside the leader's control. It is interesting to note that match (i.e., the interaction of LPC and Situational Control) is a better predictor of subordinate satisfaction than is the leader's score on the leader-member relations scale, indicating the importance of multiple, independent measures of group effects.

Although the validity of the contingency model in the prediction of group performance seems well established and its utility for predicting subordinate satisfaction is promising, many gaps in understanding remain which reduce the model's explanatory value. The model continues, however, to instigate research that may enrich our understanding of the processes that underlie match effects. The next section will briefly describe some new directions in contingency model research involving efforts at the individual level to understand the phenomenological and emotional effects of match; at the dyadic level to predict performance and satisfaction; and multi-trait approaches in which person-level variables besides the LPC are integrated into the model.

NEW DIRECTIONS

Individual-Level Analyses

A series of studies have examined the phenomenological experience of style-situation match on leaders. Garcia (1983) compared high and low LPC persons working on individual tasks that varied in the degree of certainty. Certainty was manipulated by providing half of the subjects with task-relevant training that increased task structure and subjective reports of certainty. Garcia reported that low LPC persons in the high-certainty condition (training) and high LPC persons in the low-certainty (no training) condition made stronger attributions to their own ability as the cause of performance than did low LPC persons in the low-certainty condition or high LPCs in the high-certainty condition. In a laboratory experiment on group leadership, Nahavandi (1983) found that "in-match" leaders, as defined by contingency model variables, reported higher levels of involvement and interest in the experience than did "out-of-match" leaders.

Chemers, Hays, Rhodewalt, and Wysocki (1985) measured the relationship of contingency model match to job stress and stress-related illness among university administrators. Department chairs who were out of match reported significantly higher levels of stress and stress-related illness than did their in-match counterparts. These findings were replicated in a follow-up study (Chemers, Hill, & Sorod, 1986) of high school administrators. As in the earlier studies, in-match leaders reported less stress and illness, as well as higher levels of job satisfaction, than did out-of-match leaders. Shirakashi (1991) closely replicated the results of these match-stress studies using a sample of managers in Japan.

A laboratory experiment by Chemers, Sorod, and Akimoto (reported in Chemers, 1993) found that in-match leaders as compared to out-of-match leaders reported: (1) more positive mood states, (2) greater confidence in their ability to lead, and (3) more internal attributions to their own ability and effort to explain group performance. A number of theorists and researchers have recently focused on the role of positive affective states, such as confidence and mood, on leadership performance (e.g., Murphy, 1992; May, 1993; Staw & Barsade, 1993; Bennis & Nanus, 1985; House & Shamir, 1993). Leadership match may be a powerful moderator of contemporaneous situational factors affecting such affective states.

Dyadic-Level Analyses

The study of dyads in the contingency model has not received much attention. Two studies that have examined dyads have shown trends that indicate that the nature of the task may interact with different compositions of leader's and follower's LPC score to predict subordinate satisfaction and performance.

Chemers, Goza, and Plumer (1978) conducted an experiment in which three-person groups solved a problem for which the leader and one follower had been given contradictory information in a pre-session briefing. The dyads that were most effective in solving the problem were those with a high LPC leader and low LPC follower, while the most ineffective dyads were those that were homogeneous with respect to leader and follower LPC. Tobey (1992) also found the high-LPC-leader/low-LPC-subordinate dyads to be most effective in performance on a similarly unstructured task. However, Tobey (1992) also found that dyads led by low LPCs outperformed dyads led by high LPCs when the task was more structured. It seems reasonable to expect that the effects of dyadic composition on both performance and satisfaction would be most productively addressed in a contingency framework.

Multi-Trait Approach

Weiss and Adler (1984) have suggested a multi-trait approach to organizational behavior theories. They advise the inclusion of traits that have a theoretical relationship to outcome criteria or have the potential for expanding the explanatory base of the theory. The most developed of the new expansions of the contingency model is the cognitive resource theory (Fiedler, 1993; Fiedler & Garcia, 1987). Fiedler and his associates have demonstrated that the leader's ability to make effective use of his or her cognitive resources (i.e., intellectual ability and job-relevant experience) depends on a number of contingencies. Job stress from any of several sources (including one's boss or subordinates, or the nature of one's task) interferes with a leader's ability to think creatively and use intellectual resources but enhances the value of the well-learned lessons of experience. The intellectual demands of the task, the cooperativeness of subordinates, and the leader's willingness to act directively also moderate the impact of cognitive resources on group productivity.

Unless the leader acts in a directive manner employing knowledge and insight to influence group activities, those cognitive resources will have little effect. Furthermore, compliant and supportive subordinates who respond positively to the leader's influence attempts increase the impact of the leader's directions on group outputs. Finally, intellectually demanding tasks that place a premium on thoughtful and creative ideas will increase the relative effects of cognitive processes.

Similar to the cognitive model, cognitive resource theory places an individual-level phenomenon (the effects of stress on cognition) in a context in which superiors, subordinates, and task influence relationships with group-level outcomes. Leadership as a group process, analyzable at the group level, seems to be the overriding emphasis of these two contingency theories.

Like the contingency model that preceded it, cognitive resource theory assesses the effects of individual-level variables (i.e., leader intelligence and experience) at a group level of analysis. Situational parameters, such as task demands, subordinate support, and environmental stress, moderate the relationships between the individual-level variables and group-level outcomes, for example, productivity. Cognitive resource theory adds the process variable of the leader's level of directiveness to tie together the leader and outcome variables. The centrality of job stress in the cognitive resource theory and in the recent work by Chemers and his associates on leadership match and job stress suggests the potential for integrating the two models. Future research in that direction seems warranted.

Another multi-trait approach to contingency-model research has investigated the moderating role of self-monitoring (Snyder, 1979). Kenny and Zaccaro (1983) have argued that a leader's flexibility in adapting to situational characteristics may be a leadership trait with broad applicability. The self-monitoring construct reflects an individual's sensitivity and responsiveness to the social expectations across varying situations. Since leadership match is based on the degree of fit between the leader's motivational orientation and situational characteristics, a leader's ability to adapt to situations might moderate the effects of match. Specifically, high self-monitors who are able to change their behavior to adjust to the expectations of others may be less susceptible to leader-situation mismatches than would be low self-monitors whose behavioral style is more rigidly determined by internal values and attitudes.

A recent study by Ayman and Chemers (1991) included the self-monitoring scale with the contingency model measures administered to 85 middle managers in Mexican companies. The predicted effects of match on several outcome measures, including subordinate satisfaction with work and the leader's effectiveness in conflict management, were moderated by self-monitoring as expected. Other measures in the same study, such as subordinate satisfaction with the leader, showed straight match effects, unaffected by self-monitoring.

These results indicate that multi-trait approaches to leadership effects have great potential. However, the choice of traits for inclusion must be theoretically driven (Weiss & Adler, 1984).

SUMMARY AND CONCLUSIONS

The contingency model of leadership has stimulated and guided research for more than 30 years. The greatest strengths of the model reside in: (1) the conceptual and statistical independence of its central constructs,

LPC and Situational Control; (2) its emphasis on independent and, where possible, objective measures of important organizational outcomes such as group productivity; (3) its relatively lesser vulnerability to the invalidation of its constructs and findings as a result of information-processing biases and methodological weaknesses; and, of course, (4) its proven predictive validity.

The model's greatest weaknesses arise from its inductive development. The LPC construct has little face or concurrent validity, and even evidence for its construct validity requires some faith. The lack of process-based explanations for performance effects makes both the understanding and application of the model more difficult.

One of the major strengths of the contingency model in practical application is that about 15 minutes worth of questionnaire administration provides a multi-level analysis of person-situation match that can be used in selection, placement, training, and organizational development. Based on the contingency model, the Leader Match training program (Fiedler & Chemers, 1984) provides a framework for organizational intervention at the individual, dyadic, and group levels.

During the last three decades, the contingency model has been the subject of extensive research and vigorous controversy, and yet it is alive and still developing. The individual and dyadic levels of analysis are being added to the traditional focus on group-level effectiveness phenomena. Multi-trait approaches may help to illuminate the factors that underlie its impact. The power of the cognitive resource theory reveals productive avenues for bridging the gap between the contingency model and other psychological theories. Finally, the model's utility in creating practical approaches to leadership training and organizational development reinforces Kurt Lewin's dictum that "There is nothing so practical as a good theory."

Through training such as Leader Match, which is based on the contingency model of leadership effectiveness, the leader uses both personal and group data to assess his or her match in the situation. The validity of this training program has been presented in numerous documents (Fiedler & Mahar, 1979; Burke & Day, 1986). Using the model's existing research, the leader can then anticipate his or her effectiveness both at a personal and dyadic level (i.e., experienced stress or subordinate satisfaction) and at a group level (i.e., performance, subordinates' satisfaction and morale). With access to such wisdom, the leader can do "job engineering." This does not require major changes in the way the work is done but, through modifying the three situational control constructs, the leader can affect all levels of work team dynamics and alter group functioning.

REFERENCES

Abdel-Halim, A. A. (1980). Effects of higher order need strength on the job perform-ance-job satisfaction relationship. *Personnel Psychology, 33*, 335–347.

Ajzen, I. (1987). Attitudes, traits, and actions: Dispositional prediction of behavior in personality and social psychology. In L. Berkowitz (Ed.), *Advances in Experimen-tal Social Psychology* (Vol. 20, pp. 1–63). New York: Academic.

Ashour, A. S. (1973). The contingency model of leadership effectiveness: An evalua-tion. *Organizational Behavior and Human Performance, 9*, 339–355.

Ayman, R., & Abenate, D. C. (1994). An expansion of the contingency model: The moderating influence of self-monitoring. Unpublished manuscript, Illinois Insti-tute of Technology, Chicago, IL.

Ayman, R., & Chemers, M. M. (1991). The effect of leadership match on subordi-nate satisfaction in Mexican organizations: Some moderating influences of self-monitoring. *Applied Psychology: An International Review, 40*, 299–314.

Bass, B. M. (1991). *Bass & Stogdill's handbook of leadership: Theory, research, and managerial applications.* 3rd edition. New York: Free Press.

Bennis, W., & Nanus, B. (1985). *Leaders: Strategies for taking charge.* New York: Harper & Row.

Bons, P. M., Bass, A. R., & Komorita, S. (1970). Changes in leadership style as a func-tion of military experience and type of command. *Personnel Psychology, 23*, 551–568.

Bons, P. M., & Fiedler, F. E. (1976). Changes in organizational leadership and the be-havior of relationship and task motivated leaders. *Administrative Science Quar-terly, 21*, 453–473.

Borden, D. F. (1980). Leader-boss stress, personality, job satisfaction and perform-ance: Another look at the inter-relationship of some old constructs in the modern large bureaucracy. Unpublished Ph.D. dissertation, University of Washington, Seattle.

Burke, W. W. (1965). Leadership behavior as a function of the leader, the follower, and situation. *Journal of Personality, 33*, 60–81.

Burke, M. J., & Day, R. R. (1986). A cumulative study of the effectiveness of manage-rial training. *Journal of Applied Psychology, 71*, 232–246.

Chemers, M. M. (1969). Cross-cultural training as a means for improving situational favorableness. *Human Relations, 22*, 531–546.

Chemers, M. M. (1993). An integrative theory of leadership. In M. M. Chemers & R. Ayman (Eds.), *Leadership theory and research: Perspectives and directions* (pp. 293–319). San Diego, CA: Academic Press.

Chemers, M. M., and Ayman, R. (1985). Leadership orientation as a moderator of the relationship between job performance and job satisfaction of Mexican managers. *Personality and Social Psychology Bulletin, 11*, 359–367.

Chemers, M. M., and Fiedler, F. E. (1986). The trouble with assumptions: A reply to Jago and Ragan. *Journal of Applied Psychology, 71*, 560–563.

Chemers, M. M., Goza, B., & Plumer, S. I. (1978). Leadership style and communication process. Paper presented at the annual meeting of the American Psychological Association, Toronto, Ontario, Canada.

Chemers, M. M., Hays, R. B., Rhodewalt, F., & Wysocki, J. (1985). A person-environment analysis of job stress: A contingency model explanation. *Journal of Personality and Social Psychology, 49*, 628–635.

Chemers, M. M., Hill, C., & Sorod, B. (1986). Personality-environment match and health: Support for the contingency model. Paper presented at the annual meetings of the American Psychological Association, Chicago, IL.

Chemers, M. M., Rice, R. W., Sundstrom, E., & Butler, W. (1975). Leader esteem for the least preferred co-worker score, training, and effectiveness: An experimental examination. *Journal of Personality and Social Psychology, 31*, 401–409.

Chemers, M. M., & Skrzypek, G. J. (1972). Experimental test of the contingency model of leadership effectiveness. *Journal of Personality and Social Psychology, 24*, 172–177.

Csoka, L. S., & Fiedler, F. E. (1972). The effect of military training: A test of the contingency model. *Organizational Behavior and Human Performance, 8*, 395–407.

Edwards, J. E., Rode, L. G., & Ayman, R. (1989). The construct validity of scales from four leadership questionnaires. *The Journal of General Psychology, 116*, 171–181.

Fazio, R. H. (1990). Multiple processes by which attitudes guide behavior: The MODE model as an integrative framework. In M. Zanna (Ed.), *Advances in Experimental Social Psychology* (Vol. 23, pp. 75–109). New York: Academic Press.

Fiedler, F. E. (1967). *A theory of leadership effectiveness.* New York: McGraw-Hill.

Fiedler, F. E. (1970). Leadership experience and leadership training—Some new answers to an old problem. *Administrative Science Quarterly, 17*, 453–470.

Fiedler, F. E. (1972). Personality, motivational systems, and the behavior of high and low LPC persons. *Human Relations, 25*, 391–412.

Fiedler, F. E. (1978). The contingency model and the dynamics of the leadership process. In L. Berkowitz (Ed.), *Advances in Experimental Social Psychology* (Vol. 11, pp. 59–96). New York: Academic Press.

Fiedler, F. E. (1993). The leadership situation and the black box in contingency theories. In M. M. Chemers & R. Ayman (Eds.), *Leadership theory and research: Perspectives and directions* (pp. 2–28). New York: Academic Press.

Fiedler, F. E., & Chemers, M. M. (1974). *Leadership and effective management.* Glenview, IL: Scott-Foresman.

Fiedler, F. E., & Chemers, M. M. (1984). *Improving leadership effectiveness: The leader match concept.* 2nd edition, New York: Wiley.

Fiedler, F. E., Chemers, M. M., & Mahar, L. (1976). *Improving leadership effectiveness: The leader match concept.* New York: Wiley.

Fiedler, F. E., & Garcia, J. E. (1987). *New approach to effective leadership: Cognitive resources and organizational performance.* New York: John Wiley & Sons.

Fiedler, F. E., & Mahar, L. (1979). A field experiment validating contingency model leadership training. *Journal of Applied Psychology, 64*, 247–254.

Fiedler, F. E., Potter, E. H., Zais, M. M., & Knowlton, W. A. (1979). Organizational stress and the use and misuse of managerial intelligence and experience. *Journal of Applied Psychology, 64*, 635–647.

French, J. R., & Raven, B. (1959). The basis of social power. In D. Cartwright (Ed.), *Studies in social power.* Ann Arbor, MI: Institute for Social Research, University of Michigan.

Frost, D. E. (1981). The effects of interpersonal stress on leadership effectiveness. Unpublished Ph.D. dissertation, University of Washington, Seattle.

Garcia, J. E. (1983). An investigation of a person-situation match interpretation of the esteem for the least preferred coworker scale (LPC). Unpublished Ph.D. dissertation, Salt Lake City, University of Utah.

Geyer, L. J., & Julian, J.W. (1973). Manipulation of situational favorability in tests of the contingency model. *Journal of Psychology, 84*, 13–21.

Giffort, D. W., & Ayman, R. (1989). Contingency model and subordinate satisfaction: Mental health organizations. Paper presented at Academy of Management Annual Conference, Anaheim, CA.

Graen, G., Alvares, K. M., Orris, J. B., & Martella, J. A. (1971). Contingency model of leadership effectiveness: Antecedent and evidential results. *Psychological Bulletin, 74*, 285–296.

Graen, G., Orris, J. B., & Alvares, K. M. (1971). Contingency model of leadership effectiveness: Some experimental results. *Journal of Applied Psychology, 55*, 196–201.

House, R. J., & Shamir, B. (1993). Toward the integration of transformational, charismatic, and visionary theories. In M. M. Chemers & R. Ayman (Eds.), *Leadership theory and research: Perspectives and directions* (pp. 81–104). New York: Academic.

Hunt, J. G. (1967). Fiedler's leadership contingency model: An empirical test in three organizations. *Organizational Behavior and Human Performance, 2*, 290–308.

Kennedy, J. K., Houston, J. M., Korsgaard, M. A., & Gallo, D. D. (1987). Construct space of the least preferred coworker (LPC) scale. *Educational and Psychological Measurement, 47*, 807–814.

Kenny, D. A., & Zaccaro, S. J. (1983). An estimate of variance due to traits in leadership. *Journal of Applied Psychology, 68*, 678–685.

Larson, L. L., & Rowland, K. M. (1973). Leadership style, stress, and behavior in performance. *Organizational Behavior and Human Performance, 9*, 407–420.

Lord, R. G., & Maher, K. J. (1991). *Leadership and information processing.* Boston: Unwin Hyman.

Markus, H., & Wurf, E. (1987). The dynamic self-concept: A social psychological perspective. *Annual Review of Psychology, 38*, 299–337.

May, S. T. (1993). Heavy mettle: The effects of confidence and optimism on leader performance. Unpublished B.A. thesis, Claremont McKenna College, Claremont, CA.

McNamara, V. D. (1968). Leadership, staff and school effectiveness. Unpublished Ph.D. dissertation, University of Alberta.

Murphy, S. E. (1992). The contribution of leadership experience and self-efficacy to group performance under evaluation apprehension. Unpublished Ph.D. dissertation, University of Washington, Seattle, WA.

Nahavandi, A. (1983). The effect of personal and situational factors on satisfaction with leadership. Unpublished Ph.D. dissertation, University of Utah, Salt Lake City, UT.

Nebeker, D. M. (1975). Situational favorability and environmental uncertainty: An integrative approach. *Administrative Science Quarterly, 20*, 281–294.

Orne, M. T. (1962). On the social psychology of the psychological experiment: With particular reference to demand characteristics and their implications. *American Psychologist, 17*, 776–783.

Peters, L. H., Hartke, D. D., & Pohlmann, J. F. (1985). Fiedler's contingency theory of leadership: An application of the meta-analysis procedures of Schmitt and Hunter. *Psychological Bulletin, 97*, 274–285.

Podsakoff, P. M., & Schriesheim, C. A. (1985). Field studies of French and Raven's bases of power: Critique, reanalysis, and suggestions for future research. *Psychological Bulletin, 97*, 387–411.

Podsakoff, P. M., & Organ, D. W. (1986). Self-reports in organizational research: Problems and prospects. *Journal of Management, 12*, 31–41.

Powell, G. N., Butterfield, D. A., & Mainiero, L. A. (1981). Sex-role identity and sex as predictors of leadership style. *Psychological Reports, 49*, 829–830.

Rice, W. R. (1978a). Construct validity of the least preferred co-worker score. *Psychological Bulletin, 85*, 1199–1237.

Rice, W. R. (1978b). Psychometric properties of the esteem for the least preferred coworker (LPC Scale). *Academy of Management Review, 3*, 106–118.

Rice, W. R. (1981). Leader LPC and follower satisfaction: A review. *Organizational Behavior and Human Performance, 28*, 1–25.

Rice, R. W., Marwick, N. J., Chemers, M. M., & Bentley, J. C. (1982). Task performance and satisfaction: Least Preferred Coworker (LPC) as a moderator. *Personality and Social Psychology Bulletin, 8*, 534–541.

Rice, R. W., & Seaman, F. J. (1981). Internal analyses of the Least Preferred Coworker (LPC) scale. *Educational and Psychological Measurement, 41*, 109–120.

Sample, J. A., & Wilson, T. R. (1965). Leader behavior, group productivity, and rating of least preferred co-worker. *Journal of Personality and Social Psychology, 1*, 266–270.

Schneier, C. E. (1978). The contingency model of leadership: An extension to emergent leadership and leader's sex. *Organizational Behavior and Human Performance, 21*, 220–239.

Schriesheim, C. A., & Kerr, S. (1977). Theories and measures of leadership: A critical appraisal of current and future directions. In J. G. Hunt and L. L. Larson (Eds.), *Leadership: The cutting edge* (pp. 9–44). Carbondale, IL: Southern Illinois University Press.

Shaw, M. E. (1963). Scaling group tasks: A method of dimensional analysis: *JSAS Catalogue of Selected Documents in Psychology, 3*(8).

Shima, H. (1968). The leadership between the leader's modes of interpersonal cognition and the performance of the group. *Japanese Psychological Research, 10*, 13–30.

Shirakashi, S. (1991). Job stress of managers: A contingency model analysis. *Organizational Science, 25*, 42–51.

Snyder, M. (1979). Self-monitoring processes. In L. Berkowitz (Ed.), *Advances in experimental social psychology* (Vol. 12, pp. 81–104). New York: Academic Press.

Spector, P. E. (1987). Method variance as an artifact in self-report affect and perceptions at work: Myth or significant problem? *Journal of Applied Psychology, 72,* 438–443.

Staw, B. M., & Barsade, S. G. (1993). Affect and managerial performance: A test of the sadder-but-wiser vs. happier and smarter hypotheses. *Administrative Science Quarterly, 38,* 304–331.

Strube, M. J., & Garcia, J. E. (1981). A meta-analytic investigation of Fiedler's contingency model of leadership effectiveness. *Psychological Bulletin, 90,* 307–321.

Tobey, A. M. (1992). Subordinate satisfaction with supervision: A dyadic or group phenomenon. Unpublished M. A. thesis, Illinois Institute of Technology, Chicago, IL.

Vecchio, R. P. (1977). An empirical examination of the validity of Fiedler's model of leadership effectiveness. *Organizational Behavior and Human Performance, 19,* 180–206.

Vecchio, R. P. (1980). Alternatives to the least preferred co-worker construct. *The Journal of Social Psychology, 112,* 21–29.

Weiss, H. M., & Adler, S. (1984). Personality and organizational behavior. In B. M. Staw & L. L. Cummings (Eds.), *Research in organizational behavior* (Vol. 6, pp. 1–50). Greenwich, CT: JAI Press.

Yukl, G. A., & Taber, T. (1983). The effective use of managerial power. *Personnel, 60,* 37–44.

PART V

Alternative Views of Leadership

If you don't say anything, you won't be called on to repeat it.

Calvin "Silent Cal" Coolidge

The people are the most important element, the land and grain are the next, and the ruler is least important.

Meng-Tse

There is no monument dedicated to the memory of a committee.

Lester J. Pourciau

A position of authority is neither necessary nor sufficient for the exercise of leadership.

Eric Werkowitz

See everything, overlook much, correct little.

Pope John XXIII

In this section, we turn our attention to views of leadership that are very recent, as well as very nontraditional. The first selection, "Substitutes for Leadership," suggests how attributes of a work setting (e.g., characteristics of subordinates, the task, the reward system, and the larger organization) may undermine the potential impact of a supervisor. These substitutes and neutralizers of leadership can virtually negate a supervisor's ability to influence a subordinate's performance. In the following article, Charles Manz and Henry Sims, Jr., offer a view of management based on the notion of "SuperLeadership," wherein the leader of today teaches others to lead themselves. Clearly, these notions have much relevance to the contemporary interest in work teams and team leadership. In keeping with this section's theme of alternative views of leadership, the article by Jim Collins asks us to consider how some of the most powerfully transformative executives possess a paradoxical mix of humility and professional will. Jim Collins is also well-known as the author of *Good to Great: Why Some Companies Make the Leap . . . And Others Don't* and as the co-author of *Built to Last: Successful Habits of Visionary Companies.*

In the last four readings of this section, we carry the notion of the "un-leader" to the next level, that of the leader as enabler or the leader as a person who sacrifices for others. This perspective is best embodied in the writings of Robert Greenleaf, in his treatment of "Servant Leadership." A real-life example of a CEO who personified the notion of a servant-leader, John F. Donnelly, Sr., is detailed in a lecture given by one of his colleagues, Robert J. Doyle, of Delta Management Group. Mr. Donnelly demonstrates that one can simultaneously devote one's life to humanistic ideals and still operate an organization in a profitable manner. Next, we consider the life of an entrepreneur who, while initially seeking a profit, came to appreciate the humanity of his workers: Oskar Schindler. In "A Man of Transactions," Terrence Rafferty provides a review of *Schindler's List* that is insightful as to why leadership must be measured in terms that are beyond the simple financial bottom line. Finally, Robert Vecchio takes us in for a closer look at how research on the topics of entrepreneurship and leadership reveal a number of overlapping issues.

Substitutes for Leadership: Effective Alternatives to Ineffective Leadership

Jon P. Howell, David E. Bowen,
Peter W. Dorfman, Steven Kerr,
and Philip M. Podsakoff

Leadership has been recognized through the ages as a primary means of influencing the behavior of others. Research into the keys to effective and ineffective leadership has also been going on for quite some time. The earliest assumption was that effective leaders possessed particular traits that distinguished them from ineffective leaders. Effective leaders were thought to be dynamic, intelligent, dependable, high-achieving individuals—so, since traits are hard to change, problems caused by poor leadership were considered best solved by *replacing the leader* with someone who possessed more of the key traits. Regrettably, researchers were unable to identify leader traits that systematically improved organizational effectiveness. Yet leader replacement continues to be a very popular tool in the executive toolkit.

Partly in response to the limitations of trait theory, research in the late 1940s began to focus on relationships between leader behaviors and employee performance, in search of behaviors exhibited by effective leaders that were not displayed by those less effective. With this approach, effective leaders need not possess magical traits but, instead, provide strong direction and support while encouraging subordinates to participate in important decisions. This emphasis on leader behaviors still permitted replacement of a weak leader but allowed an additional remedy as well: namely, *changing the leader's behavior* through some form of training. Probably the most disappointing aspect of research on leader behaviors is that no strong, consistent relationships between particular leader behaviors and organizational effectiveness have ever been found. This has not prevented many off-the-shelf training programs from becoming popular, however, nor the marketers of such programs from becoming prosperous.

SITUATIONAL THEORIES

By the late 1950s it became evident that an approach was needed that didn't depend on ideal traits and universal behaviors. One answer was "situational theory," which starts with the assumption that there are no traits, and no behaviors, that automatically constitute effective leadership. The key is the fit between a leader's style and the situation the leader faces; thus the leader who is highly effective in one situation may be totally ineffective in another. For instance, although General George Patton led the 3rd Army to outstanding performance in World War II, one could hardly imagine the effective use of his leadership style in Mahatma Gandhi's situation against the British in India.

According to situational theories, effective leaders must correctly identify the behaviors each situation requires and then be flexible enough to exhibit these behaviors. Leaders who are behaviorally inflexible, or who lack the necessary diagnostic skills, must be either trained or replaced—the same remedies identified by researchers of leader traits and behaviors. An alternative is to let the leader alone but *change the situation so that the fit is improved.*

Various situational leadership theories have spawned a large number of intervention strategies, many of them competent and some of them useful. However, an assumption underlies all these theories that is wholly unsupported by the research literature. This assumption is that, though different situations require different leadership styles, in *every* situation there is *some* leadership style that will be effective. It has been shown in numerous studies, however, that circumstances often counteract the potential power of leadership, making it virtually impossible in some situations for leaders to have much impact regardless of their style or how good the fit is between leader and situation.

SUBSTITUTES FOR LEADERSHIP

Fortunately, additional remedies for problems stemming from weak leadership—remedies not articulated in any of the earlier trait, behavioral, or situational approaches—have been identified. Such remedies derive from acceptance of the conclusion, based on the research studies referenced earlier, that many organizations contain "substitutes for leadership"—attributes of subordinates, tasks, and organizations that provide task guidance and incentives to perform to such a degree that they virtually negate the leader's ability to either improve or impair subordinate performance. To the extent that powerful leadership substitutes exist, formal leadership, however displayed, tends to be unproductive and can even be counter-productive. In comparison with situational leadership approaches, research on leadership substitutes focuses on whether subordinates are receiving needed task guidance and incentives to perform without taking it for granted that the formal leader is the primary supplier.

Closely Knit Teams of Highly Trained Individuals

Consider the positive impact of substitutes in the following example. Todd LaPorte, Gene Rochlin, and Karlene Roberts are three researchers studying such highly stressful organizational situations as those involving pilots who land jet fighters on a nuclear carrier and air-traffic controllers who direct traffic into San Francisco. They have found that directive leadership is rela-tively unimportant compared with the work experience and training of individuals in closely knit work groups. This is particularly evident ". . . in the white heat of danger, when the whole system threatens to collapse. . . . The stress creates a need for competence among colleagues who by neces-sity develop close working relationships with each other." All such individ-uals are trained extensively and daily, regardless of their position in the hierarchy, to redirect operations or bring them to an abrupt halt. This can involve ignoring orders from managers who are removed from the front line of action. Here the experience and continuous training of individuals, along with the close relationships among members of a work group, substi-tute for the manager's directive leadership.

By creating alternate sources of task guidance and incentives to perform, substitutes for leadership may have a temporary negative effect on morale among leaders who perceive a loss of power. However, leadership substi-tutes can also serve as important remedies where there are organizational problems, particularly in situations where the leader is not the source of the problems or where, if the leader is the source, replacement, training, and improving the leader-situation fit are overly expensive, politically infeas-ible, or too time-consuming to be considered.

A principal advantage of the substitutes construct is that it identifies a remedy for problems stemming from weak leadership in addition to re-placement, training, or situational engineering. The remedy is to intention-ally, systematically *create substitutes for hierarchical leadership*. In fact, whereas weak, power-hungry leaders invariably regard substitutes as frustrating and necessarily dysfunctional (when they are aware of them at all), strong leaders understand and are comfortable with the idea that effective results can be achieved when task guidance and incentives to perform emanate from sources other than themselves. When other sources are deficient, the hierarchical superior is in a position to play a dominant role; when strong incentives and guidance derive from other sources, the hierarchical superior has less opportunity, but also less need, to exert his or her influence.

Intrinsic Satisfaction

The degree of intrinsic satisfaction that employees derive from their work task is a strong leadership substitute in a large manufacturer of camping equipment in the western United States. The company produces sleeping bags that range from top-of-the-line light-weight backpackers to low-cost models filled with floor sweepings from a mattress factory. Manufacturing personnel are required to rotate among all the lines, so no one group gains a territorial claim to a particular product. Management reports that for workers on the top-quality down-filled bags, supervisory direction has become relatively unnecessary, yet output and quality typically exceed management expectations. Workers report pride in working on this line and usually solve production problems themselves or with co-workers.

The production of bottom-line bags is very different. Quality problems are commonplace, workers cooperate less to overcome the problems, and workers seem to care little about meeting output or quality standards. The constant supervision required to address these problems raises indirect costs. Consultants observing the various production lines during a typical day report that supervisors slowly gravitate away from high-quality lines toward the lowest-quality lines. Thus the workers' intrinsic satisfaction from producing a high-quality product alleviates the need for most supervisory leadership.

Computer Technology

Edward E. Lawler III has noticed that companies with computer-integrated manufacturing and networked computer systems rely on computers to take over many of the supervisor's leadership functions. Feedback is provided by computerized productivity and quality data; directions for certain tasks are entered into the information system; even error detection and goal setting are incorporated in some interactive systems. When individual workers have access to operating data and to a network that allows them to ask employees at other locations to help solve problems, they become more independent of their managers and arrive at solutions among themselves. Spans of control greater than 100 are not unheard of in these organizations. Computerized information technology is therefore providing a substitute for certain types of managerial leadership.

Effective leadership, then, depends upon a leader's ability to supply subordinates with task guidance and incentives to perform to the extent that these are not provided by other sources. The inverse of this assertion is equally valid. Leadership substitutes can contribute to organizational effectiveness by supplying subordinates with task guidance and incentives to perform that are not being provided by the hierarchical superior. From this perspective it makes sense for a leader or someone above the leader to create substitutes when, for example, the leader must be frequently absent, has a large span of control, or is saddled with time-consuming nonmanagerial duties. Substitutes are also useful when a leader departs before a successor has been identified or there is a need to manage employees who are geographically dispersed or who, as in the following example, are culturally resistant to hierarchical supervision.

Extensive Professional Education

Professional employees may come to their firms with so much formal education that they can perform most work assignments without relying upon technical guidance from their hierarchical superior. Their education also often includes a strong socialization component, instilling in them a desire for autonomous, self-controlling behavior. The result may be that they neither need nor will readily accept a leader's direction. In such instances, professional education and socialization can serve as substitutes for formal leadership: A 1981 study by Jeffrey Ford found that extensive subordinate education acted as a substitute for directive and supportive leadership in a book publishing firm, a branch bank, and a midwestern university.

USING LEADERSHIP SUBSTITUTES TO SOLVE ORGANIZATIONAL PROBLEMS

The notion that professional education and socialization can substitute for traditional formal leadership identifies an important potential problem, but it can be turned to advantage if a leader is sensitive to the situation and builds collegial systems of task-related guidance and interpersonal support. This approach can be found in most well-run hospitals and universities, where deliberately designed substitutes for leadership abound.

Thus charges of medical malfeasance are often investigated by peer review teams, and university promotion and tenure decisions depend greatly on assessments by faculty colleagues who lack formal authority. Indeed, many a dean has learned that the same criticism that would be bitterly denied if it came from him or her is grudgingly accepted if the source is a peer-review committee. The trick is to develop norms and structures that consistently produce feedback when feedback is needed, rather than merely an occasional spontaneous outburst when circumstances become intolerable.

Team Approaches

Tracy Kidder's *The Soul of a New Machine* provides an excellent account of how a key manager at Data General utilized subordinates' professional norms and standards as a substitute for leadership to produce a faster computer than the competition's. The company at that time was competitive, highly political, and resource-poor, but the computer-design engineers were young, creative, well trained, and highly motivated. Recognizing the futility of relying on directive leadership and meager financial rewards, the leader obtained work space that encouraged considerable interaction among team members and discouraged interaction outside the team. He articulated key parameters and project deadlines, stayed out of members' personal disputes, obtained resources for the team, and buffered them from organization politics. Reflecting the attitude of team members, Kidder observes, "They were building the machine all by themselves, without any significant help from their leader."

Task guidance and incentives to perform may derive from a number of sources other than the leader, including organized staff groups, internal and external consultants, and competent peers at all organizational levels. In the Columbus, Ohio Police Department, the creation of two-person patrol units and field-training officer positions effectively substituted for the guidance and support traditionally provided by hierarchical leaders, thus making time available for them to attend to other tasks. Where one-person patrols without field-training officers were utilized, leader guidance and support continued to be essential. (An ancillary benefit of substituting peer for hierarchical sources of task guidance is that it is often easier for subordinates to admit inadequacies to and request assistance from their co-workers than from their boss.)

High-Ability Independent Workers

Even when subordinates haven't much formal education, ability combined with experience can serve as a substitute for hierarchical leadership. Cummins Engine Company, General Motors Corporation, and Procter and Gamble all have reduced supervisory personnel and managerial overhead by selecting and developing high-ability, independent workers who require little or no supervision. Paul Reeves, a key production foreman for Harmon Auto Parts, taught workers to take over his job by helping them increase their ability and experience so that their responsibilities could also be increased. Each worker voluntarily spent half-days with him—asking questions, discussing his responses and, eventually, helping him perform his duties. When Reeves was promoted, the group continued to operate effectively without a foreman.

In Place of Hierarchical Feedback

Among the most important elements of task guidance is performance feedback. In the absence of feedback, ability to perform cannot be improved and motivation to perform cannot be sustained. Most organizations assign responsibility for feedback to the hierarchical superior, even in cases where the superior works at a physical distance from employees or doesn't know enough about their technical specialties to give them credible feedback.

However, many organizations have come to the realization that feedback from clients and peers, and feedback provided by the task itself, can serve as powerful substitutes for hierarchical feedback. Charles Manz and Hank Sims, two organizational researchers, described the operation of one such feedback system in a nonunion small-parts manufacturing plant. A subsidiary of a large U.S. corporation, the plant was organized around the concept of self-managed work teams from its inception in the early 1970s.

Each team of eight to twelve members is assigned a set of closely related production tasks, and the teams are buffered from each other by physical space and stores of in-process inventory. Each team prepares its own budgets, makes within-team job assignments, keeps track of quality control statistics and hours worked, and handles member absenteeism and discipline problems. Team members are trained in conducting meetings and in group problem solving. A hierarchical leader is responsible for each team, but this person is not supposed to supply either task guidance or interpersonal support, aside from encouraging self-observation, self-evaluation, and self-reinforcement. Manz and Sims found, in fact, that the most effective teams were those whose leaders did refrain from providing guidance and support. Leaders of effective teams spent much of their time representing the team to higher management, obtaining resources for the team, training new members, and coaching team members with respect to peer feedback and peer evaluation.

Substitutes by Procedure

The detailed work rules, guidelines, policies, and procedures existing in many organizations also serve to some extent as substitutes for hierarchical leadership by providing important non-leader sources of task guidance. Researchers Jon Howell and Peter Dorfman found this to be the case in a medium-size hospital, as did Robert Miles and M. M. Petty in county-level social service agencies. This type of leadership substitute can be particularly useful in situations where consistent behavior is imperative. For example, units of a firm increase the firm's legal exposure by acting inconsistently with respect to hiring, firing, leaves of absence, promotions, or other human resources actions. In other instances, such as pricing or purchasing activities, variation may be legal but cost-ineffective. It is quite common in these cases for organizations to install procedures, rules, and guidelines to replace or forestall managerial discretion.

LEADERSHIP NEUTRALIZERS

Thus far we have discussed only leadership substitutes, whose effect is to make it both less possible and less necessary for leaders to influence subordinates' satisfaction and performance, replacing the leader's impact with impact of their own. Leadership "neutralizers" are attributes of subordinates, tasks, and organizations that also interfere with a leader's attempts to influence subordinates. Unlike leadership substitutes, however, neutralizers do not replace the leader's impact over subordinates, but rather create an "influence vacuum" that can have serious negative consequences.

Physical Distances

For example, when subordinates work at a physical distance from their leader, many recommended leadership practices have limited usefulness or are nearly impossible to perform. A case in point is found at Kinko's, which provides professional copying services at widely dispersed locations nationwide. Regional managers at Kinko's are continually frustrated by not being able to provide enough direction, guidance, and personal support for the new store managers because physical distances are too great for much personal interaction. In other organizations, subordinates and leaders may not share a common time zone; indeed, they may scarcely share the same work day.

Spatial distance will be increasingly important as a potential leadership neutralizer in the future because, as the number of firms with international operations continues to rise, managers will increasingly be required to supervise subordinates across great distances. Furthermore, the growing importance of the U.S. service sector means that more and more employees will be working at home or at their client's work site.

Reward Systems

Organizational reward systems can also be important neutralizers of the hierarchical leadership's effects. Rewards may be awarded strictly according to seniority, for example, or attractive rewards may be unavailable to subordinates. Leaders tend to have little influence on corporate "rebels" because, in part, the rebels are not attracted to the typical rewards available in corporate bureaucracies. Union contracts also may mandate that all employees within a given job classification be paid the same wage rate, and civil service policies may require that promotions be based on objective examinations. In other cases, rewards may be controlled by higher management in ways that prevent the immediate supervisor from exerting influence. This occurs, for example, in firms requiring numerous one-over-one approvals before a salary recommendation takes effect. Other firms permit leaders to influence the amount of rewards, but their timing is wholly constrained by fiscal periods or employee anniversary dates.

Bypassing Management Structure

A very different type of neutralization occurs when someone at a higher level repeatedly bypasses a level of management to deal directly with that manager's subordinates. Another neutralizer is the continual countermanding by higher management of a leader's orders and instructions. These neutralizers often occur in instances where an organization's founder has finally, reluctantly, hired a subordinate manager to oversee operations and where a union's potential for mischief is so feared that supervisory efforts aimed at maintaining discipline are routinely reversed at higher levels.

Although normally dysfunctional, leadership neutralizers can occasionally be used to advantage. One such occasion occurred in a petrochemical processing firm where, because of his technical expertise and involvement in several critical projects, an interpersonally incompetent director of design engineering could not be replaced. As an interim solution until he could be phased out, his day-to-day contact with employees was sharply curtailed, he was given numerous technical (nonleader) assignments, and his influence over salary and personnel decisions was considerably reduced. In this instance the "influence vacuum" caused by creating leadership neutralizers was deemed preferable to the state of leadership that previously existed.

LEADERSHIP ENHANCERS

Leader "enhancers" are attributes of employees, tasks, and organizations that amplify a leader's impact on the employees. For example, cohesive work groups with strong norms in support of cooperation with management can crystallize ambiguous goals and role definitions, augment overly subtle leader-provided feedback, and otherwise increase the power of weak, inconsistent leaders—for better or for worse. A study of four large hospitals found that development of a culture with strong performance norms greatly enhanced the impact of the head nurse's directive leadership style.

The creation of leadership enhancers makes particular sense when a leader has both the skill to manage effectively and personal goals consonant with organizational objectives but is prevented by one or more neutralizers from being effective. One way to amplify such a leader's power is to alter the organization's reward system. For example, make additional resources available, grant more discretion concerning the distribution of existing resources, or increase subordinates' dependency on the leader for desired physical and financial resources. Another type of enhancement is to give the leader access to key information and prestigious people at high levels—for example, as a member of a visible, prestigious task force. Enhancement in this case derives from connecting the leader to sources of power and important information, as well as from signaling to others that the leader probably has considerable influence with those at the top.

STRATEGIES FOR IMPROVING
LEADERSHIP EFFECTIVENESS

Exhibit 1 outlines some typical leadership problems and effective coping strategies using leadership substitutes, neutralizers, and enhancers. Exhibit 2 provides specific information about how to implement these alternative leadership strategies.

Exhibit 1
Eleven Managerial Leadership Problems and Effective Coping Strategies*

Leadership Problems	Enhancer/Neutralizer	Substitutes
Leader doesn't keep on top of details in the department; coordination among subordinates is difficult.	Not useful.	Develop self-managed work teams; encourage team members to interact within and across departments.
Competent leadership is resisted through non-compliance or passive resistance.	*Enhancers:* Increase employees' dependence on leader through greater leader control of rewards/resources; increase their perception of leader's influence outside of work group.	Develop collegial systems of guidance for decision making.
Leader doesn't provide support or recognition for jobs well done.	Not useful	Develop a reward system that operates independently of the leader. Enrich jobs to make them inherently satisfying.
Leader doesn't set targets or goals, or clarify roles for employees.	Not useful	Emphasize experience and ability in selecting subordinates. Establish group goal-setting. Develop an organizational culture that stresses high performance expectations.

Exhibit 1 *Continued*

Leadership Problems	Enhancer/Neutralizer	Substitutes
A leader behaves inconsistently over time.	*Enhancers:* These are dysfunctional. *Neutralizer:* Remove rewards from leader's control.	Develop group goal-setting and group rewards.
An upper-level manager regularly bypasses a leader in dealing with employees, or countermands the leader's directions.	*Enhancers:* Increase leader's control over rewards and resources; build leader's image via in-house champion or visible "important" responsibilities. *Neutralizer:* Physically distance subordinates from upper-level manager.	Increase the professionalization of employees.
A unit is in disarray or out of control.	Not useful.	Develop highly formalized plans, goals, routines, and areas of responsibility.
Leadership is brutal, autocratic.	*Enhancers:* These are dysfunctional. *Neutralizer:* Physically distance subordinates; remove rewards from leader's control.	Establish group goal-setting and peer performance appraisal.
There is inconsistency across different organizational units.	Not useful.	Increase formalization. Set up a behaviorally focused reward system.
Leadership is unstable over time; leaders are rotated and/or leave office frequently.	Not useful.	Establish competent advisory staff units. Increase professionalism of employees.
Incumbent management is poor; there's no heir apparent.	*Enhancers:* These are dysfunctional. *Neutralizer:* Assign nonleader duties to problem managers.	Emphasize experience and ability in selecting employees. Give employees more training.

* The suggested solutions are examples of many possibilities for each problem.

Exhibit 2
Creative Strategies for Improving Leadership Effectiveness

Creating Substitutes for Leader Directiveness and Supportiveness	Creating Enhancers for Leader Directiveness and Supportiveness
Develop collegial systems of guidance: • Peer appraisals to increase acceptability of feedback by subordinates. • Quality circles to increase workers' control over production quality. • Peer support networks; mentor systems.	Increase subordinates' perceptions of leader's influence/expertise: • Provide a visible champion of leader. • Give leader important organizational responsibilities. • Build leader's image through in-house publications and other means.
Improve performance-oriented organizational formalization: • Automatic organization reward system (such as commissions or gainsharing). • Group management-by-objectives (MBO) program. • Company mission statements and codes of conduct (as at Johnson & Johnson).	Build organizational climate: • Reward small wins to increase subordinates' confidence. • Emphasize ceremony and myth to encourage team spirit. • Develop superordinate goals to encourage cohesiveness and high performance norms.
Increase administrative staff availability: • Specialized training personnel. • Troubleshooters for human relations problems. • Technical advisors to assist production operators.	Increase subordinates' dependence on leader: • Create crises requiring immediate action. • Increase leader centrality in providing information. • Eliminate one-over-one approvals.
Increase professionalism of subordinates: • Staffing based on employee professionalism. • Development plans to increase employees' abilities and experience. • Encourage active participation in professional associations.	Increase leader's position power: • Change title to increase status. • Increase reward power. • Increase resource base.

Exhibit 2   *Continued*

Creating Substitutes for Leader Directiveness and Supportiveness	Creating Enhancers for Leader Directiveness and Supportiveness
Redesign jobs to increase: • Performance feedback from the task. • Ideological importance of jobs.	Create cohesive work groups with high performance norms: • Provide physical setting conducive to teamwork. • Encourage subordinates' participation in group problem solving. • Increase group's status. • Create intergroup competition.
Start team-building activities to develop group self-management skills such as: • Solving work-related problems on their own. • Resolving interpersonal conflicts among members. • Providing interpersonal support to members.	

SuperLeadership: Beyond the Myth of Heroic Leadership

Charles C. Manz and Henry P. Sims, Jr.

When most of us think of leadership, we think of one person doing something to another person. This is "influence," and a leader is someone who has the capacity to influence another. Words like "charismatic" and "heroic" are sometimes used to describe a leader. The word "leader" itself conjures up visions of a striking figure on a rearing white horse who is crying "Follow me!" The leader is the one who has either the power or the authority to command others.

Many historical figures fit this mold: Alexander, Caesar, Napoleon, Washington, Churchill. Even today, the turnaround of Chrysler Corporation by Lee Iacocca might be thought of as an act of contemporary heroic leadership. It's not difficult to think of Iacocca astride a white horse, and he is frequently thought of as "charismatic."

But is this heroic figure of the leader the most appropriate image of the organizational leader of today? Is there another model? We believe there is. In many modern situations, *the most appropriate leader is one who can lead others to lead themselves.* We call this powerful new kind of leadership "SuperLeadership."

Our viewpoint represents a departure from the dominant and, we think, incomplete view of leadership. Our position is that true leadership comes mainly from within a person, not from outside. At its best, external leadership provides a spark and supports the flame of the true inner leadership that dwells within each person. At its worst, it disrupts this internal process, causing damage to the person and the constituencies he or she serves.

Our focus is on a new form of leadership that is designed to facilitate the self-leadership energy within each person. This perspective suggests a new measure of a leader's strength—one's ability to maximize the contributions of others through recognition of their right to guide their own destiny, rather than the leader's ability to bend the will of others to his or her own. The challenge for organizations is to understand how to go about bringing out the wealth of talent that each employee possesses. Many still operate under a quasi-military model that encourages conformity and adherence rather than one that emphasizes how leaders can lead others to lead themselves.

WHY IS SUPERLEADERSHIP
AN IMPORTANT PERSPECTIVE?

This SuperLeadership perspective is especially important today because of several recent trends facing American businesses. First, the challenge to United States corporations from world competition has pressured companies to utilize more fully their human resources. Second, the workforce itself has changed a great deal in recent decades—for instance, "baby boomers" have carried into their organization roles elevated expectations and a need for greater meaning in their work lives.

As a consequence of these kinds of pressures, organizations have increasingly experimented with innovative work designs. Widespread introduction of modern management techniques, such as quality circles, self-managed work teams, Japanese business practices, and flatter organization structures, has led to the inherent dilemma of trying to provide strong leadership for workers who are being encouraged and allowed to become increasingly self-managed. The result is a major knowledge gap about appropriate new leadership approaches under conditions of increasing employee participation. The SuperLeadership approach is designed to meet these kinds of challenges.

Before presenting specific steps for becoming a SuperLeader, it is useful to contrast SuperLeadership with other views of leadership.

Viewpoints on what constitutes successful leadership in organizations have changed significantly over time. A simplified historical perspective on different approaches to leadership is presented in Figure 1. As it suggests, four different types of leader can be distinguished: the "strong man," the "transactor," the "visionary hero," and the "SuperLeader."

The *strong-man view* of leadership is perhaps the earliest dominant form in our culture. The emphasis with this autocratic view is on the strength of the leader. We use the masculine noun purposely because when this leadership approach was most prevalent it was almost a completely male-dominated process.

The strong-man view of leadership still exists today in many organizations (and is still widely reserved for males), although it is not as highly regarded as it once was.

Figure 1
Four Types of Leaders

	Strong Man	Transactor	Visionary Hero	SuperLeader
Focus	Commands	Rewards	Visions	Self-leadership
Type of power	Position/authority	Rewards	Relational/inspirational	Shared
Source of leader's wisdom and direction	Leader	Leader	Leader	Most followers (self-leaders) and then leaders
Followers' response	Fear-based compliance	Calculative compliance	Emotional commitment based on leader's vision	Commitment based on ownership
Typical leader behaviors	Direction/command	Interactive goal setting	Communication of leader's vision	Becoming an effective self-leader
	Assigned goals	Contingent personal reward	Emphasis on leader's values	Modeling self-leadership
	Intimidation	Contingent material reward	Exhortation	Creating positive thought patterns
	Reprimand	Contingent reprimand	Inspirational persuasion	Developing self-leadership through reward & constructive reprimand
				Promoting self-leading teams
				Facilitating a self-leadership culture

The strong-man view of leadership creates an image of a John Wayne type who is not afraid to "knock some heads" to get followers to do what he wants done. The expertise for knowing what should be done rests almost entirely in the leader. It is he who sizes up the situation and, based on some seemingly superior strength, skill, and courage, delivers firm commands to the workers. If the job is not performed as commanded, inevitably some significant form of punishment will be delivered by the leader to the guilty party. The focus is on the leader whose power stems primarily from his position in the organization. He is the primary source of wisdom and direction—strong direction. Subordinates simply comply.

One would think that the day of the strong-man leader has passed, but one apparently managed to work his way up the corporate hierarchy at Kellogg Co. This venerable Battle Creek cereal maker recently terminated its president in an unusual action. Accounts printed in the *Wall Street Journal* described this person as "abrasive and often unwilling to listen . . . , very abrupt . . . , more inclined to manage without being questioned." He was known for deriding unimpressive presentations as a "CE"—career ending—performance. As another example, we suspect that the majority of employees at Eastern Airlines would describe CEO Frank Lorenzo as a prototypical strong man.

The second view of leadership is that of a *transactor*.

As time passed in our culture, the dominance of the strong-man view of leadership lessened somewhat. Women began to find themselves more frequently in leadership positions. With the development of knowledge of the power of rewards (such as that coming from research on behavior modification), a different view of influence began to emerge. With this view, the emphasis was increasingly placed on a rational exchange approach (exchange of rewards for work performed) in order to get workers to do their work. Even Taylor's views on scientific management, which still influence significantly many organizations in many industries, emphasized the importance of providing incentives to get workers to do work.

With the transactor type of leader, the focus is on goals and rewards; the leader's power stems from the ability to provide rewards for followers doing what the leader thinks should be done. The source of wisdom and direction still rests with the leader. Subordinates will tend to take a calculative view of their work. "I will do what he (or she) asks as long as the rewards keep coming."

Perhaps one of the most prototypical (and successful) transactor organizations in the world today is PEPSICO. *Fortune* described the company with phrases like ". . . boot camp, . . . sixty-hour weeks . . . , back breaking standards that are methodically raised." Those who can't compete are washed out. Those who do compete successfully are rewarded very handsomely—first-class air travel, fully loaded company cars, stock options, bonuses that can hit 90% of salary. Those who are comfortable and effective in this culture receive the spoils. Those who are not comfortable tend to leave early in their career.

Perhaps the ultimate transactor leader is Chairman Larry Phillips of Phillips-Van Heusen, manufacturer of shirts, sweaters, and casual shoes. Phillips has set up a scheme whereby the 11 senior executives will each earn a $1 million bonus if the company's earnings per share grow at a 35% compound annual rate during the four years ending in January 1992. Not surprisingly, company executives are actively absorbed in striving to meet this goal.

The next type of leader, which probably represents the most popular view today, is that of the *visionary hero*. Here the focus is on the leader's ability to create highly motivating and absorbing visions. The leader represents a kind of heroic figure who is somehow able to create an almost larger-than-life vision for the workforce to follow. The promise is that if organizations can just find those leaders that are able to capture what's important in the world and wrap it up into some kind of purposeful vision, then the rest of the workforce will have the clarifying beacon that will light the way to the promised land.

With the visionary hero, the focus is on the leader's vision, and the leader's power is based on followers' desire to relate to the vision and to the leader himself or herself. Once again, the leader represents the source of wisdom and direction. Followers, at least in theory, are expected to commit to the vision and the leader.

The notion of the visionary hero seems to have received considerable attention lately, but the idea has not gone without criticism. Peter Drucker, for example, believes that charisma becomes the undoing of leaders. He believes they become inflexible, convinced of their own infallibility, and slow to really change. Instead, Drucker suggests that the most effective leaders are those not afraid of developing strength in their subordinates and associates. One wonders how Chrysler will fare when Iacocca is gone.

The final view of leadership included in our figure represents the focus of this article—the *SuperLeader*. We do not use the word "Super" to create an image of a larger-than-life figure who has all the answers and is able to bend others' wills to his or her own. On the contrary, with this type of leader, the focus is largely on the followers. Leaders become "super"— that is, can possess the strength and wisdom of many persons—by helping to unleash the abilities of the "followers" (self-leaders) that surround them.

The focus of this leadership view is on the followers who become self-leaders. Power is more evenly shared by leaders and followers. The leader's task becomes largely that of helping followers to develop the necessary skills for work, especially self-leadership, to be able to contribute more fully to the organization. Thus, leaders and subordinates (that are becoming strong self-leaders) together represent the source of wisdom and direction. Followers (self-leaders), in turn, experience commitment and ownership of their work.

SEVEN STEPS TO SUPERLEADERSHIP

For the SuperLeader, the essence of the challenge is to lead followers to discover the potentialities that lie within themselves. How can a SuperLeader lead others to become positive, effective self-leaders? How can a Super-Leader lead others to lead themselves?

We will present seven steps to accomplish these ends. As we will see, some of the elements included in the other leadership views summarized above are a part of SuperLeadership (for instance, the use of rewards), but as Figure 1 indicates, the focus of the leadership process and the basis of power and the relationship of the SuperLeader with followers are very different.

Step 1—Becoming a Self-Leader

Before learning how to lead others, it is important—make that essential— to first learn how to lead ourselves. Consequently, the first step to becoming a SuperLeader is to become an effective self-leader.

In a taped interview from the historical files of Hewlett-Packard, David Packard, co-founder of Hewlett-Packard, described how, as a young man, he used a daily schedule as a strategy to organize his own efforts. "I was resolved that I was going to have everything organized so, when I was a freshman, I had a schedule set for every day . . . what I was going to do every hour of the day . . . and times set up in the morning to study certain things. . . . You did have to allocate your time. . . ." At a very young age, David Packard was developing the self-leadership skills that became so critical to his later success as an executive.

Self-leadership is the influence we exert on ourselves to achieve the self-motivation and self-direction we need to perform. The process of self-leadership consists of an array of behavioral and cognitive strategies for enhancing our own personal effectiveness.

Self-leadership is also the essence of effective followership. As one Ford Motor Co. executive exclaimed to us, "We started participative management, but we didn't know what that meant for the subordinate!" What are the responsibilities of the follower? How does he or she behave in a participative management situation? Developing self-leadership skills is the answer to this question. From a SuperLeadership perspective, effective followers are leaders in their own right—they are skilled at leading themselves.

We will address two classes of self-leadership strategies. The first focuses mainly on effective behavior and action—"behavioral focused strategies;" the second focuses on effective thinking and feeling—"cognitive focused strategies." A summary of these strategies is provided in Figure 2.

Behavioral Focused Strategies

These self-leadership actions are designed to help individuals organize and direct their own work lives more effectively. Specifically, these strategies include self-observation, self-goal setting, cue management, self-reward, constructive self-punishment or self-criticism, and rehearsal.

The necessity for self-observation, for example, was dramatically brought forward at Harley Davidson, when the American motorcycle manufacturer instituted a Just-in-Time/employee involvement program. Management had to train workers to use statistical tools to monitor and control the quality of their own work—an effective prerequisite for helping employees to design and conduct their own self-observation system. The Harley story is a resounding success. This is one American company that has been extraordinarily successful in dealing with the Japanese incursion into their markets.

Each of these strategies, with the exception of self-criticism, when practiced consistently and effectively, has been found to be significantly related to higher performance. While self-criticism can at times serve a useful purpose, it tends to have a demoralizing and destructive impact when overused. Nevertheless, constructive self-criticism can sometimes send a signal to others that we are ready to accept responsibility for our own actions—

Figure 2
Self-Leadership Strategies

Behavior-Focused Strategies

Self-observation—observing and gathering information about specific behaviors
that you have targeted for change

Self-Set Goals—setting goals for your own work efforts

Management of Cues—arranging and altering cues in the work environment to
facilitate your desired personal behaviors

Rehearsal—physical or mental practice of work activities before you actually
perform them

Self-Reward—providing yourself with personally valued rewards for completing
desirable behaviors

Self-Punishment/Criticism—administering punishments to yourself for behaving in
undesirable ways

Cognitive-Focused Strategies

Building Natural Rewards into Tasks—self-redesign of where and how you do your
work to increase the level of natural rewards in your job. Natural rewards that are
part of, rather than separate from, the work (i.e., the work, like a hobby, becomes
the reward) result from activities that cause you to feel:

    a sense of competence

    a sense of self-control

    a sense of purpose

Focusing Thinking on Natural Rewards—purposely focusing your thinking on the
naturally rewarding features of your work

Establishment of Effective Thought Patterns—establishing constructive and effective
habits or patterns in your thinking (e.g., a tendency to search for opportunities
rather than obstacles embedded in challenges) by managing your:

    beliefs and assumptions

    mental imagery

    internal self-talk

---

and that we are sometimes human and make a mistake. Recently, basketball
coach John Thompson of Georgetown University was ejected from a game
when he protested too vigorously to game officials. Later he commented,
"It was probably my fault more than the officials' fault. I have respect for all
three of those men. I probably let my competitive juices overflow. . . . I
made a mistake." Thompson's willingness to recognize some of his own
flaws is one reason he is so widely respected.

Cognitive-Focused Strategies

In addition to behaviorally focused strategies, we can help ourselves to become more effective through the application of self-leadership strategies that promote effective thinking.

First, effective self-leaders can both physically and mentally redesign their own tasks to make them more naturally rewarding; that is, they can create ways to do tasks so that significant natural reward value is obtained from the enjoyment of doing the job itself. Natural rewards are derived from performing tasks in a way that allows us to experience (1) a sense of competence, (2) a sense of self-control, and (3) a sense of purpose. An example of this notion is embodied in the reply of a young girl featured in a recent news story who was asked why she had made a rock collection, and why she had tried to understand all about rocks. She replied, "Because it makes me feel good in my mind."

Other cognitive strategies help us by establishing constructive and effective habits or patterns of thinking—such as "opportunity thinking" as opposed to "obstacle thinking." For example, by studying and managing our beliefs and assumptions, we can begin to develop the ability to find opportunities in each new work challenge. Until managers began to believe that employees could be important participating partners in the success of American industry, much opportunity for progress was being wasted.

In summary, it's important to remember that if we want to lead others to be self-leaders, we must first practice self-leadership ourselves. If you want to lead somebody, the first critical step is to lead yourself.

Step 2—Modeling Self-Leadership

Once we have mastered self-leadership ourselves, the next step is to demonstrate these skills to subordinate employees; that is, our own self-leadership behaviors serve as a model from which others can learn. As Max DePree, chairman of Herman Miller, the office furniture maker, says, "It's not what you preach, but how you behave."

Modeling can be used to develop subordinate self-leadership on a day-to-day basis in two ways. The first use is to establish new behaviors—specifically self-leadership behaviors. The main point is that an employee can learn an entirely new behavior, especially self-leadership, without actually performing it. Executives that are self-starters and well-organized are likely to have subordinates who, in turn, are self-starters and well-organized. Executives, in particular, have a special responsibility to serve as the kind of self-leadership example that they wish subordinate employees to emulate.

The second use involves strengthening the probability of previously learned self-leadership behaviors. Self-leadership behaviors can be enhanced through observation of positive rewards received by others for desired behaviors. We observed, for example, an older woman react with delight when presented with a special achievement award for developing a new inspection procedure at Tandem Computer. She had developed this procedure using her own initiative—she had acted as a self-leader.

This incident served as a symbolic model for other employees at Tandem. Management made it clear that initiating the development of innovative cuing strategies (the inspection procedure) is desirable and that these types of actions are encouraged and rewarded. The hope and intention are that other employees will perceive innovative behavior to be desirable and potentially rewarding. Over time, the objective is to encourage and stimulate widespread incidents of innovative self-leadership.

The lesson from the Tandem incident is straightforward. Employees learn from and are motivated when they see rewards given to others for the performance of self-leadership behaviors. Public recognition to enhance a self-leadership model can be a powerful motivating force for others to initiate self-leadership actions.

Many learn the art of self-leadership from senior executives whom they admire and respect. The book *Eisenhower: Portrait of a Hero* by Peter Lyon (Little Brown, 1974) suggests that General Dwight Eisenhower formulated his own self-leadership style under the guidance of General George Marshall. "What General Marshall wanted most . . . were senior officers who would take the responsibility for action in their own areas of competence without coming to him for the final decision; officers who in their turn would have enough sense to delegate the details of their decisions to their subordinates." Learning to lead from those above him, Ike later carried this sense of delegation and control into his own military leadership style.

Sometimes a model of self-leadership can be inspiring. Who can forget the image of Jimmy Carter as he humbly went about building low-cost housing with his own hammer and nails. The sight of a former U.S. President actually engaging in a relatively minor self-leadership behavior had more influence than anything he could have said. Carter seems to be garnering more admiration as a former President than he acquired as a President.

Step 3—Encouraging Self-Set Goals

Goal setting, in general, has been one of the most actively investigated aspects of employee behavior and performance. Several general principles have been derived from this extensive research.

First, virtually any kind of goal setting seems to be better than none at all. The mere existence of a goal serves to focus employee attention and energy. This is one of the most pervasive findings of all organizational psychological research. Further, specific goals seem to be better than ambiguous or "fuzzy" ones. Also, in general, more difficult goals result in higher performance—provided the goals are accepted by the employee.

Last but not least, many believe that participation in setting goals will also enhance performance. The logic is that if an employee sees the goal as his or her own, the employee is more likely to give the effort required to attain the goal. Of course, the idea of participation is very closely connected with the essence of SuperLeadership.

Since the main aim of the SuperLeader is to improve the performance of subordinates through the development of their own self-leadership capabilities, employee self-goal setting is a key element. An important point to note is that goal setting is a *learned behavior;* that is, it is a skill or sequence of actions that an employee can develop over a period of time, not an innate behavior that every new employee brings to the job. Since self-goal setting is something to be learned, the role of the SuperLeader is to serve as a model, coach, and teacher. The SuperLeader helps employees learn to effectively set specific challenging goals for themselves.

Among the more interesting and extreme examples of institutionalized self-set goals is the "Research Fellows" program at IBM. These high-status, high-performing scientists make their own decisions about how substantial resources will be allocated. Obviously, IBM believes its investment in the self-leadership capabilities of these eminent scientists will pay off in the long run. Other organizations would do well to learn from their example.

These ideas also have currency at the level of the shop floor. In a recent *Business Week* article (August 21, 1989), Alvin K. Allison, leader of a team of mechanics at Monsanto's Greenwood, South Carolina plant, says, "I knew 20 years ago that I could direct my own job, but nobody wanted to hear what I had to say." Today, Allison is a part of the upside-down revolution that seems to be driving dramatic improvements in quality and productivity at the Greenwood plant.

Step 4—Create Positive Thought Patterns

Constructive thought patterns are an important element in successful self-leadership. Part of the SuperLeader role is to transmit positive thought patterns to subordinates. Especially important is the process of facilitating positive self-expectation in subordinates.

Sometimes, but especially in the early stages of a new job, employees do not have adequate natural habits of constructive thinking about themselves. They have doubts and fears—a general lack of confidence in themselves. At this stage, the actions of the SuperLeader are critical: His or her positive comments must serve as a temporary surrogate for the employee's own constructive thought patterns. As indicated in a recent *Fortune* article (March 26, 1990), Jack Welch, CEO of General Electric, thinks this issue is critical: "We need to drive self-confidence deep into the organization. . . . We have to undo a 100-year-old concept and convince our managers that their role is not to control people and stay 'on top' of things but rather to guide, energize, and excite."

The notion of constructing positive thought patterns may also be particularly critical when things are not going well. In the book *Joe Paterno: Football My Way* by Hyman & White (Collier, 1971), the very successful football coach emphasized that enhancing self-esteem is an important part of the equation: "When the staff is down . . . when the squad is down . . . when they are starting to doubt themselves . . . then it's gotta be a positive approach. The minute I have the feeling they have doubts concerning . . . [their] ability to do it . . . then I immediately want to jump in there and . . . talk about how good the kids are and what a great job they've done." He emphasizes confidence and pride: "A coach must be able to develop three things [in a team member] . . . pride, poise, and confidence in himself."

The SuperLeader creates productive thought patterns by carefully expressing confidence in the employee's ability to extend his or her present level of competence. Support and encouragement are necessary. In many ways, this expression of confidence is the essence of the "guided-participation" phase in which SuperLeaders teach each employee to lead himself or herself.

This SuperLeadership behavior is well founded in the results of research on the self-fulfilling prophecy: If a person believes something can be done, that belief makes it more likely that it *will* be done. Perhaps the SuperLeader plays "Professor Higgins" to an employee's "Eliza." Most of all, through expressions of confidence, the SuperLeader helps to create productive patterns of thinking—new constructive thought habits.

Step 5—Develop Self-Leadership Through Reward and Constructive Reprimand

One of the SuperLeader's most potent strategies in developing employee self-leadership is reward and reinforcement. For the most part, conventional viewpoints about using organizational rewards tend to focus on so-called extrinsic rewards as a means of reinforcing performance. One example is incentive pay systems.

We are basically in sympathy with this behavioral-management viewpoint and generally believe that material rewards should be used to reinforce desirable job-related behaviors. However, rewards take on a new perspective when seen through the eyes of the SuperLeader. If the purpose of the SuperLeader is to lead others to self-leadership, then an essential ingredient is to teach employees how to reward themselves and to build natural rewards into their own work. The SuperLeader attempts to construct a reward system that emphasizes self-administered and natural rewards and, in a comparative sense, de-emphasizes externally administered rewards. Thus the focus shifts from material types of rewards to a stronger emphasis on natural rewards that stem more from the task itself and on self-administration of rewards.

This usually means that people need to have the freedom to do their jobs in the ways they most value and can thrive in; that is, in the ways that they find most naturally rewarding. In the book *Our Story So Far* (3M Co., 1977), William McKnight, former CEO of 3M Company during perhaps 3M's most critical years in becoming an organizational success story, was quoted on the need for employees to do their jobs the way they want to do them. He stated, "Those men and women to whom we delegate authority and responsibility, if they are good people, are going to want to do their jobs in their own way. These are characteristics we want and should be encouraging."

In addition, a new type of reprimand is appropriate to develop employee self-leadership. We know that reprimand, in the short term, can keep somebody's nose to the grindstone, but the effectiveness of this mode of behavior is limited. Author Ken Blanchard was quoted in the *Minneapolis Star and Tribune* (May 27, 1987) as saying, "Most managers can get things done when they are around to nag and push. However, the real test of leadership is when management isn't present . . . which is about 70 percent of the time."

From a behavioral viewpoint, reprimand *should* be easy to understand. When an employee does something wrong, the manager provides a contingent aversive consequence, and the undesirable employee behavior *should* be reduced or eliminated. However, the long-term efficacy of reprimand is much more complex and leaves much to be desired. Most of all, a complex and sometimes confusing set of emotions typically accompanies reprimand, sometimes even leading to aggressive and disruptive behavior.

Reprimand is usually the opposite of what needs to be done to develop productive thought patterns in others. One objective of the SuperLeader is to encourage constructive self-confidence as an important part of the transition to self-leadership, but reprimand induces guilt and depression and diminishes self-confidence. On the other hand, if a SuperLeader treats a mistake as a learning opportunity, then employee self-esteem can be enhanced. After all, one sign of self-confidence is an individual objectively realizing that he has "made every mistake in the book" and has the experience and confidence to handle surprising situations.

We do recognize that reprimand is sometimes a necessary element in a SuperLeader's repertoire of behaviors, especially with careless or chronic underperformers. The most important lesson to remember is that the careless use of reprimand can be very discouraging to employees who are in their transition to self-leadership. The main focus should be to treat a mistake as a learning opportunity, to provide positive acceptance of the *person* despite the mistake, and to remember how the opportunity to make mistakes was a critical element in the SuperLeader's own development. Following these tips will result in a *constructive* feedback process that is more effective than the traditional use of reprimand and that positively influences employee self-leadership and long-term effectiveness.

Step 6—Promote Self-Leadership Through Teamwork

One of the more interesting examples of self-leadership systems is the team-oriented system of Volvo. Volvo has considerable experience with team assembly concepts, which were pioneered at its Kalmar plant. Further, the automobile assembly approach has been completely scrapped in the design of the new $315 million plant at Uddevalla. The key organizational philosophy at this plant is the work team, and the technical system has been designed to match the team concept. As Peter Gyllenhammar, Volvo's CEO, says, "I want the people in a team to be able to go home at night and really say, 'I built that car.'"

In the U.S., the self-managing team concept has had a slow but steady start. More recent media interest seems to indicate that the team idea is about to take off. The dramatic success of the team approach at the GM-

Toyota joint venture in Fremont, California has been instructive to the U.S. automotive industry in general. In our own research, we have documented the leader characteristics that are necessary to make a team effort successful, the core of which are the basic principles of SuperLeadership.

Top-management teams are also important, as represented by this quote that appeared in *Fortune* (August, 1987) from Tom Watson, Jr., former CEO of IBM: "My most important contribution to IBM was my ability to pick strong and intelligent men and then hold the team together. . . ."

One of the more interesting indicators of a self-leadership culture is the presence of quite a few teams. The types of teams (not all work groups are called teams) include product teams, top-executive teams, ad hoc teams, and shop-floor self-managing teams. Of course, teams require a good deal of self-leadership at the group level to function correctly.

Teamwork is important at Hewlett-Packard when it comes to the precision timing and integration required for successful new product release. At H-P, a committee called "board of directors" serves to drive the process to completion. Representatives from every department involved in the project serve on these committees.

Step 7—Facilitate a Self-Leadership Culture

A major factor in developing SuperLeadership is the challenge of designing an integrated organizational culture that is conducive to high performance. Organizations will find it difficult to obtain initiative and innovation from employees without providing a pervasive environment that facilitates those elements of self-leadership.

For the most part, we focus on the one-on-one relationship between a SuperLeader and an employee: How can an executive lead that employee to lead himself or herself? For an organization, however, the best results derive from a total integrated system that is deliberately intended to encourage, support, and reinforce self-leadership *throughout* the system. Most of all, this is an issue that addresses the question of how top executives can create self-leadership cultures.

One company that has shown demonstrable results of an effort to develop a self-leadership culture is Xerox Corporation, recent winner of the Malcolm Baldrige National Quality Award. The award recognizes companies that attain preeminent leadership in quality control. At Xerox, the quality effort includes plant-level employee "family groups" that work with little direct supervision. But most of all, the award recognizes the effort of

Xerox to build a total quality culture based on bottom-up employee involvement.

At another company, Dana Corporation, highly visible symbolic acts
were instrumental in turning the organizational culture around. One of
Rene McPherson's first concerns was to indicate the importance of giving
discretion to make decisions down through the ranks. The most famous
story is about one of his first actions: eliminating the procedures manual.
According to one account, the procedures manual had risen to a height of
22.5 inches. McPherson was said to have dumped it in a wastebasket and
replaced it with a one-page policy statement.

Rene McPherson used the following metaphor to describe his philosophy of a decentralized self-leadership culture at Dana as reported in an article in *Management Review* entitled "Hell Week—Or How Dana Makes its
Managers Money Conscious" (1984). "You can control a business in one of
two ways: You can institute a kind of martial law, with troops stationed in
each hamlet or village standing guard; or you can sit back and let each village be self-governing. . . . What we are after is to help that person [the division manager] to be [his own] . . . manager." McPherson said of his division
managers, "We didn't tell the guys what they were gonna do—they came in
and told us!"

Through his radical change in culture, McPherson has left a meaningful
legacy for Dana Corporation. He transformed a top-heavy, bureaucratic,
sluggish organization into one of the most successful and competitive
manufacturing businesses in the United States today. Self-leadership was a
key ingredient: Rene McPherson demonstrated a special capacity to lead
others to lead themselves.

SuperLeadership at the top requires the creation of positive organizational cultures within which self-leadership can flourish. Such environments consist of a host of factors, some observable and concrete, others
more subtle and symbolic. Culture becomes particularly important when it
comes to balancing the needs of individualism with the need for organized,
coordinated effort. As Peter Drucker put it in the July 3, 1989 issue of *Fortune* ". . . it is important to build up the oboist as an oboist, but it is even
more important to build up the oboist's pride in the performance of the orchestra . . . it puts a tremendous premium on having very clear goals and a
very clear and demanding mission for the enterprise." Overreaching organizational values that support self-leadership are perhaps the most important factor.

Ford Motor Company, for example, has developed a set of guidelines
that is widely circulated throughout the corporation and known as its

"Mission, Values and Guiding Principles." Among other things, they identify employee involvement and teamwork as Ford's "core human values."

In addition, training and development efforts that equip employees with both task-performance and self-leadership capabilities are important means of stimulating cultures based on leading others to lead themselves. Thus the SuperLeader's challenge is not limited to direct one-on-one leadership; the SuperLeader must also foster an integrated world in which self-leadership can survive and grow; in which self-leadership becomes an exciting, motivating, and accepted way of life. At lower levels, the challenge for aspiring SuperLeaders is to develop subcultures within their own control that stimulate the unique self-leadership strengths of subordinates.

Level 5 Leadership: The Triumph of Humility and Fierce Resolve

Jim Collins

In 1971, a seemingly ordinary man named Darwin E. Smith was named chief executive of Kimberly-Clark, a stodgy old paper company whose stock had fallen 36% behind the general market during the previous 20 years. Smith, the company's mild-mannered in-house lawyer, wasn't so sure the board had made the right choice—a feeling that was reinforced when a Kimberly-Clark director pulled him aside and reminded him that he lacked some of the qualifications for the position. But CEO he was, and CEO he remained for 20 years.

What a 20 years it was. In that period, Smith created a stunning transformation at Kimberly-Clark, turning it into the leading consumer paper products company in the world. Under his stewardship, the company beat its rivals Scott Paper and Procter & Gamble. And in doing so, Kimberly-Clark generated cumulative stock returns that were 4.1 times greater than those of the general market, outperforming venerable companies such as Hewlett-Packard, 3M, Coca-Cola, and General Electric.

Smith's turnaround of Kimberly-Clark is one of the best examples in the twentieth century of a leader taking a company from merely good to truly great. And yet few people—even ardent students of business history—have heard of Darwin Smith. He probably would have liked it that way. Smith is a classic example of a *Level 5 leader*—an individual who blends extreme personal humility with intense professional will. According to our five-year research study, executives who possess this paradoxical combination of traits are catalysts for the statistically rare event of transforming a good company into a great one.

"Level 5" refers to the highest level in a hierarchy of executive capabilities that we identified during our research. Leaders at the other four levels in the hierarchy can produce high degrees of success but not enough to elevate companies from mediocrity to sustained excellence. (For more details about this concept, see the exhibit "The Level 5 Hierarchy.") And while Level 5 leadership is not the only requirement for transforming a good company into a great one—other factors include getting the right

The Level 5 Hierarchy

Level 5 *Level 5 Executive*
Builds enduring greatness through a paradoxical combination of personal humility plus professional will.

Level 4 *Effective Leader*
Catalyzes commitment to and vigorous pursuit of a clear and compelling vision; stimulates the group to high performance standards.

Level 3 *Competent Manager*
Organizes people and resources toward the effective and efficient pursuit of predetermined objectives.

Level 2 *Contributing Team Member*
Contributes to the achievement of group objectives; works effectively with others in a group setting.

Level 1 *Highly Capable Individual*
Makes productive contributions through talent, knowledge, skill, and good work habits.

---

people on the bus (and the wrong people off the bus) and creating a culture of discipline—our research shows it to be essential. Good-to-great transformations don't happen without Level 5 leaders at the helm. They just don't.

NOT WHAT YOU WOULD EXPECT

Our discovery of Level 5 leadership is counterintuitive. Indeed, it is countercultural. People generally assume that transforming companies from good to great requires larger-than-life leaders—big personalities like Iacocca, Dunlap, Welch, and Gault, who make headlines and become celebrities.

Compared with those CEOs, Darwin Smith seems to have come from Mars. Shy, unpretentious, even awkward, Smith shunned attention. When a journalist asked him to describe his management style, Smith just stared back at the scribe from the other side of his thick black-rimmed glasses. He was dressed unfashionably, like a farm boy wearing his first J. C. Penney suit. Finally, after a long and uncomfortable silence, he said, "Eccentric." Needless to say, the *Wall Street Journal* did not publish a splashy feature on Darwin Smith.

But if you were to consider Smith soft or meek, you would be terribly mistaken. His lack of pretense was coupled with a fierce, even stoic, resolve toward life. Smith grew up on an Indiana farm and put himself through night school at Indiana University by working the day shift at International Harvester. One day, he lost a finger on the job. The story goes that he went to class that evening and returned to work the very next day. Eventually, the poor but determined Indiana farm boy earned admission to Harvard Law School.

He showed the same iron will when he was at the helm of Kimberly-Clark. Indeed, two months after Smith became CEO, doctors diagnosed him with nose and throat cancer and told him he had less than a year to live. He duly informed the board of his illness but said he had no plans to die anytime soon. Smith held to his demanding work schedule while commuting weekly from Wisconsin to Houston for radiation therapy. He lived 25 more years, 20 of them as CEO.

Smith's ferocious resolve was crucial to the rebuilding of Kimberly-Clark, especially when he made the most dramatic decision in the company's history: sell the mills.

To explain: shortly after he took over, Smith and his team had concluded that the company's traditional core business—coated paper—was doomed to mediocrity. Its economics were bad and the competition weak. But, they reasoned, if Kimberly-Clark was thrust into the fire of the *consumer* paper products business, better economics and world-class competition like Procter & Gamble would force it to achieve greatness or perish.

And so, like the general who burned the boats upon landing on enemy soil, leaving his troops to succeed or die, Smith announced that Kimberly-Clark would sell its mills—even the namesake mill in Kimberly, Wisconsin. All proceeds would be thrown into the consumer business, with investments in brands like Huggies diapers and Kleenex tissues. The business media called the move stupid, and Wall Street analysts downgraded the stock. But Smith never wavered. Twenty-five years later, Kimberly-Clark owned Scott Paper and beat Procter & Gamble in six of eight product categories. In retirement, Smith reflected on his exceptional performance, saying simply, "I never stopped trying to become qualified for the job."

NOT WHAT WE EXPECTED EITHER

We'll look in depth at Level 5 leadership, but first let's set an important context for our findings: we were not looking for Level 5 or anything like it. Our original question was can a good company become a great one, and, if so, how? In fact, I gave the research teams explicit instructions to downplay the role of top executives in their analyses of this question so we wouldn't slip into the simplistic "credit the leader" or "blame the leader" thinking that is so common today.

But Level 5 found us. Over the course of the study, research teams kept saying, "We can't ignore the top executives even if we want to. There is something consistently unusual about them." I would push back, arguing, "The comparison companies also had leaders. So what's different here?" Back and forth the debate raged. Finally, as should always be the case, the data won. The executives at companies that went from good to great and sustained that performance for 15 years or more were all cut from the same cloth—one remarkably different from that which produced executives at the comparison companies in our study. It didn't matter whether the company was in crisis or steady state, consumer or industrial, offering services or products. It didn't matter when the transition took place or how big the company. The successful organizations all had a Level 5 leader at the time of transition.

Furthermore, the absence of Level 5 leadership showed up consistently across the comparison companies. The point: Level 5 is an empirical finding, not an ideological one. And that's important to note, given how much the Level 5 finding contradicts not only conventional wisdom but much of management theory to date.

HUMILITY + WILL ≐ LEVEL 5

Level 5 leaders are a study in duality: modest and willful, shy and fearless. To grasp this concept, consider Abraham Lincoln, who never let his ego get in the way of his ambition to create an enduring great nation. Author Henry Adams called him "a quiet, peaceful, shy figure." But those who thought Lincoln's understated manner signaled weakness in the man found themselves terribly mistaken—to the scale of 250,000 Confederate and 360,000 Union lives, including Lincoln's own.

It might be a stretch to compare the 11 Level 5 CEOs in our research to Lincoln, but they did display the same kind of duality. Take Colman M.

Mockler, CEO of Gillette from 1975 to 1991. Mockler, who faced down three takeover attempts, was a reserved, gracious man with a gentle, almost patrician manner. Despite epic battles with raiders—he took on Ronald Perelman twice and the former Coniston Partners once—he never lost his shy, courteous style. At the height of the crisis, he maintained a calm business-as-usual demeanor, dispensing first with ongoing business before turning to the takeover.

And yet, those who mistook Mockler's outward modesty as a sign of inner weakness were beaten in the end. In one proxy battle, Mockler and other senior executives called thousands of investors, one by one, to win their votes. Mockler simply would not give in. He chose to fight for the future greatness of Gillette even though he could have pocketed millions by flipping his stock.

Consider the consequences had Mockler capitulated. If a share-flipper had accepted the full 44% price premium offered by Perelman and then invested those shares in the general market for ten years, he still would have come out 64% behind a shareholder who stayed with Mockler and Gillette. If Mockler had given up the fight, it's likely that none of us would be shaving with Sensor, Lady Sensor, or the Mach III—and hundreds of millions of people would have a more painful battle with daily stubble.

Sadly, Mockler never had the chance to enjoy the full fruits of his efforts. In January 1991, Gillette received an advance copy of *Forbes*. The cover featured an artist's rendition of the publicity-shy Mockler standing on a mountaintop, holding a giant razor above his head in a triumphant pose. Walking back to his office, just minutes after seeing this public acknowledgment of his 16 years of struggle, Mockler crumpled to the floor and died from a massive heart attack.

Even if Mockler had known he would die in office, he could not have changed his approach. His placid person hid an inner intensity, a dedication to making anything he touched the best—not just because of what he would get but because he couldn't imagine doing it any other way. Mockler could not give up the company to those who would destroy it, any more than Lincoln would risk losing the chance to build an enduring great nation.

A COMPELLING MODESTY

The Mockler story illustrates the modesty typical of Level 5 leaders. Indeed, throughout our interviews with such executives, we were struck by the way they talked about themselves—or rather, didn't talk about themselves. They'd go on and on about the company and the contributions of other executives, but they would instinctively deflect discussion about their own role. When pressed to talk about themselves, they'd say things like, "I hope I'm not sounding like a big shot," or "I don't think I can take much credit for what happened. We were blessed with marvelous people." One Level 5 leader even asserted, "There are a lot of people in this company who could do my job better than I do."

By contrast, consider the courtship of personal celebrity by the comparison CEOs. Scott Paper, the comparison company to Kimberly-Clark, hired Al Dunlap as CEO—a man who would tell anyone who would listen (and many who would have preferred not to) about his accomplishments. After 19 months atop Scott Paper, Dunlap said in *BusinessWeek*: "The Scott story will go down in the annals of American business history as one of the most successful, quickest turnarounds ever. It makes other turnarounds pale by comparison." He personally accrued $100 million for 603 days of work at Scott Paper—about $165,000 per day—largely by slashing the workforce, halving the R&D budget, and putting the company on growth steroids in preparation for sale. After selling off the company and pocketing his quick millions, Dunlap wrote an autobiography in which he boastfully dubbed himself "Rambo in pinstripes." It's hard to imagine Darwin Smith thinking, "Hey, that Rambo character reminds me of me," let alone stating it publicly.

Granted, the Scott Paper story is one of the more dramatic in our study, but it's not an isolated case. In more than two-thirds of the comparison companies, we noted the presence of a gargantuan ego that contributed to the demise or continued mediocrity of the company. We found this pattern particularly strong in the unsustained comparison companies—the companies that would show a shift in performance under a talented yet egocentric Level 4 leader, only to decline in later years.

Lee Iacocca, for example, saved Chrysler from the brink of catastrophe, performing one the most celebrated (and deservedly so) turnarounds in U.S. business history. The automaker's stock rose 2.9 times higher than the general market about halfway through his tenure. But then Iacocca diverted his attention to transforming himself. He appeared regularly on talk shows like the *Today Show* and *Larry King Live*, starred in more than 80 commercials, entertained the idea of running for president of the United States, and promoted his autobiography, which sold 7 million copies worldwide. Iacocca's personal stock soared, but Chrysler's stock fell 31% below the market in the second half of his tenure.

And once Iacocca had accumulated all the fame and perks, he found it difficult to leave center stage. He postponed his retirement so many times that Chrysler's insiders began to joke that Iacocca stood for "I Am Chairman of Chrysler Corporation Always." When he finally retired, he demanded that the board continue to provide a private jet and stock options. Later, he joined forces with noted takeover artist Kirk Kerkorian to launch a hostile bid for Chrysler. (It failed.) Iacocca did make one final brilliant decision: he picked a modest yet determined man—perhaps even a Level 5— as his successor. Bob Eaton rescued Chrysler from its second near-death crisis in a decade and set the foundation for a more enduring corporate transition.

AN UNWAVERING RESOLVE

Besides extreme humility, Level 5 leaders also display tremendous professional will. When George Cain became CEO of Abbott Laboratories, it was a drowsy family-controlled business, sitting at the bottom quartile of the pharmaceutical industry, living off its cash cow, erythromycin. Cain was a typical Level 5 leader in his lack of pretense; he didn't have the kind of inspiring personality that would galvanize the company. But he had something much more powerful: inspired standards. He could not stand mediocrity in any form and was utterly intolerant of anyone who would accept the idea that good is good enough. For the next 14 years, he relentlessly imposed his will for greatness on Abbott Labs.

Among Cain's first tasks was to destroy one of the root causes of Abbott's middling performance: nepotism. By systematically rebuilding both the board and the executive team with the best people he could find, Cain made his statement. Family ties no longer mattered. If you couldn't become the best executive in the industry, within your span of responsibility, you would lose your paycheck.

Such near-ruthless rebuilding might be expected from an outsider brought in to turn the company around, but Cain was an 18-year insider— and a part of the family, the son of a previous president. Holiday gatherings were probably tense for a few years in the Cain clan—"Sorry I had to fire you. Want another slice of turkey?"—but in the end, family members were pleased with the performance of their stock. Cain had set in motion a profitable growth machine. From its transition in 1974 to 2000, Abbott created shareholder returns that beat the market 4.5:1, outperforming industry superstars Merck and Pfizer by a factor of two.

Another good example of iron-willed Level 5 leadership comes from Charles R. "Cork" Walgreen III, who transformed dowdy Walgreens into a company that outperformed the stock market 16:1 from its transition in 1975 to 2000. After years of dialogue and debate within his executive team about what to do with Walgreens' food-service operations, this CEO sensed the team had finally reached a watershed: the company's brightest future lay in convenient drugstores, not in food service. Dan Jorndt, who succeeded Walgreen in 1988, describes what happened next:

> Cork said at one of our planning committee meetings, "Okay, now I am going to draw the line in the sand. We are going to be out of the restaurant business completely in five years." At the time we had more than 500 restaurants. You could have heard a pin drop. He said, "I want to let everybody know the clock is ticking." Six months later we were at our next planning committee meeting and someone mentioned just in passing that we had only five years to be out of the restaurant business. Cork was not a real vociferous fellow. He sort of tapped on the table and said, "Listen, you now have four and a half years. I said you had five years six months ago. Now you've got four and a half years." Well, that next day things really clicked into gear for winding down our restaurant business. Cork never wavered. He never doubted. He never second-guessed.

Like Darwin Smith selling the mills at Kimberly-Clark, Cork Walgreen required stoic resolve to make his decisions. Food service was not the largest part of the business, although it did add substantial profits to the bottom line. The real problem was more emotional than financial. Walgreens had, after all, invented the malted milk shake, and food service had been a long-standing family tradition dating back to Cork's grandfather. Not only that, some food-service outlets were even named after the CEO—for example, a restaurant chain named Corky's. But no matter, if Walgreen had to fly in the face of family tradition in order to refocus on the one arena in which Walgreens could be the best in the world—convenient drugstores—and terminate everything else that would not produce great results, than Cork would do it. Quietly, doggedly, simply.

One final, yet compelling, note on our findings about Level 5: because Level 5 leaders have ambition not for themselves but for their companies, they routinely select superb successors. Level 5 leaders want to see their companies become even more successful in the next generation, comfortable with the idea that most people won't even know that the roots of the success trace back to them. As one Level 5 CEO said, "I want to look from my porch, see the company as one of the great companies in the world someday, and be able to say, 'I used to work there.'" By contrast, Level 4 leaders often fail to set up the company for enduring success—after all, what better testament to your own personal greatness than that the place falls apart after you leave?

In more than three-quarters of the comparison companies, we found executives who set up their successors for failure, chose weak successors, or both. Consider the case of Rubbermaid, which grew from obscurity to become one of *Fortune*'s most admired companies—and then, just as quickly, disintegrated into such sorry shape that it had to be acquired by Newell.

The architect of this remarkable story was a charismatic and brilliant leader named Stanley C. Gault, whose name became synonymous in the late 1980s with the company's success. Across the 312 articles collected by our research team about Rubbermaid, Gault comes through as a hard-driving, egocentric executive. In one article, he responds to the accusation of being a tyrant with the statement, "Yes, but I'm a sincere tyrant." In another, drawn directly from his own comments on leading change, the word "I" appears 44 times, while the word "we" appears 16 times. Of course, Gault had every reason to be proud of his executive success: Rubbermaid generated 40 consecutive quarters of earnings growth under his leadership—an impressive performance, to be sure, and one that deserves respect.

But Gault did not leave behind a company that would be great without him. His chosen successor lasted a year on the job and the next in line faced a management team so shallow that he had to temporarily shoulder four jobs while scrambling to identify a new number-two executive. Gault's successors struggled not only with a management void but also with strategic voids that would eventually bring the company to its knees.

Of course, you might say—as one *Fortune* article did—that the fact that Rubbermaid fell apart after Gault left proves his greatness as a leader. Gault was a tremendous Level 4 leader, perhaps one of the best in the last 50 years. But he was not at Level 5, and that is one crucial reason why Rubbermaid went from good to great for a brief, shining moment and then just as quickly went from great to irrelevant.

THE WINDOW AND THE MIRROR

As part of our research, we interviewed Alan L. Wurtzel, the Level 5 leader responsible for turning Circuit City from a ramshackle company on the edge of bankruptcy into one of America's most successful electronics retailers. In the 15 years after its transition date in 1982, Circuit City outperformed the market 18.5:1.

We asked Wurtzel to list the top five factors in his company's transformation, ranked by importance. His number one factor? Luck. "We were in a great industry, with the wind at our backs." But wait a minute, we retorted, Silo—your comparison company—was in the same industry, with the same wind, and bigger sails. The conversation went back and forth, with Wurtzel refusing to take much credit for the transition, preferring to attribute it largely to just being in the right place at the right time. Later, when we asked him to discuss the factors that would sustain a good-to-great transformation, he said, "The first thing that comes to mind is luck. I was lucky to find the right successor."

Luck. What an odd factor to talk about. Yet the Level 5 leaders we identified invoked it frequently. We asked an executive at steel company Nucor why it had such a remarkable track record of making good decisions. His response? "I guess we were just lucky." Joseph F. Cullman III, the Level 5 CEO of Philip Morris, flat out refused to take credit for his company's success, citing his good fortune to have great colleagues, successors, and predecessors. Even the book he wrote about his career—which he penned at the urging of his colleagues and which he never intended to distribute widely outside the company—had the unusual title *I'm a Lucky Guy*.

At first, we were puzzled by the Level 5 leaders' emphasis on good luck. After all, there is no evidence that the companies that had progressed from good to great were blessed with more good luck (or more bad luck for that matter) than the comparison companies. But then we began to notice an interesting pattern in the executives at the comparison companies: they often blamed their situations on bad luck, bemoaning the difficulties of the environment they faced.

Compare Bethlehem Steel and Nucor, for example. Both steel companies operated with products that are hard to differentiate, and both faced a competitive challenge from cheap imported steel. Both companies paid significantly higher wages than most of their foreign competitors. And yet executives at the two companies held completely different views of the same environment.

Bethlehem Steel's CEO summed up the company's problems in 1983 by blaming the imports: "Our first, second, and third problems are imports." Meanwhile, Ken Iverson and his crew at Nucor saw the imports as a blessing: "Aren't we lucky; steel is heavy, and they have to ship it all the way across the ocean, giving us a huge advantage." Indeed, Iverson saw the first, second, and third problems facing the U.S. steel industry not in imports but in management. He even went so far as to speak out publicly against government protection against imports, telling a gathering of stunned steel executives in 1977 that the real problems facing the industry lay in the fact that management had failed to keep pace with technology.

The emphasis on luck turns out to be part of a broader pattern that we came to call *the window and the mirror*. Level 5 leaders, inherently humble, look out the window to apportion credit—even undue credit—to factors outside themselves. If they can't find a specific person or event to give credit to, they credit good luck. At the same time, they look in the mirror to assign responsibility, never citing bad luck or external factors when things go poorly. Conversely, the comparison executives frequently looked out the window for factors to blame but preened in the mirror to credit themselves when things went well.

The funny thing about the window-and-mirror concept is that it does not reflect reality. According to our research, the Level 5 leaders *were* responsible for their companies' transformations. But they would never admit that. We can't climb inside their heads and assess whether they deeply believed what they saw in the window and the mirror. But it doesn't really matter, because they acted as if they believed it, and they acted with such consistency that it produced exceptional results.

BORN OR BRED?

Not long ago, I shared the Level 5 finding with a gathering of senior executives. A woman who had recently become chief executive of her company raised her hand. "I believe what you've told us about Level 5 leadership," she said, "but I'm disturbed because I know I'm not there yet, and maybe I never will be. Part of the reason I got this job is because of my strong ego. Are you telling me that I can't make my company great if I'm not a Level 5?"

"Let me return to the data," I responded. "Of 1,435 companies that appeared on the *Fortune 500* since 1965, only 11 made it into our study. In those 11, all of them had Level 5 leaders in key positions, including the CEO role, at the pivotal time of transition. Now, to reiterate, we're not saying that Level 5 is the only element required for the move from good to great, but it appears to be essential."

She sat there, quiet for a moment, and you could guess what many people in the room were thinking. Finally, she raised her hand again. "Can you learn to become Level 5?" I still do not know the answer to that question. Our research, frankly, did not delve into how Level 5 leaders come to be, nor did we attempt to explain or codify the nature of their emotional lives. We speculated on the unique psychology of Level 5 leaders. Were they "guilty" of displacement—shifting their own raw ambition onto something other than themselves? Were they sublimating their egos for dark and complex reasons rooted in childhood trauma? Who knows? And perhaps more important, do the psychological roots of Level 5 leadership matter any more than do the roots of charisma or intelligence? The question remains: Can Level 5 be developed?

My preliminary hypothesis is that there are two categories of people: those who don't have the Level 5 seed within them and those who do. The first category consists of people who could never in a million years bring themselves to subjugate their own needs to the greater ambition of something larger and more lasting than themselves. For those people, work will always be first and foremost about what they get—the fame, fortune, power, adulation, and so on. Work will never be about what they build, create, and contribute. The great irony is that the animus and personal ambition that often drives people to become a Level 4 leader stands at odds with the humility required to rise to Level 5.

When you combine that irony with the fact that boards of directors frequently operate under the false belief that a larger-than-life, egocentric leader is required to make a company great, you can quickly see why Level 5 leaders rarely appear at the top of our institutions. We keep putting people in positions of power who lack the seed to become a Level 5 leader, and that is one major reason why there are so few companies that make a sustained and verifiable shift from good to great.

The second category consists of people who could evolve to Level 5; the capability resides within them, perhaps buried or ignored or simply nascent. Under the right circumstances—with self-reflection, a mentor, loving parents, a significant life experience, or other factors—the seed can begin to develop. Some of the Level 5 leaders in our study had significant life experiences that might have sparked development of the seed. Darwin Smith fully blossomed as a Level 5 after his near-death experience with cancer. Joe Cullman was profoundly affected by his World War II experiences, particularly the last-minute change of orders that took him off a doomed ship on which he surely would have died; he considered the next 60-odd years a great gift. A strong religious belief or conversion might also nurture the seed. Colman Mockler, for example, converted to evangelical Christianity while getting his MBA at Harvard, and later, according to the book *Cutting Edge*, he became a prime mover in a group of Boston business executives that met frequently over breakfast to discuss the carryover of religious values to corporate life.

We would love to be able to give you a list of steps for getting to Level 5—other than contracting cancer, going through a religious conversion, or getting different parents—but we have no solid research data that would support a credible list. Our research exposed Level 5 as a key component inside the black box of what it takes to shift a company from good to great. Yet inside that black box is another—the inner development of a person to Level 5 leadership. We could speculate on what that inner box might hold, but it would mostly be just that, speculation.

In short, Level 5 is a very satisfying idea, a truthful idea, a powerful idea, and, to make the move from good to great, very likely an essential idea. But to provide "ten steps to Level 5 leadership" would trivialize the concept.

My best advice, based on the research, is to practice the other good-to-great disciplines that we discovered. Since we found a tight symbiotic relationship between each of the other findings and Level 5, we suspect that conscientiously trying to lead using the other disciplines can help you move in the right direction. There is no guarantee that doing so will turn executives into full-fledged Level 5 leaders, but it gives them a tangible place to begin, especially if they have the seed within.

We cannot say for sure what percentage of people have the seed within, nor how many of those can nurture it enough to become Level 5. Even those of us on the research team who identified Level 5 do not know whether we will succeed in evolving to its heights. And yet all of us who worked on the finding have been inspired by the idea of trying to move toward Level 5. Darwin Smith, Colman Mockler, Alan Wurtzel, and all the other Level 5 leaders we learned about have become role models for us. Whether or not we make it to Level 5, it is worth trying. For like all basic truths about what is best in human beings, when we catch a glimpse of that truth, we know that our own lives and all that we touch will be the better for making the effort to get there.

The Servant as Leader

Robert K. Greenleaf

Servant and leader—can these two roles be fused in one real person, in all levels of status or calling? If so, can that person live and be productive in the real world of the present? My sense of the present leads me to say yes to both questions. This chapter is an attempt to explain why and to suggest how.

The idea of *The Servant as Leader* came out of reading Hermann Hesse's *Journey to the East*. In this story we see a band of men on a mythical journey, probably also Hesse's own journey. The central figure of the story is Leo who accompanies the party as the *servant* who does their menial chores, but who also sustains them with his spirit and his song. He is a person of extraordinary presence. All goes well until Leo disappears. Then the group falls into disarray and the journey is abandoned. They cannot make it without the servant Leo. The narrator, one of the party, after some years of wandering finds Leo and is taken into the Order that had sponsored the journey. There he discovers that Leo, whom he had known first as *servant,* was in fact the titular head of the Order, its guiding spirit, a great and noble *leader.*

One can muse on what Hesse was trying to say when he wrote this story. We know that most of his fiction was autobiographical, that he led a tortured life, and that *Journey to the East* suggests a turn toward the serenity he achieved in his old age. There has been much speculation by critics on Hesse's life and work, some of it centering on this story which they find the most puzzling. But to me, this story clearly says that *the great leader is seen as servant first,* and that simple fact is the key to his greatness. Leo was actually the leader all of the time, but he was servant first because that was what he was, *deep down inside.* Leadership was bestowed upon a man who was by nature a servant. It was something given, or assumed, that could be taken away. His servant nature was the real man, not bestowed, not assumed, and not to be taken away. He was servant first.

I mention Hesse and *Journey to the East* for two reasons. First, I want to acknowledge the source of the idea of *The Servant as Leader.* Then I want to use this reference as an introduction to a brief discussion of prophecy.

Fifteen years ago when I first read about Leo, if I had been listening to contemporary prophecy as intently as I do now, the first draft of this piece might have been written then. As it was, the idea lay dormant for eleven years until, four years ago, I concluded that we in this country were in a leadership crisis and that I should do what I could about it. I became painfully aware of how dull my sense of contemporary prophecy had been. And I have reflected much on why we do not hear and heed the prophetic voices in our midst (not a new question in our times, nor more critical than heretofore).

I now embrace the theory of prophecy which holds that prophetic voices of great clarity, and with a quality of insight equal to that of any age, are speaking cogently all of the time. Men and women of a stature equal to the greatest of the past are with us now addressing the problems of the day and pointing to a better way and to a personeity better able to live fully and serenely in these times.

The variable that marks some periods as barren and some as rich in prophetic vision is in the interest, the level of seeking, the responsiveness of the hearers. The variable is not in the presence or absence or the relative quality and force of the prophetic voices. Prophets grow in stature as people respond to their message. If their early attempts are ignored or spurned, their talent may wither away.

It is *seekers*, then, who make prophets, and the initiative of any one of us in searching for and responding to the voice of contemporary prophets may mark the turning point in their growth and service. But since we are the product of our own history, we see current prophecy within the context of past wisdom. We listen to as wide a range of contemporary thought as we can attend to. Then we *choose* those we elect to heed as prophets—*both old and new*—and meld their advice with our own leadings. This we test in real-life experiences to establish our own position.

Some who have difficulty with this theory assert that their faith rests on one or more of the prophets of old having given the "word" for all time and that the contemporary ones do not speak to their condition as the older ones do. But if one really believes that the "word" has been given for all time, how can one be a seeker? How can one hear the contemporary voice when one has decided not to live in the present and has turned that voice off?

Neither this hypothesis nor its opposite can be proved. But I submit that the one given here is the more hopeful choice, one that offers a significant role in prophecy to every individual. One cannot interact with and build strength in a dead prophet, but one can do it with a living one. "Faith," Dean Inge has said, "is the choice of the nobler hypothesis."

One does not, of course, ignore the great voices of the past. One does not awaken each morning with the compulsion to reinvent the wheel. But if one is *servant,* either leader or follower, one is always searching, listening, expecting that a better wheel for these times is in the making. It may emerge any day. Any one of us may find it out from personal experience. I am hopeful.

I am hopeful for these times, despite the tension and conflict, because more natural servants are trying to see clearly the world as it is and are listening carefully to prophetic voices that are speaking *now.* They are challenging the pervasive injustice with greater force and they are taking sharper issue with the wide disparity between the quality of society they know is reasonable and possible with available resources, and, on the other hand, the actual performance of the whole range of institutions that exist to serve society.

A fresh critical look is being taken at the issues of power and authority, and people are beginning to learn, however haltingly, to relate to one another in less coercive and more creatively supporting ways. A new moral principle is emerging which holds that the only authority deserving one's allegiance is that which is freely and knowingly granted by the led to the leader in response to, and in proportion to, the clearly evident servant stature of the leader. Those who choose to follow this principle will not casually accept the authority of existing institutions. *Rather, they will freely respond only to individuals who are chosen as leaders because they are proven and trusted as servants.* To the extent that this principle prevails in the future, the only truly viable institutions will be those that are predominantly servant-led.

I am mindful of the long road ahead before these trends, which I see so clearly, become a major society-shaping force. We are not there yet. But I see encouraging movement on the horizon.

What direction will the movement take? Much depends on whether those who stir the ferment will come to grips with the age-old problem of how to live in a human society. I say this because so many, having made their awesome decision for autonomy and independence from tradition, and having taken their firm stand against injustice and hypocrisy, find it hard to convert themselves into *affirmative builders* of a better society. How many of them will seek their personal fulfillment by making the hard choices, and by undertaking the rigorous preparation that building a better society requires? It all depends on what kind of leaders emerge and how they—we—respond to them.

My thesis, that more servants should emerge as leaders, or should follow only servant-leaders, is not a popular one. It is much more comfortable to go with a less demanding point of view about what is expected of one now. There are several undemanding, plausibly-argued alternatives to choose. One, since society seems corrupt, is to seek to avoid the center of it by retreating to an idyllic existence that minimizes involvement with the "system" (with the "system" that makes such withdrawal possible). Then there is the assumption that since the effort to reform existing institutions has not brought instant perfection, the remedy is to destroy them completely so that fresh new perfect ones can grow. Not much thought seems to be given to the problem of where the new seed will come from or who the gardener to tend them will be. The concept of the servant-leader stands in sharp contrast to this kind of thinking.

Yet it is understandable that the easier alternatives would be chosen, especially by young people. By extending education for so many so far into the adult years, the normal participation in society is effectively denied when young people are ready for it. With education that is preponderantly abstract and analytical it is no wonder that there is a preoccupation with criticism and that not much thought is given to "What can *I* do about it?"

Criticism has its place, but as a total preoccupation it is sterile. In a time of crisis, like the leadership crisis we are now in, if too many potential builders are taken in by a complete absorption with dissecting the wrong and by a zeal for instant perfection, then the movement so many of us want to see will be set back. The danger, perhaps, is to hear the analyst too much and the artist too little.

Albert Camus stands apart from other great artists of his time, in my view, and deserves the title of *prophet,* because of his unrelenting demand that each of us confront the exacting terms of our own existence, and, like Sisyphus, *accept our rock and find our happiness in dealing with it.* Camus sums up the relevance of his position to our concern for the servant as leader in the last paragraph of his last published lecture, entitled *Create Dangerously:*

One may long, as I do, for a gentler flame, a respite, a pause for musing. But perhaps there is no other peace for the artist than what he finds in the heat of combat. "Every wall is a door," Emerson correctly said. Let us not look for the door, and the way out, anywhere but in the wall against which we are living. Instead, let us seek the respite where it is—in the very thick of battle. For in my opinion, and this is where I shall close, it *is* there. Great ideas, it has been said, come into the world as gently as doves. Perhaps, then, if we listen attentively, we shall hear, amid the uproar of empires and nations, a faint flutter of wings, the gentle stirring of life and hope. Some will say that this hope lies in a nation, others, in a man. 1 believe rather that it is awakened, revived, nourished by millions of solitary individuals whose deeds and works every day negate frontiers and the crudest implications of history. As a result, there shines forth fleetingly the ever-threatened truth that each and every man, on the foundations of his own sufferings and joys, builds for them all.

One is asked, then, to accept the human condition, its sufferings and its joys, and to work with its imperfections as the foundation upon which the individual will build wholeness through adventurous creative achievement. For the person with creative potential there is no wholeness except in using it. And, as Camus explained, the going is rough and the respite is brief. It is significant that he would title his last university lecture *Create Dangerously*. And, as I ponder the fusing of servant and leader, it seems a dangerous creation: dangerous for the natural servant to become a leader, dangerous for the leader to be servant first, and dangerous for a follower to insist on being led by a servant. There are safer and easier alternatives available to all three. But why take them?

As I respond to the challenge of dealing with this question in the ensuing discourse I am faced with two problems.

First, I did not get the notion of the servant as leader from conscious logic. Rather it came to me as an intuitive insight as I contemplated Leo. And I do not see what is relevant from my own searching and experience in terms of a logical progression from premise to conclusion. Rather I see it as fragments of data to be fed into my internal computer from which intuitive insights come. Serving and leading are still mostly intuition-based concepts in my thinking.

The second problem, and related to the first, is that, just as there may be a real contradiction in the servant as leader, so my perceptual world is full of contradictions. Some examples: I believe in order, and I want creation out of chaos. My good society will have strong individualism amidst community. It will have elitism along with populism. I listen to the old and to the young and find myself baffled and heartened by both. Reason and intuition, each in its own way, both comfort and dismay me. There are many more. Yet, with all of this, I believe that I live with as much serenity as do my contemporaries who venture into controversy as freely as I do but whose natural bent is to tie up the essentials of life in neat bundles of logic and consistency. But I am deeply grateful to the people who are logical and consistent because some of them, out of their natures, render invaluable services for which I am not capable.

My resolution of these two problems is to offer the relevant gleanings of my experience in the form of a series of unconnected little essays, some developed more fully than others, with the suggestion that they be read and pondered on separately within the context of this opening section.

WHO IS THE SERVANT-LEADER?

The servant-leader *is* servant first—as Leo was portrayed. It begins with the natural feeling that one wants to serve, to serve *first*. Then conscious choice brings one to aspire to lead. That person is sharply different from one who is *leader* first, perhaps because of the need to assuage an unusual power drive or to acquire material possessions. For such it will be a later choice to serve—after leadership is established. The leader-first and the servant-first are two extreme types. Between them there are shadings and blends that are part of the infinite variety of human nature.

The difference manifests itself in the care taken by the servant-first to make sure that other people's highest priority needs are being served. The best test, and difficult to administer, is: Do those served grow as persons? Do they, *while being served,* become healthier, wiser, freer, more autonomous, more likely themselves to become servants? *And,* what is the effect on the least privileged in society; will they benefit, or, at least, not be further deprived?

As one sets out to serve, how can one know that this will be the result? This is part of the human dilemma; one cannot know for sure. One must, after some study and experience, hypothesize—but leave the hypothesis under a shadow of doubt. Then one acts on the hypothesis and examines the result. One continues to study and learn and periodically one reexamines the hypothesis itself.

Finally, one chooses again. Perhaps one chooses the same hypothesis again and again. But it is always a fresh open choice. And it is always an hypothesis under a shadow of doubt. "Faith is the choice of the nobler hypothesis." Not the *noblest;* one never knows what that is. But the *nobler,* the best one can see when the choice is made. Since the test of results of one's actions is usually long delayed, the faith that sustains the choice of the nobler hypothesis is psychological self-insight. This is the most dependable part of the true servant.

The natural servant, the person who is *servant first*, is more likely to persevere and refine a particular hypothesis on what serves another's highest priority needs than is the person who is *leader first* and who later serves out of promptings of conscience or in conformity with normative expectations.

My hope for the future rests in part on my belief that among the legions of deprived and unsophisticated people are many true servants who will lead, and that most of them can learn to discriminate among those who presume to serve them and identify the true servants whom they will follow.

EVERYTHING BEGINS WITH THE INITIATIVE OF AN INDIVIDUAL

The forces for good and evil in the world are propelled by the thoughts, attitudes, and actions of individual beings. What happens to our values, and therefore to the quality of our civilization in the future, will be shaped by the conceptions of individuals that are born of inspiration. Perhaps only a few will receive this inspiration (insight) and the rest will learn from them. The very essence of leadership, going out ahead to show the way, derives from more than usual openness to inspiration. Why would anybody accept the leadership of another except that the other sees more clearly where it is best to go? Perhaps this is the current problem: too many who presume to lead do not see more clearly and, in defense of their inadequacy, they all the more strongly argue that the "system" must be preserved—a fatal error in this day of candor.

But the leader needs more than inspiration. A leader ventures to say: "I will go; come with me!" A leader initiates, provides the ideas and the structure, and takes the risk of failure along with the chance of success. A leader says: "I will go; follow me!" while knowing that the path is uncertain, even dangerous. One then trusts those who go with one's leadership.

Paul Goodman, speaking through a character in *Making Do*, has said, "If there is no community for you, young man, young man, make it yourself."

WHAT ARE YOU TRYING TO DO?

"What are you trying to do?" is one of the easiest to ask and most difficult to answer of questions.

A mark of leaders, an attribute that puts them in a position to show the way for others, is that they are better than most at pointing the direction. As long as one is leading, one always has a goal. It may be a goal arrived at by group consensus, or the leader, acting on inspiration, may simply have said, "Let's go this way." But the leader always knows what it is and can articulate it for any who are unsure. By clearly stating and restating the goal the leader gives certainty and purpose to others who may have difficulty in achieving it for themselves.

The word *goal* is used here in the special sense of the overarching purpose, the big dream, the visionary concept, the ultimate consummation which one approaches but never really achieves. It is something presently out of reach; it is something to strive for, to move toward, or become. It is so stated that it excites the imagination and challenges people to work for something they do not yet know how to do, something they can be proud of as they move toward it.

Every achievement starts with a goal—but not just any goal and not just anybody stating it. The one who states the goal must elicit trust, especially if it is a high risk or visionary goal, because those who follow are asked to accept the risk along with the leader. Leaders do not elicit trust unless one has confidence in their values and competence (including judgment) and unless they have a sustaining spirit (entheos) that will support the tenacious pursuit of a goal.

Not much happens without a dream. And for something great to happen, there must be a great dream. Behind every great achievement is a dreamer of great dreams. Much more than a dreamer is required to bring it to reality; but the dream must be there first.

LISTENING AND UNDERSTANDING

One of our very able leaders recently was made the head of a large, important, and difficult-to-administer public institution. After a short time he realized that he was not happy with the way things were going. His approach to the problem was a bit unusual. For three months he stopped reading newspapers and listening to news broadcasts; and for this period he relied wholly upon those he met in the course of his work to tell him what was going on. In three months his administrative problems were resolved. No miracles were wrought; but out of a sustained intentness of listening that was produced by this unusual decision, this able man learned and received the insights needed to set the right course. And he strengthened his team by so doing.

Why is there so little listening? What makes this example so exceptional? Part of it, I believe, with those who lead, is that the usual leader in the face of a difficulty tends to react by trying to find someone else on whom to pin the problem, rather than by automatically responding: "I have a problem. What is it? What can *I* do about *my* problem?" The sensible person who takes the latter course will probably react by listening, and somebody in the situation is likely to say what the problem is and what should be done about it. Or enough will be heard that there will be an intuitive insight that resolves it.

I have a bias about this which suggests that only a true natural servant automatically responds to any problem by listening *first*. When one is a leader, this disposition causes one to be *seen* as servant first. This suggests that a non-servant who wants to be a servant might become a *natural* servant through a long arduous discipline of learning to listen, a discipline sufficiently sustained that the automatic response to any problem is to listen first. I have seen enough remarkable transformations in people who have been trained to listen to have some confidence in this approach. It is because true listening builds strength in other people.

Most of us at one time or another, some of us a good deal of the time, would really like to communicate, really get through to a significant level of meaning in the hearer's experience. It can be terribly important. The best test of whether we are communicating at this depth is to ask ourselves first: Are we really listening? Are we listening to the one we want to communicate to? Is our basic attitude, as we approach the confrontation, one of wanting to understand? Remember that great line from the prayer of St. Francis, "Lord, grant that I may not seek so much to be understood as to understand."

One must not be afraid of a little silence. Some find silence awkward or oppressive, but a relaxed approach to dialogue will include the welcoming of some silence. It is often a devastating question to ask oneself—but it is sometimes important to ask it—"In saying what I have in mind will I really improve on the silence?"

The Case of a Servant Leader: John F. Donnelly, Sr.

Robert J. Doyle

From a lecture presented at the University of Notre Dame,
October 4, 1996

I would like to tell you a story; a story of a businessman, a story of a very successful CEO. There are, of course, lots of stories about successful CEO's. But this one was unique among his peers in two ways; unique in the way he defined success: service to others rather than profit; and unique in his personal driving force: love of neighbor rather than competition. John Fenlon Donnelly's story hasn't ended yet and, if you should find it interesting, you may help to write it. It is my hope that you will find it of sufficient value that you will be inspired to pick up the story line and add a new sentence, a new paragraph, a new chapter, or even a whole new volume.

To give you just a bit of background, Donnelly Corporation is the world's leading supplier of automotive glass parts such as rear view mirrors, windows and specialty glass parts. Because of their quality and reliability, they are one of the very few suppliers who are the single source of supply for the major auto companies. They have been listed in both editions of *The 100 Best Companies to Work For in America* and, in a recent edition, they are in the top 10 of the 100 best. Several years ago, they were voted one of the most admired companies in America by an association of human resource executives. They receive a steady stream of visitors, which over the years has included General Motors, Meade Corporation and Volvo, wanting to learn about their management and human resources systems. Using any criteria, this has been a very successful company.

I worked closely with John for 7 years as Personnel Director and we continued a correspondence on the subject for an additional 12 years. Of the more than 100 CEO's with whom I have worked, John's story is the most interesting, and the one most worthy of your careful examination and your emulation.

416

I want to tell you about John Donnelly, the man, because one can not fully appreciate his work unless one knows who he was and why he did the things he did. Then I will describe some of his work to establish participative management in his company and, finally, I will explain some of the things I have made of his legacy and encourage you to take his lessons to heart and in your own way continue to expand these efforts to make work and organizations serve the best interests of people.

John spent his entire adult life as the President and CEO of the Donnelly Corporation. He attended the University of Notre Dame in the late 1920s and early 1930s, where he studied engineering and, more importantly, was introduced to Thomistic philosophy by such great men as G.K. Chesterton and Jacques Maritain. He then entered the seminary in Baltimore, Maryland to study for the priesthood, but soon returned to Holland, Michigan to manage the family business when his father suddenly and unexpectedly died.

He applied himself diligently to the task of learning how to manage a business but he never gave up his drive to study philosophy, the arts, history and the natural and physical sciences. He was a voracious reader and the scope of his knowledge, as far as the rest of us could determine, was without limit.

A colleague, Jim Knister, and I used to lunch frequently with John at the Warm Friend Hotel and other restaurants in downtown Holland. We were amazed at the range of his understanding and knowledge. One day we decided to try to find a topic outside of his expertise. During lunch I began a conversation about offshore oil drilling in the Gulf of Mexico and Jim, according to our conspiracy, picked up the discussion. In no time, John had joined the discussion and neatly summarized the economic dimension, the environmental threat, and the technical difficulties of drilling under water. We were both stunned and, as you can well imagine, neither of us ever tried a stunt like that again. Typical of John, he did not enter the discussion to dominate it or to show how smart he was, he was just participating.

John was a leader and he wore the mantle of leadership with grace and charm in many roles. After his father's death he was needed to manage the company and he accepted that leadership responsibility willingly and continued it for more than fifty years. He was a community leader. He helped the Holland Chamber of Commerce become the first chartered Chamber in their size category in the U.S. He was a leader in his church at the parish and diocesan level and, in the early 1960s, he was elected President of the National Council of Catholic Men. He was a leader in his family, a responsibility more dear to him than anything else in his life. John gave great energy to his business and to a variety of social action causes but there was never a doubt that his primary responsibility and interest was the happiness and welfare of his wife, Kay, his children, and his brother and sisters and their families.

Michael Novak has written an excellent new book entitled *Business as a Calling.* By which he means business as a vocation. Novak didn't know John Donnelly but if he had, he could have written his book as a biography of John. In his book, Novak makes the point that human capital is the most important resource of a business. This is a point Rensis Likert made in 1960 which attracted John to Likert. Likert would ask CEO's: "What would happen to your business if I left you every asset that shows up on your balance sheet (land, buildings, machines, vehicles, computers, tools, inventory, cash and so on) but took away every one of your people? How long would it take, and what would be the cost to rebuild your company?" Likert, a social scientist, was thinking of human capital as the technical skills and organizational skills required by a business.

Novak, a theologian, takes this idea to a much higher level and points out that virtue and character are the important components of a business' human capital. Virtue and character, not technical and organizational skills, build the internal and external relationships of trust and service necessary to a successful business enterprise.

Novak applies the four cardinal virtues to the vocation of the modern businessman. These, he says, are the virtues upon which the good character of the business and business people must be built. By good character, he means the classic Greek philosophical ideal of good-Kalos, meaning a goal to aspire to, with a power of attraction and beauty drawing us onward by its radiance. We don't usually talk about business goals and strategic plans that draw us onward by their radiance, their goodness. But John was able to see things in that dimension, he had the good character hinged on the cardinal virtues. His goal was always Kalos—the good as he knew it and he worked hard to discover that which was truly good.

Novak names the cardinal virtues: tempered passions, the courage to quiet fears and inner terrors, practical wisdom, and the right touch in giving to each person and each matter its due. If you have an old catechism, the cardinal virtues were called temperance, fortitude, wisdom and justice.

John Donnelly would receive a pretty good score on the cardinal virtues. He was temperate in his passions; the first cardinal virtue. I've seen him angry, but not out of control. His absence of visible vices and his modesty were reasons he was so trusted and respected. I can remember production employees of the company saying about a new policy or program or decision: "I don't really understand it but if John says it's okay, that's good enough for me." That testimonial alone would set John apart from most business leaders, indeed from leaders in almost all professions.

The second virtue, his courage and ability to face adversity with calmness was a product of his strong faith in a divine providence. One Friday afternoon just before Christmas in the late 1950s, John received a call from the Purchasing Department of General Motors. He was told that beginning January 1st the company must lower the price of each rear view mirror by 5 cents. That was about a 5% cut in revenues and enough to wipe out any profit the company would make on GM's business. He was very upset with the harsh way the company was being treated by its best customer: no warning, no discussion, no opportunity to protect the company. He decided to keep this information to himself rather than spoil everyone's Christmas holiday. He walked downstairs to the factory and visited with the people on the floor. While talking with the workers on the silvering line, he asked if anyone had ideas about how they might take some cost out of production. One of the ideas that came up was to purchase plate glass in a slightly larger size and get five mirrors out of each blank rather than four. As soon as possible, he had Purchasing check on the availability of the larger size. The answer came back that the larger size was available and cheaper because the larger size was a standard size. The company had been paying a premium for the smaller non-standard size. This amounted to a savings of 5 cents per mirror in material and labor costs. Incidents such as this formed the rock-solid conviction John held about the power and benefits of employee participation.

In addition to his encyclopedic knowledge, he had the gift of practical wisdom, the third cardinal virtue. This enabled him to see the practical value of the Scanlon Plan as a management tool to establish the value of financial equity for the employees of the company. It was his practical wisdom that caused him to say yes when Rensis Likert asked the company to participate in a major research project on the use of employee diagnostic surveys as an organization development tool. It was his practical wisdom that prompted him to decline another Likert invitation to join a research project on Human Asset Accounting. John knew instinctively that the true value of the human organization could not be reduced to a mathematical fact. Likert's first project, Survey Guided Development, is alive and well. I use it often in my consulting. The Donnelly Corporation uses it to this day, 30 years later. Human Asset Accounting was tried for a few years in other companies and abandoned to the graveyard of intriguing, but unworkable, projects.

Another example of John's practical wisdom occurred in a discussion he was having with Art Thornbury, the Production and Manufacturing Engineering Manager for the then new Donnelly Mirrors, Ltd. factory in Ireland. John wanted to know Art's opinion of one of the more technical manufacturing processes. Art said the process had been explained to him in a way that contradicted what he considered to be good engineering practice, but he said he would withhold his concerns and see how the process worked out. John encouraged him not to acquiesce and not to withhold his knowledge and experience but to challenge everything until it made good practical sense to him. John not only possessed the virtue of practical wisdom but he encouraged it in others. This was a key element of John's idea of participation.

The fourth cardinal virtue, Novak describes as the right touch in giving each person and each matter its due; this is the virtue of justice. John was able to talk as easily with employees on the factory floor as with senior managers, major customers, government officials or even a council of bishops. He did not respect people of great status more than those with blue collars. He respected everyone very highly. He had a keen sense of justice and examined every aspect of his business to be sure that justice and equity were being served. Long before the environmental movement developed a head of steam, he moved at considerable expense to clean up a water discharge that was not toxic but was an esthetic problem. The water discolored a very minute portion of Lake Macatawa where the factory waste water emptied into the lake. No Department of Environmental Quality forced him to do it. The community loved its lake and it didn't look good, and that was enough for him to act.

Under John's leadership we never hesitated to act on a matter of social justice. We attempted a variety of affirmative action plans and participated in programs to employ the unemployable. John viewed the company as an institution of society and the community and, therefore, an institution with a responsibility to and for the community. His support of the Scanlon Plan was prompted by his sense of justice. His desire to see justice done was also the reason why he was so eager to promote the Scanlon Plan to other companies. In 1966, while I was Training Director of another Scanlon company, I convened a meeting of several western Michigan Scanlon companies and it was there that I first met John. John picked up on the idea and provided the leadership that changed that meeting into an association which, 30 years later, is still actively promoting the ideas of the Scanlon Plan.

John was not unique among CEO's in his extensive knowledge or in his practice of the cardinal virtues I have described, rare but not unique. Still he was considerably more successful than most in creating an organization whose hallmarks were participation, equity and trust. John had one more special ingredient that went beyond the cardinal virtues, a force that enabled him to be more consistent and more successful in his practice of management.

And, this is the major point I wish to make today: what made John Donnelly unique among business leaders, and the reason for his successes as a CEO, was his religion. For John, religion was not something saved for Sundays, it was the driving force in his life and in everything he did, including managing a manufacturing company. You cannot possibly understand John's actions and his successes without understanding his very strong religious motivations.

On the surface, we can characterize him as a typical devout American Irish Catholic. He attended church regularly and participated fully in the sacramental life of the Catholic Church. He was well read in philosophy and theology. In these, he was better educated than 99% of Catholic lay people and more than half of the clergy. He was very much a Thomist and strongly attracted to Aquinas' zealous pursuit of the truth. He was a serious student of two prominent 20th century Thomists: Jacques Maritain and Bernard Lonergan. He was first introduced to Thomistic philosophy by Maritain while he was a student here at Notre Dame. Later he became a fan of Lonergan. In 1977, he wrote telling me of a new book by the Jesuit, Bernard Tyrell, entitled *Bernard Lonergan's Philosophy of God*. And I quote from John's letter:

"Lonergan, in my estimation, has done more for Thomism and truth seeking than any person since Aquinas. He is developing a following among philosophers and theologians both Catholic and Protestant. While he does not often address questions of the application of philosophy to life's problems, he is very much aware that the future of mankind depends on having a sound basis for our knowing."

He has what he calls the transcendental imperatives:

Be attentive
Be intelligent
Be reasonable
Be responsible
Be loving
Develop and, if necessary, change

These imperatives he says are the way to truth. They are also the way to love, to social justice and to the Omega point."

John's reference to the Omega point refers to the writing of Teilard de Chardin. John was very familiar with the work of Chardin and often made reference to Chardin's Omega point, that state of perfection toward which evolution is aimed.

The preceding list of John's intellectual interests is not exhaustive, but it does cover his major interests and I cite it to show that he was neither your average Catholic layman nor your average businessman. What I described above was the visible and intellectual side of his religious life, but it was the spiritual side of his religion that really set John part.

As we explore this, let's listen to some of John's own words. In a company and family history John describes the religious character of his grandmother and of his father. About his grandmother he said: "Her outstanding trait, perhaps the source of her cheerfulness, was an abiding faith in God. Indeed, she appeared to live with Christ as a constant companion." And commenting on his father, he said: "Like his mother, he seemed to have God unobtrusively near."

Both of these statements could be made about John himself. He did not preach religion to his business associates, and many with whom he worked were never aware of the depth of his religious faith. Those who did not understand his deepest motivation simply saw a man who was kind, trustworthy, respectful, polite, and very smart. But today I cannot fully describe his legacy without explaining his religious motivation.

I discussed religion often with John and had the good fortune to be exposed to this powerful side of his character. John did live with Christ as a constant companion. John's religion was not a religion about Jesus, it was the religion of Jesus. Being a Christian to him meant very simply trying to live his life as Christ lived: serving others and in all matters, living the prayer "Thy will be done." Love one another is a basic tenet in all religions. John heard the whole of Jesus' message at the Last Supper: Love one another as I have loved you. It isn't enough to love on our terms. The ideal which John tried to practice was to love on Christ's terms.

Like all businessmen, John studied and practiced management, marketing, finance and technology, but as he did, he sought to use the knowledge and skills of the businessman in a Christlike manner. This was the dimension that gave John his edge.

For him, participation was not a search for a popular decision. It was always the search for truth, justice and excellence, popular or not. If you hadn't done your homework, you could be in trouble participating with John. Once an employee challenged John, asking him: "How much more improvement do you want? Aren't you ever satisfied?" John's answer was: "I won't ask for more improvement if you promise not to ask for more pay." On the other hand, if your position was sound, John would gladly support it. John's concept of participation was not a game to make people feel good. It was a way to discover truth and better ways of doing things. He expected participation to be a struggle. Achieving good things usually requires a struggle.

So now we have a CEO who was smart, who was virtuous, and whose secret ingredient was a very deep Christian faith.

So what's my point? Am I suggesting that you must be a Thomistic philosopher in order to succeed in business? No, I am not. Am I suggesting you must be a devout Catholic to be able to do the things John Donnelly did? No, I am not. But I don't want to get ahead of myself, so before I make my point, let's talk about John Donnelly's work and his achievements on the frontier of participative management.

In his first 20 years as President of Donnelly Mirrors, most of his attention was focused on the survival of the business. He took over at the depth of the Great Depression when things were anything but stable. During WWII, he was able to get some war production which kept the company alive and provided a new product technology that put them into the automotive supply business following the war. This was the foundation upon which the current company is built.

In 1952, John installed the Scanlon Plan. The Scanlon Plan was then and still is a cutting-edge program that has three principal components: a highly participative management system, a formal employee involvement process, and an employee bonus to equitably share increases in productivity and profit with all of the company's employees. This was to be his first formal experience with participative management, but participative management was not his reason for adopting the Scanlon Plan. His main reason for adopting the Scanlon Plan was his sense of equity and fairness. Following WWII, Donnelly Mirrors, like many companies, had a myriad of out-of-control individual incentive plans. These, he said, were inequitable and divisive, and to replace the many individual incentive plans with one Scanlon bonus was more equitable and unifying. It was also practical in that it was more cost effective and administratively simpler. So he installed the Scanlon Plan to correct a compensation problem and then he began to discover and learn about participative management. Apparently he didn't learn fast enough because in 1960, he was shocked when the employees petitioned for a union election. He recognized immediately that the employees' interest in a union expressed their need to have a greater say in matters that affected them, their desire for greater participation. He opposed the union, but not in a typical competitive or adversarial way. He agreed that employees should have more say in matters of interest to them but he considered it management's responsibility to provide the means for appropriate participation. He was not willing to abdicate that responsibility to any outside third party. The employees voted not to have a union and John responded by becoming a much more serious student and practitioner of participative management.

He heard and understood de Tocqueville's observation that the more a people control their own government, the more it frees them to engage in cooperative efforts to improve their life situation. He created the Donnelly Committee, a representative group to review company policies and issues affecting the work community. And, as the Donnelly Committee gave people more influence in the company, they did participate and cooperate more in improving company performance.

He heard and learned from other authorities such as Drucker, McGregor, Likert, and Maslow. Before I started working for Donnelly Mirrors, I told John about Blake and Mouton's Managerial Grid; an intensive week-long training program in participative management. John saw value in this training and sent every Donnelly salaried employee, about 50 employees, to the week-long course. At that time this one decision resulted in an expenditure equal to about 20% of the company's annual profit. This was an example of his commitment and willingness to put his money where his heart was.

This also led to my joining the company. I had been unable to get anyone from my previous company to take an interest in Managerial Grid training. When I realized I was having more influence and success at Donnelly's, I asked John for a job.

With his guidance and support we made great strides in expanding employee participation. We pioneered the use of work teams in production and at all levels of the company. Work teams met regularly to solve problems and find ways to improve work. Prior to work teams, there was a traditional Scanlon production committee suggestion process. In its first year, work teams generated cost savings three times greater than under the old system. During this period employee bonuses averaged about 15% of their pay each month. The company consistently lowered product prices and profits grew to very healthy levels.

With a good participation process in place and good bonuses satisfying people's equity concerns, John turned his attention to the planning process as he felt this was a better source of motivation than the Scanlon bonuses. In a 1981 letter, he wrote:

> I believe a strong distinction should be drawn between incentives and motivation. Incentives encourage people to concentrate on the reward, not the work to be done. They encourage many non-productive behaviors. Motivation, on the other hand, is an internal drive that is released by worthwhile goals. Goals ought to start the process for humans. People will willingly work toward organizational goals if they believe them to be worthwhile. Providing a livelihood is a minimum goal. If the work involved is creative or helpful to others, the motivational forces become stronger. The more the CEO can provide a wholesome standard for the worth of company objectives, the more willingly the people will support these objectives.

He gave a great deal of attention to the whole planning process. Most business management planning processes are only concerned with the 'what' and 'how-to' of the company's work; the 'what' being sales and revenue goals, quality and customer satisfaction goals, and so on. The 'how-to' of planning includes budgets, staffing requirements, sales programs, etc. These, of course, are necessary for efficiency and productivity. The element John began to add was the 'why' of the company's work, the real meaning in human terms for all of the company's constituents. For John the 'why' was always defined as service to others, helping others. In religious terms it is: love one another. As John said in the preceding quote—when work is helpful to others, the motivation forces become stronger.

In the terms of the Maslow five-level motivation model, pay, benefits and job security address levels 1, 2 and 3. And, for most non-management workers, companies give very little attention to any needs beyond level 3. Interesting and challenging work, which is a component of most managerial and professional work, satisfies the self-esteem needs of Maslow's level 4. Maslow's level-5 needs get an honorable mention in management training programs but are not seriously addressed in the world of work. We have had several generations of managers who believe that people, at least the people they hire, are motivated solely by economic needs. Because John believed that people had a need for meaning in their lives well beyond economic needs, he tried to put more meaning into their work and the work of the company. He believed, with Victor Frankl, the author of *Man's Search for Meaning,* that the desire for meaning was more true to human nature than the desire for pleasure. He agreed with Maslow that the best managers help workers satisfy their needs for truth and beauty and goodness, as Maslow defined level 5. This was no easy task and I doubt that John was ever satisfied with his results in this area because his expectations were so high. However, his interest and efforts are there for us to see and they are part of the legacy he left for us to build upon. In a paper he wrote in 1977 to clarify the purpose and work of the company, he started with this John Ruskin quote: "The highest reward for man's work is not what he gets for it but what he becomes by it."

His interest in meaningfulness was not limited to employees of the company. Another thing that troubled John was the role of shareholders in the modern corporation. He felt that shareholders should be active and responsible participants in the business. He saw modern shareholders as investors with no more interest in the company, its affairs or its products than the financial return on their investment. Because he believed so strongly that people are much more than the wealth they might accumulate he felt that shareholders should be interested in more than how many dollars their investment might bring them. He tried to involve his own shareholders with more regular communications and special meetings. These efforts were somewhat successful and he never ceased to encourage responsible ownership or trusteeship.

It is a pity that John did not meet Robert Greenleaf while they were both alive. John was on the same "servant leadership" wave length as Greenleaf and I'm sure they could have been great collaborators on issues such as the stewardship responsibilities of boards, owners and managers. For those of you who are attracted to the Donnelly legacy, I recommend that you also look into the work of the Greenleaf Center for Servant Leadership located in Indianapolis. They are an advocacy and educational institute promoting the same kind of service to others and responsible business leadership that characterized the work of John Donnelly.

Using Greenleaf's concept of servant leadership I can now give you a simple model that puts John Donnelly's character and motivation into perspective.

Servant leader <—> Predatory leader

Starting with servant leadership or servant business management as an ideal of Christian service, as one pole of a continuum, we can identify its polar opposite as predator leadership or predatory business management. You can use this continuum from servant to predator to analyze company cultures, business practices and specific decisions. Every day we see examples of predatory business practices. Some are truly mean, most are petty. We see downsizing, excessive executive pay, exploitation of third-world workers and petty office politics. We even have books entitled "How to Swim with Sharks." But John Donnelly was as far from the predator pole and as close to the servant pole as any CEO I have ever known. And this is my point in telling you about his very deep religious motivation. I believe his model of servant leadership to be the very essence of his legacy.

We have been trying to solve the problems of people at work with secular, humanistic behavioral science approaches for the past 50 years with very limited success. I don't believe we will make real progress until we recognize that man is truly a spiritual and religious being, and take the approach modeled by John Donnelly.

I am an unrepentant optimist and I see a shift away from predatory leadership and to servant leadership. I am encouraged by the Novak book, the Greenleaf Center, and by this lecture series. But I also want to make the point that John Donnelly was doing servant leadership when servant leadership wasn't cool. Predatory practices were the norm during most of John's career. He chose to break with the norm and move to higher ground. His courage and commitment are also part of his legacy.

The specifics of other activities to advance participative management at Donnelly's are not unique, they are typical of the many organizational changes and organizational development efforts of the past 30 years. As I have said repeatedly, the difference was the driving force, John's spirituality. Some of you may have seen and read the *Harvard Business Review* article that reports an interview with John, and contains additional details of the Donnelly experience.* As you follow the interview, note the number of changes mentioned in the article. He was learning as he went, so changes were frequent as new insights developed. What the article does not touch on is why he was so persistent in creating a human organization. I can tell you from my consulting experience that it is much more common for managers to fold when they encounter resistance or failure. Remember the transcendental imperatives from the Lonergan quote. The last one was: "Develop and, if necessary, change." John believed this imperative and he 'walked his talk.'

---

* Ewing, D. W., "Participative Management at Work: An interview with John F. Donnelly," *Harvard Business Review,* Jan–Feb. 1977, pp. 117–127.

What we have covered are these major elements in John Donnelly's efforts to implement participative management.

- He first put the company on a sound product/financial foundation.
- He introduced the Scanlon Plan, developed it into one of the most successful and enduring of Scanlon Plans and contributed to the spread of this pioneering program of equity and participation to other companies.
- He encouraged the development of highly participative work teams which increased employee participation five-fold.
- He then turned his attention to better planning and creating meaningful work for the company, its workers and shareholders.

These were his major thrusts and the more visible features of his legacy.

I also want to share a few ideas that I have been working on over the past few years. The first is a model of how management has evolved through the 20th century and where it appears to be headed in the 21st.

This model is based on the work of Rensis Likert. When John and I began working with Likert on survey-guided development, Likert had identified an evolving model of 4 systems of management. He observed that management practices were progressing from System 1–Authoritarian to System 4–Participative. His model is similar to McGregor's famous Theory X, Theory Y model. Likert was more of a scientist than McGregor and so his model is more detailed and precise. I think it was Likert's scientific precision that attracted John.

By systems of management, we mean the whole complex array of interacting and inter-related activities and practices of management in an organization. These include values, strategies, structure, policies, goals, standards, controls, communications, decision-making processes, rewards, relationships, responsibilities and authority.

There is a schematic of the evolution of management systems in the 20th century and approximate dates of their emergence.

System 1	System 2	System 3	System 4	System 5
Authoritarian →	Paternalistic →	Consultative →	Participative →	Partnership
1910	1930	1950	1970	1990

System 1, the authoritarian model, is characterized by a few leaders who have and exercise all authority because they alone are educated and know all the answers. Authoritarian business management was appropriate in 1900 for an illiterate, inexperienced, immigrant workforce and it still works in emergencies and, of course, in most of the classrooms of the world. System 1, in business, does not always respect people and it led to abusive practices.

As the workforce developed knowledge, skills and experience, they demanded better physical working conditions and forced management to System 2, which we call paternalistic. Workers forced this change by forming unions to bargain with management and by using the political process to enact government regulations more favorable to workers. The Great Depression and Roosevelt's New Deal made great changes in the world of work and made paternalistic management the norm. System 2 is still very authoritarian but it is nicer, hence the term, paternalistic. Paternalism has a pejorative connotation which always bothered John. He would remind me that paternalism wasn't all bad, for instance, the good father in a family and especially God the Father. He wished that Likert would have used a term such as benevolent despotism.

Once that plateau had been reached and, with the economic expansion following WWII, we saw the emergence of System 3. The education and experience level of the workforce had grown substantially and people had ideas which they wanted heard. System 3 is consultative. This is when the manager says: "Before I make my decision on this, I'd like to get your input." The manager agrees to consult with the employees but doesn't really give up much authority. Richard Hackman, who spoke in this series in 1992, calls this transitional management. He sees it as the transition from authoritarian to participative, from Theory X to Theory Y. The problem is that System 3 has not been a transitional system. Most managers today are stuck at System 3: consulting but not really sharing authority. It was System 3 that caused the Quality Circle initiative to fizzle in the United States. It is System 3 that is responsible for most employee discontent and lack of commitment today.

Beyond consultative is System 4 which is participative. In this system real authority is shared with people. Decision making is pushed down to levels where good information is available. To really delegate, management must be sure that everyone knows and is committed to the goals of the organization. That is why John Donnelly turned his attention to the planning process. Setting and communicating direction is essential to significant employee participation. Likert discovered System 4 in small units and departments in larger organizations. He did not find an entire System 4 organization, not even Donnelly Mirrors, although this was John's conscious goal.

Once, John and I and Ren Likert met with the Donnelly production foremen. I think it was Nick Lindsay who said that he liked Likert's idea of System 4, and believed that John truly supported it and that the foremen were trying to make it work on the factory floor. But, Nick said, there didn't seem to be much support for the idea between the President and the foremen. We had a good laugh—but Nick was right. The middle managers at Donnelly were having just as much trouble getting to System 4 as were managers in other companies. It is a struggle to make organizations more human. This is why we can call it a frontier. In the Harvard article I mentioned, John's first observation was that the greatest obstacle on the frontier of participative management was the managers' unwillingness to give up authority.

As I worked with the ideas of System 4, I began to realize that this evolution would continue to System 5 and beyond. We don't know very much yet about System 5. We know enough to say that it will be a progressive step beyond System 4; a system where what is right is more important than who is right; where the operating principle is partnership; partnerships within work groups and partnerships between shifts, between sales and engineering and production, home office and field, and partnerships with customers and suppliers. We see hints of System 5 in certain spikes in organizational performance as when the employees of Delta Airlines took up a collection and bought the company an airplane as an expression of their satisfaction and commitment to the company. Seven thousand employees showed up to christen the plane "The Spirit of Delta." Or, at another Scanlon company, when an entire engineering department postponed their summer vacations to complete a product design and save several hundred production employees from a temporary layoff. We also see evidence of System 5 in volunteer organizations such as the Peace Corps and many service organizations. We saw it in the city of Portland last winter during some serious flooding. People are capable of marvelous acts of cooperation and joint effort. When we learn how to manage in ways that stimulate high levels of consistent cooperation, we will have discovered System 5. Then we can begin to look for System 6.

Another issue I have been working on is the development of participative leaders. We have a program that helps managers and teams learn participative management practices. We don't agree with the popular notion of leaderless work groups. We don't think the solution to poor leadership is the elimination of leaders. We believe that participative management requires a new type of leadership which can be learned. Participative leadership is the responsibility of all members of the work group, not just the boss. The formal leader has certain tasks to perform as do the members. Participative leadership has four major areas of responsibility:

- to develop people as individuals
- to develop work teams and teamwork between teams
- to guide and facilitate the work of the team and individual members
- to focus and coordinate all work on the operating goals of the department and the strategic goals of the company

We have constructed a questionnaire which a team administers to itself. This survey measures the status of team leadership in the four responsibility areas and generates information the team needs to improve its leadership practices and teamwork. It is a process as old as Socrates where we help the team ask itself the right questions, and they are responsible for their answers and any change that might be required.

Remember Lonergan's transcendental imperatives. This leadership program employs all six of them:

- be attentive (the survey)
- be intelligent (analyze and learn from the survey results)
- be reasonable (take appropriate actions)
- be responsible (follow through on planned actions)
- be loving (cooperate and encourage each other)
- develop and, if necessary, change (continuous improvement)

Finally, I want to discuss the planning process. I have always been persuaded, as John was, of the primacy of planning in any system of management. But only recently, as I struggle to understand System 5 and my imagination teases me with thoughts of System 6, have I begun to see a new dimension to business planning. This comes from the essence of System 5 which is partnership. If, as System 5 suggests, a business is a partnership, then it should be operated for the mutual benefit of all partners.

The partners can be conceptualized as a 5-point star-shaped model, involving customers, shareholders, employees, suppliers, and the community. Each of the partners contributes to the success of the company and each has needs they wish to satisfy as their reason for joining in the partnership.

Customers need and are willing to pay for food or TVs or tax advice. For this, they want value. *Shareholders* have a capital surplus which they are willing to invest. For this, they want a return sufficient to cover their risk. *Employees* have knowledge and skills and are willing to work. For this, they want satisfaction of needs that span the whole Maslow hierarchy from survival to service. *Suppliers* have goods and services for sale for which they want payment and a continuing relationship. *Communities* need employment for their citizens and are willing to provide the necessary physical, societal and economic infrastructure. System 5 holds that the business should be managed in a way that *balances* this galaxy of inputs and outputs. So the planning process should include this criteria of balance. If managers would apply themselves diligently to discovering the needs of all five constituents, we would see real meaning begin to surface and guide businesses and the world of work.

For me, this idea has powerful possibilities beyond our imagination. Management must occupy a position in the center of this model and manage the partnership. Management must provide the leadership that will enable all partners to understand and support the full partnership. If management tips the balance to any one partner, all other partners suffer. Currently, we are seeing an imbalance toward shareholders driven by pressures from Wall Street and the big investment firms. Every authority I can find agrees that quarterly financial reports and pressure for short-term performance is hurting business. I think this partnership orientation to planning is a way to restore the system to balance, and the way to put real meaning into the world of work. It would certainly be more just and I believe a very sound long-term business strategy. A partnership planning process would give the business a much healthier strategic perspective: that for the business to grow it must meet the needs of all partners. A business that fails to meet the needs of one partner risks the withdrawal of that partner's contribution and ultimately the survival of the business. For instance, when a business fails to meet the legitimate needs of its workers, we see a decline in performance and customer service, followed by a decline in sales and profit. This then reduces the ability of the business to serve shareholders, suppliers and the community.

A business that satisfies all partners will be able to attract a greater contribution from all partners, which causes the business to grow. A management team that creates a culture where all of the partners are actively looking for ways to serve one another may very well discover the most powerful motivational force ever seen in business. I believe this approach, which John seemed to follow intuitively, to be one of the causes of the 90-year success of the Donnelly Corporation.

These are some of the ideas I have developed from the legacy I received from John Donnelly. I invite you to consider this rich legacy and help expand this important frontier. We must continue to refine the practices and techniques of business leadership just as we must continue to develop new products and technologies. But I am convinced that we won't fully solve the human problem of people at work unless and until we, like John Donnelly, choose servant leadership, servant management, and servant business practices.

A Man of Transactions

Terrence Rafferty

Steven Spielberg's "Schindler's List" is a great movie, and, like all great works, it feels both impossible and inevitable. In the opening pages of the 1982 book (of the same name) on which the film is based, the author, Thomas Keneally, tells the reader, "This is the story of the pragmatic triumph of good over evil, a triumph in eminently measurable, statistical, unsubtle terms," and then confesses to an odd sort of trepidation: "It is a risky enterprise to have to write of virtue." The writer's admission is staggering, because "Schindler's List" is a true story about the Holocaust: you would think that an artist who has taken on the task of portraying that unimaginably monstrous event wouldn't consider the representation of virtue his most daunting challenge. But the story of Oskar Schindler—a dashing and resourceful German Catholic businessman who saved over a thousand Polish Jews from almost certain annihilation—is extraordinary even by the standards of Holocaust literature, in which every kind of human behavior *except* the merely ordinary can be found. And, in a sense, Schindler's goodness really is more mysterious—tougher to account for intellectually—than the Nazis' evil, because his actions seem not to have been determined by anything resembling a conscious political, religious, or social principle. He wasn't an idealist (much less an ideologue), but he took the sort of risks that a fanatic or a willful martyr might take, and never troubled to explain himself. According to Keneally, many of the people Schindler rescued still say, "I don't know why he did it."

The triumph of the book is that Keneally's faithful, exhaustively detailed chronicle of Schindler's wartime activities never fully answers the question "Why?" and, besides, persuades us that it would be foolish to try: heroism of this magnitude is, at its heart, inexplicable. Spielberg also respects the mystery of Schindler's personality, and part of what makes the film so moving is that an ambiguous, complex hero is something entirely new in this director's work. The sheer unexpectedness of Spielberg's rigorous refusal to simplify his protagonist's motives seems to connect him, in a minor but distinct way, to Schindler himself; this character is, after all, a man whose dedication and commitment to righteous action simply could not have been predicted from the evidence of his prewar life. That's the beauty of the story. What Schindler does during the years of Nazi oppression appears to constitute a kind of self-transcendence, but it's really more like an improbable self-fulfillment: in the unique, deranged circumstances of occupied Poland, his shortcomings, and even his vices, somehow turn into instruments of virtue.

Spielberg introduces Schindler with a scene of his preparations for an evening out in Kraków. Before we're shown the hero's face, we see his elegant clothes and the swastika pin that gleams in his lapel. Schindler (Liam Neeson) arrives at a swank night club filled with Nazi officials and expensively dressed women, and looks as if he were right at home. He's handsome, confident, and worldly—the very image of the man of affairs. It doesn't take him long to become the center of attention: he drinks and laughs with the Nazis, and appears to be having the time of his life. The only hint that there might be something unusual about this prosperous-looking backslapper is provided by a handful of closeups of Schindler's watchful face in the moments just before he moves in on the Nazis. He gazes at them coldly, clinically, and it's impossible to tell whether the look in his eyes reflects deep-seated disdain or merely the pragmatic attitude of a businessman plotting his social tactics as he prepares to initiate a potentially advantageous contact. The uncertainty about the protagonist's character which Spielberg creates in this superbly directed sequence establishes the tone of the movie's treatment of Schindler, and, precarious as it is, it's precisely the right tone. Schindler, having failed at several businesses in Germany, has come to Kraków with the intention of making some easy money in the wartime economy. Poland, he feels, offers tremendous opportunities for someone like him—an energetic entrepreneur who knows how to get things done and isn't burdened by an overscrupulous sense of business ethics. The best opportunities, of course, have been created by the Reich's systematic destruction of the Jewish community, and in the film's first hour we see Schindler, apparently without qualms, buying a Jewish-owned factory for next to nothing, staffing it entirely with Jewish workers (because their labor costs far less than that of Polish Gentiles), and taking possession of a large, airy apartment vacated by a family that has been forced to move into the city's ghetto. And in these swift and sometimes darkly funny early passages Spielberg gives us glimpses of several other somewhat unsavory aspects of Schindler's character: the movie's hero, we learn, is also an enthusiastic participant in the city's black market and an inveterate philanderer. (His wife has remained in their prewar home, in Moravia, and, prudently, doesn't pay him many visits while he's in Poland.)

Schindler, nestled in a fur-collared coat, strides through this ugly world with a curious air of innocence. He's a war profiteer, but he obviously sees no harm in the way he's making his fortune. He treats the workers at his factory, which makes pots and pans for the German Army, reasonably well, and although they're basically slave labor, their employment provides them some tangible benefit: they can be considered essential to the war effort, and therefore (they hope) a little less likely to be deported to a concentration camp. Schindler is the sort of wheeler-dealer who closes even his most outrageous business propositions with a cheerful "And everybody's happy!"—and seems to actually mean it. The grotesque disparity in the degrees of "happiness" enjoyed by the Nazi occupiers and his Jewish employees doesn't appear to trouble him much; he's not gifted with a keen sense of irony. And, besides, he's just an entrepreneurial capitalist, doing what such men have always done—making money according to the conditions of whatever social system happens to obtain, without passing judgment on the system's fairness.

The hero's evolution from an unreflective profiteer to a conscious and daring rescuer of the Jews is portrayed, both in the book and in the film, with extraordinary subtlety. Keneally provides more detail, but Neeson's quietly brilliant performance makes up for the movie's elisions: this is nuanced and utterly unsentimental acting—exactly what the role requires. Schindler, who is no philosopher, never delivers the sort of high minded speech that tells us how he made the decision to use his friendly relations with the Nazis for the purpose of resistance rather than of profit. A speech of that sort would violate the nature of Schindler's heroism, which is instinctual, unpremeditated; like a soldier in the heat of battle, he's just responding as quickly and as effectively as he can to the chaotic events around him.

In the movie, however, it's possible to identify a turning point in the hero's consciousness—not because Spielberg crudely signals a change but because he uses the resources of film so powerfully that we, in the audience, feel a profound transformation in our relation to the historical drama we're witnessing. About an hour into the film, Spielberg stages the liquidation of the Krakow ghetto, and in this turbulent and almost unbearably vivid fifteen-minute sequence, the Holocaust, fifty years removed from our contemporary consciousness, suddenly becomes overwhelmingly immediate, undeniable. Spielberg, using his prodigious visual skills with an urgency and an imaginative intensity that he hasn't shown in a long time, creates images that have the force of intimate experience, the terrible clarity of your own most indelible memories. Summary executions are performed, in chillingly objective medium shots, on Kraków's beautiful streets; the narrow corridors of the ghetto's tenements become nightmarishly claustrophobic as the Jewish families rousted out of their apartments try to move quickly enough to satisfy the armed, shooting S.S. men; flashes of machine-gun fire light up the dark stairwells; abandoned suitcases litter the alleys and courtyards; soldiers fire into the walls and ceilings, to dispose of anyone who might be hiding on the other side; thousands of Jews are herded brutally through the old city, and Schindler, watching from a hilltop, tries to track the progress of a little girl in a red coat as she makes her way, alone, through the smoke-filled streets. Sights like these make us feel—viscerally, and in the most concrete terms—the obscenity of the Reich's treatment of the Jews, and the strength of our own reactions tells us that this must be the moment in which amiable Oskar Schindler begins to entertain the idea of subverting the system that has enriched him.

For the rest of the film—which runs better than three hours and doesn't seem a minute too long—Schindler's cunning manipulations of high-level Nazis play out against the background of the increasingly horrific experiences of Kraków's Jews. As the Final Solution gathers momentum, the people who survived the liquidation of the ghetto are sent to the Plaszów labor camp, and there they live under the constant threat of slow death from exhaustion or hunger, and of sudden, violent death at the hands of their captors: the camp's sadistic commandant, Amon Goeth, takes target practice from the balcony of his villa, picking off prisoners at random as they walk across the compound. Schindler puts his disreputable talents to good use, cozying up to the psychotic Goeth and bribing and cajoling him—one man of the world to another—into granting the businessman the most unlikely concessions. Not only is Schindler allowed to continue operating his factory, with the same workforce, but he obtains permission to turn the plant into a sub-camp and move "his" Jews onto its premises. And, late in the war, when deportations to the extermination camps are occurring at an accelerated rate, Schindler contrives to establish a new factory, in Czechoslovakia, and to have eleven hundred Jewish workers who were scheduled for transport to the camps diverted to his facility. He purchases the reprieve of each of the Jews on his list individually, out of his (rapidly dwindling) profits; and then he has to pay yet again, to liberate three hundred women who wind up, mistakenly, at Auschwitz-Birkeneau. "It was Oskar's nature," Keneally writes, "to believe that you could drink with the devil and adjust the balance of evil over a snifter of cognac. It was not that he found more radical methods frightening. It was that they did not occur to him. He'd always been a man of transactions."

The irony of Schindler's methods is that his temperamental indifference to ethical niceties is precisely what makes him an effective champion of the powerless Jews he employs. If he had been a more scrupulous man, he couldn't have done what he did. An idealist would never have dreamed, in the first place, of setting up a business to profit from the misfortune of the Polish Jews; and an idealist would have been sickened to the point of incapacity at having to spend so much time drinking and schmoozing with the likes of Amon Goeth. The people who work for Schindler are lucky to be under the protection of a man who combines the recklessness of a pirate and the oily mendacity of a confidence man; a Gandhi couldn't have served them nearly so well. What's genuinely inspiring about Schindler is that in one crucial respect he did diverge, spontaneously and unquestioningly, from his instincts as "a man of transactions": when his financial interests stopped coinciding with the single, urgent interest of his workers, which was survival, he chose to dedicate himself to *their* interest. By the end of the war, he had spent so much money implementing the ever more elaborate schemes necessary to save the Jews that he was totally wiped out. From the prospective of our own rapacious times, a businessman who values his workers' lives over his own profits seems almost inconceivably noble.

Entrepreneurship and Leadership: Common Trends and Common Threads

Robert P. Vecchio

INTRODUCTION

In recent years, a challenging question has re-emerged: Does the study of entrepreneurship constitute a separate and distinct field of inquiry within the social sciences? As noted by Shane and Venkataraman (2000), one can ask whether research in entrepreneurship predicts phenomena beyond what is known in other fields (p. 217). If the constructs and results of such research are not sufficiently unique, then knowledge related to both the birth of firms and the management of small businesses should be subsumed under the heading of other fields (e.g., leadership or interpersonal influence). Arguably, entrepreneurship needs to be defined with reference to a setting or context (e.g., start-up firms) and in terms of actions taken by an individual within such a specific setting. These actions fall under two broad headings: attempts at influencing others and exploiting opportunities. Efforts to influence others and gain advantage from opportunities can be justifiably aligned with the established areas of leadership and interpersonal influence. Hence, the essence of entrepreneurship's potential uniqueness stems from its focus on small-business ownership or firm start-up. Of course, this represents merely a narrow, specific context for studying the manifestation of social influence. The key question remains: Are social dynamics so distinctly different in these contexts that the broader field of leadership cannot adequately incorporate available empirical results? Further, what (if any) are the unique implications of available evidence on entrepreneurial individuals for human resources training and development?

In the present article, the above questions will be explored, along with the further issue of integrating entrepreneurship research and theory into the more established traditions of leadership and management. It is hoped that such an integration will aid the design of future research in these areas by highlighting the common trends and common threads of thought that underlie these scholarship streams. Finally, a model is delineated that joins process dynamics with micro- (psychological) and macro- (contextual) influences.

WHY THE SPLIT?

It is difficult to determine the processes that led to the emergence of entrepreneurship as a relatively distinct field within the organizational sciences.[1] One explanation is that its dual footings in psychology and economics have contributed to the creation of a separate character or identity. That is to say, the economics basis of the field (with its emphasis on rationality and the study of societal aggregates; Schumpeter, 1934, 1939, 1947) could not easily merge with the psychological foundation (with its emphasis on traits, personal drives, and social dynamics). Perhaps these parent disciplinary perspectives prompted ambivalent attitudes among the majority of researchers toward the topics within entrepreneurship and, thereby, encourage the emergence of a separate field of study. Furthermore, research in the economics tradition tends to focus on observable outcomes, while research in the psychological tradition tends to focus on intervening, unobservable processes as well as observable outcomes. Moreover, it has been often noted that data on many aspects of entrepreneurs are possibly more difficult to obtain (Shane & Venkataraman, 2000, p. 219). For example, response rates in entrepreneurship survey studies are notably low (for the studies cited in this review, (a) the median response rate was only 37%, (b) none of the studies reported the results of statistical power analysis, and (c) few of the studies examined response bias by comparing respondents with non-respondents). In addition, there is an openness to studying student samples as proxies for entrepreneurs (presumably, because of the trade-off of sample convenience for sample relevance). Perhaps not too surprisingly, empirical results within the area of entrepreneurship are often mixed and inconclusive.

---

1. In the following discussion, a conventional distinction is adopted among entrepreneurs (i.e., people who founded a firm), small-business operators/owners (i.e., people who manage, but did not found, a firm), and traditional managers (people who direct and are expected to display leadership within corporate settings). These three classifications are, at the outset, expected to be associated with differences in backgrounds, personal goals, and openness to innovation (Stewart, Watson, Carland, & Carland, 1998).

The distinctly different academic footings of entrepreneurship are also evident in the divergent research streams of "entrepreneurial traits" and "entrepreneurial rates." Entrepreneurial trait research (a major division of the empirical work in the field) focuses on the individual differences of entrepreneurs. For example, this approach examines personality dimensions and psychological drive states as potential explanations of entrepreneurial activity. Entrepreneurial rate research, in contrast, examines environmental influences (often economic conditions) on the propensity to start a business or to innovate. By and large, the rate approach ignores the constructs used by trait researchers, and the trait approach does not incorporate the constructs used by rate researchers. Rate researchers are more likely to be interested in studying changes in the rate of firm formation over time and, therefore, more commonly make use of longitudinal designs (e.g., Shane, 1996). Trait researchers, while praising longitudinal research, more typically adopt cross-sectional designs as part of a survey-based approach. Because of these differences in focus and preferred study design, the two approaches are not particularly informative or instructive to each other. Instead, each approach fosters a knowledge base that may be cumulative within its own orientation, but that also is not amenable to integration.

The distinction between the traits and rates approaches may be best viewed as a distinction between a supply-side perspective and a demand-side perspective (Thornton, 1999). The supply-side approach examines the propensity and availability of individuals for entrepreneurial roles, while the demand-side approach focuses on the number and nature of entrepreneurial roles that need to be filled. The supply-side approach examines the psychology of the individual, while the demand-side focuses on the context. Supply-side, or trait, research takes the context as a given and seeks to explain variation in behaviors and attitudes through examination of individual differences. In contrast, demand-side researchers regard individual differences as being of less importance than the impact of changes in contextual attributes on changes in collective behavior.

An interesting parallel can also be drawn between the traits-supply versus rates-demand approaches, and the trait versus situationalism approaches in the field of leadership. The trait approach to leadership (after failing to establish strong associations) was recognized as being limited because of its exclusion of contextual factors. At present, leadership research acknowledges the importance of (and seeks the integration of) individual-level factors and contextual factors in explaining the differences in effectiveness. A similar rapprochement seems essential for the study of entrepreneurial research.

THE ARGUMENTS FOR A SEPARATE FIELD
OF ENTREPRENEURSHIP

Recently, Shane and Venkataraman (2000) reviewed three arguments for the treatment of entrepreneurship as a distinct field. First, entrepreneurship can be viewed as a societal mechanism that converts technical information into products and services (Arrow, 1962). Second, entrepreneurship is a mechanism that enables the discovery and mitigation of temporal and spatial economic inefficiencies (Kirzner, 1997). Third, entrepreneurially-based innovation drives change in products and services (Schumpeter, 1934).

All of these arguments are economically grounded justifications, rather than behaviorally based. A reliance on an economics-based focus can lead, for example, to the study of such macro influences as economic regional attributes on the rate of new firm creation (Thornton, 1999). Of course, a focus on the influence of regional attributes misses the critical point that regions do not create firms, individuals do. Further, "entrepreneurship" serves as a vague, over-arching term that actually encompasses a fairly wide range of settings (Low & MacMillan, 1988). While generally intended to have reference to a specific setting, the term lacks precision because contexts tend to be broadly aggregated. For example, does entrepreneurship have the same meaning in solo ventures as it does in partnership or team ventures? Does it have the same meaning if personal funds are at stake? Does it have the same meaning for franchise owners versus other arrangements? Does it have the same meaning for Mom-and-Pop stores as for more growth-oriented ventures, etc.? As these contextual distinctions tend to be ignored in many research reports where "entrepreneurs" are aggregated for study, the use of the term entrepreneurship can be expected to contain much imprecision and, thereby, inexactness in prediction.

If entrepreneurship comprises a distinctly different set of phenomena that lies beyond current knowledge in the areas of leadership and social influence, then the published literature on entrepreneurship should provide us with examples of counter-intuitive findings. For instance, we should find patterns of results that indicate that trends or relationships are different or nonexistent in entrepreneurial settings. In essence, certain work settings should serve as moderators of various findings. Small-business settings, firm start-ups, and the like should define the "boundary limits" for our available knowledge. Therefore, the "burden of proof" lies with establishing distinctly different relationships and patterns of results within unique and definable settings. From a psychological perspective, the maintenance of a separate identity for such a line of research is difficult to justify without empirical evidence that the dynamics within specific settings warrant a separate treatment. With this concern as our back-drop, let us now consider the published literature on entrepreneurial behavior.

THE ARGUMENTS AGAINST A SEPARATE FIELD OF ENTREPRENEURSHIP

The scholarly literature on entrepreneurial behavior, attitudes, and predispositions is fairly substantial. Efforts to develop profiles of entrepreneurs and small-business owners (both successful and not) have been numerous. The fruit of these efforts is a set of five attributes that invariably is at the forefront of discussion of entrepreneurial profiles: risk-taking, need for achievement, need for autonomy, self-efficacy, and locus of control (Begley, 1995; Stewart et al., 1998). Arguably, these attributes comprise the "Big Five" personality dimensions within the realm of research on entrepreneurs. In addition to these five dimensions, personal demographics and person–system fit have also received substantial attention. Plus, there is a growing literature on cognitive framing and biases that may be of relevance to entrepreneurs and small-business owners. These cognitive attributes and dynamics include overconfidence, hubris, escalation of commitment, and counterfactual thinking. In the following sections, the findings in these areas are reviewed with an eye toward determining whether the findings are especially unique to founders/managers of firms or if the findings reveal unexpected patterns of results that indicate the need for separate treatment of entrepreneurship. Following a review of these research streams, we will examine neglected topics and consider several new directions for entrepreneurship research.

ENTREPRENEURSHIP'S "BIG FIVE"

Risk-Taking Propensity

On an intuitive level, risk-taking propensity (i.e., a decision-making orientation toward accepting greater likelihood of loss in exchange for greater potential reward) can reasonably be expected to be included in any profile of what might make entrepreneurs distinctly different. However, research on risk-taking propensity has not yielded clear evidence of a relationship. For example, a series of studies by Brockhaus failed to find differences on risk-taking orientation between entrepreneurs and manager groups, as well as the general population (Brockhaus, 1976, 1980a; Brockhaus & Nord, 1979). Similar results were reported by Litzinger (1965) and Masters and Meier (1988). In addition, successful entrepreneurs could not be distinguished from unsuccessful entrepreneurs on risk-taking (Brockhaus, 1980b; Peacock, 1986). In contrast, other studies reported greater risk-taking propensity among entrepreneurs versus managers (Carland, Carland, Carland, & Pierce, 1995; Hull, Bosley, & Udell, 1980; Stewart et al., 1998), and versus the larger population (Broehl, 1978; Liles, 1974; Stewart et al., 1998). Generally, the search for differences has been more successful with measures of personality (such as the Risk-Taking Scale of the Jackson Personality Inventory; Jackson, 1976) than with decision-making exercises (such as Wallach & Kogan's, 1961, Choice Dilemma Questionnaire).

In an effort to reconcile this diversity of findings, Palich and Bagby (1995) used a cognitive-based approach to argue that entrepreneurs may not perceive or accept risk more than non-entrepreneurial counterparts, but rather that they are merely predisposed to access categories that suggest greater potential within business scenarios. Although Palich and Bagby did not find evidence that entrepreneurial "types" were more predisposed to take risks than non-entrepreneurs, they did report that entrepreneurial types categorized equivocal business scenarios more positively than non-entrepreneurial individuals. This finding suggests that the entrepreneurially inclined may tend to view some situations as opportunities, when others perceive similar circumstances as having low potential. On reflection, this interpretation seems somewhat closer to an alternative dimension of optimism or confidence (Cooper, Woo, & Dunkelberg, 1988). Also, this result is not particularly surprising, as findings from lab studies indicate that individuals who are led to believe that they are highly competent at decision-making perceive greater opportunities in a risky choice situation and take more risks. Those who believe they are less competent see greater threats and take fewer risks (Krueger & Dickson, 1994).

Need for Achievement

Studies of McClelland's classic conceptions of basic needs (McClelland & Winter, 1969) have yielded relatively more supportive findings of certain expected differences. For example, high achievement motivation has been associated with some aspects of venture performance (Begly & Boyd, 1987; Carsrud & Olm, 1986). Plus, Stewart et al. (1998) also reported that entrepreneurs were higher in achievement motivation than both corporate managers and small-business owners-managers. Nonetheless, the results have not been uniformly supportive (Brockhaus & Horwitz, 1986; Johnson, 1990). Alternative interpretations of achievement motivation and entrepreneurship that rely on configural notions (i.e., that high, moderate, or low levels of need for achievement should be examined in conjunction with levels of other needs, such as power and affiliation) have not yet been convincingly linked to entrepreneurial activity or success.

Need for Autonomy

As with need for achievement, need for autonomy has often been assumed to be related to entrepreneurial motivation. Definable as the desire to be independent and self-directing (Harrell & Alpert, 1979; McClelland, 1975), need for autonomy has been offered as (a) an underlying motive for why some MBA students may be interested in working for smaller firms (Harrell & Alpert, 1979, p. 260) and (b) a predictor of the successful "fit" of an individual with an entrepreneurial position (Harrell & Alpert, 1979, p. 264). These arguments are based on the premise that larger firms suppress personal freedom and the potential for entrepreneurial initiative. Empirical evidence in support of these contentions, however, is lacking. The intuitive appeal of this reasoning suggests that alternative opportunities for personal expression at work and individual adaptability may be of some consequence. The question of whether need for autonomy operates in a configural manner with other needs has been similarly neglected. In short, the rhetoric surrounding the drive for independence as a core element of entrepreneurial interest, despite its self-evident character, needs to be empirically demonstrated.

Self-Efficacy

Borrowing from Bandura's work on social learning theory (Bandura, 1982; Wood & Bandura, 1989), we can expect that individuals will prefer situations in which they anticipate high personal control, but avoid situations in which low control is anticipated. Following this logic, individual career paths should reflect personal assessments of capabilities for various occupations. Extending these ideas to entrepreneurial activity suggests that those individuals who believe they are capable of performing the roles and tasks of an entrepreneur (i.e., who have strong beliefs in their entrepreneurial self-efficacy) will engage in activities associated with firm start-ups (Boyd & Vozikis, 1994; Scherer, Adams, Carley, & Wiche, 1989). People who are comparatively high on the dimensions of entrepreneurial self-efficacy should perceive more opportunities in a given situation, while people who are low on self-efficacy should perceive more costs and risks. People who are higher on self-efficacy should also feel more competent to cope with perceived obstacles, and should anticipate more positive outcomes. In addition to lab studies that show that people who are led to believe they are very competent will see greater opportunity in a risky choice and take more risks (Krueger & Dickson, 1994), a comparison of small-business founders versus non-founders revealed that founders scored higher on a measure of entrepreneurial self-efficacy (Chen, Greene, & Crick, 1998). Along with explaining why some people avoid entrepreneurial actions (i.e., due to a lack of personal belief in possessing necessary skills, or low self-efficacy), this approach may also help to account for why some entrepreneurs avoid certain critical entrepreneurial activities (e.g., deliberately avoiding company growth because of a fear of losing one's sense of control, due to low self-efficacy concerning specific essential skills).

Locus of Control

Related to research on self-efficacy is work on the broader concept of locus of control (Rotter, 1966). While self-efficacy and locus of control are both cognitive dimensions that are based on notions of control, locus of control is a much broader concept that may be independent of one's sense of task-specific efficacy. Perhaps not surprisingly, studies of locus of control relative to entrepreneurship have had a poor record. For example, Engle, Mah, and Sadri (1997) were not able to distinguish between small-business owners and a sample of employees based on Rotter's (1966) scale, nor could Chen et. al. (1998) distinguish between founders and non-founders of current businesses using a scale developed by Levinson (1973). Gatewood, Shaver, and Gartner (1995) also employed an alternative to Rotter's scale that focused on personal efficacy (a subscale of Paulhus's Spheres of Control Scale, 1983). Their results yielded a mixed pattern of results suggesting that female potential entrepreneurs held more internal/stable attributions (e.g., "I have always wanted to be my own boss"), while male potential entrepreneurs held more external/stable attributions (e.g., "I had identified a market need"). Although these results were statistically significant, the moderating role of gender is not easily interpretable, as the items for internal/stable attributions (e.g., "I want the autonomy and independence to do what I like through self-employment") seem closer to the aforementioned construct of need for autonomy than internal locus of control. Evidence from confirmatory factor analysis would be particularly valuable for determining what the scales in this study, and the scales in many other studies in this domain, were assessing. Although conceptual arguments for the role of locus of control in entrepreneurship can be compelling (Gilad, 1982), the evidential base is not strong.

THE "BIG FIVE" FROM A MACRO-LEVEL PERSPECTIVE

Entrepreneurial Orientation

Although one might think that "entrepreneurial orientation" would represent an individual's overall propensity to engage in firm start-up activities, the term has come to refer to a macro- (or firm-) level concept. Based on a nine-item scale developed by Khandwalla (1977), corporate members are asked to assess aspects of perceived corporate innovation and proactiveness. The items pertain to the perception of top managers' inclinations, and attributes of products and services. When responses are combined, these assessments are taken as an index of a firm's degree of entrepreneurship (Covin & Slevin, 1989). While the scale has adequate internal reliability, it appears to have two underlying factors (innovativeness and proactive disposition), such that combining the items into a single score is a questionable practice (Knight, 1997). Continued interest in a macro-level aggregated construct of entrepreneurial orientation is demonstrated in a review article by Lumpkin and Dess (1996), wherein they contend that entrepreneurial orientation should be defined as a firm's propensity to display autonomy, innovativeness, risk-taking, proactiveness, and competitive aggressiveness. Of course, these five dimensions overlap with many of the aforementioned individual differences attributes. As is common with much macro scholarship, the tendency is to discuss firms as if individuals' actions were of relatively little consequence (while micro approaches, to be sure, tend to view larger contextual features as being relatively fixed).

At this juncture in the development of entrepreneurship research, it must be acknowledged that the creation of a composite construct, termed *orientation*, at either the macro or micro level is essentially a subjective, discretionary exercise (e.g., we are more likely to include subconstructs that receive much attention and exclude subconstructs that are less well researched). Different scholars may reach different conclusions concerning which dimensions should be included or excluded. Hence, attempts at defining an orientation (or constellation of factors) based on subdimensions must be tied empirically to evidence that the subdimensions are highly useful and that inclusion/exclusion is empirically (and not merely intuitively) justified. As noted earlier in the present review, such evidence on the predictive utility of dimensions is not readily identifiable, nor can convincing evidence be provided for inclusion of some dimensions over others (other than the suspect practice of relying on a dimension's frequency of study or its frequency of discussion).

PERSONAL DEMOGRAPHICS

Personal demographics comprise a further set of individual differences attributes that does not fit under the heading of psychological attributes. The study of demographics in relation to entrepreneurial activity, however, has been largely atheoretical. One consequence of this heavily empirical approach is that the available findings, while often intriguing, cannot be easily interpreted. For example, is an observed association more reflective of demographics being a surrogate for a causal process, or is an observed association the result of unspecified processes producing a selection or filtering on some demographic dimension? A review of the published literature suggests that differences do exist on a variety of dimensions.

In an analysis of U.S. Census data, Fairlie and Meyer (1996) found that education was an important positive correlate of whether someone was self-employed. Also, after making statistical adjustments for differences in age, education, immigrant status, and time in country, they found significant differences in the likelihood of being self-employed across 60 ethnic and racial groupings. For example, Korean and other Asian-Americans had comparatively high rates of self-employment, while African-Americans had comparatively low rates of self-employment. Contrary to stereotypic explanations that difficulty in speaking English drives minorities into self-employment, Fairlie and Meyer found that having a problem speaking English was negatively related to self-employment. Additionally, these researchers also reported that although male and female rates of self-employment varied across ethnic and racial groupings, the gender rates were similarly ranked within groupings such that female rates of self-employment, in the aggregate, were 55% of the rate of male self-employment.[2] Further, they reported that the more advantaged ethnic/racial groupings (as measured by wage/salary earnings, self-employment earnings, and unearned income) had the highest rates of self-employment. This finding is contrary to a popular expectation that relatively disadvantaged racial/ethnic groupings would have a higher rate of self-employment.

Other research, from the United Kingdom, suggests that the probability of self-employment depends positively on whether an individual ever received an inheritance or gift (Blanchflower & Oswald, 1998), suggesting that the availability of start-up capital is paramount. A study conducted in Korea found that profitability as an entrepreneur, however, may be a function of whether an entrepreneur has prior experience in a relevant line of business and more education (Jo & Lee, 1996). In addition, actual involvement in starting a new firm (as distinct from personal descriptions of being simply self-employed) was found to be far more prevalent among younger individuals, aged 25–34 years, in the United States (Reynolds, 1997).

In two best-selling books (*The Millionaire Next Door*, Stanley & Danko, 1996; *The Millionaire Mind*, Stanley, 2000), Thomas Stanley reported survey results for individuals who were unquestionably wealthy (i.e., with an average household net worth of $9.2 million). High on the list of self-reported success factors were being well-disciplined and having a supportive spouse. Of special relevancy to the present review are the results for a segment of survey participants who were business owners/entrepreneurs (32% of the total sample of 733 individuals). Compared to the other occupational groupings of senior corporate executives, attorneys, physicians, and others, the business owners/entrepreneurs revealed the lowest percentage of those who indicated having a high IQ/superior intellect as an important success factor. In addition, this same job category had the highest relative percentages indicating the following factors as being important: getting along with people, having strong leadership qualities, having an ability to sell ideas and products, ignoring the criticism of detractors, and seeing opportunities others do not see. Interestingly, the same job grouping did not differ from the others on attending a top-rated college, loving my career/business, having a very competitive spirit, and having good mentors. Business owners/entrepreneurs had the lowest percentage reporting that

2. The only exception being Vietnamese women, who had a higher rate of self-employment than Vietnamese men.

they graduated near/at the top of their class. The factors that influenced the choice of a vocation were also assessed. For business owners/entrepreneurs, the most distinguishing factors were a chance to be financially independent, greater profit/income potential, and a legacy as part of a family's business. The lowest percentage for these same respondents was obtained on having one's vocation suggested by aptitude test results.

PERSON-SYSTEM FIT

Based on role motivation theory, John Miner (1990) has offered a framework for identifying individual orientations that match with organizational systems. Of the various organizational systems he described, two are most relevant to the present discussion. Specifically, Miner identified a hierarchic (or bureaucratic) system wherein managers are the key agents, and a task system wherein people are attracted to intrinsic rewards offered by task accomplishment. In a hierarchic system, there are six essential motives that a manager should possess. These are a desire to (1) maintain positive relations with authority figures, (2) exercise power by imposing sanctions and attempting to influence subordinates, (3) model one's actions after a parental role, (4) compete with peers to attain such extrinsic rewards as promotions and salary increases, (5) accept responsibility for routine administrative tasks, and (6) assume a distinctive position of status that involves being highly visible while remaining apart from subordinates. By contrast, a task system requires essential motives for (1) obtaining feedback on the results of one's efforts, (2) having greater control of outcomes so as to reduce risk, (3) engaging in tasks that can satisfy an intrinsic desire to achieve, (4) being personally innovative, and (5) planning and goal setting. As noted by Miner, these system requirements should map into different motivational patterns such that individuals who have primary desires that align with these system features will be more successful in specific settings.

In a series of studies that spanned 15 years, Miner (1986) developed measures of both hierarchic (managerial) motivation and task (entrepreneurial) motivation, and conducted a number of comparisons of managers and entrepreneurs. In general, these results indicated that entrepreneurs scored lower on hierarchic motivations than middle- and lower-level managers (Smith & Miner, 1983), or top-level corporate executives (Berman & Miner, 1985). Research with the task measure revealed that entrepreneurial founders of a firm scored higher on task motivation than manager-scientists in small firms who were not founders (Miner, Smith, & Bracker, 1989). In a comparison of entrepreneurs with managers in small firms, Bellu found that entrepreneurs were consistently more task motivated (Bellu, 1988; Bellu, Davidson, & Goldfarb, 1989). Similar results were reported by Bracker, Keats, Miner, and Pearson (1988). Finally, Miner (1990) found that entrepreneurs who head high-growth firms could be distinguished, in accordance with the theory, from a comparison group of managers.

In general, the results for Miner's (1990) theory have been consistently supportive of the view that different types of people may be drawn to different types of organizational systems. However, it could be more cautiously stated that different types of people are simply more likely to be identified within different systems, as we do not know whether people might modify their responses to role theory measures based on the normative definitions for the role that they presently occupy when completing the measures. Miner also noted that the entrepreneurial aspects of his theory may be limited to founders who head firms slated for growth (Miner, 1990), and the theory may have less relevance for small organizations where there is never an intention to achieve significant growth (e.g., Mom-and-Pop stores). The fact that many prior studies of entrepreneurial differences have failed to sort out whether firms were growth-oriented or not, may partially account for difficulties in reliably identifying a consistent pattern of meaningful entrepreneurial traits.

COGNITIVE FRAMING AND BIASES

As noted earlier, there is a growing literature on cognitive framing and biases that may pertain to entrepreneurs and small-business owners. The findings in this area are generally more consistent than the findings for personality measures. However, the comparison of managerial groups with entrepreneurial groups is somewhat less common.

Overconfidence and Hubris

Entrepreneurs and small-business managers have been found to be highly confident—perhaps, even to a fault. In an early study in this vein, Cooper et al. (1988) surveyed entrepreneurs (who recently had become business owners) to determine their self-perceptions concerning chances of being successful. Overall, these individuals expressed an extremely high degree of confidence in being successful when compared to data for the actual base rate of firm survival after the first 5 years. Cooper et al. concluded that entrepreneurs display a remarkable degree of optimism, and may experience a type of "euphoria" associated with the start-up of a firm.

While entrepreneurs do not believe they are more predisposed to taking risks than non-entrepreneurs, entrepreneurs do categorize equivocal business scenarios more positively than other individuals (Palich & Bagby, 1995). This does not mean that entrepreneurs perceive and accept greater risk than non-entrepreneurs, but rather that they may be predisposed to categorize situations more positively if they suggest greater potential for gain and opportunity. Further, the perception of risk may be influenced by one's degree of confidence (Simon, Houghton, & Aquino, 1999), such that overconfident individuals will perceive less risk associated with starting a new venture. In a supportive study, Busenitz and Barney (1997) compared founders of new firms with managers in large organizations. While their measure of overconfidence (a set of five questions, developed by Lichtenstein & Fischoff, 1997, that asks for confidence estimates of death rates from various diseases and accidents) correlated with occupational grouping, the magnitude of this association was not appreciably greater than that found with various personality measures. Although intriguing, this link has not yet been convincingly established, perhaps because of difficulties associated with defining and measuring overconfidence.

A further question surrounds whether overconfidence should be properly considered as a manifestation of self-esteem (i.e., a personality construct). Although overconfidence is typically categorized as a cognitive or decision-making bias, the manner in which it is typically assessed (cf. Simon et al., 1999) does not involve confidence in decision making as much as a stylistic response that is possibly reflective of high self-esteem. Future work on overconfidence should, therefore, include measures of general self-esteem to determine whether self-esteem is a comparable predictor and whether self-esteem is strongly correlated with the commonly-used measures of overconfidence.

Overconfidence may be an important ingredient in providing the wherewithal to move into risky territory. It can also be of help in convincing others (e.g., investors, customers, and employees) that a venture will be successful, and thereby aid in enlisting and sustaining their support. Overconfidence may also, somewhat ironically, be a major factor in a venture's failure. When overconfidence leads to failure, it is frequently labeled as hubris. Recently, Kroll, Toombs, & Wright (2000) reviewed theory and examples of hubris in political and management history. They define hubris as exaggerated self-confidence, pride or arrogance that frequently generates circumstances that lead, ultimately, to failure. The familiar prototypical examples of leaders who rose from humble origins to great power, and ultimate ruin, because of their hubris are Napoleon and Hitler. In these and other instances, over-arching self-confidence enlisted a strong following and led to a series of early successes, but eventually led to a disregard of warning signs of impending failure.[3] Kroll et al. (2000) provide a number of suggestions for guarding against hubris. These suggestions include listening to naysayers, appointing an alter ego or devil's advocate, basing one's actions on a role model who is relevant to the unit's mission, and engaging in exercises that involve deliberate reflection on personal performance. They also argue that board members who oversee executives should take on a greater monitoring role in confronting potential hubris in senior executives. In addition, views that are counter to the dominant perspective of top executives should be tolerated via the active promotion of a more heterogeneous organizational culture.

In a related vein, Manfred Kets de Vries (1996) contends, based on a series of interviews, that entrepreneurs have a need for control, a sense of distrust, a desire for "applause," and a propensity for action. A number of entrepreneurs, he argues, may also have a narcissistic tendency that is reflective of difficulties in regulating self-esteem. Dysfunctional consequences of these tendencies include propensities to be impulsive and dramatically venturesome, and to micro-manage others' activities. While Kets de Vries' conjectures on dysfunctional tendencies are intuitively appealing and do tie in with examples of hubris, they remain open for empirical validation.

Additional evidence in support of the notion that entrepreneurs possess greater relative confidence can be found in Robert Baron's research on counterfactual thinking. Counterfactual thinking refers to the emotional response that results from reflections on "what might have been." Evidence of this type of regret, for example, has been found for second-place finishers in Olympic events relative to third-place finishers. Specifically, third-place (bronze medal) winners reported greater happiness relative to second-place (silver medal) winners due to the awareness that the counterfactual alternative to winning third place was to win no medal, while the

---

3. Overconfidence may also lead to a ruinous outcome because of its likely association with tendencies to escalate commitment to a clearly failed course of action (Baron, 1998; Staw & Ross, 1987). For a more organizational/cultural level discussion of dysfunctional dynamics, see Miller (1990).

counterfactual alternative to winning second place was to win the gold medal for first place (Medvec, Madey, & Gilovich, 1995). Recent research by Baron (1999) indicates that entrepreneurs are less likely to engage in counterfactual thinking than other persons and are, as a result, less likely to experience feelings of regret over disappointing results. In addition, Baron found that entrepreneurs, perhaps because of a reduced tendency to engage in counterfactual thinking, found it easier to admit past mistakes to themselves and others (i.e., they were less susceptible to hindsight bias). As noted by Baron (p. 88), the cross-sectional nature of this research does not permit the determination of whether counterfactual thinking is more a cause than a consequence of becoming an entrepreneur. Also, there is much continuing debate on whether engaging in counterfactual thinking is an inherently detrimental or beneficial process. For example, such social comparisons may lead to envy (cf. Vecchio, 1995, 2000) and dissatisfaction (Medvec et al., 1995). Alternatively, it may lead to an analysis of the causes of failure and, thereby, lead to improved future performance (Roese, 1997). A challenge for future research is the specification of the settings in which these differing processes can be expected.

NEGLECTED TOPICS AND NEW DIRECTIONS: TYING ENTREPRENEURSHIP TO LEADERSHIP

A number of opportunities exist for new research directions in the study of entrepreneurship. Some of these directions have been previously explored within the field of leadership. Four promising avenues that relate largely to an entrepreneur's relations with others are followership, social intelligence, substitutes and neutralizers, and training and development.

Followership

The ability to inspire and motivate subordinates, especially in light of the risky character that surrounds early start-up conditions, is a critical attribute for a founder. Research on leader charisma and vision has particular relevance to entrepreneurship. The ability to capture subordinate interest and to communicate an appealing vision has been the subject of recent work in the domain of leadership (Baum, Locke, & Kirkpatrick, 1998; Kirkpatrick & Locke, 1996). However, beyond what a leader/entrepreneur can offer as interpersonal inducements to subordinates, there is a need to consider the attributes of followers in such a social process. With the notable exception of an article by Pearce, Kramer, and Robbins (1997) that found entrepreneurially-oriented managers in a change setting had subordinates who expressed greater satisfaction with supervision, the topic of followers has been neglected within the field of entrepreneurship. Within the field of leadership, followership has been long recognized as the *ying* to leadership's *yang*. However, no compelling theory of followership has, as yet, generated a significant research stream. Perhaps the most widely known view on follower attributes is to be found in Hersey and Blanchard's Situational Leadership Model (Hersey, Blanchard, & Johnson, 1996), wherein followers are assessed for "readiness" or "maturity" on the dimensions of task knowledge and commitment. These assessments, in turn, dictate appropriate styles of supervisor behavior. While the empirical validity of the theory is far from clearly established (Fernandez & Vecchio, 1997; Graeff, 1997), the intuitive appeal of the theory's underlying principles is not in dispute.

Given that followers who work for an entrepreneur/founder are likely to have more opportunities for greater interpersonal contact with the leader/founder, it is also worth considering what this increased contact may mean to each follower. For many people, the opportunity to interact with the top person in a firm represents a significant opportunity to receive approval or affirmation from an authority figure. As suggested by Gabriel (1997) in an article entitled "Meeting God: When Organizational Members Come Face to Face with the Supreme Leader," followers can draw two types of psychological support from a top person's approval: charismatic and messianic. Charismatic approval derives from the followers' feelings of being rewarded for who they are rather than what they have achieved, while messianic approval derives from feelings of being approved for actual contributions and achievements. Gabriel argues that these two basic views of approval from authority figures have their origin in earlier family experiences, wherein maternal (unconditional approval) and paternal (relatively more conditional approval) roles are first encountered, and then extended as a template to viewing and interpreting later relations with authority figures.

Another promising avenue for entrepreneur research relative to followers can be found in the theory and research related to leader-member exchange theory. First proposed in the early 1970s (Dansereau, Cashman, & Graen, 1973; Graen, Dansereau, & Minami, 1972), the theory has produced a reasonably consistent set of findings (for a recent review, see

Schriesheim, Castro, & Cogliser, 1999). The theory, in essence, argues that leaders and followers negotiate specific social exchange relationships wherein leaders offer such inducements as salary and opportunities for input on decision-making, and followers offer their effort and loyalty. Following early "try-out" experiences, the leader develops a unique working relationship with each subordinate. For subordinates who display a desire to be treated within the confines of a relatively limited psychological contract of exchanging effort for wages, the relationship becomes somewhat formal; while for subordinates who display a desire to be treated as confidants and supporters, the relationship takes on a special quality that involves a high degree of interpersonal trust and mutual support. Over time, subordinates are categorizable as members of the leader's "out-group" or "in-group." Research suggests that in-group followers, relative to out-group followers, enjoy greater job satisfaction, higher ratings of performance, more enriched job assignments, and possibly greater length of employment. The extension of these principles to the small-business setting seems straightforward as it is not clear that the principles of social-exchange would not operate there as well.

Finally, the dysfunctional features of being in the role of follower/subordinate within a small-business setting are deserving of study. Although most claims of abuse at the hands of small-business operators are anecdotal, the reality cannot be ignored that small-business owners/managers have greater latitude in disciplining and dismissing their subordinates, relative to subordinates in larger firms where requests for transfers or appeal procedures often exist. Further, a number of labor laws do not extend to small businesses (with "small" being legally defined by the number of employees). Hence, followers in small-business settings are in a more dependent position. Moreover, dysfunctional entrepreneurial styles, such as the aforementioned construct of narcissism, may be related to the abuse of others. Specifically, narcissism (defined by grandiose views of personal superiority, inflated sense of personal entitlement, low empathy for others, and fantasies of personal greatness, American Psychiatric Association, 1994) has been empirically linked to high, but unstable, self-esteem. In turn, this pattern has been tied to the manifestation of aggression against others (Baumeister, Bushman, & Campbell, 2000; Bushman & Baumeister, 1998). As suggested by Baumeister et al. (2000), the dangerous aspects of narcissism lie not so much with simple vanity or high self-esteem per se, as with the inflated sense of being superior to others and, therefore, entitled to privileges that allow reprisals against perceived threats to self-image. Given that a substantial portion of the workforce is employed in settings that are definable as small-business settings (i.e., less than 50 employees), the magnitude of such potential abuse is of some importance. Further, subordinates' claims of being "betrayed" by founders/small-business managers, even after years of loyal service, are worthy of study (Elangovan & Shapiro, 1998; Tepper, 2000).

Social Intelligence and Social Capital

It is often observed that conventional measures of analytical reasoning such as IQ test scores (Sternberg, Wagner, Williams, & Horvath, 1995), as well as grades in school (Stanley, 2000), do not correlate strongly with measures of success in later life. In response to this, Sternberg (1988) has offered a triarchic model of intelligence that proposes that intellectual functioning is best viewed as consisting of analytical reasoning ability, social intelligence, and creativity. Analytical reasoning refers to the ability to use deductive thinking, social intelligence covers the ability to accurately interpret the actions of others and interact effectively with them (sometimes referred to as "street smarts"), and creativity refers to the ability to generate many possible solutions to a particular problem. Sternberg's model is particularly interesting because it suggests the existence of an optimal combination of abilities for predicting effectiveness in a specific real-world setting. That is to say, some jobs may require relatively more analytical reasoning ability (e.g., financial analysts), while others likely require greater social intelligence (e.g., sales) or creativity (e.g., research-and-development). While Sternberg and Horvath (1999) and Sternberg, Wagner, and Okagaki (1993) have developed instruments to assess tacit knowledge (i.e., action-oriented knowledge that is practical, and acquired often through experience) for such occupations as law, medicine, traditional management, sales, and teaching, they have not, as yet, tackled the role of entrepreneurship. The application of their measures of managerial tacit knowledge to entrepreneurial samples may yield interesting insights in comparison to traditional managers. In addition, the development of uniquely tailored measures for understanding entrepreneurial tacit knowledge would be of great practical value for identifying and nurturing entrepreneurial interests.

Perhaps a good starting point for developing a model of entrepreneurial "street smarts" (social intelligence) can be found in the work of Robert Baron on social skills that relate to entrepreneurial success. Baron (2000a,b) has identified specific social competencies that are likely to play a role in an entrepreneur's success. These competencies encompass the ability to correctly gauge the current moods or emotions of others, proficiency in inducing positive reactions in others by enhancing one's own appearance and image (i.e., impression management), effectiveness in persuasion, and the ability to adjust to a range of social situations with a range of individuals (social adaptability). These interpersonal skills contribute to the accumulation of personal social capital. Social capital is defined as the actual and potential resources that individuals gain from knowing others, being included in social networks, and possessing a positive reputation. All things being equal, entrepreneurs with greater social capital should be more successful relative to other entrepreneurs. Although no published work has, as yet, appeared on this critical contrast, two observations are immediately apparent. First, the overlap with Sternberg's concept of social intelligence is striking, and suggests that these points of view can be informative to each other. Second, arguments (and evidence) that demonstrate that social capital is uniquely important to entrepreneurs relative to traditional managers and other professions need to be generated. For example, it seems reasonable that attorneys and faculty members would also be more successful in advancing their careers if they are comparably stronger on social capital. Therefore, social capital may be a general "life skill," rather than a uniquely entrepreneurial skill. Nonetheless, the parallel approaches offered by Baron and Sternberg merit serious consideration in any comprehensive model of entrepreneurial success.

Substitutes and Neutralizers of Entrepreneurship

Kerr and Jermier (1978) have proposed that, in some circumstances, a leader's behavior becomes unnecessary or superfluous. The essential aspects of these circumstances are termed substitutes or neutralizers for leadership. The characteristics that contribute to these substitution or neutralization effects are features of the task (e.g., if it is structured and routine, provides feedback, and is intrinsically satisfying), features of the subordinates (e.g., if they are experienced, highly trained, or have a professional orientation), and features of the firm (e.g., physical distance between the subordinates and supervisor, and detailed procedures). By and large, the features that Kerr and Jermier have identified should extend readily to start-up firms and the ability of owners/founders to influence subordinate behaviors. As the arguments for extending their view to small businesses are compelling, an empirical test seems warranted.

Training and Development

Training and development has a long and relatively well-accepted tradition in the developed nations. Many large organizations invest substantial dollars in supervisory and managerial training and development programs. Probably less clearly defined or widely accepted is the notion of entrepreneurial training and development. David McClelland's early efforts at raising achievement motivation notwithstanding (Durand, 1975; McClelland, 1965), the most prevalent and implicitly popular perspective is probably that entrepreneurs are "born, not made." Entrepreneurial interest is thought to reflect a "type" and requires a self-selection or self-nomination process. In addition, the responsibility of identifying and developing such individuals is not clearly an assigned social responsibility (excluding various government assistance programs or large firms that seek to develop an internal entrepreneurial spirit). Nonetheless, some individuals (taking responsibility for their own careers) do seek out entrepreneurial training opportunities. It is difficult to specify how such training programs should differ from traditional leadership/managerial training programs (beyond, of course, studying such practical techniques as developing a business plan and securing venture capital). Generally, the topics pertaining to interpersonal relations can be largely borrowed from available social science evidence relating to techniques in social persuasion, power and politics, social skill training, and established models of leadership (e.g., LMX, Situational Leadership Theory, charismatic perspectives, managerial grid). Determining the effectiveness of such training programs raises another set of interesting questions. Beyond the reasonable outcome measures of whether individuals subsequently pursue a start-up and are successful (as measured by longevity, growth, etc.), assessments of the impact of such programs should also demonstrate gains in personal beliefs of entrepreneurial self-efficacy (Chen et al., 1998) and confidence of success (Cooper, et al., 1988).

As suggested by Baron (2000a), a social skills training emphasis for entrepreneurs should include giving feedback on current social skills (e.g., by creating videotapes, with critiques, of interactions with others) and training in active rehearsal techniques (e.g., on public speaking and interviewing). Additionally, the effectiveness of entrepreneurial training may be enhanced by incorporating techniques from the domain of assessment centers. For example, techniques such as in-depth interviews, decision-making exercises (such as modified in-baskets that reveal decision-making style), test batteries, role-plays (that reveal interpersonal tendencies), and situational tests (that can reveal preferred responses to stress), can be employed to assess an individual's strengths and weaknesses, and to suggest areas where a person needs counseling or greater skill development. The benefits of such extensive assessment and subsequent skills training should be of particular value to minorities and women, who will continue to grow as a proportion of the U.S. workforce (Judy & D'Amico, 1997), but who have comparatively lower rates of entrepreneurial involvement and who may lack role models and understanding of how best to launch new firms (Anna, Chandler, Jansen, & Mero, 2000; Fairlie & Meyer, 1996).

MERGING DYNAMIC AND LEVEL ISSUES: A MODEL OF ENTREPRENEURIAL LEADERSHIP

A number of writers (cf. Gartner, 1985; Low & MacMillan, 1988) have suggested that firm start-ups move through specific sequential stages. These stages often include identifying an opportunity, amassing resources, delivery of services or products, responding to internal and external forces, etc. Stevenson, Roberts, and Grousback's (1995) five-stage model provides a useful foundation for the present discussion. Specifically, they proposed that start-ups involve the following stages: evaluating the opportunity, developing the firm's concept, assessing required resources, acquiring needed resources, and managing/harvesting the business. With some modification, these stages can be incorporated into a model as portrayed in Fig. 1. The present extension of their model includes a recognition that founders also serve as leader/managers during the entire process, and are engaged continuously in the creation of the firm's culture (Schein, 1983; Smith & Vecchio, 1993). Further, a discussion of the life cycle of a firm should recognize that the role of founder also necessarily involves an exit event (planned or otherwise).

Beyond merely laying out or describing these stages, the model proposes that certain psychological factors may be more critical at some stages than others. Further, certain economic factors may be of greater importance at specific stages as well. Prior efforts to relate psychological factors to entrepreneurship have failed to consider that factors may vary in importance according to the stage of a firm's existence. In addition to ignoring process issues, prior psychological research has ignored the role of broader contextual or economic factors. Therefore, a more comprehensive model that incorporates both process and context in attempting to explain entrepre-

Figure 1.
A model of entrepreneurial leadership that integrates process and level influences.

	Stages of Firm Start-Up		
	Pre-launch and Launch →	On-going Concern →	Exiting
Actions	Develop Concept Evaluate Opportunities Assess Resources Acquire Resources	Manage Resources Harvest Results Culture Creation	Disengage Depart
<u>Relevant Micro-Macro Factors</u>			
Psychological Factors	Big Five Social Capital Deomographics (as surrogates)	Big Five Social Capital Follower Attributes Strategic Response Person-Systems Fit Framing & Biases	Fatigue Family
Economic Factors	Capital Availability Alternative Opportunities Support Mechanisms	External Threats (competitors, market exhaustion, innovations)	Financials Firings

neurial behavior would likely be of the type portrayed in Fig. 1. This model suggests that the process of firm start-up must recognize at least three phases: prelaunch and launch, the ongoing concern, and exiting. The critical actions that define each phase (listed below the headings in the model) do not necessarily fit neatly into these columns, to be sure, as the creation of culture, for example, can begin even during the pre-launch phase. Nonetheless, this basic three-part process acknowledges that dynamics and focus will vary depending on stage of development. Admittedly, it is rare to include the topic of entrepreneurial exiting in a model of a firm start-up. Relatively little has been written on this topic (Carroll & Delacroix, 1982), and often discussions of exiting deal mostly with dysfunctional aspects of departure. Yet, the reality of founders eventually exiting or transferring control at some point should be attended to in any full model of the entre-preneurial process. For example, factors such as overconfidence that may enhance the likelihood of a successful start-up (as noted earlier) may also contribute to later difficulties for the firm's viability.

At each of the three stages in the model, micro- and macro-level variables can be identified as being potentially more important in accounting for relative success/failure. At the earliest phase, the entrepreneurial Big Five are arguably all relevant. Unfortunately, efforts to relate these five dimensions have not revealed strong evidence. Perhaps, this weak set of results is partly due to the prior failure to incorporate (a) a broader set of critical psychological factors (such as social capital, and demographic surrogates that may be important as controls for other influences) and (b) contextual-economic factors (e.g., the use of support mechanisms such as incubators and mentors). The key point is that research on relative success at the early stage of a firm start-up should recognize the need to study more than unitary-level and univariate typologies.

As the start-up process moves to the establishment and management of the more routine aspects of an ongoing concern, the critical psychological and economic influences will change as well. For example, various dimensions of the Big Five may be of relatively less importance, while issues traditionally related to effective leadership/management may be of greater relevance (e.g., managing followers' attitudes and behaviors, crisis management, designing a strategic response to environmental change). Because founders have the freedom to modify the larger system to accommodate their preferred style (be it hierarchic/bureaucratic versus task), issues of person-fit also become more critical to success. Founders who change or introduce system features to match their style (e.g., a hierarchic founder who creates greater routinization) may be at a relative advantage, ceteris paribus. Cognitive framing and biases may also have differential impact at this stage of a firm's life as, for example, the down-side cost of hubris and narcissism may increase because of the potential for turning accumulated successes into substantial failure. At the ongoing concern stage, economic factors are a significant source of external threats. For example, the entry of competitors, changes in technology, and the exhaustion of a market exemplify threats that require an effective strategic response. However, the critical point that merits restating is that relative success at this second stage is a function of contextual-economic factors, individual-psychological factors, and their interaction.

Ultimately, entrepreneurs do disengage and depart from their firms (even if only via their own deaths). Although comparatively little academic discussion has been devoted to the topic of entrepreneurial exiting, it seems likely that psychological and economic factors can again have relatively distinct, as well as interactive, influences on entrepreneurial withdrawal. Problems of fatigue (declining health, loss of interest) and family succession (when later generational members do not wish to take over the firm or when they actively resent the firm's claim on parental time and attention) are commonly reported by otherwise successful founders. Beyond personal psychological factors that influence the decision to withdraw as the owner/manager, financial exigencies may dictate a founder's departure (e.g., impending bankruptcy, legal distress, foreclosure, or an attractive buy-out opportunity). Again, the interplay of economic and psychological factors (e.g., what types of entrepreneurs are more likely to be enticed by a buy-out offer?) has not received serious attention in the social science journals. Moreover, the dynamic process aspects of entrepreneurial activity (from pre-launch through exit) should be integrated with individual and contextual factors when attempting to explain entrepreneurial activity and success. The past tendency to ignore both process and level/contextual influences has generated a pattern of fragmented and mixed empirical findings. A more comprehensive, integrated approach to the study of entrepreneurship holds the promise of refining the theoretical base with a broader measurement approach, while encouraging the cross-fertilization of otherwise exclusive academic perspectives.

CONCLUSION

While casual observation leads many of us to believe that people who start firms are inherently different from people who seek employment in large existing firms, studies of entrepreneurs have not yet offered a convincing profile of factors that clearly make entrepreneurs different from others. While some tantalizing, suggestive results have been found, the reliability and magnitude of these associations have not been impressive. In addition, some issues are severely under-researched (such as personal need for independence), while others that are more heavily researched (such as risk-taking propensity) do not yield a consistent pattern of findings. Further, Miner's theory of person-system fit (perhaps, one of the more promising avenues of research, in terms of theory and strength of findings) has not received much attention in recent years. This neglect may partially stem from reliance on measures (role sentence completions) that involve more elaborate scoring procedures in comparison to other paper-and-pencil measures.

At the outset of this review, the question was posed: Does entrepreneurship offer theory and findings that are so distinctly different that they justify a separate status, outside the area of leadership? Following our examination of the available literature, it seems reasonable to conclude that: (a) many of the constructs used in the area of entrepreneurship are also found within the mainstream of leadership theory; (b) the findings are not beyond being incorporated within available scholarship on leadership and interpersonal influence (i.e., entrepreneurship is leadership within a narrow, specific context); (c) the findings in entrepreneurship have not yet identified nonlinear associations or disjointed patterns of results that are clearly context-specific; and (d) there is a lack of (as well as a critical need for) study of so-called entrepreneurial types when they are employed in traditional work settings that would establish whether they are in any way distinguishable from other employees (post hoc, or retrospective recall, reports suggest they may be relatively dissatisfied when employed in such settings, but empirical evidence of their in-place sentiments and the opinions of their supervisors and peers have not been reported). Until these concluding points are empirically refuted, perhaps, it is more cogent and parsimonious to view entrepreneurship as simply a type of leadership that occurs in a specific setting, and, like many other small group manifestations of leadership (e.g., coaching sports teams, organizing volunteer work ers, etc.), a type of leadership that is not beyond the reach or understanding of available theory in the areas of leadership and interpersonal influence. While some might contend that there is instructional value in treating entrepreneurship as a specialized topic, it is important (and more honest) to acknowledge that the phenomenon is less clearly unique or distinctive than it is a specific instance of a more general social process.

REFERENCES

American Psychiatric Association (1994). *Diagnostic and statistical manual disorders* (4th ed.). Washington, DC: Author.

Anna, A. L., Chandler, G. N., Jansen, E., & Mero, N. P. (2000). Women business owners in traditional and non-traditional industries. *Journal of Business Venturing, 15,* 279–303.

Arrow, K. (1962). Economic welfare and the allocation of resources for invention. In R. Nelson (Ed.), *The rate direction of incentive activity: economic and social factors* (pp. 609–625). Princeton, NJ: Princeton University Press.

Bandura, A. (1982). Self-efficacy mechanism in human agency. *American Psychologist, 37*, 122–147.

Baron, R. A. (1998). Cognitive mechanisms in entrepreneurship: why and when entrepreneurs think differently than other people. *Journal of Business Venturing, 13*, 275–294.

Baron, R. A. (1999). Counterfactual thinking and venture formation: the potential effects of thinking about "what might have been". *Journal of Business Venturing, 15*, 79–91.

Baron, R. A. (2000a). Beyond social capital: how social skills can enhance entrepreneurs' success. *Academy of Management Executive, 14*, 106–115.

Baron, R. A. (2000b). Psychological perspectives on entrepreneurship: cognitive and social factors in entrepreneurs' success. *Current Directions in Psychological Science, 9*, 15–18.

Baum, J. R., Locke, E. A., & Kirkpatrick, S. A. (1998). A longitudinal study of the relation of vision and vision communication to venture growth in entrepreneurial firms. *Journal of Applied Psychology, 83*, 43–54.

Baumeister, R. F., Bushman, B. J., & Campbell, W. K. (2000). Self-esteem, narcissism, and aggression: does violence result from low self-esteem or from threatened egoism? *Current Directions in Psychological Science, 9*, 26–29.

Begley, J. M. (1995). Using founder status, age of firm, and company growth rate as the basis for distinguishing entrepreneurs from managers of smaller businesses. *Journal of Business Venturing, 10*, 249–263.

Begly, T., & Boyd, D. (1987). Psychological characteristics associated with performance in entrepreneurial firms and small business. *Journal of Business Venturing, 2*, 79–93.

Bellu, R. R. (1988). Entrepreneurs and managers: are they different? *Frontiers of Entrepreneurship Research, 8*, 16–30.

Bellu, R. R., Davidson, P., & Goldfarb, C. (1989). Motivational characteristics of small firm entrepreneurs in Israel, Italy, and Sweden. *Proceedings of the International Council for Small Business, 34*, 349–364.

Berman, F. E., & Miner, J. B. (1985). Motivation to manage at the top executive level: a test of the hierarchic role-motivation theory. *Personnel Psychology, 38*, 377–391.

Blanchflower, D. G., & Oswald, A. J. (1998). What makes an entrepreneur? *Journal of Labor Economics, 16*, 26–60.

Boyd, N. G., & Vozikis, G. S. (1994). The influence of self-efficacy in the development of entrepreneurial intentions and actions. *Entrepreneurship Theory and Practice, 18*, 63–90.

Bracker, J. S., Keats, B., Miner, J. B., & Pearson, J. N. (1988). *Task motivation, planning orientation and firm performance.* Working paper, Arizona State University (cited in Miner, 1990).

Brockhaus, R. H. (1976). Risk-taking propensity of entrepreneurs. *Proceedings of the Academy of Management*, 457–460.

Brockhaus, R. H. (1980a). Risk taking propensity of entrepreneurs. *Academy of Management Journal, 23*, 509–520.

Brockhaus, R. H. (1980b). Psychological and environmental factors which distinguish the successful from the unsuccessful entrepreneur: a longitudinal study. *Proceedings of the Academy of Management*, 368–372.

Brockhaus, R. H., & Horwitz, P. S. (1986). The psychology of the entrepreneur. In D. Sexton, & R. Smilor (Eds.), *The art and science of entrepreneurship* (pp. 25–48). Cambridge, MA: Ballinger.

Brockhaus, R. H., & Nord, W. R. (1979). An exploration of factors affecting the entrepreneurial decision: personal characteristics versus environmental conditions. *Proceedings of the Academy of Management*, 364–368.

Broehl, W. G. (1978). *The village entrepreneur.* Cambridge, MA: Harvard University Press.

Busenitz, L. W., & Barney, J. B. (1997). Differences between entrepreneurs and managers in large organizations: biases and heuristics in strategic decision-making. *Journal of Business Venturing, 12*, 9–30.

Bushman, B., & Baumeister, R. (1998). Threatened egotism, narcissism, self-esteem, and direct and displaced aggression: does self-love or self-hate lead to violence? *Journal of Personality and Social Psychology, 75*, 219–229.

Carland III, J. W., Carland, J. W., Carland, J. A., & Pearce, J. W. (1995). Risk-taking propensity among entrepreneurs, small business owners, and managers. *Journal of Business and Entrepreneurship, 7*, 15–23.

Carroll, G. R., & Delacroix, J. (1982). Organizational mortality in the newspaper industry of Argentina and Ireland: an ecological approach. *Administrative Science Quarterly, 27*, 169–198.

Carsrud, A., & Olm, K. (1986). The success of male and female entrepreneurs: a comparative analysis of the effects of multidimensional achievement motivation and personality traits. In R. W. Smilor, & R. I. Kuhn (Eds.), *Managing take-off in fast-growth companies* (pp. 147–162). New York: Praeger.

Chen, C. C., Greene, P. G., & Crick, A. (1998). Does entrepreneurial self-efficacy distinguish entrepreneurs from managers? *Journal of Business Venturing, 13*, 295–316.

Cooper, A. C., Woo, C. Y. & Dunkelberg, W. C. (1988). Enterpreneurs' perceived chances for success. *Journal of Business Venturing, 3*, 97–108.

Covin, J., & Slevin, D. (1989). Stategic management of small firms in hostile and benign environments. *Strategic Management Journal, 10*, 75–87.

Dansereau, F., Cashman, J., & Graen, G. (1973). Instrumentality theory and equity theory as complementary approaches in mediating the relationship of leadership and turnover among managers. *Organizational Behavior and Human Performance, 10*, 184–220.

Durand, D. E. (1975). Effects of achievement motivation and skill training on the entrepreneurial behavior of black businessmen. *Organizational Behavior and Human Performance, 14*, 76–90.

Elangovan, A. R., & Shapiro, D. L. (1998). Betrayal of trust in organizations. *Academy of Management Review, 23,* 547–566.

Engle, D. E., Mah, J. J., & Sadri, G. (1997). An empirical comparison of entrepreneurs and employees: implications for innovation. *Creative Research Journal, 10,* 45–49.

Fairlie, R. W., & Meyer, B. D. (1996). Ethnic and racial self-employment differences and possible explanations. *Journal of Human Resources, 31,* 757–793.

Fernandez, C., & Vecchio, R. P. (1997). Situational Leadership Theory revisited: a test of an across-jobs perspective. *Leadership Quarterly, 8,* 67–84.

Gabriel, Y. (1997). Meeting God: when organizational members come face to face with the Supreme Leader. *Human Relations, 50,* 315–352.

Gartner, W. B. (1985). A conceptual framework for describing the phenomenon of new venture creation. *Academy of Management Review, 10,* 696–706.

Gatewood, E. J., Shaver, K. G., & Gartner, W. B. (1995). A longitudinal study of cognitive factors influencing start-up behaviors and success at venture creation. *Journal of Business Venturing, 10,* 371–391.

Gilad, B. (1982). On encouraging entrepreneurship: an interdisciplinary analysis. *Journal of Behavioral Economics, 11,* 132–163.

Graeff, C. L. (1997). Evolution of Situational Leadership Theory: a critical review. *Leadership Quarterly, 8,* 153–170.

Graen, G., Dansereau, F., & Minami, Y. (1972). Dysfunctional leadership styles. *Organizational Behavior and Human Performance, 7,* 216–236.

Harrell, T., & Alpert, B. (1979). The need for autonomy among managers. *Academy of Management Review, 4,* 259–267.

Hersey, P., Blanchard, K. H., & Johnson, D. E. (1996). *Management of organizational behavior: utilizing human resources* (7th ed.). Englewood Cliffs, NJ: Prentice-Hall.

Hull, D., Bosley, J., & Udell, G. (1980). Reviewing the heffalump: identifying potential entrepreneurs by personality characteristics. *Journal of Small Business Management, 18,* 11–18.

Jackson, D. N. (1976). *Personality inventory manual.* Goshen, NY: Research Psychologists Press.

Jo, H., & Lee, J. (1996). The relationship between entrepreneur's background and performance in a new venture. *Technovation, 16,* 161–171.

Johnson, B. (1990). Toward a multidimensional model of entrepreneurship: the case of achievement motivation and the entrepreneur. *Entrepreneurship Theory and Practice, 14,* 39–54.

Judy, R. W., & D'Amico, C. (1997). *Workforce 2020.* Indianapolis, IN: Hudson Institute.

Kerr, S., & Jermier, J. M. (1978). Substitutes for leadership: their meaning and measurement. *Organizational Behavior and Human Performance, 22,* 375–403.

Kets de Vries, M. F. R. (1996). The anatomy of the entrepreneur: clinical observations. *Human Relations, 49,* 853–883.

Khandwalla, P. (1977). *The design of organizations.* New York: Harcourt Brace Jovanovich.

Kirkpatrick, S. A., & Locke, E. A. (1996). Direct and indirect effects of three core charismatic leadership components on performance and attitudes. *Journal of Applied Psychology, 81,* 36–51.

Kirzner, I. (1997). Entrepreneurial discovery and the competitive market process: an Austrian approach. *Journal of Economic Literature, 35,* 60–85.

Knight, G. A. (1997). Cross-cultural reliability and validity of a scale to measure firm entrepreneurial orientation. *Journal of Business Venturing, 12,* 213–252.

Kroll, M. J., Toombs, L. A., & Wright, P. (2000). Napoleon's tragic march home from Moscow: lessons in hubris. *Academy of Management Executive, 14,* 117–128.

Krueger, N., & Dickson, P. R. (1994). How believing in ourselves increases risk-taking: perceived self-efficacy and opportunity recognition. *Decision Sciences, 25,* 385–400.

Levinson, H. (1973). Multidimensional locus of control in psychiatric patients. *Journal of Consulting and Clinical Psychology, 41,* 397–404.

Lichtenstein, S., & Fischhoff, B. (1977). Do those who know more also know more about how much they know? *Organizational Behavior and Human Performance, 20,* 159–183.

Liles, P. R. (1974). *New business ventures and the entrepreneur.* Homewood, IL: Irwin.

Litzinger, W. (1965). The motel entrepreneur and the motel manager. *Academy of Management Journal, 8,* 268–281.

Low, M. B., & MacMillan, I. C. (1988). Entrepreneurship: past research and future challenges. *Journal of Management, 14,* 139–161.

Lumpkin, G. T., & Dess, G. G. (1996). Clarifying the entrepreneurial orientation construct and linking it to performance. *Academy of Management Review, 21,* 135–172.

Masters, R., & Meier, R. (1988). Sex differences and risk-taking propensity of entrepreneurs. *Journal of Small Business Management, 26,* 31–35.

McClelland, D. C. (1965). Toward a theory of motive acquisition. *American Psychologist, 23,* 321–333.

McClelland, D. C. (1975). *Power: the inner experience.* New York: Irvington.

McClelland, D. C., & Winter, D. G. (1969). *Motivating economic achievement.* New York: Free Press.

Medvec, V. H., Madey, S. F., & Gilovich, T. (1995). When less is more: counterfactual thinking and satisfaction among Olympic medalists. *Journal of Personality and Social Psychology, 69,* 603–610.

Miller, D. (1990). *The Icarus paradox: how successful companies bring about their own downfall.* New York: Harper Business.

Miner, J. B. (1986). *Scoring guide for the Miner Sentence Completion Scale-Form T.* Buffalo, NY: Organizational Measurement Systems Press.

Miner, J. B. (1990). Entrepreneurs, high growth entrepreneurs, and managers: contrasting and overlapping motivational patterns. *Journal of Business Venturing, 5,* 221–234.

Miner, J. B., Smith, N. R., & Bracker, J. S. (1989). Role of entrepreneurial task motivation in the growth of technologically innovative firms. *Journal of Applied Psychology, 74,* 554–560.

Palich, L. E., & Bagby, D. R. (1995). Using cognitive theory to explain entrepreneurial risk-taking: challenging conventional wisdom. *Journal of Business Venturing, 10,* 425–438.

Paulhus, D. (1983). Sphere-specific measures of perceived control. *Journal of Personality and Social Psychology, 44,* 1253–65.

Peacock, P. (1986). The influence of risk-taking as a cognitive behavior of small business success. In R. Ronstadt, J. Hornaday, R. Peterson, & K. Vesper (Eds.), *Frontiers of entrepreneurship research* (pp. 110–118). Wellesley, MA: Babson College.

Pearce, J. A., Kramer, T. R., & Robbins, D. K. (1997). Effects of managers' entrepreneurial behavior on subordinates. *Journal of Business Venturing, 12,* 147–160.

Reynolds, P. D. (1997). Who starts new firms?—Preliminary explorations of firms-in-gestation. *Small Business Economics, 9,* 449–462.

Roese, N. J. (1997). Counterfactual thinking. *Psychological Bulletin, 121,* 133–148.

Rotter, J. (1966). Generalized experiences for internal versus external control of reinforcement. *Psychological Monographs, 80* (1, Whole No. 609), 1–28.

Schein, E. H. (1983). The role of the founder in creating organizational culture. *Organizational Dynamics, 12,* 13–28.

Scherer, R. F., Adams, J. S., Carley, S. S., & Wiche, F. A. (1989). Role model performance effects on development of entrepreneurial career preference. *Entrepreneurship Theory and Practice, 13,* 53–71.

Schriesheim, C. A., Castro, S. L., & Cogliser, C. C. (1999). Leader-member exchange (LMX) research: a comprehensive review of theory, measurement, and data-analytic practices. *Leadership Quarterly, 10,* 63–113.

Schumpeter, J. (1934). *The theory of economic development: an inquiry into profits, capital, interest, and the business cycle.* Cambridge: Harvard University Press.

Schumpeter, J. (1939). *Business cycles: a theoretical, historical, and statistical analysis of the capitalist process.* New York: McGraw-Hill.

Schumpeter, J. (1947). *Capitalism, socialism, and democracy.* London: Allen & Unwin.

Shane, S. (1996). Explaining variation in rates of entrepreneurship in the United States: 1899–1988. *Journal of Management, 22,* 747–781.

Shane, S., & Venkataraman, S. (2000). The promise of entrepreneurship as a field of research. *Academy of Management Review, 25,* 217–226.

Simon, M., Houghton, S. M., & Aquino, K. (1999). Cognitive biases, risk perception, and venture formation: how individuals decide to start companies. *Journal of Business Venturing, 15,* 113–134.

Smith, C. G., & Vecchio, R. P. (1993). Organizational culture and strategic management: issues in the management of strategic change. *Journal of Managerial Issues, 5,* 53–70.

Smith, N. R., & Miner, J. B. (1983). Type of entrepreneur, type of firm, and managerial motivation: implications for organizational life cycle theory. *Strategic Management Journal, 4,* 325–340.

Stanley, T. J. (2000). *The millionaire mind.* Kansas City, KS: Andrews McMeel.

Stanley, T. J., & Danko, W. D. (1996). *The millionaire next door.* Kansas City, KS: Andrews McMeel.

Staw, B. M., & Ross, J. (1987). Behavior in escalation situations: antecedents, prototypes, and solutions. In L. Cummings, & B. M. Staw (Eds.), *Research in organizational behavior, vol. 9.* Greenwich, CT: JAI Press.

Sternberg, R. J. (1988). *The triarchic mind: a new theory of human intelligence.* New York: Viking.

Sternberg, R. J., & Horvath, J. A. (1999). *Tacit knowledge in professional practice: researcher and practitioner perspectives.* Mahwah, NJ: Erlbaum.

Sternberg, R. J., Wagner, R. K., & Okagaki, L. (1993). Practical intelligence: the nature and role of tacit knowledge in work and at school. In H. Reese, & J. Puckett (Eds.), *Advances in lifespan development* (pp. 205–227). Hillsdale, NJ: Erlbaum.

Sternberg, R. J., Wagner, R. K., Williams, W. M., & Horvath, J. A. (1995). Testing common sense. *American Psychologist, 50,* 912–927.

Stevenson, H. H., Roberts, M. J., & Grousback, H. I. (1985). *New business ventures and the entrepreneur.* Homewood, IL: Irwin.

Stewart, W. H., Watson, W. E., Carland, J. C., & Carland, J. W. (1998). A proclivity for entrepreneurship: a comparison of entrepreneurs, small business owners, and corporate managers. *Journal of Business Venturing, 14,* 189–214.

Tepper, B. J. (2000). Consequences of abusive supervision. *Academy of Management Journal, 43,* 178–190.

Thornton, P. H. (1999). The sociology of entrepreneurship. *Annual Review of Sociology, 25,* 19–46.

Vecchio, R. P. (1995). It's not easy being green: jealousy and envy in the workplace. In G. R. Ferris (Ed.), *Research in personnel and human resources management, vol. 13* (pp. 201–244). Greenwich, CT: JAI Press.

Vecchio, R. P. (2000). Negative emotion in the workplace: employee jealousy and envy. *International Journal of Stress Management, 7,* 161–179.

Wallach, M. A., & Kogan, N. (1961). Aspects of judgment and decision-making: interrelationships and changes with age. *Behavioral Science, 6,* 23–36.

Wood, R., & Bandura, A. (1989). Social cognitive theory of organizational management. *Academy of Management Review, 14,* 361–384.

PART VI

Emerging Issues

My job as leader is to keep the five guys who hate me away from the five guys who haven't yet made up their mind.

Casey Stengal

Nice guys finish last.

Leo Durocher

Contrary to the cliche, genuinely nice guys most often finish first, or very near it.

Malcolm Forbes

Officers (and mothers) always eat last.

Colin Powell

Be awful nice to 'em goin' up, 'cause you're gonna meet 'em all comin' down.

Jimmy Durante

In our final section, we explore macro-level issues that impact on the process of leadership. The first article, by Geert Hofstede, considers how other cultures have different views of leadership and management. He asks us to consider how our Westernized models may be of limited value in understanding social dynamics in other cultures and offers a model in which cultural dimensions can be categorized in order to explain differences we might observe. The following article, by Clayton Smith and Robert Vecchio, examines the topic of organizational culture and suggests that organizational culture influences the process of organizational strategic management by influencing leader perception, interpretation, and response to the external environment. Mary Zalesny and Robert Vecchio, in the next reading, consider factors that affect technological change in an organization and specifically examine the key role played by supervisors in impeding or facilitating change.

Women are entering leadership positions in increasing numbers. The article "Leadership and Gender Advantage" reviews research on the question of whether a leader's sex is related to leader effectiveness.

The experience of extreme emotion at work is a relatively new and important topic which has been neglected in the past. In the article "It's Not Easy Being Green," Robert Vecchio reviews the sparse information on jealousy and envy in the workplace and offers specific techniques for managing negative emotion at work. While extreme negative emotion is readily recognized as a potential source of problems at work, it is sometimes forgotten that extreme positive emotion at work can also be a source of difficulties.

Cultural Constraints
in Management Theories

Geert Hofstede

Lewis Carroll's *Alice in Wonderland* contains the famous story of Alice's croquet game with the Queen of Hearts.

Alice thought she had never seen such a curious croquet-ground in all her life; it was all ridges and furrows; the balls were live hedgehogs, the mallets live flamingoes, and the soldiers had to double themselves up and to stand on their hands and feet, to make the arches.

You probably know how the story goes: Alice's flamingo mallet turns its head whenever she wants to strike with it; her hedgehog ball runs away; and the doubled-up soldier arches walk around all the time. The only rule seems to be that the Queen of Hearts always wins.

Alice's croquet playing problems are good analogies to attempts to build culture-free theories of management. Concepts available for this purpose are themselves alive with culture, having been developed within a particular cultural context. They have a tendency to guide our thinking toward our desired conclusion.

As the same reasoning may also be applied to the arguments in this article, I better tell you my conclusion before I continue—so that the rules of my game are understood. In this article we take a trip around the world to demonstrate that there are no such things as universal management theories.

Diversity in management *practices* as we go around the world has been recognized in U.S. management literature for more than thirty years. The term "comparative management" has been used since the 1960s. However, it has taken much longer for the U.S. academic community to accept that not only practices but also the validity of *theories* may stop at national borders, and I wonder whether even today everybody would agree with this statement.

An article I published in *Organizational Dynamics* in 1980 entitled "Do American Theories Apply Abroad?" created more controversy than I expected. The article argued, with empirical support, that generally accepted

473

U.S. theories like those of Maslow, Herzberg, McClelland, Vroom, Mc-Gregor, Likert, Blake and Mouton may not or only very partly apply outside the borders of their country of origin—assuming they do apply within those borders. Among the requests for reprints, a larger number were from Canada than from the United States.

MANAGEMENT THEORISTS ARE HUMAN

Employees and managers are human. Employees as humans was "discovered" in the 1930s, with the Human Relations school. Managers as humans, was introduced in the late 40s by Herbert Simon's "bounded rationality" and elaborated in Richard Cyert and James March's *Behavioral Theory* of *the Firm* (1963, and recently re-published in a second edition). My argument is that management scientists, theorists, and writers are human too: they grew up in a particular society in a particular period, and their ideas cannot help but reflect the constraints of their environment.

The idea that the validity of a theory is constrained by national borders is more obvious in Europe, with all its borders, than in a huge borderless country like the U.S. Already in the sixteenth century Michel de Montaigne, a Frenchman, wrote a statement which was made famous by Blaise Pascal about a century later: *"Vérite en-deça des Pyrenées, erreur au-delà"*— There are truths on this side of the Pyrenées which are falsehoods on the other.

FROM DON ARMADO'S LOVE TO TAYLOR'S SCIENCE

According to the comprehensive ten-volume Oxford English Dictionary (1971), the words "manage," "management," and "manager" appeared in the English language in the 16th century. The oldest recorded use of the word "manager" is in Shakespeare's "Love's Labour's Lost," dating from 1588, in which Don Adriano de Armado, "a fantastical Spaniard," exclaims (Act I, scene ii, 188):

"Adieu, valour! rust, rapier! be still, drum! for your manager is in love; yea, he loveth".

The linguistic origin of the word is from Latin *manus*, hand, via the Italian *maneggiare*, which is the training of horses in the *manege*; subsequently its meaning was extended to skillful handling in general, like of arms and musical instruments, as Don Armado illustrates. However, the word also became associated with the French *menage,* household, as an equivalent of "husbandry" in its sense of the art of running a household. The theatre of present-day management contains elements of both *manege* and *menage* and different managers and cultures may use different accents.

The founder of the science of economics, the Scot Adam Smith, in his 1776 book *The Wealth of Nations,* used "manage," "management" (even "bad management") and "manager" when dealing with the process and the persons involved in operating joint stock companies (Smith, V., i.e.). British economist John Stuart Mill (1806–1873) followed Smith in this use and clearly expressed his distrust of such hired people who were not driven by ownership. Since the 1880s the word "management" appeared occasionally in writings by American engineers, until it was canonized as a modern science by Frederick W. Taylor in *Shop Management* in 1903 and in *The Principles of Scientific Management* in 1911.

While Smith and Mill used "management" to describe a process and "managers" for the persons involved, "management" in the American sense—which has since been taken back by the British—refers not only to the process but also to the managers as a class of people. This class (1) does not own a business but sells its skills to act on behalf of the owners and (2) does not produce personally but is indispensable for making others produce, through motivation. Members of this class carry a high status and many American boys and girls aspire to the role. In the U.S., the manager is a cultural hero.

Let us now turn to other parts of the world. We will look at management in its context in other successful modern economies: Germany, Japan, France, Holland, and among the Overseas Chinese. Then we will examine management in the much larger part of the world that is still poor, especially South-East Asia and Africa, and in the new political configurations of Eastern Europe, and Russia in particular. We will then return to the U.S. via mainland China.

Germany

The manager is not a cultural hero in Germany. If anybody, it is the engineer who fills the hero role. Frederick Taylor's *Scientific Management* was conceived in a society of immigrants—where a large number of workers with diverse backgrounds and skills had to work together. In Germany this heterogeneity never existed.

Elements of the mediaeval guild system have survived in historical continuity in Germany until the present day. In particular, a very effective apprenticeship system exists both on the shop floor and in the office, which alternates practical work and classroom courses. At the end of the apprenticeship the worker receives a certificate, the *Facharbeiterbrief,* which is recognized throughout the country. About two-thirds of the German worker population holds such a certificate and a corresponding occupational pride. In fact, quite a few German company presidents have worked their way up from the ranks through an apprenticeship. In comparison, two thirds of the worker population in Britain have no occupational qualification at all.

The highly skilled and responsible German workers do not necessarily need a manager, American-style, to "motivate" them. They expect their boss or *Meister* to assign their tasks and to be the expert in resolving technical problems. Comparisons of similar German, British, and French organizations show the Germans as having the highest rate of personnel in productive roles and the lowest both in leadership and staff roles.

Business schools are virtually unknown in Germany. Native German management theories concentrate on formal systems. The inapplicability of American concepts of management was quite apparent in 1973 when the U.S. consulting firm of Booz, Allen and Hamilton, commissioned by the German Ministry of Economic Affairs, wrote a study of German management from an American view point. The report is highly critical and writes among other things that "Germans simply do not have a very strong concept of management." Since 1973, from my personal experience, the situation has not changed much. However, during this period the German economy has performed in a superior fashion to the U.S. in virtually all respects, so a strong concept of management might have been a liability rather than an asset.

Japan

The American type of manager is also missing in Japan. In the United States, the core of the enterprise is the managerial class. The core of the Japanese enterprise is the permanent worker group; workers who for all practical purposes are tenured and who aspire at life-long employment. They are distinct from the non-permanent employees—mostly women and subcontracted teams led by gang bosses, to be laid off in slack periods. University graduates in Japan first join the permanent worker group and subsequently fill various positions, moving from line to staff as the need occurs while paid according to seniority rather than position. They take part in Japanese-style group consultation sessions for important decisions, which extend the decision-making period but guarantee fast implementation afterwards. Japanese are to a large extent controlled by their peer group rather than by their manager.

Three researchers from the East-West Center of the University of Hawaii, Joseph Tobin, David Wu, and Dana Danielson, did an observational study of typical preschools in three countries: China, Japan, and the United States. Their results have been published both as a book and as a video. In the Japanese preschool, one teacher handled twenty-eight four-year-olds. The video shows one particularly obnoxious boy, Hiroki, who fights with other children and throws teaching materials down from the balcony. When a little girl tries to alarm the teacher, the latter answers "What are you calling me for? Do something about it!" In the U.S. preschool, there is one adult for every nine children. This class has its problem child too, Glen, who refuses to clear away his toys. One of the teachers has a long talk with him and isolates him in a corner, until he changes his mind. It doesn't take much imagination to realize that managing Hiroki thirty years later will be a different process from managing Glen.

American theories of leadership are ill-suited for the Japanese group-controlled situation. During the past two decades, the Japanese have developed their own "PM" theory of leadership, in which P stands for performance and M for maintenance. The latter is less a concern for individual employees than for maintaining social stability. In view of the amazing success of the Japanese economy in the past thirty years, many Americans have sought for the secrets of Japanese management hoping to copy them.

France

The manager, U.S. style, does not exist in France either. In a very enlightening book, unfortunately not yet translated into English, the French researcher Philippe d'Iribarne (1989) describes the results of in-depth observation and interview studies of management methods in three subsidiary plants of the same French multinational: in France, the United States, and Holland. He relates what he finds to information about the three societies in general. Where necessary, he goes back in history to trace the roots of the strikingly different behaviors in the completion of the same tasks. He identifies three kinds of basic principles *(logiques)* of management. In the USA, the principle is the *fair contract* between employer and employee, which gives the manager considerable prerogatives, but within its limits. This is really a labor *market* in which the worker sells his or her labor for a price. In France, the principle is the *honor* of each class in a society which has always been and remains extremely stratified, in which superiors behave as superior beings and subordinates accept and expect this, conscious of their own lower level in the national hierarchy but also of the honor of their own class. The French do not think in terms of managers versus nonmanagers but in terms of *cadres* versus *non-cadres;* one becomes cadre by attending the proper schools and one remains it forever; regardless of their actual task, cadres have the privileges of a higher social class, and it is very rare for a non-cadre to cross the ranks.

The conflict between French and American theories of management became apparent in the beginning of the twentieth century, in a criticism by the great French management pioneer Henri Fayol (1841–1925) on his U.S. colleague and contemporary Frederick W. Taylor (1856–1915). The difference in career paths of the two men is striking. Fayol was a French engineer whose career as a *cadre supérieur* culminated in the position of Président-Directeur-Général of a mining company. After his retirement he formulated his experiences in a pathbreaking text on organization: *Administration industrielle et générale,* in which he focused on the sources of authority. Taylor was an American engineer who started his career in industry as a worker and attained his academic qualifications through evening studies. From chief engineer in a steel company he became one of the first management consultants. Taylor was not really concerned with the issue of authority at all; his focus was on efficiency. He proposed to split the task of the first-line boss into eight specialisms, each exercised by a different person; an idea which eventually led to the idea of a matrix organization.

Taylor's work appeared in a French translation in 1913, and Fayol read it and showed himself generally impressed but shocked by Taylor's "denial of the principle of the Unity of Command" in the case of the eight-boss-system.

Seventy years later Andre Laurent, another of Fayol's compatriots, found that French managers in a survey reacted very strongly against a suggestion that one employee could report to two different bosses, while U.S. managers in the same survey showed fewer misgivings. Matrix organization has never become popular in France as it has in the United States.

Holland

In my own country, Holland or as it is officially called, the Netherlands, the study by Philippe d'Iribarne found the management principle to be a need for *consensus* among all parties, neither predetermined by a contractual relationship nor by class distinctions, but based on an open-ended exchange of views and a balancing of interests. In terms of the different origins of the word "manager," the organization in Holland is more *menage* (household), while in the United States it is more *manege* (horse drill).

At my university, the University of Limburg at Maastricht, every semester we receive a class of American business students who take a program in European Studies. We asked both the Americans and a matched group of Dutch students to describe their ideal job after graduation, using a list of twenty-two job characteristics. The Americans attached significantly more importance than the Dutch to earnings, advancement, benefits, a good working relationship with their boss, and security of employment. The Dutch attached more importance to freedom to adopt their own approach to the job, being consulted by their boss in his or her decisions, training opportunities, contributing to the success of their organization, fully using their skills and abilities, and helping others. This list confirms d'Iribarne's findings of a contractual employment relationship in the United States, based on earnings and career opportunities, against a consensual relationship in Holland. The latter has centuries-old roots; the Netherlands were the first republic in Western Europe (1609–1810), and a model for the American republic. The country has been and still is governed by a careful balancing of interests in a multi-party system.

In terms of management theories, both motivation and leadership in Holland are different from what they are in the United States. Leadership in Holland presupposes modesty, as opposed to assertiveness in the United States. No U.S. leadership theory has room for that. Working in Holland is not a constant feast, however. There is a built-in premium on mediocrity and jealousy, as well as time-consuming ritual consultations to maintain the appearance of consensus and the pretense of modesty. There is unfortunately another side to every coin.

The Overseas Chinese

Among the champions of economic development in the past thirty years we find three countries mainly populated by Chinese living outside the Chinese mainland: Taiwan, Hong Kong and Singapore. Moreover, overseas Chinese play a very important role in the economies of Indonesia, Malaysia, the Philippines and Thailand, where they form an ethnic minority. If anything, the little dragons—Taiwan, Hong Kong and Singapore—have been more economically successful than Japan, moving from rags to riches and now counted among the world's wealthy industrial countries. Yet very little attention has been paid to the way in which their enterprises have been managed. *The Spirit* of *Chinese Capitalism* by Gordon Redding (1990), the British dean of the Hong Kong Business School, is an excellent book about Chinese business. He bases his insights on personal acquaintance and in-depth discussions with a large number of overseas Chinese businesspeople.

Overseas Chinese American enterprises lack almost all characteristics of modern management. They tend to be small, cooperating for essential functions with other small organizations through networks based on personal relations. They are family-owned, without the separation between ownership and management typical in the West, or even in Japan and Korea. They normally focus on one product or market, with growth by opportunistic diversification; in this, they are extremely flexible. Decision making is centralized in the hands of one dominant family member, but other family members may be given new ventures to try their skills on. They are low-profile and extremely cost-conscious, applying Confucian virtues of thrift and persistence. Their size is kept small by the assumed lack of loyalty of non-family employees, who, if they are any good, will just wait and save until they can start their own family business.

Overseas Chinese prefer economic activities in which great gains can be made with little manpower, like commodity trading and real estate. They employ few professional managers, except their sons and sometimes daughters who have been sent to prestigious business schools abroad, but who upon return continue to run the family business the Chinese way.

The origin of this system, or—in the Western view—this lack of system, is found in the history of Chinese society, in which there were no formal laws, only formal networks of powerful people guided by general principles of Confucian virtue. The favors of the authorities could change daily, so nobody could be trusted except one's kinfolk—of whom, fortunately, there used to be many, in an extended family structure. The overseas Chinese way of doing business is also very well adapted to their position in the countries in which they form ethnic minorities, often envied and threatened by ethnic violence.

Overseas Chinese businesses following this unprofessional approach command a collective gross national product of some 200 to 300 billion US dollars, exceeding the GNP of Australia. There is no denying that it works.

MANAGEMENT TRANSFER TO POOR COUNTRIES

Four-fifths of the world population live in countries that are not rich but poor. After World War II and decolonization, the stated purpose of the United Nations and the World Bank has been to promote the development of all the world's countries in a war on poverty. After forty years it looks very much like we are losing this war. If one thing has become clear, it is that the export of Western—mostly American—management practices *and* theories to poor countries has contributed little to nothing to their development. There has been no lack of effort and money spent for this purpose: students from poor countries have been trained in this country, and teachers and Peace Corps workers have been sent to the poor countries. If nothing else, the general lack of success in economic development of other countries should be sufficient argument to doubt the validity of Western management theories in non-Western environments.

If we examine different parts of the world, the development picture is not equally bleak, and history is often a better predictor than economic factors for what happens today. There is a broad regional pecking order with East Asia leading. The little dragons have passed into the camp of the wealthy; then follow South-East Asia (with its overseas Chinese minorities), Latin America (in spite of the debt crisis). South Asia, and Africa always trails behind. Several African countries have only become poorer since decolonization.

Regions of the world with a history of large-scale political integration and civilization generally have done better than regions in which no large-scale political and cultural infrastructure existed, even if the old civilizations had decayed or been suppressed by colonizers. It has become painfully clear that development cannot be pressure-cooked; it presumes a cultural infrastructure that takes time to grow. Local management is part of this infrastructure; it cannot be imported in package form. Assuming that with so-called modern management techniques and theories outsiders can develop a country has proven a deplorable arrogance. At best, one can hope for a dialogue between equals with the locals, in which the Western partner acts as the expert in Western technology and the local partner as the expert in local culture, habits, and feelings.

Russia and China

The crumbling of the former Eastern bloc has left us with a scattering of states and would-be states of which the political and economic future is extremely uncertain. The best predictions are those based on a knowledge of history, because historical trends have taken revenge on the arrogance of the Soviet rulers who believed they could turn them around by brute power. One obvious fact is that the former bloc is extremely heterogeneous, including countries traditionally closely linked with the West by trade and travel, like Czechia, Hungary, Slovenia, and the Baltic states, as well as others with a Byzantine or Turkish past; some having been prosperous, others always extremely poor.

Let me limit myself to the Russian republic, a huge territory with some 140 million inhabitants, mainly Russians. We know quite a bit about the Russians as their country was a world power for several hundreds of years before communism, and in the nineteenth century it has produced some of the greatest writers in world literature. If I want to understand the Russians—including how they could so long support the Soviet regime—I tend to re-read Lev Nikolayevich Tolstoy. In his most famous novel, *Anna Karenina* (1876), one of the main characters is a landowner, Levin, whom Tolstoy uses to express his own views and convictions about his people. Russian peasants used to be serfs; serfdom had been abolished in 1861, but the peasants, now tenants, remained as passive as before. Levin wanted to break this passivity by dividing the land among his peasants in exchange for a share of the crops; but the peasants only let the land deteriorate further. Here follows a quote:

"(Levin) read political economy and socialistic works . . . but, as he had expected, found nothing in them related to his undertaking. In the political economy books—in (John Stuart) Mill, for instance, whom he studied first and with great ardour, hoping every minute to find an answer to the questions that were engrossing him—he found only certain laws deduced from the state of agriculture in Europe; but he could not for the life of him see why these laws, which did not apply to Russia, should be considered universal. . . . Political economy told him that the laws by which Europe had developed and was developing her wealth were universal and absolute. Socialist teaching told him that development along those lines leads to ruin. And neither of them offered the smallest enlightenment as to what he, Levin, and all the Russian peasants and landowners were to do with their millions of hands and millions of acres, to make them as productive as possible for the common good."

In the summer of 1991, the Russian lands yielded a record harvest, but a large share of it rotted in the fields because no people were to be found for harvesting. The passivity is still there, and not only among the peasants.

And the heirs of John Stuart Mill (whom we met before as one of the early analysts of "management") again present their universal recipes which simply do not apply.

Citing Tolstoy, I implicitly suggest that management theorists cannot neglect the great literature of the countries they want their ideas to apply to. The greatest novel in the Chinese literature is considered Cao Xueqin's *The Story of the Stone,* also known as *The Dream of the Red Chamber* which appeared around 1760. It describes the rise and fall of two branches of an aristocratic family in Beijing, who live in adjacent plots in the capital. Their plots are joined by a magnificent garden with several pavillions in it, and the young, mostly female members of both families are allowed to live in them. One day the management of the garden is taken over by a young woman, Tan-Chun, who states:

"I think we ought to pick out a few experienced trust-worthy old women from among the ones who work in the Garden—women who know something about gardening already—and put the upkeep of the Garden into their hands. We needn't ask them to pay us rent, all we need ask them for is an annual share of the produce. There would be four advantages in this arrangement. In the first place, if we have people whose sole occupation is to look after trees and flowers and so on, the condition of the Garden will improve gradually year after year and there will be no more of those long periods of neglect followed by bursts of feverish activity when things have been allowed to get out of hand. Secondly there won't be the spoiling and wastage we get at present. Thirdly the women themselves will gain a little extra to add to their incomes which will compensate them for the hard work they put in throughout the year. And fourthly, there's no reason why we shouldn't use the money we should other-wise have spent on nurserymen, rockery specialists, horticultural cleaners and so on for other purposes."

As the story goes on, the capitalist privatization—because that is what it is—of the Garden is carried through, and it works. When in the 1980s Deng Xiaoping allowed privatization in the Chinese villages, it also worked. It worked so well that its effects started to be felt in politics and threatened the existing political order; hence the knockdown at Tienanmen Square of June 1989. But it seems that the forces of privatization are getting the upper hand again in China. If we remember what Chinese entrepreneurs are able to do once they have become Overseas Chinese, we shouldn't be too sur-prised. But what works in China—and worked two centuries ago—does not have to work in Russia, not in Tolstoy's days and not today. I am not of-fering a solution; I only protest against a naive universalism that knows only one recipe for development, the one supposed to have worked in the United States.

A THEORY OF CULTURE IN MANAGEMENT

Our trip around the world is over and we are back in the United States. What have we learned? There is something in all countries called "management," but its meaning differs to a larger or smaller extent from one country to the other, and it takes considerable historical and cultural insight into local conditions to understand its processes, philosophies, and problems. If already the word may mean so many different things, how can we expect one country's theories of management to apply abroad? One should be extremely careful in making this assumption, and test it before considering it proven. Management is not a phenomenon that can be isolated from other processes taking place in a society. During our trip around the world we saw that it interacts with what happens in the family, at school, in politics, and government. It is obviously also related to religion and to beliefs about science. Theories of management always had to be interdisciplinary, but if we cross national borders they should become more interdisciplinary than ever.

Cultural differences between nations can be, to some extent, described using first four, and now five, bipolar *dimensions*. The position of a country on these dimensions allows us to make some predictions on the way their society operates, including their management processes and the kind of theories applicable to their management.

As the word culture plays such an important role in my theory, let me give you my definition, which differs from some other very respectable definitions. Culture to me is *the collective programming of the mind which distinguishes one group or category of people from another*. In the part of my work I am referring to now, the category of people is the nation.

Culture is a *construct*, that means it is "not directly accessible to observation but inferable from verbal statements and other behaviors and useful in predicting still other observable and measurable verbal and nonverbal behavior." It should not be reified; it is an auxiliary concept that should be used as long as it proves useful but bypassed where we can predict behaviors without it.

The same applies to the *dimensions* I introduced. They are constructs too that should not be reified. They do not "exist;" they are tools for analysis which may or may not clarify a situation. In my statistical analysis of empirical data the first four dimensions together explain forty-nine percent of the variance in the data. The other fifty-one percent remain specific to individual countries.

The first four dimensions were initially detected through a comparison of the values of similar people (employees and managers) in sixty-four national subsidiaries of the IBM Corporation. People working for the same multinational, but in different countries, represent very well-matched samples from the populations of their countries, similar in all respects except nationality.

The first dimension is labelled *Power Distance,* and it can be defined as the degree of inequality among people which the population of a country considers as normal: from relatively equal (that is, small power distance) to extremely unequal (large power distance). All societies are unequal, but some are more unequal than others.

The second dimension is labelled *Individualism,* and it is the degree to which people in a country prefer to act as individuals rather than as members of groups. The opposite of individualism can be called *Collectivism,* so collectivism is low individualism. The way I use the word it has no political connotations. In collectivist societies a child learns to respect the group to which it belongs, usually the family, and to differentiate between in-group members and out-group members (that is, all other people). When children grow up they remain members of their group, and they expect the group to protect them when they are in trouble. In return, they have to remain loyal to their group throughout life. In individualist societies, a child learns very early to think of itself as "I" instead of as part of "we." It expects one day to have to stand on its own feet and not to get protection from its group any more; and therefore it also does not feel a need for strong loyalty.

The third dimension is called *Masculinity* and its opposite pole *Femininity.* It is the degree to which tough values like assertiveness, performance, success and competition, which in nearly all societies are associated with the role of men, prevail over tender values like the quality of life, maintaining warm personal relationships, service, care for the weak, and solidarity, which in nearly all societies are more associated with women's roles. Women's roles differ from men's roles in all countries; but in tough societies, the differences are larger than in tender ones.

The fourth dimension is labelled *Uncertainty Avoidance,* and it can be defined as the degree to which people in a country prefer structured over unstructured situations. Structured situations are those in which there are clear rules as to how one should behave. These rules can be written down, but they can also be unwritten and imposed by tradition. In countries which score high on uncertainty avoidance, people tend to show more nervous energy, while in countries which score low, people are more easy-going. A (national) society with strong uncertainty avoidance can be called rigid; one with weak uncertainty avoidance, flexible. In countries where uncertainty avoidance is strong a feeling prevails of "what is different, is dangerous." In weak uncertainty avoidance societies, the feeling would rather be "what is different, is curious."

The fifth dimension was added on the basis of a study of the values of students in twenty-three countries carried out by Michael Harris Bond, a Canadian working in Hong Kong. He and I had cooperated in another study of students' values which had yielded the same four dimensions as the IBM data. However, we wondered to what extent our common findings in two studies could be the effect of a Western bias introduced by the common Western background of the researchers: remember Alice's croquet game. Michael Bond resolved this dilemma by deliberately introducing an Eastern bias. He used a questionnaire prepared at his request by his Chinese colleagues, the *Chinese Value Survey* (CVS), which was translated from Chinese into different languages and answered by fifty male and fifty female students in each of twenty-three countries in all five continents. Analysis of the CVS data produced three dimensions significantly correlated with the three IBM dimensions of power distance, individualism, and masculinity. There was also a fourth dimension, but it did not resemble uncertainty avoidance. It was composed, both on the positive and on the negative side, from items that had not been included in the IBM studies but were present in the Chinese Value Survey because they were rooted in the teachings of Confucius. I labelled this dimension: *Long-term* versus *Short-term Orientation.* On the long-term side one finds values oriented towards the future, like thrift (saving) and persistence. On the short-term side one finds values rather oriented towards the past and present, like respect for tradition and fulfilling social obligations.

Table 1 lists the scores on all five dimensions for the United States and for the other countries we just discussed. The table shows that each country has its own configuration on the four dimensions. Some of the values in the table have been estimated based on imperfect replications or personal impressions. The different dimension scores do not "explain" all the differences in management I described earlier. To understand management in a country, one should have both knowledge of and empathy with the entire local scene. However, the scores should make us aware that people in other countries may think, feel, and act very differently from us when confronted with basic problems of society.

IDIOSYNCRACIES OF AMERICAN MANAGEMENT THEORIES

In comparison to other countries, the U.S. culture profile presents itself as below average on power distance and uncertainty avoidance, highly individualistic, fairly masculine, and short-term oriented. The Germans show a stronger uncertainty avoidance and less extreme individualism; the Japanese are different on all dimensions, least on power distance; the French show larger power distance and uncertainty avoidance, but are less individualistic and somewhat feminine; the Dutch resemble the Americans on the first three dimensions, but score extremely feminine and relatively long-term oriented; Hong Kong Chinese combine large power distance with

Table 1

Culture Dimension Scores for Ten Countries

PD = Power Distance; ID = Individualism; MA = Masculinity; UA = Uncertainty
Avoidance; LT = Long Term Orientation; H = top third, M = medium third,
L = bottom third (among 53 countries and regions for the first four dimensions;
among 23 countries for the fifth)

	PD	*ID*	*MA*	*UA*	*LT*
USA	40L	91H	62H	46L	29L
Germany	35L	67H	66H	65M	31M
Japan	54M	46M	95H	92H	80H
France	68H	71H	43M	86H	30˚L
Netherlands	38L	80H	14L	53M	44M
Hong Kong	68H	25L	57H	29L	96H
Indonesia	78H	14L	46M	48L	25˚L
West Africa	77H	20L	46M	54M	16L
Russia	95˚H	50˚M	40˚L	90˚H	10˚L
China	80˚H	20˚L	50˚M	60˚M	118H

* estimated

weak uncertainty avoidance, collectivism, and are very long-term oriented, and so on.

The American culture profile is reflected in American management theories. I will just mention three elements not necessarily present in other countries: the stress on market processes, the stress on the individual, and the focus on managers rather than on workers.

The Stress on Market Processes

During the 1970s and 80s it has become fashionable in the United States to look at organizations from a "transaction costs" viewpoint. Economist Oliver Williamson has opposed "hierarchies" to "markets." The reasoning is that human social life consists of economic transactions between individuals. We found the same in d'Iribarne's description of the U.S. principle of the contract between employer and employee, the labor market in which the worker sells his or her labor for a price. These individuals will form hierarchical organizations when the cost of the economic transactions (such as getting information, finding out whom to trust, etc.) is lower in a hierarchy than when all transactions would take place in a free market.

From a cultural perspective the important point is that *the "market" is the point of departure or base model,* and the organization is explained from market failure. A culture that produces such a theory is likely to prefer organizations that internally resemble markets to organizations that internally resemble more structured models, like those in Germany or France. The ideal principle of control in organizations in the market philosophy is *competition* between individuals. This philosophy fits a society that combines a not-too-large power distance with a not-too-strong uncertainty avoidance and individualism; besides the USA, it will fit all other Anglo countries.

The Stress on the Individual

I find this constantly in the design of research projects and hypotheses; also in the fact that in the U.S. psychology is clearly a more respectable discipline in management circles than sociology. Culture however is a collective phenomenon. Although we may get our information about culture from individuals, we have to interpret it at the level of collectivities. There are snags here known as the "ecological fallacy" and the "reverse ecological fallacy." None of the U.S. college textbooks on methodology I know deals sufficiently with the problem of multilevel analysis.

A striking example is found in the otherwise excellent book *Organizational Culture and Leadership* by Edgar H. Schein (1985). On the basis of his consulting experience he compares two large companies, nicknamed "Action" and "Multi." He explains the differences in culture between these companies by the group dynamics in their respective boardrooms. Nowhere in the book are any conclusions drawn from the fact that the first company is an American-based computer firm, and the second a Swiss-based pharmaceutics firm. This information is not even mentioned. A stress on interactions among individuals obviously fits a culture identified as the most individualistic in the world, but it will not be so well understood by the four-fifths of the world population for whom the group prevails over the individual.

One of the conclusions of my own multilevel research has been that culture at the national level and culture at the organizational level—corporate culture—are two very different phenomena and that the use of a common term for both is confusing. If we do use the common term, we should also pay attention to the occupational and the gender level of culture. National cultures differ primarily in the fundamental, invisible values held by a majority of their members, acquired in early childhood, whereas organizational cultures are a much more superficial phenomenon residing mainly in the visible practices of the organization, acquired by socialization of the new members who join as young adults. National cultures change only very slowly if at all; organizational cultures may be consciously changed, although this isn't necessarily easy. This difference between the two types of culture is the secret of the existence of multinational corporations that employ, as I showed in the IBM case, employees with extremely different national cultural values. What keeps them together is a corporate culture based on common practices.

The Stress on Managers Rather than Workers

The core element of a work organization around the world is the people who do the work. All the rest is superstructure, and I hope to have demonstrated to you that it may take many different shapes. In the U.S. literature on work organization, however, the core element, if not explicitly then implicitly, is considered the manager. This may well be the result of the combination of extreme individualism with fairly strong masculinity, which has turned the manager into a culture hero of almost mythical proportions. For example, he—not really she—is supposed to make decisions all the time. Those of you who are or have been managers must know that this is a fable. Very few management decisions are just "made" as the myth suggests it. Managers are much more involved in maintaining networks; if anything, it is the rank-and-file worker who can really make decisions on his or her own, albeit on a relatively simple level.

An amusing effect of the U.S. focus on managers is that in at least ten American books and articles on management I have been misquoted as having studied IBM *managers* in my research, whereas the book clearly describes that the answers were from IBM *employees*. My observation may be biased, but I get the impression that compared to twenty or thirty years ago less research in this country is done among employees and more on managers. But managers derive their *raison d'etre* from the people managed: culturally, they are the followers of the people they lead, and their effectiveness depends on the latter. In other parts of the world, this exclusive focus on the manager is less strong, with Japan as the supreme example.

CONCLUSION

This article started with *Alice in Wonderland*. In fact, the management theorist who ventures outside his or her own country into other parts of the world is like Alice in Wonderland. He or she will meet strange beings, customs, ways of organizing or disorganizing and theories that are clearly stupid, old-fashioned or even immoral—yet they may work, or at least they may not fail more frequently than corresponding theories do at home. Then, after the first culture shock, the traveller to Wonderland will feel enlightened, and may be able to take his or her experiences home and use them advantageously. All great ideas in science, politics and management have travelled from one country to another, and been enriched by foreign influences. The roots of American management theories are mainly in Europe: with Adam Smith, John Stuart Mill, Lev Tolstoy, Max Weber, Henri Fayol, Sigmund Freud, Kurt Lewin and many others. These theories were re-planted here and they developed and bore fruit. The same may happen again. The last thing we need is a Monroe doctrine for management ideas.

Organizational Culture and Strategic Leadership: Issues in the Management of Strategic Change

Clayton G. Smith and Robert P. Vecchio

The concept of organizational culture is certainly not new. The successes of many companies are frequently attributed to their cultures (or to similar terms, such as climate). Likewise, the failure of mergers is often explained in terms of the difficulties of marrying two business organizations with differing cultures (Chatterjee et al., 1992). But while it is generally accepted that organizations may be described in cultural terms, the foundations of organizational culture have proven to be somewhat elusive (Sackmann, 1992). Further, the ways in which organizational culture influences the effectiveness of an organization are not fully understood. As will be discussed below, an organization's culture can greatly influence its strategic management processes—both in terms of the options that are generated in the formation of strategy, and in how effectively a given strategy is implemented.

In this article, we explore the construct of organizational culture and relate it to the process of strategic management. Following an overview of the concept of organizational culture and its significance, a framework is proposed for analyzing the culture of an organization. Six central elements of organizational culture are identified and discussed: (a) critical decisions of founding members, (b) guiding ideas, (c) social structure, (d) norms, values, and premises, (e) remembered history and symbolism, and (f) institutionalized arrangements. The issue of how culture influences the ability of an established company to institute effective strategic change is then considered.

ORGANIZATIONAL CULTURE AND ASSESSMENTS OF "WHAT WORKS"

In the collective literatures of anthropology, sociology, and social psychology, many definitions of the term "culture" can be found. Social psychologists Krech et al. defined culture as:

... the pattern of all those arrangements, material and behavioral, which have been adopted by a society as the traditional ways of solving problems of its members. Culture includes all the institutionalized ways and the implicit cultural beliefs, norms, values, and premises which underlie and govern conduct (1962: 380).

And according to anthropologist C. S. Ford,

Culture is composed of responses which have been accepted because they have met with success (as quoted in Kroeber and Kluckhohn, 1952: 55).

Similarly, the core of an organization's culture is composed of the norms[1] and the shared values[2] and premises (taken-for-granted assumptions) of its members (Schein, 1984; Smircich, 1983; Wiener, 1988). Norms, values, and premises are reflected in the informal systems that emerge within the company over time—the habits and routines that develop, and the unwritten understandings that people gain about "how business gets done around here," and "what it's like out there." As discussed below, norms, values, and premises are also reflected in the firm's institutionalized arrangements, which include formal management systems (measurement and reward systems, information systems, planning systems, and training systems, etc.), and written policies covering common situations that occur (Peters, 1980). Taken together, these aspects of an organization's culture result from the firm's accumulated experience, experience which gives rise to assessments about "what works" when handling problems concerning the organization and its environment.

Through organizational experience and the emergence of social processes, people develop common ways of interpreting events, and attitudes about what is important and what actions should be taken under given conditions (Wilkins, 1979). This orientation provides members with an ordered approach to routine problems that arise—a way of responding to events according to approved perspectives. Moreover, the company's management systems and policies orient attention and decision making toward "important" issues and information. For example, reward systems gauge performance according to measures that are regarded as important (such as market share at Pepsico). Likewise, formal information systems commu-

---

1. Norms are typically viewed as rules or standards that define what people should or should not do in given situations.
2. A value is usually defined as a belief concerning what is good, right, wise, or beneficial.

nicate "valuable" information. In their operation, management systems and policies reinforce norms, values, and premises by directing and constraining the attention of individual members. And the decisions that are made by members "continually reaffirm the corporation's culture and reinforce expected behavior across the organization" (Schwartz and Davis, 1981: 35).

The orientation that develops helps to produce a homogeneous organization, which is a particularly important aid to communication; shared understandings facilitate the flow of information and the making of decisions. However, the cost of these commitments is a loss of creativity, flexibility, and adaptability. They tie the organization to traditional customers; they bind the company to established marketing practices and technologies; and they constrain the firm from altering long-standing patterns of resource allocation. Rooted in the authority of experience and, often, a history of success, organizational culture tends to be inertial (Tushman and Romanelli, 1985). While a company's culture can make the organization more livable, more orderly, and in important respects, stronger, it can also reduce the firm's capacity to adapt and survive under new conditions. Thus, it is important to understand how a firm develops and maintains a "culture," and how an established culture can influence the effectiveness of efforts to institute strategic change. It is to these issues that our focus now turns.

A FRAMEWORK OF ORGANIZATION CULTURE

In this section, a framework is developed for analyzing organizational culture and its foundations. Issues that were briefly introduced in the previous section are examined further, and other aspects of organizational culture are also developed. As shown in Figure 1, an organization's culture can be

Figure 1
A Framework for Analyzing Organizational Culture

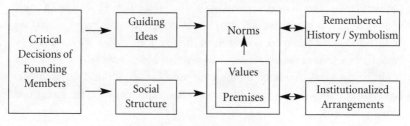

viewed in terms of a set of six central elements. Through an exploration of these elements, it is possible to gain an understanding of how an organization develops a culture, or in Selznick's (1957) words, a "distinctive identity." The framework also helps to explain the forces that sustain an organization's culture over time.

Critical Decisions of Founding Members

The founder of a company, or a small group of founding members who start a firm, can play a particularly important role in the development of an organization's culture. Such individuals bring their personal goals, values, and dreams to the fledgling organization. Frequently, it is their goals and values, and their conception of the organization's mission, that define the initial commitments of the enterprise. Strategic decisions that are made by the company's founding members concerning the firm's product market scope define the task environment and provide the focus for organizational learning. The nature of that environment—how competitive it is, how rapid the rate of change is, how high the degree of risk is, and so forth—will profoundly shape the organization's experience and its character. Similarly, decisions that are made within this environment to employ certain technologies and methods of manufacturing and marketing shape the organization's experience and character as well (Gordon, 1991).

The recruiting decisions of founding members often fill the organization with individuals who share particular ideas and values, and thereby affect the capacity of the company to control its future behavior. Such decisions help to foster organizational commitment to goals and policies. But at the same time, the values of the new recruits can restrain the firm from making subsequent decisions that would be inconsistent with those values.

In sum, the initial impact of the firm's founding members will be through the making of such decisions, decisions that can be of critical importance in the formation of the organization's culture (Kets de Vries and Miller, 1986). As will be described in the next section, the impact of a company's founding members will also come through the guiding ideas that are conceived and developed as a result of their actions (Clark, 1972). Eventually, their activities will affect other important aspects of the organization's culture, and the character of the company that the founding members build may remain intact long after new leaders and members have assumed their positions.

Guiding Ideas

One of the key functions of an entrepreneur, or any leader, is the creation and maintenance of a system of shared values. A leader performs this function, in part, by articulating a small number of guiding ideas. A guiding idea (referred to as a "superordinate goal" by Waterman et al., 1980) is a statement of purpose or mission that embodies fundamental aspects of the organization's existing character, or the character that a company's leadership seeks to build. A guiding idea is usually set forth by the organization's founder or founding members when the firm is young. However, it is also possible that a subsequent leader or coalition may conceive a guiding idea, or that it may simply evolve. For societies, an example of a guiding idea is "The American Dream." For companies, examples of guiding ideas include "IBM Means Service" and, at 3M, "The 11th commandment is never kill a new product idea." Guiding ideas serve to shape and communicate values and premises; they also serve to foster norms.

Over time, a guiding idea may become a source of direction for thinking and behavior, as members come to share a common experience within the organization, and as the company's efforts meet with success. As a guiding idea is followed, and as it is validated by accomplishments in the marketplace, the firm becomes predictable with respect to that aspect of organizational life. As a result, the company may take on a distinctive identity (Clark, 1972). In most instances, this identity cannot be readily abandoned. An organization's history may be interpreted to show that it has adhered to its guiding ideas, and that they are the basis of the firm's success, thereby giving legitimacy to established practices. Moreover, these commitments may be highly valued by members, and the historical interpretation may take on an emotional loading. Thus, a story of past commitments may influence current conceptions and expectations, and create pressures to continue to fulfill these expectations (Wilkins, 1979).

Social Structure

The social structure that emerges and is sustained within an organization reflects a pattern of interactions that develops among people, between people and their jobs, and among groups. Over time, people develop attitudes about themselves and what they are doing, about others in the company, and about the organization and its environment. The pattern is historical in that it reflects the specific experiences of the organization. It is also dynamic, because it generates social forces, especially internal interest groups made up of people committed to particular aims and policies (Selznick, 1957).

Selznick argues that while the organization begins as a tool, it may subsequently take on added meaning from the psychological and social functions that it performs, and from the unique way in which it comes to fulfill personal and group needs. Because of this, the organization may become valued for itself as members come to see it as a source of personal satisfaction. Some members will value the organization more than others. But the more an organization's social structure develops, the more it is likely to become valued for its own sake. In essence, the organization becomes an institutional fulfillment of group integrity and aspiration.

A measure of the extent to which an organization has become valued for itself is the degree to which it is viewed as being expendable. If an organization is seen as expendable, members will offer little resistance to actions that would alter its character. When value infusion occurs, however, such actions will cause members to feel a sense of personal loss. They may feel that the "identity" of the group has been violated. As a result, members may offer significant resistance, and yield to economic or technological considerations only as a last resort. Their resistance becomes a struggle to preserve the uniqueness of the group in the face of change.

Norms, Values, and Premises

Through organizational experience and the emergence of a social structure, individuals will (within the context of their "location" in the organization) develop norms, or expectations about what the company, its constituent units, and its members should or should not do in particular situations. In essence, norms constitute expectations about what actions are called for under given conditions. People will also develop values, or explicit beliefs concerning what is good, right, or beneficial for the enterprise and its members. And finally, they will develop a set of premises, or taken-for-granted assumptions, that they will use unconsciously when interpreting events that occur in the organization and its environment. In other words, members become sensitized to certain ways of perceiving events that take place, as individuals, as members of parochial groups, and as members of the organization. As with norms, values and premises are shaped by the company's historic experience and the personal involvement of individuals in the organization over time. But it should be noted that values and premises also affect the formation and maintenance of norms as well.

Remembered History and Symbolism

The history of a company, whether informally remembered or officially recorded, is not an integrated flow of events. Rather, certain aspects of history are noted, while others are ignored or forgotten, and still others are exaggerated or distorted. This selective perception of history is tied to the norms, values, and premises of the organization, and can play a very important role in maintaining and enhancing its culture. Clark (1972), Pettigrew (1979), and Wilkins (1979) discuss several social phenomena that are related to the remembered history of an organization, including symbols, sagas, myths, folklore, and rituals. As will become apparent, these phenomena are associated with emotional or attitudinal functions, and information processing functions. They also are important means of organizational control, because they help to shape the understandings people have about what they should do under given conditions.

Symbols

Symbols are objects, acts, concepts, or language that members use to express feelings, images, or values. They may evoke emotions and impel people to action (Dandridge et al., 1980: Pettigrew, 1979). Among the concepts that are important for the remembered history of an organization, "symbols" is the most inclusive category (encompassing myths and rituals for example), and symbols help to express the character of the organization to members and outsiders. Efforts to change the direction of an organization that threaten to erode or destroy important symbols may meet with substantial resistance. However, the effective use of symbols can also be a valuable tool in the successful implementation of fundamental change. The qualities that symbols possess for communicating values and legitimizing practices suggest their importance in the analysis of organizational culture.

Sagas

According to Clark (1972), an organizational saga is a collective understanding of a unique accomplishment of the formal organization. A saga often begins as a strongly stated purpose (a guiding idea), conceived by a single person or a small group. The usual setting is the autonomous, new organization. However, it is also possible that a saga may be initiated in an established organization in the midst of crisis and suffering from years of decay, or sometimes, in an organization that is sound but facing the need for substantial change. A saga typically explores the key events (e.g., the organization's founding, critical incidents, etc.) that helped to shape the character of the organization, and describes how the guiding idea was followed and fulfilled by the actions of its members. In so doing, a saga provides a connection between history and purposes or values, and it serves as an important means of maintaining an image of distinctiveness about the organization.

It may take years (even decades) for a saga to become firmly established. And, while based on historical events, it is often embellished through retelling and rewriting. But a saga that is well-developed will affect the definition of the organization, and will be protected from participants who might wish to relegate it to the past. Usually a saga will prove to be very long-lasting and stable, and will be abandoned only after years of steady organizational decline. By appealing to shared values, sagas serve as a powerful means of producing unity and attachment to the organization and its policies. "It makes links across internal divisions and organizational boundaries as groups share their common beliefs" (Clark, 1972: 183). At the same time, it should be noted that the unique identity that is fostered can suggest differences between the organization and external groups.

Myths, Folklore, and Rituals

Myths are sacred narratives of events that depart from the objective world, and explore (in dramatic form) issues of origin and transformation (Pettigrew, 1979). In so doing, they help to communicate values, and legitimize current organizational practices by offering explanations of past events. Pettigrew briefly discusses the role of myths in supporting stability and unity in the organization. He also argues that myths can be created and used by interest groups to further their causes. It is suggested that myths can be used by individuals and groups to justify their stances "and affirm wavering or aspiring power positions . . . [Myths may] justify and sustain values that underlie political interests, explain, and thereby reconcile the contradictions between professed values and actual behavior, and legitimize established leadership systems faced with threats" (Pettigrew, 1979: 576).

Wilkins notes that studies of folklore indicate that stories are often used to teach the consequences of behavior. "Among the Jicarilla Apache, for example, grandparents or other relatives use stories (isolated episodes) to instruct the young about appropriate behavior" (Wilkins, 1979: 6). Fables and folk tales with morals are also used to instill attitudes and principles into new members of an organization. Rituals are important because of the messages that they contain. They can indicate which are important or marginal values, which goals are most important and which take a lower priority, who the key people of the organization are, and which organizational units have the most power. "It is partially through rituals that social relationships become stylized, conventionalized, and prescribed" (Pettigrew, 1979: 576). And like myths and folklore, rituals help to communicate and reinforce what is valued (Trice and Beyer, 1984).

To summarize what has been said so far, the remembered history of an organization (whether realistic or exaggerated) serves to help maintain and enhance its culture. The concepts that have been discussed can connect history with purposes and shared values, and thereby foster commitment and unity. They can also be used to encourage conformity with social norms, to direct individual action toward common goals, to legitimize established practice and status arrangements, and to reconcile differences between expressed values and actual behavior. By encouraging conformity and serving as a source of shared values and premises, these elements of an organization's culture also guide and limit decision making; the information that they contain about selective aspects of the organization's accumulated experience will often be abstracted and used to handle present situations in an "appropriate" manner. This leads us to consider the social information processing function of sagas and other concepts.

Social Information Processing Function

Because the number of factors that people can consider in decision making is limited, they often make decisions by using what amount to learned "programs" (March and Simon, 1958; Wilkins, 1979). These programs, which are used as though the person is performing a script, will be evoked by stimuli contained in mundane, everyday activities, or in critical situations that have occurred before. Scripts include routines that pertain to the independent actions of individuals, as well as routines that concern the coordinated efforts of members and groups (Stinchcombe, 1990). Since most of the problems that people face pertain to recurring activities, the use of scripts is usually an efficient and effective means of problem solving; it helps individuals to avoid a separate decision process each time a problem occurs. "People simply reduce the problem to one that has been satisfactorily solved in the past and use that program again" (Wilkins, 1979: 7–8).

For example, stories from organizational history may become scriptural and be applied in subsequent situations of a similar nature. Wilkins reported on an organization where there was a story concerning how the firm had avoided a layoff. It was called the "Nine-Day Fortnight" by participants. Wilkins paraphrased the story, which was told to him by company executives:

> In the early 1970s, the entire electronics industry suffered a drop in orders and most companies had begun to lay people off in significant numbers. Our calculations suggested the need to cut back 10% in our output and our salary level to match the decline in orders. However, an essential part of our company tradition is to avoid layoffs. After considerable discussion, we decided (who actually made the decision and how it was announced are points upon which informants differed) to require everyone from the president to the lowest-paid employee to take a 10% cut in pay and to stay home every other Friday. At first we worried about whether people in the company would go along with us, and there were a few critics, but most people thought it was a great idea. In fact, a good number of our employees got so used to having Friday off every other week that they were reluctant to go back to a full schedule. It took about six months to build up our orders again, but we didn't ever have to lay off our people (Wilkins, 1979: 10).

When a similar situation arose three years later, the scheme was again employed. It was also used at a plant in the Far East which experienced a sharp drop in orders. "Apparently, the nine-day fortnight has become a script in the company, not only because almost everybody remembers the story and thinks it was significant, but also because it continues to be evoked and applied in similar situations" (Wilkins, 1979: 10). In addition to its social information processing and decision-making functions, the story has an emotional appeal in that it helps to communicate the fact that the company cares for the well-being of its members. The story is also used to help indoctrinate new employees, and it is invoked by executives who wish to defend or illustrate existing and proposed personnel policies.

Although only stories have been related to the function of social information processing, the other concepts that have been discussed aid in this regard as well. Each facilitates communication and decision making within the organization. But it should be noted that people who have absorbed a way of perceiving and evaluating experience may apply traditional scripts to non-routine or novel problems where they are not effective. They may do this partly out of habituation and partly out of the desire to conform to established norms. This can make it more difficult for the organization to deal with environmental change.

Institutionalized Arrangements

Beyond the influence of remembered history, the decisions of individuals and groups are also guided by institutionalized arrangements, which encompass formal management systems and written policies. Management systems include measurement and reward, information, planning, and training systems. Policies are "decision rules that are used in recognizable, repetitive, structured problem-solving situations" (Schendel, 1977: 11). To some degree, an organization's management systems and policies reflect its remembered history. The "nine-day fortnight," for instance, reveals how remembered history can come to be manifested in company policy. But fundamentally, policies and systems reflect the adaptation of the organization to its environment (Stinchcombe, 1990) and the norms, values, and premises that develop in the process.[3] Policies and systems embody suppositions about events that routinely occur, and attitudes about what is important and what actions should be taken under given conditions.

An important point to understand is that an organization's institutionalized arrangements exert a powerful form of control, because they fundamentally influence behavior (Bower, 1970; Peters, 1980). Formal information systems, for instance, orient attention and decision making toward certain issues and types of information, since people tend to respond to what they actually see. Similarly, people will consider how their performance is gauged by the company's reward system as they make decisions and take action. Written policies, of course, provide more explicit control by setting rules for such things as (e.g.) customer service. Because norms, values, and premises are embedded in the reports people read, the incentive systems under which they operate, the training they receive, the forms they fill out, and the policies within which they work, institutionalized arrangements serve to reinforce and thereby perpetuate the culture of an organization.

Studying Organizational Culture

The framework that we have outlined incorporates the central elements of

---

3. For example, if servicing the customer's needs was an important value of an office equipment company, this might be reflected in a policy of providing additional customer training at no extra charge if a customer had trouble learning how to use the equipment.

an organization's culture. Each of the identified elements can be ascertained in any formal organization—through personal interviews with members and leaders, through "partial membership" by the researcher in the organization, through self-administered questionnaires, through materials produced by the company pertaining to its history, and through articles and books written about the firm over time (Gregory, 1983; Wilkins, 1983). If the concepts discussed above are utilized as an analytical lens, all of these methods and sources can help to reveal the "makeup" of a company's culture and the dynamics of its cultural development. Indeed, as Duncan (1989) suggests, "triangulation" (the use of multiple approaches) can be a particularly effective means of studying the culture of an organization. While culture is often seen as being a rather nebulous aspect of organizations, it is possible to "get one's arms around it" to a considerable degree.

ORGANIZATIONAL CULTURE AND STRATEGIC RESPONSES TO ENVIRONMENTAL CHANGE

The effectiveness of an organization is substantially influenced by the assessments of members and leaders regarding "what works." These assessments depend to a great extent on the outlook and habits—the patterns of emphasis and judgment—that people develop over time. Such an orientation can be a tremendous source of strength when it is congruent with the firm's traditional strategy. Indeed, a strong culture is sometimes seen as one of the central characteristics of an "excellent" organization (Dennison, 1984; Peters and Waterman, 1982). But where environmental change calls for substantial changes in strategy—as has been true for the major U.S. auto producers for example—an established orientation can become a major liability (Gordon, 1991; Halberstam, 1986; Womack et al., 1990). And even when a firm is not faced with serious environmental threats, the established orientation of the organization may reduce its ability to perceive and take advantage of emerging opportunities.

In 1979, Roy Ash commented about the troubles of AM International, which he then headed. His comments help to illustrate how assessments of "what works," and the orientation on which they are based, can hinder organizational effectiveness.

> We have diagnosed our main challenge here at AM International not as sales or manufacturing or cost problems, but rather as cultural problems.

Our problems have been mindsets and prejudices. I'm not using these terms in a pejorative sense; it's simply that everyone here knew the decisions that had been made long ago. Those decisions, those prejudgments, guided the organization. Very few questions were being asked. People had stopped raising questions. And any questions that were being asked were answered with responses developed years ago (*Organizational Dynamics,* 1979: 53).

Subsequently, Ash was forced to step down because of the company's poor financial performance under his leadership. This poor performance record was partially due to his failure to build a solid foundation of profits before making acquisitions. Nevertheless, his comments still suggest how the culture of a company can hinder its effectiveness.

Influences on Strategy Formulation

An organization's culture may be viewed as a factor that moderates the reciprocal influence of the environment and strategy formulation. (This "moderating influence" of culture is depicted in Figure 2.) Strategies are built on the beliefs and assumptions that managers make about the enterprise and its environment (Weick, 1985). However, an organization's culture filters the perspective of its members, and affects their ability to *ask the right questions.* Frequently, the questions that are asked and the strategic options that are generated are tied to the organization's general outlook—a tacit image of the company and its mission. At the same time, the normative element of culture circumscribes the range of options that are acceptable.

Figure 2
The Reciprocal Influence of Strategy and Environment as
Moderated by Organizational Culture

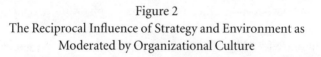

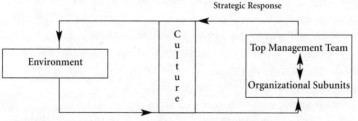

And when a firm has had a history of success, its success reaffirms the soundness of past practices in the minds of the company's leaders and other members (Argyris and Schön, 1978). The net result is that the options generated are inherently limited and may be inadequate to deal with threats that the company faces or opportunities that it could exploit.

Organizational culture can also influence the politics of strategic decisions. Members of organizational subunits usually hold unit-specific values and, among members of various subunits, there will be different viewpoints of "what works" for the company (Cyert and March, 1963; Van Cauwenbergh and Cool, 1982). Out of these varying perspectives, debates will ensue, and individuals and subunits may engage in bureaucratic maneuvering to defend their interests and steer decisions about strategy in what they believe is the right direction. The top management team will also make assessments regarding what strategies are most likely to succeed. These appraisals will depend not only on their perception of the company's resources and the conditions in the firm's environment, but also on how they believe different individuals and subunits will react to the strategy that is decided upon. In making these assessments, senior managers must consider who will support and who will resist a given alternative, as well as whether their support is vital for that strategy (Quinn, 1980).

Influences on Strategy Implementation

Issues such as the ones described above also raise questions regarding the implementation of strategic change. As individuals and as members of particular subunits, people will decide how organizational choices of strategy will affect them and the well-being of the company as a whole. These judgments will depend on their personal needs, on the norms and values of their units, and on the norms and values of the entire company. Perhaps more importantly, they will depend on the degree to which members personally identify with and are committed to the organization. Based on these judgments, individuals will choose to support the strategic decisions that are made, to remain neutral, or to actively resist them. Generally, when a new strategy threatens to substantially alter the character of an organization, members will offer resistance; the larger the intended change, the greater the resistance is likely to be (Huse, 1975).

There is a less tangible issue involved in the implementation of strategic change as well. Beyond new methods of manufacturing, marketing, and servicing, a new strategy may require an orientation—a way of thinking and processing information—that differs from the one that the organization and its members are geared to. Differing rates of market growth and rates of change, and differing types of uncertainty (e.g., unstable markets or technology) all require different approaches to business management. If a new strategy takes the company into areas that require an approach that is incompatible with the firm's traditional orientation, the organization may be ill-equipped to meet the needs and challenges of that strategy (Prahalad and Bettis, 1986; Stinchcombe, 1990). For this reason, the firm's attempts at implementing a new strategy may meet with limited success, even if little active resistance is met.

REFERENCES

Argyris, C., and D. Schön. 1978. *Organizational Learning.* Reading MA: Addison-Wesley.

Bower, J. L. 1970. *Managing the Resource Allocation Process: A Study of Corporate Planning and Investment.* Boston, MA: Graduate School of Business Administration, Harvard University.

Chatterjee, S., M. H. Lubatkin, D. M. Schweiger, and Y. Weber. 1992. "Cultural Differences and Shareholder Value in Related Mergers: Linking Equity and Human Capital." *Strategic Management Journal* 13: 319–334.

Clark, B. 1972. "The Organizational Saga in Higher Education." *Administrative Science Quarterly* 17: 178–184.

Cyert, R., and J. March. 1963. *A Behavioral Theory of the Firm.* Englewood Cliffs: Prentice-Hall.

Dandridge, T. C., I. Mitroff, and W. F. Joyce. 1980. "Organization Symbolism: A Topic to Expand Organizational Analysis." *Academy of Management Review* 5(1): 77–82.

Dennison, D. 1984. "Bringing Corporate Culture to the Bottom Line." *Organizational Dynamics* 13(2): 5–22.

Duncan, W. J. 1989. "Organizational Culture: 'Getting a Fix' on an Elusive Concept." *Academy of Management Executive* 3(3): 229–236.

Gordon, G. G. 1991. "Industry Determinants of Organizational Culture." *Academy of Management Review* 16(2): 396–415.

Gregory, K. L. 1983. "Native-View Paradigms: Multiple Cultures and Culture Conflicts in Organizations." *Administrative Science Quarterly* 28: 359–376.

Halberstam, D. 1986. *The Reckoning.* New York: William Morrow.

Huse, E. F. 1975. *Organization Development and Change.* St. Paul: West.

Kets de Vries, M. E. R., and D. Miller. 1986. "Personality, Culture, and Organization." *Academy of Management Review* 11(2): 266–279.

Krech, D., R. S. Crutchfield, and E. L. Ballachey. 1962. *Individual in Society.* New York: McGraw-Hill.

Kroeber, A. L., and C. Kluckhohn. 1952. *Culture: A Critical Review of Concepts and Definitions.* Cambridge: Harvard University Printing Office.

March, J., and H. Simon. 1958. *Organizations*. New York: Wiley.

Organizational Dynamics. 1979. "Conversation: An Interview with Roy L. Ash" (Autumn): 49–67.

Peters, T. J. 1980. "Management Systems: The Language of Character and Competence." *Organizational Dynamics* (Summer): 3–26.

———, and R. H. Waterman, Jr. 1982. *In Search of Excellence: Lessons from America's Best-Run Companies*. New York: Warner Books.

Pettigrew, A. M. 1979. "On Studying Organizational Cultures." *Administrative Science Quarterly* 24: 570–580.

Prahalad, C. K., and R. A. Bettis. 1986. "The Dominant Logic: A New Linkage between Diversity and Performance." *Strategic Management Journal* 7: 485–501.

Quinn, J. B. 1980. *Strategies for Change: Logical Incrementalism*. Homewood, IL: Irwin.

Sackmann, S. A. 1992. "Culture and Subcultures: An Analysis of Organizational Knowledge." *Administrative Science Quarterly* 37: 140–161.

Schein, E. H. 1984. "Coming to a New Awareness of Organizational Culture." *Sloan Management Review* (Winter): 3–16.

Schendel, D. 1977. "Goals, Strategy, and Environment." Unpublished Working Paper. Purdue University.

Schwartz, H., and S. M. Davis. 1981. "Matching Corporate Culture and Business Strategy." *Organizational Dynamics* (Summer): 30–48.

Selznick, P. 1957. *Leadership in Administration: A Sociological Interpretation*. Evanston: Row, Peterson.

Smircich, L. 1983. "Concepts of Culture and Organizational Analysis." *Administrative Science Quarterly* 28: 339–358.

Stinchcombe, A. L. 1990. *Information and Organizations*. Berkeley: University of California Press.

Trice, H. M., and J. M. Beyer. 1984. "Studying Organizational Cultures Through Rites and Ceremonials." *Academy of Management Review* 9(4): 653–669.

Tushman, M. L., and E. Romanelli. 1985. "Organizational Evolution: A Metamorphosis Model of Convergence and Reorientation." In *Research in Organizational Behavior*. Ed. L. L. Cummings and B. M. Staw. Greenwich, CT: JAI Press.

Van Cauwenbergh, A., and K. Cool. 1982. "Strategic Management in a New Framework." *Strategic Management Journal* 3: 245–264.

Waterman, R. H., Jr., T. J. Peters, and J. R. Phillips. 1980. "Structure is Not Organization." *Business Horizons* (June): 14–26.

Weick, K. E. 1985. "The Significance of Corporate Culture." In *Organizational Culture*. Ed. P. J. Frost et al. Beverly Hills: Sage.

Wiener, Y. 1988. "Forms of Value Systems: A Focus on Organizational Effectiveness and Cultural Change and Maintenance." *Academy of Management Review* 13(4): 534–545.

Wilkins, A. L. 1979. "Organizational History, Legends and Control." Unpublished Working Paper. Brigham Young University.

———. 1983. "The Culture Audit: A Tool for Understanding Organizations." *Organizational Dynamics* (Autumn): 24–38.

Womack, J. P., D. T. Jones, and D. Roos. 1990. *The Machine that Changed that World*. New York: Macmillan.

Challenges to Leadership in the Implementation of Technological Change

Mary D. Zalesny and Robert P. Vecchio

This article examines influences on and consequences of the introduction of new technology at the level of the functional work unit and of the organization. In the following sections, the roles of critical variables in technological innovation, spanning both unit and organizational levels of analysis, are described. Also, propositions are offered that tie innovation to culture, and "subordinate acceptance of change" to the neglected topic of leadership influence at the interface of the first-level supervisor with nonsupervisory organizational members. Finally, implications are presented for the management of change in organizations confronted with technological change decisions.

Although the "technological imperative" implies that technology drives structural variation in organizations, changes in structure and modifications in technology frequently are influenced by the actions of first-level supervisors within organizations. The role of supervisors is therefore a critical, but often neglected, element in theorizing about the relation of structure and technology. We argue that leadership can impact on openness to innovation and that the favorability of this impact will be dependent on the nature of or need for supervision, and the extent to which the first-level supervisor's actions are congruent with employees' expectations for the management of change (Lord and Maher, 1990). The structural design features of an organization also are likely to be influenced by higher management's propensity to support change and innovations as a consequence of both inertial and pro-change processes (Gersick, 1994).

LEADERSHIP, TECHNOLOGICAL CHANGE, AND CULTURE

Some individuals, more than others, are likely to play a key role in successful implementation of technological and administrative innovations. In addition, at different stages of the implementation process, specific front-line individuals assume greater importance in achieving successful implementation. In some cultures (most notably in Western countries), first-level supervisors are in critical positions for impacting an innovation as they can directly affect the goal setting, feedback, and performance monitoring that are crucial to successful innovative efforts (Drucker, 1985).

Because these leaders frequently hold key positions with respect to the implementation process, it is important to obtain their commitment to ensure a successful change effort. Overcoming employee resistance to change and increasing employee openness often require the continued attention of immediate supervisors. Supervisors, as well, may understandably resist change as it may threaten their status and, therefore, their political power bases (Staw, Sandelands, and Dutton, 1981). Additionally, supervisors may fear that increases in unit efficiency may translate into a reduction in the ranks of supervisors.

Seven factors can be identified that influence the extent to which leaders at the frontline of an organization can influence and maintain change in organizations, such as the changes occurring contemporaneously with attempts to implement a new technology. First, the nature of the work to be performed and the abilities and competencies of the workers will partly determine the *extent to which first-level supervisors are needed to provide feedback, direction, and rewards.* Various views of group leadership have posited roles for task and subordinate attributes in the explanation of supervisory effectiveness (Fiedler and Chemers, 1984; Evans, 1974; House, 1971). For example, if there are standard operating procedures outlined for task completion and task-related indicators for performance feedback, a supervisor's ability to influence workgroup effectiveness may be limited. In their model of substitutes for leadership, Kerr and Jermier (1978) proposed that task, employee, and organizational characteristics can either substitute or neutralize supervisor attempts to influence employees either through support or through initiation of structure. For example, Hofstede (1992) has observed that the expertise of skilled German workers eliminates the need for task direction from supervisors who function, therefore, primarily as task consultants.

Hulin and Roznowski (1985) discussed the effects of advanced technology on tasks that shift some management control and information to technical employees who have the expertise to understand and use both the technology and the information it generates. Through its effects on task characteristics, advanced technology indirectly affects group composition and structure by changing the knowledge and skill requirements of the work. The adage that knowledge is power has particular relevance for supervisors faced with new technologies. To the extent that first-level supervisors lack the technological expertise to make credible pronouncements about the usefulness or appropriateness of a new technology, they may lose some of their credibility and power in their work groups.

Second, the *dominant social culture* surrounding the organization will influence the role and style of leadership that exists in the organization. In discussing three decades of research on leadership in Japan, Misumi and Peterson (1985) identified several cultural factors that may partially account for differences between Japanese and U.S. leaders in the reported effectiveness of performance (or structuring) and maintenance (or consideration) leadership styles. Among these factors are: (a) career patterns in Japan that encourage greater employee reliance on their formal supervisors for career guidance, (b) greater physical proximity of Japanese supervisors to their workgroup members, and (c) greater legitimate, reward, and coercive power of Japanese supervisors compared to their U.S. counterparts (leading to greater employee dependence on their supervisor for valued rewards). These factors, individually or jointly, are likely to contribute to differences between Japanese and U.S. supervisors and subordinates in openness to change and the determination of an optimal change strategy.

Cognitive approaches to group leadership suggest that leadership status is attributed to an individual on the basis of employee perceptions about leadership (Lord and Maher, 1990). Different cultures (and subcultures) are likely to possess differing sets of "criterial attributes" that are associated with ideal leadership. Employees whose definition of ideal leadership includes certain roles, behaviors, or characteristics (e.g., participative, accessible) are unlikely to accept the influence attempts of a supervisor whose perceived attributes do not encompass these criterial attributes, regardless of the formal title assigned to that individual. For example, Hofstede (1992) has observed that in the Netherlands, "modesty" is highly rated as a desired attribute of an ideal supervisor. However, among U.S. respondents, "modesty" is not regarded as an important feature of leadership.

Third, the existence *of formal representation of workers* (and of the government, in certain nations) may constrain a leader's authority and ability to facilitate change engendered by technological innovation. Where management shares responsibility and control with representatives of the employees and society, decisions to implement a new technology are also likely to be shared. Attempts to adopt a new technology that threatens specific jobs or the continued existence of entire organizational units may be seen as a danger to the established management-worker relationships and may result in strong employee or government action to protect the status quo (see, for example, Brett, 1980a, 1980b).

Fourth, *a leaders personal beliefs about employees and the process of leadership* may influence his or her willingness to become involved in the implementation of technological innovation, and to involve his or her subordinates in the implementation process. The Vertical Dyad Linkage model or Leader-member Exchange Theory (LMX) of work unit leadership (Graen and Cashman, 1975; Graen and Uhl-Bien, 1991) describes how leaders at all levels in an organization enter into differential exchange relationships with their subordinates. By their loyalty, effort, and performance, members of one subgroup of subordinates establish close and trusted relationships with the leader (in-group). These individuals function as informal assistants to the leader in accomplishing organizationally relevant tasks, and in return receive special rewards (e.g., greater autonomy, visibility, compensation, personal development opportunities, etc.). Members of the other subgroup of subordinates (the out-group) generally contribute, and receive in return, little more than what their explicit contract with the organization specifies.

Leaders with a broader base of support (i.e., with a comparatively higher percentage of their subordinates being members of their in-group) should be better able to initiate and accomplish successful adoption of a new technology as they have already established a social mechanism through which the acceptance of change by the workgroup may be enhanced. Moreover, leaders who are themselves members of their leader's in-group (i.e., who possess upward influence) will have access to more rewards and inducements for distribution among their own subordinates. Leaders who are in their supervisor's out-group may find it difficult to access and provide sufficient special rewards and benefits to their in-groups so as to succeed in their attempts at implementing new technology. To the extent that exchange transactions described in the LMX model are found to vary in importance across cultures (and there is evidence that LMX exchanges do exist in other cultures, Wakabayashi and Graen, 1984; Wakabayashi, Graen, Graen and Graen, 1988), the quality of exchange relationships may be an especially important avenue for the introduction and acceptance of innovations.

Fifth, supervisors who exhibit *behaviors characteristic of transformational leaders* may also engender greater acceptance of technological innovations among their subordinates than supervisors who do not exhibit such behaviors. Bass (1985) has described transformational leaders as those who can affect their subordinates by (a) increasing their awareness of the importance and value associated with desired outcomes (here, the successful implementation of a new technology), (b) influencing them to consider the greater interests of their workgroup and the organization rather than only their own self-interests, and (c) addressing their needs for personal growth and development. Proposed innovations that have "champions" (i.e., personal sponsors) who display attributes of transformational leadership are more likely to be adopted and effectively implemented. As part of a social process that may be similar in some ways to that used by supervisors to motivate in-group members, transformational leaders rely on special rewards to facilitate their influence attempts (Yukl, 1989). Reliance on transformational leaders for successful innovations may be effective to the extent that the characteristics of transformational leaders are valued within a culture.

Sixth, leaders may differ in the extent to which they are supportive of change in their units as a function of the stage that they occupy in their careers. That is, *more recently appointed first-level supervisors may be more open to innovation* than first-level supervisors with greater seniority. More established supervisors may have greater investments in the status quo, whereas newer supervisors may be less committed to past policies and procedures and are more likely to be seeking ways to distinguish themselves by improving unit performance (Damanpour, 1991; Kimberly and Evanisko, 1981). The primary loyalty of supervisors may also shift over time, such that newly appointed supervisors may be more desirous of implementing change that is apparently mandated by higher management, than supporting subordinates who may be offering resistance to change. This suggests that there may be an "optimal time" for attempting to introduce change that is influenced by a supervisor's willingness to support innovation which, in turn, is based on career stage issues.

In addition, the collectivism-individualism dimension (i.e., the valuing of "working together" versus "working alone") underlies differences in managerial openness to change (Hofstede, 1980). For example, proposing a new idea that does not originate from one's group may be viewed as selfish in a relatively collectivist country, such as Japan (Hornstein, 1986). Similarly, one can hypothesize that the collectivism-individualism dimensions may be associated with employee and supervisor willingness to accept the principles of semi-autonomous (i.e., relatively self-directed) work arrangements, such that team-based approaches to work may be more readily accepted in collectivist cultures.

Seventh, *aversion to risk-taking* (which can play an important role in influencing openness to innovation at a micro level) has also been found to vary by nationality (Bass, Burger, Doktor, and McPherson, 1979). For example, a sample of managers from the United States was found to be the least risk averse in comparison with other nationalities. In a comparison of Far Eastern (Singapore Chinese) and Anglo (North American and British) managers on Cattell's 16 Personal Factors Questionnaire, Gill (1983) reported that Far Eastern managers described themselves as relatively more reserved, conservative, serious, trusting, assertive, expedient, group dependent, and relaxed than did Anglo managers. In addition, the Far Eastern managers viewed themselves as less imaginative and tough-minded. Furthermore, supervisory openness to change and innovation is influenced by the larger culture's endorsement of change. For example, Americans are concerned with a need to control their environment or circumstances, while Hindus are inclined to believe that they cannot drastically alter the nature of personal circumstances (Adler, Doktor, and Redding, 1989). In a related view, the Japanese tend to discourage aspects of competitiveness (Hall and Hall, 1988).[1] Finally, differences may exist between cultures in terms of subordinates' willingness to accept authority as a source of truth versus observation (Solo, 1975).

In summary, we propose that specific leadership and contextual characteristics are expected to be associated with subordinate acceptance of change. Acceptance will be greater with:

(a) tasks that require supervisory feedback, direction, and rewards;
(b) a dominant social culture that espouses employee dependence on supervisors for guidance;
(c) cooperative, versus confrontational, forms of employer-employee sharing of responsibility and control;
(d) supervisors who hold personal beliefs that employees should be involved in the implementation process, thereby increasing their base of support;
(e) supervisors who exhibit behaviors that are characteristic of transformational leaders;
(f) supervisors who are more recently appointed; and
(g) supervisors who are comparatively low on aversion to risk-taking.

STRUCTURE AND TECHNOLOGY

In comparing successful organizations in industrialized and developing countries, Kiggundu (1989) observed that all the organizations followed a rational model of organizing. That is, they accomplished their critical operating tasks (i.e., the basic tasks through which the organization accomplished its objectives) by relying on rational principles of organization and management. However, it appears that highly successful economies (e.g., Japan) adopt, then adapt or modify, a rational model of organizing so as to achieve alignment with the dominant social values within the culture. This process should hold regardless of whether the culture is defined by national boundaries or by the shared history and experiences of a social group.

Societal culture should delimit the extent to which the adoption (and adaptation) of any new technology will alter the existing social systems within an organization to maximize the technology's effectiveness. Highly successful technological innovations developed in one culture may be less successful in another culture if they are simply imported without any modification (Ricks, 1983), and in doing so, may disrupt the established core cultural values among employees (Kiggundu, 1989). Also, it is almost a cliched notion to argue that flexible structures (i.e., structures with greater degrees of decentralization of knowledge and power, less formality or adherence to rules, and little hierarchical communication and authority) are advantageous for enhancing openness to change (Aiken and Hage, 1971; Kimberly and Evanisko, 1981; Pierce and Delbecq, 1977). As the predisposition to create flexible organizational structures is likely to be associated with societal cultural values regarding openness to change, the larger culture can be viewed as having the ability to act as a facilitating or impeding factor.

Hulin and Roznowski (1985) have proposed that technology, in addition to influencing organizational structure, is jointly influenced by the organization's size and developments in the basic industry of which the organization is a member. Larger organizations will certainly have more extensive resources than smaller organizations from which to draw upon when incorporating technological developments (Ford and Slocum, 1977; Dewar and Hage, 1978). Similarly, Barley (1986) and Burkhardt and Brass (1990) have argued that new technologies may actually alter the organizational structure by altering institutionalized roles and patterns of interaction. To be sure, the processes associated with diffusion of innovation within an industry, as well as the capacity of the industry's members to

absorb innovation, are central to any complete explanation of technological change (Czepiel, 1975). For example, in centrally planned economies,
diffusion of an innovation is more likely when there is ample technical capacity for adopting the innovation and when the necessary labor resources
are available (Bornstein, 1985). Also, organizations in industries that are
experiencing considerable technological growth will have greater opportunities and pressures to implement new technology than will organizations
in declining industries.

THE ROLE OF SOCIETAL CULTURE
IN TECHNOLOGICAL CHANGE

Societal Culture, Technology, and Structure

Organizational researchers have come to view technology (i.e., the types
and patterns of activity, equipment, material, and knowledge used to perform tasks) as a powerful influence in determining organizational structure
(Spacapan and Oskamp, 1990; Gillespie and Mileti, 1977). This view is so
widely assumed that it is termed the "technological imperative" (Grimes
and Klein, 1973). While accepting the proposed influence of technology
on structure, it can be reasonably argued that culture plays a similarly powerful role in determining structure *and* technology. That is to say, societal
culture influences the creation and nature of relationships between organizational members and units, as well as the decision to adopt specific forms
of technology. In essence, one can argue for the existence of a "cultural imperative." Although the "technological imperative" and the "cultural imperative" do not necessarily oppose one another, an area of special interest
arises when imperatives are in opposition. Such is the state of affairs when
the "technological imperative" meets opposition from firmly held cultural
values. In the West, cultural values have tended to give ground in many
areas of technological change. However, in parts of the world where traditional values are being reaffirmed, conflict between the imperatives may be
manifest (consider the confrontation of imperatives that has arisen as a
consequence of the Islamic fundamentalist movement, wherein, e.g., the
technology for birth control and organ transplant is available in certain
countries, yet it is outlawed because of conservative religious values).[2]

Bamber and Lambury (1989) suggest an even broader view emphasizing
a general "contextual imperative." Here, culture and technology are only
two of several factors (e.g., politics, economics) influencing openness to

and decisions regarding organizational change, including the adoption of new technologies. However, among these context factors, technology and culture appear to be more critical than the other factors for initiating and sustaining organizational change.

We propose that the "technological imperative" drives structural change in organizations. However, the "cultural imperative" determines the openness to change within organizations. The "cultural imperative," therefore, acts as a moderator of the impact of the "technological imperative."

Temporal Issues

An important factor to consider when conceptualizing technological change is the temporal element of the innovation process. Neither the decision to adopt an innovation nor the implementation of the innovation are discrete events (Rogers, 1983). Rather they are "time dependent processes" (Pennings, 1985) which are characterized by relatively discrete stages that result in innovation adoption (see also, Mohr, 1982). However, this is not to imply that there is a linear relation between the amount of time taken to innovate and the acceptance of an innovation. Each innovation and its context may dictate an "optimal span of time" required for effective implementation. The time that it takes an innovation to move through various stages of acceptance and implementation may determine partly its chances for actual acceptance and successful implementation. Administrative innovations that are rushed through the organization without sufficient opportunity for analysis, debate, and consensus-building are less likely to receive the support necessary to maintain them once they are in place. Technological innovations that are similarly installed without due consideration as to how they might affect existing organizational practices and work routines, or without ensuring that required support structures are available (e.g., training in new equipment, expert advice for trouble-shooting problems, etc.), are likely to be similarly handicapped from the start. A complete analysis of successful and unsuccessful innovations, then, necessitates documenting the processes through which an innovation traverses the organization (McGrath and Rotchford, 1983).

Cultural Value Shifts

Cultural change (i.e., shifts in shared values and norms) represents an important process that, depending on the direction and nature of the change, can influence openness to technological innovation. Hofstede (1980) has suggested that affluence may be a major determinant of a culture's shift from collectivism to individualism (e.g., he reported a strong correlation between the individualism score of a country and its per capita gross national product). Also, the mass media may contribute to cultural shifts toward individualism as most media programming (e.g., television, music, and films) originates in individualistic cultures. Cultural change in itself may be the result of societal shifts that reflect continual testing of basic beliefs concerning the nature of reality (Sorokin, 1941).

In order to examine cultural change in a rigorous fashion, longitudinal data are needed (Hofstede, 1980). Shifts in values and norms can be cautiously attributed to several possible causal processes based on the configuration of data across the age of the respondent (individuals or social units) and time. Maturation, generation, and zeitgeist are three possible influences on cultural shifts (Hofstede, 1980). Maturation effects refer to respondent values changing because of an aging process. Across respondents at the same stage of development, no differences are expected. Generation effects are reflected in the maintenance of values that were established during an earlier, formative period. These established values remain unchanged over time for members of a given cohort. Zeitgeist effects refer to dramatic changes in values or norms that occur for everyone regardless of age because of sudden system-wide shifts. Figures 1a, 1b, and 1c portray the patterns of results that reflect maturational, generational, and zeitgeist changes in values or norms.

The three patterns of change can be viewed from organizational and workgroup perspectives, as well as from an individual perspective. That is to say, the age of groups and organizations can be understood as a correlate of change in a manner similar to individuals. The three patterns of results can be taken as suggesting various underlying processes. The maturational effect for an organization is somewhat parallel to the view offered by Greiner (1972; Greiner and Bhambri, 1989) of organizations undergoing changes as they develop. The generational effect in an organizational context may be seen as parallel to cohort differences in organizational commitment of employees that reflect unique experiences, shifts in hiring practices, and changes in work ethic. Organizational zeitgeist effects might be exemplified by shifts in the way in which work is viewed because of dramatic events (e.g., a war-time economy, a severe economic depression, or the emergence of an "economic-bloc warfare" perspective). To complicate matters further, these three patterns can operate simultaneously. To the ex-

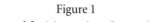
Figure 1
Patterns of Results Expected for Maturation, Generation and Zeitgeist Effects

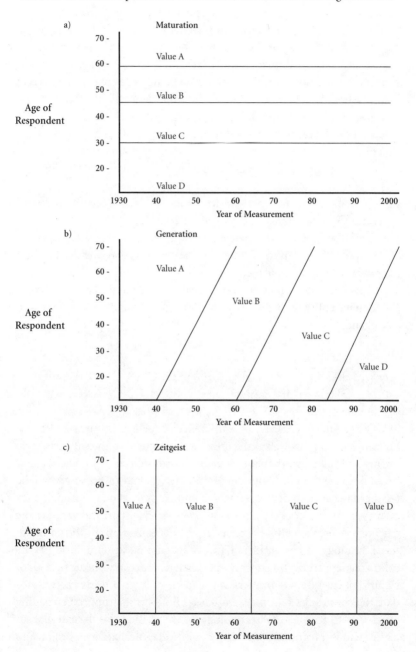

tent that a particular pattern is of interest as a "main effect," the operation of any additional patterns would be viewed as confounds. Nonetheless, a search for such patterns, especially the possible result that one pattern may be predominant for a given domain, seems worthwhile. Certainly, cross-cultural differences should be expected when one culture experiences a relatively placid environment and another is experiencing tumultuous change. Furthermore, seemingly equivalent employee cohorts in different cultures should not be assumed to exhibit equivalent attitudinal and behavioral responses to a proposed change. For example, flex-time may be a more valued or desirable innovation within a workforce that has a higher proportion of dual-career employees.

To summarize the above points, we offer the following propositions:

(a) An examination of "openness to change" must take account of maturational, generational, and zeitgeist effects;
(b) Degree of "openness to change" will be correlated with certain specific, yet potentially universal, cultural values (e.g., small power distance and low uncertainty avoidance, Hofstede, 1980); and
(c) Tracking historical events associated with revolutionary and evolutionary cultural change may aid in predicting shifts in "openness to change."[3]

INTEGRATING CULTURE, TECHNOLOGY, SUPERVISION, STRUCTURE, AND OPENNESS TO CHANGE

Thus far, we have focused on the influence of societal culture on technology and structure, as well as the influence of culture on the supervisor via norms for leadership behavior in relations with subordinates. The successful adoption and implementation of a new technology (especially when the technology has been developed in one culture and is being considered for adoption into another culture) requires that certain critical variables be considered: (a) the culture external to the organization, (b) the nature of the technology being considered, (c) organizational structure, and (d) the role of leaders in affecting openness to change. Especially during periods of significant change, organizations must adapt their structures to accommodate the core values that their employees hold most strongly. Persuading employees to accept a new technology will be facilitated if the external social system is integrated with the organization's internal social system and process. This may mean modifying the new technology or adopting only a portion of it so as to jointly maximize the integration of the technology with the existing and prevailing social system.

The more advanced and complex the technology, the more it will impose changes in tasks, in organizational structure, and in role requirements. Technology may cause shifts in the existing status and power relationships that may be disruptive to organizational functioning. By taking the existing internal social system into account, cumbersome procedural changes and duplication of effort may result, but these may help to ensure an alignment of the organizational culture with the values of the larger external culture. Organizations that are relatively successful in managing such an alignment may enjoy a comparative advantage over competitors.

Finally, first-level supervisors may represent an underutilized resource in the implementation and maintenance of technological innovations. To the extent that leaders are able to make use of relationships with their subordinates (especially subordinates with critical skills and expertise), they may be able to influence the acceptance of change through informal means within their workgroups. The role of leaders, however, cannot be fully understood without a consideration of the influences of societal culture and the organization's internal social system.

IMPLICATIONS FOR THE MANAGEMENT OF TECHNOLOGICAL CHANGE

Organizational decisions regarding the implementation of a technological innovation generally begin with an analysis of the feasibility and cost-benefit trade-offs of adopting the innovation. Often, this analysis is largely restricted to economic considerations. We propose that the decision to adopt a technological innovation should be based on a broader assessment that goes beyond the economic utility of the innovation to consider the impact on a wider range of aspects of organizational functioning (Wall, Corbett, Martin, Clegg, and Jackson, 1990; Wall, Clegg, and Kemp, 1987). In addition to the economic impact of an innovation, there are five issues that decision-makers contemplating a technological innovation should consider.

First, is the need for an *extensive analysis of the current state of the organization* (Prasad, 1993). This analysis should accomplish several goals. Initially, it should identify the existing, salient contextual factors likely to facilitate or hinder acceptance and implementation of the innovation. Then, by tracking relevant events, both internal and external to the organization, areas of support and resistance can be determined and appropriate strategies developed. Here, a candid assessment of employee perceptions of the climate and culture of the organization is critical for providing an accurate estimate of the reception the innovation will receive. Also, an organizational analysis should identify and plan for obtaining the material resources necessary to accomplish the technological change. Delays brought about by poor planning and failure to anticipate organizational needs may engender negative attitudes toward the innovation among employees who are tasked with its implementation.

Second, is the need to conduct a *detailed analysis of the proposed technology's consequences,* both intended and potentially unintended, for the organization's formal and informal operating structure. Restructuring of functional areas may result in redundancy of positions, or new skill requirements that will require time and resources to address. Where workforce reductions are anticipated, decisions must be made about how they should be accomplished. Also, layoffs, early retirement incentives, and attrition due to normal requirements can have a differential impact on the remaining workforce (see, for example, Brockner, Grover, Reed, DeWitt, and O'Malley, 1987). Where new skills will be required, decisions must be made about retraining current employees (or hiring appropriately skilled personnel) and possibly modifying the existing compensation scheme.

Third, *organizational structures should be developed to facilitate the technological change.* One strategy would involve the formation of a change committee consisting of representatives drawn from all relevant constituency groups (e.g., functional area representatives, managerial and nonmanagerial employees, clients/customers, suppliers, etc.). Broad representation on the committee would provide one mechanism for employee participation in the innovation process. The committee would develop recommendations for adapting the innovation to fit the organization's particular configuration of societal norms. Existing lines of communication should be used to ensure unrestricted two-way flow of information between top management and all employee groups. An especially critical link is that between the lowest level of supervision and its workgroups. If necessary, other communication networks, specific to the innovation process, should be established. Assessment of the network of leader-member exchanges across organizational work units should identify the subgroup members most likely to be instrumental in introducing and maintaining change.

Fourth, in addition to the innovation-specific training that will be required, organizations would benefit from *establishing and conducting training programs* that seek to facilitate acceptance and implementation of the technological innovation by influencing the change process. Training strategies that rely on contracting outside trainers, training in-house with Human Resource Development (HRD) staff, or adding training responsibilities to the role of the immediate supervisor, possess inherent relative advantages and disadvantages (Osigweh and Segalla, 1992). At a minimum, training programs should include (a) an orientation to the innovation for all affected employees that delineates the expected benefits to the organization and its employees, and (b) the development of a support group within the work unit that will provide assistance for facilitating changes within the unit. Here again, organizations can rely upon in-group exchanges between leaders and members to establish a core of support within each work unit.

Fifth, the *level of commitment of immediate work unit supervisors* to a proposed technological innovation should be appraised and accounted for in the development of an implementation strategy. Before subordinates are likely to commit themselves to an objective (i.e., an innovation), their immediate supervisors must give unambiguous indications of their own personal commitment to the suggested end-state. As noted previously, there are specific, identifiable supervisory-related factors that are likely to be related to subordinate acceptance of change (e.g., stage of career, supervisor's aversion to risk-taking, etc.).

Although the above implications suggest considerable additional work for organizations, their benefits should significantly outweigh their costs in time and resources. Rather than being unusual or unique approaches to implementing technological innovations, these implications largely reflect the analysis and preplanning that distinguish successful from unsuccessful change attempts.

NOTES

The authors express their appreciation to Peter Dorfman for his comments on an earlier version of this paper.

1. This is illustrated in the Japanese saying that "the nail that sticks up invites hammering down."

2. It is important to recognize that technology is, in a basic sense, value-neutral. However, the parentage of a technology may arouse suspicion and resistance (e.g., a product of Western origin may not be readily adopted in certain cultures because of

standing in opposition to Western values). Therefore, it is more often the intended use, application, or perceived consequences of a technology that arouses cultural resistance. For example, television and audio-video recording are not inherently opposed in conservative Islamic countries. Rather, it is the content of programs conveyed via these technologies (i.e., Western value-based programming) that may be opposed. As noted by Madu (1992, p. 19), technology also has the complementary capacity to strengthen cultural values.

3. Tracking critical, historical events may also be useful to an organization for determining the impact of various contextual factors and formulating appropriate interventions for the acceptance of change. For example, the end of a collectively bargained agreement may heighten employee concern about issues of job security and changes in job skill requirements that result from a technological innovation, thereby intensifying the stance of an employee union concerning openness versus resistance to change.

REFERENCES

Adler, N. J., Doktor, R., and Redding, S. G. (1989). From the Atlantic to the Pacific century. In C. A. B. Osigweh (Ed.), *Organizational science abroad* (pp. 27–54). New York: Plenum.

Aiken, M. and Hage, J. (1971). The organic organization and innovation, *Sociology, 5*, 63–82.

Bamber, G. and Lambury, R. (1989). *New technology: International perspectives on human resources and industrial relations*. London: Unwin Hyman.

Barley, S. R. (1986). Technology as an occasion for structuring: Evidence from observations of CT scanners and the social order of radiology departments, *Administrative Science Quarterly, 31*, 78–108.

Bass, B. M. (1985). *Leadership and performance beyond expectations*. New York: Free Press.

Bass, B. M., Burger, W. F., Docktor, R., and McPherson, J. W. (1979). *Assessment of managers: An international comparison*. New York: Free Press.

Bornstein, M. (1985). *East-west technology transfer: The transfer of western technology to the USSR* (pp. 91–94). Paris: OECD (Org. for Econ. Cooperation Development).

Brockner, J., Grover, S., Reed, T., DeWitt, R. and O'Malley, M. (1987). Survivors' reactions to layoffs: We got by with a little help from our friends, *Administrative Science Quarterly, 32*, 526–541.

Brett, J. M. (1980a). Behavioral research on unions and union management systems. In B. M. Staw and L. L. Cummings (Eds.), *Research in organizational behavior, 2*, 177-213. Greenwich: JAI Press.

Brett, J. M. (1980b). Why employees want unions, *Organizational Dynamics*, Spring, 847–859.

Burkhardt, M. E. and Brass, D. J. (1990). Changing patterns or patterns of change: The effects of a change in technology on social network structure and power, *Administrative Science Quarterly, 35*, 104–127.

Czepiel, J. A. (1975). Patterns of interorganizational communication and diffusion of a major technological innovation in a competitive industrial community, *Academy of Management Journal, 18,* 6–24.

Damanpour, F. (1991). Organizational innovation: A meta-analysis of effects of determinants and moderators, *Academy of Management Journal, 36,* 555–590.

Dewar, R. and Hage, J. (1978). Size, technology, complexity, and structural differentiation: Toward a theoretical synthesis, *Administrative Science Quarterly, 23,* 111–136.

Drucker, P. F. (1985). *Innovation and entrepreneurship: Practice and principles.* New York: Harper & Row.

Evans, M. G. (1974). Extensions of a Path-Goal theory of motivation, *Journal of Applied Psychology, 59,* 172–178.

Fiedler, F. E. and Chemers, M. M. (1984). *Improving leadership effectiveness: The Leader Match concept* (Rev. ed.). New York: Wiley.

Ford, J. D. and Slocum, J. W. Jr. (1977). Size, technology, environment and the structure of organizations, *Academy of Management Review, 2,* 561–575.

Gersick, C. J. G. (1994). Pacing strategic change: The case of a new venture, *Academy of Management Journal, 37,* 9–45.

Gill, R. W. (1983). Personality profiles of Singapore-Chinese, British, and American managers: A cross-cultural comparison. Paper presented at Third Asian Regional Conference on Cross-Cultural Psychology, Bangi, Malaysia.

Gillespie, D. F. and Mileti, D. S. (1977). Technology and the study of organizations: An overview and appraisal, *Academy of Management Review, 2,* 7–16.

Graen, G. and Cashman, J. F. (1975). A role-making model of leadership in formal organizations: A developmental approach. In J. G. Hunt and L. L. Larson (Eds.), *Leadership frontiers.* Kent, OH: Kent State University Press.

Graen, G. B. and Uhl-Bien, M. (1991). The transformation of professionals into self-managing and partially self-designing contributors: Toward a theory of leadership-making, *Journal of Management Systems, 3,* 25–30.

Greiner, L. E. (1972). Evolution and revolution as organizations grow, *Harvard Business Review, 50,* 37–46.

Greiner, L. E. and Bhambri, A. (1989). New CEO intervention and dynamics of deliberate strategic change, *Strategic Management Journal, 10,* 67–86.

Grimes, A. J. and Klein, S. M. (1973). The technological imperative: The relative impact of task unit, modal technology, and hierarchy on structure, *Academy of Management Journal, 16,* 583–597.

Hall, E. T. and Hall, M. (1988). *Hidden differences: Doing business with the Japanese.* New York: Prentice-Hall.

Hofstede, G. (1980). *Culture's consequences.* New York: Sage Publications.

Hofstede, G. (1992). Cultural constraints on management theories. Distinguished International Scholar Lecture presented at National Meeting of Academy of Management, Las Vegas.

Hornstein, H. (1 986). *Managerial courage: Revitalizing your company without sacrificing your job.* New York: Wiley.

House, R. J. (1971). A path-goal theory of leader effectiveness, *Administrative Science Quarterly, 16,* 321–338.

Hulin, C. L. and Roznowski, M. (1985). Organizational technologies: Effects on organizations' characteristics and individuals' responses. In L. L. Cummings and B. M. Staw (Eds.), *Research in Organizational Behavior,* Vol. 7 (pp. 39–85). Greenwich, CT: JAI Press.

Kerr, S. and Jermier, J. M. (1978). Substitutes for leadership: Their meaning and measurement, *Organizational Behavior and Human Performance, 22,* 375–403.

Kiggundu, M. N. (1989). *Managing organizations in developing countries.* West Hartford, CT: Kumarian Press.

Kimberly, J. R. and Evanisko, M. (1981). Organizational innovation: The influence of individual, organizational and contextual factors on hospital adoption of technological and administrative innovations, *Academy of Management Journal, 24,* 689–713.

Lord, R. G. and Maher, K. J. (1990). Alternative information-processing models and their implications for theory, research, and practice, *Academy of Management Review, 15,* 9–28.

Madu, C. N. (1992). *Strategic planning in technology transfer to less developed countries.* New York: Greenwood Publishers.

McGrath, J. E. and Rotchford, N. L. (1983). Time and behavior in organizations. In B. Staw and L. Cummings (Eds.), *Research in Organizational Behavior,* Vol. 5. Greenwich, CT: JAI Press.

Misumi, J. and Peterson, M. F. (1985). The performance-maintenance theory of leadership: Review of a Japanese research program, *Administrative Science Quarterly, 30,* 198–223.

Mohr, L. B. (1982). *Explaining organizational behavior.* San Francisco: Jossey-Bass.

Osigweh, C. A. B. and Segalla, M. (1992). Managing innovative technologies. In C. Madu (Ed.), *The management of new manufacturing technologies for global competitiveness.* New York: Greenwood Press.

Pennings, J. M. (1985). *Organizational strategy and change: New views on formulating and implementing strategic decisions.* San Francisco: Jossey-Bass.

Pierce, J. L. and Delbecq, A. L. (1977). Organizational structure, individual attitudes, and innovation, *Academy of Management Review, 2,* 26–37.

Prasad, P. (1993). Symbolic processes in the implementation of technological change: A symbolic interactionist study of work computerization, *Academy of Management Journal, 36,* 1400–1429.

Ricks, D. A. (1983). *Big business blunders.* Homewood, IL: Dow Jones-Irwin.

Rogers, E. M. (1983). *Diffusion of innovation.* New York: Free Press.

Solo, R. A. (1975). *Organizing science for technology transfer in economic development* (pp. 37–40). Lansing, MI: Michigan State University Press.

Sorokin, P. A. (1941). *The crisis of our age: the social and cultural outlook.* New York: Dutton.

Spacapan, S. and Oskamp, S. (1990). People's reaction to technology. In S. Oskamp and S. Spacapan (Eds.), *People's reaction to technology.* Newbury Park: Sage.

Staw, B. M., Sandelands, L. E., and Dutton, J. E. (1981). Threat-rigidity effects in organizational behavior: A multilevel analysis, *Administrative Science Quarterly, 26,* 501–524.

Wakabayashi, M. and Graen, G. B. (1984). The Japanese career progress study: A 7-year follow-up, *Journal of Applied Psychology, 69,* 603–614.

Wakabayashi, M., Graen, G., Graen, M., and Graen, M. (1988). Japanese management progress: Mobility into middle management, *Journal of Applied Psychology, 73,* 217–227.

Wall, T. D., Corbett, J. M., Martin, R., Clegg, C. W., and Jackson, P. R. (1990). Advanced manufacturing technology, work design, and performance: A change study, *Journal of Applied Psychology, 75,* 691–697.

Wall, T. D., Clegg, C. W., and Kemp, N. J. (1987). *The human side of advanced manufacturing technology.* New York: Wiley.

Yukl, G. A. (1989). *Leadership in organizations,* Second edition. Englewood Cliffs, NJ: Prentice-Hall.

Leadership and
Gender Advantage

Robert P. Vecchio

INTRODUCTION

Several distinct trends document the increased involvement of women in leadership positions. For example, the proportion of women in executive, managerial, and administrative roles nearly tripled during the last three decades of the 20th century (US Dept. of Labor, Labor Statistics, 1998). Women-owned small businesses employ a growing portion of the US workforce (Moore, 1999). Plus, roughly one-third of all American businesses are owned by women. Although percentages vary widely from country to country, the worldwide participation of women in the labor force, as well as in managerial positions, also has been expanding (International Labour Office, 1996).

Another clear trend is the entry of women into positions of global political leadership. Over the last 40 years, the number of women in top or senior political leader positions (e.g., president or prime minister posts) has been increasing exponentially. The rate of entry into political positions is so rapid that Adler (1996) contends that the world is witnessing the "feminization" of governmental leadership roles (feminization being definable as when women disproportionately enter a traditionally male occupation). Increased openness to women in positions of political leadership is also manifest in Gallup poll results that show a steady increase of the US population's willingness to vote for a woman as president (from 33% in the 1930s to 92% in 1999; Gallup Special Reports, 1999).

Female entry into top corporate leadership roles (e.g., CEO positions in large firms) has been far less rapid. However, the presence of women in top management teams and executive positions has also expanded during recent years. One study of matched samples of female and male executives suggests that the experience of women in executive positions may be best characterized as "mixed" (with evidence of similarities to men on compensation and attitudes, but also evidence of smaller spans of control and less international mobility; Lyness & Thompson, 1997).

The increase in female entry into leadership ranks has been accompanied by an increase in social science research on the topic of sex/gender and leadership. The related empirical issues are numerous and varied, from differences in career guidance, to pay equity, to work-family conflict, to mentoring and workplace romance (Bass, 1990; Hooijberg & DiTomaso, 1996). However, the present article reviews only a specific facet of this sizable research domain and seeks to identify recurring themes, methodological concerns, major findings, and new directions for research relative to the topic of sex/gender and leader behavior. More specifically, four issues related to research on gender and leadership are examined: Do males and females differ in the forms of leader behavior they exhibit? Do the two groups differ in effectiveness in managerial positions? Do the groups differ in terms of being effective followers? What critical issues have been neglected in leadership research relative to sex/gender?

SHIFTING VIEWS OF GENDER AND LEADERSHIP

The conceptualizations of key constructs in both gender and leadership have undergone comparable change. Of particular interest is the parallel nature of their shifting views. Specifically, gender was conceptualized early on as one-dimensional, with femininity and masculinity as opposite ends of a single dimension (Constantinople, 1973; Lenney, 1991).[1] Initial attempts to measure gender with this approach involved one-dimensional personality scales (e.g., the MMPI, Hathaway & McKinley, 1951), with many items relating to preferred activities and interests (Hoffman, 2001; Morawski, 1985, 1987). This view was replaced with an independent two-dimensional view of gender, wherein an individual could be judged to be relatively high, moderate, or low on separate dimensions of femininity and masculinity. Leading examples of scales that embody this bi-dimensional view are the Bem Sex-Role Inventory (Bem, 1974) and the Personal Attributes Questionnaire

---

1. While it is important to recognize that sex refers to biological differences and gender refers to role behaviors and psychological processes/identity, much of the research in this domain readily mixes the two terms. Often, sex is what is actually measured, but gender is what is discussed. For some writers, gender appears to be a polite version of the word sex. Interestingly, a liberal mixing of two key terms also occurs among researchers who study "management" and "leadership."

(Spence & Helmreich, 1978). One result of this bi-dimensional conceptualization was the suggestion that there is an "ideal" combination of these constructs. The optimal combination came to be known as the "androgynous person" (Marsh & Myers, 1986). However, evidence that an androgynous style is an optimal managerial style has not been clearly shown (Powell & Butterfield, 1979, 1989; Powell, Butterfield, & Parent, 2002).

An alternative approach is to view gender role as a social construction that resides more in observer attribution than in the object of study. Hence, feminine or masculine labels can be overlaid on a set of relatively separate and distinct behavioral dimensions. Such a view suggests that individuals be assessed on a variety of dimensions. Whether these dimensions could be considered as being more feminine or more masculine is a separate judgment. For example, we might obtain assessments on such individual behaviors as being directive, evaluative, caring, nurturant, etc. Efforts to group these behaviors as being "masculine" or "feminine" may add less to an understanding of individual behavior than to an understanding of the labeling process. Questions of leader effectiveness are well beyond these grouping issues, and involve examining main and interactive effects of potential predictor dimensions with a set of outcome criteria. In light of theory and research in leadership, situational attributes likely determine what an optimal combination of behaviors (or optimal profile) would be.

Interestingly, a comparable and parallel shift has occurred in the dominant scholarly view of leadership dimensions. A one-dimensional view of leadership (wherein "concern with people" versus "concern with production" were seen as mutually exclusive leader options) is today regarded as simplistic and inappropriate. When Fiedler's (1967) construct of the Least-Preferred Coworker (which embodies this bi-polar view) was first offered, it was already something of a step backward in that the bi-dimensional view of the Ohio State University approach was widely recognized as a superior approach (Schriesheim & Klich, 1991; Schriesheim & Stogdill, 1975). One result of the bi-dimensional approach was the suggestion that there is an "ideal" combination of levels of these constructs. Like the search for the androgynous manager, evidence has not clearly shown that a particular ("high-high") leader style is optimal (Larson, Hunt, & Osburn, 1976; Nystrom, 1978; Schriesheim, 1982).

In recent years, researchers have generated a large number of additional leader behavior dimensions. Arguably, these dimensions could be subsumed under the broader Ohio State dimensions of consideration and structuring. However, such factoring exercises may reveal more about the categorizing or labeling process of the researchers than the object under study. If we add the goal of predicting leader effectiveness, then it must be acknowledged that no single profile is "best" for all settings, and that situational attributes likely play a major role as moderators (Kerr & Jermier, 1978).

The parallel development of these shifting conceptualizations of gender and leadership has coincided with attempts to merge the major dimensions of these conceptualizations by equating "femininity" with consideration and "masculinity" with structuring (Table 1). At an intuitive but superficial level, one can see how a stereotypic view of gender-based behaviors may merge with a stereotypic view of leader behaviors. For example, Maier (1992, 1999) argued that the theories of managerial leadership could be configured around a purportedly inherent incompatibility in the task-people dimension. As illustrations, Maier highlighted such "masculine/feminine models" as McGregor's (1960) Theory X–Theory Y, Likert's (1967) Systems 1–4, the Ohio State approach's (Stogdill, 1974) structure-consideration, Managerial Grid's (Blake & Mouton, 1978) concern for production-people, the Contingency Model of Leadership's (Fiedler, 1967; Fiedler & Chemers, 1982) task-relationship motivated, Vroom-Yetton-Jago decision model's (Vroom & Jago, 1978, 1988; Vroom & Yetton, 1973)

Table 1
Shifting Views

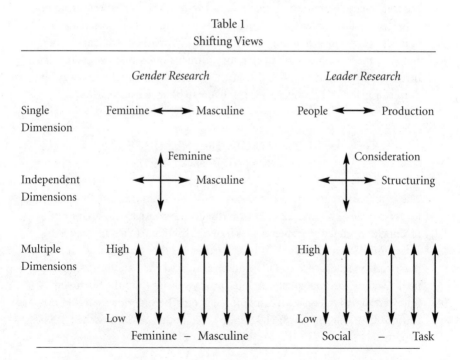

autocratic-consultative/group responses, and Situational Leadership Theory's (Hersey & Blanchard, 1977, 1982) task-relationship behavior.

A notable omission from this list is the vertical dyad linkage model (Gerstner & Day, 1997; Graen & Scandura, 1986; Graen & Uhl-Bien, 1995; Schriesheim, Castro, & Cogliser, 1999), which focuses on the social exchange process that develops between a leader and each follower rather than on a stylistic caricature of a leader. However, the forced femininity-masculinity dichotomy could easily be extended to make the claim that female leaders should have larger in-groups than male leaders due to the presumed female tendency to foster greater social inclusion and power sharing. Units headed by women should, as a consequence, have higher subordinate satisfaction, higher performance, and lower employee turnover. In essence, the creation of in-groups is an arguably feminine tendency, while the creation of out-groups is a presumptively masculine tendency.

As is the case with other superficial and simplistic approaches, the equating of major dimensions of leadership with gender stereotypes has not demonstrably advanced understanding. Furthermore, Maier's claim of an inherent incompatibility of a task-versus-people dimension is actually a return to a one-dimensional view of leadership (and is, therefore, not an accurate characterization of most major models). An honest reflection on behaviors witnessed in work settings forces us to admit that both males and females are capable of acting assertively and sympathetically, that leaders can vary their actions across behavioral dimensions while being effective through different avenues, and that the search for a "single best way" of prescribing leader effectiveness is not likely to be successful.

GENDER ADVANTAGE: THE RESURRECTION OF A DORMANT CONTROVERSY

The core question of whether the sexes differ in aptitudes and abilities for leadership deserves special attention due to the controversy surrounding recent claims that one gender role is inherently better skilled for leadership in organizational settings. This position, labeled the "feminine advantage" perspective (Yukl, 2002, p. 412), contends that women are more skilled at inclusiveness, interpersonal relations, power sharing, and the nurturing of followers; and as a consequence, women should be superior leaders (Carr-Rufino, 1993; Grant, 1988; Helgeson, 1990; Loden, 1985; Rosener, 1990, 1995).

The proposed female propensity to prefer frequent contact and information sharing should result in "webs of inclusion" (Helgeson, 1990) that foster greater effectiveness. Evidence for the "webs of inclusion" thesis is derived from a diary study of four women, two of whom were entrepreneurs (Helgeson, 1990, pp. 16–18). While no comparable males were assessed in this ideographic approach, contrasts were drawn to Mintzberg's (1973) early diary study.[2] Females, it is also contended (Loden, 1985), are inclined to a cooperative leadership style that includes team structure, while males are inclined to a competitive leadership style that includes hierarchical structure. This contention, that males and females operate out of distinctly different leadership models (cf. Loden, 1985, pp. 26 and 63 for a summary that contrasts suggested sex-related leadership differences), is based on interviews with 200 women and 50 men. An unreported number of these women, however, refused to participate and/or insisted that no differences existed. The remaining women (who agreed with the starting thesis that differences do exist) provided the information on which the book is based. The males who provided data were selected by their women colleagues because they were described as "enlightened" (p. 13).

Other versions of the feminine advantage position (Rosener, 1990, 1995) argue that males prefer an alpha-style of leadership based on command-and-control, whereas females prefer a beta-style of leadership based on social interaction. The empirical base of Rosener's argument is taken from a survey of an unreported number of women who were members of the Independent Women's Forum (a reported 31% response rate). These respondents also provided the names of an unreported number of comparable males who received the same questionnaire (1990, p. 121). From these survey data and interviews, it was concluded that women's self-descriptions frequently referred to aspects of interactive leadership (e.g., participation, power sharing, and inclusion).

Recent claims of gender advantage often cite Gilligan's (1982) arguments that there are distinct psychological differences between the sexes (particularly in the domain of moral reasoning, cf. the moral stage theory of Lawrence Kohlberg, 1969). A recently published meta-analysis (Jaffee & Hyde, 2000), however, concluded that observed sex differences in moral orientation were "small" and that the meta-analytic results did "not offer

---

2. As noted by Martinko and Garder (1985), ideographic studies offer the opportunity to generate new insights. However, nomothetic studies (that examine large samples) offer greater assurance for making normative appraisals and comparisons.

strong support for the claim" that females predominantly employ a caring orientation while males predominantly employ a justice orientation. Other challenges to Gilligan's work have been put forward by Christina Hoff Sommers (2000a, 2000b, 2000c), who contends that Gilligan has (1) not been willing to produce her original data, (2) relied heavily on anecdotal evidence, and (3) employed small samples. For a further critique of Gilligan's work, see Tavris' (1992, pp. 80–90) *The Mismeasure of Women.*

Claims of gender superiority are certainly not new. Historically, such preferential claims have been based on exaggerated gender stereotyping (i.e., the "masculine advantage" perspective that presumes men are inherently better skilled for leadership due to greater task focus, lower emotionality, and a propensity to be directive). Arguably, the more recent claims of female advantage constitute a modified reincarnation (or resurrection) of a previously dormant debate. Regardless of how it is framed, the gender advantage position rests on assumptions that strong polarities exist and that specific poles are to be valued. Rather than relying on stereotypic assumptions favoring either sex, empirical tests are required to determine whether claims of relative superiority are valid.

ARE THERE DIFFERENCES IN LEADER BEHAVIOR AS A FUNCTION OF GENDER?

We might first ask a very basic question: Do females and males differ in displayed behavior? The answer of course is that, in the aggregate, the sexes do differ with respect to social actions (Archer, 1996; Eagly, 1995; Eagly & Wood, 1999).[3] Men have been found to be somewhat more self-assertive, aggressive, and coarse in their manner and language than women. Females, in contrast, have been found to be more expressive of emotion and compassion (although also quite capable of behaving aggressively; Chesler, 2001; Simmons, 2002).

In an analysis of tapes of mixed-sex groups of management students (Case, 1985), comparisons of conversations suggested that males more typically employ an imperative tone, slang, and use of the third person, whereas females more typically use passive agreement, tag questions, and intensi-

---

3. Although mean differences on physiological dimensions (e.g., height and physical abilities) and aptitudes (e.g., test score differences on math, visual-spatial, and verbal tests) are widely recognized (see Deaux & La France, 1998; Feingold, 1988, for reviews), it is important to emphasize that the present discussion focuses on the domain of social behavior.

fiers. When men and women address each other and try to influence each other, they may also modify their speech, with women using more tag questions and hesitation so as to be liked more and perceived as more trustworthy by men (Carli, 1990). Although men and women may engage in gossip with comparable frequency, females use more animated tones, detail, and feedback (Fox, 2002). Women and men may also differ in the way they convey power and status (Cashdan, 1998), such that male body posture tends to be more "open" (suggesting greater social ease, relaxation, or potential assertiveness). However, a high degree of extraversion predicts elevated social status for both sexes (Anderson, John, Keltner, & Kring, 2001). Whether these differences are largely a result of innate dispositions versus social-structural processes, or the product of the interplay of these forces, is a subject that continues to draw attention and debate (Buss, 1996; Eagly & Wood, 1999). It is important to underscore, however, that these findings are of an aggregate, or mean, differences nature and that the ranges for the groups overlap substantially (i.e., there are males who are quite expressive of emotion, and there are females who are quite self-assertive). It is perhaps even more important to emphasize that evidence of aggregate differences does not mean evidence of aggregate deficiencies.

A highly practical question, however, is whether these identifiable aggregate differences are likely to be job-relevant. By and large, it is difficult to conceive of positions where job descriptions would include these specific attributes. Furthermore, even if jobs were created that did explicitly include these attributes, it would still be a questionable practice (in fact it would be illegal) to hire only one type of applicant because that applicant's group membership is generally higher, on average, on that particular attribute. Recall that decisions about individuals are to be made based on individual (not group) abilities and aptitudes in order to conform to current legal guidelines. For example, evidence that one sex is, on average, taller or can float in water for longer periods of time (McLean & Hinrich, 2000), even if highly job-relevant, would not justify the preferential hiring of only members of one group (i.e., each individual would have to be assessed on the particular dimension). Despite this practical legal limit on the potential usefulness of findings of sex differences relative to employment decision making, research on this topic has sought to identify stylistic differences in females and males in leadership roles in laboratory and organizational settings. Presumably, the practical value of any findings in this vein would be for developmental insights related to the understanding of others and one's self.

Lab studies of sex/gender differences offer the clear advantage of substantial experimenter control. However, one obvious down-side is that the contrived circumstances are of relatively short duration. Plus, strangers in groups with assigned leaders or presented with videotaped or written vignettes may rely heavily on stereotypic responses as lab settings are usually informationally-impoverished situations. It is also possible that the hypothesis under examination may be somewhat transparent.

In spite of these factors and the potential of stereotypic responses emerging in such limited circumstances, evidence of sex/gender effects in lab studies and simulations has been difficult to obtain (Butterfield & Powell, 1981; Trempe, Rigny, & Haccoun, 1985). Also, Ragins (1991) observed that sex/gender effects did not exist when power-related variables were controlled (i.e., lab scenarios omit information on leader power and thereby allow respondents to introduce sex-role stereotypes when judging another's behavior).

Greg Dobbins and Stephanie Platz (1986) reported the results of a meta-analysis of 17 studies that examined sex differences in leadership. They selected only studies that had observers as raters of leaders (i.e., they did not include studies that relied on leader self-reports). Their analyses revealed that male and female leaders did not differ on consideration and initiating structure.

In a subsequent meta-analysis, Alice Eagly and Blair Johnson (1990) examined a much broader sample of studies ($n = 370$) that included unpublished documents and dissertations. Moreover, they included leader self-ratings in their analyses (despite the fact that this type of assessment is presently regarded as highly suspect in the field of leadership research). In fact, roughly half of the leader style measures were self-report in nature. Also, the variety of leadership scales they included was extremely inclusive and encompassed such scales as the Leadership Opinion Questionnaire (Fleishman, 1957), the Leadership Effectiveness and Adaptability Description Scale (Hersey & Blanchard, 1982), and the Least-Preferred Coworker Scale (Fiedler, 1967).

The LOQ is recognized for providing inflated self-reports and is of little value compared to alternative rating sources. The LEAD Scale has not demonstrated adequate psychometric properties (Graeff, 1983, 1997). Plus, the LPC Scale has not been shown to correlate with the Ohio State dimensions or other widely used measures and has doubtful construct validity (in fact, it may actually provide a measure of what it precisely proclaims to be, a description of one's least-preferred coworker, but an index of little else). Moreover, the bi-polar character of the LPC Scale is at odds with the orthogonal view of task and social behaviors offered by other leadership frameworks (Schriesheim & Kerr, 1977a, 1977b; Vecchio, 1979).

Yet, despite this generous inclusion of a broad range of studies, Eagly and Johnson (p. 233) concluded "female and male leaders did not differ" in the two leader styles of interpersonal orientation and task orientation within organizational studies. However, these two aspects of leader style were found to be "somewhat gender stereotypic" in lab experiments and assessment studies (defined as studies wherein the styles of individuals are assessed, but individuals are not selected for leader roles). It is worth restating that the lab studies involved short-term duration experiences employing undergraduates and are of, understandably, limited practical relevance.

Eagly and Johnson (1990) then concluded that there was a tendency for women to be more democratic and for men to be more autocratic. The measures of democratic-autocratic orientation were mostly (16 of 28 comparisons) "unique measures" or measures "constructed by authors from components" in the document. The remaining comparisons (12 of 28) involved unusual indices of democratic-autocratic style. Specifically, six comparisons used the Vroom and Yetton's (1973) problem set. This problem set involves hypothetical scenarios that may reveal gender-based propensity but do not provide an index of actual behavior. Two of the remaining comparisons used Sargent and Miller's (1971) leader questionnaire. This ten-item forced-choice self-descriptive scale has little evidence of construct validity in the organizational behavior literature beyond Sargent and Miller's scale development study based on 42 4-H club leaders. Four of the remaining comparisons employed the Grobman and Hines (1956) Principal Behavior Checklist. The checklist involves responses to 86 hypothetical situations. Importantly, responses to the F scale index of authoritarianism were unrelated to Principal Behavior Checklist scores, for both males and females (p. 13). Also of great relevance is the revelation (p. 14) that "virtually all the women principals studied were in elementary schools," where it may be "that the situation lends itself more readily to what were considered democratic practices." Males were more typically operating in high school settings.

Eagly and Johnson's (1990) statements that women and men differ in their tendency to "adopt" different styles (p. 247) and "to lead" in autocratic or democratic fashion (p. 233) seem to be overstatements in that these conclusions are based largely on nonstandardized measures of leader behavior and clearly include self-reports rather than independent observer ratings. Again, it is worth noting that the overall results of Eagly and Johnson are essentially equivocal and that reported differences are of the weak aggregate/

mean differences type that requires a restatement of the overlap of the two distributions. Further, Eagly and Johnson also concluded that both sexes were inclined toward a task-oriented style when in a gender-congruent (or gender-congenial) context. This conclusion suggests that, regardless of sex, individuals are inclined to be work-focused. Interestingly, Eagly and Johnson also found that female researchers obtained more stereotypic gender findings, thus replicating an earlier "sex of researcher effect" (Eagly & Carli, 1981). In a later study, Eagly, Makhijani, and Klonsky (1992) concluded that females were judged to be more task-oriented than males. This finding actually runs counter to the traditional stereotypic view of sex roles.

In summary, the search for sex differences in the behavior of leaders has yielded results that are highly equivocal. The relatively select literature review by Dobbins and Platz (1986) concluded that sexes do not differ. Moreover, Dobbins and Platz went so far as to call for a halt to sex differences studies of managerial leadership. The relatively inclusive literature review of Eagly and Johnson (1990) also concluded that the search for sex differences has not demonstrated substantial differences. While Dobbins and Platz can be applauded for focusing their analysis on more rigorous, published studies, Eagly and Johnson can also be applauded for striving to address Rosenthal's (1991) and Rosenthal and DiMatteo's (2001) "file drawer problem" by trying to identify less visible studies (i.e., studies that may have obtained null effects and, hence, were less likely to be published).

ARE THERE DIFFERENCES IN LEADER EVALUATIONS AND EFFECTIVENESS AS A FUNCTION OF GENDER?

As with the prior question of whether there are differences in leader behavior, we might again begin by asking another more basic question: Is there a tendency to pre-judge males as being more effective managers? This question has been examined in a stream of research that compares gender stereotypes with managerial stereotypes. In an early study, Powell and Butterfield (1979) asked evening MBA students and undergraduates to describe themselves and a "good manager" on the Bem Sex-Role Inventory instrument (Bem, 1974). Their results indicated a "good manager" was viewed as having "masculine" characteristics by both groups of respondents, as well as by males and females. These characteristics included assertiveness, independence, and willingness to take risks. More "feminine" characteristics included sensitivity, compassion, and understanding.

Even though the proportion of women in managerial positions has increased since their initial study, replications of their methods (Heilman, Block, Martell, & Simon, 1989; Powell & Butterfield, 1989; Powell, Butterfield, & Parent, 2002) have continued to show that the "agentic" stereotypic male qualities (of competitiveness, daring, assertiveness) are more aligned with stereotypic views of managerial roles, versus "communal" stereotypic female qualities (of kindness, supportiveness, and affection). Research in cultures outside of the United States has also replicated this tendency to view successful managers in relatively masculine terms (Schein & Mueller, 1992; Schein, Mueller, Lituchy, & Liu, 1996).

While this line of research is intriguing for offering insights on the stability of gender stereotypes and managerial stereotypes, as well as their overlap, this research is understandably limited due to the omission of contextual dimensions. In essence, subjects are asked to respond to very limited information; and in so doing, they reveal thumbnail stereotypic responses. If subjects had been asked to envision specific positions with which they were familiar or positions involving (e.g.) greater requirements of nurturing and mentoring, it seems likely that the results would have differed. Studies of differences in leader effectiveness, therefore, require the use of objective indices of performance within organizational settings.

An interesting related question is whether there is a tendency for students to pre-judge male professors as being more effective classroom instructors. Substantial data from anonymous student evaluations of faculty have been collected over the years. Although a meta-analysis by Feldman (1993) showed no overall main effect for teacher sex/gender, other evidence suggests that women instructors fare better than men on questions reflecting warmth and concern for students, while male instructors fare better on ratings of enthusiasm and knowledge of subject matter (Basow, 1995; Marsh & Ware, 1982; Bernstein & Burke, 1995). An interesting question that is analogous to the study of managerial stereotypes is whether ratings of the stereotypic "good professor" would be more characteristically feminine, masculine, or a mix. If the stereotypic "good professor" were found to be characteristically feminine or masculine, the aforementioned meta-analytic findings of no main effect for teacher sex/gender would suggest that while stereotypes may exist, they have little bearing on evaluators who are asked to describe a real stimulus person.

As suggested previously, organizational studies allow for the examination of potential sex differences within settings of greater relevance. However, observed ranges of behavior style may not be maximal due to the use of organizational selection criteria and subsequent attrition processes.

Also, the sexes actually self-select into occupations due to differences in vocational interest. Further, individual propensities to speak in characteristically masculine or feminine styles (noted earlier as aggregate differences in the use of language) may be greatly curtailed in many employment settings. That is to say, there is a societally preferred style of communication when one is "on the job." This preferred style results in job incumbents dropping the more extreme forms of masculine or feminine styles of communication in favor of a type of "office-speak" that involves "putting on one's business face." This more professional, job-focused style of communicating may minimize potential gender effects. Of course, employee communication does not always conform to this workplace expectation, with results that can contribute to interpersonal conflict or heightened emotion.

Despite these limitations (which would perhaps lead one to anticipate truncated ranges and less likelihood of finding associations), some evidence of gender effects on leader effectiveness criteria has been found in organizational studies. Ragins' (1991) comparison of organizational studies on the added dimension of control for power-related variables, however, indicated that gender effects were more likely when no control for power exists; and no gender effects were identified when control for power did exist. Similarly, lab studies that used written scenarios to describe leaders and that did not control for power-related variables did report gender effects (Bartol & Butterfield, 1976; Haccoun, Haccoun, & Sallay, 1978; Jacobsen & Effertz, 1974; Rosen & Jerdee, 1973).

Dobbins and Platz (1986) examined studies of "satisfaction with supervision" as a function of supervisor sex. They concluded that no evidence of meaningful differences existed. Eagly et al. (1992) reviewed research on sex and evaluations of leaders. The great majority of the studies that they reviewed, however, presented subjects with written descriptions of leaders' behaviors. As a result, the only difference in leader portrayals were changes in the leaders' names and the personal pronouns used in the vignettes. Their comparison of experimental data showed only a small nonsignificant overall tendency of subjects to evaluate female leaders less favorably than male leaders. Specifically, 56% of the reports favored male leaders and 44% favored female leaders (a nonsignificant difference from a 50% null hypothesis expectation). This difference was somewhat greater when leaders occupied male-dominated roles and the evaluators were male. Differences favoring males were most pronounced in the context of college or school athletics. In an examination of the sex of the subordinates, male subordinates favored female leaders over male leaders with male subordinates, while female subordinates favored male leaders over female leaders with female subordinates. Eagly et al. suggest that this reversal may reflect the subjects' viewing the mixed parings of women and men as more interesting or provocative. Unlike their prior meta-analysis, Eagly et al. did not report on a test for "sex of researchers" in relation to magnitude or direction of observed gender effects.

From these studies, Eagly et al. concluded that their analyses produced evidence of only a slight tendency for females and males to differ in their evaluations, with some evidence of selective devaluation by sex. Specifically, gender-role expectations for specific positions may operate against individual leaders when their behavior is not congruent. It is, of course, difficult to generalize this evidence from hypothetical scenarios to actual organizations, given that much greater information on leader performance is available to evaluators in real-world settings.

In a further meta-analytic effort, Eagly, Karau, and Makhijani (1995) compared studies that examined effectiveness and leader sex. A comparison of the "effectiveness" of leaders differs from a comparison of the "evaluation" of leaders in that "effectiveness" implies greater attention to measurable outcomes, whereas "evaluation" implies a comprehensive, but largely subjective, judgment of performance. In a comparison of 14 studies that employed objective measures of performance versus 57 studies that employed subjective measures, no evidence of a sex effect was found. Also, the confidence interval for the mean weighted effect size for objective measures of performance bracketed 0.0 (mean effect size = -0.02, 95% CI = -0.17 to 0.14).

In a comprehensive meta-analytic test of all studies, no evidence of a sex effect was found. However, a test of the homogeneity of the effect sizes indicated a lack of homogeneity. Hence, 12 studies were removed from subsequent analyses because they were relative outliers. All of the 12 outlier effect sizes favored male leaders over female leaders. Half of these outlier cases involved military settings and two involved leaders in a sport and an Outward Bound program. The removal of these outlier cases resulted in an overall effect size that slightly favored females over males as leaders. Yet the proportion of remaining cases favoring males (43% of the effect sizes) did not differ significantly from the .50 proportion expected under the null hypothesis. Eagly et al. (p. 134), therefore, concluded "that women and men did not differ in general in their effectiveness as leaders."

Despite this overall finding of no differences, Eagly et al. contended that the specific setting played a role in determining relative effectiveness in conjunction with leader sex. Specifically, Eagly et al. pointed to the military study outliers as evidence that males were favored in some settings, while females were somewhat favored in other settings (i.e., education and government/social service). Interestingly, neither sex was favored in business organizations (p. 136). These results suggest that female and male leaders may be differentially effective in particular settings. A key condition associated with relative advantage was whether leadership roles could be characterized as gender-congenial.

Because gender congeniality was assessed via undergraduate students' ratings of brief job descriptions of various leadership roles (e.g., principal of an elementary school, middle manager in a manufacturing firm, coach of a boys' high-school basketball team) rather then actual job-analytic techniques concerning specific requirements taken from incumbents, supervisors, customers, peers, or subordinates, the question is open as to whether gender-congeniality is largely a reflection of societal experiences and general expectations. That is to say, the undergraduate ratings may simply have reflected their general impressions and likely experiences in dealing with leaders; effectiveness measures may also have reflected impressions based on the relative frequency of past experiences in dealing with leaders; and hence, the two indices may co-vary due to common, impressionistic bases rather than actual matching of talents to objective job requirements.

GENDER ADVANTAGE VERSUS THE CONTINGENCY VIEW

Finally, it is worth considering how the gender advantage perspective compares with the widely-held view of the merits of a contingency perspective. According to a contingency perspective, there are few easy answers to seemingly simple social science questions. For example, consider the simple question: Is it better for someone in a leadership position to be autocratic or democratic? While we might be inclined to quickly endorse one side of this question based on experience or preference, the most accurate answer is that the better style "depends" on other contingent factors. For instance, if the task involves time pressure (such as a strict deadline), then the autocratic style may be superior to the democratic; if the work group is quite large, then logistics may dictate an autocratic style for the leader; if the followers have strong expectations for an ideal style of leadership (such as when one is leading a group of neo-fascists or urban terrorists), then again an autocratic style may be the better response; if the larger societal culture places a strong value on autocratic leadership (as seems true for some non-Western cultures), then an autocratic style may be more appropriate; and if the leader lacks the skills or confidence to enact a particular style, then the leader may necessarily rely on one style over another.

Clearly, there is no simple answer to a seemingly simple question. Yet, the gender advantage perspective implies that one gender is superior at enacting a preferred style—a preferred style that is useful across settings. Advocates of a gender advantage perspective offer a simplistic, stereotypic view that largely ignores the importance of contextual contingencies. In essence, a gender advantage perspective is a step backward in explaining social behavior in work settings.

A superior approach to tackling the simplistic question of "autocratic versus democratic" style would be to investigate whether leaders who are able to enact a range of behaviors (encompassing autocratic and democratic behaviors), and who are able to effectively integrate and balance a variety of leader behaviors, are judged to be comparatively more effective. In addition to being able to competently enact these roles, a more effective leader should be able to recognize *when* to enact each role. Such enaction involves issues of social intelligence (i.e., being able to "read" people and situations; Sternberg, 1988, 1997; Sternberg & Horvath, 1999; Sternberg, Wagner, Williams, & Horvath, 1995) and leader flexibility (i.e., being able to enact differing roles; Hooijberg, Hunt, & Dodge, 1997). Leader flexibility is a topic that has received relatively little empirical attention (Zaccaro, Foti, & Kenny, 1991), while leader social intelligence has only received significant attention in recent years (Baron, 2000a, 2000b).

Sternberg's work on "tacit" intelligence has emphasized how job "know-how" is domain-specific, and has not focused on sex/gender differences. Similarly, proposals concerning leader flexibility have not considered whether the genders would differ in such an ability. Potential arguments for sex/gneder differences in these areas are difficult to sustain. Leader flexibility is also recognized as important by Hooijberg et al. (1997), who highlighted the construct of "social differentiation" as the ability of a leader to discriminate among facets and aspects of social settings over time, including differentiating emotions in one's self and others. Hooijberg et al. also proposed the related concept of "behavior differentiation" as the ability of a leader to perform roles adaptively in response to aspects of organizational settings. These promising constructs await empirical testing.

In summary, it has not been demonstrated that either sex is clearly advantaged with respect to operating as a leader. Strong claims of masculine or feminine advantage do not have the data to support them. While the behaviors of the sexes differ stylistically, the overlap of the two groups should not be ignored in favor of claims based on small mean differences in these distributions. The argument that including setting in "gender advantage" discussions allows one to make strong claims is also suspect. The strongest evidence of setting-based "gender advantage" is from military and coaching settings. Yet, these results have been discounted as being "outliers." Evidence from business organizations does not substantiate the gender advantage claims of either perspective.

The best evidence in support of a possible female advantage is a weak effect for education and government/social service settings. However, highly "feminized" job settings (such as nursing or child care) do not have much published data relative to sex differences. This is somewhat surprising as a sizable empirical literature has developed for the nursing profession, with journals devoted exclusively to such research (e.g., *Nursing Research, Journal of Clinical Nursing, Journal of Advanced Nursing, Journal of Nursing Administration, Research in Nursing and Health, International Journal of Nursing Studies,* and *Journal of Professional Nursing*). The relatively low number of male head nurses or male clinical directors has perhaps contributed to this lack of data (males presently comprise only 6% of the nursing profession; Evans, 1997; Hilton, 2001).

Potential influences of sex/gender differences in preferred aggregate styles are probably muted by organizational emphasis on (and the tendency of leaders toward) being task-focused (rather than engaging in highly gender-stylized behaviors). Individual supervisors who engage in the worst aspects of each stereotypic style (e.g., by over-socializing or being overly directive) may be advised by their supervisors to change their style (or they may be less likely to be placed in positions involving responsibility for others). Furthermore, obstacles to leader effectiveness, that are fundamentally gender-based, need to be better understood. The study of subordinate acceptance of a leader based on gender similarity, length of association, and initial preferences may provide additional insights to the potential impact of leader gender on unit outcomes.

GENDER ADVANTAGE AND GENDER SIMILARITY

The gender advantage perspective is arguably an "average-leadership style" perspective that ignores the unique social exchange that occurs at the dyadic level (Dansereau, Graen, & Haga, 1975; Dienesch & Liden, 1986).

The gender advantage persepective implies that sex/gender dictates leader behavior and that all group members will be subjected to or experience the manifested appropriate (or relatively less appropriate) leader style. A superior approach that recognizes the potential influence of dyadic diversity is embodied in a "fine-grained" analytic approach (Williams & O'Reilly, 1998). This approach explores the potentially unique influences of specific types of leader-follower demographic differences and acknowledges that various forms of demographic differences are not equivalent. Hence, the demographic similarity of each supervisor-subordinate pair becomes the focus of study in order to describe more precisely how differing forms of demographic dimensions might be differentially related to outcomes.

In addition to the value of studying sex/gender similarity (rather than merely studying leader sex/gender), further insights may be gained by incorporating temporality and tolerance/support of diversity into leader research (Harrison, Price, & Bell, 1998; McGrath, 1991). The length of time that a leader and subordinate interact likely plays a role in explaining how leader-subordinate gender similarity may influence outcomes. Sex/gender is a superficial (or surface) attribute, as is sex/gender similarity. Surface-level similarity/diversity may convey information of limited value. However, surface-level information is all that unit members may be able to rely on during the initial period of a working relationship. One consequence is that stereotypic influences may be invoked during this early phase of contact. As time passes and involvement increases, interpersonal assessments will be based more on specific observed behaviors and less on stereotypes. Sociologists, who have termed this process "the contact hypothesis" (Ellison & Powers, 1994; Pettigrew, 1998; Sigelman & Welch, 1993), argue that interpersonal attraction and group cohesion should build over time, while prejudice and interpersonal conflict should decrease as relationships mature and people come to recognize their common humanity. A further moderator of potential importance to gender similarity is whether the leader is perceived to be tolerant of surface-level differences. That is to say, if one differs from a leader, then a key concern for the subordinate is likely to be whether the leader is seen as being supportive of diversity (versus less tolerant of demographic differences).

One recent study, that employed a "fine-grained" approach to studying gender similarity and also incorporated the moderators of length of relationship and leader's perceived tolerance of diversity, reported several interesting findings. Specifically, Vecchio and Bullis (2001) analyzed subordinate survey data from 2883 US Army officers who described their relationships with their supervising officers. Separate analyses were run for males supervising males, males supervising females, females supervising males, and females supervising females. When subordinate appraisal of satisfaction with supervisors was examined as the dependent variable, satisfaction with one's supervisor was found to decrease generally over time. Plus, there was a significant interaction of length of relationship with gender similarity. More specifically, the largest drop occurred for females who were supervised by females, while the most consistently satisfied pairing over time was males who were supervised by males. Also of interest was the finding that the range of mean responses increased across length of relationship. This "fanning-out" pattern of average satisfaction over time, coupled with the declines in average satisfaction, is contrary to what the "contact hypothesis" would lead us to expect.

According to the contact hypothesis, the pattern of means early on in relationships should have been more variable but also in alignment with sex/gender similarity/dissimilarity. This initial pattern of responses should have been followed by improved levels of average satisfaction, due to deep-level similarity replacing surface-level similarity as a more important influence on subordinate attitudes. In the Vecchio and Bullis (2001) results, the pattern of means reflected an early positive level of satisfaction via a tightly clustered set of means for all four gender-similarity combinations. This pattern then fanned-out and declined over the length of working relationships.

The same study also identified a significant interaction involving gender similarity (of supervisor and subordinate) and perceived supervisor tolerance of diversity for predicting subordinate satisfaction with supervision. This interaction was of the form that support for diversity was regarded as a positive feature by all gender pairings. However, nonsupport of diversity was viewed as a positive feature of a supervisor if the subordinate and supervisor were both males.

These results are of importance for illustrating how a fine-grained analytical approach (where various mixes of supervisor-subordinate demographics are not combined but are treated as unique, and supervisor sex is not examined as a simple aggregate-level grouping variable) can yield insights on how differing forms of demographic pairings may not have comparable or equivalent effects. They also suggest there are limits to broad generalizations concerning the likelihood that increased length of contact between diverse individuals will lead to improved social relations (i.e., the contention that increased contact between diverse dyads enhances positive regard). On the plus side, the magnitudes of the observed effects were not particularly strong. This suggests that demographic similarity/dissimilarity is a weak contributing, but far from controlling, factor in the affective reactions of subordinates.

GENDER DIFFERENCES, GENDER STEREOTYPES, AND GENDER HEURISTICS

In light of the empirical evidence on gender differences, a deeper question arises: Is the belief in gender advantage (feminine or masculine) a social construction that is based on learned heuristics? That is to say, do gender stereotypes function as a heuristic device that is employed in retrospective or prospective judgments? Gender stereotyping may be used as a "rule of thumb" when judging others, especially in the absence of target-specific and setting-specific information, as well as when judging one's self. Such a heuristic would be based on a societally-popular, learned perspective concerning aggregate sex group differences. Evidence that a gender heuristic may be operative in some instances can be discerned from recent research on the common stereotype that females are "more emotional" than males.

To be more precise, the "emotionality stereotype" maintains that females are more emotional within certain affective domains (e.g., love, sadness, guilt, shame, and compassion), while males are inclined to be more emotional within other specific domains (e.g., anger and pride/ego). The stereotype holds that the intensity of these emotional experiences and their public display differs according to an individual's sex. Intriguingly, evidence on this fairly simple and widespread stereotype is inconsistent. When individuals report past emotions or a general tendency toward an emotion, then the data support the stereotype. Yet, when individuals report ongoing specific emotions or recent experienced emotions, the stereotype is not substantiated (Fischer, 1993; LaFrance & Banaji, 1992; Shields, 1991, 1995). This evidence suggests that the stereotype is false, and that people invoke the stereotype to estimate emotions in others or to estimate emotions in themselves when emotions are not immediate within themselves.

One interesting demonstration of this gender heuristic comes from a study by Robinson, Johnson, and Shields (1998). Specifically, they reported that when participants rated their own emotions immediately after playing a timed cooperative-competitive word-game that was designed to arouse moderate levels of emotion, no stereotypic gender differences were observed. However, stereotypic gender differences did appear in ratings collected after a week-long delay. Also, people who merely observed the game-playing showed no gender differences in their ratings of others. Yet, when the observers were asked to imagine a game involving themselves and an average man or average women, the ratings matched the gender-based stereotypes.

While these results neither prove nor disprove gender differences in emotional reaction, they do suggest that stereotypic differences were not perceived unless the circumstances were recalled at a later time or were imagined by the respondent. Of further interest is the failure of Robinson et al. (1998) to find evidence that gender stereotypes were influenced by the sex of the observers themselves. Both male and females, therefore, appear to share the same gender stereotype and to use the same gender heuristic. This absence of participant-sex X target-sex interaction has also been reported in other research (Birnbaum, Nosanchuk, & Croll, 1980; Fabes & Martin, 1991; Johnson & Shulman, 1988).

Other evidence (Shields, 1991, 1995) suggests that gender differences in emotional self-reports are more likely when these reports are global and retrospective rather than specific and concurrent with events. Global retrospective reports of feeling angry typically yield a gender effect (i.e., males report feeling anger more frequently than females). However, a study that had males and females maintain diaries of immediate experiences of anger revealed that the sexes experience anger with equivalent frequency (Averill, 1983).

Extending the logic of the gender heuristic argument to judgment in work settings is a straightforward exercise. The heuristic hypothesis suggests that when respondents are asked to describe their own behavior in a job setting, stereotypic gender differences in anticipated leader inclinations may be difficult to identify. Yet, when subjects/respondents are asked to envision whether gender differences may exist or are asked to generalize over past work experiences, they may be more likely to invoke a gender heuristic to characterize differences among leaders. Furthermore, increases in temporal distance between work experiences and reporting may facilitate stereotypic inferences, while the availability of specific episodic information may eliminate stereotypic inferences.

GENDER AND FOLLOWERSHIP

Discussions of leadership often recognize the dependency of leaders on subordinates for unit effectiveness (Heller & VanTil, 1982; Litzinger &

Schaeffer, 1982). To be sure, leadership cannot exist without some degree of followership (Hollander & Kelly, 1992; Lundin & Lancaster, 1990; Vecchio, 1987). Effective leadership implies or requires effective followership, in a ying-yang sense of interdependency. Yet, our views of leadership are far more developed than our views of followership (Kelley, 1988). While we have a number of models that detail styles or dimensions of leadership, we have no formal models that detail styles or dimensions of followership. Extending the gender advantage perspective to followership, one could argue that sex/gender differences exist with respect to being an effective subordinate. This argument implies that one gender should be relatively more loyal, more self-sacrificing, more obedient to authority, more devoted to a leader, etc.

An argument that females are better followers can be raised from two positions: First, it can be argued that women are socialized to be more co-operative and that (from feminist arguments) women's inferior social standing predisposes them to be cooperative. Second, one can also raise the "women are wonderful" argument that stems from the general ascription that females possess such admired qualities as being communally-oriented, self-sacrificing, and devoted to the well-being of others (Eagly & Mladinic, 1989, 1994; Eagly, Mladinic, & Otto, 1991).

An argument that males are better followers can be offered on the grounds that males are socialized (especially via involvement in team sports experiences) to fall into place within a hierarchal social order and to accept one's social standing for the benefit of a higher goal (team victory). Further, the notion that "maleness" is compatible with self-sacrifice has re-gained national recognition following the actions of the "first responders" to the September 11 terrorist attacks on New York and Washington, DC. This argument that "men are wonderful" has been dormant and has only recently reemerged within the popular culture, as reflected in various media commentary (Allen, 2002; Noonan, 2001a, 2001b).

Since competing arguments can be raised in support of gender advantage relative to followership, it is instructive to move beyond the rhetoric of gender stereotypes to identify available empirical evidence. Leaving aside extreme examples of risking personal safety to rescue others or instances of suicidal devotion to a cause, followership per se has not received substantial investigation, especially along gender lines. One notable exception is the famous work of Milgram on obedience to authority (Milgram, 1963).

In his classic studies, Stanley Milgram's subjects were instructed to follow orders in circumstances that pitted personal conscience against moral objections. Competing gender arguments concerning likely degree of obedience (measured by how far a subject would go in administering electric shock to another individual) can be raised as follows: (1) females should be more obedient because of social conditioning that emphasizes compliance with directions; (2) females should be less compliant because of social permission to feel compassionate toward a person in suffering; (3) males should be more obedient because of social conditioning to ignore issues of compassion concerning others; and (4) males should be less compliant because of social permission to be assertive and to defy authority.

In recent years, Blass (1999) reexamined data collected on male and female subjects from various Milgram and Milgram-based studies to determine whether sex/gender differences existed. Blass concluded that the sexes displayed equivalent levels of obedience to authority. Like many sex/gender studies, however, it is not possible to rule out (or rule in) any of the four proposed dynamics (or to conclude whether differing processes cancel each other out).

In the more mundane aspects of routine work-related followership, evidence of gender differences in subordinate performance has been sought in lab and organizational studies. These studies have employed ratings, rather than "hard" performance measures. Therefore, issues of rater sex/gender, as well as ratee sex/gender are of some importance. Bartol's (1999) narrative review of sex/gender influences on evaluations of men and women concluded that findings from a variety of lab studies indicate little or no impact of rater sex/gender on performance evaluations.

Field studies (which are much fewer in number because of the difficulty of finding comparable numbers of evaluators from both sexes), however, also have not shown convincing evidence of gender bias (although contextual and gender similarity issues deserve further exploration). Evaluations received by subordinates of both sexes have shown equivocal results (Bartol, 1999). Plus, research on sex/gender differences in assessment center evaluations has failed to identify differences in the ratings received by nonmanagerial and low-level supervisory personnel who were assessed for purposes of identifying management potential (Ritchie & Moses, 1983).

Insights on sex/gender differences may also be gained from research on intraorganizational influence tactics. If the sexes differ in propensity to use certain interpersonal influence tactics "to get their way" with others, then the variety of identified social tactics should yield clear differences. For example, we might expect males to use assertiveness more frequently, while females would make greater use of friendliness and ingratiation. Some tactics that have been labeled as relatively "hard" may be more characteristic of males, while tactics that have been labeled as relatively "soft" may be more characteristic of females.

Major studies of the use of influence tactics in organizations (Kipnis, Schmidt, Swaffin-Smith, & Wilkinson, 1984; Kipnis, Schmidt, & Wilkinson, 1980; Schmidt & Kipnis, 1987) have examined the varieties of influence that employees utilize and the factor structure of these tactics. The factors that they identified include assertiveness, ingratiation, rationality, sanctions, exchange, upward appeal, blocking, and coalition formation.

Of particular interest to our present discussion, Kipnis et al. reported no significant relations associated with sex of respondent or the sex of the respondent's boss in terms of frequency of use of the eight influence dimensions. These authors concluded that men and women chose similar social tactics when attempting to "get their way." Moreover, highly assertive employees (termed "shotgun" employees who refused to take "no" for an answer and who used all the above social tactics to obtain their goals) received the lowest evaluations from their supervisors. This low evaluation held for both males and females. Hence, the popular rhetoric that assertiveness is tolerated or valued when displayed by males, but criticized when displayed by females, is probably in error. In general, being viewed as highly assertive is not judged favorably for either group within organizational settings.

Subsequent important research that sought to replicate and refine the influence tactics work of Schmidt, Kipnis, and Wilkinson (Farmer & Maslyn, 1999; Schriesheim & Hinkin, 1990) and to extend their research to lateral and upward influence (Yukl & Falbe, 1990) did not explicitly report differences on sex/gender. However, it seems likely that had significant differences been identified in this later research (with their great variety of samples), it would have been noted by these authors.

Notwithstanding these findings, the possibility remains that the sexes may yet be found to differ in the aggregate, along various dimensions of follower style. Also, the sexes may differ with respect to followership dimensions as a function of contextual factors. That is to say, we may find that the sexes differ in commitment to a leader as a function of different external factors (such as differences in commitment to, or identification with, a leader's principles or cause). The specificity of these moderating contextual dimensions, as well as the identification of dimensions of followership, are two major directions for future research.[4]

---

4. Research on the construct of organizational commitment may have some bearing on followership, in terms of affective, continuance, and normative commitment (Meyer, Allen, & Smith, 1993). So, too, findings on organizational citizenship behavior may have some relevance (Kidder & Parks, 2001; LePine, Erez, & Johnson, 2002; Organ, 1977).

AN AGENDA FOR GENDER RESEARCH

While any suggested abandonment of research on sex differences seems quite extreme (Baumeister, 1988), any predisposition to accept claims of dramatic differences also seems quite extreme. Although claims of relative gender advantage with respect to leadership remain suspect and legal hurdles prohibit the utility of possible evidence of leadership-related sex differences, other research streams devoted to gender dynamics in organizational contexts may offer additional insights. For these research efforts to be most fruitful, evidence should be gathered from research designs that are more than simple main effect cross-sectional examinations of sex/gender. Main effect studies have generally ignored contextual dimensions (e.g., the association of sex proportion on performance evaluations, cf. Kanter, 1977; Pazy & Oron, 2001) and often ignored temporal dynamics (e.g., the sequencing of specific leader behaviors, cf. Casimer, 2001). Also, the study of leadership and sex/gender in short-term contact settings (lab studies) should be curtailed in favor of the study of intact, continuously performing groups.

There is a further need to specify the processes that link individual sex/gender with anticipated outcomes. Without the specification and measurement of these intervening dynamic connections, much of the theoretical grounding is decidedly lacking or, at best, post-hoc (Lawrence, 1997). One consequence is that sex is often treated as a "proxy" for supposed underlying variables. As noted by Wallston (1987), a fair amount of research on sex/gender has been atheoretical in nature, with a consequence that results are often difficult to integrate.

Findings that the sexes differ with respect to preferences for idealized styles of leadership (i.e., that females prefer leaders who are more considerate) are also of limited value, as the underlying dynamics that foster differences are not fully understood (Vecchio & Boatwright, 2002). As noted by Yukl (2002, p. 413), sex differences in leader behavior and effectiveness may be driven by biologically-based differences that are reinforced by socialization processes, and/or differing gender stereotypes that influence role expectations, perceptions and evaluations (i.e., these processes are not mutually exclusive). Perhaps, because it is not feasible to manipulate biological factors or socialization experiences, research on sex/gender differences in leadership has not been able to address underlying causes of potentially observable differences.

It is a common practice among social scientists to treat hypothesis tests of sex differences as something of a "freebie." That is to say, researchers will often run tests on the variable of sex because the data are so routinely and easily obtained. Although a given study will not necessarily be designed to study sex differences as a primary focus, when sex differences are identified it becomes, essentially, a "bonus" for the researcher in that it provides more material for the write-up and the selling of the manuscript in the journal review process. Considering how many times sex differences must be tested in the normal conduct of social science (especially survey) research (i.e., by simply checking the correlations between sex and all other variables or by treating sex as a moderator/mediator), it is instructive that significant sex differences are not frequently reported in management journals or conference proceedings. The reality that researchers do not widely advise each other that "sex is so critical to examine because it is so commonly found to reveal differences" is itself insightful.

The relative absence of strong evidence of sex differences is probably reflective of the influence of societal and organizational influences. Two major *societal* dynamics that likely contribute to the difficulty of identifying sex/gender differences in the domain of leadership are (a) the growing openness to women in leadership positions (see Gallup Special Reports, 1999) as a consequence of cultural values that emphasize equal opportunity for individuals and (b) the socialization of young men and women by teachers and administrators of both sexes (i.e., the West does not segregate the sexes for educational purposes, and many people have substantial experience with authority figures of both sexes beginning in their earliest employment years).[5]

Major *organizational* dynamics that likely contribute to the difficulty of identifying sex/gender differences in the domain of leadership are embodied in Ben Schneider's (1983, 1987) attraction-selection-attrition framework. Schneider's A-S-A framework suggests that job incumbents tend to have a high degree of homogeneity because certain types of people are (a) drawn to specific positions, (b) selected by the employing organization, and (c) adequately socialized to position/role expectations so as to be effective and less likely to quit or be terminated.

Cultures wherein these societal and organizational dynamics are not operative (i.e., where there is cultural resistance to women in leadership roles, the sexes are segregated in their education and various employment

5. While young people (both female and male) have substantial exposure to authority figures of both sexes (including parents), one difference that is far more consistent in their employment experiences, and that is widely perpetuated in society, is the maintenance of a clear age differential between supervisors and the people they supervise. This norm is so readily accepted that it is seldom studied in work organizations (cf. Lawrence, 1984, 1996).

settings, individuals are not free to pursue occupational interests, and job performance and socialization norms are not clear or enforced) should reveal relatively greater sex/gender differences on work-related dimensions.

While the magnitude of within-culture sex differences should vary in a systematic fashion across cultures, it is important to not be seduced by stereotypes of cultural differences (even when couched in elegant theoretical frameworks). For example, consider the following (reasonably accurate) description of a culture wherein the "core values" include "femininity—in the sense of being more relationship-oriented than task-oriented and highly and demonstrably communicative; driven by traditions of emoting and verbal eloquence" (Scarborough, 1998, p. 121). We might think that this culture would (at least compared to the West) be quite open to female involvement in leadership because of this "core value" and be economically successful (in accordance with the pro-female version of the gender advantage viewpoint). Yet, it is actually a description of the Arab culture. Clearly, we should not rely heavily on our stereotypic views of the world's cultures or the simple exportation of Western constructs and theories. It might be quite an eye-opener to discover how a theory of culture developed in the Arab world could be used to analyze issues surrounding sex/gender differences in the West.

Simplistic claims that increased unit diversity or increased contact promotes positive outcomes should also be regarded as suspect (Keller, 2001; Vecchio & Bullis, 2001; Williams & O'Reilly, 1998). Instead, research should focus on how to effectively manage the nature of the contact that occurs between diverse peoples in order to minimize the possibility of dysfunctional conflict and maximize the likelihood of collaboration and unification. Furthermore, attempts to move beyond simple demographic effects by studying "relational demography" through the combination of superior and subordinate differences along a set of demographic dimensions may add little to understanding sex/gender issues (Roberson & Block, 2001; Tsui, Egan, & O'Reilly, 1992; Tsui & O'Reilly, 1989).

Our knowledge of leadership techniques that facilitate a sense of commonality or mutual fate (common identity and common goals) is still limited, yet urgently needed to better integrate an increasingly diverse workforce. Rallying others to a sense of mission or the instillment of an attractive vision is in the realm of charismatic leadership (Bass, 1998; Conger & Kanungo, 1998). Heretofore, the study of sex/gender differences in charismatic leadership has been minimal. Yet, recent research on sex differences in charismatic leadership suggests that differences, if they exist, are not great (Bass, Avolio, & Atwater, 1996; Komives, 1991; Maher, 1997; van Engen, van der Leeden, & Willemsen, 2001).

For example, one study (Carless, 1998) reported no difference in subordinate evaluations of transformational leadership for female and male managers (although female managers self-reported greater interpersonal-oriented behavior than male managers). Eagly and Johannesen-Schmidt (2001) reported that a comparison of male and female managers (that included ratings by superiors, subordinates, peers, or the managers themselves) indicated that males were more transactional, while females were more transformational in style. However, critical breakdowns of these analyses by job type and organizational context, or by rating source, in order to ensure comparability were not reported.

Leadership techniques that promote the development of a strong sense of unity have received little attention. Perhaps, this stems from an academic aversion to studying certain aspects of leadership due to major historical instances where leaders who advocated unity were later determined to be manipulative and exploitative of their followers. Cynicism concerning people in power also seems to have been at comparatively high levels following the Vietnam War era and the near impeachment of two US presidents. The emerging era of terrorist threats may be rekindling interest in the study of leadership techniques targeted toward the promotion of inclusion, unity, and allegiance, and less toward the emphasis of division and separateness (Bloom, 2002; Tavris, 2001).

REFERENCES

Adler, N. J. (1996). Global women political leaders: an invisible history, an increasingly important future. *Leadership Quarterly, 7*, 133–161.

Allen, C. (2002). Return of the guy. *The Women's Quarterly* (Winter), http://www.iwf.org/pubs/twq/Winter2002d.shtml.

Anderson, C., John, O. P., Keltner, D., & Kring, A. M. (2001). Who attains social status? Effects of personality and physical attractiveness in social groups. *Journal of Personality and Social Psychology, 1*, 116–132.

Archer, J. (1996). Sex differences in social behavior: are the social role and evolutionary explanations compatible? *American Psychologist, 51*, 909–917.

Averill, J. R. (1983). Studies on anger and aggression: implications for theories of emotion. *American Psychologist, 38*, 1145–1160.

Baron, R. A. (2000a). Beyond social capital: how social skills can enhance entrepreneurs' success. *Academy of Management Executive, 14*, 106–115.

Baron, R. A. (2000b). Psychological perspectives on entrepreneurship: cognitive and social factors in entrepreneurs' success. *Current Directions in Psychological Science, 9*, 15–18.

Bartol, K. M. (1999). Gender influences on performance evaluations. In G. N. Powell (Ed.), *Handbook of gender and work* (pp. 168–178). Thousand Oaks, CA: Sage Publ.

Bartol, K. M., & Butterfield, D. A. (1976). Sex effects in evaluating leaders. *Journal of Applied Psychology, 61*, 446–454.

Basow, S. A. (1995). Student evaluations of college professors: when gender matters. *Journal of Educational Psychology, 77*, 656–665.

Bass, B. M. (1990). *Bass and Stogdill's handbook of leadership*. New York, NY: Free Press.

Bass, B. M. (1998). *Transformational leadership: industrial, military, and educational impact*. Mahwah, NJ: Erlbaum.

Bass, B. M., Avolio, B. J., & Atwater, L. (1996). The transformational and transactional leadership of men and women. *Applied Psychology: An International Review, 45*, 5–34.

Baumeister, R. F. (1988). Should we stop studying sex differences altogether? *American Psychologist, 43*, 1092–1095.

Bem, S. (1974). The measurement of psychological androgyny. *Journal of Consulting and Clinical Psychology, 42*, 155–162.

Bernstein, B., & Burke, L. (1995). *Report on student evaluations of female and male faculty at Arizona State University*. Tempe: Arizona State University Graduate College.

Birnbaum, D. W., Nosanchuk, J. A., & Croll, W. L. (1980). Children's stereotypes about sex differences in emotionality. *Sex Roles, 6*, 435–443.

Blake, R., & Mouton, J. (1978). *The new managerial grid*. Houston, TX: Gulf.

Blass, T. (1999). The Milgram paradigm after 35 years: some things we now know about obedience to authority. *Journal of Applied Social Psychology, 29*, 955–978.

Bloom, H. (2002, March/April). Can the United States export diversity? *Across the Board*, 47–51.

Buss, D. M. (1996). The evolutionary psychology of human social strategies. In E. T. Higgins, & A. W. Kruglanski (Eds.), *Social Psychology: handbook of basic principles* (pp. 3–38). New York: Guilford Press.

Butterfield, D. A., & Powell, G. N. (1981). Effect of group performance, leader sex, and rater sex on ratings of leader behavior. *Organizational Behavior and Human Performance, 28*, 129–141.

Carless, S. A. (1998). Gender differences in transformational leadership: an examination of superior, leader, and subordinate perspectives. *Sex Roles, 39*, 887–902.

Carli, L. L. (1990). Gender, language, and influence. *Journal of Personality and Social Psychology, 59*, 941–951.

Carr-Rufino, N. (1993) *The promotable woman: advancing through leadership skills*. Belmont, CA: Wadsworth.

Case, S. S. (1985) A sociolinguistic analysis of the language of gender relations, deviance, and influence in managerial groups (intergroup language differences). *Dissertation Abstracts International, 46*(7A), 2006.

Cashdan, E. (1998). Smiles, speech, and body posture: how women and men display sociometric status and power. *Journal of Nonverbal Behavior, 22*, 209–228.

Casimer, G. (2001). Combinative aspects of leadership style: the ordering and temporal spacing of leadership behaviors. *Leadership Quarterly, 12*, 245–278.

Chesler, P. (2001). *Woman's inhumanity to woman*. New York, NY: Nation Books.

Conger, J. A., & Kanungo, R. (1998). *Charismatic leadership in organizations*. Thousand Oaks, CA: Sage Publ.

Constantinople, A. (1973). Masculinity-femininity. *Psychological Bulletin, 80*, 389–407.

Dansereau, F., Graen, G., & Haga, W. J. (1975). A vertical dyad linkage approach to leadership within formal organizations: a longitudinal investigation of the role-making process. *Organizational Behavior and Human Performance, 15*, 46–78.

Deaux, K., & La France, M. (1998). Gender. In D. J. Gilbert, S. T. Fiske, & G. Lindzey (Eds.), *The handbook of social psychology, 4th ed., vol. 1* (pp. 788–827). Boston: McGraw-Hill.

Dienisch, R. M., & Liden, R. C. (1986). Leader-member exchange model of leadership: a critique and further developments. *Academy of Management Review, 11*, 118–134.

Dobbins, G. H., & Platz, S. J. (1986). Sex-differences in leadership—how real are they? *Academy of Management Review, 11*, 118–127.

Eagly, A. H. (1995). The science and politics of comparing women and men. *American Psychologist, 50*, 145–158.

Eagly, A. H., & Carli, L. L. (1981). Sex of researchers and sex-typed communications as determinants of sex differences in influenceability: a meta-analysis of social influence studies. *Psychological Bulletin, 90*, 1–20.

Eagly, A. H., & Johannesen-Schmidt, M. C. (2001). The leadership styles of women and men. *Journal of Social Issues, 57*, 781–797.

Eagly, A. H., & Johnson, B. T. (1990). Gender and leadership-style: a meta-analysis. *Psychological Bulletin, 108*, 233–256.

Eagly, A. H., Karau, S. J., & Makhijani, M. G. (1995). Gender and the effectiveness of leaders: a meta-analysis. *Psychological Bulletin, 117*, 125–145.

Eagly, A. H., Makhijani, M. G., & Klonsky, B. G. (1992). Gender and the evaluation of leaders: a meta-analysis. *Psychological Bulletin, 111*, 3–22.

Eagly, A. H., & Mladinic, A. (1989). Gender stereotypes and attitudes toward women and men. *Personality and Social Psychology Bulletin, 15*, 543–558.

Eagly, A. H., & Mladinic, A. (1994). Are people prejudiced against women? Some answers from research on attitude, gender stereotypes, and judgments of competence. In W. Strobe, & M. Hewstone (Eds.), *European review of social psychology, vol. 5* (pp. 1–35). New York, NY: Wiley.

Eagly, A. H., Mladinic, A., & Otto, S. (1991). Are women evaluated more favorably than men? An analysis of attitudes, beliefs, and emotions. *Psychology of Women Quarterly, 15*, 203–216.

Eagly, A. H., & Wood, W. (1999). The origins of sex differences in human behavior: evolved dispositions versus social roles. *American Psychologist, 54*, 408–423.

Ellison, C. G., & Powers, D. A. (1994). The contact hypothesis and racial attitudes among Black Americans. *Social Science Quarterly, 75*, 385–400.

Evans, J. (1997). Men in nursing: issues of gender segregation and hidden advantage. *Journal of Advanced Nursing, 26*, 226–231.

Fabes, R. A., & Martin, C. L. (1991). Gender and age stereotypes of emotionality. *Personality and Social Psychology Bulletin, 17*, 532–540.

Farmer, S. M., & Maslyn, J. M. (1999). Why are styles of upward influence neglected? Making the case for a configurational approach to influences. *Journal of Management, 25*, 653–682.

Feingold, A. (1988). Cognitive gender differences are disappearing. *American Psychologist, 43*, 95–103.

Feldman, K. (1993). College students' views of male and female college teachers: Part II. Evidence from student evaluations of their classroom teachers. *Research in Higher Education, 34*, 151–211.

Fiedler, F. E. (1967). *A theory of leadership effectiveness.* New York: McGraw-Hill.

Fiedler, F. E., & Chemers, M. M. (1982). *Improving leader effectiveness: the leader match concept* (2nd ed.). New York, NY: Wiley.

Fischer, A. (1993). Sex differences in emotionality: fact or stereotype? *Feminism and Psychology, 3*, 303–318.

Fleishman, E. A. (1957). The leadership opinion questionnaire. In R. M. Stogdill, & A. E. Coons (Eds.), *Leader behavior: its description and measurement* (pp. 120–133). Columbus, OH: Bureau of Business Research, Ohio State University.

Fox, K. (2002). Evolution, alienation, and gossip. *Social Issues Research Group*, www.sirc.org/publik/gossip.shtml.

Gallup Special Reports (1999). The Gallup poll: 65 years of polling history, www.gallup.com/poll/specialReports/pollSummaries/polls_this_century_QuizQ. asp.

Gerstner, C. R., & Day, D. V. (1997). Meta-analytic review of leader-member exchange theory: correlates and construct issues. *Journal of Applied Psychology, 82*, 827–844.

Gilligan, C. (1982). *In a different voice: psychological theory and women's development.* Cambridge, MA: Harvard Univ. Press.

Graeff, C. L. (1983). The situational leadership theory: a critical view. *Academy of Management Review, 8*, 285–291.

Graeff, C. L. (1997). Evolution of situational leadership theory: a critical review. *Leadership Quarterly, 8*, 153–170.

Graen, G., & Scandura, T. A. (1986). Toward a psychology of dyadic organizing. *Research in Organizational Behavior, 9*, 175–208.

Graen, G., & Uhl-Bien, M. (1995). Relationship-based approach to leadership: development of leader-member exchange (LMX) theory of leadership over 25 years: applying a multi-level multi-domain perspective. *Leadership Quarterly, 6*, 219–247.

Grant, J. (1988). Women as managers: what they can offer to organizations. *Organizational Dynamics*, 56–63.

Grobman, H., & Hines, V. A. (1956). What makes a good principal? *Bulletin of the National Association of Secondary-School Principals, 40*, 5–16.

Haccoun, D. M., Haccoun, R. R., & Sallay, G. (1978). Sex differences in the appropriateness of supervisory styles: a non-management view. *Journal of Applied Psychology, 63*, 124–127.

Harrison, D. A., Price, K. H., & Bell, M. P. (1998). Beyond relational demography: time and the effects of surface-level and deep-level diversity on work group cohesion. *Academy of Management Journal, 41*, 96–107.

Hathaway, S. R., & McKinley, J. C. (1951). *The Minnesota Multiphasic Personality Inventory (revised).* Minneapolis, MN: University of Minnesota.

Heilman, M. E., Block, C. J., Martell, R. F., & Simon, M. C. (1989). Has anything changed? Current characterizations of men, women, and managers. *Journal of Applied Psychology, 74*, 935–942.

Helgeson, S. (1990). *The female advantage: women's ways of leadership.* New York: Doubleday/Currency.

Heller, T., & VanTil, J. V. (1982). Leadership and followership: some summary propositions. *Journal of Applied Behavioral Science, 18*, 405–414.

Hersey, P., & Blanchard, K. H. (1977). *Management of organizational behavior: utilizing human resources* (4th ed.). Englewood Cliffs, NJ: Prentice-Hall.

Hersey, P., & Blanchard, K. H. (1982). *Management of organizational behavior: utilizing human resources* (3rd ed.). Englewood Cliffs, NJ: Prentice-Hall.

Hilton, L. (2001). A few good men: male nurses defy stereotypes and discrimination to find satisfaction in female-dominated profession. *Nurse Week*, www.nurseweek.com/news/features/01-05/men.html.

Hoffman, R. M. (2001). The measurement of masculinity and femininity: historical perspective and implications for counseling. *Journal of Counseling and Development, 79*, 472–485.

Hollander, E. P., & Kelly, D. R. (1992). Appraising relational qualities of leadership and followership. *International Journal of Psychology, 27*, 289–290.

Hooijberg, R., & DiTomaso, N. (1996). Leadership in and of demographically diverse organizations. *Leadership Quarterly, 7*, 1–19.

Hooijberg, R., Hunt, J. G., & Dodge, G. E. (1997). Leadership complexity and development of the Leaderplex Model. *Journal of Management, 23*, 375–408.

International Labour Office (1996). *Yearbook of labour statistics* (55th ed.) (pp. 73–84). Geneva: ILO.

Jacobsen, M. B., & Effertz, J. (1974). Sex roles and leadership: perceptions of the leaders and the led. *Organizational Behavior and Human Performance, 12*, 383–396.

Jafee, S., & Hyde, J. S. (2000). Gender differences in moral orientation: a meta-analysis. *Psychological Bulletin, 126*, 703–726.

Johnson, I. T., & Shulman, G. A. (1988). More alike than meets the eye: perceived gender differences in subjective experience and its display. *Sex Roles, 19*, 67–79.

Kanter, R. M. (1977). Some effects of proportions on group life: skewed sex ratios and responses to token women. *American Journal of Sociology, 82*, 965–990.

Keller, R. T. (2001). Cross-functional project groups in research and new product development: diversity, communications, job stress, and outcomes. *Academy of Management Journal, 44*, 547–555.

Kelley, R. E. (1988). In praise of followers. *Harvard Business Review, 66*, 142–148.

Kerr, S., & Jermier, J. M. (1978). Substitutes for leadership: their meaning and measurement. *Organizational Behavior and Human Performance, 22*, 375–403.

Kidder, D. L., & Parks, J. M. (2001). The good soldier: who is s(he)? *Journal of Organizational Behavior, 22*, 939–959.

Kipnis, D., Schmidt, S. M., Swaffin-Smith, C., & Wilkinson, I. (1984). Patterns of managerial influence: shotgun managers, tacticians, and bystanders. *Organizational Dynamics, 12*, 58–67.

Kipnis, D., Schmidt, S. M., & Wilkinson, I. (1980). Intraorganizational influence tactics: explorations in getting one's way. *Journal of Applied Psychology, 65,* 440–452.

Kohlberg, L. (1969). Stage and sequence: the cognitive-developmental approach to socialization. In D. A. Goslin (Ed.), *Handbook of socialization theory and research* (pp. 347–400). Chicago, IL: Rand-McNally.

Komives, S. R. (1991). The relationship of same- and cross-gender work pairs to staff performance and supervisory leadership in residence hall units. *Sex Roles, 29,* 405–420.

LaFrance, M., & Banaji, M. (1992). Toward a reconsideration of the gender-emotion relationship. In M. S. Clark (Ed.), *Emotion and social behavior. Review of personality and social psychology, vol. 14* (pp. 178–201). Newbury Park, CA: Sage.

Larson, L. L., Hunt, J. G., & Osburn, R. (1976). The great Hi-Hi leader behavior myth: a lesson from Occam's razor. *Academy of Management Journal, 19,* 628–641.

Lawrence, B. S. (1984). Age grading: the implicit organizational timetable. *Journal of Occupational Behavior, 5,* 25–35.

Lawrence, B. S. (1996). Organizational age norms: why is it so hard to know one when you see one? *Gerontologist, 36,* 209–220.

Lawrence, B. S. (1997). The black box of organizational demography. *Organizational Sciences, 8,* 1–22.

Lenney, E. (1991). Sex roles: masculinity, femininity, and androgyny. In J. P. Robinson, P. R. Shaver, & L. S. Wrightsman (Eds.), *Measures of personality and social psychological attitudes, vol. 1* (pp. 573–660). San Diego, CA: Academic Press.

LePine, J. A., Erez, A., & Johnson, D. E. (2002). The nature and dimensionality of organizational citizenship behavior: a critical review and meta-analysis. *Journal of Applied Psychology, 87,* 52–65.

Likert, R. (1967). *The human organization.* New York, NY: McGraw-Hill.

Litzinger, W., & Schaeffer, T. (1982). Leadership through followership. *Business Horizons, 25,* 78–81.

Loden, M. (1985). *Feminine leadership: or how to succeed in business without being one of the boys.* New York, NY: Times Books.

Lundin, S. C., & Lancaster, L. C. (1990). Beyond leadership: the importance of followership. *Futurist, 24,* 18–22.

Lyness, K. S., & Thompson, D. E. (1997). Above the glass ceiling? A comparison of matched samples of female and male executives. *Journal of Applied Psychology, 82,* 359–375.

Maher, K. J. (1997). Gender-related stereotypes of transformational and transactional leadership. *Sex Roles, 37,* 209–225.

Maier, M. (1992). Evolving paradigms of management in organizations: a gendered analysis. *Journal of Management Studies, 4,* 29–45.

Maier, M. (1999). On the gendered substructure of organizations: dimensions and dilemmas of corporate masculinity. In G. Powell (Ed.), *Handbook of gender and work* (pp. 69–93). Thousand Oaks, CA: Sage Publ.

Marsh, H. W., & Myers, M. (1986). Masculinity, femininity, and androgyny. A methodological and theoretical critique. *Sex Roles, 14,* 397–431.

Marsh, H. W., & Ware, J. E. (1982). Effects of expressiveness, content coverage, and incentive on multidimensional student rating scales: new interpretations of the Dr. Fox effect. *Journal of Educational Psychology, 74,* 126–134.

Martinko, M. J., & Gardner, W. L. (1985). Beyond structural observation: methodological issues and new directions. *Academy of Management Review, 10,* 676–695.

McGrath, J. E. (1991). Time, interaction, and performance (TIP): a theory of groups. *Small Group Research, 22,* 147–174.

McGregor, D. (1960). *The human side of enterprise.* New York: McGraw-Hill.

McLean, S. R., & Hinrich, R. N. (2000). Buoyancy, gender, and swimming performance. *Journal of Applied Biomechanics, 16,* 248–263.

Meyer, J. P., Allen, N. J., & Smith, C. A. (1993). Commitment to organizations and occupations: extension and test of a three-component conceptualization. *Journal of Applied Psychology, 78,* 538–551.

Milgram, S. (1963). Behavioral study of obedience. *Journal of Abnormal and Social Psychology, 67,* 371–378.

Mintzberg, H. (1973). *The nature of managerial work.* New York: Harper and Row.

Moore, D. P. (1999). Women entrepreneurs. In G. N. Powell (Ed.), *Handbook of gender and work* (pp. 371–390). Thousand Oaks, CA: Sage Publ.

Morawski, J. G. (1985). The measurement of masculinity and feminity: engendering categorical realities. *Journal of Personality, 53,* 196–233.

Morawski, J. G. (1987). The troubled quest for masculinity, femininity, and androgyny. In P. Shaver, & C. Hendrick (Eds.), *Sex and gender* (pp. 44–69). Newbury Park, CA: Sage.

Noonan, P. (2001a, Oct. 5). Courage under fire. *Wall Street Journal,* http://www.opinionjournal.com/columnists/pnoonan/?id=95001272.

Noonan, P. (2001b, Oct. 12). Welcome back, Duke. *Wall Street Journal,* http://www.opinionjournal.com/columnists/pnoonan/?id=95001309.

Nystrom, P. C. (1978). Managers and the hi-hi myth. *Academy of Management Journal, 21,* 325–331.

Organ, D. W. (1977). Organizational citizenship behavior: it's construct clean up time. *Human Performance, 10,* 85–97.

Pazy, A., & Oron, I. (2001). Sex proportion and performance evaluation among high-ranking military officers. *Journal of Organizational Behavior, 22,* 689–702.

Pettigrew, T. F. (1998). Intergroup contact theory. *Annual Review of Psychology, 49,* 65–85.

Powell, G. N., & Butterfield, D. A. (1979). The "good manager:" masculine or androgynous. *Academy of Management Journal, 22,* 395–403.

Powell, G. N., & Butterfield, D. A. (1989). The "good manager": did androgyny fare better in the 1980's? *Group and Organization Studies, 14,* 216–233.

Powell, G. N., Butterfield, D. A., & Parent, J. D. (2002). Gender and managerial stereotypes: have the times changed? *Journal of Management, 28,* 177–193.

Ragins, B. R. (1991). Gender effects in subordinate evaluations of leaders: real or artifact. *Journal of Organizational Behavior, 12,* 259–268.

Ritchie, R. J., & Moses, J. L. (1983). Assessment center correlates of women's advancement into middle management: a 7-year longitudinal analysis. *Journal of Applied Psychology, 68,* 227–231.

Roberson, L., & Block, C. J. (2001). Racioethnicity and job performance: a review and critique of theoretical perspectives on the causes of group differences. *Research in Organizational Behavior, 23,* 247–325.

Robinson, M. D., Johnson, J. T., & Shields, S. A. (1998). The gender heuristic and the database: factors affecting the perception of gender-related differences in the experience and display of emotions. *Basic and Applied Social Psychology, 20,* 206–219.

Rosen, B., & Jerdee, J. H. (1973). The influence of sex-role stereotypes on evaluations of male and female supervisory behavior. *Journal of Applied Psychology, 57,* 44–48.

Rosener, J. B. (1990). Ways women lead. *Harvard Business Review, 68*(6), 119–125.

Rosener, J. B. (1995). *America's competitive secret: utilizing women as a management strategy.* New York, NY: Oxford Univ. Press.

Rosenthal, R. (1991). *Meta-analytic procedures for social research.* Newbury Park, CA: Sage.

Rosenthal, R., & DiMatteo, M. R. (2001). Meta-analysis: recent developments in quantitative methods for literature reviews. *Annual Review of Psychology, 52,* 59–82.

Sargent, J. F., & Miller, G. R. (1971). Some differences in certain communication behaviors of autocratic and democratic group leaders. *Journal of Communication, 21,* 233–252.

Scarborough, J. (1998). *The origins of cultural differences and their impact on management.* Westport, CT: Quorum Books.

Schein, V. E., & Mueller, R. (1992). Sex-role stereotyping and requisite management characteristics: a cross-cultural look. *Journal of Organizational Behavior, 13,* 439–447.

Schein, V. E., Mueller, R., Lituchy, T., & Liu, J. (1996). Think manager—think male: a global phenomenon? *Journal of Organizational Behavior, 17,* 33–41.

Schmidt, S. M., & Kipnis, D. (1987, Nov.). The perils of persistency. *Psychology Today,* 32–34.

Schneider, B. (1983). Interactional psychology and organizational behavior. *Research in Organizational Behavior, 5,* 1–31.

Schneider, B. (1987). The people make the place. *Personnel Psychology, 40,* 437–453.

Schriesheim, C. A. (1982). The great high consideration–high initiating structure myth: evidence on its generalizability. *Journal of Social Psychology, 116,* 221–228.

Schriesheim, C. A., Castro, S. L., & Coglister, C. C. (1999). Leader-member exchange (LMX) research: a comprehensive review of theory, measurement, and data-analytic practices. *Leadership Quarterly, 10,* 63–113.

Schriesheim, C. A., & Hinkin, T. R. (1990). Influence tactics used by subordinates: a theoretical and empirical analysis and refinement of the Kipnis, Schmidt, and Wilkinson subscales. *Journal of Applied Psychology, 75,* 246–257.

Schriesheim, C. A., & Kerr, S. (1977a). Theories and measures of leadership: a critical appraisal. In J. G. Hunt, & L. L. Larson (Eds.), *Leadership: the cutting edge* (pp. 9–45). Carbondale, IL: Southern Illinois Univ. Press.

Schriesheim, C. A., & Kerr, S. (1977b). R. I. P. LPC: a reply to Fiedler. In J. G. Hunt, & L. L. Larson (Eds.), *Leadership: the cutting edge* (pp. 51–56). Carbondale, IL: Southern Illinois Univ. Press.

Schriesheim, C. A., & Klich, N. R. (1991). Fiedler's least preferred coworker (LPC) instrument: an investigation of its true bipolarity. *Education and Psychological Measurement, 51,* 305–315.

Schriesheim, C. A., & Stogdill, R. M. (1975). Differences in factor structure across three versions of Ohio State Leadership Scales. *Personnel Psychology, 28,* 189–206.

Shields, S. A. (1991). Gender in the psychology of emotion: a selective research review. In K. T. Strongman (Ed.), *International review of studies on emotion, vol. 1* (pp. 227–245). New York, NY: Wiley.

Shields, S. A. (1995). The role of emotion, beliefs, and values in gender development. In N. Eisenberg (Ed.), *Review of personality and social psychology, vol. 15* (pp. 212–232). Thousand Oaks, CA: Sage Publ.

Sigelman, L., & Welch, S. (1993). The contact hypothesis revisited: intersocial contact and positive racial attitudes. *Social Forces, 71,* 781–795.

Simmons, R. (2002). *Odd girl out: the hidden culture of aggression in girls.* New York, NY: Harcourt Brace.

Sommers, C. H. (2000a). *The war against boys: how misguided feminism is harming our young men.* New York, NY: Simon and Schuster.

Sommers, C. H. (2000b). The war against boys. *Atlantic Monthly,* www.theatlantic.com/issues/2000/05/sommers.htm.

Sommers, C. H. (2000c). Letters: Christina Hoff Sommers replies to Carol Gilligan. *Atlantic Monthly,* www.theatlanticmonthly.com/issues/2000/08/letters.htm.

Spence, J. T., & Helmreich, R. L. (1978). *Masculinity and femininity: their psychological dimensions, correlates, and antecedents.* Austin, TX: University of Texas Press.

Sternberg, R. J. (1988). *The triarchic mind: a new theory of human intelligence.* New York, NY: Viking.

Sternberg, R. J. (1997). Managerial intelligence: why IQ isn't enough. *Journal of Management, 23,* 475–493.

Sternberg, R. J., & Horvath, J. A. (1999). *Tacit knowledge in professional practice: researcher and practitioner perspectives.* Mahwah, NJ: Lawrence Erlbaum Associates.

Sternberg, R. J., Wagner, R. K., Williams, W., & Horvath, J. (1995). Testing common sense. *American Psychologist, 50,* 912–927.

Stogdill, R. M. (1974). *Handbook of leadership.* New York, NY: Free Press.

Tavris, C. (1992). *The mismeasure of woman: why women are not the better sex, the inferior sex, or the opposite sex.* New York, NY: Touchstone.

Tavris, C. (2001). The politics and science of gender research. In C. Tavris (Ed.), *Psychobabble and biobunk* (pp. 43–60). Upper Saddle River, NJ: Prentice-Hall.

Trempe, J., Rigny, A., & Haccoun, R. (1985). Subordinate satisfaction with male and female managers: role of perceived supervisory influence. *Journal of Applied Psychology, 70,* 44–47.

Tsui, A. S., Egan, T. D., & O'Reilly, C. A. (1992). Being different: relational demography and organizational commitment. *Administrative Science Quarterly, 37,* 549–579.

Tsui, A. S., & O'Reilly, C. A. (1989). Beyond simple demographic effects: the importance of relational demography in superior-subordinate dyads. *Academy of Management Journal, 32,* 402–423.

US Dept. of Labor, Labor Statistics (1998). *Employment and Earnings, 45*(1), 163; (9), 7.

van Engen, M. L., van der Leeden, R., & Willemsen, T. M. (2001). Gender, context and leadership styles: a field study. *Journal of Occupational and Organizational Psychology, 74,* 581–598.

Vecchio, R. P. (1979). A test of the cognitive complexity interpretation of the least preferred coworker scale. *Educational and Psychological Measurement, 39,* 523–526.

Vecchio, R. P. (1987). Effective followership: leadership turned upside down. *Journal of Business Strategies, 4*, 39–47.

Vecchio, R. P., & Boatwright, K. J. (2002). Preferences for idealized styles of supervision. *Leadership Quarterly, 13*, 327–342.

Vecchio, R. P., & Bullis, R. G. (2001). Moderators of the influence of supervisor-subordinate similarity on subordinate outcomes. *Journal of Applied Psychology, 86*, 884–896.

Vroom, V. H., & Jago, A. G. (1978). On the validity of the Vroom-Yetton model. *Journal of Applied Psychology, 63*, 151–162.

Vroom, V. H., & Jago, A. G. (1988). *The new leadership: managing participation in organizations*. Englewood Cliffs, NJ: Prentice-Hall.

Vroom, V. H., Yetton, P. C. (1973). *Leadership and decision making*. Pittsburgh, PA: University of Pittsburgh Press.

Wallston, B. S. (1987). Social psychology of women and gender. *Journal of Applied Psychology, 17*, 1025–1050.

Williams, K. Y., & O'Reilly, C. A. (1998). Demographic diversity in organizations: a review of 40 years of research. *Research in Organizational Behavior, 20*, 77–140.

Yukl, G., (2002). *Leadership in organizations*. Upper Saddle River, NJ: Prentice-Hall.

Yukl, G., & Falbe, C. M. (1990). Influence tactics and objectives in upward, downward, and lateral influence attempts. *Journal of Applied Psychology, 75*, 132–140.

Zaccaro, S. J., Foti, R. J., & Kenny, D. A. (1991). Self-monitoring and trait-based variance in leadership: an investigation of leader flexibility across multiple group situations. *Journal of Applied Psychology, 76*, 308–315.

It's Not Easy Being Green: Jealousy and Envy in the Workplace

Robert P. Vecchio

Given the inherent competitiveness of a great deal of organizational life, it may be reasonable to claim that the experience of jealousy and envy by employees ranks among the more common emotional experiences in organizational settings. In recent years, I have begun my graduate-level courses by asking students to provide confidential examples of jealousy and/or envy that they have experienced in the workplace, either as an observer or as the person who felt a strong negative reaction. Using this approach as part of an anonymous written exercise, I have found that respondents have no difficulty citing at least several instances of jealousy and/or envy. One confidential survey of the frequency of the experience of employee jealousy (Miner, 1990) revealed that 77% of a sample of 278 employees had observed an instance of jealousy during the prior month, with 58% of the respondents being directly involved in the event. These instances were reported to occur with a mean frequency of 3.6 events per month, and, perhaps more importantly, with a majority of the respondents reporting that managers were not effectively handling these situations.

Despite the fairly commonplace nature of this experience, surprisingly little systematic research on employee affect and behavior has directly addressed these topics (Vecchio, 1993a). Although popular magazines have shown a continuing increase in discussing the topic of jealousy since 1945 (Clanton, 1989), only during the late 1980s and into the 1990s has interest in jealousy and envy begun to receive serious attention from social science researchers (Salovey, 1991; Stearns, 1989; White & Mullen, 1989). The absence of empirically-based attention to these topics may be partly due to the difficulties associated with studying an issue that is inherently distasteful. Many people are simply embarrassed to publicly acknowledge strong, negative emotions. In a study of the likableness ratings of 555 personality-trait words, Norman Anderson (1968) reported that "jealousy" ranked 502nd on "favorableness or desirability," below the traits of "cold" (496th) and "unfair" (498th). "Envious" ranked 425th, comparable to "short-tempered"

(422nd) and "weak" (429th). In essence, these emotions are regarded as noxious and unpleasant, as well as potentially inevitable, yet inappropriate for social display. Moreover, there is a tendency on the part of many supervisors to dismiss employee complaints concerning pay allocations, promotions, performance evaluations, and task assignments as "merely" reflecting jealousy and/or envy.

The absence of research on jealousy and envy, particularly in work settings, may stem also from difficulties in measuring these psychological experiences and associated behavioral manifestations. Additionally, the lack of a distinct theoretical framework for defining employee jealousy and envy, and deducing predictions within the organizational domain, may have served to limit work on the topic.

This paper seeks to begin discussion concerning the role of employee jealousy and envy. In the following sections, we consider the definition of jealousy and envy in the workplace, consequences of these emotions, the utility of existing organizational theories for understanding these emotions, their measurement, the generation of specific hypotheses that pertain to these emotional experiences, some preliminary evidence on several of the hypotheses, the management of negative emotions, and further issues associated with the organizational and cross-cultural aspects of these emotions.

DEFINING EMPLOYEE JEALOUSY AND ENVY

Although feelings of jealousy and envy at work are generally denigrated, they have been traditionally recognized in literature and the arts as a powerful influence on behavior. For example, in Shakespeare's *Othello*, Iago is passed over for promotion in favor of Cassio (despite the fact that Iago has a stronger service record than Cassio). Resentment of Cassio's advancement prompts Iago to contrive events so as to lead Othello to suspect his wife of infidelity with Cassio, and ultimately to murder her (Todd & Dewhurst, 1955). A contributing factor to Iago's malice is his prior admiration of Othello. In Shaffer's play *Amadeus* (1981), Mozart's creative genius and personal style spark bitterness and rancor on the part of a colleague, Salieri. The level of resentment is so great that Salieri conspires to limit Mozart's success as a composer and to ensure Mozart's early demise, while simultaneously feigning admiration and friendship.[1] In a number of respects, these literary works highlight some basic elements and processes of jealousy and envy in that the aggrieved adopt courses of action that seek a form of vengeance while concealing their true feelings.

Jealousy

In order to study the phenomenon of jealousy more systematically, social scientists have recently sought to define jealousy. Based on White and Mullen's (1989, p. 9) examination of romantic jealousy, we can more generically define jealousy as a pattern of thoughts, emotions, and behaviors that results from the loss of self-esteem and/or the loss of outcomes associated with a relationship. This perceived loss, or threat, is due to the perception of a real (or potential) attraction between a significant other and a (potentially imagined) rival.[2] This definition suggests that the pattern is a response to an initial perception of the perceived intrusion of a rival, and the likelihood that the rival will reduce one's self-esteem or threaten an existing valued relationship. The definition identifies three essential participants (i.e., the phenomenon is inherently triadic) for whom the relations among the elements form the basis of a "social tension." Also, the definition recognizes that jealousy may be: (1) largely illusory, but that the impact of such illusions for the participants is real, and (2) anticipatory in nature (i.e., a response to expected threats as well as existing threats). Last, the definition recognizes the central role of self-esteem in the experience.

Although the above definition emphasizes cognitive-perceptual processes in the experience, it is nonetheless important to recognize the physiological base of the experience. As is true of other emotions, visceral reactions (a stress "fight or flight" response) serve to define the experience on a personal level (Selye, 1976).[3] In some instances, the initial emotional reaction is quite strong—being referred to as a "flash" of jealousy. This initial strong reaction tends to be recalled vividly and over a long span of time (Clanton & Smith, 1977).

While jealousy may be examined in a fairly generic fashion, it is important to recognize the unique varieties or types of jealousy that exist. Two major types that have received the most attention from researchers are romantic jealousy (White, 1981a) and sibling jealousy (Banks & Kahn, 1982; Dunn, 1983). In the work setting (a largely unexplored social arena), jealousy may exist for an employee toward a coworker who poses as a rival to a valued relationship with a supervisor or another co-worker. Although probably less commonly observed, a supervisor may also experience jealousy toward a subordinate who poses as a rival to a valued relationship with another subordinate. However, the following discussion primarily focuses on jealousy and envy experienced by employees toward peers.

Although jealousy can be examined in generic terms, aspects of working relationships are sufficiently unique to qualify for a separate discussion. For example, the norms that govern social relations in work settings are distinct from those that operate in family units (i.e., among siblings and parents) and between lovers. The difficulty of terminating relations, and the acceptability of recourse to physical violence are generally lower in work settings versus other contexts, while social pressure to deliberately ignore rivals is greater in work settings (Gayford, 1979; Stets & Pirog-Good, 1987). These differences in norms pose unique constraints on responses to the experience of jealousy. Additionally, the nature of the rewards that are exchanged in working relationships differ from those that are used in other social relations (Foa & Foa, 1980). For example, the ability of a supervisor to confer status via public recognition of a subordinate's efforts and to alter tangible extrinsic outcomes, are rewards that are fairly unique to working relations.

Envy

After stating what employee jealousy is, it is also important to state what it is not. Jealousy is probably most frequently confused with the experience of envy. However, the experiences are, upon scrutiny, recognizable as distinct (Parrott, 1991). Jealousy pertains to the loss of an existing relationship, while envy pertains to another possessing what one desires for oneself. Succinctly stated, envy concerns what we would like to have, but do not have, while jealousy concerns what we have, but fear we may lose (Van Sommers, 1988). Employee jealousy involves a win/lose outcome relative to a rival, while in employee envy, another's gain need not be at one's own personal expense. Moreover, hostility that accompanies employee jealousy is relatively more socially approved than hostility or ill will that may accompany feelings of employee envy. That is to say, many people believe that it is acceptable to feel anger or resentment in response to the intrusion of a specific rival, more so than to feel resentment of the success of others in general. Furthermore, subjects report that jealousy produces more intense affective response than does envy (Salovey & Rodin, 1986). Individuals also report that envy is more characterized by a sense of inferiority, self-criticism, and a desire to improve, while jealousy is more characterized by suspicion, fear of loss, anger, rejection, and a desire to get even (Parrott & Smith, 1993; Smith, Kim, & Parrott, 1988). One reason that envy may be especially difficult for people to admit to is that in recognizing it in oneself, a person acknowledges inferiority with respect to another (Foster, 1972). In so doing, there is a loss of self-esteem. A further issue that contributes to the confusion of jealousy and envy is the reality that envy can exist without feelings of jealousy, while jealousy may often be accompanied by feelings of envy.

Both envy and jealousy are similar in terms of involving a loss of self-esteem that is derived from social comparison. As a result, both envy and jealousy may coexist in a specific social instance, in that a rival in a jealousy-invoking situation may arouse envy via an unfavorable social comparison. In essence, the experience of jealousy that is derived from an unfavorable comparative appraisal made by a valued or admired other, can lead to a negative self-appraisal or self-dissatisfaction and, hence, envy. Like workplace jealousy, employee envy is a neglected topic in organizational research, despite the unquestioned occurrence of the experience by employees. Envy and jealousy can be viewed as deriving from two fundamental realities of organizational life: competition and hierarchy. It may be said that envy is to competition what jealousy is to hierarchy (Simmel, 1955). Both emotions can be seen as deriving from an inability to control events, in that jealousy reflects an inability to control (or influence) the target member of a valued relationship, while envy reflects an inability to control (or influence) the allocation of outcomes. In a more basic sense, the desire to control events is a component of jealousy and envy (i.e., in order to maintain an extreme form of attachment, and in order to influence the assignment of rewards, respectively). Furthermore, both jealousy and envy can be understood as an emergent concern with the perceived erosion of one's social standing. For purposes of discussion, envy can be formally defined as a pattern of thoughts, emotions, and behaviors that results from the loss of self-esteem in response to another obtaining outcomes that one strongly desires.

A useful distinction of the types of negative emotions that are found in organizational settings lies in the level of threat. Hupka (1984) has offered the terms *"fait accompli"* and *"suspicious"* to define, respectively, the incontrovertible and accepted reality that a rival or competitor is now receiving the type of attention or rewards that the protagonist values, versus a condition where the threat is only suspected and the nature of the threat is not clear. The condition of "suspiciousness" carries a greater sense of anxiety concerning the status of the situation, and offers the prediction that information-gathering behaviors on the part of the protagonist are far more likely (e.g., monitoring the actions of others, and the questioning of others). In some instances, "fait accompli" may lead to cognitive reappraisals of the relationship, and a form of begrudging resignation. The two forms of threat can be viewed as representing two levels of jealousy and envy, with each level predisposing different emotional and behavioral responses.

CONSEQUENCES OF WORKPLACE JEALOUSY AND ENVY

As social emotions possessing negative connotations and sources of stress, there is a tendency to view workplace jealousy and envy as necessarily dysfunctional. From one perspective, employee jealousy and envy can be, in fact, quite functional in that they can energize behavior and act as discriminative cues for eliciting coping responses. Essentially, employee jealousy and envy can serve the social function of protecting highly valued relationships and circumstances. This is not to argue that jealousy and envy are not potentially pathological. In the extreme, they certainly can be precisely that. Recent reports of increased violence in the work setting (including the murder of co-workers and supervisors) and the more commonplace forms of harassment of rivals indicate that work settings are not exempt from pathological reactions (Sprouse, 1992).[4] Short of the range of responses (which includes preoccupation or obsessive thinking) that mark the pathological realm of behavioral response, workplace jealousy and envy can be viewed as sources of "cognitive tension" that activate coping responses (Festinger, 1954). From this perspective, workplace jealousy and envy can serve socially useful purposes for an individual by focusing attention and action on the resolution of a threat.

The available literature on the topic of coping with emotions has some relevance to work settings. White and Mullen (1989) have identified nine major coping strategies, in addition to a variety of minor coping responses (e.g., humor, projection, and fantasy). "Strategy," in this context, means a cognitive structure organized in terms of superordinate goals, and associated representations of the cognitive and behavioral steps that are required to achieve the desired goals. As superordinate goals, the cognitions and actions of the protagonist are directed at either altering the situation (to reduce the threat), managing the associated affect, or both. Tables 1 and 2 list the coping strategies and the superordinate goals of each strategy, and provides organizational examples.

RESEARCH OF POTENTIAL RELEVANCE
TO WORKPLACE JEALOUSY AND ENVY:
SEARCHING FOR GENERALIZABLE PRINCIPLES

As noted earlier, empirical research on jealousy, per se, among family members is still in an early stage, while research on jealousy in organizational settings is essentially nonexistent. Nonetheless, some of the findings from the existing literature may have relevance for individuals in organizations. Therefore, it can be instructive to review some of these potentially pertinent findings.

One stream of research has begun to examine whether patterns of jealousy in adulthood can be linked to childhood experiences with parental or sibling rivals. A critical argument for studying adult jealousy in this fashion is that work group settings resemble sibling situations as group members vie for the primary attention of the idealized group leader (i.e., the equivalent of a parental figure). Also, it can be reasonably argued that the manner in which people learn to relate to authority figures and peers is influenced by early socialization experiences within the family unit. Interestingly, sibling jealousy has been found to be less common in larger families (Dunn, 1983), suggesting, thereby, that other family unit members can satisfy the needs of an individual beyond the parents. By extension, we might expect to find that employee jealousy is less severe, with respect to relations with a supervisor, in larger work units.

Gender differences have also received study, with the debate focusing on whether one gender is more prone to a jealous response. In a review of research on gender and job values, Nieva and Gutek (1981) argued that women, relative to men, value promotions and salary less, while valuing interpersonal relationships more. Other research suggests that women strive for interpersonal or social success, while men strive for exploitive or competitive success (Buss, Larsen, Westen, & Semmelroth, 1992; Kahn, O'Leary, Krulewitz, & Lamm, 1980; Nadler & Dotan, 1992). Therefore, it seems reasonable to expect differences in response by the genders to threats to relationships and competitive standing. Thus far, the majority of the results of this research has not found reliable gender differences in the level of self-reported jealousy (Bringle & Buunk, 1985; White, 1984). The genders may differ, however, in preferences for coping strategies. Bryson (1976) observed that females predicted they would more likely seek social support, engage in denial, and try to get even, while males predicted they would more likely drink to excess, be sexually aggressive with others, and ask a mutual friend

Table 1
Features of Major Coping Strategies: Primary Focus on Jealousy

Strategy	Superordinate Goal(s)	Organizational Examples
Improve relationship with target	Situation	Project image of loyalty or offer praise
		Take on greater work load and responsibility
Interfere with rival's relationship	Situation	Display resentment or hostility
		Arouse guilt
Demand commitment	Situation, affect	Seek assignment to more critical/desirable tasks
Derogation of target	Affect	Come to accept that target is not one's ideal
		Provoke the target to rejection
Develop alternatives	Affect, situation	Seek social rewards in other co-workers
		Become more involved in the work itself
Denial/Avoidance	Affect	Pretend to be unaffected
		Use of alcohol or drugs
Self-assessment	Situation, affect	Alter one's approach to the work setting
Seek support	Affect	Commiserating with a colleague
Appraise challenge	Affect, situation	Renegotiate the relationship
		Use outsider (consultant) to air grievances and manage conflict
Bolstering one's self-image	Affect	Dwelling on one's own positive attributes
		Indulging one's own interests

Source: Adopted from White and Mullen (1989)

to talk to the target. More recently, Brockner and Adsit (1986) found that satisfaction within a relationship is more strongly related to perceptions of equity among men than women. Kahn (1972) also found that men are more likely than women to distribute income to individuals in direct proportion to their input. Hence, the issue of gender differences remains open to study.

Finally, other research has found that relative dependence is positively related to feelings of jealousy (White, 1981a). Also, a person who is in a

Table 2
Features of Major Coping Strategies: Primary Focus on Envy

Strategy	Superordinate Goal(s)	Organizational Examples
Improve relationship with rival	Situation	Recognizing rival's superior position, but engaging the rival as a friend in hopes of improving one's later rewards.
Diminish rival's outcomes	Situation, Affect	Display resentment or hostility Sabotage rival's work Harassment or ostracism of rival
Demand greater, alternative outcomes from superior	Situation, Affect	Seek assignment to more rewarding/desirable tasks
Derogation of rival	Affect	"Back-stabbing" of competitor to supervisor Spreading slanderous gossip, misinformation and disinformation
Develop alternatives	Affect, Situation	Seek alternative rewards in other co-workers, or the work itself
Denial/avoidance	Affect	Pretend to be disinterested in rival Use of alcohol or drugs Compel rival to offer reciprocal compliments
Self-assessment	Situation, Affect	Alter one's approach to the work setting
Seek support	Affect	Commiserating with a colleague
Appraise challenge	Affect, Situation	Renegotiate the relationship Use outsider (consultant) to air grievances and manage conflict
Bolstering one's self-image	Affect	Dwelling on one's own positive attributes Indulging one's own interests
Seek "sop" behavior	Situation, Affect	Encourage rival to offer tokens of symbolic sharing
Seek true sharing	Situation	Encourage rival or rival's superior to genuinely share resources (e.g., rotating tasks, or work schedules)
Seek creation of redistributive mechanism	Situation	Seek imposition of a "taxation" system (e.g., shifting financial resources and adjustments in budgets) Support collective bargaining efforts
Seek encapsulation	Situation	Request separate facilities to reduce social contact

more powerful social position is likely to respond to a jealous threat with anger, while a person who is in a more dependent position is likely to respond with depression. This suggests that supervisors are more likely to respond to a threat to a relationship involving a subordinate with anger, while subordinates may experience depression in a reverse of the situation (White, 1985).

IDENTIFIABLE RESEARCH QUESTIONS

Despite its comparative infancy as a topic of scientific inquiry, there are a number of testable hypotheses concerning workplace jealousy and envy that can be generated both deductively (from prior theory in the domain of negative emotional reactions) and intuitively (from experience with social dynamics in the workplace).

The following is a list of questions that forms an agenda for research on workplace jealousy and envy:

1. Do supervisors who display high levels of consideration (i.e., in the Ohio State leadership sense of the term) have units with higher levels of employee jealousy (jealousy among children has been found to be greater in families with intensely affectionate mothers, Stearns, 1989, p. 76)?
2. Are the levels of employee jealousy and envy in smaller work units lower than in larger work units?
3. Are there differences between the genders in reports of jealousy and envy (Kahn et al., 1980) such that females respond more strongly to threats to relationships (jealousy), while males respond more strongly to threats to competitive standing (envy)?
4. Are employee jealousy and envy correlated with such organizational constructs as:
   a. individual in-group/out-group status (Graen & Cashman, 1975)— we should expect to find that out-group members report more jealousy and envy relative to in-group members because they are aware of differences in the quality of supervisor-subordinate working relations, and they are aware of differences in reward allocations;
   b. subscription to the work ethic (Kanungo, 1982; Mathieu & Zajac, 1990)—individuals who value the work ethic may be more attuned to differences in reward allocations and working relationships and hence may report greater feelings of envy and jealousy, relative to others who do not place a high value on the work ethic;

c. general job satisfaction (Brayfield & Rothe, 1951)—employees who report higher levels of such negative feelings as jealousy and envy could reasonably be expected to report lower levels of overall job satisfaction;

d. satisfaction with supervision (Smith, Kendall, & Hulin, 1969)—because supervisors play a role in deciding who is in/out in working relationships, and also influence reward allocation decisions, reports of jealousy and envy should be inversely related with satisfaction with one's supervisor; and

e. predisposition to quit (Dittrich & Carrell, 1979; Spencer & Steers, 1980)—employees who report higher levels of jealousy and envy should also report a relatively stronger predisposition to find alternative employment.

Before the above hypotheses can be tested, measures of employee jealousy and envy are required. As noted previously, people are reluctant to admit to negative social emotions (Sommers, 1984). Jealousy and envy, in particular, are denigrated emotions because they are presumed to reflect insecurity and immaturity. Prior efforts to develop measures of jealousy have produced a number of instruments that require the assumption that self-reports are an accurate reflection of reality, while other instruments rely on "what-if" hypothetical scenarios to obtain individual predispositions. Hypothetical-scenario instruments essentially require a type of role-playing exercise. The construct validity of each of these various scales is far from satisfactorily demonstrated. However, there are some creative illustrations of validation efforts. Specifically, Mathes, Phillips, Skowran, and Dick (1982) investigated the validity of the Interpersonal Jealousy Scale (a paper-and-pencil questionnaire wherein respondents indicate how they would behave in response to various social situations involving a target and a rival) by having dating couples complete the scale, and then having a confederate (of the same sex) call each member of the couple to ask for permission to date the respondent's partner. Tape-recordings of the phone conversations were rated by judges with respect to granting permission. Scores on the Interpersonal Jealousy Scale were significantly negatively correlated with obtained permission for both men and women respondents. Unfortunately, many other instruments in the area do not have comparable validation data, but instead rely largely on evidence of factorial validity and internal consistency. While theoretical definitions of jealousy and envy have viewed it as a complex construct, composed of feelings, cognitions, and behaviors aroused by threat-evoking situations, measures have tended to be fairly simplistic (yielding single, univariate indices). More complex measures might deliberately incorporate separate affective, cognitive, and behavioral dimensions (Bringle & Buunk, 1985).

Studying jealousy and envy in organizational settings may impose other unique problems. For example, one would ideally hope to find agreement in actor (protagonist) and observer's ratings. Yet, impression management of feelings by employees would likely cause observers to have difficulty in making accurate assessments. Also, it seems critical that employees who are experiencing negative emotions be the object of study in order to more accurately determine what protagonists, targets, and rivals actually do, feel, and think (White & Mullen, 1989).

As noted earlier, the emotions of jealousy and envy may be viewed as being related to a feeling that one lacks control over events (i.e., control over valued relationships and reward allocations). Self-esteem is related to one's sense of being able to control events. One of the more frequently studied correlates of jealousy has been the trait of self-esteem. While one would expect that people who are low in self-esteem may feel more vulnerable to threats by rivals, it is also possible that people who are high in self-esteem may be more sensitive to esteem threats (Tetlock & Manstead, 1985). Perhaps not surprisingly, therefore, evidence for an association between measures of jealousy and global self-esteem has been mixed (Bringle, 1981; Buunk, 1982; Hansen, 1982; White, 1981a, 1981b; Melamed, 1991; Salovey & Rodin, 1991), with reported relationships ranging from zero to moderately negative. In one study (Hansen, 1985), low self-esteem was found to be associated with jealousy for females, but not for males. White and Mullen (1989) argue that global self-esteem measures are not sufficiently related to relevant aspects of self to be useful, and that future research employ more focused measures of relevant aspects of self-esteem. In our present concern with organizational extensions of these prior findings, we would anticipate that work-related aspects of self-esteem (i.e., Brockner, 1988; Pierce, Gardner, Cummings, & Dunham, 1989) would likely be more predictive of jealous reactions than global measures of self-esteem. In a study of the effects of co-worker turnover on the attitudes of those who remain (i.e., stayers), Brockner and Kim (1987) found that low self-esteem co-workers (relative to their high self-esteem counterparts) felt more dissatisfied when the departed co-worker took a better job, and less dissatisfied when the co-worker had left for a worse job. Also, low self-esteem employees are more reactive than their counterparts to role conflict, ambiguity, overload, and poor supervisory support (Pierce, Gardner, Dunham, &

Cummings, 1993). These findings suggest that employee attitudes, self-esteem, and social comparison processes are intricately linked.

Finally, another stream of work that is worthy of consideration is the search for other personality correlates of jealousy and envy. Some evidence suggests that individuals who are characterizable as external on locus of control, dispositionally dogmatic, or highly insecure tend to be more jealous, while Machiavellianism is not clearly related to jealousy (Bringle & Buunk, 1985; De Moja, 1986; Mathes, Roter, & Joerger, 1982; White, 1984). Evidence on personality correlates of envy is essentially nonexistent. However, highly competitive individuals and highly Machiavellian individuals may experience stronger feelings of envy. Machiavellians, however, may be better able to hide their envious feelings and thereby be better able to maintain effective working relationships. A similar line of reasoning applies to the personality construct of self-monitoring (Snyder, 1974). Individuals who can be characterized as "high" self-monitors, relative to "low" self-monitors, are more attentive to the images that others may form of them through social interactions. Because of their concern with the impression they may convey, they tend to tailor their behavior to fit the constraint of social appropriateness. We would predict, therefore, that self-monitoring would be correlated positively with individual ability to conceal jealous and envious feelings.

MANAGERIAL RESPONSES TO NEGATIVE EMOTIONS

From a practical perspective, it is important to consider how an organization might seek to manage negative social emotions. Deliberate statements by managers of concern for equity and fair treatment may help to create a climate that emphasizes sensitivity to the impact of behaviors (Greenberg, Bies, & Eskew, 1991). Also, providing a forum for discussing how decisions are made, and policies are formulated, may be of value. Additionally, it may be possible to ameliorate feelings of jealousy and envy by boosting an individual's self-esteem. Managers who can foresee that a subordinate may react negatively to an upcoming event, may be in a position to reduce or avert ill will by the administration of praise and recognition. Such a tactic would likely backfire, however, if the subordinate felt that the praise and recognition were deliberately calculated to soothe negative feelings. Esteem-raising tactics may also be effective following the experience of jealousy or envy, perhaps in part because of the distracting quality of esteem-enhancement. Furthermore, the experience of low self-esteem may be qualitatively different for men and women. Research on the relation of self-esteem and ease of persuasability has found that low self-esteem females appear to be alienated from, and rejecting of, attitude-influence attempts, whereas an inverse relationship was found for males (Gergen & Bauer, 1967). This suggests that influence attempts may need to be qualitatively different for males and females.

The assisting of subordinates who may be experiencing jealousy and envy may also be accomplished by giving such subordinates a greater sense of inclusivity in unit activities. As one of the consequences of these negative emotions tends to be brooding and a feeling of being left out, it may be possible to minimize negative consequences by deliberately involving affected subordinates in a broader range of ongoing unit activities.

Subordinates who may be most resistant to feelings of envy and jealousy may be those who are able to engage in self-bolstering and selective ignoring (Salovey & Rodin, 1988). Self-bolstering enables individuals to raise their own esteem by focusing thoughts on personal strengths and positive attributes. Selective ignoring enables individuals to focus thoughts on alternative issues and thereby ignore potentially troubling events. It is questionable, from a human resources development standpoint, as to whether such broad socially adaptive traits can be actively developed in the work setting. Perhaps, from a personnel selection standpoint, it may be possible to identify individuals who display sufficient self-confidence so that they are less likely to be troubled by feelings of jealousy and envy. One can imagine such individuals in terms of being highly mature psychologically, in the sense of being "at peace" with themselves and their surroundings. Attempting to specify the nature of such interpersonally nontroubled individuals brings to mind the prototype of the self-actualized individual who has found personal fulfillment and is not easily troubled by (petty) social conflicts because of having attained a more transcendent view of social dynamics.

The relatively recent approach to fostering employee commitment via self-managed work teams may offer a practical device for minimizing workplace jealousy and envy (Osborn, Moran, Musselwhite, & Zenger, 1990). In self-managed teams, employees have a reduced sense of possessiveness concerning work assignments (as a consequence of mandatory job rotation and limitations on job titles/levels) and working relationships (as a consequence of job rotation, as well as a diminished role for the supervisor as a central authority figure). With shared responsibility for task completion and the deliberate elimination of "turf," self-managed teams provide a model that is distinct from traditional, hierarchical work systems. As a consequence, the magnitude of workplace jealousy and envy that may be found in self-managed or semiautonomous teams may be significantly lower than in traditional settings. Lessened dependency of the subordinates on their supervisor for information, direction, job assignments, and other job benefits should also aid in the formation of mutual dependency linkages among team members. Jealousy on the part of supervisors toward preferred subordinates could also be lessened because of the diminished attachment/dependency of supervisors on a select subset of dependable subordinates. Because of reduced levels of jealousy, members of self-managed teams would also engage in less coping-strategy behaviors (cf. Tables 1 and 2). That is to say, one would expect to find less derogation of coworkers, or projection of resentment and hostility derived from employee jealousy. Employee envy may also be at lower levels in self-managed teams as the compensation system is often of a skill-based nature, and job rotation eliminates the creation of fiefdoms and the holding of "cushy" jobs by select employees.

It should be noted that the creation of an utopian-type of work environment, where feelings of employee possessiveness toward others are essentially eliminated, is highly unlikely. As observed by James (1890) and Kinsey, Pomeroy, Martin, and Gebhard (1953), jealousy and envy are fairly innate reactions.[5] This view, however, does not negate the study of employee negative emotion as a socially conditioned phenomenon. Moreover, the results of efforts to create utopian social units (communes), where nonpossessiveness or openness to sharing includes sharing spouses, have shown that jealousy and competitiveness are persistent social problems (Stearns, 1989, p. 35).

CONCLUDING COMMENT

Not that many years ago the suggestion that one would seriously attempt to study jealousy or envy in the workplace would probably have brought snickers or jeers from an academic audience.[6] The topic was seen as trivial, perhaps somewhat suggestive of employee infantilism, and certainly an issue that the proper application of "rational problem-solving logic" could easily overcome.

Today, jealousy and envy are less likely to be seen as reflective of infantilism or as inherently abnormal responses, which might be viewed as indications of a defective personality. Fortunately, most day-to-day experiences of workplace jealousy and envy are relatively more "benign" than pathological in nature. However, the cumulative effects of experiencing such negative emotions would not necessarily be benign. Therefore, negative emotion at work needs to be better understood, and not ignored. As the antecedents and consequences of negative emotion at work are not fully understood, the study of negative emotion offers a rich ground for original research. For the near-term, we need to expand our understanding of the immediate reality of felt emotion at work, and its impact on work relations. For the long term, our goals, however, should include the creation of techniques for effectively managing and constructively channeling negative emotion at work.

NOTES

1. It must be noted that the real Salieri's alleged complicity in Mozart's death is, in fact, rejected by historians (Kupferberg, 1986), although there is a substantial amount of written correspondence by members of the Mozart family which attests to rivalry and intrigue between the two composers (Stafford, 1991).

2. Although a number of alternative definitions of jealousy have been offered, they differ from the above by emphasizing either threat to self-esteem (Mead, 1931; Farber, 1973), threat to the valued relationship (Neu, 1980; Vuyk, 1959), or a sense of exclusivity or possessiveness (Ausubel, Sullivan, & Ives, 1980).

3. For the sake of clarity, it is necessary to note that an "emotion," strictly speaking, occurs when sympathetic arousal is noticeable, while "feelings" are evaluative cognitive states that have a low level of arousal. "Affect" is a broader term that encompasses both emotion and feeling (Berscheid, 1983).

4. Somewhat surprisingly, even minimal contact between individuals can result in extreme violence. In an examination of the topic of malicious behavior, Berke (1988) reports a case of a security guard in London who murdered a visiting American banker who was out for a stroll. When arrested by police, the guard responded that he had felt lonely, degraded—an outcast from society—and that he felt cheated upon meeting a man who looked "rich and comfortable."

5. The neurological base of jealousy is suggested by examples of the sudden onset of pathological delusional jealousy (aptly termed, Othello's syndrome) that results from right hemispheric pathology (e.g., a right-middle cerebral artery infarction). Treatment of pathological delusional jealousy is successfully accomplished with the application or withdrawal of certain drugs (pimozide and amantadine, respectively), thereby underscoring the link of neuropharmacology and behavior (McNamar & Durso, 1991).

6. I am not as certain that a candid group of managers would have dismissed the topic as readily, if at all.

REFERENCES

Anderson, N. H. (1968). Likableness ratings of 555 personality-trait words. *Journal of Personality and Social Psychology, 9*, 272–279.

Ausubel, D. P., Sullivan, E. V., Freeman, W. H., & Ives, S. W. (1980). *Theory and problems of child development.* New York: Grune and Stratton.

Banks, S. P., & Kahn, M.D. (1982). *The sibling bond.* New York: Basic Books.

Berscheid, E. (1983). Emotion. In H. H. Kelley, E. Berscheid, A. Christensen, J. H. Harvey, T. L. Huston, G. Levinger, E. McClintock, L. A. Peplan, & O. R. Peterson (Eds.), *Close relationships* (pp. 110–168). San Francisco: W. H. Freeman.

Brayfield, A. H., & Rothe, H. F. (1951). An index of job satisfaction. *Journal of Applied Psychology, 35*, 307–311.

Bringle, R. G. (1981). Conceptualizing jealousy as a disposition. *Alternative Lifestyles, 4*, 274–290.

Bringle, R. G., & Buunk, B. (1985). Jealousy and social behavior. *Review of Personality and Social Psychology, 6*, 241–264.

Brockner, J. (1988). *Self-esteem at work: Research, theory, and practice.* Lexington, MA: Lexington.

Brockner, J., & Adsit, L. (1986). The moderating effect of sex on the equity-satisfaction relationship. *Journal of Applied Psychology, 71*, 585–590.

Brockner, J., & Kim, D. (1987). *The effects of turnover on those who stay: A social comparison analysis.* Unpublished manuscript. [Cited in Brockner, J. (1988). *Self-esteem at work: Research theory and practice* (pp. 80–81). Lexington, MA: Lexington.

Bryson, J. B. (1976). *The nature of sexual jealousy: An exploratory paper.* Paper presented at annual meeting of the American Psychological Association.

Buunk, R. (1982). Anticipated sexual jealousy: Its relationship to self-esteem, dependence and reciprocity. *Personality and Social Psychology Bulletin, 8*, 310–316.

Buss, D., Larsen, R., Westen, D., & Semmelroth, J. (1992). Sex differences in jealousy: Evolution, physiology, and psychology. *Psychological Science, 3*, 251–255.

Clanton, G. (1989). Jealousy in American culture, 1945–1985: Reflections from popular literature. In D.D. Franks & E.D. McCarthy (Eds.), *The sociology of emotions: Original essays and research papers.* Greenwich, CT: JAI Press.

Clanton, G., & Smith, L. G. (1977). *Jealousy.* Englewood Cliffs, NJ: Prentice-Hall.

De Moja, C. A. (1986). Anxiety, self-confidence, jealousy, and romantic attitudes toward love in Italian undergraduates. *Psychological Reports, 58*, 138.

Dittrich, J., & Carrell. M. (1979). Organizational equity perceptions, employee job satisfaction, and departmental absence and turnover rates. *Organizational Behavior and Human Performance, 24*, 29–40.

Dunn, J. (1983). Sibling relationships in early childhood. *Child Development, 54*, 787–811.

Farber, L. H. (1973). On jealousy. *Commentary, 55*, 180–202.

Festinger, L. (1954). A theory of social comparison. *Human Relations, 7*, 117–140.

Foa, E. B., & Foa, U. G. (1980). Resource Theory: Interpersonal behavior as exchange. In M. K. Gergen, M. S. Greenberg, & R. H. Willis (Eds.), *Social exchange* (pp. 77–102). New York: Plenum.

Foster, G. (1972). The anatomy of envy: A study of symbolic behavior. *Current Anthropology, 13*, 165–202.

Gayford, J. J. (1979). Battered wives. *British Journal of Hospital Medicine, 22*, 496–503.

Gergen, K., & Bauer, R. (1967). The interactive effects of self-esteem and task difficulty in social conformity. *Journal of Personality and Social Psychology, 6*, 16–22.

Graen, G., & Cashman, J. F. (1975). A role-making model of leadership in formal organizations: A developmental approach. In J. G. Hunt & L. L. Larson (Eds.), *Leadership frontiers* (pp. 143–165). Kent, OH: Kent State University Press.

Greenberg, J., Bies, R. J., & Eskew, D. E. (1991). Establishing fairness in the eye of the beholder. In R. Giacalone & P. Rosenfeld (Eds.), *Applied impression management* (pp. 111–132). Newbury Park, CA: Sage.

Hansen, G. L. (1982). Reactions to hypothetical jealousy. *Alternative Lifestyles, 4*, 310–356.

Hansen, G. (1985). Perceived threats and marital jealousy. *Social Psychology Quarterly, 48*, 262–268.

Hupka, R. B. (1984). Jealousy: Compound emotion or label for a particular situation? *Motivation and Emotion, 8*, 141–155.

James, W. (1890). *Principles of psychology.* New York: Henry Holt.

Kahn, A. (1972). Reactions to the generosity or stinginess of an intelligent or stupid work partner: A test of equity theory on a direct exchange relationship. *Journal of Personality and Social Psychology, 21*, 116–123.

Kahn, A., O'Leary, V., Krulewitz, J. E., & Lamm, H. (1980). Equity and equality: Men and women means to a just end. *Basic and Applied Social Psychology, 1*, 173–197.

Kanungo, R. (1982). Measurement of job and work involvement. *Journal of Applied Psychology, 67*, 341–349.

Kinsey, A. C., Pomeroy, W. B., Martin, C. E., & Gebhard, P. H. (1953). *Sexual behavior in the human female.* Philadelphia: W.B. Saunders.

Kupferberg, H. (1986). *Amadeus: A Mozart mosaic.* New York: McGraw-Hill.

Mathes, E. W., Phillips, J. T., Skowran, J., & Dick, W. E. (1982). Behavioral correlates of the Interpersonal Jealousy Scale. *Educational and Psychological Measurement, 42*, 1227–1230.

Mathes, E. W., Roter, P. M., & Joerger, S. M. (1982). A convergent validity study of six jealousy scales. *Psychological Reports, 50*, 1143–1147.

Mathieu, J., & Zajac, D. (1990). A review and meta-analysis of the antecedents, correlates, and consequences of organizational commitment. *Psychological Bulletin, 108*, 171–194.

McNamar, P., & Durso, R. (1991). Reversible pathologic jealousy (Othello syndrome) associated with amantadine. *Journal of Geriatric Psychiatry and Neurology, 4*, 157–159.

Mead, M. (1931). Jealousy: Primitive and civilized. In S. D. Schmalhauser & V. F. Calverton (Eds.), *Woman's coming of age* (pp. 35–48). New York: Horace Liverlight.

Melamed, T. (1991). Individual differences in romantic jealousy: The moderating effect of relationship characteristics. *European Journal of Social Psychology, 21*, 455–461.

Miner, F. C. (1990, April). Jealousy on the job. *Personnel*, pp. 89–95.

Nadler, A., & Dotan, I. (1992). Commitment and rival attractiveness: Their effects on male and female reactions to jealousy-arousing situations. *Sex Roles, 26*, 293–310.

Nieva, V. F., & Gutek, B. A. (1981). *Women and work: A psychological perspective.* New York: Praeger.

Osburn, J. D., Moran, L., Musselwhite, E., & Zenger, J. H. (1990). *Self-directed work teams.* Homewood, IL: Irwin.

Parrott, W. G. (1991). The emotional experiences of envy and jealousy. In P. Salovey (Ed.), *The psychology of jealousy and envy* (pp. 3–30). New York: Guilford Press.

Parrott, W. G., & Smith, R. H. (1993). Distinguishing the experiences of envy and jealousy. *Journal of Personality and Social Psychology, 64,* 906–920.

Pierce, J. L., Gardner, D. G., Cummings, L. L., & Dunham, R. B. (1989). Organization-based self-esteem: Construct definition, measurement, and validation. *Academy of Management Journal, 32,* 622–648.

Pierce, J., Gardner, D., Dunham, R., & Cummings, L. (1993). Moderation by organization-based self-esteem of role condition-employee response relationships. *Academy of Management Journal, 36,* 271–288.

Salovey, P. (1991). *The psychology of jealousy and envy.* New York: Guilford Press.

Salovey, P., & Rodin, J. (1986). The differentiation of social-comparison jealousy and romantic jealousy. *Journal of Personality and Social Psychology, 50,* 1100–1112.

Salovey, P., & Rodin, J. (1988). Coping with envy and jealousy. *Journal of Social and Clinical Psychology, 7,* 15–33.

Salovey, P., & Rodin, J. (1991). Provoking jealousy and envy: Domain relevance and self-esteem threat. *Journal of Social and Clinical Psychology, 10,* 395–413.

Selye, H. (1976). *The stress of life.* New York: McGraw-Hill.

Shaffer, P. (1981). *Amadeus: A play.* New York: Harper and Row.

Simmel, G. (1955). *Conflict and the web of group affiliation.* Glencoe, IL: Free Press.

Smith, P. C., Kendall, L. N., & Hulin, C. L. (1969). *The measurement of satisfaction in work and retirement.* Chicago: Rand-McNally.

Smith, R. H., Kim, S. H., & Parrott, W. F. (1988). Envy and jealousy: Semantic problems and experimental distinctions. *Personality and Social Psychology Bulletin, 14,* 401–409.

Snyder, M. (1974). The self-monitoring of expressive behavior. *Journal of Personality and Social Psychology. 30,* 526–537.

Sommers, S. (1984). Adults evaluating their emotions. A cross-cultural perspective. In C. Malatesta & C. Izard (Eds.), *Emotion in adult development* (pp. 161–185). Beverly Hills, CA: Sage.

Spencer, D. G., & Steers, R. M. (1980). The influence of personal factors and perceived work experiences on employee turnover and absenteeism. *Academy of Management Journal, 23,* 567–572.

Sprouse, M. (1992). *Sabotage in the American workplace.* San Francisco: Pressure Drop Press.

Stafford, W. (1991). *The Mozart myths: A critical reassessment.* Stanford, CA: Stanford University Press.

Stearns, P. N. (1989). *Jealousy: The evolution of an emotion in American history.* New York: New York University Press.

Stets, J., & Pirog-Good, M. A. (1987). Violence in dating relationships. *Social Psychology Quarterly, 50,* 237–246.

Tetlock, P. E., & Manstead, A. S. R. (1985). Impression management versus intra-psychic exploration in social psychology: A useful dichotomy? *Psychological Review, 92,* 59–77.

Todd, J., & Dewhurst, K. (1955). The Othello syndrome: A study of the psychopathology of sexual jealousy. *Journal of Nervous and Mental Disease, 112,* 367–374.

Van Sommers, P. (1988). *Jealousy.* London: Penguin Books.

Vecchio, R. P. (1993a). *Employee jealousy: Antecedents, consequences, and testable hypotheses.* Paper presented at 1993 Meeting of the Western Academy of Management, San Jose, CA.

White, G. L. (1981a). A model of romantic jealousy. *Motivation and Emotion, 5,* 295–310.

White, G. L. (1981b). Some correlates of romantic jealousy. *Journal of Personality, 49,* 129–147.

White, G. L. (1984). Comparison of four jealousy scales. *Journal of Research in Personality, 18,* 115–130.

White, G. L. (1985). Gender, power, and romantic jealousy. Unpublished manuscript. University of Auckland, Auckland, New Zealand.

White, G. L., & Mullen, P. E. (1989). *Jealousy: Theory, research, and clinical strategies.* New York: Guilford Press.

About the Editor

Robert P. Vecchio (Ph.D., University of Illinois) holds the Franklin D. Schurz Chair in Management at the University of Notre Dame. Since joining the university in 1976, Professor Vecchio has taught and conducted research on organizational behavior and human resources management, with special emphasis on leadership. Currently, Professor Vecchio teaches an undergraduate and MBA class devoted exclusively to the topic of leadership and effective supervision. He also served as an instructor in the university's Supervisory Development Program for over 25 years. From 1983 to 1990, Professor Vecchio was head of the Department of Management and Administrative Sciences at Notre Dame. He has served on the editorial boards of the *Academy of Management Review, Leadership Quarterly,* the *Academy of Management Learning and Education Journal,* the *Journal of Management,* the *Journal of Occupational and Organizational Psychology,* the *Journal of Managerial Inquiry, Employee Responsibilities and Rights Journal,* the *International Journal of Applied Quality Management,* and the *International Journal of Organizational Analysis.* In 1995 he assumed the role of Editor-in-Chief of the *Journal of Management,* the first journal to be headquarderd in the College of Business Administration at the University of Notre Dame. The *Journal* is a broad-gauge outlet that publishes rigorous empirical research in all aspects of management, with special emphasis on issues surrounding effective management and leadership. Professor Vecchio was selected as a Fellow of the Center for Creative Leadership in 1974. In 1975 he was awarded a grant from the U.S. Department of Labor to study the leadership process. He has published numerous articles in such journals as the *Journal of Applied Psychology,* the *Academy of Management Journal,* the *Academy of Management Review, Organizational Behavior and Human Performance,* the *Journal of Management,* the *Journal of Organizational Behavior, Leadership Quarterly,* and *Human Relations.* He is also the author of *Organizational Behavior,* a book published by Thomson Learning, which is now in its sixth edition, as well as international editions. Professor Vecchio has served as a consultant to both for-profit and not-for-profit organizations. He is a Fellow of the American Psychological Association, the Society for Industrial and Organizational Psychology, the American Psychological Society, and the Southern Management Association. He is listed in *Who's Who in America* and *Who's Who in the World.*